Frommer's®

Kenya & Tanzania

1st Edition

by Keith Bain, Pippa de Bruyn, Philip Briggs & Lizzie Williams

Wiley Publishing, Inc.

Published by:

WILEY PUBLISHING, INC.

111 River St.
Hoboken, NJ 07030-5774

ISBN 978-0-470-28558-9

Editor: Anuja Madar & Marc Nadeau
Production Editor: Katie Robinson
Cartographer: Andrew Murphy
Photo Editor: Richard Fox
Production by Wiley Indianapolis Composition Services

Front cover photo: Kenya, Masai Mara National Reserve: African Elephant full length portrait on savannah. ©Andy Rouse/Corbis
Back cover photo: Maasai Tribes people portrait. ©Eric Meola/Getty Images

For information on our other products and services or to obtain technical support, please contact our Customer Care Department within the U.S. at 877/762-2974, outside the U.S. at 317/572-3993 or fax 317/572-4002.

Wiley also publishes its books in a variety of electronic formats. Some content that appears in print may not be available in electronic formats.

Manufactured in the United States of America

5 4 3 2 1

CONTENTS

5 NAIROBI 70

6 SOUTHERN KENYA 102

7 THE CENTRAL HIGHLANDS 125

8 THE RIFT VALLEY 143

9 THE MASAI MARA & WESTERN KENYA 165

LIST OF MAPS

ABOUT THE AUTHOR

Born and bred in the South African coastal city of Durban, **Keith Bain** has a doctoral degree in drama. Now he's quit academia to explore and write about the world. Besides his safari adventures in Kenya, his assignments for Frommer's have taken him to India, Italy, Botswana, Romania, Slovenia, Ireland, and even out onto the streets of Johannesburg. Most recently, he's been writing about the most beautiful city on earth—Cape Town, which he calls home.

Pippa de Bruyn was born in Durban, raised in Johannesburg, and has now settled in Cape Town. She is an award-winning journalist and is the author of *Frommer's South Africa* and the coauthor of *Frommer's India.*

Philip Briggs has been exploring the highways, byways, and backwaters of Africa since 1986, when he backpacked from Nairobi to Cape Town. In the 1990s, he wrote a series of pioneering Bradt Guides to destinations that were then—and in some cases still are—otherwise practically uncharted by the travel publishing industry, including the first dedicated guidebooks to Tanzania, Uganda, Ethiopia, Malawi, Mozambique, Ghana, and Rwanda. He contributes regularly to guidebooks by other publishers and to specialist travel and wildlife magazines including *Africa Birds & Birding, Africa Geographic, BBC Wildlife, Travel Africa,* and *Wanderlust.* He still spends about half his time on the road, accompanied by his wife, the travel photographer Ariadne Van Zandbergen, and the rest of it cloistered behind a keyboard at home in the uKhahlamba-Drakensberg region of South Africa.

Lizzie Williams, who originally hails from the U.K., is a freelance travel writer based in Cape Town. She is the author of more than 20 guidebooks on African countries for Footprint, Bradt, the AA, and Dorling Kindersley, and regularly writes for magazines and travel websites. She is also the author of *Frommer's Cape Town Day By Day* and the online guide to Kenya and Tanzania.

ACKNOWLEDGMENTS

Thanks to all tourism partners in East Africa for constantly keeping me in the loop of new developments in the region and readily giving out information. Also thanks to long-term friends Bruce and Sparky in Dar, and Wendy and Thommo in Nairobi for their ever present hospitality. Finally thanks to Marc and Anuja for putting it all together.

—Lizzie Williams

HOW TO CONTACT US

In researching this book, we discovered many wonderful places—hotels, restaurants, shops, and more. We're sure you'll find others. Please tell us about them, so we can share the information with your fellow travelers in upcoming editions. If you were disappointed with a recommendation, we'd love to know that, too. Please write to:

Frommer's Kenya & Tanzania, 1st Edition
Wiley Publishing, Inc. • 111 River St. • Hoboken, NJ 07030-5774

AN ADDITIONAL NOTE

Please be advised that travel information is subject to change at any time—and this is especially true of prices. We therefore suggest that you write or call ahead for confirmation when making your travel plans. The authors, editors, and publisher cannot be held responsible for the experiences of readers while traveling. Your safety is important to us, however, so we encourage you to stay alert and be aware of your surroundings. Keep a close eye on cameras, purses, and wallets, all favorite targets of thieves and pickpockets.

FROMMER'S STAR RATINGS, ICONS & ABBREVIATIONS

Every hotel, restaurant, and attraction listing in this guide has been ranked for quality, value, service, amenities, and special features using a **star-rating system.** In country, state, and regional guides, we also rate towns and regions to help you narrow down your choices and budget your time accordingly. Hotels and restaurants are rated on a scale of zero (recommended) to three stars (exceptional). Attractions, shopping, nightlife, towns, and regions are rated according to the following scale: zero stars (recommended), one star (highly recommended), two stars (very highly recommended), and three stars (must-see).

In addition to the star-rating system, we also use **eight feature icons** that point you to the great deals, in-the-know advice, and unique experiences that separate travelers from tourists. Throughout the book, look for:

Finds	Special finds—those places only insiders know about
Fun Facts	Fun facts—details that make travelers more informed and their trips more fun
Kids	Best bets for kids, and advice for the whole family
Moments	Special moments—those experiences that memories are made of
Overrated	Places or experiences not worth your time or money
Tips	Insider tips—great ways to save time and money
Value	Great values—where to get the best deals
Warning!	Warning—traveler's advisories are usually in effect

The following **abbreviations** are used for credit cards:

AE American Express
DISC Discover
V Visa
DC Diners Club
MC MasterCard

TRAVEL RESOURCES AT FROMMERS.COM

Frommer's travel resources don't end with this guide. Frommer's website, **www.frommers.com**, has travel information on more than 4,000 destinations. We update features regularly, giving you access to the most current trip-planning information and the best airfare, lodging, and car-rental bargains. You can also listen to podcasts, connect with other Frommers.com members through our active-reader forums, share your travel photos, read blogs from guidebook editors and fellow travelers, and much more.

The Best of Kenya & Tanzania

Safari means "journey" in Swahili, and it's quintessential to the East Africa experience: a transformative trip through some of the continent's most extraordinary landscapes, wild and untouched, much of it teeming with Africa's densest concentrations of wildlife. The coastline is equally blessed, with exotic islands surrounded by an extraordinary variety of hard and soft corals, home to myriad species of gemlike fish that flit just below the surface. Add to this pristine beaches, cuisine and architecture that reflects a fascinating blend of Arabic and African influences, a host of very special places to stay, the warm embrace of ever-temperate climes, and a laid-back and welcoming atmosphere, and you'll see why East Africa is one of those destinations that never disappoints.

1 THE MOST ROMANTIC SAFARI DESTINATIONS

- **Borana—Cottage No. 8** (Laikipia, Kenya): As the country's very first boutique lodge, Borana revolutionized the way travelers bed down while on safari in Kenya. First built in the early 1990s, Borana's urbane owners chose a brilliant cliff-edge location and ensured that each of the beautifully rustic stone cottages enjoys amazing views. They also brought a high level of wilderness-appropriate luxury, unparalleled exclusivity, and hands-on hosting to rejuvenate the safari experience. Upping the design ante, though, are the newly added open-to-the-elements suites. Built directly into the rocks, the Moroccan-influenced rooms are, in fact, nothing short of breathtaking, with lime-washed floors, views framed by natural wooden beams, and eye-catching furnishings. Cottage 8 is the most desirable of all—with a shower carved from massive boulders, glass doors that open onto wooden decks stretching down to your private plunge pool, and a bathroom that's as massive as the bedroom; the overall look is chic, cool, and sexy. It's simply one of the most romantic spaces in Kenya. See p. 214.
- **Dodo's Tower at Hippo Point** (Lake Naivasha, Kenya): This unusual and decadent folly near the shores of Lake Naivasha breaks the rules of any dwelling you've ever laid eyes on. Each on a different floor of this majestic fairytale tower, the five elegant bedrooms offer increasingly splendid views—and from the upper level you'll spy pink flamingoes in the thousands and half-submerged hippos wallowing in the lake. Built of cedar, cypress, mahogany, ebony, and black granite, the interior is a marvelous gallery of astonishing antiques, artfully displayed alongside Maasai handicrafts. There's every chance you'll forget where in the world you are, but when you're not swooning over the fantastical design, you can arrange game drives, boat rides, or a muscle-tingling massage in the lakeside

gazebo—and the animals you'll see will bring you back to the heart of Africa. See p. 149.

- **Ngorongoro Crater Lodge** (Ngorongoro Conservation Area, Tanzania): Built right on the lip of the crater, this is Africa's most over-the-top lodge, a wonderful mix of hobbitlike styling and baronial splendor famously described as "Versailles meets Maasai." As such, it is a destination in its own right, and every vantage quite stunning—the view of the vast crater below is an added bonus. It's a real exercise in pampering, too: Return from your game drive, and you're likely to find a crackling fire lit in your room (it's cold up on the crater rim) and a rose-strewn bubble bath; settle in and drink in the view, along with a glass of bubbly. See p. 418.
- **Olerai and Elephant Watch** (Rift Valley and Samburu National Reserve, Kenya): These shabby chic properties are two very distinctive creations by the effervescent conservationist Oria Douglas-Hamilton. One is on the shores of the Rift Valley's Lake Naivasha, near the family mansion where Oria grew up, and the other in the heart of the elephant-rich Samburu game preserve. Both are defined by slick bohemian styling and superbly intimate hosting. At **Olerai** you'll enjoy the gentlest possible introduction to East Africa, in lovely colonial-era quarters; hippos trim the lawn through the night (perhaps munching right outside your window), and you can watch all kinds of plains game while you breakfast on the vast lawns. From Olerai, you can arrange to be flown to the popular Samburu game park, where **Elephant Watch**—not far from the elephant research facility started by Oria and her husband, Ian—is far and away the best place to stay inside the reserve. It's also arguably the finest place in Kenya to get up close and personal with pachyderms, perhaps watching them from your beautifully decorated tent or from beneath the open-air shower where you wash with water from a hand-painted bucket. Never was rusticity so elegant. See p. 151 and 234.
- **The Sanctuary at Ol Lentille** (Northern Laikipia, Kenya): Each of the four villas at this fabulous boutique "resort" is magnificently attired and comes with a private butler, personal Maasai guide, and housekeeper. With its far-flung location creating a sense of absolute privacy and remoteness, there's no disputing that this is East Africa's most exclusive and alluring hideaway (and one of Africa's most luxurious). Even if the surrounding territory is not yet bustling with animals, the real thrill here is the splendid luxury in the midst of a sweltering semi-arid landscape—on a clear morning, you can spy Mount Kenya across the dry plains strewn with rocks and studded with termite mounds. The visual beauty will hold you in its awe. For pure romance, the retro-style Eyrie is ideal for sensualists—after waking up to wraparound cinemascope views on your circular, shagadelic bed, you can dine at your convenience, anytime, anywhere, and sign up for decadent spa treatments, all included in the reasonable rate. Secluded from the world, you'll be hard-pressed to imagine a higher degree of pampering—or why you'd ever want to leave. See p. 221.
- **Saruni Samburu** (near Samburu National Park, Kenya): Inspired by the arid, rock-strewn surrounds, Italian author Riccardo Orizio's second Kenyan camp is a splendid mix of Moorish influences and elements drawn from nomadic Samburu tribal homesteads. Savvy minimalist design works surprisingly well in the sweltering heat of Northern Kenya and the large, beautiful accommodations blend magnificently

into the rugged, rocky surrounds. Positioned on the lip of a cliff, and affording show-stopping views from al fresco showers, these dreamy spaces are a perfect spot from whence to commence a love affair with Africa in its more arid avatar. Returning to your quarters at the end of a busy day of game drives or bush walks, you'll find the light of the stars, flickering candles, and a leopard calling in the dead of night all combine to set the scene for another sort of romantic magic. See p. 232.

- **SaSaab** (near Samburu National Park, Kenya): This chic addition to Kenya's safari scene is—like Saruni Samburu—a firm signal that tony, design-centric properties are the country's future trendsetters. Each of the beautiful open-fronted living quarters comes standard with wonderful views from the bedroom, the bathroom, and the plunge pool on your private terrace overlooking the Ewaso Nyiro River and distant plains beyond. With their Moroccan-inspired good looks and generous proportions, you'll have no trouble thinking up excuses to spend entire days in your suite, but with excellent game drives into the game-rich Samburu National Reserve and the chance to visit tribal homesteads or picnic on boulders in the arid wilderness, don't forget that this is a perfect location to combine sensual pleasure with a top-drawer safari experience. See p. 228.
- **Serengeti Under Canvas** (Serengeti, Tanzania): There's little to beat the romance of having nothing but canvas between you and the bush (hence "The Best Tented Camps" reviewed below). The semi-permanent tented camps that follow the Migration offer great game viewing with a level of luxury—carpets, plush sofas, table lamps, and small libraries—not normally associated with camping. There are four excellent operators (reviewed in chapter 15), but only &Beyond comes with the luxury of a private butler to see to your every need, from delivering piping hot water, warmed over a fire and carried to your private bucket shower, to remembering that you like your G&T with crushed ice and mint. See p. 432.
- **Shompole** (Southern Rift, Kenya): Sitting pretty on a cliff in one of the haziest, hottest parts of Kenya, this is another innovatively designed designer lodge, this time overlooking the volcanic hills and breathtaking plains of the Great Rift Valley. The thatched, whitewashed accommodations are bright, light-filled, breezy, and beautiful—to compensate for the heat, they're open to the elements and feature running water in the rooms. You'll be mesmerized by the exotic design and drawn to the relatively undiscovered location; not far from the Tanzanian border, this is an ideal spot if you want to escape the hordes. From here, you can easily nip across the border to witness millions of flamingoes carpeting the Lake of Fire's crimson-colored surface, or take a plane ride to get a better view of Kilimanjaro. See p. 146.
- **Singita's Grumeti Camps** (Grumeti Reserve, Serengeti, Tanzania): Singita has been wowing followers of the world's glossiest travel tomes with their South Africa camps for years, and they regularly vote Singita SA Best Destination on Earth (a record-setting 5 consecutive years)—with Grumeti sure to follow suit. Well, given the landscape, Singita's East Africa camps—a choice of three, each so different you'll feel as if you've arrived at a totally new destination—are even better. Whether you're on honeymoon or have been married "forever," this is where you come to feel like the world's first couple. See p. 440.
- **Tassia** (Laikipia, Kenya): The multi-talented architect-cum-builder (and now pilot with Kenya's Tropic Air) who

designed this community-owned lodge legendarily spent 2 years living in a tree while he conjured each of the unique wood and rock cottages. Balancing on a rocky bluff that protrudes from the Mokogodo Escarpment in a remote corner of the vast Laikipia Plateau, each of the imaginatively crafted spaces overlooks a scene of devastating beauty—especially lovely when troops of elephants come bounding through the wilderness below. Pachyderms, in fact, are frequent visitors to the salt lick just below the lodge, and you can spend hours watching them from behind a nearby gigantic rock. For more active pursuits, your hosts will take you on exciting adventures—up sacred mountains, into caves once used by tribal hunters, and on foot through an animal-rich wilderness. It's a magical place to lose yourself for a few days and experience a life unimpeded by modernity—solar energy powers the entire lodge, and the only contact with the outside world is from a satellite hotspot under a tree down near the airstrip. See p. 224.

2 THE WILDEST ANIMAL ENCOUNTERS

- **Wondering exactly where that roaring lion is** (Most game preserves in Kenya and Tanzania): In any national park or concession with a relatively high lion population, your slumber will more than likely be disturbed by the distant but still powerful roar of a lion announcing jurisdiction over its kingdom. Reaching 115 decibels, the sound is carried across the plains 8km (5 miles) or more and remains one of the most powerful, thrilling sounds on Earth. See chapters 9 and 15.
- **Watching a cheetah beat a Ferrari** (Serengeti/Masai Mara): The fastest animal on land, the cheetah can reach a top speed of 110km (68 miles) an hour; more impressively, it can reach this top speed from a stationary position in 3 seconds flat—0.2 seconds faster than a Formula 1 car! Despite occurring in vastly reduced numbers, your chances of seeing this critically endangered cat hunt in the Serengeti are probably higher than that of seeing a leopard stalk, as cheetahs are diurnal, preferring to hunt at sunrise and sunset, and usually on the open plains, where they can approach stragglers by running them down with a short burst of speed within a 400m (1,312 ft.) range. See chapters 9 and 15.
- **Witnessing crocs snacking on easy pickings** (Serengeti/Masai Mara): The sight of thousands of animals plunging into waters infested with some of the biggest crocodiles in Africa is, for many, the eponymous moment of the "greatest wildlife spectacle on Earth." The Migration usually crosses the Grumeti River sometime during June or July (timing depends on rainfall during that particular year), while the Mara River can see continual crossings from June to September as the herds seek out fresh pastures on either side of the river. See chapters 9 and 15.
- **Tracking rhino with a Maasai warrior** (Laikipia, Kenya): By all accounts, walking into the wilderness can be extremely dangerous, and those who do it without expert guidance put themselves at risk—from elephants, rhinos, buffaloes, hippos, and predators, too. Typically when you head into the bush, you'll be accompanied by a rifle-carrying ranger or tracker who will—if push comes to shove—shoot an animal to save your life. At **Lewa Wilderness** in Kenya's Laikipia Plateau, it's possible to

head out with a Maasai warrior (or elder) whose intimate, expert knowledge of the animals means that you could find yourself within 20m (66 ft.) of rhino and closer to an elephant than you ever imagined possible in the wild. As you discover how to study the ground for tracks and stay upwind in order to avoid detection, you'll feel yourself marveling by the untamed splendor of a world far removed from the relative security of a tented camp or fenced-off lodge. If you're seeking a profoundly intimate encounter with the wilds, jump at the chance to head out and track the animals on foot. See p. 218.

- **Counting coins with a whale shark** (Mafia Island): It's humbling swimming alongside the planet's biggest fish. Whale sharks weigh in at around 15 tons and can reach a length of 14m (46 ft.); the oldest is estimated to be 150 years old. While classified as a shark (not least because its huge mouth has around 3,000 teeth), these gentle giants—their dappled skins giving rise to the Swahili name *papa shillingi,* which means "shark covered in shillings"—are harmless and feed on enormous amounts of plankton sieved through their gills. Whale sharks tend to arrive in Mafia's waters around November and usually stay until February. See chapter 14.
- **Being serenaded by a million wildebeest** (Serengeti, Tanzania, and Masai Mara, Kenya): East Africa's most abundant antelope is charmingly vocal at night, with a harmonious array of snorts and honks that sound not unlike a composition by Stockhausen, best appreciated when sleeping underneath the thin "walls" of a canvas tent. The Migration happens year-round, so find out where the herds are likely to be before deciding where to book; alternatively, time your visit for December/January, when some 1.5 million wildebeest descend on the short-grass plains near Lake Ndutu, birthing—at their peak—8,000 calves daily. See chapter 15.
- **Swimming with endorphins** (Zanzibar, Pemba, and Mafia islands): Plunging into the waters above the coral reefs of Mnemba (Zanzibar), Misali (Pemba), and Mafia is a little like a good dose of shock therapy—guaranteed to cauterize depression. Floating above this parallel universe, swarming with magnificently patterned and brightly colored fish, even the most committed skeptic cannot help but experience something like a religious awakening. See chapter 14.
- **Tracking chimpanzees on the shores of Lake Tanganyika** (Southern Tanzania): Gombe National Park, famed for the research undertaken there by Jane Goodall in the 1960s, vies with nearby Mahale Mountains National Park as Africa's best chimp-tracking destination. The hiking can be tough, but the reward—touching base with a totally habituated community of man's closest relative in its forested home—is utterly thrilling and engaging. If you're choosing between the two, the tracking is generally less demanding in Gombe, but Mahale is a wilder and more scenic location. See chapter 17.

3 THE BEST NATIONAL PARKS

- **Meru National Park** (Kenya): Experiencing a massive renaissance after poachers decimated animal numbers and waged all-out war on park wardens, Meru is not only a beautiful reserve where you can spot the Big Five among increasingly good numbers of plains game and slightly rarer animals, but because it was virtually off-limits for so many years, it's seen relatively little development and consequently draws few visitors. Such alluring potential solitude is unlikely to last, though, so make this a priority if you'd like to get a glimpse of African wilderness before the developers step in. See chapter 7.

- **Mafia Marine Park** (Mafia Island): Lapping the largely uninhabited archipelago that lies 200km (124 miles) south of Zanzibar, Mafia Marine Park's waters hold some of the richest reefs in the world, with more than 400 species of fish flitting along its shallow reefs and plummeting walls, including the whale shark, found in the shallow waters on the northwestern side of the island, facing Kilondoni. With a grand total of six accommodation options in the entire archipelago, diving these clear waters is also a pretty exclusive experience. See chapter 14.
- **Serengeti National Park** (Tanzania, Northern Circuit): The Serengeti is the greatest game park on the continent. It's not just the wildlife (the sight of more than two million animals moving across the plains is quite a sight), nor is it the actual size (almost that of a small country), but rather the expansive views you find at every turn. It was the Maasai who called it Siringitu—"the place where the land moves on forever"—and it is precisely this sense of vastness that will blow you away: the sheer expanse of the short-grass plains like a yellow sea, broken only by occasional rocky outcrops and elegant acacia trees. And above it all, always the high noble arc of the African sky. See chapter 15.
- **Tarangire National Park** (Northern Circuit): While the focus for most travelers to Tanzania is nearby Serengeti, many come away claiming lesser-known Tarangire as the real highlight of their trip. It can't compete in terms of size, but it is a beautiful park, typified by century-old baobabs that stand sentinel above the open grass plains and riverbeds, and home to a vast array of animal and bird species, attracted by the permanently flowing waters of the Tarangire River. In fact, given its dense concentrations of animals—second only to Ngorongoro—there is every chance you will enjoy a higher incidence of sightings here than in Serengeti; elephants, in particular, are common. See chapter 15.
- **Kilimanjaro National Park** (Tanzania): Kilimanjaro is unique in the pantheon of great mountains, in that it can be scaled by virtually anyone with the drive to do so—no mountaineering skills or special preparations are needed, and most people entering this park are intent on conquering the summit (though only some 60% actually make it). Even if you're not interested in ascending Africa's highest mountain, the sight of Kili's snowcapped dome—when she deigns to appear from behind the clouds that swaddle her for much of the day—is a source of amazement; a result, perhaps, of the viewer being physically immersed in equatorial heat, while towering 5,895m (19,336 ft.) above the plains is the other-worldly glow of snow and ice. See chapter 16.

4 THE BEST PRIVATE CONCESSIONS

- **Ranches throughout the Laikipia Plateau** (Kenya): Kenya's Laikipia Plateau is the country's hottest destination for enlightened safari enthusiasts looking to escape the crowds and experience a less commercial, more authentic brush with the wilds. This is also where you'll find the greatest number of smart, well-managed, conservation-savvy ranches, many of them with intimate and exclusive camps or lodges (or both) where top-notch game-viewing opportunities are available day and night. Because the ranches and privately managed game reserves exist without the rules and strictures of the state-run parks, here you'll have the chance to set out on foot, on horseback, on mountain bike, and in the company of camels—there are chances to sleep under the stars (at **Loisaba**) or strike camp in the middle of an untamed wilderness. Laikipia may not offer the same kind of dramatic high-density game viewing experienced in the popular Masai Mara, but it offers the seductive allure of an African wilderness completely free of the press of mass tourism. See chapter 10.

- **Grumeti Private Reserve** (Adjoining Serengeti, Tanzania): If you're fortunate enough to have a rather cavalier attitude toward budget constraints, make a beeline for the Grumeti Private Reserve, bordering Serengeti in the northwest. A beautiful concession, it offers classic East African landscapes explored with exceptional guides, both informative and charming, who are allowed to go off-road to approach the game up-close in open-topped vehicles. Accommodations are also unparalleled, but perhaps the real luxury is the fact that only a handful of guests enjoy access to the Grumeti's 138,000 game-rich hectares (340,860 acres). Also the best place for horseback safaris. See chapter 15.
- **Klein's** (Adjoining Serengeti, Tanzania): Like Grumeti, Klein's offers off-road game drives, allowing visitors the chance to get really close to animals, as well as night drives and guided walks, accompanied by an armed guide. Guides here are also top-class (typical of &Beyond's stringent selection and training), and the experience is similarly exclusive to the handful of guests overnighting at the camp. Hardly surprising that Klein's is one of the most popular destinations in the Serengeti, despite the fact that accommodations are not quite up to &Beyond standards. See chapter 15.
- **Ol Donyo Wuas and Campi ya Kanzi** (Chyulu Hills, Kenya): Although lovingly described by Hemingway, the Chyulu Hills in Southern Kenya remain an undiscovered paradise—visually among the most satisfying stretches of real estate in East Africa. The rolling volcanic hills and vast swaths of lushly vegetated lava flow have hardly seen any development, and views are magnificent no matter what way you look at it—not to mention the spectacular vistas of nearby Mount Kilimanjaro, best appreciated at dawn or, if you're lucky, with a sundowner from atop a rocky hill. There are just two remote and wonderful places to bed down in this region, and both of them offer the thrill of being surrounded by Africa at its most pristine. **Ol Donyo Wuas** is one of the most luxurious places to stay in Kenya—enormous, lavish suites overlook a vast plain and every imaginable activity is on offer, including light aircraft flights at sunrise and a chance to compare your jumping skills with Maasai warriors. Far less lavish, but with a no less magnificent setting (and some incredible views of Mount Kili), **Campi ya Kanzi** is a conservation-focused project with emphasis on community empowerment, and it's a good place to better understand the ways of the Maasai. See p. 112.

5 THE BEST TENTED CAMPS

- **Bateleur Camp** (Masai Mara, Kenya): For pure luxury, this is one of Kenya's top-drawer offerings, with chicly styled tents (and state-of-the-art built-in stone-and-glass bathrooms) and imaginative public areas filled with intriguing artifacts and artworks. In fact, tents are so smart—with dark wood furniture, built-in wardrobes, rare Maasai beaded leather, and Egyptian cotton linens—that you'll probably find yourself checking the walls to make sure they're canvas. Over and above the pampering you get from your butler, whose job it is to take care of your every whim (including sorting out your daily schedule), you'll be treated to exceptional guiding by some of the best in the business. And all this within striking distance of some famous *Out of Africa* film locations—if that doesn't stir your imagination, there's always the prospect of witnessing an episode from the Great Migration directly from your private porch, complete with a butler-mixed G&T at your beck and call. See p. 176.
- **Cottar's 1920s Safari Camp** (Masai Mara, Kenya): A regular backdrop for fashionable magazine shoots and a popular destination with safari-loving celebrities, this evocative camp just outside the Masai Mara harks back to another era. Re-created here, in fact, is a time when the Cottars established their reputation as the First Family of the safari business, setting up the first fixed camps in Kenya. The big, breezy tented accommodations are beautiful and private, and there's a small wing of two-bedroom suites especially for families. Colonial-era antiques, family heirlooms, and nostalgic *objets* re-create an era of sublime, gentle luxury—although game drives are now in modern 4×4s and most guests arrive by light aircraft. Meals are served by waiters in period costume, with candles and lanterns setting a romantic scene. The camp is beyond the reach of the multitudes that drive around the southern part of the Masai Mara, so apart from local tribespeople and cattle herders from across the Tanzanian border, you'll seldom catch a glimpse of another soul. See p. 193.
- **Joy's Camp** (Shaba National Reserve, Kenya): Kenya has recently seen the establishment of several new tented camps that have broken an older mold of generally bland and functional canvas operations. Set within the peaceful, little-visited Shaba reserve (where authoress Joy Adamson lived out her final years), this elegant camp—with pretty Bedouin-style tents surrounded by a quintessential African wilderness and distant volcanic hills—is a relaxing place to get attuned to the rhythm of the continent. Whether from your private terrace, the pool, the open-air dining area, or your cleverly positioned shower, you'll be able to watch elephants and buffaloes grazing just beyond the edge of the camp—and in the morning you might discover evidence that the animals have been tasting the grass just outside your sleeping quarters. See p. 234.
- **Ngare Serian** (Masai Mara, Kenya): Renowned Kenyan safari guide and filmmaker Alex Walker offers a wide range of game-viewing activities from his exclusive new riverside camp that—with just four smart, simple tents—is jam-packed with charm and elegance, yet without any over-the-top grandeur. There's no in-room electricity, for example, but your large, multilevel accommodations (including open-plan bathrooms with tub and shower)

overlook a stretch of water populated by comical hippos that will keep you entertained all day long. Not that they'll need to, though, since you'll be out discovering the local wildlife on totally private game drives, picnicking in the bush, or tracking animals on foot. And if that sounds like too much effort, you can always settle into the breezy mess tent—designed like someone's posh indoor-outdoor lounge—while being served by cool, disarming Maasai butlers. See p. 182.

- **Oliver's Camp** (Tarangire National Park, Tanzania): Located in a remote wilderness area in the eastern section of Tarangire, Oliver's lies at the end of a dirt track that has scenery and game that will have you stopping to take pictures every few minutes. The camp itself is just as beautiful, combining thoughtful and luxurious furnishings with authentic camping facilities (composting toilets, bucket showers), and is one of only two camps that offers walking safaris inside the park; visitors can either complete a few hours' circuit or head off across the plains to overnight at a specially set up (and more rudimentary) fly-camp. See p. 402.
- **Rekero** (Masai Mara, Kenya): In the heart of Kenya's most popular wildlife preserve, there's little to beat the river's-edge location of this rustic, thoroughly authentic camp. Secreted away from the Mara's often-hectic crowds, and almost indistinguishable from the bush upon approach, here you can breakfast in full view of one of the Great Migration's best fording points. Add to this intimate service and impeccable guiding by some of the Mara's most respected Maasai—professional, articulate gentlemen who not only introduce you to the abundant animals you'll spot within close quarters of this unfenced camp, but also share a deep knowledge of their culture. Your tented digs will be neat, simple, and functional, but the pared accommodations only help make the experience more memorable. See p. 192.
- **Sabora Plains Tented Camp** (Grumeti Private Reserve, Tanzania): "Camping" doesn't get better than this. Each tented "suite" comprises a huge bedroom tent furnished with antiques and custom-made articles, all with brass hinges to indicate mobility (in keeping with its Victorian safari theme), Persian carpets, and cut-glass vases brimful with roses. This is linked to a separate bathroom and dressing room tent to one side, and a separate lounge/library tent to the other, the latter filled with books and games; beyond your wrought-iron outdoor bed is a shaded umbrella-thorn acacia tree. Quite simply the most opulent and beautifully furnished tented camp on Earth. See p. 441.
- **Sayari Camp** (Serengeti, Tanzania): Located on the south bank of the Mara River, in the remote northwest of the Serengeti, Sayari Camp enjoys an unusually lush location in the Serengeti, with rolling parkland interspersed with riverine woodlands, and the river a permanent magnet for a variety of game. After a full refurbishment in 2009, furnishings in Sayari's public spaces are cool and modern—more urban bar than Hemingway safari—and the tents now have bathtubs in addition to showers and double basins. With the completion of the pool, this is now—along with Singita's Sabora Plains—the best tented camp in the Serengeti. See p. 437.

6 MOST MEMORABLE MOMENTS

- **Waiting out a storm on Lake Baringo** (Rift Valley): You see it coming, the weather that—inexplicably and without any real warning—besieges gorgeous Lake Baringo. Surrounded by cliff-edged escarpments, tea-colored Baringo is usually a peaceful oasis supporting canoe-riding fishermen and serene island communities. But the lake is subject to tremendous climactic mood swings, and when the winds suddenly kick up, the scene can be exciting and spectacular—particularly when seen from the inside. Although usually short-lived, the storms that blow in are pure, epic theater—brilliant tempests that bring welcome relief from the sweltering heat. Best place to witness the drama? From your water's-edge bedroom at the intimate Samatian Island "resort," or from the porch of your wooden lakeside cottage at Roberts' Camp, where you'll sometimes catch glimpses of crocodiles poking their snouts above the choppy waters. See chapter 8.
- **Hot-air ballooning over the Masai Mara** (Masai Mara, Kenya): The most memorable way of seeing the Masai Mara—Kenya's most popular wildlife preserve—is from a hot-air balloon that launches at dawn and flies just above Earth's surface, from where terrestrial animals and splendid topography combine to create a marvelous bird's-eye drama. Gather for the predawn ritual of watching the balloon being inflated, and you'll be swept off your feet—spoilt with compelling vistas as you float above the plains and forests, following the contours of the Mara River enjoying a compelling perspective on an enchanting animal kingdom. Book well in advance if you want to fly during the Great Migration, when your view of tens of thousands of wildebeest and zebra will be without comparison. See p. 183.
- **Flying the Waco** (Laikipia Plateau): Here you have the rare opportunity of reliving the romance and thrill-ride fun of flying in an open-cockpit Waco. Piloted by Will Craig, owner of the superb **Lewa Wilderness** safari lodge, the bright yellow Waco is a replica 1930s biplane. During your exhilarating flight, you'll feel the wind on your face as you check out the ant-size animals down below and get the ultimate, definitive feel for the lay of the land. Because there's just the one biplane and only Will is able to pilot it, it's worth booking your flight *before* leaving for Kenya—and prepare to encounter the African wilderness in a truly unforgettable way. See p. 218.
- **Setting sail with a *taarab* orchestra** (Zanzibar, Tanzania): Listening to a live performance of *taraab* (roughly translated as "to be moved by music")—preferably on the sea-facing terrace of the Serena Inn—is wonderful. Like so much of the island's architecture and cuisine, this Zanzibari music form is a blend of styles from Africa, India, and the Middle East, and dates to the 19th century during the sybaritic rule of Sultan Barghash. The Ikhwani Safaa Musical Club, which his court musician established, remains one of the leading Zanzibari *taarab* orchestras, with 35 active members playing a variety of instruments. See chapter 13.
- **Taxying up to Mafia's "airport"** (Mafia Island, Tanzania): Having run the sandy palm-lined strip that passes for a runway, the Cessna's pilot taxis up to a whitewashed shed, juddering to a halt near a neatly placed row of white plastic chairs behind a hand-painted sign that

reads DEPARTURE LOUNGE. Mafia airport is the most charming we have yet arrived at (or, sadly, departed from). Step inside the whitewashed shack to have your luggage weighed on an old stainless steel scale; it's as if you've traveled back 50 years, to a time when air travel was exotic and thrilling, and it was actually possible to find yourself marooned on a tropical island. See chapter 14.

- **Driving the road to Ol Doinyo L'Engai** (Ngorongoro Conservation Area, Tanzania): If you like getting off the beaten track and revere stark and desolate landscapes, a trip to Lake Natron, which takes you past the last active volcano in the Rift Valley, is a must. Aside from the volcano's spiritual significance (rumblings emitted by the mountain are believed by the Maasai to be the voice of their female deity), Ol Doinyo L'Engai is one of the most arresting sights in East Africa. Entirely barren, its single-cone peak dusted in white ash, the triangulated shape rises from flat plains that are blackened and strewn with volcanic rock; hot and hostile, it is as humbling as any of Earth's great natural wonders, a truly surreal and post-apocalyptic vision that will have you stopping your vehicle every few minutes to try, yet again, to capture it all on film. See chapter 15.
- **Walking with camels** (Laikipia, Kenya): You'll need time and stamina to explore the arid expanses of the sweltering northern wildernesses. Traveling on foot in desertlike conditions under blazing sun and intense heat can be physically and mentally challenging. Camels will accompany you to carry your gear—tents, food, and other supplies—but you'll enjoy an intimate encounter with the bush that's without parallel. Typically you'll be guided by local tribespeople—keen trackers and experts at surviving some of the harshest conditions known to humankind—who'll share intimate secrets of the terrain and show you wild creatures not only in their natural habitat, but light-years away from the nearest vehicle or sign of Western civilization. At night you'll sleep under canvas or beneath the stars in a temporary campsite, and you'll feel as if you are one of Africa's original explorers. See chapter 10.
- **Gazing into the Ngorongoro Crater** (Ngorongoro Conservation Area, Tanzania): Like Victoria Falls or the Taj Mahal, the world's largest unbroken volcanic caldera is one of those wonders that does not disappoint. Created some 2 million to 3 million years ago, the crater walls drop a sheer 610m (2,001 ft.)—a circular embrace enclosing a 260-sq.-km (101-sq.-mile) valley, in which even a 6-ton elephant appears no larger than an ant. Standing on the lip and gazing into this vast natural arena, the opposite walls of which rise almost 20km (12 miles) away, one is struck not only by the sheer size and symmetry, but by the visible ecosystems: From the dark montane forests that clad the southern crater walls, to the open yellow grassland and acacia thickets, intersected by veins of freshwater streams and the tell-tale white crust of its very own salt lake, Ngorongoro's great caldera falls into the archetypal realm of an isolated "Lost World." See chapter 15.
- **Boating the Rufiji** (Southern Tanzania): The Rufiji is Tanzania's largest river and the lifeblood of the vast Selous Game Reserve, its wide, sluggish waters feeding a labyrinth of small lakes and reed-lined channels. Boat trips along this riverine wilderness provide a thrilling variation on the conventional game drive—the indignant harrumphing of hippos, outsized crocodiles basking gape-hawed on the sandbanks, buffalo and giraffes filing down to the riverbank to drink, and elephants cavorting

playfully in the shallows. The birdlife is fantastic, too: Storks and skimmer wade close to shore, colorful bee-eaters and kingfishers nest seasonally along the mud banks, and pairs of African fish eagles deliver their piercing trademark call from high in the palms. See chapter 17.

7 THE BEST PLACES FOR CULTURE & HISTORY

- **Lamu** (Kenyan Coast): Discovered as part of the hippy circuit just a few decades ago, this ancient Muslim town has become a favored getaway for celebs and royalty keen to escape the gaze of the media. Remote and relatively isolated, Lamu is also an intriguing repository for a culture and way of life that's seen little impact from the outside world, and many visitors spend their days wandering through the narrow laneways gazing up at the multistory stone houses trying to make sense of a world where donkeys and dhows are the principal means of transport. When the sense of déjà vu from continually cruising the same tight spaces gets too much, you can sail off to even more remote islands, such as Pate and Kiwayu, discovering deserted beaches, mingling with villagers, and picking through ruins of towns mysteriously abandoned centuries ago. And when the sense of stepping back in time starts to overwhelm, you can revel in the natural beauty of the Lamu archipelago, swimming with dolphins, tackling the warm water surf, or venturing across majestic sandy dunes. See chapter 11.
- **Stone Town** (Zanzibar, Tanzania): The history and atmosphere of the old city surrounding Zanzibar's port—declared a UNESCO site in 2000—is tangible, its town planning almost medieval. Get lost in its labyrinth of narrow, winding lanes lined with tall crumbling buildings, where turning a corner can produce the sparkling ocean or a courtyard of local schoolchildren intoning the Koran. While it is a popular tourist destination, Stone Town is no sanitized historical re-creation, and you'll cross paths with (or observe, from your spot on the sand or on the balcony of the House of Wonders) African men in long dresses, women draped in black, and bare-backed men on the seashore sweating beneath huge bags of spices. See chapter 13.
- **Ngorongoro Conservation Area** (Northern Circuit, Tanzania): Ngorongoro was, and still is, the only conservation area in Africa to provide full protection status for resident wildlife as well as the interests of its indigenous pastoralists, the Maasai, who traded their rights to live in the Serengeti and pursued their traditional lifestyle in the neighboring Ngorongoro Conservation Area half a century ago. There are a number of villages within easy striking distance of the crater, but these see heavy tourist traffic; the best encounters are off the beaten track, such as the road to Lake Natron, where you will see Maasai men striding like kings before their cattle, their tall, lean frames draped in artful shades of red—a startling contrast against the parched backdrop of seemingly barren valleys; similarly, the women usually are wrapped in blue, their white beaded manacles gleaming against their elongated necks and slim wrists. Despite the innate beauty of these scenes, trigger-happy photographers are urged to practice restraint; some Maasai prefer not to

have their photographs taken, others will expect to be paid; always ask first, and respect the response. See chapter 15.

- **Kilwa Ruins** (Southern Tanzania): Set on the small offshore island of Kilwa Kisiwani, on the remote south coast of Tanzania, are the extensive ruins of the medieval port that the 14th-century globetrotter Ibn Buttata described as "one of the most beautiful and well-constructed towns in the world." For 300 years, Kilwa Kisiwani was the hub of a trade network that linked the goldfields of present-day Zimbabwe to Arabia and Asia, and the haunted ruins—dome-roofed mosques, sprawling palaces, and ornate graves—form a peerless example of medieval Swahili architecture, recognized as a UNESCO World Heritage Site in 1981. See chapter 17.

8 THE BEST ISLAND LODGINGS

- **Baraza** (Zanzibar, Tanzania): We're not fond of resorts, but this is a real beauty, and if you like space, opulence, modern conveniences, and great service, this is definitely the number-one choice on Zanzibar. It's also the top choice for spa junkies, with the best-looking spa in East Africa, and treatments to match. See p. 365.
- **Chole Mjini Lodge** (Chole Island, Tanzania): The ideal destination for anyone harboring a castaway fantasy (and wanting the best diving experience in Mafia waters), tiny Chole Island has no roads, electricity, or water mains, and this intimate ecolodge, the only on the island, is accessible only by boat. Accommodations are, in some ways, relatively spartan, but if you think real luxury is living in a large stilted tree-house, open to the sea breeze but private enough to enjoy the view naked, and near enough to the water's edge to be lulled by the sound of the tide trickling back through mangrove roots, this is for you. See p. 380.
- **Delta Dunes** (Tana River Delta, Kenya): Spread across the tops of high dunes and affording indescribably beautiful views over river, ocean, and yet more dunes, this is a Robinson Crusoe–style fantasy comprising a unique combination of beach and bush. The location makes it possible to spend the day getting the adrenaline pumping and then, with G&T in hand, witnessing wildlife at sunset while lazily cruising through the delta's water channels. The big appeal is being sequestered among the naturally, organically designed spaces and with an endless, wild beach at your disposal (if you're lucky, you'll spot elephants swimming across the river or lion tracks on the beach). See p. 281.
- **Fundu Lagoon** (Pemba Island, Tanzania): Just getting to this aptly described "beach safari camp" is an adventure. Located on the isolated west coast of Pemba Island, here you will do nothing but dive, snorkel, canoe, and relax—there are plenty of places to do so. It's both a romantic hideaway and a serious divers' destination. See p. 373.
- **Funzi Keys** (South Coast, Kenya): At the northern edge of Kenya's southernmost marine park, a maze of water channels spreads between a patchwork of pretty mangroves and forested islands, one of which has been transformed into this exceptionally laid-back and relaxing hideaway, with palm trees and handsome, beautifully designed and decorated *makuti*-roofed bungalows ranged

along a private beach. Everything here is designed to make you feel spoiled and pampered, whether you're taking a Jacuzzi bath in your massive open-plan room, having a romantic breakfast for two on the sand island that appears and disappears with the tides, or taking a languid sunset cruise between the islands. Come here to feast on spectacularly fresh seafood and discover new ways to do very little at all. See p. 268.

- **Kiwayu Safari Village** (Lamu, Kenya): Spread across the beach just a few steps from the gently breaking surf, the huge, beautiful, open-plan bungalows at this ultimate toes-in-the-sand hideaway are the final word in beachcomber chic. Just about everything is made from natural materials, and there's hardly a hint of concrete to be seen. Vivid Swahili colors bring a simple elegance to the interiors, while outside, the gleaming white sands offset the sea's turquoise palette brilliantly. Besides marveling at the sense of solitude and remoteness—you're lodged at the northernmost enclave along the Kenyan coast with only a tiny village for neighbors—there's an endless line-up of waterborne activities to keep you active, and the endless supply of fresh, fresh seafood at mealtimes will have you in rapture. And if sharing paradise with a few other guests seems unfair, you can always opt for the ultimate in privacy at the very exclusive **Baobabs of Kitangani,** where a single couple can indulge their castaway fantasies while being waited on hand and foot in a dreamy setting. See p. 295.
- **A private villa in Lamu** (Lamu, Kenyan Coast): The conversion of Lamu's *medina*-style stone houses into chic contemporary holiday homes has created some of the most sumptuous and romantic lodgings in the archipelago. Although the houses are generally suitable for families, they also make decadently spacious retreats for anyone who values their privacy and wants a sense of being part of the daily life of this ancient settlement. There are now dozens of sophisticated and lovely villas that you can rent, either on Lamu Island or on Manda, its neighbor to the north. Those in Lamu town and Shela village are mostly restored originals, done up in a flattering style that's reminiscent of authentic Swahili design, while there is also a selection of newly built houses (the best is Leslie Duckworth's beautifully innovative creations at **Kizingoni Beach**). See p. 288.
- **Mnemba Island Lodge** (Mnemba Island, Tanzania): This small, chic resort, carefully tucked into its picture-perfect island, is arguably the most romantic escape in Africa. The island is tiny (it takes about 10 min. to stroll its circumference), with a coastal forest that sticks out from the powder-soft beaches and is surrounded by a conservation area. Plunge into the ocean to have the most amazing snorkeling experience; diving farther afield is stellar. See p. 363.
- **Pongwe Beach Hotel** (Zanzibar, Tanzania): This unpretentious, laid-back beach retreat is located on a particularly stunning piece of coast and enjoys one of the most remote locations in increasingly developed Zanzibar. This is still easily the most romantic barefoot beach hotel on Zanzibar's east coast and offers exceptionally good value. See p. 369.
- **Shooting Star** (Zanzibar, Tanzania): This intimate, personally managed beach resort offers a rustic, pared island style that resonates with island-hoppers from across the globe. The spa, a single whitewashed room, is within earshot of the ocean. See p. 369.

2

Planning Your Safari

The regional chapters cover why it's worth getting there, where to stay, and how to make the most of your time, but if this is your first safari, there are a number of questions that will arise while trying to plan your itinerary that are not covered there. The following are frequently asked questions we've come across when helping people come to grips with what a safari in East Africa entails. If you have any more, please write to us, and we'll try to include these online or in the next edition.

WHAT WILL AN EAST AFRICAN SAFARI COST?

Although we have supplied the rack rates to lodges and camps, actual prices are very different when you factor in transfers, park fees, and game drives, which is why you will inevitably have to deal with a tour operator/agent or a company that has camps or lodges throughout the area you want to visit in order to get a realistic price quote on the whole safari. It's best to choose a few operators and compare quotes: **www.africatravelresource.com** and **www.expertafrica.com** are two excellent online agents and a good place to start. To give you an idea, a private Land Rover safari staying in the midrange Serena chain costs around $600 per person, per night, with full board. Ultimately, you get what you pay for; if possible, aim for a more exclusive experience and—if you're visiting the Serengeti—book somewhere near the Migration. A fly-in safari to the Northern Circuit, staying at semi-permanent tented camps, costs from $700 to $1,500 per person, per night, all-inclusive, depending on the company, time of year, and number of people and nights. In the 1970s, Kenya became a focal point for a great deal of mass-market safari tourism, and we've tended to highlight the alternatives to large lodges and volume-driven experiences throughout the Kenya regional chapters. Where larger lodges and camps can't be avoided, or represent really good value, we've included them, but have also pointed out the downside of staying in these types of places. Tanzania has a number of excellent safari operators, all based in Arusha; for recommendations, refer to chapter 15. Kenya's best one-stop safari operator, based in the U.S., is **Uncharted Outposts** (www.unchartedoutposts.com), which works with local outfit **Bush and Beyond** (www.bush-and-beyond.com) to provide an airport-to-airport service where the lack of hassle, the personal attention to detail, and the quality of the entire experience (they use only small, intimate camps and lodges) will make up for the upmarket price tag.

IS IT POSSIBLE TO CUT COSTS?

There's no getting around it: An East African safari will take a relatively hefty chunk out of your budget. Just as daily park fees add significantly to your daily costs ($35–$100 per person per day in Tanzania; $20–$80 in Kenya), so do concession or operating rights within the park to your accommodations—no bad thing if all profits raised are poured back into conservation. Aside from this, running a tourist operation miles from the nearest town is incredibly costly—fresh supplies need to be trucked or flown in, often at great expense (on inquiry, one camp informed us that they were currently paying $4 per orange, which made us appreciate the freshly squeezed juice all the more). You can reduce costs by staying in large lodges, such as those run by Sopa (www.sopalodges.com), and joining group package tours, such as those offered by **Simba Safaris** (www.simbasafaris.com). Even if you settle for a large lodge to save money, we still strongly advise you, if possible, to budget for a private vehicle, as this will enhance your safari immeasurably. If necessary, put together your own group. Better still is to cut short the safari by a few days (but you will need to spend at least 3–4 nights in the bush to really experience it).

WHEN IS THE BEST TIME TO GO?

April and May are the rainy months and best avoided; many camps choose to close over this period. The rest of the year is good, though where you choose to book is then of equal importance as when, particularly in the Serengeti, where much of game viewing is dependent on rainfall and attendant migration pattern. See chapter 15 for more advice on this.

CAN I HIRE A CAR AND SELF-DRIVE?

Not really. Aside from Nairobi National Park, which is as well signposted as you'd expect from a national park bordering a capital city, operators will insist on supplying a driver with your vehicle. This is because local drivers know the vehicles and terrain better, and roads are not only virtually impassable in certain areas, but rarely marked. The driver also doubles as a guide, pointing out wildlife, birds, or plants you may otherwise miss and giving you a bit of background on the species. This knowledge can be very rudimentary, however; if you want a really good guide (and if this is your first safari, you should definitely try to budget for this), you should choose a company that prides itself on the quality of its guiding and invests in specialized training (**&Beyond, Singita, Nomad**). As a result, these companies tend to insist on having guests use their guides and vehicles, and won't accommodate another company guide, making it difficult to include them in overland safaris that comprise a number of destinations. You know you are dealing with a company like this when they offer only "game package" and no "full board" options (refer to rates located below each review). Camps and lodges that offer full board options have separate accommodation and dining for guides and pilots (this is more often than not included in your price); alternatively, expect to pay around $150 per night full board. Guides may take meals with you at your table, but only at your request and at an additional cost.

WHAT DOES THE "GAME PACKAGE" INCLUDE?

All meals, drinks, laundry, transfers to and from the nearest airstrip, daytime game drives in 4×4 vehicles with trained driver/guide (bush walks and night game if available), and camping fees (if applicable). Cigars and private cellar items are available at supplementary costs, as are medical insurance, tips, and personal items. Game package rates exclude park fees, but tour agents/operators factor these in.

ARE MOSQUITOES A REAL PROBLEM?

You won't be bothered much in the dry seasons (usually Jan–Feb and May–Sept) or at sufficiently high altitude unless you are near stagnant water, but malaria is a real risk. If you are entering a high-risk zone for the first time, a course of antimalarial pills is essential. What is prescribed will depend on your health profile, but Malarone (or Malanil, as it also known) is the most effective (98%) and has the fewest side effects. You take it only 1 day before entering a malarial area and continue the course for only 7 days after you leave the area. The downside? It's pretty expensive! Larium and its later version, Mefliam, are cheaper and are weekly doses, but these have strong potential side effects for certain people (including night sweats, bouts of depression, anxiety hallucinations, nausea exacerbated by alcohol, and sometimes intense headaches that will obviously spoil any holiday). They should be started 1 week prior to entering the area (2 weeks to give yourself time to switch), and you need to take them for 4 weeks after leaving the area. Doxycycline is the other choice; it's also a schedule 4 drug (a category of drugs with less potential for abuse), taken once daily, but we have heard that it is possible to find it without prescription in East Africa, should you forget your tabs at home (but we strongly advise you to get—and pack—your malaria prophylaxis in your home country). Doxycycline is an antibiotic (not great for the immune system) and needs to be taken for 4 weeks after leaving the area. Needless to say, none of these should be taken if you are pregnant. Chloroquine, a once commonly prescribed antimalaria drug, has been proven to be completely ineffective.

WHAT ABOUT OTHER INSECTS?

Some people will criticize a lodge or—heavens above—a tented camp because they encountered a few "bugs" in their room or tent. Really, you're in the middle of a massive wilderness area, and aside from mosquitoes, the resident insects mean you no harm (and count yourself lucky if you're sharing a room with a gecko or a lizard, as mosquitoes are a favored part of their diet). If you have a real bug phobia, we gently suggest that you reconsider your holiday destination. Most camps and lodges will spray your tent or room while you are at dinner, rendering the space bug-free for much of the night; there's usually some kind of bug spray in every room, and mosquito nets are so common that a lot of places admit that they're mainly for decorative effect. Tsetse flies can be a problem during game drives when windows are open or the vehicle's top is up. To deal with these, don't wear dark clothes and consider packing a fly swatter; the tsetse fly is a relatively slow mover and very satisfying to swat. See "The Tsetse Fly: Guardian of the Wilderness," on p. 398.

AM I SAFE FROM WILD ANIMALS WHILE ON SAFARI?

It is not in any operator, camp, or lodge's interest to lose a client, so they don't. Driver/guides will look out for you and inform you of the rules (such as not alighting from the vehicle in a national park for any reason). Upon arrival at your destination, you will—once the sun has gone down—be asked what time you want to dine, then told to wait in your room or tent until an *askari* (usually a brightly garbed Maasai carrying a spear or machete) knocks on your door or calls out to escort you to the dining room and then back again after dinner. (The exception to this is at the large hotel-like lodges, which is yet another reason to avoid these.) Some find it an exciting ritual, others rather tedious, but given that you are in an unfenced wilderness area where predators roam at will, it's best to follow the rules and move around only with an escort after dark. Tents (and many rooms) do not have telephones—you will be given a whistle for emergencies or a two-way radio (obviously not to be used to place a drinks order).

WHAT HAPPENS IF I HAVE SPECIAL DIETARY REQUIREMENTS?

This is not a problem as long as you let your camps or lodges know well in advance—bear in mind that everything

Staying Safe

The time to be especially vigilant and alert to the potential dangers in the wilds is while out on bush walks or hiking safaris. Whatever the case, you will always be with an experienced (hopefully, armed) ranger, guide, or Maasai tracker. It is absolutely in your best interest to follow his or her instructions very clearly and be on full alert at all times. This is not the place to let your guard down for even a moment. By way of example, seven people (including one tourist) were killed by elephant in the Masai Mara in Western Kenya in 2007, so never become too lax about anticipating any potential danger. Some of the most frightening stories (including a recent *National Geographic* article about a life-threatening attack on expert elephant man Ian Douglas-Hamilton) involve victims who have plenty of experience in the bush. Under no circumstances should you ever wander off alone—even in broad daylight—and when you are out walking, always inform your guide or ranger if you need to use the toilet or are going to stop for a moment to take a photograph. If a dangerous animal—elephant, buffalo, rhino, hippo, or any predator—should chance upon you (or you upon it), the chance of survival without the aid of your ranger or guide is close to zero. Most precautions in the bush are actually linked to common sense, but it's easy, when staying in sophisticated lodges and camps, to forget that you're in the middle of a different world—one where the beasts still rule. Unless you've been given an absolute thumbs up, do not swim in dams, lakes, or rivers. Hippos may be grass eaters, but they're Africa's biggest killers (after mosquitoes) and are known to snap humans in half with their powerful jaws. In 2007, one of Kenya's top professional guides was taken by a crocodile when he stupidly decided to take a dip in a river. And just because you feel safe and cosseted in your safari vehicle, don't think the animals aren't sensitive enough to know if they're being teased, taunted, or cajoled. A Range Rover is no match for an angry elephant. Always treat any and all wildlife with respect, and encourage your driver to keep a safe, respectful distance when viewing and tracking animals.

has to be trucked or flown in, and stock has to be micromanaged to avoid waste, so it's hard to deal with last-minute requests (though it is incredible what the top-end camps are capable of). As a general rule, make sure your operator takes note of your food requirements (and—in the case of the high-end lodges—your drinks preferences, too) at the time of booking.

SHOULD I BRING MY HAIR DRYER? ADAPTOR PLUGS?

Although many lodges don't have a hair dryer in the room, they will have one or two at reception. This is hardly convenient or practical, so if you're dependent on one, bring it. That said, if you want to visit semi-permanent tented camps, leave it in the suitcase, or check first that you are not overloading the system, as they use a lot of power. The power systems that operate at many camps and lodges (notably the eco-friendly ones) will malfunction if you plug in your hairdryer, and there are even a handful of high-end facilities that don't supply power to the tents out of principle. Some camps offer 24-hour solar power, but many are still powered with a generator that is switched off at night. Flashlights and candles are supplied in this case. Every camp or lodge has adaptor plugs, but to save the hassle of going to reception (and, on occasion, being forced to hand over a deposit), bring your own. If having access to power is likely to be a deal breaker when choosing where to stay, be sure to investigate this issue thoroughly.

WILL I HAVE INTERNET & CELLPHONE RECEPTION?

For better or worse, cellphone reception is remarkably good throughout Tanzania's Northern Circuit. With a few exceptions in specific lodges and camps, reception is also very good in much of Kenya's safari territory—although it must be said that the private conservancies in places such as Laikipia and the Masai Mara are far better covered than the national parks; in some of the large parks, such as Tsavo, it's possible to drop out of contact with the outside world completely for a few days (which is not necessarily a bad thing). Internet is available at the big lodges; count on around $10 for 30 minutes. In Kenya, many of the smaller camps and lodges have Wi-Fi (or some access to an Internet facility)—of course, limited electricity may make it difficult to power up your laptop, and there's every chance that the server won't be working (as we experienced all over Kenya in late 2008).

CAN I USE MY CREDIT CARD WHILE ON SAFARI?

Ideally, no. Many places don't take cards; others convert all the charges to U.S. dollars at a very unfavorable exchange rate. Try to prepay for as much as possible and carry cash (U.S. dollars) on you for tipping and small purchases. Traveler's checks are useful for big purchases, but there is often a surcharge for using them, just as there is for using a credit card. If you are not American, change your currency into dollars before arriving in Tanzania or Kenya, and try to grab a handful of the local currency for smaller payments at the airport (using an ATM) when you arrive. A growing trend in Kenya is to quote prices (and accept payment) in euros or British pounds in addition to U.S. dollars; Kenyan shillings (Ksh) are also widely quoted.

Throughout this book, our accommodation reviews carry credit card information; we've listed those cards that can be accepted for payment on-site. For the most part, when it comes to booking a safari, you'll have paid for your accommodations and safari package well in advance (operators won't secure your reservation until payment is received). Most places will have a minimum amount for credit card payments, but unless we've listed them as a "no credit cards" operation, you should be able to pay for extras (drinks, additional specialist activities, balloon rides) using a card.

HOW IMPORTANT IS THE LODGING ON SAFARI?

With no nightlife, restaurants, or shopping experiences, and usually no TV, where you stay is very important. If you can afford it, select a private lodge or camp that takes no more than 18 guests—this means you are given very personal service and the peace to absorb your surroundings. Privacy is paramount—units should be set far apart, particularly in tented camps where canvas does nothing to insulate sound. If you don't mind living out of a suitcase, moving from camp to camp is the ideal way to see different environments as well as plentiful game.

SHOULD I OPT FOR A TENTED CAMP OR A LODGE EXPERIENCE?

There are many who say you haven't been on safari until you've heard the roar of a lion through canvas. We strongly recommend that you stay in at least one tented camp, and regular safari-goers will not set foot in a lodge

The Argument for Tented Camps

If the idea of sleeping in a tent leaves you cold (or even claustrophobic), you haven't been on an exclusive safari to East Africa. Journalist Henry Morton Stanley (sent by the *New York Herald* to find Dr. David Livingstone, which he did at Lake Tanganyika in 1871) thought nothing of going on safari with 200 porters to ensure he enjoyed all the comforts he was accustomed to. Today's safaris tend to have fewer staff, but the comforts are still great.

The classic East African safari tent is a great deal more spacious than the kind of tent you'll come across at your average campsite—big enough to comfortably stand up in, with adequate space to move around your king-size bed; some are even furnished with comfortable chairs and a writing desk. There's almost always a separate dressing area behind the bedroom, which, in turn, leads through to the bathroom—the walk-in shower privately cordoned off and often open to the stars, the wash basin (often two) dropped in a marble or timber vanity, and a separate toilet.

Plumbing varies from camp to camp, but permanent camps always have flushing toilets. Mobile camps vary between flushing (usually chemical) and a short-drop, but are always comfortably outfitted. Bucket showers are provided as and when you wish; staff discreetly hook up a plastic "geyser"—20 to 40 liters (5–10 gallons) of hot water heated in a bucket over a fire. Imbued with the subtle smell of wood smoke, the traditional safari shower is one of our favorite experiences. Plumbed showers in the bush are somehow less successful, perhaps because you expect more: Water pressure is usually not high, and it can often take up to 10 minutes for water to heat properly (sometimes not at all). Basins are always provided, with jugs of cold and hot water in mobile camps; taps are plumbed in permanent camps.

or any concrete structure in the wilds. If you're edgy about sleeping in a tent, be assured, this is camping, but not as you know it. There are also an increasing number of small lodges that, in their design, eschew traditional distinctions between different kinds of building material. So a cottage may have part-stone, part-canvas walls—or, in some sections, no walls at all. And it's long been typical of high-end safari tents to come with attached stone-walled bathrooms.

WHAT ABOUT TIPPING?

Bring plenty of low-denomination dollars for tipping at each camp or lodge; the best camps have a communal box so that tips are shared equitably between front- and back-of-house (or tent) staff. Specialized services such as a private butler or your driver/guide are usually tipped at $10 a day per person. You may, of course, tip more, or not at all, depending on service rendered.

WHAT SHOULD I WEAR?

Loose cotton clothing tends to be the most comfortable and protects your limbs from mosquitoes. If you intend to walk, you'll need long pants to protect you from prickly vegetation and ticks, as well as comfortable hiking boots, but given that walking in the national parks is usually not allowed, keep your feet cool and pack sandals for the game drives. A warm sweater and pants are essential if you're going to visit the escarpment

Electricity is best when it's 100% solar generated; many camps, however, still rely on oil-fueled generators, which are buried and located far away. Although there is no noise pollution, the generator still has to be switched off, usually between 11pm and 6am.

Furnishings are always practical and often luxurious, with the best tents romantically lit with solar-powered lamps that wouldn't look out of place in a five-star hotel. Most tents have shaded verandas, furnished with comfortable chairs or daybeds from which to enjoy the view. What they often don't have is adequate hanging space, and not all tents have luggage racks.

Aside from this minor irritation, the East African tent is—within reason—a wonderfully luxurious experience, and while not to everyone's taste (the designer John Galliano famously erupted from his tent in Amboseli, shouting "Who invented this, this 'thing' called canvas?!"), the thrill of having nothing but canvas between you and the wilderness is unbeatable. If you're lucky enough to have the wildebeest move past, you will be serenaded by a symphony of snorts and calls, one of the most harmonious and beautiful "languages" in nature; if you're near a koppie, rock hyraxes will use your canvas roof as a slide, a baboon may opt to take a rest on your veranda, or you may be woken by the "scrunch, scrunch" of tearing grass and exit to startle a grazing zebra. And when the night is rent by the roar of a lion, you will curl as close to your partner as you did on your wedding night, no matter that the lion is probably miles away, or that no one has ever been attacked in a zipped tent. It's simply the best of Africa—wild and untamed—experienced under 400-thread-count linen.

areas (such as Ngorongoro), and you'll need cold-resistant clothing for places such Mount Kenya and something to keep you dry should the heavens decide to open during the rainy season (and they will).

WHAT ELSE SHOULD I PACK?

Pack light, particularly if you are taking a charter plane, which currently allows only one soft-sided bag per person weighing a maximum 15kg (33 lbs.)—they're not as strict as in, say, Botswana and often don't even bother weighing the bags, but if they do you may be forced to leave something you value behind. Bear in mind that game packages include free laundry, so packing light shouldn't be a problem. A fitted broad-brimmed hat, swimwear, good sunglasses, and sunscreen are essential. Though some lodges supply insect repellent, pack your own, as well as every other malaria precaution. If you take any special medication or prescription drugs, bring them along with you, as you're unlikely to find exact matches, even in the city pharmacies. Dust can affect the durability of contact lenses, so bring a pair of glasses as a backup, as well as sufficient cleaning solution for your lenses. And, of course, don't forget binoculars and a camera (and, if you're not using digital, plenty of film.) A fly swatter, kept in your vehicle, is useful for dealing with the tsetse flies.

3

Planning Your Trip to Kenya & Tanzania

Plenty of amazing wildlife destinations exist on the continent, but few can combine endless plains studded with umbrella-shape acacia trees and herds so vast they appear as ants; dormant volcanoes carpeted with dense, lush jungle; clouds of butterflies and gemlike birds that flit in their wake; salt-lined soda lakes that tinge the feathers of flamingoes that feed and breed there a deep pink; rivers in which huge pods of hippo wallow, indifferent to the baleful glare of crocodiles on their banks—all lapped by an ocean that hides a treasure trove of color just beneath the surface. This is East Africa's promise, and Kenya has the oldest, best-developed tourism infrastructure in it.

Aside from the huge number of professional tourism operators, best browsed on www.katokenya.org or www.tatotz.org, which list operators according to the activities they specialize in and provide annual turnovers to indicates their size and success (though not necessarily the quality), Kenya also has a huge choice of accommodations catering to varied budgets. Relative to Tanzania, however, parks such as the Masai Mara can feel pretty crowded, so if you're looking for a more exclusive experience, you'd do well to focus your time in the lesser-known and relatively underutilized Kenyan reserves or splash out on a semi-permanent camp in the Masai Mara's southern neighbor, the borderless Serengeti, in Tanzania.

Tanzania contains some of the world's greatest natural wonders, but due to a socialist government that more or less shunned contact with the outside world, much of it remained relatively inaccessible until the 1980s, when major reforms to its foreign tourism policies were finally implemented. Since then, Tanzania has played an impressive game of catch-up with Kenya, though it has consciously pursued a low-density, high-quality tourism policy, making it a far more exclusive (and pricey) destination than its northern neighbor. This means that Tanzania, with the exception of Zanzibar and the coast, is not a budget destination, and from park fees to lodgings, you'll need to prepare yourself for a relatively hefty price tag. It's also worth being forewarned that unless you are traveling at the very top end of the market (which companies such as &Beyond and Singita typify), the facilities, infrastructure, and service levels seldom measure up to the rates charged (then again, the untouched beauty of Tanzania's landscapes, the most awe-inspiring on the continent, more than make up for this).

The most popular safari destinations in Tanzania are located in the north, on what is commonly referred to as the Northern Circuit. From Arusha, the country's "safari capital" and a short hop by plane or bus from Nairobi, the famous parks of Kilimanjaro, Ngorongoro, and Serengeti beckon, and there are numerous operators who cater to the ever-increasing number of visitors keen to explore this spectacular region. Regular visitors to Tanzania shun this well-trod circuit for the wilder Southern Circuit, which is best reached from Dar es Salaam, though there are also direct air connections from Arusha. Certainly, the first-time visitor will—and should—make a beeline for the Northern Circuit, but time and budget allowing, a sojourn in the south is recommended as an add-on or as an alternative on a repeat visit. Active travelers may choose to conquer

Kilimanjaro, the tallest mountain in Africa but one of the most accessible ascents in the world. Depending on the route, you'll need to allow 5 to 7 days for this.

Having spent 3 to 5 days on safari, most visitors head for some downtime on the beach. Aside from an undulating coastline of white sands, lined with family-friendly resorts, Kenya offers the little-known Lamu archipelago, a stunning string of isles with chic lodgings that global island-hoppers in the know have tried in vain to keep a secret. Alternatively, there's Zanzibar and Pemba off the coast of Tanzania (see chapter 13), both relatively easy to access from Kenya and offering a greater variety of lodgings than the Kenyan coast. Zanzibar, the largest and most atmospheric, is understandably the most popular, with a plethora of accommodations options as a result, but if you're looking for a castaway fantasy come true, head for little-known Mafia Island, which offers some of the best snorkeling and diving sites on the African coast.

The main potential obstacle to your trip is getting around on a budget, as the infrastructure is not designed to make completely independent travel a viable option for vacationers. If you have relatively unlimited time—assuming you're up for a serious adventure—it's possible to piece together a holiday without the aid of a ground operator and use local transport between destinations, but you are likely to miss out on the real safari experience, surely the main reason to travel here. Self-drive holidays are also not recommended, except for the hardiest adventurers (roads are rough, routes are unpredictable and often poorly marked, and local drivers can be quite dangerous). Even with a driver, you'll have to endure long, dusty, and bumpy rides in Land Rovers, which is why travelers with limited time prefer to fly between destinations. Kenyan and Tanzanian parks are well connected by light aircraft companies, which link the parks and reserves, as well as the coast and cities, on daily scheduled flights; although these can be pricey, they are well worth budgeting for, as you save so much time (and the views from the air can be pretty spectacular). You'll need to weigh costs and plan accordingly, but it's crucial to have your holiday properly mapped and booked in advance of your arrival.

The sensible way of organizing a hassle-free holiday is to arrange everything through a reputable, reliable operator. Aside from the peace of mind this brings, the advantage of such thorough planning is that your operator will be able to tell you the entire cost of your trip in advance. The best international agents have direct relationships with ground operators; some foreign agents travel here regularly to familiarize themselves with the destination (www.africatravelresource.com and www.expertafrica.com are good examples), but many rely completely on their local operator, and you can save a lot money dealing direct with a local operator. Note, however, that many operators, foreign and local, tend to stick with lodgings where they have negotiated the best commissions; when it comes to accommodations, the independent advice you receive in this book will prove invaluable, and you should use these to set your own lodging itinerary.

The only other major considerations will be getting yourself immunized against tropical diseases and taking malaria prophylactics. If you are traveling via a country where yellow fever is present, you will need to produce a certificate proving that you have been inoculated or have it done at the border ($50); this is the only legal requirement, but there are a few other inoculations we recommend, discussed below.

Finally, it's worth noting that, for some, Africa requires some amount of emotional preparation; even if you spend the majority of your time in luxurious safari camps, you will encounter human poverty, as well as ways of life that you might never have imagined still exist. Prepare to have your reality turned on its head—for many, Africa represents an unforgettable shift of consciousness.

For additional help in planning your trip and for more on-the-ground resources in Kenya and Tanzania, please turn to "Fast Facts," on p. 484.

1 WHEN TO GO

Sitting on the equator, Kenya and Tanzania enjoy temperate climates and are pretty much year-round destinations; as you'll notice from the charts below, there is remarkably little fluctuation in monthly temperatures. However, temperatures on the rim of the Tanzania's Ngorongoro Crater drop dramatically at night, particularly June to August, so pack a warm layer or two. Temperatures drop below freezing on Mount Kilimanjaro (and Mount Meru at certain times), where there is permanent snow on the highest peaks. To keep an eye on local weather patterns, visit www.africanweather.net.

Seasonal fluctuations mostly relate to rainfall, which—in game-viewing regions—can have a dramatic impact on animal populations and accessibility, and consequently also on accommodations prices. Generally there are two seasons, dry and rainy. The best months for game viewing are generally the dry seasons, which are January to March and June to September. At these times, vegetation is light and there is no surface water created by the rains that disperse the animals, and instead they congregate around the remaining rivers and waterholes. Drier weather also means less hassle by mosquitoes. Many safari lodges and camps will close during the "long rains" in April and May—considered low season—and this is when you'll score the best deals on lodging and are least likely to feel besieged by other travelers. However, getting around at this time (as well as in Oct and Nov, during the so-called "short rains") can be difficult, as dirt roads turn to mud, and many become impassable.

Top season to visit Kenya's Masai Mara and Tanzania's Serengeti is during the Migration, which starts as early as July and can continue through November (though Aug–Oct are the most productive months); however, this period is generally marred by popularity, as visitor numbers soar and the best viewing areas are mobbed by *homo sapiens.* Note also that the Migration continues year-round, with most of the movement happening in Tanzania's Serengeti, so you can plan to incorporate the Migration pretty much any time of the year, as long as you're flexible about where to go. Toward the end of May, when the rains abate, the Migration moves north and/or into the western corridor, and the river crossings usually happen in July. Between August and October, the herds are at the Mara River (in the far northern Serengeti), and over these months they cross backward and forward, in and out of Kenya, drawn by localized rain showers. In November, when the rain clouds usually gather to green the south, they again cross the Mara, passing through the eastern Serengeti to return to the short-grass plains of the southern Serengeti in December.

Bird-watchers will want to visit in the winter months from October to April, when many birds migrate to East Africa from Europe.

Calving season usually occurs January to March in Tanzania's southern plains. This is an incredible time to be in the Serengeti, with thousands of calves being born every day, and—thanks to the short-grass plains—the riveting predator action in clear view.

Kenya and Tanzania's coasts and Zanzibar can be visited at any time of year, although again the rainy seasons may hamper beach time. They enjoy a tropical climate with average daytime temperatures of 30°C (86°F) and long hours of sunshine, making them a perfect destination for a beach vacation. During the day the humidity is tamed by sea breezes, but it can feel sultry at night. High season on the Kenyan and Tanzanian coasts is November to February, when it's a popular winter sun destination from the Northern Hemisphere.

Average Monthly High/Low Temperatures & Rainfall

Dar es Salaam	Jan	Feb	Mar	Apr	May	June	July	Aug	Sept	Oct	Nov	Dec
Temp. (°F)	77/54	79/55	77/57	77/57	72/55	72/54	70/61	70/61	75/61	77/55	75/55	75/55
Temp. (°C)	25/15	26/13	25/14	24/24	22/13	21/12	21/11	21/11	24/11	24/13	23/13	23/13
Rainfall (in.)	1.5	1.3	4.9	8.2	6.2	1.7	0.5	0.9	3.5	2.1	4.3	3.5
Zanzibar	**Jan**	**Feb**	**Mar**	**Apr**	**May**	**June**	**July**	**Aug**	**Sept**	**Oct**	**Nov**	**Dec**
Temp. (°F)	90/75	90/75	90/73	88/73	86/72	84/68	84/64	84/64	86/66	88/68	88/72	90/73
Temp. (°C)	32/24	32/24	32/23	31/23	30/22	29/20	29/18	29/18	30/19	31/20	31/22	32/23
Rainfall (in.)	2.1	2.1	4.5	7	5.2	1.4	1.1	0.9	0.5	2.0	3	3.1
Nairobi	**Jan**	**Feb**	**Mar**	**Apr**	**May**	**June**	**July**	**Aug**	**Sept**	**Oct**	**Nov**	**Dec**
Temp. (°F)	77/54	79/55	77/57	77/57	72/55	72/54	70/61	70/61	75/61	77/55	75/55	75/55
Temp. (°C)	25/12	26/13	25/14	24/14	22/13	21/12	21/11	21/11	24/11	24/13	23/13	23/13
Rainfall (in.)	1.5	1.3	4.9	8.2	6.2	1.7	0.5	0.9	3.5	2.1	4.3	3.5
Laikipia (Nanyuki)	**Jan**	**Feb**	**Mar**	**Apr**	**May**	**June**	**July**	**Aug**	**Sept**	**Oct**	**Nov**	**De**
Temp. (°F)	61/45	63/47	63/49	62/51	61/50	61/48	59/47	60/47	61/46	61/47	61/49	60/47
Temp. (°C)	25/7	26/8	25/9	23/10	22/10	23/8	22/8	22/8	24/7	23/8	22/9	23/8
Rainfall (in.)	0.5	0.9	1.8	4.7	3.2	2.0	2.7	2.6	1.9	2.5	3.4	1.5
Lake Victoria (Kisumu)	**Jan**	**Feb**	**Mar**	**Apr**	**May**	**June**	**July**	**Aug**	**Sept**	**Oct**	**Nov**	**Dec**
Temp. (°F)	85/66	85/67	85/67	82/67	81/66	80/64	81/63	82/64	83/64	84/66	83/66	84/66
Temp. (°C)	29/18	29/19	29/19	27/19	27/18	26/17	27/17	27/17	28/17	28/18	28/18	28/18
Rainfall (in.)	1.9	3.2	5.5	7.5	6.1	3.3	2.3	3.0	2.5	2.2	3.4	4.0
Southern Kenya (Voi)	**Jan**	**Feb**	**Mar**	**Apr**	**May**	**June**	**July**	**Aug**	**Sept**	**Oct**	**Nov**	**Dec**
Temp. (°F)	90/69	92/69	91/70	88/70	85/68	83/65	82/63	82/63	84/63	88/66	88/68	88/69
Temp. (°C)	32/20	33/20	32/21	31/21	29/20	28/18	27/17	27/17	28/17	31/18	31/20	31/20
Rainfall (in.)	1.3	1.2	3.0	3.8	1.3	0.3	0.1	0.3	0.5	0.9	3.8	5.1
Nakuru	**Jan**	**Feb**	**Mar**	**Apr**	**May**	**June**	**July**	**Aug**	**Sept**	**Oct**	**Nov**	**Dec**
Temp. (°F)	38/46	69/47	69/47	67/48	65/48	63/47	60/47	61/46	64/46	66/46	65/47	65/46
Temp. (°C)	20/7	20/8	20/8	19/8	18/8	17/8	15/8	16/7	17/7	18/7	18/8	18/7
Rainfall (in.)	0.9	1.1	2.6	7.1	5.7	5.0	6.3	7.6	4.3	2.1	2.2	1.9
Mombasa	**Jan**	**Feb**	**Mar**	**Apr**	**May**	**June**	**July**	**Aug**	**Sept**	**Oct**	**Nov**	**Dec**
Temp. (°F)	89/75	89/75	89/75	86/74	82/73	82/73	81/72	81/72	81/72	84/73	86/75	86/75
Temp. (°C)	31/24	31/24	31/25	30/24	28/23	28/23	27/22	27/22	28/22	29/23	29/24	30/24
Rainfall (in.)	1.0	0.7	2.5	7.7	12.6	4.7	3.5	2.5	2.5	3.5	3.8	2.4
Northern Frontier District (Lodwar)	**Jan**	**Feb**	**Mar**	**Apr**	**May**	**June**	**July**	**Aug**	**Sept**	**Oct**	**Nov**	**Dec**
Temp. (°F)	94/77	96/78	96/80	93/80	93/80	91/79	90/78	91/78	94/79	95/80	93/78	93/77
Temp. (°C)	34/25	35/25	35/26	33/26	33/26	32/26	32/25	32/25	34/26	35/26	33/25	33/25
Rainfall (in.)	0.3	0.3	0.9	1.9	1.1	0.3	0.7	0.4	0.2	0.3	0.7	0.5

CALENDAR OF EVENTS

For an exhaustive list of events beyond those listed here, check http://events.frommers.com, where you'll find a searchable, up-to-the-minute roster of what's happening in cities all over the world. For public holidays, see p. 484 and 488.

Maulidi Festival, third month of the Muslim calendar, Lamu (http://lamuheritage.org/Maulidi.htm). Maulidi, or Milad-un-Nabii, is the Islamic celebration of the birth of Prophet Muhammad. It is celebrated throughout the world, but Lamu's 4-day Maulidi Festival combines traditional prayer with popular entertainment such as swimming; donkey and dhow races; a henna body-painting competition; tug-of war; football matches; a traditional board game, *bao,* contest; and performances of Swahili music and dance. The event attracts up to 20,000 people, and the narrow alleyways are transformed with twinkling lights and brightly colored banners, while the dhows on the waterfront are decorated with flags.

January to April

Sauti za Busara, February, Stone Town (www.busaramusic.com). *Sauti za Busara* means "songs of wisdom" in Kiswahili, and this annual festival of Swahili music attracts the best musicians and performers from all over East Africa, as well as visiting groups from West Africa. Most performances and workshops are held in Stone Town's Old Fort and Beit el Ajaib (House of Wonders) over 4 days, and there's a final night's party with DJs on the beach at Kendwa on the north coast. Music is varied, from traditional *taarab* (which combines African percussion and Arabic rhythms, and uses large numbers of musicians and Arabian instruments) to *bongo flava,* a local take on hip-hop and R&B.

May & June

Rhino Charge, May or June, Laikipia Plateau (www.rhinoark.org). This is an annual four-wheel off-road endurance car event organized by the charity Rhino Ark Trust, dedicated to protecting Kenya's rhinos. In recent years, they have funded the ongoing project to fence the Aberdare National Park, to protect it from poaching. The course goes cross-country for more than 200km (124 miles), and it's a grueling race through rugged terrain of dense bush, ditches, and boulders. The winner of the event is the team that manages to complete the course with the least distance recorded.

Lewa Marathon, June, Lewa Wildlife Conservancy, Laikipia Plateau (www.lewa.org). The Safaricom Marathon and Half-Marathon was established in 1999 by Tusk Trust, a London-based charity dedicated to preserving wildlife in its natural habitat, and runners are asked to pledge a donation to take part. It's run on dirt roads within the Lewa Wildlife Conservancy and is the only marathon in the world to go through a game park. Lewa is home to black and white rhinos, elephants, a variety of plains animals, and big cats. The runners are escorted by helicopters and armed rangers, to avoid any confrontations with the four-legged residents—it's a very exciting race. It's hugely popular with Kenyans, who are known as world-class runners, and recently it's attracted more international participants.

Zanzibar International Film Festival of the Dhow Countries, July, Stone Town. This festival celebrates and promotes the unique culture that grew as a result of the ancient trade route around the Indian Ocean and the dhow, which for centuries crossed Africa, Arabia, and

Asia on the monsoon winds. All nations around the Indian Ocean participate in the festival, and films are judged, critiqued, and shown in venues along Stone Town's waterfront. Additionally, there are contemporary artists, musicians, cultural troupes, and photo exhibitions, and an arts-related program to creatively empower women and children.

August to October

International Camel Derby, August or September, Maralal (www.yaresafaris.co.ke). This annual camel-racing event is held over a weekend around the small town of Maralal in Northern Kenya. There's a short amateur race, when camels and riders are assisted by a handler who runs alongside. Anyone can compete in this, camels are available for hire, and for complete amateurs, it's very amusing as they try to persuade their reluctant charges to even move forward, never mind cross the finish line. Then there's the more serious 42km (26-mile) professional race that circles the town, when local riders don colorful traditional dress.

Africa Concours D'Elegance, September, Nairobi Racecourse (www.concourskenya.com). This is the equivalent of a beauty contest in the classic car world and a competition for quality for restored cars and motorbikes. There's plenty of other entertainment, too, and the day ends with a drive-by of the vehicles.

2 ENTRY REQUIREMENTS

PASSPORTS

Your passport must be valid for at least 6 months from date of entry to Kenya or Tanzania and with sufficient blank pages for any visa stamps. If your passport does not meet the requirements, you must renew your passport or obtain a new one prior to obtaining the visa.

VISAS

Most visitors can purchase a visa from the airport or land border immigration desk upon entry. Alternatively, you can get a visa from an embassy or high commission overseas (p. 486), but it's easier to get one on arrival. Visas are valid for 3 months from the time of entry and cost $50 (U.S. and Irish citizens pay $100). If you are only transiting through Kenya, say, from a safari in Tanzania or Uganda to the airport in Nairobi, a transit visa valid for 7 days is $20. Visas are paid for in cash (in dollars, British pounds, or euros). In theory, there is a similar transit visa available in Tanzania, though this is not always enforced.

Kenya, Tanzania, and Uganda have an agreement that you can cross into each and back again without purchasing a new visa, as long as each visa is within its 3-month validity. For example, you can go from Kenya to Uganda, to see the mountain gorillas, and return to Kenya on the visa you acquired on first entry to the country.

Up-to-date requirements can be found at Kenya's **Ministry of Home Affairs** website (www.homeaffairs.go.ke) and Tanzania's **Ministry of Home Affairs** website (www.moha.go.tz).

CUSTOMS

What You Can Bring into Kenya

Every visitor aged 18 and older may bring 200 cigarettes, 50 cigars, or no more than 250g of tobacco, and 1 liter of liquor (or 2 liters of wine) into Kenya, duty-free. Additionally, everyone entering the country is entitled to bring up to Ksh5,000 worth of gifts and souvenirs and 500 milliliters of perfume. The import of fruit, plants and seeds, and imitation firearms is prohibited. For more information, visit www.revenue.go.ke.

What You Can Bring into Tanzania

The import and export of firearms, narcotics, and pornography is illegal. The government has the right to charge duties on items brought in intended for resale, but personal items such as jewelry, laptops, and cameras can be brought in duty-free. There are no restrictions on the import or export of foreign currency, but as the Tanzanian shilling (Tsh) is not a hard currency, it cannot be taken in and out of the country. Every visitor aged 18 and older may bring 200 cigarettes, 50 cigars, or no more than 250g of tobacco, and 1 liter of liquor (or 2L of wine) into Tanzania, duty-free.

What You Can Take Home from Kenya & Tanzania

The export of gold, diamonds, or game trophies not obtained from the authorized government departments is prohibited. It is illegal to export elephant ivory, wildlife skins, and sea turtle products.

For information on what you're allowed to bring home, contact one of the following agencies:

U.S. Citizens: U.S. Customs & Border Protection (CBP), 1300 Pennsylvania Ave., NW, Washington, DC 20229 (✆ **877/287-8667;** www.cbp.gov).

Canadian Citizens: Canada Border Services Agency (✆ **800/461-9999** in Canada, or 204/983-3500; www.cbsa-asfc.gc.ca).

U.K. Citizens: HM Customs & Excise, at ✆ **0845/010-9000** (from outside the U.K., 020/8929-0152), or consult their website at **www.hmce.gov.uk**.

Australian Citizens: Australian Customs Service, at ✆ **1300/363-263,** or log on to **www.customs.gov.au**.

New Zealand Citizens: New Zealand Customs, The Customhouse, 17–21 Whitmore St., Box 2218, Wellington (✆ **0800/428-786** or 04/473-6099; **www.customs.govt.nz**).

MEDICAL REQUIREMENTS

Consult your physician ahead of any trip to Africa. The Centers for Disease Control and Prevention (CDC; www.cdc.gov/travel) has details of required and recommended immunizations for international travelers as compiled by the World Health Organization. The CDC also regularly updates its website with news of outbreaks that affect specific areas and destinations; it's worth checking out their travel advisory and following up by consulting your doctor. You will certainly need to take some prophylaxis against **malaria,** and there are other immunizations that are highly recommended.

Both Kenya and Tanzania are endemic for contracting **yellow fever,** so it is essential you have a yellow fever vaccination; you may be denied entry without one. We also highly recommend immunizing yourself against **typhoid, hepatitis A and B, meningitis, rabies,** and—if you're going to be in East Africa for an extended period—**cholera.** Booster shots, although not mandatory, are suggested for **tetanus-diphtheria, measles-mumps-rubella, polio,** and **varicella.**

Certain immunizations must be administered over a period of time, while others cannot be given at the same time. Consult your doctor at least 4 to 6 weeks prior to your trip, especially since some vaccines require time to take effect. Vaccinations should be recorded and stamped in a yellow international immunization card, which you will be given when your first shots are administered; take this with you whenever you go for booster shots or new immunizations.

If you use any prescription drugs (and, for that matter, contact lenses), be sure to take adequate supplies with you. Also take the original prescription along, as brand names of drugs may be different in drugstores. When it comes to medical needs, do not leave anything to chance, and if you have any specific conditions, consult your physician well ahead of your scheduled departure.

Note: Anyone who has recently undergone surgery (up to 18 months prior to traveling in Africa) should consult their doctor or surgeon to discuss the need for antibacterial drugs to stave off any risk of infection.

3 GETTING THERE & GETTING AROUND

GETTING TO KENYA

By Plane

Nairobi's Jomo Kenyatta International Airport (NBO) is the main point of arrival for most visitors; Mombasa's Moi International Airport (MBA), on the coast, also sees some international arrivals, although this is generally restricted to package tour groups on charter flights from Europe aiming for a beach vacation. Both airports have banks with ATMs and exchange facilities, car-hire desks, duty-free shops, and restaurants. For more information about the airports, visit www.kenyaairports.com. Nairobi is East Africa's air travel hub and is served by several international airlines. It's also served by just about all of the African airlines and so is a good destination to move on to other countries in Africa. For information about airlines with routes to Kenya, see "Airline, Hotel & Car Rental Websites," p. 489.

By Road

Kenya's busiest border crossing is with Tanzania at Namanga. Arusha (p. 384) is the nearest large town on the Tanzanian side and is the springboard for the Northern Circuit parks (chapter 15). It is 270km (167 miles) south of Nairobi. Moshi is 80km (50 miles) to the east of Arusha and is the base for climbing Mount Kilimanjaro (chapter 16). Regular daily shuttle buses run between Arusha and Moshi and Nairobi, which take 6 or 8 hours via the Namanga border crossing; drivers assist passengers with border formalities. Timetables and prices can be found on the following websites: **AA Shuttles** (www.aashuttles.com), **Impala Shuttles** (www.impalashuttle.com), and **Riverside Shuttles** (www.riverside-shuttle.com).

There are other border crossings with Tanzania at Taveta near Voi (p. 384), which is served by local buses. Lunga Lunga, south of Mombasa, and Isebania, on the Lake Victoria side of the country, are served by cross-border buses that link Nairobi with cities in Tanzania. The best bus company to use these routes is the Tanzanian company **Scandinavian Express** (www.scandinaviagroup.com).

Kenya has two border crossings with Uganda at Malaba and Busia, and there are regular cross-border bus services between Kampala and Nairobi. Kenya has one border crossing with Ethiopia at Moyale in the extreme north of the country, but there is no public transport.

If you are crossing any of these borders in your own vehicle, you must have vehicle registration and a Carnet de Passage issued from your own country, and will need to take out third-party insurance at the border.

By Boat

Though cruise ships do dock in Mombasa Harbor, there are no other passenger ferry services to Kenya. Except for short excursions for snorkeling or sightseeing, it is illegal for foreigners to travel by dhow along the East African coast.

Tips Coping with Jet Lag

Jet lag is a pitfall of traveling across time zones. If you're flying north–south and you feel sluggish when you touch down, your symptoms will be the result of dehydration and the general stress of air travel. When you travel east–west or vice-versa, your body becomes confused about what time it is, and everything from your digestive system to your brain is knocked for a loop. Traveling east is more difficult on your internal clock than traveling west because most peoples' bodies are more inclined to stay up late than to fall asleep early.

Here are some tips for combating jet lag:

- **Reset your watch** to your destination time before you board the plane.
- **Drink lots of water** before, during, and after your flight. Avoid alcohol.
- **Exercise and sleep well** for a few days before your trip.
- If you have trouble sleeping on planes, **fly eastward on morning flights.**
- **Daylight** is the key to resetting your body clock. At the website for **Outside In** (www.bodyclock.com), you can get a customized plan of when to seek and avoid light.

GETTING TO TANZANIA

By Plane

Dar es Salaam's Julius Nyerere International Airport (JNIA), ideal for accessing the Southern Circuit or Mafia Island, is served by a number of airlines, some of which also touch down at Kilimanjaro International Airport (KIA), which is the preferred airport for the Northern Circuit. Zanzibar International Airport (ZIA) has flights linking the regional airports and is a popular destination for charter flights for visitors from Europe on package holidays. All Tanzanian airports have banks with ATMs and exchange facilities, car-hire desks, duty-free shops, and restaurants. For those visiting only the national parks in Tanzania's Northern Circuit; another option is to fly to Nairobi (p. 70), though you'll need a yellow fever vaccination certificate and visas for both countries. Shuttle bus services operate between Nairobi and Arusha, the closest town to the parks (p. 446).

For information about airlines with routes to Tanzania, see "Airline, Hotel & Car Rental Websites," p. 489.

By Road

Tanzania's busiest border crossing is with Kenya at Namanga. (www.riversideshuttle.com). See "Getting There By Road," above, for information about accessing Arusha and Moshi and requirements for crossing the border in your own vehicle.

By Boat

There are no passenger ferry services to Tanzania. Except for short excursions for snorkeling or sightseeing from Zanzibar and the coast, it is illegal for foreigners to travel by dhow in East Africa. However, there are ferry services from mainland Tanzania to Zanzibar and Pemba (p. 341) and on Lake Victoria.

GETTING AROUND KENYA

If you are visiting a number of parks and reserves in Kenya, the option is to either drive or fly between them. Roads in most of the wilderness areas are extremely rough and difficult, and self-drive is, in our opinion, not recommended (unless you have good off-road experience and are a talented and adventurous map reader). Instead, consider joining an organized safari and then decide whether you will fly or be driven between destinations, considering your budget and amount of time you have.

Elsewhere, all the towns in Kenya are linked by a steady stream of buses and *matatus* (minibuses), and in the cities there is public transport in the way of buses, *matatus,* taxis, and, in some places, bicycle or *tuk-tuk* taxis.

By Plane

If you can afford it, getting around Kenya by plane is the quickest and most comfortable option. There are a few domestic airlines to choose from that link the most popular safari destinations and provide services to the coast. Some of the more up-market safari lodges have their own airstrips and use small planes operated by private air charter companies to ferry their guests in from Nairobi or Mombasa. In Nairobi, flights go from Jomo Kenyatta International Airport (p. 71), and some operators fly from Wilson Airport, 6.4km (4 miles) from the city center off the Langata Road. **Kenya Airways** (© **020/327-4747;** www.kenya-airways.com) provides regular services between Nairobi, Mombasa, Malindi, and Lamu on the coast, and Kisumu in Western Kenya. They also operate a useful service between Nairobi and Zanzibar in Tanzania. **AirKenya** (© **020/606-539;** www.airkenya.com) flies from Nairobi's Wilson Airport and links the more popular safari destinations. They fly to several airstrips in the Masai Mara, as well as Amboseli and Samburu, and Lewa, Nanyuki, and Meru; the latter three offer access to the game ranches on the Laikipia Plateau. They also fly from Nairobi to Lamu, Malindi, and Mombasa on the coast. Additionally, as they code share with Tanzania's **Regional Air,** they offer flights from Nairobi to Kilimanjaro, Dar es Salam, and Zanzibar. **Mombasa Air Safari** (© **0734/400400,** 0734/500500, 0722/791509, or 0722/202559; www.mombasaairsafari.com), based on the coast, links the coastal resorts and Amboseli and the Masai Mara. **Safarilink** (© **020/600-777;** www.safarilink-kenya.com), also based at Wilson Airport, links the parks and, from Nairobi, touches down in the Masai Mara, Amboseli, Tsavo, Lewa Downs (for the Laikipia Plateau), Samburu, and Lamu on the coast. **Fly 540** (© **020/827-521;** www.fly540.com) is Kenya's newest "no frills" airline and flies from Nairobi to Eldoret, Kitale, Kisumu, Lamu, Malindi, Mombasa, and the lodges in the Masai Mara, as well as to Kilimanjaro and Zanzibar in Tanzania and Entebbe in Uganda.

If you're headed for less-visited parks, or simply prefer to set your own schedule, the best charter airline is **Boskovic Air Charters** (© **020/602-026;** www.boskovicaircharters.com), although some lodges and safari operators may have their own preferred charter company. It's expensive to charter a plane and probably worthwhile only if you can fill the entire plane with your family or friends.

On some flights using small planes, luggage is restricted to 15kg (33 lbs.) per person, but you can leave excess luggage at hotels in Nairobi for a small fee. Don't schedule any domestic flights too close to your international departure from Kenya, in the event internal flights are delayed or canceled.

By Car

Unless you are familiar with African driving culture and have great road instinct, profound map-reading skills, and an ability to know the way almost intuitively, our advice is that you avoid driving in Kenya. Many of the roads in rural areas and in the parks and reserves are not tarred, so a four-wheel-drive vehicle is essential, particularly in the wet seasons when these roads often become impassable. Besides the bone-rattling that you'll experience as you careen along potholed roads and over dirt tracks in various states of repair, you need to be wary of Kenyan drivers. Road accidents are frequent, and deaths on the roads occur frequently. Overtaking is extremely hazardous and can make being on the roads quite frightening. During traffic jams (which occur frequently, often thanks to accidents), it is a common habit for drivers to cross the median strip and drive unflinchingly toward oncoming traffic. Buses (including long-distance buses) and *matatus* are frequently involved in (and often the cause of) fatal accidents. *Matatus,* in particular, are a hazard, thanks to speeding and erratic driving.

Vehicular travel outside major cities at night should be avoided—roads are poor, as is street lighting, where it exists at all. Also be aware that, in some areas, the roads are the only place where people have adequate room to walk, and domestic and wild animals are also regularly encountered on the roads. ***Warning:*** Carjackings are a reality in Kenya, so try not to carry valuables around with you, and make yourself aware of what's happening on the roads around you. Do not leave anything in plain sight when leaving a vehicle unattended, as this might tempt would-be thieves. In certain areas, particularly in Northern Kenya, there is a threat of banditry.

If you think you're tough enough to tackle Kenya's largely appalling roads, you can consider the following 4WD vehicle-hire companies. Rates start at $140 per day:

Roving Rovers (www.rovingrovers.com) has a fleet of well-maintained Land Rover Defenders that can be rented for self-drive expeditions. They cost $165 per day (including tax) with unlimited mileage and come fully equipped with camping equipment. There is also the option to hire a driver/cook/guide.

Avis (www.avis.com) is well stocked with vehicles catering to off-road needs, as is **Hertz** (www.hertz.com). **Central Rent-a-Car** (www.carhirekenya.com) is a Nairobi-based firm with a fleet of 4×4s and SUVs.

If you've got the time and the desire to self-drive, we recommend you first spend a few days with one of the instructors at the **Glen Edmunds Performance Driving School** (www.glenedmunds.com) in Nairobi, which offers training in 4WD-driving, high-performance driving, anti-carjacking, and other useful techniques for surviving Kenya's roads.

To hire a car, you must be over 23, and while you don't necessarily need an international driver's license, your license must be in English. Driving is on the left, though on badly potholed roads it is customary to drive all over the road to avoid them. Parking in the towns usually involves paying a parking attendant on the street a small fee, and they will display a ticket on your windshield. Nairobi also has some multistory car parks.

By Train

For decades, the overnight Nairobi-to-Mombasa railway was one of the world's most famous and pleasant rail journeys. However, in the last few years, and thanks to chronic underinvestment, the railway today is close to financial collapse and suffers from frequent breakdowns and derailments, making it lengthy and unsafe. In addition, much of the rolling stock (some of the carriages are 80 years old) needs to be maintained or replaced. Nevertheless, the service is still running, although the 530km (330 mile) overnight trip, which should take 13 hours, often takes a lot longer, and in the extreme, local people have been known to get off the train and take a bus for the rest of their journey. If you are a tolerant traveler and still want to take the train, first class is recommended, which is in two-bed compartments and includes dinner and breakfast in the restaurant car for around $65 per person. Tickets can be bought from Nairobi's and Mombasa's railway stations or booked through local travel agencies. Railways in the rest of the country are restricted to freight.

By Bus

If you're on a budget, buses are the best and cheapest way to travel. Large buses and *matatus* crisscross the country and link the major towns. Longer routes link Nairobi and Mombasa with cities in neighboring Uganda and Tanzania. Some of the vehicles are quite old and can be driven rather recklessly, but recent legislation has curbed overcrowding and ensured that each seat has a seatbelt and that the vehicles are speed governed. The buses are reasonably efficient and comfortable, but exercise caution around the bus stations, as petty theft can be a problem. The best bus company to use on long routes is the Tanzanian company **Scandinavian Express** (www.scandinaviagroup.com).

By Taxi, Tuk-Tuk & Boda-Boda

Regular taxis are found easily on the street and outside hotels. *Tuk-tuks* are three-wheeled vehicles with a back seat that sits three passengers and can be used over short distances in the beach resorts along the coast. *Boda-bodas,* meaning "border-border," as they originated in East Africa's border towns to ferry people across no-man's land, are bicycle taxis with one seat over the back wheel. These are cheap and fun over short distances, but you need to hang on tightly. With all these, prices should be negotiated before setting off.

GETTING AROUND TANZANIA

If you are visiting a number of parks and reserves in Tanzania, you can either drive or fly between them. Roads in most of the wilderness areas are in poor condition and unmarked, and self-driving is not recommended. Operators will supply you with a driver who doubles as an informal guide; alternatively, you can arrange to fly to your destination and utilize a car and driver supplied by the lodgings. Elsewhere in Tanzania, towns and cities are linked by a steady stream of buses and *dala-dalas* (minibuses), and in the cities, there is public transport in the way of buses, *dala-dalas,* taxis, and, in some places, bicycles or *tuk-tuks.*

By Plane

If you can afford it, getting around Tanzania by plane is the quickest and most comfortable option. There are a few domestic airlines that link the most popular safari destinations and provide services to the coast. Some of the more upmarket safari lodges have their own airstrips and use small planes operated by private air charter companies to ferry their guests in, which is a good alternative to long drives on dusty roads. The national airline, **Air Tanzania** (www.airtanzania.com), was grounded in 2008 because of issues over maintenance. Since then, they have resumed some domestic flights between Dar es Salaam, Zanzibar, Kilimanjaro, and Mwanza. However, the airline desperately needs new planes, timetables frequently change, and there can be long delays. In most cases, the private airlines offer much more reliable service, with aircrafts in good shape and excellent pilots. **Precision Air** (© **022/286-0701;** www.precisionairtz.com) links the major cities and towns and flies between Dar es Salaam, Bukoba, Mwanza, Kigoma, Tabora, Lindi, Mtwara, Arusha, Kilimanjaro, Zanzibar, and Seronera and Grumeti in the Serengeti National Park. They also fly to Nairobi. **Coastal Aviation** (© **075/262-7825;** www.coastal.cc) links the upmarket lodges in the game parks and reserves, as well as the islands, flying between Dar es Salaam, Mwanza, Arusha, Selous, Ruaha, Mikumi, Lake Manyara, and to several airstrips in the Serengeti, as well as to Zanzibar, Pemba, and Mafia islands. **Air Excel** (© **027/254-8429;** www.airexcelonline.com) links the parks with the coast and flies between Dar es Salaam, Arusha, several airstrips in the Serengeti, Lake Manyara, Kilimanjaro, and Zanzibar. **Zan Air** (© **024/223-3670;** www.zanair.com) links Arusha and Dar es Salaam with Selous, Zanzibar, Pemba, Mafia, and Mombasa in Kenya. **Regional Air** (© **027/250-2541;** www.regionaltanzania.com) links eight airstrips in the Northern Circuit with Arusha, Dar es Salaam, and Zanzibar.

If you're headed for less-visited parks or simply prefer to set your own schedule, then air charter is the best option. Companies at Dar es Salaam Airport include **Flightlink** (© **022/2137885;** www.flightlinkaircharters.com) **Zantas Air** (© **022/2137181;** www.zantasair.com); and at Kilimanjaro International Airport, **Kilimanjaro Air Safaris** (© **027/275-0523;** www.kiliair.com).

On some flights using small planes, luggage is restricted to 15kg (33 lbs.) per person, but you can leave excess luggage at hotels in Arusha or Dar es Salaam, for example, for a small fee (if you are returning to these destinations). Don't schedule any domestic flights too close to your international departure from Tanzania, in the event internal flights are delayed or canceled.

By Car

Driving in Tanzania can be dangerous because everyone does pretty much as they please, and traffic in Dar es Salaam is especially chaotic. The roads are not always well maintained and frequent potholes are a problem, so keep your speed down and avoid driving at night because of the danger of domestic and wild animals on the road. Many of the roads in rural areas and in the parks and reserves are not tarred, so a four-wheel-drive vehicle is essential, particularly in the wet seasons, when these roads often become impassable. If you're confident that you can hold your own on Tanzanian roads, you can either book a car at your country of origin from one of the large agencies or contact them once you arrive. **Avis** (www.avis.com), **Budget** (www.budget.com), and **Hertz** (www.hertz.com) have several offices in Dar es Salaam and Arusha. A popular way for independent travelers to reach the north or west coasts of Zanzibar from Stone Town is to hire a jeep or motorbike from a travel agent in Stone Town.

To hire a car, you must be over 23, and while you don't necessarily need an international driver's license, your license must be in English. Driving is on the left, though on badly potholed roads it is customary to drive all over the road to avoid them. Parking in the towns usually involves paying a parking attendant on the street a small fee, and they will display a ticket on your windshield. Dar es Salaam also has some multistory car parks.

By Train

There are two railways that cross Tanzania and offer three to four services per week. Clean bedding is provided for cars with sleeping berths, and there are dining cars. However, the rolling stock is very old and dirty, and the trains get very crowded with not only people, but sacks of vegetables and livestock. Thefts are common (stewards even hand you a piece of wood to jam your window so it can't be opened from outside during night stops), and it takes an inordinate amount of time to get around. Traveling by bus is generally safer, quicker, and cheaper. If you insist on traveling by rail, you should opt for first class, always lock your door, and never leave your possessions unguarded.

Tazara (Tanzania-Zambia Railway Authority; © **022/226-2191**) runs from Dar es Salaam through the south of the country and on to Kapiri Mposhi in Zambia. The average journey from Dar es Salaam to Mbeya in the southwest of Tanzania is 23 hours. However, we have heard recently that this company is close to financial collapse and not all the trains have been running, so inquire locally at

Dar es Salaam's railway station. **Tanzania Railway Corporation's Central Line** (✆ **022/211-7833;** www.trctz.com) runs from Dar es Salaam across the middle of the country to Tabora, where it splits into two lines that end in Kigoma on Lake Tanganyika and Mwanza on Lake Victoria. It takes 36 hours to get from Dar es Salaam to Kigoma.

By Bus

If you're on a budget, buses are the best and cheapest way to travel. Large buses and *dala-dala* crisscross the country and link the major towns, and longer routes link Dar es Salaam with Nairobi and Mombasa in Kenya. Some of the vehicles are quite old, can be driven rather recklessly, and can be overcrowded. The most reasonably efficient and comfortable buses are operated by **Scandinavian Express** (www.scandinaviagroup.com). They have modern ticket offices in each of the towns and cities, you can choose your seat onscreen, buses are speed governed, most have air-conditioning, and complimentary drinks and biscuits/cookies are offered onboard. The only other reputable bus company is **Royal Coach** (✆ **022/212-4073** or 075/488-5778), which runs a dedicated route between Dar es Salaam and Arusha. Always exercise caution around the bus stations, as petty theft can be a problem.

By Taxi, Tuk-Tuk & Boda-Boda

Regular taxis are found easily on the street and outside hotels. *Tuk-tuks* can be used over short distances in the beach resorts along the coast. *Boda-bodas* are a cheap and fun way to travel over short distances, but you need to hang on tightly. With all of these, prices should be negotiated before setting off.

4 MONEY & COSTS

The Value of the Kenyan Shilling vs. Other Popular Currencies

Ksh	US$	Can$	UK£	Euro (€)	Aus$	NZ$
1	.01¢	.01C¢	.008p	.009€	.02A¢	.02NZ¢

The Value of the Tanzanian Shilling vs. Other Popular Currencies

Tsh	US$	Can$	UK£	Euro (€)	Aus$	NZ$
1	.0008¢	.0008C¢	.0005p	.0005€	.0008A¢	.001NZ¢

In this book, we list exact prices in the local currency only where it is actually quoted; the vast majority of safari destinations and upmarket resorts and hotels in Kenya and Tanzania quote their prices in dollars (and, in some instances, euros or sterling). Visitors generally pay a higher rate for accommodations and game park entrance fees than East African residents; in such instances, you can always expect to be charged in one of the three major Western currencies. You will always have the option of paying in local currency, but the exchange rate will work against you. The currency conversions quoted above were correct at press time. However, rates fluctuate, so before departing, consult a currency exchange website such as **www.oanda.com/convert/classic** or **www.xe.com** to check up-to-the-minute rates.

What Things Cost in Kenya & Tanzania

Kenya and Tanzania are relatively affordable, which does not mean to imply that they are cheap. Safaris are big business, and maintaining a business (of any kind) in the wilderness is implicitly costly and those expenses will obviously filter down to you, the paying customer. Additionally, park entry fees add to the cost. Although everyone is going to have a similar game-viewing experience, a safari holiday could set you back anywhere between $150 and $2,000 per person per day, depending on the level of comfort you want. At the top end of the spectrum, you can expect luxury accommodations and service in sublime locations, while at the lower end, you'll be looking at a camping safari in basic camp sites, with a cook to prepare simple meals.

Away from the parks and reserves, upmarket hotels and coastal resorts cost about $250 to $300 per night, although a number of exclusive luxury spots on the coast aimed at honeymooners cost more. Budget travelers utilizing midrange hotels and using public transport can get by on $60 to $100 a day.

The cost of eating varies from a $3 portion of chicken and chips or fries from a local canteen to a $60 meal for two with wine in a good restaurant. Often on safaris and in the coastal resorts, meals are inclusive of the rates. A bottle of beer is about $2. Wine is expensive (as it's imported), but is readily available. Bottles of water and sodas are less than $1.

Allow for additional funds if you think you may want to do extra activities in Kenya—watersports on the coast or the balloon ride over the Masai Mara, for example.

The official currency in Kenya is the Kenyan shilling, not to be confused with the Tanzania and Ugandan shillings, which are different currencies. The written abbreviation of the Kenyan shilling is either Ksh or /= (which you will see on handwritten receipts). Notes are 50, 100, 200, 500, and 1,000, whereas coins are 5, 10, and 20. Kenyan shillings can be used to pay for most things, though dollars are accepted by airlines and some large hotels, and can be used to pay national park entry fees.

The official currency in Tanzania is the Tanzanian shilling. The written abbreviation is either Tsh or /=. Notes are 200, 500, 1,000, 5,000, and 10,000, while coins are 50, 10, and 20, but these are virtually worthless and rarely used. Tanzanian shillings can be used to pay for most things, though U.S. dollars *only* are accepted by airlines, for national park entry fees, and for ferry tickets to Zanzibar and the other islands. The exchange rate has been pretty steady against the U.S. dollar in recent years.

Generally, you will have paid all lodging and transport costs in advance in order to secure your reservation at safari lodges, camps, and resorts; you'll also usually need to pay for any tours or operator costs in advance. That will take much of the burden off you when it comes to thinking about money. However, you will need to carry some Kenyan and Tanzanian shillings with you for tipping, shopping, restaurant and bar visits, and incidental expenses that might occur.

Plan your safari so you are left with as little local currency as possible before your departure home, since neither country allows you to export currency.

CURRENCY EXCHANGE

Currency and traveler's checks can be exchanged at the major banks, exchange bureaus, and some hotels. Airports in Nairobi, Mombasa, Dar es Salaam, and Zanzibar have 24-hour exchange services. The easiest currencies to exchange are U.S. dollars, British pounds, and euros. Try to carry bills that are relatively new, as banks in Kenya have been known not to accept older U.S. bills. Do not change money on the black market; it is illegal and you risk going to a jail or being swindled. The easiest and best way to get cash away from home is from an **ATM** (automated teller machine). Most banks in Kenya and Tanzania have ATMs, and they are increasingly being installed in petrol stations in Nairobi and Mombasa. They take four-digit PINs. However, remember that in remote regions, they are few and far between. ***Note:*** Overseas withdrawals may charge an additional fee by your home bank. **Credit cards** are a safe alternative to cash and are widely accepted in hotels, upscale souvenir stores, and restaurants, and can be used to pay for safaris. However, some small camps do not have credit card facilities and you will be asked to settle your outstanding account in cash, so it's always wise to make inquires first. If you are carrying plastic, make sure one of your cards is a Visa or MasterCard, as these are most commonly accepted. Diners Club is unheard of, and American Express is accepted at only a few establishments. Upmarket restaurants in Arusha or Moshi have been known to refuse credit card payments under \$50 (or even \$80). Note that there will also be a 5% to 7.5% surcharge on the bill (and for any other credit card purchases in either Kenya or Tanzania, for that matter).

In Kenya, dollars are largely used in business with airlines and large hotels, while everyone in Tanzania accepts them as payment rather than local currency (parks in both countries will, in fact, only accept U.S. dollars in cash or traveler's checks), so it's worth bringing a certain amount of dollars in cash and/or traveler's checks. Note that if you bring euros or sterling, you will have to convert them to shillings and then to dollars (a big hassle), and most street vendors and even some hotels take a very relaxed attitude to actual conversation rates and will simply knock off three zeros (Tsh 1,000 = \$1).

5 HEALTH

STAYING HEALTHY

General Availability of Health Care

For details on what shots you need to take before your trip, see "Medical Requirements," under "Entry Requirements," earlier. For information on what medications you should take if heading out on safari, refer to chapter 2.

COMMON AILMENTS

TROPICAL ILLNESSES **Malaria** is responsible for more than one million deaths in Africa each year, so it is imperative to take malaria precautions seriously. The threat of infection—the result of a bite from a disease-carrying mosquito—is present throughout the country, though the risk reduces at higher altitudes such as the Kenyan Highlands and Nairobi.

Avoiding "Economy Class Syndrome"

Deep vein thrombosis, or as it's know in the world of flying, "economy-class syndrome," is a blood clot that develops in a deep vein. It's a potentially deadly condition that can be caused by sitting in cramped conditions—such as an airplane cabin—for too long. During a flight (especially a long-haul flight), get up, walk around, and stretch your legs every 60 to 90 minutes to keep your blood flowing. Other preventative measures include frequent flexing of the legs while sitting, drinking lots of water, and avoiding alcohol and sleeping pills. If you have a history of deep vein thrombosis, heart disease, or another condition that puts you at high risk, some experts recommend wearing compression stockings or taking anticoagulants when you fly; always ask your physician about the best course for you. Symptoms of deep vein thrombosis include leg pain or swelling, or even shortness of breath.

Besides using **prophylaxis medication,** such as Malarone or Larium, arm yourself with strong mosquito repellents that can be safely sprayed or rubbed onto exposed skin, and make use of mosquito nets (these are a standard feature of nearly every property we've reviewed in this book) when you retire at night. Mosquitoes generally appear the moment the sun goes down, and just because you cannot see or hear them does not mean that they aren't buzzing around your ankles—stay alert and do everything in your power to prevent being bitten (even if you have taken medication). Bear in mind, too, that children are more at risk of contracting the disease. For a more in-depth discussion of the different prophylactic medications available, see chapter 2. Note that prophylactics have intense side effects on a small percentage of people, including forms of psychosis and depression—it's worth taking the medication a few days before you leave. If you become ill with either a fever or flulike symptoms while traveling—or up to 1 year after returning home—you should seek medical attention at once and let your physician know the details of your travel history, along with details of the prophylactics you've been taking. For additional information on malaria, protection from insect bites, and antimalarial drugs, visit the CDC Travelers' Health website at **www.cdc.gov/malaria**.

Although mosquito bites are responsible for the greatest number of deaths in Africa, **HIV/AIDS** is obviously a major health concern in both countries, and you should remain cautious of this fact if you intend to have sexual relations with locals or if you come into contact with human blood.

Less prominent, but occasionally reported, risks in Kenya include **tick bite fever, Rift Valley fever, typhus** (usually the result of a tick bite), **African sleeping sickness, plague,** and **relapsing fever.** None of these pose as great a threat as chloroquine-resistant malaria, but it pays to be vigilant and try to protect yourself against bites.

Cholera has been reported in certain parts of Kenya and Tanzania, but you are unlikely to encounter it on safari. **Bilharzia** or **schistosomiasis** (which spends part of its life cycle in snails and the other part in humans) is a concern in and around Lake Victoria, so it's best not to swim there or in any other lakes. **Rabies** is prevalent in Kenya. Avoid touching any feral animals; if you are bitten by a domestic or wild animal, clean the wound immediately and seek medical treatment. This involves taking a vaccine, and the dose depends on whether you have already been vaccinated against rabies—not necessary for a one-off visit, but it should be considered for lengthy stays in developing countries.

For general information about outbreaks of infectious diseases abroad, consult the website of the World Health Organization (www.who.int/en), and get more health information for travelers from www.who.int/ith/en.

DIETARY RED FLAGS Never drink water from any tap unless you have been assured that it is completely safe to do so (and only if the assurance comes from someone you can trust). On the whole, at every single lodge and camp you'll encounter while on safari, you'll be briefed on the quality of the water and whether it's drinkable. Most places will provide bottled or filtered water in your room or tent; this may be free or chargeable. Also see "Water" in "Fast Facts." Most food in Kenya and Tanzania is safe to eat, but be wary of ice in drinks and washed salads and fruits, and always ask where the water has come from. Also avoid reheated food or food that has been sitting around for awhile—equally relevant to a street stall and a hotel buffet.

Kenyans and Tanzanians are big meat-eaters, but that doesn't mean that **vegetarians** should go hungry. When making reservations for safari lodges and camps, make your hosts aware of your dietary predilections. You can do this either directly or through your operator or travel agent. Bear in mind that many of these lodges are a great distance away from towns where special foodstuffs can be purchased, so supplies need to be purchased in advance. If there are vegetarian guests, they need to make adjustments to their shopping list ahead of schedule, and you'll enjoy a more exciting culinary experience if you give prior warning.

BITES & OTHER WILDLIFE CONCERNS Although unlikely while on safari, there is a chance of encountering snakes, spiders, or scorpions, and on the coast a variety of sea creatures that can sting. Most snakes will clear off before you have a chance to tread on them, and the old tale that snakes are more scared of humans is generally true. The most worrisome snake is the puff adder, considered too lazy to move off when they sense you coming. In the event that you are bitten, stay calm and seek medical assistance immediately. Remember, the majority of snake bites are not poisonous. Spiders and scorpions may be spotted but are unlikely to pose a threat; the general rule is to leave them alone. At the coast, certain tropical sea creatures can inject venom into bathers' feet, which can be very painful. Wear plastic shoes if such creatures are reported in the area.

For information on staying safe in areas inhabited by wildlife, see chapter 2.

HIGH-ALTITUDE HAZARDS **Altitude sickness** can be a risk for anyone heading to altitudes above 3,000m (9,840 ft.) above sea level, so hikers and climbers tackling Mount Kenya and Kilimanjaro should take adequate precautions and prepare properly for the ascent. Symptoms include shortness of breath, nausea, vomiting, headaches, and dizziness. Mild altitude sickness requires rest before ascending higher; severe altitude sickness requires medication and a slow descent in stages. It's best not to attempt a climb if you have a bad cold or chest infection, or within 48 hours of going scuba diving. It's also a good idea not to go straight from the coast to Mount Kenya or Kilimanjaro, but to acclimatize at a midway altitude, such as Nairobi or the foothills around Moshi, for a couple of days.

SUN/ELEMENTS/EXTREME WEATHER EXPOSURE It can get incredibly hot under the African sun—particularly in arid and semi-arid areas. Arm yourself with a high-factor sunscreen, a hat that will protect your face, and good sunglasses, and be vigilant to prevent overexposure to the sun. Be especially cautious of children. At the other extreme, many people are surprised by the prevalence of extreme cold in certain parts of the country. Mount Kenya and Kilimanjaro may lie on the equator, but temperatures, particularly at higher altitudes, are freezing. If you're going to climb, you'll need special protective clothing. Temperature fluctuations are known to take travelers by surprise; because the countries are on the equator, the sun disappears rather suddenly (at more or less the same time throughout the year), and nightfall can bring quick temperature changes.

WHAT TO DO IF YOU GET SICK AWAY FROM HOME

While in the tourist areas, you'll have access to good medical facilities, and Nairobi has the best hospitals and private clinics in East Africa. The coast, too, has top-class facilities, which in some cases even offer cosmetic procedures to vacationers. If you are going to more remote regions, be aware that medical facilities (including drugstores) are few and far between. There may be occasional clinics, but these are poorly equipped and may not be able to dispense medicines that you might require. For minor ailments, pharmacists can assist and recommend a doctor, if necessary. Expect to pay for any medical services either upfront or immediately after treatment. If you have international medical insurance, keep the receipts so your company can reimburse you. However, if you become seriously ill and require advanced medical attention or surgery, you should definitely fly home, as local equipment and training standards are still far below those in the West. Your travel insurance should include repatriation to your home country in an emergency. Within Kenya and based at Nairobi's Wilson Airport, the **Flying Doctor Service** (www.amref.org) provides evacuation from remote areas in both Kenya and Tanzania to the nearest hospital. You may want to consider a temporary membership ($50) if you are going off the beaten track, but for the more popular parks and reserves, there are adequate medical provisions in case of an emergency.

We list additional **emergency numbers** in "Fast Facts" on p. 484.

6 SAFETY

In countries with rampant **poverty** and police departments that are often seen to be ineffective, **crime** can be a problem. However, much of the crime around Kenya and Tanzania is not directed at tourists and is in areas most tourists wouldn't visit or are in transit through (the north of Kenya and Nairobi, or Dar es Salaam and Arusha). The biggest threat to visitors is **petty theft,** particularly in Nairobi, Mombasa, and Kisumu; along the Kenyan coast; and in Tanzania, Dar es Salaam, and Zanzibar. In Nairobi and Dar es Salaam, **theft** is sometimes accompanied by an **armed threat** and **violence,** and **carjacking** is a particular problem (although, to put this in context, this particular crime is usually targeted at expats with expensive four-wheel-drive vehicles). Nevertheless, if driving, be alert and vigilant at all times. **Pickpockets** operate in cities and crowded areas, and travelers should be wary of "snatch and run" thieves who routinely snatch jewelry and other objects from people in the street or through open vehicle windows. Vehicle windows should be kept up and doors locked regardless of the time of day or weather. Thieves on *matatus,* buses, and trains may steal valuables from inattentive passengers.

Never leave any luggage unattended. It is safer not to carry valuables—store them in your hotel room safe—and try to limit the amount of cash and valuables that you carry with you. Make every effort not to flaunt items such as cameras and mobile phones. Walking alone or at night, especially in downtown areas, in public parks, along footpaths, on beaches, and in poorly lit areas, is dangerous and discouraged.

In the remote and sparsely populated northern parts of Kenya (which include much of the Northeastern Province, the Eastern Province, the northern part of the Coast Province, and the northern part of the Rift Valley Province), there are a number of security issues. Police escorts or convoys are a requirement in certain parts of Northern Kenya (p. 239); for visitors here, air travel is the recommended means of transportation. Here, **highway banditry** remains an ongoing problem, and also be aware that localized violence can occur in the form of **cattle rustling** (a cultural tradition for a number of tribes), which is often reciprocated by counter-raids. Such activity can also precipitate **ethnic or tribal conflict** and even small-scale warfare. **Cross-border violence** is also prevalent. A key problem zone is near Kenya's border with Somalia, where criminal acts, including **kidnappings,** have occurred. Travelers should be aware of the dangers and seek current status updates before heading to Northern Kenya.

Be aware that **political demonstrations** occur from time to time in East Africa. In late 2007 and early 2008, following the presidential and parliamentary elections held on December 27, Kenya was hit by intense unrest and violence. The violence, which made its way into news headlines around the world and portrayed a situation that many believe was far worse than the reality, followed the announcement by the Electoral Commission that incumbent candidate Mwai Kibaki had retained the presidency. Violence flared up in opposition strongholds and most heavily impacted the Nyanza, Rift Valley, and western provinces, as well as Nairobi and parts of Coast Province; more than 1,000 people were killed in the conflict and 300,000 were displaced. In previous general elections in Tanzania, there were some violent protests on Zanzibar and Pemba between supporters of varying political parties, but elections have passed peacefully in recent years. That said, safari destinations are not affected in any way during political elections, and as long as you avoid lengthy stays in populated areas (and, naturally, public demonstrations, which tend to happen in public parks, near government buildings, and around university campuses), protest activity is unlikely to affect tourist attractions outside Nairobi. For up-to-date information, contact the **State Department** (© **202/501-4444;** www.state.gov/travelandbusiness). For more safety tips, download the Department of State's pamphlet "Tips for Travelers Abroad," at **http://travel.state.gov**.

7 SPECIALIZED TRAVEL RESOURCES

In addition to the destination-specific resources listed below, please visit Frommers.com for specialized travel resources.

GAY & LESBIAN TRAVELERS

Homosexuality is illegal in Kenya and Tanzania and carries a hefty jail sentence. Generally, being gay is still largely a taboo subject, lesbianism doubly so, and many locals take the attitude that it's a foreign, un-African practice. Nevertheless, because of this, most locals in the tourism industry do accept that non-African visitors may be gay, so you'll receive no discrimination. However, complete discretion is advised—

even public displays of affection between a heterosexual couple are frowned upon on the Muslim coast and Zanzibar. Although in saying that, platonic affection between African males, such as holding hands or, by Muslims, kissing on the cheek, is common and a sign of friendship and respect. **Behind the Mask** (www.mask.org.za) is an organization that reports on gay and lesbian issues throughout Africa.

TRAVELERS WITH DISABILITIES

Kenya and Tanzania are not the most friendly travel destinations for those with disabilities. Few places are wheelchair accessible, and sidewalks and roads are in such dilapidated condition that even those without disabilities can find them challenging. Nevertheless, safaris should not pose too much of a problem, given that much of the time is spent in a vehicle, and you can choose one where accommodations are in a tent or a ground-floor room. Level-entry flat-floored showers, ramps, and grab handles do exist, but only in a few safari lodges and resorts; by doing a bit of research, most disabled travelers should be able to find an itinerary that suits their needs. You should also check with each lodge to be sure they have game-viewing vehicles that can accommodate passengers with special needs—some vehicles may be too cramped or difficult to climb into to make them worth considering. **Access-Able Travel Source** (www.access-able.com) offers extensive access information and advice for traveling around the world with disabilities. **Accessible Journeys** (www.disabilitytravel.com) caters specifically to slow walkers and wheelchair travelers and their families and friends, and organizes safaris in Kenya and Tanzania to the more popular parks. In Kenya, **Southern Cross Safaris** (www.southerncrosssafaris.com) can organize itineraries for wheelchair users.

FAMILY TRAVEL

Generally speaking, game-viewing safaris are not ideal for very young children, and many smaller, more intimate (and, consequently, peaceful) camps and lodges will place a moratorium on kids below a certain age. Certainly, you should think twice before taking children under 12 on game drives with other passengers—for children under 8, it's an absolute no-no. The problem is that young children get bored (game drives can go on for hours), and boredom leads to listless noisemaking, which annoys other passengers, interferes with the game-viewing experience, and may even frighten the animals away. One option for smaller kids is to organize a game-viewing vehicle for exclusive use for your family, which means you can return to your lodge when you want. Also keep kids occupied with animal and bird checklists, and perhaps give them their own binoculars or cameras.

Conversely, taking teenagers on safari is a perfect introduction to the African bush. They have the patience and enthusiasm to look for animals on a long game drive, and it can't be more exciting for them (and their parents) when they spot their first elephant or lion. Besides considering how the behavior of your children will impact the people, animals, and environment around you, it's vital to think carefully about the natural dangers posed by the wilderness and its inhabitants. While on safari, you are always at some kind of risk of attack by wild animals, and while adults usually understand the importance of following simple safety instructions, children may take a lot of convincing. Many of the safari lodges and camps reviewed and recommended in this book are unfenced, and it's relatively easy to imagine younger children wandering off into the bush. Many families do travel on safari, but unless you want to have sleepless nights, you'll want to ensure that your younger offspring are accommodated in the same room or in a suite with a bedroom adjoining yours.

Heritage Hotels (www.heritage-eastafrica.com) runs their very popular Adventurer's Club for children 4 to 12 and Young Rangers Club for those 12 to 17 at some of their Intrepids and Voyager safari lodges, which keep kids occupied while parents go on game drives. The lodges themselves have family rooms/tents.

The coastal resorts are very child-friendly, and good discounts can be had if you opt for a family or adjoining room. In some cases, children under 6 are free. Other considerations are that children are prone to sunburn or falling ill with minor stomach upsets and must be protected from contracting malaria at all times. Items such as diapers, powdered milk, and pureed food are available only in Kenya and Tanzania's major city supermarkets, and they are expensive. You may want to consider bringing enough for the length of your vacation. To locate accommodations, restaurants, and attractions that are particularly kid-friendly, refer to the "Kids" icon throughout this guide.

WOMEN TRAVELERS

Kenya and Tanzania are not problematic countries for women (even those traveling alone) to visit, although the normal precautions should be taken. You shouldn't go anywhere alone at night, and be wary of unsolicited male interest, especially in the coastal resorts, where foreign women looking for sexual adventure have encouraged pestering by local men. This can be dealt with if you are assertive. Women travelers should dress modestly, as both countries have a wide range of cultural differences. The islands and the coast are predominantly Muslim, so a modest dress code will help you blend in. Wear skirts or pants that reach below the knee and tops that cover shoulders and upper arms. Avoid see-through or overly tight clothing. In beach areas, where there are a lot of tourists, it's acceptable to wear beachwear, but going topless is considered taboo. Lamu and Zanzibar are particularly conservative, so it's important to heed this dress advice so as not to insult the local people. Most of the women on these islands and much of the Muslim coast in both Kenya and Tanzania wear *bui-buis,* head-to-toe black Islamic dress. Also be aware that public displays of affection are severely frowned upon in Zanzibar, and previously visitors have been arrested for kissing in public. Local women themselves are highly respected, especially older women, so a sharp word from them will help diffuse any number of situations. On public transport, try to get a seat next to other local women. You may be rewarded with good conversation, too.

For general travel resources for women, go to www.frommers.com/planning.

SENIOR TRAVEL

Age incurs great respect among Kenyans and Tanzanians—*mzee* means "old man" in Kiswahili but is actually an honored title of respect—so older travelers are generally treated with politeness. However, there are no special discounts or provision for senior travelers. The countries don't have any specific restrictions aside from health risks, which can be avoided with the right preparation (p. 37).

SINGLE TRAVELERS

The main disadvantage to traveling alone while on safari is cost. The per-person rate of a room or tent will invariably work out much more expensive if there's only one occupant. The same principle applies to the cost of charter flights and car hire; if you're looking to spread costs a little, it's a good idea to partner up for your trip. **Ranger Safaris** (www.rangersafaris.com), the biggest operator in Tanzania, deals with big catalog operators but also offers a large selection of scheduled small-group "seat in vehicle" itineraries, making this a good value option for singles.

Of course, if you're planning a totally budget-oriented adventure where you'll be jumping on buses, making use of relatively inexpensive tour operators, and shacking up in cheap local places, you can have a perfectly good time on your own, with great flexibility to do what you want, when you want. There is some price to pay for such independence, though, such as never having someone to watch your bags at airports and the like, or keep an eye on your drink if you need to visit the washroom. Hopefully, if you're planning to explore on your own, you'll be sufficiently outgoing and gregarious to make friends and acquaintances along the way. The other alternative is to join an overland truck safari, which can be ideal for single travelers. For details of routes through East Africa, visit www.overlandafrica.com. For more information on traveling alone, go to www.frommers.com/planning.

8 SUSTAINABLE TOURISM

You can help reduce your personal impact and lower your carbon footprint by choosing accommodations that make at least some attempt to be eco-friendly. The large concrete game lodges and beach resorts were built many decades ago without much thought about their impact to the environment. But these days, new camps are being built in a way that they can be completely removed and won't leave a lasting trace on the land. A number of camps have attained some eco-rating, and there is a big trend (particularly by the smaller places) to implement environmentally sensitive measures. Seek out places that have aimed to avoid the use of felled timber—many responsible designers use only wood from trees that have been knocked over by elephants, for example, and the keenest architects are careful to use local materials as much as possible and create accommodations that blend organically with the landscape in which they're located.

Many camps make use of solar power (for electricity and hot water), and some restrict their use of generators, helping reduce their use of fuel. Game-drive vehicles are a necessary evil in the wilderness, but you can at least try to encourage your guides and drivers to be responsible and considerate toward the environment; discourage off-road driving wherever possible.

Choose lodges and camps that employ local people (not just in menial positions, but in posts that matter, such as guiding and management), and look for evidence of involvement in community projects (you'll usually get a sense of how involved a property is from its website). Often there's evidence of sustainable, responsible tourism practices in small details, such as how a curio shop is stocked. Is it filled with mass-produced goods with widely distributed brands? Or can your host show you the workshop where local communities are actively employed in the craft trade?

You can also make a difference in small ways. Where your room or tent has a bathtub, first find out about the availability of water before going ahead and thoughtlessly squandering a scarce resource. If your lodge or camp still provides drinking water in plastic bottles, make strong suggestions that they change over to using reusable glass bottles or—better still—provide filtered water in glass jugs in your room.

Another issue to consider is that many locals are involved in the tourism industry, and some, like the Maasai and Samburu,

General Resources for Green Travel

In addition to the resources listed above, the following websites provide valuable wide-ranging information on sustainable travel. For a list of even more sustainable resources, as well as tips and explanations on how to travel greener, visit www.frommers.com/planning.

- **Responsible Travel** (www.responsibletravel.com) is a great source of sustainable travel ideas; the site is run by a spokesperson for ethical tourism in the travel industry. **Sustainable Travel International** (www.sustainable travelinternational.org) promotes ethical tourism practices and manages an extensive directory of sustainable properties and tour operators around the world.
- In the U.K., **Tourism Concern** (www.tourismconcern.org.uk) works to reduce social and environmental problems connected to tourism. The **Association of Independent Tour Operators** (**AITO;** www.aito.co.uk) is a group of specialist operators leading the field in making holidays sustainable.
- In Canada, **www.greenlivingonline.com** offers extensive content on how to travel sustainably.
- In Australia, the national body that sets guidelines and standards for ecotourism is **Ecotourism Australia** (www.ecotourism.org.au). **The Green Directory** (www.thegreendirectory.com.au), **Green Pages** (www.thegreen pages.com.au), and **Eco Directory** (www.ecodirectory.com.au) offer sustainable travel tips and directories of green businesses.
- **Carbonfund** (www.carbonfund.org), **TerraPass** (www.terrapass.org), and **Carbon Neutral** (www.carbonneutral.org) provide info on "carbon offsetting," or offsetting the greenhouse gas emitted during flights.
- **Greenhotels** (www.greenhotels.com) recommends green-rated member hotels around the world that fulfill the company's stringent environmental requirements. **Environmentally Friendly Hotels** (www.environmentally friendlyhotels.com) offers more green accommodation ratings.
- For information on animal-friendly issues throughout the world, visit **Tread Lightly** (www.treadlightly.org).
- **Volunteer International** (www.volunteerinternational.org) has a list of questions to help you determine the intentions and the nature of a volunteer program. For general info on volunteer travel, visit **www.volunteer abroad.org** and **www.idealist.org**.

do so while maintaining their traditional lifestyles, customs, and dress. When encountering these people, do not stop and stare, but interact and share. And it is the local people who act as guides that can best show you their country. On another note, never take a photograph of a person without first asking permission.

For further guidance on operators that practice sustainable safari tourism, contact the **Ecotourism Society of Kenya** (www. ecotourismkenya.org).

9 SAFARI & TOUR OPERATORS

There are a plethora of operators, and it's worth obtaining a quote from a few of them before deciding. Note that almost all operators will usually stick to their preferred lodges and camps, not always to the benefit of the guest. Use the accommodations reviews in the relevant chapters to help inform your final overnight itinerary, as all operators will book the recommendations you discover in this book if specifically requested, with the exception of those that offer only a full game package (your own driver and vehicle). Also see chapter 2.

Top operators and travel agents for planning your safaris in Kenya include the following:

- Although based in Atlanta, Georgia, **Uncharted Outposts** ★★★ (✆ **505/795-7710;** www.unchartedoutposts.com) specializes in safaris, and its proprietors have first-hand knowledge of many of the camps and lodges in East Africa. They have handpicked most of the properties in their portfolio and have a close working relationship with people on the ground. If you want assurance of the best in the business, contact Sandy Cunningham, who was not only born in Africa and lived in Kenya for many years (where she worked at one of the country's finest lodges), but is on first-name terms with most of the best hosts and guides at the more exclusive and intimate places to stay.
- **The Africa Adventure Co.** ★ (✆ **800/882-9453;** www.africa-adventure.com) operates out of Fort Lauderdale and is a much-lauded operation with more than 2 decades of experience.
- South African-based **Uyaphi.com** ★ (www.uyaphi.com) puts together reliable packages according to clients' needs; their agents have access to a

broad base of Kenyan safari properties and ground operators.

- **Abercrombie & Kent** ★ (✆ **800/554-7016;** www.abercrombiekent.com) and New York–based **Micato Safaris** ★★★ (✆ **800/642-2861;** www.micato.com) both have good reputations as safari operators; Micato, in fact, was recently voted the world's top tour operator and safari outfitter by *Travel + Leisure,* an accolade they've earned every year since 2003.
- U.K.–based **Black Tomato** ★★★ (www.blacktomato.co.uk) is an award-winning travel agency that specializes in putting together off-the-beaten-track holiday experiences that are always above the norm. They don't have a huge roster of tours in East Africa, but their staff are imaginative enough to put something extraordinary together for you.

Top operators and travel agents for planning your safaris in Tanzania include the following:

- **Albatros Travel** (www.albatros-africa.com) is an internationally respected company that's had an office in Arusha for more than a decade. Their dedicated team, headed by Julian Camm (East Africa Manager for Albatros Travel), knows what quality and service are all about.
- **&Beyond** (formerly CC Africa; www.andbeyond.com) prides itself on offering superb luxury safaris aimed at the mid- to high-end traveler. Of course, there is a bias toward their own camps, but they also offer independent advice and bookings to other lodges and camps in East Africa, and their all-inclusive packages can be surprisingly good values.
- Jeroen Harderwijk and Bas Hochstenbach are the cofounders of **Asilia** (www.asilialodges.com), with a focus on areas away from large concentrations of tourists in the Northern Circuit. They operate Oliver's Camp in Tarangire, the mobile Suyan Camp in Loliondo, the Sayari Camp and mobile Olakira Camp in the Serengeti, as well as Matemwe in Zanzibar. Asilia lodges and camps are as high-end and comfortable as you can get on a mobile safari, but the real luxury, they believe, is "bringing you closer to the overwhelming beauty of Africa." They do not make bookings outside of the Asilia family.
- **Awaken to Africa** (www.awakentoafrica.com) is jointly owned by a Tanzanian naturalist guide, David Mshana, with more than 18 years of experience in leading safaris in Tanzania (including professional photographic safaris), and Grace Evans, a veteran traveler and accomplished photographer from the U.S. This is both a tour operator and a ground operator company. The combination means no middle man and solid service.
- **Planet Africa Safaris** (formerly Green Footprint Adventures; www.planetafricasafaris.com) is led by veteran guide and Animal Planet celeb Jean du Plessis, Mary Rijnberg, and an enthusiastic team. They are particularly recommended for tailor-made private, active (canoe, cycling), and yoga safaris. "You get what you pay for" is their motto, and while they are not the cheapest, you sure do get a lot.
- A leading tour operator in Tanzania, **Leopard Tours** (www.leopard-tours.com) is a slick operator dealing in high volumes and receives literally thousands of visitors a year. They operate safaris from midmarket to high-end, but accommodations are usually skewed toward the big lodge category.
- **Nomad Safaris** (www.nomad-tanzania.com) operates some of the most stylish and exciting safari camps in Tanzania: Sand Rivers Selous, Kiba Point, Rhino House, Greystoke Mahale, Chada Katavi, Nduara Loliondo, Serengeti Safari

Camp, and Nomad Tarangire. Like Asilia, they don't make bookings outside the family, but what a family.

- **Renaissance Safaris** (http://renaissancesafaris.com) is an excellent high-end exclusive operator specializing in private safaris, with only the best lodges on their books. Björn, the cofounder, never gets it wrong.
- Based in Arusha, **Simba Safaris** (www.simbasafaris.com), a 35-year-old family operation, offers solid support with 50 4×4 vehicles, 40 drivers, and excellent service. Tours are often biased toward the big lodges, but the company is flexible and able to arrange more intricate itineraries. Highly recommended for their commitment and their ability to produce the best itinerary for your budget. Africa specialist Julian Harrison, owner of U.S.–based **Premier Tours** (www.premiertours.com), works closely with Simba to ensure a 100% match between incoming travelers and on-the-ground experiences.
- Operating since 1984, **Wildlife Explorer** (www.wildlife-explorer.co.uk) owner Gary Strand has outfitted luxury tented safaris in Tanzania for National Geographic, the BBC Natural History Unit, Sir Anthony Hopkins, Sir David Attenborough, Rod Stewart, and Penny Lancaster—enough said.
- Osman runs **Ultimate Safaris Ltd.** (www.ultimatesafarisltd.com), a small, successful, and personally run tour company offering value-for-money to high-end tours, with a modern fleet of custom-made Land Cruisers and experienced driver/guides.

SPECIAL-INTEREST TRIPS

In Kenya

- **Insider's Africa** ★★★ (www.insidersafrica.com) is a small, low-key safari operation now based in the Ol Pejeta Conservancy in the Central Highlands, just outside Nanyuki. Alex Hunter has long been known for his walking safaris and now runs a small tented camp where—in addition to the usual safari experiences—guests can sign up for an interactive **conservation safari course,** which offers a much deeper understanding of the African bush, with hands-on experience. Alex also tailors special-interest safaris catering to individual requests, whether you have a penchant for culture and history or a fascination with flora and fauna.
- If you're looking to get a firsthand look at some of Kenya's diverse cultures, **Origins Safaris** ★★★ (www.originsafaris.info) is a top choice. They specialize in experiential cultural discovery tours that allow you to meet some of the various tribal groups that live here, learning about and even participating in some astonishing activities, including ceremonies that are rarely witnessed by the outside world. Origins also offers the best **bird-watching safaris** in Kenya, bringing together the best ornithological guides and exclusive accommodations.
- Offering both trekking and cultural trips, **IntoAfrica** ★★ (www.intoafrica.co.uk) is a good choice if you want to tackle Mount Kenya or spend time getting to know the people of Kenya—or combine both. The company offers scheduled and tailored trips.

In Tanzania

- **Matembezi Safaris** (www.matembezi.co.tz) is a multilanguage safari company (with guides who speak English, French, Italian, Spanish, and Hebrew) that offers a range of specialized safaris, as well as no-frills wilderness camping, including the Lake Natron–to–northern Serengeti haul.
- **InTanzania** (http://birds.intanzania.com) is the top choice for birders. Run by James Wolstencrof, known affectionately as the Birdman, a lifelong naturalist

(and very keen birder) whose first East African safari was in 1976.

If you're looking to **climb Kilimanjaro,** the following are recommended:

- The family-run **Marangu Hotel** (www.maranguhotel.com) offered the first commercial climbs from their farmhouse in the 1930s, and their most senior guides have been working with the hotel for more than 40 years. Their climbs are not the cheapest (though they are certainly competitive), but they provide highly professional service with experienced guides and porters who queue up to work here (Marangu Hotel is a partner with the Kilimanjaro Porters Assistance Project). You have to stay at the Marangu Hotel (p. 449) to utilize their climbs.
- Owned by the dynamic Zainab, **Zara Tours** (www.zaratours.com) has been cornering the budget market for 2 decades and is, in this sense, by far the most successful outfit in Moshi, proudly claiming to put more people on the summit than anyone else. Zara offers a very competitive package, including airport transfers and 2 nights at their hotel (Springlands, p. 451), with add-on tours elsewhere in Tanzania, though, again, these are very much focused on the budget mass end of the market. You do not need to stay at Springlands to utilize Zara Tours, but it makes sense to, given that the accommodations are also geared to saving money.
- **Nature Discovery** (www.naturediscovery.com) is a highly ethical company that's been climbing since 1992 and focuses on top-end personalized expeditions. Kili climbs are only via the Machame and Shira routes and include the Western Breach ascent with all safety precautions. Their cooks are said to be the best on the mountain, and their equipment is tip-top, from the modern mountaineering tents with ground sheets and cold-weather sleeping mats to large mess tents furnished with aluminum tables and chairs (with backs and armrests) and sanitary portable flush toilets inside enclosed tents. All guides are fluent in English and receive ongoing training. Their camping and lodge safaris are also highly rated.
- **Chagga Tours** (www.chagga-tours.com) was founded by mountain guide Michael Nelson Ntiyu of Tanzania and investor-hiker Christina Helbig of Germany. Michael, a Chagga who grew up on the mountain, has successfully guided hundreds of groups up the mountain (he has also climbed Mt. Everest) and is very attuned to the needs of climbers. Christina climbed with him twice and was so impressed by his leadership skills that she decided to partner with him. Tours are not just mountain treks, but can include stops at the cultural achievements of the Chagga, such as the irrigation canals, built hundreds of years ago, which seem to flow uphill, and the terraced cultivation of plants in the Chagga farmlands.
- Jo Anderson, a keen botanist who, after 50 climbs, is well versed on Kili flora, runs **Jo Anderson Safaris** (www.jo-anderson.com). He, along with three guides he's trained, make the journey as special as the arrival at the summit. Safety is a top priority, and his team carries oxygen, a high-altitude pressure chamber, and a full wilderness medical kit on every climb; all support staff have first-aid qualifications and have practical experience in wilderness first aid. Flowers bloom at different times, but March through May is great (low season on the mountain), as are September and October.
- The Arusha-based **Hoopoe Adventure** (www.hoopoe.com) won the Condé Nast Ecotourism Award for best tour operator in 2004. Hoopoe offers relatively inexpensive tours, with a bias to

their own camps and other eco-friendly lodges.

- **Ranger Safaris** (www.rangersafaris.com) is the biggest operator in Tanzania and deals with big catalog operators, but also offers a large selection of scheduled small-group "seat in vehicle" itineraries, a good-value option for singles and couples who don't mind sharing their experiences. The company also provides custom safaris where you have complete flexibility.

Details of recommended adventure and specialist safari operators are provided in chapter 15.

MOBILE SAFARIS

Mobile safaris can be like advanced camping expeditions, where you overnight in a different spot each night, either in smart tents (the best companies erect these for you and put on fabulous meals, too) or at a string of lodges or permanent camps. The level of luxury will be reflected in the price, and the type of transport (you can go by 4×4, camel, horse, foot, or even plane) will determine the manner in which you encounter the wilderness, its wildlife, and its people. Two of the top mobile safari operators in Kenya are **Robert & William Carr-Hartley Safaris** ★★★ (✆ **254/722-510-673;** www.carrhartley.com) and **Bill Winter Safaris** ★★★ (✆ **254/20/88-3369,** or 832/585-0042 in the U.S.; www.bwsafaris.com), which both offer luxurious standards and years of experience.

In Tanzania, &Beyond, Nomad, Lemala, and Asilia (p. 46) are the best choices (other top-end safari operators are likely to be booking through these four).

ADVENTURE & WELLNESS TRIPS

For details of some of Kenya's best specialist operators—offering packages specializing in safaris with camels, on foot or horseback, and even dedicated photographic tours—see p. 46. Note that some of these companies also operate in other parts of the country.

One of the top operators for adventure holidays is the country's lone white-water-rafting company, **Savage Wilderness Safaris** (www.whitewaterkenya.com). They also put together mountain-climbing, hiking, and caving trips.

VOLUNTEER & WORKING TRIPS

Some of the smaller, privately owned lodges and camps will take on volunteers who express a genuine interest in either conservation, community work, or—in the case of working ranches—farming. Please don't volunteer yourself if you're not fully committed to putting in substantial efforts, earning your keep (you'll generally receive full board and lodging), and engaging with your hosts, their guests, and their staff fully. The volunteers we've met have been young (often taking time out on a gap year) and exceptionally enthusiastic. You can expect to work hard, get up early each day, experience multiple facets of a new and fascinating way of life, learn Kiswahili (or a local tribal language), and develop a close working relationship with your hosts. You have a better chance of landing such a special opportunity if you have previously been to Africa or have visited the lodge or camp you're interested in. Potential volunteers should have good people skills and should be prepared to interact with paying guests. Start by contacting Richard Bonham of **Ol Donyo Wuas** (www.oldonyowuas.com), Colin and Rocky Francombe of **Ol Malo** (www.olmalo.com), or the management at **Lewa Wildlife Conservancy** (www.lewa.org) to begin your search for a volunteering opportunity.

You can also go the institutional route, starting out by investigating opportunities at the **Kenya Voluntary & Community Development Project** (www.kvcdp.org), a good grassroots organization that places volunteers in anything from planting trees, building schools, and promoting AIDS awareness to constructing roads, making bricks, and providing reproductive health education. A 2-week work camp costs $350, while a 2-month program will set you back $950, which covers airport transfers, orientation, participation in the program, and transport to the volunteer location. Accommodations and food are provided, but volunteers take turns preparing meals.

Volunteer Kenya (www.volunteerkenya.org) is the international name for ICODEI (Inter-Community Development Involvement), which runs volunteer programs mainly in education, health care, AIDS education, and micro-enterprise development. Their programs are based in Western Kenya, where the organization also began the first public library in the region. Volunteers pay $1,185 per month to participate, and the fee covers airport pick-up, all meals, and accommodations in a four-person hut situated on a former sugar cane farm in rural Kenya.

Eco-Resorts (www.eco-resorts.com) is worth investigating for their tailor-made safaris that combine interactive cultural experiences with opportunities to participate in volunteer activities and programs.

Tanzania Volunteer Experience (www.volunteertanzania.org) places volunteers in day-care centers and orphanages around Arusha as teachers or HIV/AIDS educators. A 2-week work camp costs $495, while a 2-month program will set you back $1,495, which covers airport transfers, orientation, participation in the program, and transport to the volunteer location. Accommodation and food are provided, but volunteers take turns to prepare meals.

ESCORTED SAFARIS

You'll get the most out of your safari with an experienced and knowledgeable guide who understands the bush and should be able to discuss the flora and fauna with you in detail. Often your guide will be available to join you for meals (indicate whether you'd like this) and regale you with tales of past adventures. Note that the safari companies recommended above all provide a guide/driver along with their vehicle, but often they are more drivers than guides. Companies that provide guides as well as drivers (&Beyond, for example) usually take the whole safari experience to a new level.

In Kenya, guides employed by legendary high-end safari company **Ker & Downey** ★★★ (www.kerdowneysafaris.com)—don't muddle them with the similarly named tour company that's based in Houston—are renowned for their professionalism and know-how. Ker & Downey was established in 1946 and is considered the world's oldest safari company, making use of luxury lodges and camps, yet giving clients a real sense of adventure and an excellent insight into the bush. On similar footing is **Royal African Safaris** ★★★ (www.royalafricansafaris.com), which organizes highly individualized bespoke tours, matching up clients with their ideal guide.

If you want the most informative Tanzanian safari ever—a veritable crash course in fascinating animal facts—arrange your trip with **Lee Fuller** ★★★. Lee acts as a private guide to select clients traveling in East Africa, but is also the trainer to all Singita's guides in East Africa; his knowledge, commitment, and passion for his subject are unbeatable. He's also excellent company. With limited time at his disposal, it's best to book Lee well in advance (LeeF@grumeti.singita.com). Lee tends to work in the north, including Kenya, in safari itineraries. If you're interested in combining a trip to the south and west, including gorilla tracking in Rwanda, Leslie Nevison, sole proprietor of **Mama Tembo Tours** ★★★ (leslie@mamatembottours.com; www.mamatembotours.com), offers personal custom tours on Tanzania's less-trodden routes.

For more information on escorted general-interest tours, including questions to ask before booking your trip, see www.frommers.com/planning.

10 STAYING CONNECTED

TELEPHONES

In the cities there are public coin and card phones on the street. Phone cards can be bought from post offices, street vendors, or small shops. You can make direct international calls from these. Phoning from hotels is expensive, as they add a hefty premium.

To call Kenya or Tanzania from another country: Dial the international access code: 011 from the U.S.; 00 from the U.K., Ireland, or New Zealand; or 0011 from Australia. Dial the country code 254 (Kenya) or 255 (Tanzania) and then the local number minus the first 0.

To make domestic calls within Kenya or Tanzania: For all calls within the countries, drop the country code, but the full area code (including the first 0) must be dialed along with the number. All numbers begin with a three-digit area code.**To make international calls from Kenya or Tanzania:** First dial 000 and then the country code (U.S. or Canada 1, U.K. 44, Ireland 353, Australia 61, New Zealand 64). Next dial the area code (drop the first 0 if there is one) and number. For international operator-assisted calls, dial 0196. Note that calls between Kenya and Tanzania and Uganda are charged at long-distance tariffs and not international. To call Kenya from Tanzania and Uganda, dial 005 followed by the area code and number. To call Uganda from Kenya, dial 006 followed by the area code and number, while calls to Tanzania require the prefix 007. Kenya and Tanzania have discontinued their "collect call" facilities. Toll-free numbers in the U.S. cannot be accessed from Kenya or Tanzania. Use of international long-distance calling cards is very limited.

CELLPHONES

Kenya and Tanzania are awash with mobile phone operators; you'll spot advertisements for Safaricom, Zain, Celtel, and several others in even the most remote corners of the country. Surprisingly, there may be mobile services even in far-flung wilderness areas (where cellular connectivity is the only means of communicating with the outside world), but limited coverage in national parks that are relatively close to major towns or cities. Most of the local operators have partnerships with international service providers—if you want to investigate these services, it's best to make inquiries through your home operator before departure. Using a mobile phone to call internationally is very expensive, so try to avoid doing so. You'll also pay dearly for international roaming through your service provider back home. The simplest way to have mobile phone access is to purchase a SIM card when you arrive and stock up on prepaid charge cards, which are available everywhere from formal phone shops to street vendors. If you are traveling to other African countries, opt for a Zain SIM card. They operate borderless roaming across 22 African countries, and call costs are local, not international. International calls from a Kenyan or Tanzania SIM card are about 50¢ a minute and local calls cost about 20¢ a minute.

Online Traveler's Toolbox

Veteran travelers usually carry some essential items to make their trips easier. Following is a selection of handy online tools to bookmark and use.

- **Airplane Food** (www.airlinemeals.net)
- **Airplane Seating** (www.seatguru.com; and www.airlinequality.com)
- **Foreign Languages for Travelers** (www.travlang.com)
- **Maps** (www.mapquest.com)
- **Time and Date** (www.timeanddate.com)
- **Travel Warnings** (http://travel.state.gov, www.fco.gov.uk/travel, www.voyage.gc.ca, www.smartraveller.gov.au)
- **Universal Currency Converter** (www.oanda.com)
- **Weather** (www.intellicast.com; and www.weather.com)

Cellular Abroad (✆ **800/287-5072;** www.cellularabroad.com) has a number of services that are handy for travelers to Kenya; these include satellite phone rentals and various conventional cellphone and SIM card rental packages that can be tailored to your specific needs. Although their SIM cards are not as cost-effective as buying one locally, they'll be more useful if you're visiting Kenya as part of a multi-destination trip and wish to continue using the same card. They also sell the National Geographic Travel Phone, which enables you to keep the same number no matter where in the world you're visiting and save on international calls; the per-minute rate for a call from Kenya to the U.S., the U.K., or Australia, for example, is $1.55.

INTERNET & E-MAIL

Internet cafes in major tourist spots and in the towns and cities are easy to find. The Kenya Post Office now offers access in almost all of their branches, even in the small towns. Hotels and lodges, too, are increasingly offering Internet access to their guests, though this is usually more expensive than a street-side cafe. Generally, you won't find Internet access in remote safari destinations. Although speed connections from landlines can be slow, satellite connections are continually increasing and the cost is lowering; expect to pay little more than $1 per hour. Wi-Fi is catching on in Kenya and Tanzania (Arusha's International Conference Center), and the airports and some hotels and coffee shops (such as the Java chain) now have Wi-Fi.

11 TIPS ON ACCOMMODATIONS

Accommodations in Kenya and Tanzania range from high-end luxury safari lodges or tented camps and beach resorts with a full range of facilities and entertainment to flea-ridden $10-a-night local town hotels with simple beds and a shared bathroom. Camping is also popular in the parks and brings down the price of an organized safari considerably. Kenya and Tanzania do operate a star grading system for accommodations, although it is below par to what you would expect from the U.S.

or Europe. Generally, you can assume four- and five-star hotels are of a good standard. There are also a clutch of world-class, luxurious, and intimate settings in the parks or on the coast.

HOTELS Nairobi has a good selection of international chain hotels and cheaper three- and four-star individual establishments. The coast leans toward places where vacationers rarely venture out of the confines of their resort except to go on a short safari to one of the closer parks, such as Tsavo. There are a few individual hotels that have a lot of either history or character. For example, the Norfolk in Nairobi has been a Kenyan institution since the colonial days. If you stick to three stars or higher, you can expect clean rooms, a private bathroom with a shower, a swimming pool, and one or more decent restaurants. At the lower end of the scale, the towns offer basic lodgings in one- or two-star hotels that are predominantly used by locals. Budget travelers should look at a room to ensure that the sheets are clean and the plumbing works before committing.

Zanzibar has places on the beach where vacationers rarely venture out of the confines of their resort, but also has some wonderful hotels in Stone Town housed in historic Arabian-style buildings that feature unique Zanzibar-style four-poster beds, Persian rugs, and antique furniture, even at the cheaper end of the scale.

SAFARI ACCOMMODATIONS For all budgets, entrance fees to the parks are the same, and you can expect to have the same sort of game-viewing experience. But what you pay for an organized safari depends on the standard of accommodations and whether you choose to get to the parks by road or air. Generally, accommodations in the parks fall into three categories: top-end luxury tented camps, midrange large lodges, and campsites. Intimate tented camps usually comprise a dozen or so spacious tents under a thatched or wooden roof with their own terrace and sometimes extras such as a private plunge pool or outside shower. Cuisine and service are excellent, and game drives and other activities are all-inclusive. The benefit of these is that you are sleeping in the wild with animals close by, and you'll have the personal service of knowledgeable guides. The large safari lodges in the parks also offer good service and are mostly in scenic locations, but with a large number of rooms in either hotel-like blocks or individual chalets, they can feel a little impersonal. Nevertheless, they offer reasonable value and have a full range of facilities such as restaurants, bars, and swimming pools. Camping safaris offer the best value but are the least comfortable, with cold showers, primitive toilets, and hard ground to sleep on. But the advantage is sleeping in unfenced campsites where you may hear the roar of a lion at night. Camping safaris usually have a cook who prepares meals over an open fire.

Generally, you get what you pay for, and if you avoid peak seasons (see "When to Go," earlier in this chapter), you'll score fantastic deals. Another source for discounted stays (sometimes in top accommodations) is the online booking service **www.kenyalastminute.com**. Kenya has several reputable hotel and safari accommodation chains; some of these deal in large, good-value lodging, with a focus on packing in as many guests as possible, whereas the better ventures are boutique companies that are not so much chains as associations of smaller, intimate, and personalized operations that are marketed under a particular banner.

When it comes to safari destinations, we favor **Bush and Beyond** ★★★ (www.bush-and-beyond.com and www.bush-homes.co.ke), which has an assortment of excellent lodges and camps on its books (the majority of which are in the game-rich Masai Mara and on private concessions on the Laikipia Plateau), and **Cheli**

& Peacock ★★★ (www.chelipeacock.com), which also has a substantial portfolio of similarly lovely properties. Both companies will arrange all accommodations, ground and air transport, and pick-ups and transfers, and will tailor your experience according to your preferences. Of the two companies, Bush and Beyond offers greater flexibility and is better equipped to customizing your holiday. They work closely with U.S.–based travel operator **Uncharted Outposts** ★★★ (www.unchartedoutposts.com), which specializes in top-drawer accommodations that are intimate, sustainable, often family- or community-owned, and as untouristy as possible. U.K. travel agency **Carrier** ★★ (www.carrier.co.uk) also works with a highly commendable selection of camps and lodges, with an emphasis on exclusivity and hassle-free comfort.

The main "luxury" hotel chain in East Africa is **Serena** (www.serenahotels.com), which has a mix of upmarket city hotels, fine beach resorts, and safari lodges that range from comfortable-but-unattractive to decent-yet-affordable. The biggest problem with their safari properties, however, is their size. A high number of bedrooms means that they are able to keep rates down, but that also takes away from the level of exclusivity, and you'll see plenty of package groups taking up large tables. Serena's service standards are, however, fairly high, and the accommodation standards are the best in the chain resort category, thereby offering the best value despite the slightly higher price tag (in comparison to, say, Sopa). Serena's main competitor, although often with properties in areas not challenged by Serena, is **Sarova** (www.sarovahotels.com), although we don't recommend them unless there really is nowhere else to stay. Even less to our taste is **Sopa** (www.sopalodges.com), a frankly outdated chain that draws chiefly groups arranged by operators attracted to the hefty commissions Sopa offers them. If you're exploring these two options because of a tight budget, try **Wildlife Lodges** (www.hotelsandlodges-tanzania.com), which offers similar or lower rates but often in better locations.

Still owned by the family of one of Kenya's former presidents, **Heritage Hotels** (www.heritage-eastafrica.com) runs eight Kenyan safari lodges and camps (the smaller ones are good, the large properties much less so) under three marginally distinct brands, namely Explorer, Intrepids, and Voyager—of the three, the Explorer properties tend to offer greater exclusivity. One advantage of the Heritage properties is that some offer kids clubs (p. 43) both on safari and at the beach, so they appeal to families. Heritage is represented in the U.S. by Sarah Fazendin's **The Fazendin Portfolio** (**© 303/993-7906;** www.FazendinPortfolio.com), worth contacting to find out about any special deals on Heritage packages.

Tented camps, particularly the so-called mobile camps (those that move to two to three locations depending on animals' movement), are ideal for those who want to be in the midst of the Migration or simply want to experience the thrilling experience of sleeping in the wild with animals close by while enjoying luxuries such as quality linen and en suite toilets. For both of these options, you'll have the personal service of knowledgeable guides. Tanzania's **Nomad** (www.nomad-tanzania.com) is highly recommended in this category; see relevant chapters for more.

Kenya also has a growing number of boutique "chains" comprising personally managed smaller properties. **Porini** ★★★ (www.porini.com) comprises four different safari camps and focuses on providing eco-friendly lodgings. **Offbeat Safaris** ★★ (www.offbeatsafaris.com) grew out of a slick horseback safari operation and now has four different lodging options in prime game-viewing areas. **Governors** ★★ (www.governorscamp.com) is a family-run operation based in the Masai Mara; they have a growing number of camps, lodges, and resorts, including their new Sabyinyo Silverback Lodge in Rwanda, which is set to become a prime base for gorilla trekking safaris. Governors also has the best hot-air ballooning operation in Kenya and has its own air service. One more operation to consider if you're seeing Southern Kenya and the coast is **Southern Cross Safaris** (www.southerncrosssafaris.com), which handles bookings for a small number of camps in Tsavo and represents many resorts on the beach.

Major international players that have set their sights on Kenya include **Fairmont** ★ (www.fairmont.com), which has recently taken over several prestigious hotels and lodges and is steadily transforming them into ultra-luxurious destinations for the well-heeled. Unfortunately, while they generally provide quality accommodations and efficient service, their properties suffer from a lack of local community involvement, and you'll often find that they employ city-based personnel at their safari destinations. Best of the international players for wildlife enthusiasts is South African–based **&Beyond** ★★★ (formerly CC Africa; www.andbeyond.com), which has the added advantage of a better spread of properties in East Africa (including one in the Masai Mara and one on Pemba), and their guides are among the very best in the business.

4

Suggested Kenya & Tanzania Itineraries

Visitors to Kenya are either going on safari or taking a beach break, or looking to combine the two.

Most people arrive in Nairobi, where the majority of game parks and reserves are within a day's drive. Popular safari circuits include a couple of nights in the Masai Mara, combined with a night or two in Lake Nakuru National Park or Samburu National Reserve, or a combination of 1 or 2 nights in both Amboseli and Tsavo. Longer safaris combine the Kenyan parks with those in Tanzania's Northern Circuit. Adventure-seekers will want to explore the northern deserts or climb Mount Kenya. And just because you want to lounge on the beach in Mombasa doesn't mean you have to forgo your safari; a night or two can be spent at nearby parks such as Tsavo.

To see more than one park or game reserve in Kenya, you'll need at least a week, with a couple of nights at each to make the most out of early-morning and late-afternoon game drives, when animals are most active.

Tanzania is one of the greatest safari destinations in Africa, covering a diverse selection of landscapes. It's home to the Big Five (elephant, lion, leopard, buffalo, and rhino), which were trophies for game hunters in the past but today are popular sights on a game drive. About 25% of Tanzania is occupied by parks and reserves, and ocean life is protected in a number of marine parks.

The country's most popular parks, known as the Northern Circuit—Serengeti, Ngorongoro Crater, Tarangire, and Lake Manyara—and the two big mountains, Kilimanjaro and Meru, are most easily accessed from the town of Arusha, dubbed the safari capital of Tanzania. Almost all Northern Circuit safaris start and finish here. Arusha is actually closer to Nairobi than Dar, so visitors going to only the Northern Circuit may want to consider flying into Nairobi instead, from where there are regular shuttle buses or flights to Tanzania.

Tanzania is also home to archaeological sites such as the Olduvai Gorge, where traces of early man were discovered, as well as historical coastal towns where the Swahili way of life can be experienced. The impossibly atmospheric island of Zanzibar is steeped in culture and history and has unpolluted beaches, and there is excellent diving on the reefs around the islands of Pemba and Mafia. Tanzania is also home to Kilimanjaro, the tallest mountain in Africa and the tallest in the world that can be walked up.

KENYA REGIONS IN BRIEF

Nairobi, Kenya's capital, has grown from a swampy railway camp in 1899 into the largest city between Johannesburg and Cairo, and is today a thriving city with a clamoring street life. Although not a prime tourist destination, Nairobi does have a number of good attractions, including the **Nairobi National Park** and other wildlife centers and museums.

The **Rift Valley** is a vast geological feature created by tectonic forces in Earth's crust, which runs approximately 6,000km (3,720 miles) from Syria, under the Red Sea, through East Africa to Mozambique. In Kenya, the valley is at its deepest just north of Nairobi, and there are viewpoints on the Nairobi-Naivasha road. This region is dotted with lakes such as **Elmenteita, Baringo, Bogoria,** and **Nakuru.**

Western Kenya is one of the least visited areas of the country, as there are no big game parks to attract visitors. The hilly, fertile scenery, characterized by strikingly green tea plantations, is pretty and has some impressive geographical features. **Mount Elgon** is the second-tallest mountain in Kenya, and **Lake Victoria** is the second-largest freshwater lake in the world. The **Kakamega Forest** is the last patch of tropical rainforest left in East Africa, while the tiny **Saiwa Swamp National Park** protects the rare and shy sitatunga antelope.

Roughly covering the region north of Nairobi to Isiolo, the **central highlands** are dominated by **Mount Kenya,** which can be climbed on an organized 5-day hike. To the north of the mountain is the **Laikipia Plateau,** a former region for ranching that has now been restocked with wild animals. To the west of Mount Kenya is the **Aberdare National Park,** which is not your typical African game park, as the terrain is moorlike, forested, and often shrouded with fog, though it has plentiful wildlife.

Kenya's **coast** is a playground for mostly European package tourists on sun, sea, and sand holidays, and for good reason. The 480km (298 miles) of Indian Ocean shoreline boasts sublime white-sand beaches, shady palm trees, sunny weather, warm water for swimming, and a colorful chain of offshore fringing coral reefs. Away from the beach, the historical towns remain a testament to the Swahili culture that has been on the coast for thousands of years.

No trip to Kenya is complete without visiting one or more of the major parks and reserves, located along the border with Tanzania in **southern Kenya.** The **Masai Mara Game Reserve** is an extension of Tanzania's Serengeti National Park, and this region of well-watered grassland plains stages the spectacular annual wildebeest migration. Kilimanjaro provides a stunning backdrop to **Amboseli National Park,** while the combined **Tsavo East** and **Tsavo West national parks** are the biggest protected wildlife refuge in Kenya and home to large herds of game, especially elephants.

The vast parched and stony deserts of **Northern Kenya** are remote and isolated, access is difficult, and in recent years the area has suffered from drought and parts have been occupied by refugees from war-torn Somali and Sudan. Much of the area is also troubled by intertribal violence and banditry, and tourists should take local advice before traveling in the region. **Samburu National Reserve** is the only stop on the traditional tourist circuit in this region, although **Lake Turkana** and **Marsabit national parks** are other rarely visited options.

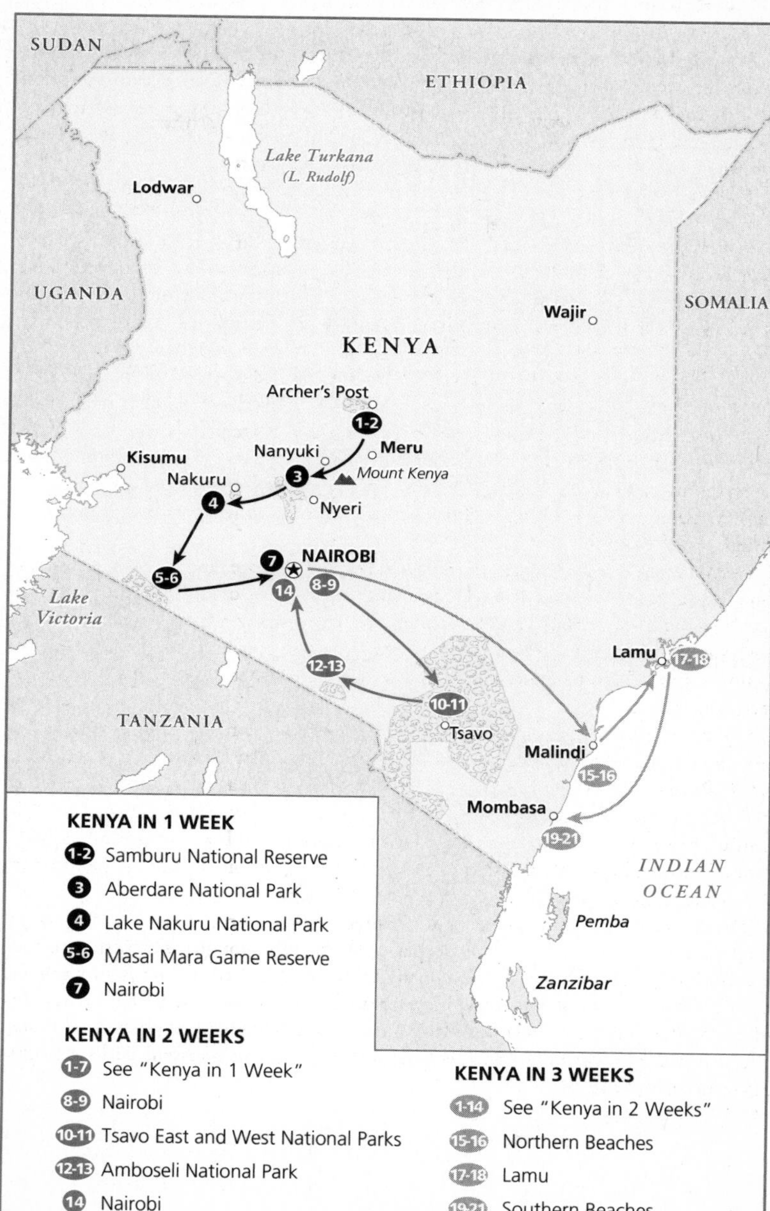
SUDAN
ETHIOPIA
Lake Turkana
(L. Rudolf)
Lodwar
UGANDA
SOMALIA
Wajir
KENYA
Archer's Post
1-2
Nanyuki
Meru
Kisumu
3
Mount Kenya
Nakuru
4
Nyeri
7
NAIROBI
5-6
14
8-9
Lake
Victoria
12-13
Lamu
17-18
10-11
TANZANIA
Tsavo
Malindi
15-16
Mombasa
19-21
INDIAN
OCEAN
Pemba
Zanzibar
KENYA IN 1 WEEK
1-2 Samburu National Reserve
3 Aberdare National Park
4 Lake Nakuru National Park
5-6 Masai Mara Game Reserve
7 Nairobi
KENYA IN 2 WEEKS
1-7 See "Kenya in 1 Week"
8-9 Nairobi
10-11 Tsavo East and West National Parks
12-13 Amboseli National Park
14 Nairobi
KENYA IN 3 WEEKS
1-14 See "Kenya in 2 Weeks"
15-16 Northern Beaches
17-18 Lamu
19-21 Southern Beaches

1 KENYA IN 1 WEEK

You can easily combine two or three parks and reserves in a week. This is a sample itinerary, but tour operators can offer other combinations with other parks. On some safaris you may find yourself rerouting through Nairobi between the parks.

Days ❶ & ❷: Samburu National Reserve ★★★

From **Nairobi,** safaris head north to the **Samburu National Reserve** for a couple of nights at one of the lodges on the banks of the Ewaso Ng'iro River, where most of the game is concentrated. Animals include giraffes, elephants, hippos, crocodiles, buffalos, lions, leopards, cheetahs, and hyenas, and more than 365 types of birds. Look out for species here not seen farther south, such as Grevy's zebra, Somali ostrich, and gerenuk, an unusual antelope that can reach up the trees on its hind legs.

Day ❸: Aberdare National Park ★★

Heading south, the option is to spend a night in one of the two unusual lodges in the Aberdare National Park: **Treetops,** where Princess Elizabeth stayed in 1952 on the night her father died and she became queen, or the **Ark** built in the shape of Noah's Ark. At night, stay up to watch the game activities over the floodlit waterholes. This park is unusual in that it lies above 21,000m (68,880 ft.) and so has a more alpine feel, with mountains, streams, valleys, and moorland.

Day ❹: Lake Nakuru National Park ★★★

After another morning game drive, your safari will head to Nakuru. Situated just a stone's throw from the town, the attractive **Lake Nakuru National Park** surrounds the lake of the same name, which is a haven for the pink lesser flamingo as well as hippo. Other species include various antelope, giraffe, zebra, lion, rhino, and leopard (which can actually be spotted during daylight hours in the arms of the giant yellow acacia trees near the entrance). Enjoy the great views from the park's rocky escarpments and ridges. Accommodation can be found at several lodges and campsites.

Days ❺ & ❻: Masai Mara Game Reserve ★★★

You will spend at least 2 nights in the **Masai Mara Game Reserve,** Kenya's most famous park with an extraordinary density of animals, including the Big Five. In July and August, it's also the scene of the Migration, when hundreds of thousands of wildebeest, plus smaller numbers of zebra and antelope, arrive in search of fresh grazing from Tanzania's Serengeti National park to the south. The predators follow the herds, so this is the best time to witness plenty of animal action, especially if you get the opportunity to see the wildebeest cross the Mara River, where they have to dodge crocodiles, too. There are dozens of places to stay, from hotel-style lodges to tented camps.

Day ❼: Nairobi ★

After an early morning game drive, you'll head back to Nairobi, a 6-hour drive away.

2 KENYA IN 2 WEEKS

After a few days on bumpy and dusty roads, have a break in Nairobi to recharge your batteries and see the urban sights, as well as enjoy the good shopping and restaurants. Then consider a short safari to the southern parks; Amboseli and Tsavo can also be visited from the coast.

Days 1–7:

See "Kenya in 1 Week," above.

Days 8 & 9: Nairobi ★★★

Spend at least half a day on a game drive in the **Nairobi National Park,** which, with the city as a backdrop, is home to all of the Big Five except elephants, but these can be seen on the morning excursion to the **David Sheldrick Animal Orphanage** adjoining the park. Here you can watch baby elephants tearing around; kids will love it. They'll also enjoy feeding the giraffes at the **Langata Giraffe Centre.** The nearby **Karen Blixen Museum** looks at Kenya's colonial past. End one evening at the **Carnivore** restaurant, where meat is roasted on Maasai spears.

Days 10 & 11: Tsavo East and West National Parks ★★★

One of Kenya's oldest and largest national parks, this is split by the Nairobi-Mombasa road and railway. It's administered as Tsavo East and Tsavo West; its southern plains meet those in Tanzania's Serengeti National Park. The diverse range of habitats—mountains, river, forest, lakes, and grassland—are home to rhinos, lions, leopards, crocodiles, waterbucks, kudus, hartebeests, and zebras, as well as some of the largest herds of elephants in Kenya. There are plenty of isolated lodges and campsites to choose from.

Days 12 & 13: Amboseli National Park ★★★

Amboseli National Park is famous for its wonderful image of elephants on the grassy plains, with Kilimanjaro's snow-covered peaks in the background. Plentiful game to look for includes zebras, wildebeests, giraffes, impalas, lions, and leopards, and bird-watchers may spot pelicans, African fish eagles, and pygmy falcons. As one of Kenya's most popular parks, there's a full range of accommodations.

Day 14: Nairobi ★

After a morning game drive, return to Nairobi.

Home on the Range

The **Laikipia Plateau** is a patchwork of spacious ranches to the north of Mount Kenya, owners of which in the early 1990s got together, took down fences, and turned from farming livestock to harboring free-roaming wildlife on the shared land. This has been Kenya's greatest conservation initiative in recent years, and today has the largest concentration of game outside the Masai Mara, with exceptionally healthy populations of rhino and elephant. Visitors to this region need to be well heeled, as most of the lodges are in original farm homesteads where you will experience personal hosting by the ranch owners. Allow at least a week in the region, and if you want to climb Mount Kenya, allow another 5 days.

3 KENYA IN 3 WEEKS

After 2 weeks of game viewing, you'll be in need of a little sun and sand. Kenya's coast is well equipped for tourists with a string of resorts. Those who prefer a more traditional stay should head for the historical islands of Lamu, which are deeply religious and culturally conservative.

Days 1–14:

See "Kenya in 2 Weeks," above.

Days 15 & 16: Northern Beaches ★★★

A coastal highway runs north from **Mombasa** all the way to Kenya's northern frontier and provides access to Kenya's northern beaches. From the outskirts of Mombasa, there's a string of popular vacation resorts that finally peter out on the north side of **Malindi,** from where the road continues through coastal bush to the islands of the **Lamu Archipelago.** Each resort has access to the beach, and the Indian Ocean marine life of coral, fish, sea turtles, and dolphins can be seen by snorkeling and diving, or more sedately from a dhow or glass-bottom boat. Directly north of Mombasa, the palm-fringed **Nyali** and **Bamburi** beaches fall within the small **Mombasa Marine Park,** while beyond, the bustling town of **Mtwapa** is flanked by the sheltered **Shanzu Beach.** The beaches are then broken by the wide mouth of **Kilifi Creek,** whose azure waters are a popular port of call on the international yachting circuit. The sleepy village of **Watamu** is fronted by a wide white sandy beach with several well-established resorts and the **Watamu Marine Park,** with its small offshore islands, which has an excellent fringing coral reef that attracts a number of colorful fish. Farther up the coast, **Malindi** has another set of idyllic tropical beaches, though seaweed can be a problem here. The **Malindi Marine Park** again offers reefs full of tropical fish, and you can dive and snorkel around **Casuarina Point.**

Days 17 & 18: Lamu ★★★

From Malindi, the road continues through coastal bush to the islands of the **Lamu Archipelago,** located in the extreme north of Kenya. **Lamu** has a lovely 13km (8-mile) isolated beach at **Shela,** with perfect sand and no reef, which means substantial waves. Lamu town, with its long waterfront lined with white-sailed dhows and its intriguing network of alleyways, warrants a day's exploration to enjoy its time-warped traditional Swahili atmosphere. A few luxurious and exclusive resorts lie hidden among the islands, or you can stay in a traditional Arabic house in Lamu or Shela. Also make time to sample local cuisine; little alcohol is available in the predominantly Islamic islands, but the coconut juice is legendary, as is the Swahili-style seafood.

Days 19–21: Southern Beaches ★★★

The coastal road south of Mombasa is not as crowded with resorts as the north coast. The beaches are backed by lush green coastal forest with prolific birdlife and a variety of wildlife, including baboons and black-and-white colobus monkeys. **Tiwi Beach** is the first tourist beach south of the ferry (across Mombasa Harbor) and has some large hotels popular with families and budget travelers; when the tide goes out, kids can explore the hundreds of exposed rock pools. Farther south, **Diani Beach** is one of the nicest on the coast, with bright blue water and a long expanse of white sand. There are several reefs offshore that can be explored by snorkeling from a dhow or glass-bottom boat, and the nearest ones can be waded out to at low tide. Off the coast, **Funzi Island** is home to a luxury lodge popular with honeymooners, while the southernmost section of the Kenyan Coast falls within the **Kisite Marine National Park.** The sea here is an intense turquoise blue, and the park has a range of reefs and small islands where dolphins and turtles are regularly spotted. If you are staying at Diani Beach, day trips to the park are available that include dhow rides, snorkeling, and a seafood lunch on **Wasini Island.**

TANZANIA REGIONS IN BRIEF

Dar es Salaam, meaning "haven for peace," was founded in 1862 by Sultan Seyyid Majid of Zanzibar and was later capital of the colonial administration. Evidence of German and British architecture can be seen around the city. It also serves as a springboard to Zanzibar, only a short hop by plane or a 90-minute ferry ride away.

Zanzibar refers to the archipelago made up of **Zanzibar** and **Pemba,** and several smaller islands, roughly 40km (25 miles) off the Tanzanian coast. For centuries it was an important hub in the Indian Ocean trade route, until the colonists arrived. The island of Zanzibar is by far the most popular tourist destination, and for good reason—dazzling white beaches, an azure and warm Indian Ocean, and the wonderfully atmospheric **Stone Town.**

Tanzania's **mainland coast** has witnessed very little tourist development, though there are a couple of highlights for adventurous travelers. **Kilwa Kivinje** and **Kilwa Kisiwani** are ruined Swahili settlements dating back as far as the 12th century, where the Omanis built great forts, palaces, and mosques. Local guides give tours, and there's accommodation in nearby **Kilwa Masoko. Mafia Island,** remote with very few places to stay, is world renowned for its deep-sea fishing and scuba diving.

The region around **Moshi** is fairly attractive, thanks to Kilimanjaro, which looms above the town. On the fertile lower slopes of the mountain are the Arabica coffee plantations that Catholic missionaries introduced at the end of the 19th century. But the main reason to come to Moshi is to climb Kilimanjaro to the highest point in Africa, at Uhuru Peak.

Located in the foothills of **Mount Meru,** and the halfway point between Cairo and Cape Town, **Arusha** is a thriving city and is the access point for safaris to Tanzania's **Northern Circuit** parks. Here the vast rolling plains, trampled by herds of wildlife, are the Africa most visitors expect to see, and Tanzania's Northern Circuit parks won't disappoint. The **Serengeti** features the famous annual wildebeest migration, one of the greatest movements of animals on Earth. Equally impressive is the **Ngorongoro Crater,** a caldera created by a collapsed volcano that supports a staggering number of animals. **Lake Manyara** is known for its soda lake that supports thousands of flamingoes, while **Tarangire** has an abundance of elephants.

Lake Victoria, at 67,850 sq. km (26,462 sq. miles), is the second-largest freshwater lake in the world. The Tanzanian section of Lake Victoria is one of the least-visited parts of the country, and, admittedly, the featureless ports of **Bukoba, Musoma,** and **Mwanza** have few attractions. Most travelers head for the Kenyan and Ugandan sections of the lake.

Forming the western border of Tanzania, skinny **Lake Tanganyika** is divided among four countries: Tanzania, Burundi, Democratic Republic of the Congo (DRC), and

Zambia. The main town on the lake is **Kigoma,** a simple place and a long way from anywhere else. The main reason to come to this isolated spot is to see chimpanzees in the **Gombe Stream National Park** and the **Mahale Mountains National Park.**

Accessed from Dar es Salaam, Tanzania's **Southern Circuit** parks offer an unrivalled bush wilderness experience. **Selous, Katavi,** and **Ruaha** are way off the usual tourist itinerary and are largely accessible only to those who can afford the few high-cost, low-impact camps.

4 TANZANIA IN 1 WEEK

The route below gives a quick taste of Tanzania's most popular national parks. You'll experience a short safari and wildlife, but it'll be a busy week. Those who prefer a laid-back pace should spend an extra night or two in each park or consider flying between lodges and camps. This itinerary is not set in stone, as tour operators may visit these parks in a different order. If you're coming from Nairobi and using a tour operator that operates in both Kenya and Tanzania, it may also be possible to visit Amboseli National Park en route from Nairobi to Arusha.

Day ❶: Arusha ★

As your safari starts and ends in **Arusha,** it is essential to stay there the night before your safari departs. The busy commercial town lacks charm, but for the traveler there are a number of good souvenir shops and bustling markets where you can pick up some good-value Maasai curios. **Arusha National Park** offers good views of Mount Meru and is one of the few parks that permit walking safaris.

Day ❷: Tarangire National Park ★★★

From **Arusha,** safaris head southwest through the coffee plantations and on to the plains, where you may see the Maasai grazing their cattle, and on to the **Tarangire National Park,** which is less than 2 hours' drive from Arusha. The floodplains, grasslands, and acacia woodlands are home to a full range of animals, and the tall sausage and baobab trees are a favorite haunt of leopards and tree-climbing lions. The lodges here are a little less crowded than in the other parks.

Day ❸: Ngorongoro Crater Conservation Area ★★★

The following day, tours continue east where the road goes up the scenic escarpment overlooking **Lake Manyara.** There are viewing spots to pull over and admire the lake, tinged with pink thanks to the thousands of flamingoes. From here the road steadily climbs the foothills of the **Ngorongoro Conservation Area,** and the vegetation becomes increasingly green and lush until you are in dense forest on the Ngorongoro Crater's rim. After spending the night at a lodge or camp at the top of the crater, sink into the crater the next day for a half-day's safari, where plentiful game-watching is virtually guaranteed.

Days ❹ & ❺: Serengeti National Park ★★★

Back on the crater rim, the road spectacularly continues down the steep hill of the outer crater, where again Maasai can be seen stalking the open plains, before flattening out at the gate of the **Serengeti National Park.** Spend 2 nights here, where game drives across the sun-baked

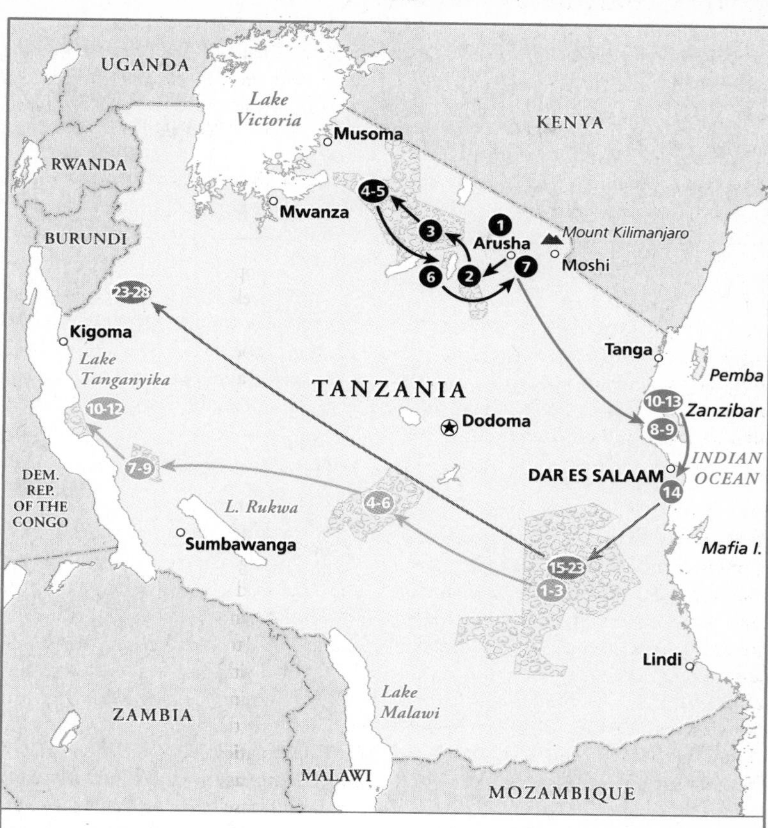

TANZANIA IN 1 WEEK

- 1 Arusha
- 2 Tarangire National Park
- 3 Ngorongoro Crater Conservation Area
- 4-5 Serengeti National Park
- 6 Lake Manyara National Park
- 7 Arusha

TANZANIA IN 2 WEEKS

- 1-7 See "Tanzania in 1 Week"
- 8-9 Stone Town, Zanzibar
- 10-13 North or East Coast Beaches
- 14 In transit

TANZANIA IN 3 TO 4 WEEKS

- 1-14 See "Tanzania in 2 Weeks"
- 15-23 Safari in the South
- 23-28 Western Circuit

SOUTHERN SAFARI CIRCUIT IN 1 TO 2 WEEKS

- 1-3 Selous Game Reserve
- 4-6 Ruaha National Park
- 7-9 Katavi National Park
- 10-12 Mahale Mountains National Park

Climbing Kili

Between Arusha and Zanzibar, visitors have the option of climbing Kilimanjaro, or Kili, as it's affectionately known, and there are plenty of tour operators to choose from in and around Moshi. The highest point in Africa is the Uhuru Peak, at 5,895m (19,336 ft.), which is one of seven summits of Kilimanjaro. There are a number of climbs to choose from, with various levels of difficulty. The three easiest routes—Marangu, Rongai, and Machame—can be climbed by anyone in good health and require no mountaineering experience, although acclimatization and altitude sickness must be taken into consideration. Allow at least 5 days for the climb, with a night on either side in Moshi (this will tack on another week to your existing schedule).

plains, dotted with piles of giant boulders, can be richly rewarding, particularly during the Migration.

Day 6: Lake Manyara National Park ★★★

Backtrack on the same road across the top of the Ngorongoro Crater and spend a final night in **Lake Manyara National Park.** Lying at the foot of the scenic Manyara Escarpment and surrounding the lake of the same name, this park features acacia woodland, some ancient gnarled teak and mahogany trees, and grass and marshland. It's home to a number of large animals and although rarely seen, is famous for its tree-climbing lions. Easily seen around the lake and on the cliffs is the rich diversity of birdlife.

Day 7: Arusha ★

On the final day, return to Arusha.

5 TANZANIA IN 2 WEEKS

The highlights of **Zanzibar** can be visited in 3 or 4 days, but to enjoy some downtime on the beach, consider going for a week after a safari. After a few days on bumpy and dusty roads, this is an ideal way to round up a vacation to Tanzania. You can fly to **Zanzibar** from Kilimanjaro International Airport or the other regional airports, or catch a 90-minute hydrofoil from Dar es Salaam.

Days 1–7:

See "Tanzania in 1 Week," above.

Days 8 & 9: Stone Town, Zanzibar ★★★

Stone Town warrants a couple of days to soak up the atmosphere in the fascinating labyrinth of narrow streets and alleyways. The elaborate 19th-century houses have impressive carved-wood doors, elegantly carved balconies, and loggias and verandas that cling precipitously overhead; many have been restored as charming hotels decorated with antiques and Persian rugs. Zanzibar is also known as the Spice Isle, thanks to the inland spice plantations with cardamom, ginger, cloves, and nutmeg, and you can sample these on an informative half-day tour. Also when in Stone Town, eat at the nightly food market, visit one of the offshore islands, and perhaps take a ride on a dhow.

Days ⑩–⑬: North or East Coast Beaches ★★★

There are more than 25 idyllic beaches to choose from on Zanzibar, all backed by palms and mangroves, where views of a white-sailed dhow slipping silently across a sinking sun are a permanent feature. The young at heart can head to the north coast for a few nights in a rustic bungalow at **Nungwi** or **Kendwa** (well known as a party destination and for its idyllic beach), while on the east coast are large family resorts spread attractively along the beaches. Watersports are on offer around the island. In the southeast, the **Jozani Forest** has excellent nature trails and is home to the rare red colobus monkey, or you can swim with dolphins off the southwest of the island.

In contrast with Zanzibar, the other island in the archipelago, **Pemba,** has a fledgling tourist industry and is hardly visited at all. It's almost completely surrounded by mangroves and so has fewer beaches than Zanzibar, though serious scuba divers should head here for some of the best diving in Africa. On the west coast, the Pemba Channel creates dramatic walls and drop-offs that are home to a variety of large marine species such as sharks, rays, and barracudas.

Day ⑭: In Transit

Depending on times of onward travel, you may need to spend another night in Stone Town before catching a flight or the ferry to Dar es Salaam to connect with international flights or continue on to other parts of Tanzania.

6 TANZANIA IN 3 TO 4 WEEKS

If your appetite for game viewing hasn't been satiated in the Northern Circuit parks, then the lesser-visited parks in the Southern and Western circuits can be accessed by flights from Dar es Salaam. The lodges and camps in these are far more remote and intimate, so this is the ideal destination for those looking for a wilderness experience away from hordes of safari-goers.

Days ①–⑭:

See "Tanzania in 2 Weeks," above.

Days ⑮–㉓: Safari in the South ★★★

The **Selous Game Reserve** and the **Ruaha** and **Kitavi** national parks in Tanzania's south are some of the wildest areas of East Africa and are fairly inaccessible except by small plane. They operate on a high-cost, low-impact system, and those who can afford it will enjoy the tremendous solitude of the bush. The three parks are connected by flights, so spend at least 2 to 3 nights in each; they can be visited in any order. The landscapes are reminiscent of what the whole of East Africa looked like when it belonged only to the wildlife. About the same size of Denmark, the vast Selous is the largest game reserve in Africa, and it's reputedly home to more than a million animals. Both Ruaha and Katavi offer untouched swathes of game-filled wilderness and receive only a handful of visitors each year. While the parks' few tented camps are isolated enough as it is, there's the additional option of going fly-camping, guided walking safaris where visitors sleep out in the open with only a mosquito net between them and the African sky. The final flight will return you to Dar es Salaam.

Days ㉓–㉘: Western Circuit ★★

For those with more time, flights (or a long and arduous train ride) connect Dar es Salaam to Kigoma on the shores of Lake Tanganyika in Western Tanzania. The main reason to come to this isolated spot is to see chimpanzees in the **Gombe Stream National Park** and the **Mahale Mountains National Park.** Both are on the lakeshore and feature very basic rest camps, as well as luxury lodges. Visitors can go on guided forest walks to see the chimpanzees. The final flight will return you to Dar es Salaam.

7 SOUTHERN SAFARI CIRCUIT IN 1 TO 2 WEEKS

As with any safari destination, Southern Tanzania is best explored at a leisurely pace and with the dictum "Less is more" firmly in mind. Put simply, visiting fewer reserves for longer periods is likely to prove more rewarding than trying to squeeze in as many different places as possible into one holiday. The best way to get around the region is by air, a minimum of 3 nights in any given reserve is recommended, and given the remoteness of the terrain, it is strongly recommended you book through an operator with regional knowledge. The itinerary below is spread over 12 days and takes in the region's top four reserves, but you could add an extra night at Selous to fly-camp, or stay on at Mahale to enjoy the beach, while those with more limited time could split off the Selous/Ruaha component or Katavi/Mahale component and do either as a 1-week safari.

Days ❶–❸: Selous Game Reserve

The short flight from Dar es Salaam to Selous is a real thriller, especially as you fly low over the swampy maze of channels and lakes fed by the Rufiji, with elephants wallowing in the swamps below and giraffe trotting nervously along the plains in response to the engine's roar. Three nights in the Selous is a must, and make sure you take advantage of the varied activities offered by most camps; this is the only place in Southern Tanzania where you can view game from a boat, and guided walks are also offered to supplement game drives. All the camps in Selous offer something special, but for those whose budget knows no limit, our pick is Sand Rivers. And think about adding a fourth night if you want to fly-camp on the lakes (highly recommended, though not for the nervous).

Days ❹–❻: Ruaha National Park

Another short but exciting plane ride takes you to Ruaha National Park, which feels even more remote than Selous and offers more varied game viewing; this is your best shot on the Southern Circuit for seeing leopards and cheetahs, and chances of sighting these elusive cats are very good if you stay 3 nights. Game drives dominate proceedings at Ruaha more than in Selous, but several camps offer guided bush walks, too. It's difficult to pick a favorite among the superb quartet of established camps here, but we're going with Mwagusi for its wonderful location, top-notch guides, unforgettable bush dinners, and the peerless quality of game viewing in the surrounding area.

Days ❼–❾: Katavi National Park

And you thought Ruaha was remote? When you land at Katavi, you really do feel like you've slipped back 100 years, staying at one of a handful of camps whose Edwardian bush ambience has you half expecting Karen Blixen and Denys Finch-Hatton to pitch up at the dinner table. The wildlife here is not as varied as Ruaha, but dry season concentrations can be staggering; try a herd of 1,000 buffalo, a group of 50 elephants, and a pride of lions in one binocular sweep of the floodplain. But for students of animal behavior, it's the hippos that steal the show at the height of the dry season, when hundreds of individuals might congregate in one pool, and bloody male dominance fights are a daily event.

Days ⑩–⑫: Mahale Mountain National Park

Another short scenic flight crosses the Mahale Mountain to bring you to the shore of Lake Tanganyika and a complete change of pace. Chimpanzee tracking is the main activity here, and at least 2 nights is required (3 or 4, even better) to be certain of coming face to face with these charismatic forest dwellers. When you're not scrambling through the undergrowth, you can pretend you're on a beach holiday; catch a tan on the sandy beach, swim in the insanely clear water, or kayak or snorkel out on the lake. Greystoke is the top camp here, but its more affordable competitor, Kungwe, is also very good and just as idyllically located.

5

Nairobi

A city of dream-chasers, Nairobi represents the modern aspirations of an increasingly Western-minded Kenya. Hard to believe, in fact, that just a century ago, the Maasai were hunting lions right here where the concrete high-rises cast their shadows. Today, in fact, when Maasai warriors walk through the city, they stick out incongruously among the suits and fashion-conscious who are working so hard to slough off outward links with tribe, tradition, and perhaps the village they've abandoned in favor of bright lights and the big city.

Like so much in Africa, Nairobi is a city of astounding paradoxes. It's infamously plagued by the worst of Third World ailments—the biggest slum in East Africa, a massive reputation for its crime, and population growth that has long outstripped urban planning—and yet is infused with a unique brand of cosmopolitanism that makes it one of the continent's buzziest capitals, stocked with shopping malls, first-rate restaurants, and an upwardly mobile middle class with money to burn. Alongside the BMWs and fuel-guzzling SUVs, beaten-up *matatus* race through the streets, and in the city's outskirts, cattle and goats graze at the side of the road. At traffic lights, hawkers sell everything from mobile phone chargers and cheap artworks to underwear and live kittens, while traditionally attired Maasai warriors cruise the streets looking for opportunities to flog their handicrafts. At the end of the day, the city sidewalks are abuzz with office workers marching to meet their transport or pausing for an after-work drink, while in suburbia, armed security guards prepare for an all-night vigil as the rich retire behind their walls and fences.

The contrasts are as startling as they are riveting; the mélange of rich and dirt-poor, empowered and down-at-heel, modern and traditional makes this a fascinating example of a city permanently in flux. After dark, much of the city center turns into a virtual nightclub, with an incessant throng for booze, dancing, misbehavior, and sex. But come Sunday, prayers and gospel music blare out from just about every second building. It's a city where strip clubs and pubs stand cheek-by-jowl with gargantuan churches and solemn-looking office blocks; restaurants occupy floor space above gas stations; and street vendors selling cigarettes, condoms, and mobile phones set up shop outside SUV showrooms and slick shopping malls.

Nairobi is today the largest city between Cairo and Johannesburg, and its rapid growth has inevitably put heavy pressure on a wholly inept infrastructure. With its people caught up in the wealth-creation ethos of Western capitalism, the resultant clamor for a part of the corporate action has meant that the city's streets are usually choked by traffic, and at peak hours, the situation is dire. Yet just a few miles from downtown Nairobi, in posh neighborhoods such as the frangipani-scented diplomatic enclaves to the north and the gentrified colonial-era farming suburbs such as Karen (named after the author of *Out in Africa*) and Langata, the scene slows down to a countryside pace. Here farm-style manor houses and enormous estates shelter the wealthy and the privileged, and many residents—mostly white Kenyans and expats—seldom set foot in the city itself, preferring to carry on their lives away from the clutter and the mayhem. This is where you'll get some idea of what Nairobi might have been like in its early days as a cool country retreat, a place where English gentry would send their sons and daughters to keep them away from the temptations of early-20th-century London. It's here, too, that some of Nairobi's favorite attractions are located—an orphanage for baby elephant and rhino, a sanctuary for endangered giraffe, and excellent artisan workshops where community involvement means you can shop with a clear conscious.

Whatever you've heard, read, or seen, first impressions aren't likely to win you over. Chances are, you're not going to be sticking around for too long anyhow—most visitors are here in anticipation of a safari far from the hustle and the bustle, or awaiting a flight home.

But with an open mind, it's easy to pick up on—and, hopefully, experience—Nairobi's zest and vitality; there's a genuine vibe if you can see through the discontent, poverty, and crime and venture beyond the cosseting barricades. It's definitely worth remembering that smack up against this bustling, sprawling, combustible, modern city is a wildlife preserve inhabited by lion and leopard, giraffe and buffalo—it's one fantastic eccentricity that makes Nairobi feel like the frontier town it started out as, with the untamed wilderness forever on its sun-drenched fringe.

1 ESSENTIALS

GETTING THERE & AWAY

BY AIR Located 15km (9¼ miles) from the city center, Nairobi's **Jomo Kenyatta International Airport** (✆ **020/82-2111;** www.kenyaairports.com) is East Africa's major air transport hub, and it sees its fair share of international air traffic, receiving large numbers of diplomatic and business travelers, not to mention many Westerners arriving for their first African safari.

Closer to the city center is the smaller **Wilson Airport** (✆ **020/50-1943**), which specializes in domestic and charter flights; it's located on Langata Road, just 6km (3¾ miles) south of the city. Wilson is a hub for flights to a string of coastal destinations, national parks, and reserves, as well as scheduled and charter flights to private airstrips on wildlife preserves throughout the country (it's also used for a few flights to neighboring countries). The main domestic airlines (which may also fly to select airports in neighboring countries) are **AirKenya** (www.airkenya.com), **SafariLink** (www.safarilinkkenya.com), **TropicAir** (www.tropicairkenya.com), and **Fly540** (www.fly540.com).

Taxis are always available at both airports, but in all likelihood, you'll feel better if you arrange a transfer in advance; this is usually done through a tour operator's ground agent (see "Tour Operators & Guided Tours," below). Someone with prior knowledge of your full itinerary will be waiting in the arrivals hall with a name board; they'll assist with luggage and get you to your Nairobi hotel or to your onward transfer in the quickest time possible, and also inform you of any amendments to your schedule. You can also arrange airport pick-up through your hotel, but if you have the patience and the will, it's relatively simple and safe (and considerably cheaper) to grab a cab at the airport; you'll discover that the fare is highly negotiable, almost always starting with an inflated suggestion from the driver; anything more than Ksh1,200 to reach downtown from the International Airport, and you're being hustled—chances are, you'll end up paying Ksh1,500. If you're going into the city, it is, theoretically, also possible to catch the no. 34 City Hoppa

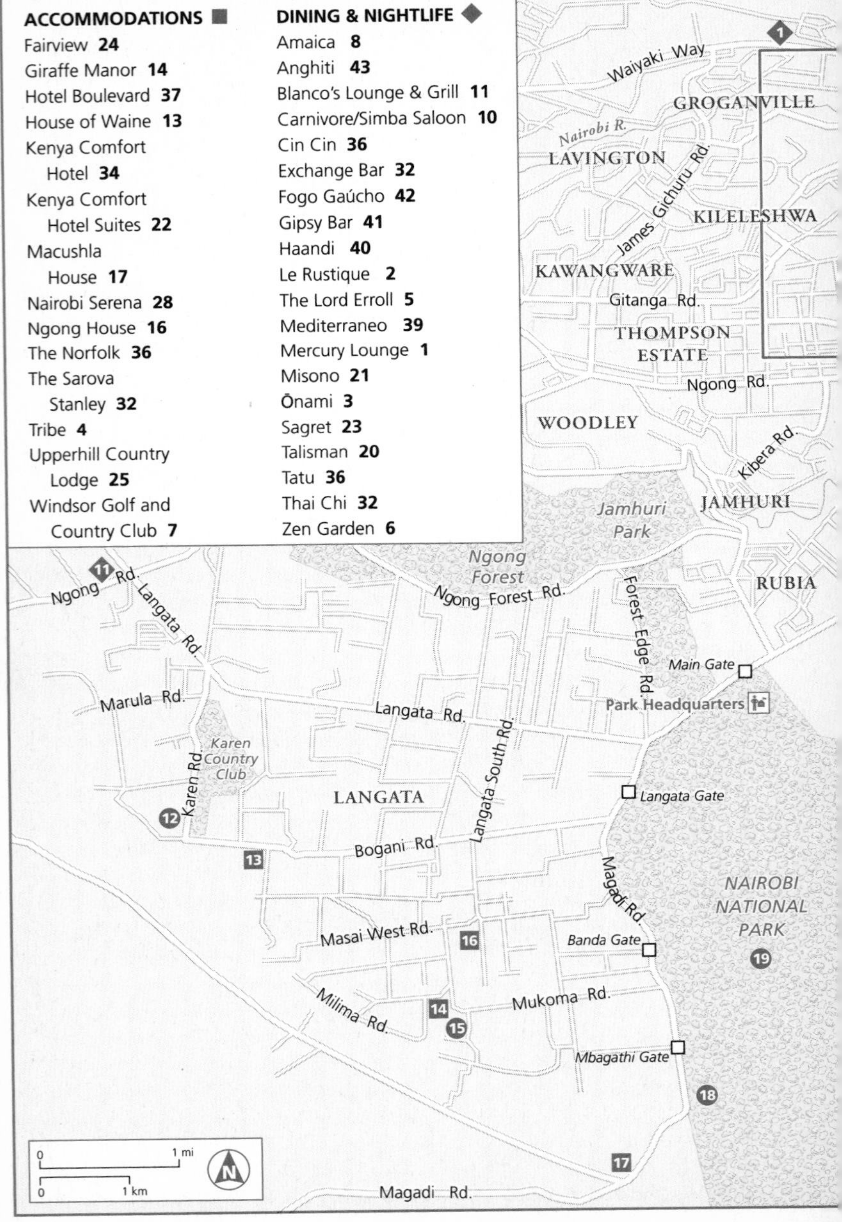

ESSENTIALS 5 NAIROBI

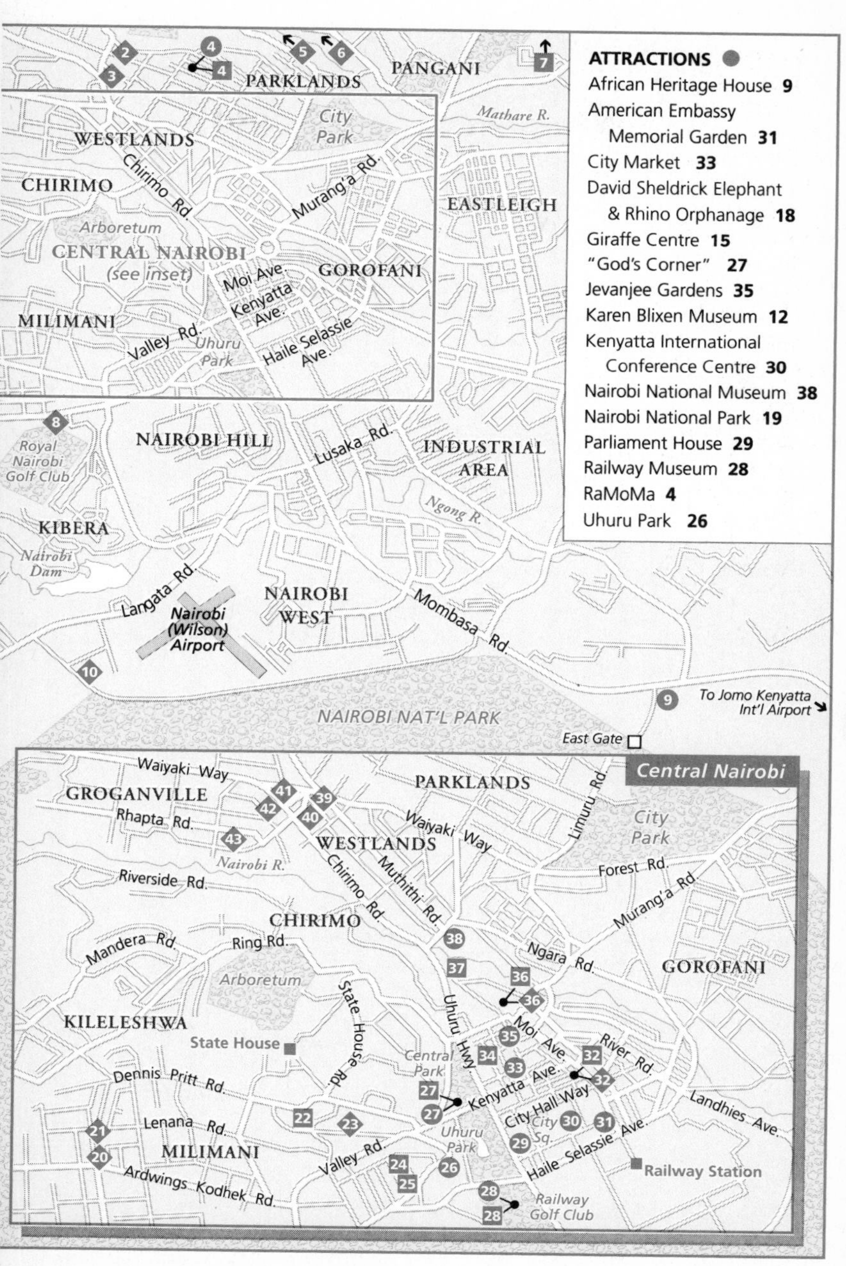

NAIROBI

5

ESSENTIALS

Tips For Safety's Sake

Even if you only occasionally tune into CNN or BBC, you'll have seen the harrowing images that almost destroyed Kenya's tourism industry in early 2008. Weeks of violent post-election rioting plagued Nairobi and other corners of the country, and burning buildings, street battles, and haphazard violence made headline news and stirred the global media into a frenzy. The pictures of looting, rioting, billowing smoke, and charging policemen in full anti-riot gear were enough to stop people from coming to Kenya; such images are hardly helped by memories of the American embassy bombing in 1998, pre-election violence in 1997, and street clashes during pro-democracy protests back in 1990. While the impression left in the minds of Westerners was of a country in tatters, Kenyans seem to agree that the flair-up was generally limited to certain quarters and had almost zero impact on areas of tourist interest. Still, the images linger and the death toll serves as a bleak reminder of the fury that exists under the surface of a nation of people who will stop you in the street to remind you, "Kenyans are very peaceful." Peace-loving Kenyans may be, but that doesn't undercut Nairobi's overwhelming reputation for crime—it's so notorious, in fact, that it's often called "Nai-robbery," while it seems almost ironic that the city headquarters a government even more notorious for its endless corruption.

Like Johannesburg, with which it draws obvious comparisons, Nairobi is a teeming city where countless destitute people rub shoulders daily with the privileged, and somewhere in that stew there's a huge propensity for all manner of crime. Don't assume for one instant that tourists are especially targeted. In 2009, during a citywide public art exhibition in which 50 artist-decorated, life-size fiberglass lions were on display in shopping centers and sidewalks, it wasn't long before at least one of the lions was stolen. Ironically, the exhibition was called *Pride of Kenya* and aimed to raise awareness about the threat facing Kenya's wildlife. But for many Nairobians, carjackings and armed home invasions (now greatly diminished) have been a far more tangible threat for many years, and you'll be astounded by the sheer extent of private security employed to protect businesses and private homes—one company protects more than 4,000 households. In the suburbs, there are electric fences and manned security posts, while *askaris* line the city streets protecting shops, banks, and offices through the night. Yet while the streets of middle-class and wealthy suburbs—such as Karen and Langata—may be deserted at night, save for a few *askari* manning the gates to vast estates, there's a totally different feeling in some of the slums. In Mathare, one the poorest areas of the city, for example, one youth leader is proud to claim that if you lose your mobile phone

bus and pay just Ksh30; the journey will take you as far as the bus "terminal" right near the Hilton Hotel, but if you've arrived with anything more than a small bag, you're going to battle stowing your luggage or, indeed, keeping an eye on it—better to take a taxi.

BY ROAD You can travel by road (including by bus or minibus) between Kenya and Tanzania. The main routes are from Mombasa or Nairobi to Dar es Salaam, and from in his neighborhood, it'll be returned by whomever finds it. It's a proud boast, perhaps, but one that certainly serves as a yardstick against which to measure perceptions of how crime and poverty really relate.

The latest panic-inducing threat is kidnapping, and several recent attacks have been on children and Western women. Security is being stepped up at schools in response to the abduction of more than 100 Nairobi residents in the first part of 2009; some "experts" have even referred to an emerging "kidnapping industry," possibly inspired by Somali pirate activity. Foreigners are not unaffected, and while single women may be especially vulnerable, there have been incidents of entire busloads of passengers being robbed, while in 2009 carjackers kidnapped a member of Parliament as well as a senior police commander; in a separate incident, the prime minister's private office was looted.

The moral of the story is that crime is a reality in Nairobi—and in Africa—and it is not bound by geographic borders or social contexts. It may take the form of a customs official trying to press you for a bribe or a taxi driver overcharging you. Such incidents don't even register against the hardships faced by many of the people living here. Vigilance and common sense are your most powerful allies. And the sooner you learn to adapt to a wholly different environment, the better. Do not wear expensive or even ostentatious-*looking* jewelry, and don't carry bags through the city with you, especially if they're loose fitting or easily snatched away. In fact, try to limit the valuables that you carry on your person. There are reports of unsuspecting tourists climbing into fake taxi cabs and being stripped naked, so it doesn't matter how well you hide your money—but obviously, concealing your wallet (which is actually best left in a hotel safe) is better than flaunting it in a bulging pocket. Exercise the same caution with cameras, often difficult to keep an eye on when in use. Be wary of whom you speak to in the street or in bars; a simple conversation may, in fact, be a planned distraction—more often than not, it's the start of a lengthy con in which you'll eventually be asked for some kind of monetary donation. Do not accept lifts with strangers or rides with unmarked, unidentifiable taxis. Be careful about sitting next to open windows in vehicles—snatch-and-grabs are common, and you're most vulnerable when sitting in a car. And don't leave valuables in any vehicle, unless your driver (and I'm not talking about taxi drivers here) has assured you that it's safe or that he'll be keeping an eye on the car. Don't walk around at night, and be sure not to step onto deserted streets. And, at all times, keep your wits about you.

Nairobi to Arusha and Moshi. Roads also, theoretically, connect Nairobi with the Ugandan capital, Kampala, and with Ethiopia, the main border crossing being at Moyale. Die-hard adventurers can ultimately travel to Nairobi by bus or 4×4 from Cape Town or Cairo—but that's another story entirely.

BY TRAIN There is an overnight train connecting Mombasa (at the coast) with Nairobi; however, use this option only if you have time and patience, as it's grown increasingly notorious for an inability to operate according to schedule.

GETTING AROUND

Your tour operator, hotel, or host can put together a sightseeing itinerary for you and will usually make all transport arrangements, so you needn't even pick up the phone or think about where you're headed. Some establishments, such as Giraffe Manor and Ngong House (both reviewed later in this chapter), have limited sightseeing included in the rate, ideal if you're in town for only a day or less but keen to explore a bit. If you prefer your independence and need a reliable **taxi,** this can also be arranged through your hotel. With an extensive network and fixed good-value rates for destinations all across Kenya, **Kenatco** (✆ **020/222-5123** or 072/183-0061; www.kenatco.com) can be relied upon to get you from A to B, or you can hire a car and driver for a specified number of hours. You can even book a pick-up online (although it's a bit laborious). Alternatively, try any of the cab companies listed in the "Fast Facts" section below, or call **Joseph Irungu** (✆ **072/183-8661**); he's based at Village Market near the UN headquarters and so is a good (and reliable) choice if you're in or around the northern suburbs, and he'll quote a price that's fair. With all cabs, you need to consider the city's heavy traffic and schedule pick-ups accordingly—a driver will inevitably take longer than expected to get to you.

For people who don't have their own vehicle in Nairobi, the main modes of transport are either **bus** or ***matatu;*** the latter is basically a minibus taxi (as it's called in South Africa, or *dala dala* in Tanzania). These can both be useful (and extremely cheap) if you have time to figure out routes and are traveling without any luggage, bags, and valuables. If you're interested in how truly local transport operates, you can start investigating the chaotic throng of vehicles that continually pull in and depart from the sprawling bus stands near the Hilton Hotel.

Warning: As a general rule, do not leave any valuables in plain sight inside any vehicle and do not carry valuables around with you; flimsy backpacks and handbags are also vulnerable. Be wary of using your mobile phone with the car window open, as snatch-and-grab scenarios are all too common. Most important, don't get into unmarked or ambiguously identified vehicles whose drivers claim to be taxi drivers—there have been reports of travelers being mugged in this way, and basically left naked in a ditch with everything taken off them.

CITY LAYOUT

Nairobi's business-oriented **city center** is actually quite compact, and you can probably walk from one end to the other in about 30 minutes. The center is also where a good number of business hotels, budget lodgings, restaurants, bars, and rather old-fashioned shopping centers are located. Kenya's Parliament is also located here, as are a handful of the city's museums. Beyond the center, Nairobi sprawls in every direction, with leafy upmarket suburbs to the north and south. **Westlands,** which is northwest of the center, has a high concentration of restaurants, bars, and upmarket shopping malls (including Westgate, the city's newest) frequented by large numbers of expats, many of whom are associated with the foreign embassies located nearby, as well as by UN representatives. Nearby, in a couple of green and unbelievably wealthy neighborhoods, many of these expats live. The areas most popular with travelers are the suburbs south of the city, notably **Karen** and adjacent **Langata,** established on what was once the coffee plantation of

Policing the Cowboys

In October 2009, as part of a bizarre attempt to make Nairobi appear better policed, the city council introduced a number of bylaws banning a number of "unacceptable" behaviors. Suddenly (and this is against a background of poverty, unchecked sewage disasters, power shortages, slums without running water, and embarrassing crime statistics), it's become an offence to spit in the street, blow your nose without a tissue, walk across the road while talking on your mobile phone, and even make loud noises. Each of the Singaporean-style laws can be enforced with either a spot fine or a pretty stiff jail sentence. Spitting in public can attract a fine of Ksh2,000 or 3 months in prison. They're probably the most controversial and slightly surreal bits of legislation to be foisted on the city, and while they might sound like an attempt to clean up Nairobi's tarnished image, most people assume this is yet another opportunity for bribery, with the city likely to employ a squadron of enforcement agents keen to have their palms greased. As a foreigner, your misdemeanor is likely to attract a lot of attention, so remember to cover up when you sneeze and think twice before using your mobile phone while walking.

Danish author Karen Blixen. These two suburbs—also referred to simply as Karengata—are the preserve of Nairobi's white Kenyan community, many of whom are loathe to ever visit the city center itself. You can hardly blame them, though, since Karengata feels nothing like a city at all—for now, it remains countryside. Here you're never too far from Wilson Airport, the main hub for scheduled domestic and charter flights to the major safari destinations, and you have a number of the city's most impressive attractions, including the main entrance for Nairobi National Park, right on your doorstep; shopping here is an adventure.

VISITOR INFORMATION

Your best bet for any sort of meaningful information and news about the city is to ask your host if you're staying in a smaller hotel or guesthouse; these people are usually passionate about Kenya and their city and know its ins and outs. If you're staying in one of the larger city hotels, speak to the hotel concierge, but be warned that many of them give pretty much standard responses about what to see and where to eat, and few have experienced any of these places for themselves; the concierge at the Tribe hotel at the Village Market in Gigiri is very thorough. If you want to surf for information before you travel, try the expat community website **Inside Nairobi** (http://insidenairobi.xemzi.com), which includes Google Earth maps for all places listed. For up-to-the-minute information on Kenya's national parks, visit **www.kws.org**.

TOUR OPERATORS & GUIDED TOURS

Nairobi does a brisk safari trade, and at times it seems that just about anyone will be able to sell you a trip to the Masai Mara, Amboseli, or just about anywhere you care to imagine. I wouldn't recommend leaving any safari planning until your arrival in Nairobi unless you have the luxury of time. For all accommodations and in-Kenya arrangements—from airport transfers to accommodations reservations and domestic flight arrangements—I rely exclusively on **Bush and Beyond** ★★★ (formerly known as Bush

Homes of East Africa; www.bush-and-beyond.com); Chris Flatt, who oversees the operation, has intimate knowledge of virtually every corner of the country, and his team is on the ball, savvy, and immensely helpful, making you feel as though you're a guest rather than a tourist. As a rule, they don't support mass-market, package tourism operations and (unless you request otherwise) will ensure that you're put up in exclusive, mostly family- or community-run lodges, camps, and guesthouses. Their network is extensive, and their itineraries generally ensure that you stay away from the crowds. What's great is that Chris will sagely recommend alternatives if he is unable to assist, or should you be looking for something a little cheaper; a safari with Bush and Beyond starts at around $600 per person per day.

Frank Whalley is one of East Africa's foremost art critics; his weekly columns in *The EastAfrican* pretty much set the tone for the region's emerging contemporary art scene. Frank's **Lenga Juu** (Kiswahili for "Aim High") is a small, personal consultancy offering specialized **art tours,** as well as tailored holidays especially geared to art lovers wanting to expand their knowledge (and perhaps ownership) of contemporary African painting. Frank arranges exclusive tours of artists' studios, where collectors and enthusiasts can interact with Kenya's leading practitioners and even acquire work before it's shown to agents or galleries. Gallery tours can be arranged, too, where you can obtain choice works at specially discounted rates; excursions in Nairobi usually start with tea and snacks in Frank's own home, where you can look at his own marvelous collection of tribal and more modern African art. Frank also puts together bespoke tours that can include painting tuition by practicing artists, as well as time at a game reserve and perhaps a break at the coast to round off. For longer trips, you should contact Frank well in advance (© **072/252-5195;** fwhalley@gmail.com).

Fast Facts Nairobi

Airlines Contact details for the main international airlines servicing Nairobi: **Kenya Airways** (© 020/320-7474), **South African Airways** (© 020/22-7486), **British Airways** (© 020/698-000 airport, or 020/327-7400 sales), **Brussels Airlines** (© 022/444-3070 Nairobi, or 020/82-2329 airport), **KLM** (© 020/327-4210, or 020/622-3509 or -3527 airport), **Turkish Airlines** (© 020/221-8720), **Emirates** (© 020/329-000 or -0404), **Qatar** (© 020/280-0000), **Swiss** (© 020/374-4045 or -4535), and **Virgin Atlantic** (© 020/278-9000). **Domestic airlines** include **Safarilink** (© 020/60-0777), **AirKenya** (© 020/60-5745), **TropicAir** (© 020/203-3032, -3033, 020/214-4405, 072/220-7300, or 071/131-1477), and **Fly540** (© 072/254-0540, 073/354-0540, or 073/754-0540).

Ambulance Dial © **999,** or contact any of the private hospitals listed below. You can also call **AAR Emergency Ambulance** (© **020/271-7374** or -7375), or the **St John Ambulance** (© **020/21-0000**).

American Express Hilton Hotel, Mama Ngina Street (© **020/22-2906**).

Area Code The dialing code for Nairobi is © **020.**

ATMs Automated bank tellers are ubiquitous; besides the myriad machines throughout the city center, you'll find ATMs in all shopping malls (where you'll undoubtedly feel safer drawing money); those belonging to **Barclays Bank** and

Standard Chartered are usually reliable. If you're nervous about using a bank machine, look for one manned by a security guard. Most machines accept Visa or MasterCard credit cards, but fewer also accept American Express cards.

Banks You'll have little trouble locating a bank in this city; **Barclays** and **Standard Chartered** are well represented.

Bookstores **Text Book Centre,** Sarit Centre, Parklands Road, Westlands (www.textbookcentre.com/index.htm), stocks a wide selection of all kinds of books, including African literature and photographic studies; plenty of magazines and newspapers, too. **Simply Books,** ABC Place, Waiyaki Way (✆ **020/444-9312**), sells a good range of fiction and nonfiction, including books on Africa and Kenya; they also sells gifts and greetings cards. **Bookstop,** 2nd floor, Yaya Centre, Argwings Kodhek Road, Hurlingham (✆ **020/271-4533**), has a good selection of second-hand books, as well as books on Africa, natural history, and gardening, and maps and guidebooks. There is also a large choice of local and international magazines. **Westland Sundries,** in the Village Market shopping center, carries wonderful novels from Africa, Africana-themed photographic tomes, and a wide range of magazines, nonfiction, and stationery.

Car Hires If you're here on vacation, I don't think it's a good idea to even consider driving a vehicle in Kenya; stick to the chauffeured options offered by your tour agency, or see the options under "Getting Around," above, and "Taxis," below.

Currency Exchange The best way to get local currency is to withdraw money from an ATM (see ATMs, above); alternatively, step inside any bank with your money and your passport. In Karen, you change currency at **Karen Connection Forex,** Lower Plains Road, off Karen Road (✆ **020/88-3535**), and **Karen Bureau de Change,** Karen Shopping Centre (✆ **020/88-4674**).

Doctors, Dentists & Drugstores Ask your host or concierge for trusted choices close to where you're staying.

Embassies & Consulates Many foreign missions tend to be located north of the city in the vicinity of the UN Headquarters: **Australian High Commission,** ICIPE House, Riverside Drive (✆ **020/444-5034** or 020/272-6958); **British High Commission,** Upper Hill Road (✆ **020/284-4000**); **Canadian High Commission,** Limuru Road, Gigiri (✆ **020/366-3000**); **Irish Consulate,** Owashika Road (✆ **020/387-8043** or 020/235-7242); **U.S. Embassy,** United Nations Avenue (✆ **020/363-6000** or 020/712-3304).

Emergencies **Flying Doctors** (✆ **020/60-0090** or -0602), **police** (✆ **122,** 112, or 999), **ambulance** (✆ **999** or 020/271-7374), **fire** (✆ **112** or 999).

Hospitals Opened in 2006, **Karen Hospital,** Langata Road, Karen (✆ **020/661-3000,** 073/620-0001 or -0003, 072/622-2001 or -0003; www.karenhospital.org), is a private general hospital serving the Karen and Langata communities. The **Aga Khan University Hospital,** 3rd Parklands Ave., off Limuru Road, about 4km (2½ miles) from downtown (✆ **020/366-2000;** www.agakhanhospitals.org), is the second-largest private hospital in Nairobi and is owned by the Aga Khan Foundation. **The Nairobi Hospital,** Argwings Kodhek Road, about 3km (1¾ miles) from downtown (✆ **020/272-2160;** www.nairobihospital.org), is the largest private hospital in the city.

Internet Access You'll inevitably have Internet (often Wi-Fi) access at your hotel or guesthouse (all those reviewed here have some kind of connectivity); alternatively, there are a good number of cybercafes in the city center, and you can usually track one down in any of the city's upmarket shopping centers.

Mobile Phones You should be able to use your own mobile phone; simply purchase a SIM card from one of the local service providers (such as Safaricom or Zain); air time can topped up by purchasing scratch cards from vendors and shops just about anywhere.

Newspapers & Magazines ***The Daily Nation*** is arguably the best Kenyan newspaper; ***The EastAfrican,*** with stories from Kenya, Tanzania, and Uganda, is a better read. These and other daily, weekly, and monthly publications from the region and around the world are available from sidewalk vendors and bookstores everywhere. Hotels generally have at least two local dailies available, one of which may be delivered to your room each morning.

Police To contact your nearest police station, dial ✆ **122.**

Post Office Post offices, or **posta,** are easy to spot; the main one in the city is on Kenyatta Avenue (✆ **020/24-3434**) and is open Monday to Friday 8am to 6pm and Saturday 9am to noon. For parcels, you're best off using a courier service.

Restrooms Stick to toilets in hotels, upmarket shopping centers, and restaurants.

Safety See the box "For Safety's Sake," above.

Taxis Cabs are fairly ubiquitous in the city and always hang around hotels, shopping centers, and many points of tourist interest. While in the city, drivers of unmarked "taxis" will often attempt to solicit your business; best to stick to vehicles that are clearly branded as taxis. If you can't find a cab, you can call one of the following companies: **On-Time Cabs** (✆ **020/271-0507,** 020/273-0995, 072/152-1322, or 073/352-1313; www.ontimecabstravel.co.ke); **Courtesy Cabs** (✆ **072/270-1291,** 072/239-0756, or 073/372-5429); or **Soaring Eagles Tours, Travel & Taxi Co.** (✆ **020/445-3996**). **Kenatco** (see "Getting Around," above) can be relied upon for fixed-rate trips to just about any point in the country.

Weather Nairobi enjoys a relatively mild climate, with warmish days averaging 24°C (75°F) and cooler nights that may require light woolens or a jumper; June and July are considerably colder, averaging 18°C (64°F) during the day, with very brisk nights. Theoretically, the short rains fall from October through December, while long rains fall between March and June.

2 WHAT TO SEE & DO

Although it's not widely marketed as a tourist destination, Nairobi sees an inordinate number of foreign visitors and definitely doesn't lack for engaging attractions. While there are museums and other references to the nation's history, you'll almost inevitably want to devote the lion's share of your time here to one or two of Nairobi's dedicated animal sanctuaries, and perhaps even head out on a brief but rewarding safari through the city's very own national park. In some ways, a cultural safari through the **city center** is even more of an adventure, even if you just spend an hour or two getting a feel for the contrasts and paradoxes and try out a local restaurant or coffee shop where you'll be surrounded by local people rather than by tourists. There's no order or singular purpose in visiting here, but it's a chance to see how modern developments have impacted an ambitious Third World capital. Many people are surprised by the sheer volume of soulless modern edifices—gleaming mirror-glass office towers that seem utterly incongruous with the bushlands that lie right on the city's doorstep. This is largely the result of a wide-reaching post-independence building spree that saw the majority of colonial-era buildings replaced. At the same time, you're likely to be as surprised by the number of open spaces and parks in the center of the city, including Central and Uhuru parks, which are hardly spaces you'd want to spend any time in. One small park you may be interested in visiting is the **American Embassy Memorial Garden,** a leafy wall-protected space on the site of the embassy that was bombed in 1998. At the other end of Moi Avenue, **Jeevanjee Gardens** is considered Nairobi's equivalent of Speaker's Corner—visit here, and you'll likely hear all kinds of weird and wonderful sermonizing by self-styled preachers-in-the-park.

While you may find that sipping a cold Tusker in one of the city's open-air bars or on the **Norfolk Hotel's terrace** is a sufficient sampling of Nairobi's day-to-day life, if you're interested, you will discover that, between the brutal business blocks, there are a few fascinating stops—the **city market** (which looks like some bizarre latter-day temple, on Mbingu St.), for one, is a whirlwind of salesmanship, worrying odors, and eye-catching crafts, while the city's over-abundant **churches** are breathtaking for the sheer quantity of concrete used in their construction. At one busy traffic roundabout, the number of bland modern church buildings (and one synagogue) has earned the moniker **"God's Corner";** ironically, in a mirror-glass high-rise nearby, the city's first male strip club has long drawn bevies of hard-partying, liberated women. Monuments and memorial statues dot the city's public spaces, and you can gawk at Kenya's **parliament,** go train-spotting at the **Railway Museum,** or bribe your way to the top floor of the **Kenyatta International Conference Centre** for the most fulfilling bird's-eye view of the entire city. None of this is likely to over-fascinate you unless you have a genuine interest in the city's dynamics, and even then you might find better rewards by going on a Sunday outing to the **Ngong Hills Racecourse,** where the mix of heavy-betting punters and horse enthusiasts ensures that there's never a dull moment—and you might even win some money if you're willing to fill out a race card.

But for the average short visit to Nairobi, you'll probably want to limit your exploration to one or two picks from the attractions below, and then cap off your day with a top-class meal at the **Talisman** or **Blanco's** (see "Where to Eat," below); then, if you have the energy (and a long-suffering taxi driver), join the party set and boogie the night away at **Mercury Lounge** (see "Nairobi After Dark").

THE TOP ATTRACTIONS

David Sheldrick Elephant & Rhino Orphanage ★★★ Kids Moments This is likely to be a highlight of your visit to Nairobi (and, for some, a high point of their time in East Africa). Seeing the parade of baby elephants—all orphaned and in critical need of human intervention—make a brief lunchtime appearance each day at this world-renowned animal orphanage will warm even the coldest heart. A small charity that's managed to have a huge impact, the trust was established in 1977 in memory of the eponymous naturalist David Sheldrick, who was also the founding warden of Kenya's Tsavo East National Park, where he worked for nearly 30 years. The Nairobi-based

East Africa's Largest Shantytown: Kibera

Kibera, the name given to Africa's largest informal settlement—commonly referred to as a slum—is a Nubian word meaning "forest." In today's urban psyche, however, *Kibera* conjures awful images of a way of life that is almost incomprehensible to Westerners or privileged Africans. Housing more than one quarter of Nairobi's population, Kibera is 5km (3 miles) southwest of downtown Nairobi and is about the same size as New York's Central Park, with a population density estimated to be 2,000 people per hectare. It was originally settled by Sudanese (Nubian) soldiers who fought in the British army during the First World War. While the British government tolerated the informal settlement for political and tactical reasons, the post-independence government made certain types of housing illegal, and Kibera was consequently deauthorized. With "legal" land beyond the means of most ordinary Kenyans, Kibera's poor tenants were forced to stay on and occupy the illegal land. They officially became squatters, and the area has continued to grow as more people immigrate to the city hoping to find their place in the sun. Kibera's rate of growth is estimated to be around 17% per annum; since its boom years at the end of the 1970s, when 62,000 people lived there, the population has grown to an estimated 1 million. In late 2009, the government finally began addressing the situation with the inaugural relocation of an initial batch of Kibera residents to a new low-cost housing scheme. Unfortunately, such a translocation hardly puts a dent in the existing problem.

Most people living in Kibera—where an average makeshift home is 3m×3m (9¾ ft.× 9¾ ft.) and most dwellings house an average of five people—are without basic amenities. Electricity, clean water, and sanitation are not readily available, and there is an average of one pit latrine for every 50 to 500 people (or, by some accounts, one for every 500–1,000 people). Two in every three residents must defecate in the open, while the river and dam into which the

center, which specializes in the rescue of orphaned animals, particularly elephant and rhino, was established by Sheldrick's widow, Daphne, who worked alongside her husband and was knighted by the Queen; among other achievements, she was the first person to perfect a milk formula that can be used to raise newborn orphan elephants. Born with a natural empathy for animals, Dame Daphne has personally hand-reared more than 30 elephants and more than a dozen black rhino calves. Today all the animals—sadly, in 2009, the orphanage had its highest-ever numbers—are hand-reared and prepared for rehabilitation into the wild.

There is also a fostering program whereby you can contribute directly to the day-to-day sustenance of an orphaned elephant that will one day be released into the wild: Visit the website to adopt right away, and when you visit the orphanage, you'll be able to visit with your very own foster elephant.

Outside Nairobi National Park, Magadi Rd., Langata. ✆ **020/89-1996.** www.sheldrickwildlifetrust.org. Minimum donation Ksh300. Mon–Fri 11am–noon.

human waste and sewerage runs are used for swimming, bathing, and laundry—cholera and typhoid are an ever-present threat. It goes without saying that the combination of poor nutrition and an overwhelming lack of sanitation contributes to widespread disease and death. There are more than 50,000 AIDS orphans in Kibera; those without grandparents or a place in one of the overcrowded orphanages are left to fend for themselves or are raised by older siblings, many of whom are themselves young children. Schooling remains a luxury.

With survival itself a miracle, it's hard to imagine the industriousness and business savvy of the people living in Kibera. Despite the hardships, there's a strong sense of community, and all kinds of entrepreneurial and business enterprises—as well as many grassroots organizations—are contributing to an evolving economy, known in Kenya as the *Jua Kali*, or "Fierce Sun." It's part of the massive informal sector that drives up to 75% of Africa's economy. For some insight into contemporary community life in Kibera, pick up a copy of Michael Holman's satirical novel *Last Orders at Harrods—An African Tale* (Abacus), which conjures some fabulous characters in a thinly veiled version of Kibera called Kireba.

Tours of Kibera are available, but they're currently the subject of mixed opinion, and I've heard too many residents express their unhappiness at the way some of the tours are run to be able to recommend them at this stage. If you're truly interested in seeing life within Kibera and feel you have something to give in return, it might be best to do so through one of the NGOs working there rather than by joining a potentially exploitative tour. Better still, contact one of the community groups started and run by people actually living there; a good place to start is the dynamic youth-oriented organization **SHOFCO** (Shining Hope for Community; www.shofco.org).

Giraffe Centre ★★ Kids Moments Unless you're fortunate enough to be put up at Giraffe Manor (p. 90), this is your best chance to get up close and personal to the pretty-faced Rothschild giraffe, looked after here by the African Fund for Endangered Wildlife. A.F.E.W. is a nonprofit organization founded in 1979 by former Baltimorean model Betty Leslie-Melville and her husband, Jock, in a bid to save the endangered giraffe, which lost its natural habitat in Western Kenya to agriculture. At the time there were only 130 left in the wild; today Kenya's Rothschild population is about 300. Established more as an educational facility concerned with exposing Kenyan schoolchildren to aspects of their rapidly disappearing natural heritage, there's nothing too sophisticated or overly touristy about the center, but you will have the chance to "kiss" a friendly giraffe as it takes a food pellet straight from between your lips. It's a moment you'll never forget, and you'll be happy to know that the slobber that accompanies the 45cm (18 in.) tongue that whips out against your mouth is a natural antiseptic designed to help heal various cuts and wounds sustained while the giraffe browse for tiny leaves among the thorns. The

Fun Facts Big Babies Looking for Love

According to Daphne Sheldrick, who founded the world-famous David Sheldrick Elephant & Rhino Orphanage in Nairobi (p. 70), blowing into an elephant's trunk is the pachyderm equivalent of saying "hello" or shaking hands. During her many years spent with the ellies, Dame Sheldrick has also learned a great deal about the vulnerabilities of what we too easily assume to be thick-skinned beasts. Elephant children depend on the nurturing atmosphere of a close-knit family, so when they lose their mothers or are torn from the herd, it takes 'round-the-clock care and attention to keep them from succumbing to depression. The elephants kept at the orphanage are looked after by 24-hour "keepers" who sleep on bales of hay alongside the elephants and wake up every 3 hours in order to feed their charges. Like human infants, baby elephants are sensitive to cold, and the orphanage welcomes donations of blankets and ladies tights, which are used to wrap the animals up snugly when they go out to play in the dirt in the early morning (the tights are used as belts to keep the blankets in place). The orphans also need to be sheltered from wind, rain (often with umbrellas), and the sun—in the wild, such protection would be provided by the presence of maternal elephants in the herd, who would also help keep the babies' body temperature stable. And, just as humans need to be protected from sunburn, elephants take regular mud baths because mud acts as a natural sunblock.

volunteers can also tell you many other interesting facts about the Rothschild, and you could easily learn how to distinguish between these and the other giraffe species just by looking at their patterning or noticing whether or not they have "white socks." Unless you're very interested in plant ecology, skip the dull Nature Sanctuary Forest Trail.

Langata. ✆ **020/89-1658** or -0952. www.giraffecenter.org. Ksh700 adults, Ksh250 children 18 and under. Daily 9am–5pm.

Karen Blixen Museum ★ Twenty minutes (traffic dependent) from downtown Nairobi is the prestigious and leafy suburb of Karen, named after Karen Blixen, the Danish baroness who wrote *Out of Africa.* She lived in Kenya from 1914 to 1931, and if you want to briefly revisit those colonial times, you can do so at her house, where some of her old things are mixed up with some of the props from the quintessential African romance film based on her book. Karen's playboy husband (from whom she claimed to have contracted syphilis; she once declared that "the world being as it is, it was worth having syphilis in order to become a Baroness") had bought a coffee farm at the foot of the Ngong Hills, and she was left to try and run the plantation. Although she failed as a coffee planter, her descriptions of the landscape and of the world she viewed from her home—then called Mbogani House (Kiswahili for "In the Forest")—suggest a love affair with the land as intense as the supposedly steamy affair she had with Denys Finch-Hatton, an English hunter and aviator (whom at least one mutual friend claimed was actually homosexual). After Finch-Hatton's death, Blixen returned to Denmark, and her land was apportioned into smaller parcels that later became the suburb named in her honor. Following Kenyan independence in 1963, the Danish government bought Mbogani House and 15 hectares (37 acres) of land, donating them to the National Museums of Kenya.

Many years later, Universal Studios, which made *Out of Africa,* paid for the house's restoration. While it's certainly evocative of the early-20th-century colonial period, and the grounds and garden are lovely (with a great view toward the Ngong Hills), there isn't much by way of deep historical insight into Nairobi or Kenya—although you may just pull together some of the soap operatic threads of Blixen's life.

Karen Rd., Karen. ✆ **020/88-2777** or -2779. www.museums.or.ke. Ksh800 adults, Ksh400 children. Daily 9:30am–6pm.

Nairobi National Museum ★★ Even the director of this, Kenya's most important museum, agrees that prior to its recent 8€-million, 2½-year revamp, this place was dull and lifeless. E.U. funding has greatly expanded the museum, updating the exhibits with more relevant and dynamic content. If you enjoy museums, you shouldn't miss the *Human Origins* exhibition, which focuses on the research done in Kenya on human evolution. Prized among the Rift Valley fossils displayed here is the 1.6-million-year-old "Turkana Boy," the most complete early hominid fossil in existence. By 2010, a new Kenyan history exhibition should be up and running, but if you're trying to understand life in Kenya today, check out the *Cycles of Life* exhibit, where you'll come to understand some of the key moments—birth, circumcision, marriage, old age, and death—that define the culture of some of the 42 different tribes that make up Kenyan society.

Museum Hill, off Chiromo St. ✆ **020/374-2161** through -2164. www.museums.or.ke. Ksh800 adults, Ksh400 children. Daily 8:30am–5:30pm.

Nairobi National Park ★★ Unbelievably close to the human bustle of the city, this is an important wildlife reserve (Kenya's first, in fact), if only because it provides an opportunity to catch a final look at lions, leopards, buffaloes, and rhinos (no elephants, I'm afraid) during those precious hours before jetting back home—this is surely one of the easiest game drive opportunities on Earth. The preserve is also an important breeding center for the endangered black rhino and home to more than 100 different sorts of mammals, with as many as 400 species of birds recorded. Incorporating important migration corridors, animal concentrations are best during the dry season, which theoretically runs from January through March but is fairly unpredictable these days. In fact, if your flight into Kenya arrives by daylight, try to spot game during those final moments before touchdown. The park incorporates the Nairobi Safari Walk, which—if you don't mind a somewhat zoolike experience—will give you a chance for close-quarters animal eyeballing.

10km (6¼ miles) south of Nairobi city center. The main gate and KWS headquarters is on Langata Rd. ✆ **020/60-2121** or 020/60-3769. www.kws.org. $40 adults, $20 children; in addition, Ksh600 per vehicle. KWS Smartcard is required for entry; this can be purchased and charged at the gate. Daily 6am–6pm.

RaMoMa ★★ Probably the biggest private gallery of art in East and Central Africa, the Rahimtulla Museum of Modern Art (RaMoMa) is Nairobi's premiere contemporary art gallery, which opened in its slick new guise (and location) in 2008. With five different exhibition spaces, including a dedicated Photographer's Gallery, it's an excellent place to get a taste of East Africa's established and emerging talent; from fine art and sculpture to furniture and graphic design, the scope of the exhibitions hints at the diversity of creative expression in contemporary Kenya. ***Tip:*** On the last Saturday of the month, the museum hosts a monthly sale of Kenyan art, and there's a very good museum shop.

2nd Parklands Ave., Parklands. ✆ **020/374-8612** or -8618, or 072/425-6136. ramoma@africaonline.co.ke. Sun–Fri 9:30am–4:30pm; Sat 9:30am–6pm.

Nairobi's Architectural Diva

It's said to be the most photographed house in Africa, rising from the parched plains of Nairobi's outskirts like an architectural mirage. Overlooking Nairobi National Park, and with views of Mount Kilimanjaro and Mount Kenya, **African Heritage House** ★★★ (www.africanheritagebook.com) was actually designed by an American, Alan Donovan, a former bureaucrat from Colorado whose love of the continent started at an early age. He made wildlife scrapbooks as a child and designed jewelry based on tribal ornaments that he encountered on his travels through Africa after he ditched his job as a bureaucrat sent to Nigeria during the Biafran War. His African Heritage House is similarly inspired by the monumental mud architecture he'd seen 20 years before in Nigeria and Mali. Naturally, the mud mosque tradition strongly influences the nine-room African mansion, but so do the architecture of coastal Kenya and the sculptural house styles of northern Nigeria and southern Morocco. And, inside, Donovan's African handicrafts make up one of the finest private collections of this kind in the world. The house, with its hand-painted ceilings and walls, and extensive African art, artifacts, and ornamentation, certainly lives up to its name; it's a look that's lavish and original enough to have graced the cover of *Marie Claire* and has long been a popular choice for fashion shoots, architecture spreads, and all kinds of television programs. It never pretends to be a traditional African house or structure, but is a fabulous (if somewhat ostentatious) homage to the building traditions and creative diversity of Africa.

If you have any desire to see how "African luxe" *should* look, then this is an essential stop during your time in Nairobi. The house is available for tours, meals (breakfast, lunch, and dinner on the rooftop or by the refreshing pool), as well as overnight stays in its luxurious rooms (with modern appointments). Accommodations cost $265 double (with breakfast and a tour of the house). Otherwise, tours must be prearranged and cost a minimum of Ksh2,500 for up to five people, including tea and coffee. You can also organize a house tour combined with rooftop lunch or sundowner dinner for Ksh2,500 per person; the chance to see the sun disappear behind the famed Ngong Hills is worth planning for. If you want to arrange this yourself, you can call Alan at ✆ **072/151-8389,** also useful if your taxi driver doesn't know the route (which has changed recently).

For some, the mélange of African textiles, masonry, wood, weaponry, pottery, art, and furnishings may prove too much, but the eclectic willfulness of what's been assembled and the dutiful manner in which the collector has paid homage to Africa is definitely worth seeing. In a way, the house is a grown-up rendition of those early scrapbooks, testament to an enduring love affair with the continent's endlessly fascinating colors, textures, patterns, and designs, synthesized and blended in a refreshing way. It'll more than likely change the way you see Africa and hopefully inspire in you a better understanding "of the irreducible modernity of African crafts."

3 WHERE TO STAY

Nairobi's accommodation scene is diverse, and there is no shortage of places to stay; what the city does lack, though, is truly good-value digs for the budget traveler. In its favor, the city has some very charming smaller guesthouses, cushioned away in the leafy suburbs to the south of the city. Many people choose to stay in the suburbs in order to avoid the congestion of the city center while being close to some of Nairobi's loveliest attractions and great restaurants and within an easy commute to either airport (Langata is about 20 min. from Wilson and 30 min. from Jomo Kenyatta International). The city center can be reached in 30 minutes, traffic dependent. All the options in the city center are larger hotels—a few come with real character (and hefty price tags), but most cater to an indistinguishable business clientele, and many of the cheapies are downright rotten.

IN & AROUND THE CITY CENTER

Expensive

Nairobi Serena ★ A reasonable alternative to The Norfolk, this city flagship of East Africa's biggest luxury hotel chain features decor that is more distinctively African, reminding you of where you are today rather than recalling a distant colonial past. You're also more likely to rub shoulders here with people from all across Africa; throughout the hotel—at the excellent poolside breakfast terrace, in the bar, and in various lounge areas—you'll witness deals being struck and business solidarities forged as corporate Kenya bares its soul. Despite the unfortunate exterior, the hotel has warm, gracious spaces inside—tribal masks and wall hangings adorn the interior, with hand-knotted rugs laid out on stone-tile floors and elaborate floral arrangements spilling out of large clay vessels. Accommodation wings, on the other hand, are a bit stuffy, cramped, and old-fashioned—textbook reminders of unimaginative 1970s hotel design. Avoid the standard rooms, which are a little depressing, with miniscule bathrooms, shin-high beds, and that modular dark-wood look that can be off-putting at the end of the day; superiors are neater and larger, and have balconies, good beds, and alright bathrooms. One definite improvement on The Norfolk is the pool area, which here feels more out in the open, without buildings peering down at you as you sunbathe or swim.

Kenyatta Ave., P.O. Box 46302, 00100 Nairobi. ✆ **020/282-2000.** Fax 020/272-5184. www.serenahotels.com. 183 units. $535 standard double; $575 superior double; $690–$1,900 suite. Rates include taxes and service charge. AE, DC, MC, V. **Amenities:** 2 restaurants; 2 bars; airport transfers ($30–$35 per person one-way); health club; spa. *In room:* A/C, TV, fax (in suites), hair dryer, minibar, free Wi-Fi.

The Norfolk ★★ Nairobi's second-oldest hotel opened in 1904 and, despite some lavish contemporary revamping in the lounge, bar, and restaurants, still bears the vestiges of its colonial heyday; it's among the few buildings to have survived the 1960s destruction of British-era buildings after independence. The colonial-style entrance, manned by porters in top hats and tails, opens into a bright lobby hung with a mix of watercolors depicting Kenyan scenes and sepia photographs recalling an earlier time. Karen Blixen honeymooned here in 1914, and besides the politicos and aristocrats, famous guests have included Robert di Niro and Mick Jagger. Despite its rich pedigree, there's a warm, friendly atmosphere and an emphasis on comfort. The hotel's new owners have invested heavily by refurbishing all the rooms—distinctive styles, all with an antique feel, define the different wings—while bringing in a luster of modernity. There's plenty of space to wander, curl up with a book, or lean back with a customary G&T. The look is decidedly colonial Africa, however, so if you're looking for a more overtly African atmosphere, check out the Serena (p. 87).

Harry Thuku Rd., P.O. Box 58581, 00200 Nairobi. © **020/226-5000.** www.fairmont.com/norfolkhotel. 165 units. The hotel operates a Best Available Rate policy; doubles from $299; suites from $529. AE, DC, MC, V. **Amenities:** 2 restaurants; bar; airport transfers ($60); babysitting; concierge; health club; pool. *In room:* A/C, TV, hair dryer, minibar, Wi-Fi ($7 per hr., $25 per day).

The Sarova Stanley ★ With the potential to be a gracious city hotel, this colonial stalwart is plagued by awkward, unreliable (and often absent) service. In all other respects—comfortable bedrooms, decent amenities, and a couple of respected dining venues—it does very well, but you somehow feel a bit cheated when you step inside the lobby and find the reception deserted and the stench of lemon-scented wood polish so thick you struggle to breathe. At times, the assortment of work uniforms, starting with the doorman's yellow coat and top hat, make this place look a lot like a dislocated circus performance rather than a high-end hotel. I quite like the distinctive look of the spacious Club rooms, though; they're plush, with bold red and blue color schemes (there's nothing subtle about the Stanley's design), great thick mattresses on high beds, and even plasma TVs with DVD players. Still, every time I step inside the closet-size bathrooms, I wish myself back at the Norfolk, where service is friendly, professional, and, well, actually happens. I also find this hotel noisy—a problem that's hard to conceal when you're bang-up against some of the busiest roads in a heaving city (although most suites face the interior courtyard atrium and are quieter).

Corner of Kimathi St. and Kenyatta Ave., P.O. Box 30680, 00100 Nairobi. © **020/275-7072,** 073/329-8540, or 020/31-6377. Fax 020/222-9388. www.sarovahotels.com. 217 units. $468 deluxe double; $503 Club double; $608–$1,135 suite. Rates include all taxes; suites rates include breakfast. AE, MC, V. **Amenities:** 3 restaurants; bar; airport transfers (Ksh1,600 per person one-way); babysitting; concierge; health club w/ massage services; pool. *In room:* A/C, TV, DVD (Club rooms and suites), hair dryer, minibar, free Wi-Fi.

Moderate

Although to my mind it's overpriced, the **Hotel Boulevard,** Harry Thuku Road (© **020/222-7567** through -7569, or 020/224-7536; www.hotelboulevardkenya.com), is widely considered the best "budget" hotel in central Nairobi. When I was last there, they were advertising $165 double, including breakfast and all taxes, and staff intimated that a discount was not out of the question. Day rooms are available at 50% the over-night rate, so this may be a reasonable choice if you want to catch a nap, shower, and stow your luggage while you wait for a flight. Still, you'll be infinitely more comfortable at the bland but thoroughly contemporary **Upperhill Country Lodge,** 2nd Ngong Ave., Upperhill (© **020/288-1600;** www.countrylodge.co.ke), situated next door to the Fair-view (reviewed below). With lovely gardens, the hotel offers straightforward, clean, severely minimalist accommodations aimed at business travelers on a budget. Expect few frills—good, clean linens on comfy beds; spotless small washrooms; and little else besides a phone, tiny TV, desk, and soundproof window. Doubles cost Ksh11,000, including breakfast, tax, and free Wi-Fi; family rooms are just Ksh13,500.

Fairview ★ Value Family-run, very comfortable, and a great value, it's nevertheless the security (including the "strongest entrance barriers in Kenya") that you'll notice first when arriving at this is efficient hotel scattered over 2 well-tended hectares (5 acres) on Nairobi Hill, a semi-suburb not too far from downtown. It may prove disconcerting if you're not used to high fences and armed guards, and you're discouraged from walking anywhere, which does make this feel a bit like Fort Knox. The name is a bit of a misnomer—there's no view, although the leafy, lovely gardens are a source of pride, so make sure you get a room that opens directly on to them. The best units are the First Class rooms, which are quite lovely and spacious and have good amenities. Breakfast here is a bit like a jovial UN gathering—a first-class spread is laid out for a mix of NGO workers, diplomats, businessfolk, and tourists—with a variety of venues, set in the original ivy-covered rough-hewn stone buildings, for dinner.

Bishops Rd., Upperhill, Nairobi. ✆ **020/288-1000.** www.fairviewkenya.com. Reservations 020/288-1419 or 020/271-1321. Fax 020/272-1320. book@fairviewkenya.com. 105 units. Ksh12,200 economy double; Ksh13,900 business double; Ksh14,900 first-class double; Ksh21,000 executive suite. Children over 12 pay Ksh5,400; children 5–12 Ksh3,900; children under 5 free. Rates include breakfast, Wi-Fi, and taxes. AE, MC, V. **Amenities:** 5 restaurants; bar; wine bar; health club; pool; room service. *In room:* A/C, TV, hair dryer, minibar, free Wi-Fi.

Inexpensive

From the brilliant value offered by the Fairview (above), it's a tremendous leap down the quality scale to find a cheap-but-clean place to stay. If you can see your way past the ghastly '80s decor and put your faith firmly in the low room price, then there are two money-saving options under the same banner that you *might* want to consider. In the city center, opposite the Jevanjee Gardens, is the 91-room **Kenya Comfort Hotel,** corner of Muindi Mbingu and Monrovia streets (✆ **020/31-7606** through -7609; www.kenya comfort.com), with cheap but livable rooms from as little as $60 double, although you may want to cough up an extra $10 for an executive room with a TV, a wardrobe, and a touch more comfort. Breakfast pushes up the price a bit, but I'd definitely skip it in favor of one of the city's more salubrious coffee shops. A slightly more expensive sister venture, **Kenya Comfort Hotel Suites** (✆ **020/271-9060** or -9061, or 022/272-3414; same website; from $70 studio double), is situated just beyond the center, in Milimani; it has the added benefit of a solar-heated pool, and despite the hideous exterior, rooms aren't quite so awful.

IN THE SUBURBS

Golfers interested in sinking a few holes rather than exploring the city might want to consider staying at the **Windsor Golf and Country Club** ★★ (www.windsorgolfresort.com), where all rooms look directly over the 18-hole golf course, so you won't even suspect that you're in Nairobi in the first place. It's a moderately sized property with 130 pastel-colored rooms, all with the standard amenities, and there are several restaurants (including one that's open 'round-the-clock), multiple bars, and a pool set amid the well-tended gardens; there's even a dinner dance–style "disco" with music from several decades ago. A double room will set you back $334, including breakfast and taxes, while a family-size cottage is $642. For Nairobi, that's pretty decent value but doesn't include the once-in-a-lifetime opportunity to smooch an endangered giraffe—that privilege is reserved for guests at **Giraffe Manor** (reviewed below), is one of my favorite guesthouses in any city. It's situated in the upmarket, countrified suburb of Langata, an extension of Karen, which is where Danish author Karen Blixen started her affair with Denys Finch-Hatton and tried unsuccessfully to run a coffee plantation. Just about every house—or mansion, rather—in Karen is surrounded by vast manicured gardens, green lawns with electric fencing, and 24-hour guards. Hotels here are usually converted country manors providing an intimate experience of life among Kenya's upper class. With the notable exception of great-value **Macushla House** (reviewed below), they tend to be pricey but often include all meals, as well as drinks and sightseeing—they all feel like places you'd like to visit for more than just a brief stopover between flights.

Giraffe Manor ★★★ Moments Giraffe really are capable of kicking and head-butting, which you learn during the safety briefing at what turns out to be one of Africa's most enchanting guesthouses. You need to know this because this is the only place on Earth where endangered Rothschild giraffe, each one known intimately and by name by your hosts (and you by the time you leave), poke their heads through the windows at breakfast time, eat from your hand, or give you endless fat, slobbering kisses on the front terrace. They may even peep in through your bedroom window. Throw in the atmospheric accommodations—the ivy-clad house was built in 1932 in the Scottish baronial style—great organic seasonal food, and all-round homey comforts, and this is one of the most memorable places to spend a night anywhere on Earth. The personal attention and cozy spaces—with fireplaces, comfy couches, nonstop bar service, and a kitchen that you can visit for a tête-à-tête with the chef—make this feel much more like a home than a hotel, albeit one where it's easy to feel yourself slipping back in time. Ask specifically for either Betty's Room (which has a one-of-a-kind Art Deco bathroom) or the Karen Blixen suite (especially useful if you have children), so named because it has furniture donated by her.

Koitobos Rd., Karen, Nairobi. P.O. Box 15665, 00503 Nairobi. ✆ **020/89-1078** or 020/89-0949. Reservations ✆ **020/251-3166** or 073/431-7992. Fax 020/89-2234. www.giraffemanor.com. 6 units (most with tub and shower). $720 double. Rates include all meals, most drinks, laundry, local sightseeing vehicle, taxes, and Giraffe Centre admission. Half-board rate and day-room rates available. No credit cards. **Amenities:** Bar; airport transfers ($30 Wilson, $40 Jomo Kenyatta International); babysitting; free Wi-Fi (in study). *In room:* No phone, hair dryer (on request), fireplace (in some), TV (in Karen Blixen suite).

House of Waine ★★ Built as a mansionlike family home in 1979, this stylish guesthouse is run with all the professionalism and sophistication of a fine hotel, yet it retains a warmth and personality seldom found in larger establishments. The landing here is amazingly gentle—staff meet and greet you in hushed tones, and when you're shown through your room, it feels like you're being welcomed home and you half expect to be tucked in later. Feeling like the VIP guest of wealthy Kenyan relatives is one thing, but the Waine household backs up its service with comfortable, extremely user-friendly rooms, each subtly themed with references to some aspect of Kenyan history or culture (be it with Maasai reds or Victorian-era colonial riffs) and loads of space. If you can afford the gorgeous Mailaka Suite, with a pretty four-poster bed, an enormous private porch from which you can survey the immaculate grounds, and one of the very best bathrooms in town, do so. After a morning of shopping, a visit to the nearby Giraffe Centre, and a humbling hour with the orphaned ellies at the Sheldrick sanctuary, you can sprawl out over one of the rattan divans on the pool pavilion and soak up the warm African sun surrounded by immaculate rolling lawns.

Masai Lane, off Bogani Rd., Karen, P.O. Box 25035, 00603 Nairobi. ✆ **020/89-1820** or 020/89-1553. Fax 020/89-2091. www.houseofwaine.co.ke. 11 units (9 with tub and shower). $450 standard double; $600 superior double. Rates include breakfast AE, MC, V. **Amenities:** Restaurant; bar; airport transfers ($40 international airport, $24 Wilson), pool. *In room:* A/C, TV, hair dryer, free Internet (cable), complimentary minibar.

Macushla House ★ Value Within walking distance of the Giraffe Centre, and convenient for all of the attractions in the Karen/Langata area, this refreshingly informal guesthouse feels as if it's at the edge of the bush—and it more or less is. Within the lovingly decorated walls of this house are plenty of peaceful nooks, with sofas, hand-knotted rugs, old photographs, wall hangings, *objets,* flowers, and fireplaces, where you can curl up with your thoughts or with a drink from the very intimate bar. It's a respite from the city and—for a short while, at least—from the prospect of onward travel (dayrooms are available at $100 per person); if you're feeling particularly lazy (or jetlagged), it's good to know that the homestyle cooking is delicious enough to make any restaurant superfluous. Bedrooms are spacious, with vague Art Nouveau touches, loads of wardrobe space, polished hardwood floors, pretty rugs, and four-poster wrought-iron beds. At night, a hot water bottle is tucked under the covers, and a glorious hush fills the entire house.

Incidentally, an excellent choice for families is **Fadhili House** ★★, a gorgeous little two-bedroom cottage at the bottom of Macushla's jungly garden. Filled with quirky and exceptional artwork created by the owner's talented sister, it's a homey, highly livable space with a fully kitted kitchen and decor reflecting a love of African culture and wildlife, but with inspiration borrowed from India and the Orient, too.

Nguruwe Rd., Langata. ✆ **020/89-1987,** 073/370-6178, or 072/232-9863. Fax 020/89-1971. www.macushla.biz. 6 units (all with tubs). $230 double. Children 2–12 pay 50% when sharing with 2 adults. Rate includes breakfast, taxes, and service charge. MC, V. **Amenities:** Restaurant; bar; Internet (office laptop; Ksh5/min.); pool.

Ngong House ★★ If you prefer the ordinariness of a standard hotel room, you may find this audacious collection of beautiful, slightly experimental stand-alone suites a bit too quirky. Spread across 4 hectares (10 acres) of lush gardens and facing the Ngong Hills, accommodations are in assorted cottages, wooden bungalows, and even tree houses on stilts. Owner-designer-architect Paul Verleysen has used all kinds of recycled material, natural woods, and organic textures in his designs (in one treehouse, a bed is fashioned from a Swahili canoe, with dugouts as bath tubs). Each space has its advantages (some have views, other are simply stylish), but all come with good four-poster beds, comfortable lounges, and many homey comforts. You take predinner drinks around the bonfire, where you'll meet UN representatives, NGO workers, tourists, businessmen, and celebrities—some recovering from safari, others about to plunge into the African bush. Meals are designed to really take your breath away: Dine just about anywhere you like—staff set you up at a privately situated table—and you choose from a small, well-considered menu. The only real drawback (besides the high price tag) is the ongoing din from rock hyraxes and suburban dogs that may go on through the night (light sleepers will need earplugs).

Ndovo Rd., Langata, P.O. Box 24963, 00502 Nairobi. ✆ **020/89-1856,** 073/360-0184, or 072/243-4965. Fax 020/89-0674. www.ngonghouse.com. 9 units. $880 double. Rate includes all meals, drinks (excluding champagne), Nairobi excursions, and airport transfers. AE, MC, V. **Amenities:** Restaurant; bar; free airport transfers; pool; free Wi-Fi. *In room:* Fireplace (in some), hair dryer, kitchenette, minibar.

Tribe ★ Located in a posh northerly suburb near the UN headquarters, this is Nairobi's first attempt at a totally contemporary "boutique" hotel. Problem is, once you step inside, it looks and feels more like a nightclub than a hotel, and despite the best efforts of the swish staff, things don't always run very smoothly (check-in was slow, accommodations average, and housekeeping slack). Rooms are very comfortable but bland and featureless by design, with that slick, modern, no-nonsense look that feels a bit hollow. Although it's clearly a business hotel, the focus in public areas is on creating "hip" little enclaves where guests can "hang out." Consequently, the place heaves with socialites, diplomats, and respectable-looking representatives from all kinds of multinationals. It's lively, and its proximity to the Village Market shopping center (next door) is useful if you want to step out for a bite or engage in a quick spending spree. They've got the best concierge in town, but they can also claim one of the most inefficient breakfast spreads I've ever witnessed.

The Village Market, 9/418 Limuru Rd., Gigiri, Nairobi. ✆ **020/720-0000.** Fax 020/720-0110. www.africanpridehotels.com/tribe. 137 units. The hotel operates a Best Available Rate policy. $290–$435 deluxe double; $330–$475 superior double; $410–$555 junior suite; $440–$1,085 suite. Rates include breakfast and taxes. AE, MC, V. **Amenities:** Restaurant; bar; airport transfers ($40–$50 per person one-way); concierge; health club and spa (under construction at press time); pool; room service. *In room:* A/C, TV, hair dryer, minibar, free Wi-Fi.

4 WHERE TO DINE

The great thing about dining in Nairobi—and most places in Kenya, for that matter—is the quality and freshness of the raw ingredients. Many people visiting Africa find the dining here remarkable simply because the foodstuffs have "more taste." Don't be surprised to find that the freshness and general tendency toward organic, "natural" produce imbues much of what you put in your mouth with an altogether different taste; you're unlikely to be disappointed. The other big surprise in Nairobi is the abundance of good restaurants, many of them catering to an elite, expat, or even passing tourist/business market, and doing a good trade. Finding a distinctively "African" eatery may prove less successful, although there are countless pub-style *nyama choma* places (where you feast on charcoal-grilled meat, usually cuts that you've chosen in their raw state, so it's like a cross between a butchery and a steakhouse) worth visiting if only for the cultural experience (although they're unlikely to interest vegetarians at all). If you're in the city center, one worthwhile *nyama choma* joint is **Sagret,** on Milimani Road (✆ **020/274-0933**). Order a couple of bottles of cold Tusker (remember that Kenyans generally prefer their beer warm, so it's important to ask for it cold, or *baridi*) and choose the cuts you want thrown on the barbecue-style grill. The upmarket version of the *nyama choma* dive is **Carnivore** (reviewed below), widely considered a quintessential dining experience (and does, in fact, cater to vegetarians), although I think it's a tourist trap. Besides **Blanco's** (reviewed below), another fine place for African cuisine is **Amaica** (✆ **020/476-5288**), located in the China Centre on Ngong Road. Try to visit on weekends, when live African music—much of it very good—accompanies the tastes of Western Kenya.

EXPENSIVE

If you don't mind traipsing through a hotel lobby, one of the city center's finest dining experiences is at the Sarova Stanley's authentic Thai restaurant, **Thai Chi** ★★ (✆ **020/31-6377** or 020/275-7000; Sun–Fri noon–2pm, daily 7–10pm), which is where the Thai ambassador likes to indulge in *hor mok ta lee,* a seafood curry served in a banana-leaf basket with vegetable rice. You can safely start with the wok-fried fish sponge cakes, and then consult with Chef Ta or Chef Poo about how to proceed—they'll prepare your main course to fit your palate.

The Lord Erroll ★★ FRENCH/SWISS/EUROPEAN The name makes it sound like a medieval country pub, but this is actually considered Nairobi's finest gourmet French restaurant—although the kitchen also dabbles in famous dishes from all over central Europe. It's the kind of place that evokes an earlier era of gentility, formality, and refinement, with dining in a choice of wood-paneled spaces such as The Conservatory and The Claremont. Choices range from Vienna Schnitzel (served with anchovy and

French fries) and *osso bucco* to veal bratwurst and Swiss fondue. There's also good seafood, but stick to Kenyan tilapia, red snapper, or spicy jumbo prawns. On the downside, it may be a touch too stuffy for some, and the atmosphere does little to evoke the spirit of the continent you're visiting—unless you consider waiters in starched jackets an apt ode to African colonialism.

89 Ruaka Rd., Runda Estate, Gigiri; off the Runda roundabout connecting United Nations Ave. and Ruaka Rd.; entrance from Ruaka Rd. ✆ **020/712-2433,** -1308, -2302, or -2636, 073/357-9903, or 072/192-0820. www.lord-erroll.com. Reservations highly recommended. Main courses Ksh900–Ksh2,450. MC, V. Daily 12:30–2:30pm and 5–11pm.

Tatu ★★★ STEAKHOUSE This sophisticated restaurant at Nairobi's longest-running hotel focuses on serving high-quality, succulent cuts of dry-aged Kenyan Angus beef. Since opening in mid-2009, the chef has been steadily refining his menu to ensure he's at the helm of nothing less than Kenya's most elegant steakhouse.

The Norfolk, Harry Thuku Rd. ✆ **020/226-5000.** Main courses Ksh750–Ksh5,000. AE, DC, MC, V. Mon–Sat 7–11pm.

MODERATE

Besides the sexy-looking **Ōnami** (reviewed below), Westlands—which probably has the greatest concentration of good restaurants and fashionable drinking establishments—has another respected Japanese restaurant, this time a branch of the Mombasa stalwart **Misono,** Lenana Road, Hurlingham (✆ **020/386-8959** or 072/253-0205; Mon–Sat 12:30–2:30pm and 7–10:30pm); see the review of the original (p. 257) if you can't make up your mind.

Anghiti ★★ Value INDIAN Although East Africa's dealings with India can be traced back many centuries, Nairobi's large and successful Indian community was spawned by the building of the Mombasa–Kampala railroad, for which the British shipped in workers from across the Indian Ocean. Today there is a marvelous profusion of excellent Indian eateries, and Anghiti (which has two branches) is one of the best. Start with a passion fruit *lassi* (a wonderfully refreshing yogurt drink) while you weigh up between Punjabi-style chicken Angiti or the *raan* Anghiti—a whole leg of mutton that's been marinated overnight. If you don't eat meat, there are plenty of excellent *paneer* (cottage cheese) and vegetarian dishes, too.

Westlands: New Rehema House, off Rhapta Rd. ✆ **020/444-1258.** Muthaiga: Muthaiga Shopping Centre. ✆ **020/374-0292** or 020/375-3296. Reservations highly recommended. Main courses Ksh325–Ksh950. MC, V. Daily noon–3pm and 7–10:30pm.

Blanco's Lounge & Grill ★★★ AFRICAN/KENYAN This is perhaps the best place in Nairobi to sample genuinely Kenyan food, albeit in a contemporary setting (and in a modern shopping center) with all the accoutrements associated with a thoroughly Western dining experience—call it "sophisticated African cuisine" if you must, but the food looks and tastes authentic, and an evening here is likely to be memorable, even without the carnivalesque atmosphere of Carnivore (see below). Start by ordering some *mishikakis* (barbecued meat skewers) and spicy fish *samosas* to share (or perhaps the lemon grass–flavored sweet potato soup, if you'd rather not share). The short selection of mains packs in a pretty broad variety of tastes: *sarara ya samaki* (fish filet) with either mild coconut or spicy-hot *pili pili hoho* sauce; slow-cooked chicken and vegetable casserole; or *matumbo ya kukaangwa,* a flavorful tripe dish with ginger, garlic, and soy sauce. Surprisingly for an African restaurant, there are even a few dishes for vegetarians—order the *viazi na muhogo wa nazi,* potatoes, sweet potatoes, and cassava cooked in fragrant coconut. For dessert, there's an interesting coconut crème brûlée, or skip dessert and head for the cocktail bar, where you should coax the barman into preparing you a *madafu* mojito.

Ground Floor, Timau Plaza, off Argwings Khodek Rd., near Yaya Centre, Hurlingham. ✆ **020/386-4670** or -4671, or 072/400-8335. www.blancos.co.ke. Main courses Ksh350–Ksh1,250. AE, MC, V. Mon–Sat noon–3pm and 5–11:30pm.

Carnivore **Overrated** STEAKHOUSE Prepare for an onslaught of barbecued meat, served by a team of roving carvers dressed in zebra-striped uniforms whose job it is to ensure that the meat (typically overdone) doesn't stop landing on your plate until you accept defeat, signaled by the dropping of a flag on your table. The meat in question is carried around on Maasai swords after being cooked over a massive charcoal pit that you'll see as you come in—there's something hypnotically medieval and primal about the experience, and it's perhaps fun to get caught up in the action, but not such a good idea if you're really looking for a fine meal. For meat eaters, the experience of dining on, among other things, crocodile, camel, ostrich meatballs, and skewered kidneys is probably as enjoyable as watching the relentless, rather heavy-handed activities that go on here. With staff busily carving up the meat, diners knocking back *dawa* cocktails, and a full force of ancillary entertainment in the attached bars and discotheque, this is no mere restaurant, but a contemporary African institution. Going strong since it opened nearly 30 years ago, Carnivore's megalithic popularity shows no signs of letting up, but it certainly doesn't score any points when it comes to good taste.

Langata Rd., Karen. ✆ **020/60-5933.** www.tamarind.co.ke/carnivore. Meat-eaters set price Ksh1,700; vegetarians set price Ksh850. AE, MC, V. Daily noon–late.

Fogo Gaúcho ★ BRAZILIAN Before the arrival of this Latin American steakhouse, who would have imagined that culinary ties exist between southern Brazil and Kenya? A love of meat, cooked and served on big skewers, certainly breaks down any divide, no matter how far apart the two countries may be geographically. Indeed, traditional *churrasco* would appear to be the Latino version of East African *nyama choma.* A bit like a low-key rendition of Carnivore (above), much of the meat is carved at the table off large skewers, only here the meat has been lightly salted and expertly grilled by the Brazilian chefs. Pork leg, braised over charcoal and drippingly juicy, is always good, and the crocodile meat is deliciously marinated. And, of course, there's the famous Brazilian *picanha,* a big, juicy rump steak, and *guacho*-cut beef ribs, grilled in flavor-preserving foil for 12 hours.

Viking House, Waiyaki Way, Westlands. ✆ **020/354-4037.** http://fogogauchonbi.com. Main courses Ksh350–Ksh1,350. MC, V. Daily noon–2:30pm and 6:30–11pm.

Haandi ★★★ **Value** INDIAN With an exhaustive menu of authentic—and usually hot—dishes, this is one of Africa's finest curry dens, serving sublime *masalas* from the North Indian Frontier region. Decor may be nondescript, but the spicy, rich tastes more than make up for this, and if you want something to look at, you can always cast your eyes toward the robust cooking going on in the glass-fronted kitchen. Everything is fresh and made in-house, usually as you order (with the obvious exception of *tandoori* dishes, which are marinated overnight). The menu can be a little overwhelming, so if you're stumped, know that you can't go wrong with the *masala* prawns—big, fleshy crustaceans packed with flavor—or the ever-popular chicken *makhani,* done in a spicy tomato sauce.

And if you're wondering, yes, this is the same Haandi now found in London, Dar es Salaam, Kampala, and Sudan.

Westlands Mall, Westlands. ✆ **020/444-8294** through -8296, 073/364-8294, or 072/356-4466. www.haandi-restaurants.com. Dinner reservations strongly recommended. Main courses Ksh485–Ksh2,325. AE, MC, V. Daily 12:30–2:30pm and 7:30–10:30pm.

Le Rustique ★★ MEDITERRANEAN/DELI/CRÊPERIE This wonderful daytime venue comprises a sweet and savory crêpe-cum-waffle section; a New York–style deli, packed with cheeses, Italian cold meats, French pâté, salads, smoked fish, and chocolates; and a Mediterranean restaurant with a menu that's reinvented on a weekly basis. The emphasis is on using fresh ingredients to create home-style dishes thought up by Le Rustique's creative owner, Maike, including duck braised in orange juice spiced with star anise, lemon grass, chili, and ginger; or fennel seed–infused slow-roasted pork belly with garlic and rosemary. On Wednesdays, Maike serves dinner and creates a slightly more formal, romantic atmosphere, complete with outdoor bonfire. If you've made it this far, you'd do well to save room for a taste of the homemade sorbets or—better still—clotted cream ice cream, served with a homemade tart.

Note: By 2010, Le Rustique should also be open for Sunday brunch.

General Mathenge Dr., Westlands. ✆ **020/375-3081.** www.lerustique.co.ke. Dinner by reservation only. Main courses Ksh700–Ksh1,000. MC, V. Mon–Sat 9:30am–7pm, Wed (during the warmer months) 7pm till last guests.

Mediterraneo ★★ ITALIAN Step inside this cozy trattoria-style eatery tucked into an unlikely shopping arcade in Westlands, and the aromas instantly take hold. Order a focaccia with gorgonzola and rocket to nibble on while you paw through the long list of wood-fired pizzas and wonderfully fresh, homemade pastas (there's a brilliant tagliatelle with Lamu crab, spinach, and rich cream). The meat and seafood selection is excellent, too. Try the veal escalopes, pan-fried with mushroom and a hint of mint, or the beef *carpaccetto,* served with artichokes, parmesan, and rocket. Or scan the long list of specials on the chalkboards. Just keep in mind that you're going to want to try out the dessert menu, too.

Note: There's a second branch of Mediterraneo in the Junction Shopping Centre on Ngong Road, which will be more convenient if you're staying in the suburbs south of the city (✆ **020/387-8608** or -3823, 073/484-5077, or 072/885-5100).

Pamstech House, Woodvale, Westlands. ✆ **020/444-7494,** 020/445-0349, 073/357-6630, or 072/554-7800. www.mediterraneoreststaurant.co.ke. Main courses Ksh880–Ksh1,990; pasta and pizza Ksh560–Ksh880. AE, MC, V. Daily noon–11pm.

Ōnami ★★ Kids JAPANESE Just in case you haven't yet witnessed any evidence of Nairobi's renaissance as a worldly, design-conscious metropole, take a look at this classy "industrial zen" space on the second floor of Westgate Shopping Centre. Good looks aside, when this place opened in January 2009, it quickly somersaulted into poll position as one of the city's trendiest eating spots. Whether it's the fashionable open kitchen, the crazy sushi and cocktail specials on Tuesday nights (try a strawberry smash, with pepper vodka, basil, and strawberries), or simply the amazing line-up of sushi, sashimi, tempura, and teppanyaki, this place has an enviable following. A highlight is the crispy *agedashi* tofu, prepared in hot nameko radish sauce, or ask for either the Ōnami Dream or Imari special salmon. They also do a good beef filet *(gyu niku)* and exceptional teppanyaki prawns and fish.

Westgate Shopping Mall, Westlands. ✆ **020/374-3244.** www.onami.co.ke. Main courses Ksh140–Ksh1,370; *teppanyaki* Ksh1,650–Ksh1,950. AE, DC, MC, V. Daily noon till last customer.

Talisman ★★★ Kids INTERNATIONAL/FUSION Among those in the know, this low-key, part-alfresco eatery that spills out of an old colonial mud and wattle bungalow is unquestionably the best restaurant in Nairobi. And somehow, despite even the *New York Times* raving about the feta and coriander *samosas,* the Talisman has retained the air of a well-hidden secret. Run by a radiant British couple, Ian and Charlotte Cameron, the Talisman is a rustic, lovely place overlooking a mature garden with space for kids to run around. Inside there are crackling log fires, cozy furnishings, and paintings by local artists. The setting is one thing, but they produce some seriously good food to back up their reputation: pan-seared fresh yellow fin tuna, grilled ostrich filet with sweet-and-sour plum sauce, prime Kenyan Highland beef grilled with red wine reduction, perfectly tender Molo lamb kebabs, smoked Lake Victoria tilapia, and even good old-fashioned fish and chips. They've successfully kept their focus on creating simple, unbeatable classics, making this a must. And, yes, the *samosas* are unforgettable.

320 Ngong Rd., Karen. ✆ **020/88-3213** or 073/376-1449. www.talismanrestaurant.com. Main courses Ksh550–Ksh1,600. MC, V. Tues–Sun noon–3pm and 6–9:30pm; starters, deserts, and tea/coffee served 3–6pm.

5 SHOPPING

For serious shoppers, Nairobi can be a revelatory adventure. Not only are the country's (and the continent's) diverse arts and crafts well represented here, but there's an abundance of exceptionally creative designers producing covetable clothing, unique accessories, Africa-inspired furniture, and downright beautiful objects to show off in your home. It's also great to know that there are so many community- and environmentally conscious endeavors, with lots of focus on sustainable, eco-friendly practices. And there are numerous opportunities to shop at informal markets, too. Some of the best places to shop are reviewed below, but there are many more, so speak to your host if you have any specific interests.

If you're looking for a more general shopping experience, or simply need to get a few mundane chores done, and want to see how locals go about their daily activities, you might want to head for one of Nairobi's many shopping centers, which, for the most part, aren't too different from a mall you might visit in Canada, Australia, or the U.S.

Tip: Be aware that when shopping at markets, you'll need to pay in cash (hawkers are usually more than keen to accept foreign currency), and some shops will not accept credit cards without some form of official identification.

A.P.D.K. Fair Trade Shop ★ An outlet for wide-ranging crafts by people with disabilities, as well as goods from other fair-trade producers. You can buy everything from Zanzibari beds, kitchenware, leather goods, and tables to stone carvings, African ornaments, jewelry, and clothing. Waiyaki Way, opposite ABC Place/OilLibya. ✆ **020/445-1523** through -1525, 072/233-4677, or 073/459-0497. www.apdk.org.

African Lily ★★ All the leather handbags, purses, and belts produced by African Lily are handmade by local crafters, while the beadwork is done by HIV-positive women who live in the Kibera slum. They work to Italian designs using cow, goat, and camel hides—the latter giving a rougher, hardier texture—and their prices are very good. You can buy from the workshop on Ngong Road or visit their second outlet, which is a mobile cart on the first floor of the Westgate Shopping Centre. 1st Floor, Adam's Arcade, Ngong Rd. Also at Westgate Shopping Centre, Westlands. ✆ **071/149-2147** or 072/510-6542.

Tips Canvas Safari: On the Hunt for Great Kenyan Art

While most visitors to East Africa know what they want when it comes to seeing wildlife—namely, to track and photograph the Big Five—most people are stumped when it comes to hunting down a worthwhile souvenir. Usually they make a beeline for the dozens of curios shops catering to popular taste—paintings or *batiks* of Maasai warriors leaning on their spears, their *shukas* a winning splash of red, or maybe a ponderously drawn lion licking its lips, or a leopard apparently asleep in a tree. But now, increasingly, there is a new breed of tourists on the prowl—shrewd art collectors who have heard whispers that Kenya is home to a growing group of painters and sculptors who are making it big on the international scene. These visitors wisely ignore the tourist tat and instead, supported by a knowledgeable local guide, head for the galleries and studios that house works by some of the country's leading artists, whose paintings and sculptures are now shown in museums throughout the world and owned by top international private collections, including those of Jean Pigozzi, the World Bank, and the Daraja Group.

Names to look out for among the young lions of Kenyan painting include Peterson Kamwathi, with his edgy animal studies and life-size charcoal drawings reflecting the country's troubled political history, and Jesse N'gang'a, whose brightly colored canvases, with their iconography of skulls, skeletons, and graffiti, express the sort of grim gaiety last seen in the works of the American neo-expressionists and European masters such as Constance Permeke and James Ensor. Other artists whose work is being snapped up include Sane Wadu, Chain Muhandi, Richard Onyango—who chronicled the life and death of his gargantuan lover, Suzie Droze—Wanyu Brush, and the Nairobi surrealist Richard Kimathi.

The extent of available talent in Kenya is truly astounding—and with major new artists appearing on the scene every few years, it is still possible to pick up a bargain. You just have to get there and spot the talent before the major collectors have moved in.

—**Frank Whalley,** art critic and expert on African art
(Whalley writes a weekly art column for The EastAfrican. *He also arranges art tours;* *see "Tour Operators & Guided Tours," earlier.)*

The Banana Box ★ You'll find interesting-looking, well-made crafts from Kenya as well as other African countries in this fine little shop in the otherwise ordinary Sarit shopping center. The key ingredient—over and above the high standard of creativity—is the commitment to community involvement and fair trade. There's choice aplenty, including dhows turned into coffee tables, beautiful carvings made from sustainable wood, and even beautiful metal items made from recycled *matatus.* Lower Ground Floor, Sarit Centre, Westlands. ✆ **020/375-3745.** www.bananaboxcrafts.com.

Fuskai ★★★ There's no shop, but do make the effort to check out the considerable talents of Sue Fusco and her daughter, Kai. They design furniture, jewelry, wrought-iron home accessories, and clothing (fashioned from some unique fabrics) for a selection of East African craft markets, but also welcome keen shoppers into their home studio. To check out their ever-changing collection, call Sue (or e-mail her at sue@fuskai.com) to arrange an appointment. ✆ **073/360-8597** or 072/628-7420. www.fuskai.com.

Kalabash ★★ A tiny space filled with beautiful objects, African art, and stylish souvenirs, this is the ultimate one-stop gift shop in case you've left all your shopping till the last minute. Village Market, Gigiri. ✆ **020/712-2169** or 072/437-2111.

Kazuri Bead Factory ★★ You can buy hand-painted ceramic jewelry, cowhide handbags, pottery tableware, and beads at this famous studio established in 1975 as a place where poor people could learn a trade. The clay, which comes from Mount Kenya, is processed on-site, and there's a short tour of the workshop where around 340 women, most of them single mothers, produce the merchandise that's sold in shops throughout Kenya. Mbagathi Ridge, Karen. ✆ **020/232-8905** or 072/095-3298. www.kazuri.com. Outlets: Village Market, Gigiri (✆ **020/712-0847**); Westgate Shopping Mall, Westlands (✆ **020/374-1917**); and The Junction Shopping Centre, Ngong Rd. (✆ **020/387-2925**).

Kiko Romeo Labeling itself "radical Nairobi chic," this fashion house is known for its sexy integration of ethnic African elements with an international haute couture feel. Expect flamboyant, eye-catching, and occasionally risqué clothing—great if you like to shop for one-of-a-kind, scene-stealing outfits. 2nd Floor, Yaya Centre, Hurlingham. ✆ **071/467-4538** or 020/386-2411.

Kitengela Glass ★★ One of Kenya's most ubiquitous design brands, Nani Croze's impressive recycled glass project runs the gamut from enormous artistic showpieces to functional kitchenware. Her sought-after blown glassware and beautiful mosaics can be found in various locations around the city (the best of which is the new store in Westlands), but it's worth visiting the workshop near Nairobi National Park, if only to wander through the fantasy gardens that are laid out with all kinds of surreal animals, figures, and imaginative designs. Magadi Rd., Kitengela. ✆ **020/675-1858** or -0602, 020/300-5126, or 073/428-7887. www.kitengela-glass.com. Outlets: General Mathenga Rd., Westlands. ✆ **020/387-2378.** Village Market, Gigiri. ✆ **020/712-5691.** The Junction, Dagoretti corner, Ngong Rd. ✆ **020/57-6150.**

MagikGrace ★★★ This highly respected brand is one of Nairobi's hottest exports, started by designer Adele Bejak. Her jewelry, clothing, belts, and sandals evoke a contemporary style that's distinctly African. I particularly like her oversize handbags, combining traditional textiles with leather (and exquisite workmanship) to produce a very special

Tips Let's Go to the Maasai Market

If you're in the mood for haggling, then by all means check out the multifangled selection of arts, crafts, jewelry, *kikois, kangas,* and assorted miscellany that's sold at the so-called **Maasai Market,** which now happens 5 days a week at a different venue each day (except Mon and Thurs)—ask your hotel concierge or manager for today's location. While you'll potentially score a bargain, the constant sales pitch and low-key harassment from some vendors can be extremely off-putting.

accessory. Bejak runs her studio from home (✆ **073/725-3862**) but has a small network of stores and outlets around Kenya. The Village Market, Gigiri. ✆ **073/380-1665** or 020/712-1798. www.magikgrace.com.

Marula Studios, the Eco Hub ★★ Eco-warriors, take note: This gathering of several different community-oriented creative ventures is one of the great success stories of Kenya's green revolution that has, in most respects, grown out of the substantive efforts of small grassroots organizations such as UniqueEco—The (Flipflop) Recycling Company (www.uniqueco-designs.com). Collected along the East African coasts, literally hundreds of thousands of flip-flops are recycled and turned into unique, colorful, handmade pieces of art—from backgammon sets to '60s-style beaded curtains and amazing life-size animal sculptures, including a 30m (98-ft.) minke whale, which starred in an anti-whaling campaign, and a life-size giraffe, which was part of a European ethical fashion event. Since they started operating in 2005, more than 90 tons of flip-flops have been collected. Marula also stocks other socially and environmentally conscious products—picture frames made from recycled *matatus,* sisal lampshades made by orphans living in Kibera, knitted children's gear made by a group of single mothers, furniture produced from recycled wood . . . I could go on and on about the clever, practical, and simply beautiful creations made here, but you're probably already wondering what to do with this guidebook once you get home. Marula Lane, Karen. ✆ **072/624-8774.** info@marulastudios.com.

Matbronze Art Gallery & Foundry ★★ You can buy anything from bronze elephant tusk sculptures, to fire-breathing dragons, to animal-themed toilet paper roll holders at this hugely popular bronze workshop done out like a faux-castle with a lovely garden; the lion paw-print ashtrays go for $146, while a small elephant mother with calf statue costs $7,440. If you don't feel like burdening your luggage, you can at least watch some of the sculptural process—from bronze smelting to lost wax casting (which happens only once a month)—and also pick up good wildlife images and landscapes in various other media, including watercolors by Karen Laurence-Rowe and captivating bird pictures by Andrew Kamiti. There's a very good cafe here with iced lattes, fresh croissants, and fab carrot cake. 2 Kifaru Lane, Karen. ✆ **073/396-9165.** www.matbronze.com.

Penny Winter ★★★ This Irish-born designer produces some of Kenya's most coveted ladies' clothing collections, which you can browse in her studio shop at Ngong House (see "Where to Stay," above), where she lives with her Belgian husband, Paul Verleysen. She has designed garments for the likes of Princess Caroline of Monaco and actress Rachel Weisz, working with a range of natural-looking fabrics, including her own hand-loomed material, and often combining different textures for a bold, imaginative look. Ngong House, Langata. ✆ **073/361-1565.** www.pennywinter.com.

Pinkopallino Design ★★★ Having worked in Nairobi for nearly 2 decades, designer Jutta Gavidia-Wilhelm has served as consultant for various hotels, luxury lodges, private homes, and even the RaMoMa (p. 85). Today she moves between Italy and Kenya, working closely with her local team to produce consistently ground-breaking, always dramatic lines in furniture that brings a European sensibility to an African-influenced look: She especially loves working with iron, challenging the inherent rigidity of the material to create pieces that are soft, almost liquid in appearance—or what has been called "whispering iron." She's also known for her hand-painted leather, and in 2010 will start working with a brand-new acrylic-type material. Her sculptural furniture must be seen to be appreciated, and at her small showroom you'll also see some beautiful jewelry and ornamental pieces by fellow artists whom she admires and respects. Village Market, Gigiri. ✆ **020/712-1192** or 072/775-5145. www.pinkopallino-design.com.

Robert Glen Gallery ★★★ Call ahead to make an appointment to view bronzes by East Africa's best-known sculptor, famed for creating one of the world's largest equine sculptures, *The Mustangs of Las Colinas,* a public commission in Irving, Texas. If you're actually able to shop here, you'll be going home with a true collector's piece—no more than 10 castings of any work are ever made; in owning a Robert Glen sculpture, you'll be joining the likes of Queen Elizabeth II and the Aga Khan. 14 Mutamaiyu Rd., Langata. ✆ **020/89-1065,** 072/275-6647, 072/183-6792, or 072/162-6630. www.robertglen.com.

Utamaduni Crafts Centre ★★ It's on just about every Nairobi itinerary, but the fact that you can work your way through such a wide variety of pan-African arts and crafts (not to mention many of the usual kitsch souvenirs) makes this an almost essential stop before heading home. Anything you've neglected to buy elsewhere—Kisii soap-stone carvings, jewelry made from recycled paper, antique Moroccan silver *khulkhal* (armbands), beaded leather sandals, Maasai-designed slippers made from recycled tires, West African antiques, frocks made from colorful Swahili *kangas,* beaded leather chairs, and children's toys—can be bought here (albeit at a marginally inflated price, but without the need to bargain). Even if you go in claiming that you're just looking, you're likely to walk out laden. ***Tip:*** If you're feeling charitable, don't miss the **Streetwise** stall on the same grounds: Everything here, from picture frames and coasters to entire table settings, is made by homeless children. Bogani East Rd., Langata. ✆ **020/89-1798** or 020/89-0464. www.utamadunicrafts.com.

Woodley Weavers ★★ Located near the Kibera shantytown, this is a breathtakingly successful community initiative that has been responsible for providing training and jobs to hundreds of single mothers who live in the slums. The hand-knotted rugs they produce are made from wool sourced in the Rift Valley and are 100% natural. This is also a good place to look for African fabrics. Corner of Ngong and Menelik rds. ✆ **020/387-3759** or 073/361-2028. www.woodleyweavers.com.

Zebu Shop ★★★ This is an essential stop for chic, upscale leather handbags and embellished belts, shoes, and clothes by designer Annabelle Thom. Her bags have graced the arms of the queens of Denmark and Jordan. Nakumatt Junction. ✆ **020/386-4665.** annabelle@africaonline.co.ke.

6 NAIROBI AFTER DARK

Hard-working by day, after-dark Nairobi is packed with a heady vibe. You'll have no problem finding a club, pub, bar, or *heng,* as the locals call a boozer; you can get fuelled up at any number of fairly lively spots in the city center, where intersecting with the after-work crowd is often a good way to meet locals. Nairobians have quite a reputation for full-on partying, and there seem to be no restrictions on when—or how—they choose to let their hair down. Music is a key ingredient in the Nairobi party culture—you can listen to everything from excellent Congolese rhythms, to cheesy '80s pop, to the latest *genge* (local music) sensation, and there seem to be few limitations on taste; this is very much a "go with the flow" nocturnal environment. You need to be wary, though, of fairly pervasive prostitution. and men are advised that the sexily dressed woman showing you affection is probably more interested in the content of your wallet than anything else. Sex workers can be pretty insistent, in-your-face, and—when you reject them—even a touch hostile; best to steer clear of their advances from the get-go (be aware, too, that 54% of people living in urban areas in Kenya either are HIV positive or have AIDS). On the other hand, striking up conversation in a social setting needn't be cause for anxiety, so don't pass up the chance to mingle.

It's also pretty seldom that food isn't available in conjunction with music and alcohol—there's an easy fluidity between restaurants and party hang-outs, **Carnivore** (see "Where to Dine," above) being the obvious example, with its lively **Simba Saloon** nightclub showcasing everything from contemporary African music to rock and jazz. International names as diverse as Maxi Priest, Salif Keta, Ismael Lo, and Hugh Masakela have performed here. To get a taste of Kenya's lingering colonial atmosphere, drop in at **The Norfolk** hotel for a drink. The once-infamous terrace bar—where hardcore colonial hunter types would cultivate magnificent hangovers while regaling whoever would listen with wild tales of their cowboy adventures—is now a slightly more elegant all-day drinking and eating venue, and one of the better (and costlier) places for a bottle of Tusker. Another old-world place for a drink is the Stanley hotel's **Exchange Bar,** done out in clubby leather with Art Nouveau overtones and electronic *pankas* overhead to keep the air fresh. It's open all day and closes around midnight.

If serious clubbing is your thing, you need to know that discos and clubs don't really get going until midnight, and then they keep going until sunrise.

Cin Cin ★★ Urbane, elegant, and decidedly contemporary, The Norfolk's prettily styled wine bar stands in striking contrast to the hotel's well-maintained colonial ambience. A lovely place to escape after the daytime chaos of downtown Nairobi, this is also a good choice if you like to sample several different vintages through the evening—it has the biggest "wine by the glass" selection in town. Italian snacks are available. Open daily 3pm until late. The Norfolk, Harry Thuku Rd. ✆ **020/225-0900.**

Gipsy Bar ★ One of the most popular bars in Nairobi, this is a dance club, cocktail lounge, and restaurant all in one; there's a full-on disco every Friday and Saturday night, and live bands occasionally perform on Thursdays. While their emphasis is on the four different theme bars, they also host regular art exhibitions. Open Monday to Saturday from 11am to 3pm and every night from 4:30pm till late. Woodvale Grove, Westlands. ✆ **020/444-0964** or 073/373-0529. www.gipsybar.com.

Mercury Lounge ★★ A young, sexy crowd of well-dressed locals bumps shoulders with tourists and expats out for a night of "New York–style" fun in a place that—by local standards—scores high in terms of cool. There's a list of clever-sounding cocktails, atmospheric lighting, and plenty of deep sofas, and on weekends you can expect to hear DJ-spun tunes. Excellent Spanish tapas (for some, the best thing about this place) help stave off hunger as you try out various liquid concoctions. Open daily 9pm till late. ABC Place, off Waiyaki Way, Lavington, Westlands. ✆ **020/445-1875** or -0364.

Zen Garden ★★ Expect a glamorous crowd, impressive jazz, and Japanese snacks at this very pleasant indoor-outdoor venue catering to a mixed, sophisticated crowd. Nothing too hectic or wild, but a lovely place for a drink, and it's easy to drift between the different venues—from the Jade teahouse, to Bamboo Oriental Restaurant, and then into the Zen Square lounge for a nightcap. Call for times and special events. Lower Kabete Rd. ✆ **020/071-474-4231,** 073/374-4231, or 020/80-3445.

6

Southern Kenya

By Keith Bain

Ironically, one of the enduring images of Kenya lies just over the border in Tanzania. There, like a gigantic pudding forming a surreal backdrop to some of Kenya's most quintessential landscapes, is Mount Kilimanjaro. Shimmering in the near-distance, its snow-capped presence looms so large you feel you could reach out and touch it—when, indeed, it can be seen at all. In Kili's shadow are several of Kenya's most important game parks, clustered within its southern tip between the coast and the Tanzanian border.

Kilimanjaro—which, had it not been for some colonial-era political wangling and suspect deal-signing, might well today have been a part of Kenya—stands out as the dominant geographical feature here. Visible on a clear day (or, at least, in the early morning), it forms the perfect backdrop to images of large elephant herds that have found their way onto swaths of Kenyan marketing material.

Southern Kenya is really southeastern Kenya and is the country's largest wildlife-intensive region—among its important preserves are **Amboseli,** known to have the most intensively studied elephants in Africa, and the enormous **Tsavo National Park,** so vast that it's divided into two distinct entities. Between these long-established parks are the little-known **Chyulu Hills,** which form a spine of undulating volcanic mounds that stretch across a magnificent, permanently green landscape. Although hardly discovered—even many decades after Hemingway wrote about them—the Chyulus stand out as one the country's most idyllically beautiful and unspoiled regions. Along with easily encountered wildlife and beautiful vistas is the immediate presence of the Maasai communities—particularly around Amboseli and the Chyulus, where many have gone into partnerships with conservationists to protect massive tracts of land in an attempt to make them safe for animals to roam freely.

Scenically diverse—with startling contrasts between dusty, arid terrain and lush, spring-fed forest—this wildlife-rich corner of Kenya is easily accessible from both Nairobi and the coast. Tsavo is particularly convenient if you're looking to break up a beach holiday with a few days of game viewing—you can drive from Mombasa to Tsavo along a good highway within hours and be ogling red elephants or stalking overly hormonal lions before lunch. Some argue that Amboseli long ago fell victim to the mass tourism market and has been overexploited, while wildlife sightings are patchy. But Amboseli's slightly ominous landscape—its parched terrain interrupted by life-giving swamps and springs—is a mesmerizing foil for Kili's looming presence. It's also quite possible to steer clear of the masses by staying in its smaller, classier camps and lodges. Chyulu Hills is the less commercial, more scenically enchanting option. But with arrival more difficult by road, and only private charters providing viable access to the region's two exclusive lodges, it remains for many an elusive, undiscovered gem—and one well worth the extra effort.

1 AMBOSELI NATIONAL PARK

260km (161 miles) SE of Nairobi, 300km (186 miles) NW from Mombasa

At the foot of Kilimanjaro, which usually floats on a big fluff of cloud just across the border, Amboseli National Park—compressed into a mere 390 sq. km (152 sq. miles)—stands out as one of Kenya's most famous wildlife preserves, second only in popularity to the Masai Mara. If you have a yen to see large agglomerations of tuskers—big, well-balanced, unthreatened families that are habituated to the presence of humans and their vehicles—then this is an essential stop, although not necessarily one where you'll escape the crowds.

Comprising several different ecosystems ranging from sulfur-rich springs, swamps, and marshes to lava-rock scrubland, open plains, acacia woodland, and a shallow lake that spends most of its life as a dry salt pan, Amboseli—which means "Salty Dust"—is a mercurial environment heavily impacted by changing weather patterns and subject to the destructive tendencies of tree-toppling elephants.

Extraordinarily flat, this often eerie, surreal landscape is given to periods of harsh drought. Dust devils dance across the plains, and the fragile circle of life hangs permanently in the balance. At its most brutal, the terrain is apocalyptic, desertlike. There's a sense of foreboding here, heightened by the helplessness of animals that traipse through the barren wilderness, stalked by death. Skeletons and carcasses litter the land. Hyenas lope across the plains scavenging for easy targets, tackling weakened wildebeest. Flesh-eating marabou storks—undertakers perched at the fringes of swamps—hover menacingly, and vultures soar not far above the ground. The scene should evoke misery, but instead it is a mesmerizing, primordial African spectacle.

Strange as all this is to witness, the real mystery of Amboseli lies in its ability to transform, to reveal itself in different guises. A dry, dusty expanse in parts, it's otherwise strewn with immense lava rocks spewed up by Kilimanjaro during its final eruption, and elsewhere—around its perennial swamps, especially Enkongo Narok (Black and Benevolent), and springs fed by life-saving melt-water runoff from Mount Kilimanjaro—it's eternally lush and green. Other bodies of water, such as the vast, alluvial, dried-up bed of Amboseli Lake, appear and disappear. A dry, shimmering mirage that's entirely dormant for much of the year, the lake fills with water only during the rainy seasons, if the rains come at all. And when the rains do come, Amboseli transforms overnight, instantly turning from brown to green, its vegetation exploding to life. But it's during the dry seasons, when Amboseli's swamplands are the only source of water for miles, that animals are most evident in the park. When these life-sustaining waters work their magic, extraordinary numbers of game do indeed flourish here; the concentration of wildlife includes

Fun Facts **A Beast by Any Other Name**

Sadly, Amboseli is devoid of rhino—the last members of the park's black rhino population were relocated to Tsavo West in 1995 when poaching finally proved too huge a threat to their continued existence. You may, however, hear occasional references to "Amboseli rhinos"—it's a total misnomer, of course, and is actually a nickname for the feisty little warthogs that call the park home.

a magnificent array of waterbirds—herons, storks, Egyptian geese—and as many as six different species of vulture. You'll also spot buffalos, zebras, wildebeest, gazelles, Maasai giraffes, lions, and cheetahs.

And then there are the elephants, Amboseli's pride and joy. They're believed to be the most studied and understood elephants in Africa—more than 1,400 of them, comprising approximately 58 matriarchal families, roam this terrain and include the oldest and biggest individuals left on the continent. However, the summer of 2009 witnessed one of the area's worst droughts, so numbers could be much smaller. Closely studied by researcher Cynthia Moss for more than 25 years, Amboseli's pachyderms are known intimately by many of the guides who work here.

The bad news is that, as one of Kenya's most popular parks, Amboseli retains reminders that it had its heyday in the '70s and '80s—essentially boom time for a number of big hotel-style operations established for an inelegant strain of mass-market tourist that spawned thoroughly unromantic images of a Kenyan safari dominated by fleets of minibuses careening through the African bush with Kilimanjaro in the background. Amboseli's credentials—and those of Kenya itself—have been a little suspect ever since. Yet while Amboseli remains a busy destination with even more titanic-size lodges today than there were 5 years ago, your experience need not be ruined by the human hordes. It'd be worth your while to stick to the intimate camps if privacy and a sense of seclusion feature among your priorities.

ESSENTIALS

VISITOR INFORMATION For up-to-date information on the park—particularly regarding current rain and drought conditions and prevalence of wildlife—contact the senior warden, P.O. Box 18, 00207, Namanga (© **045/62-2250** or -2251; amboselinp@kws.go.ke; www.kws.org).

GETTING THERE Driving all the way from either Nairobi or the coast is not recommended. The main route from Nairobi is via Namanga (240km/149 miles), beyond which the remaining stretch of road is badly potholed. It's also possible to travel via Emali (228km/141miles) on the Nairobi-Mombasa highway; from Emali, the remaining 64km (40 miles) is on difficult-but-doable dirt road. The drive from the coast is a full-day affair and definitely to be avoided. Fly instead. Amboseli has a single airstrip for light aircraft in the center of the park. **Safarilink** (www.safarilink-kenya.com) flies between Amboseli and Nairobi early each morning (either at 7:30 or 8:15am), and the trip takes around 40 minutes. The return flight is at 9:05am. One-way fares are $122 to $131; round-trip $194 to $216. **AirKenya** (www.airkenya.com) also flies there daily at either 7:30am ($105 one-way) or 8:10am ($105 one-way). **Mombasa Air Safari** (www.mombasaair safari.com) flies to Amboseli from Mombasa (via Ukanda; about 1 hr.)

GETTING AROUND Amboseli's fairly extensive road network is in a shocking state of disrepair and certainly feasible only for four-wheel-drive vehicles. Many roads are unmanageable during the rains, while during the dry season, the loose volcanic soil makes roads incredibly dusty.

PARK FEES Entry to Amboseli is by KWS Smartcard only. These cannot be bought or loaded at the park itself; your ground operator can arrange the purchase of your card and load it with sufficient credit to cover your stay. Adults are charged $60 per night; children ages 3 to 18 pay $30.

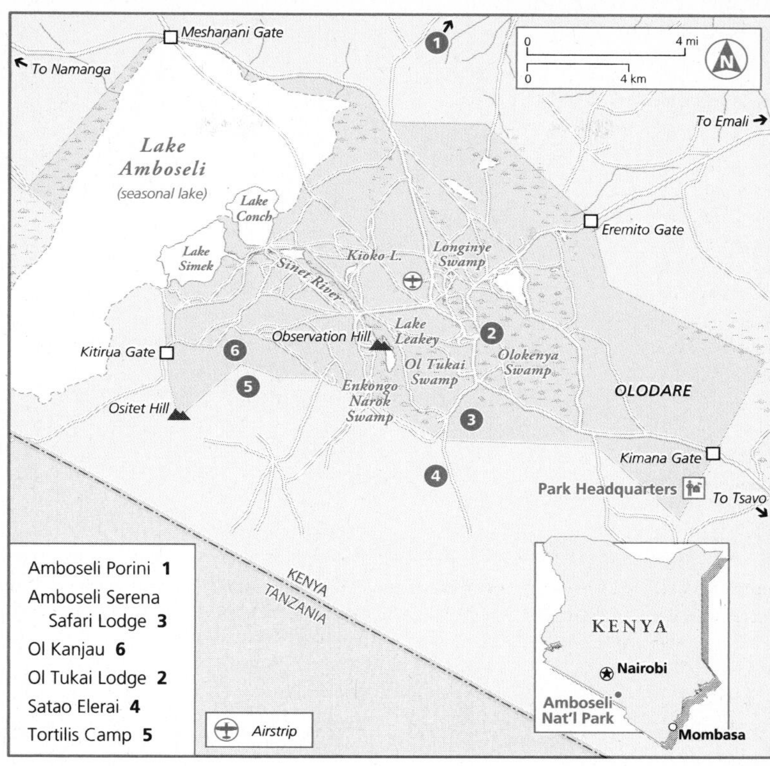

WHERE TO STAY

Amboseli's fame during the early days of independence saw the establishment of some pretty hideous concrete lodges within the park's boundaries. Adding insult to injury, these places are not only designed to accommodate large numbers of guests, but are usually protected by ugly fences and electric wires, exacerbating a sense of being in an isolated environment that's disconnected from the wilderness you've come to witness. That said, the large lodges are a good deal more affordable than the more dignified, intimate properties situated outside the park itself.

Large Lodges Within the Park

Amboseli Serena Safari Lodge (Value) Comprising a number of maroon-ocher buildings designed like enormous space-age huts (perhaps innovative when they were constructed back in 1973), this massive lodge occupies an expansive, neat, tree-studded lawn bordered by clumps of rocky bush and then surrounded by wide-open rangelands. The lodge itself looks and feels dated, and there's a slight smell of boot polish just about everywhere you go. Still, it's secure and comfortable. Guest rooms are in blocks on either

Poisoned Pride: How to Save a Lion by Buying a Cow

Like many wildlife preserves throughout Africa, the threat posed by poaching the animals of Amboseli represents an ongoing battle. In fact, conservationists fear that the park's lions risk being eradicated from Amboseli in just a few years. There are now fewer than 100 lions in the greater Amboseli region—by far the most significant threat to these animals is from pastoralists who are in the habit of taking revenge on lions and leopards for the cattle they have lost to these predators. Between 2003 and 2007, for example, 63 lions were killed in just two Maasai-owned group ranches in the region. Their crime? Straying threateningly close to domestic animals. Before the divvying-up of Africa into parcels of land for agriculture and modern development, lions were less likely to prey on livestock, but as human encroachment has restricted the movement of wildlife, it stands to reason that lions (by all accounts, lazy creatures) will target more easily accessible species, such as cows. It's a vicious circle that, if allowed to run its course, will result in the imminent decimation of all Amboseli's lions.

Conservationists have been hard at work developing schemes to reduce community anger against predators and thus cut back on the number of killings. One successful model here and elsewhere in Kenya is a program in which communities are reimbursed for livestock killed by the cats. So instead of seeking revenge on killer-predators, Maasai pastoralists can claim financial compensation. Theoretically, this should minimize the number of killings. In fact, the results have been dramatic. Successful conservancies in the Masai Mara area where the compensation scheme has been up and running since 2001 have seen lion numbers double. And on one Amboseli ranch (bordering the ranches where 63 lions were killed) where the scheme was established in 2003, just 4 lions were lost during the same time span. Funding for such programs is mostly sourced from visitor entry fees (usually called "conservation fees" on

side of the main buildings; each has a small, private terrace from which the better rooms have views of Kilimanjaro (when it is, in fact, visible)—ask specifically for one of these (nos. 1–26 and 70–86). Otherwise, despite hand-painted flora- and fauna-themed murals and beaded Maasai crafts on the walls, bedrooms have an overwhelmingly dull, "hotel" ambience with a faintly '70s decor—tiled floors, rugs, and beds that have become slightly concave over the years—despite an extensive upgrade in 2007. The bathrooms (nearly all are shower only) are particularly dinky. If you're traveling with children (or simply prefer to have a bit of extra space), reserve one of the three family suites, which come with an extra junior bedroom and also have tubs. Standard bedrooms are rather cramped. Although the lodge is larger and less attractive than Ol Tukai (below), service here is more agreeable.

Serena Hotels, Williamson House 4th Floor, 4th Ngong Ave.; P.O. Box 48690, 00100 Nairobi. © **045/62-2361,** 045/62-2622, or 0735/52-2361. Fax 045/62-2430. www.serenahotels.com. 92 units. Double high season $350; low season $185; midseason $212. Children 2–12 pay 50% if sharing with 2 adults; ages 13–17 pay 75%; under 2 free. Rates include all meals, 2 game drives per day, and airstrip transfers. AE, MC, V. **Amenities:** Restaurant; cafe; 2 bars; babysitting; room service; spa; currency exchange; in-house nurse.

private concessions), although there is always a potential shortfall for which private funding and donor money must be found. Funding for cattle compensation in the Mara Triangle fell dramatically during the post-election violence in Kenya in early 2008, when revenue dropped by $50,000 per month thanks to a dramatic dip in tourist numbers. Such financial shortfalls also impact other essential antipoaching resources such as the number of patrols by rangers because of a sudden lack of money for wages.

Sadly, while gains are being made in the saga of human-lion conflict, the dangers faced by wildlife have unexpectedly worsened, thanks to the careless interference by humans on other levels. The use of agricultural poisons, for example, is becoming a serious threat, potentially much worse than traditional poaching involving snaring and spearing. Whereas a warrior's spear might target and kill a single lion, poison works indiscriminately and unexpectedly, with the potential to decimate entire prides. In Kenya, Carbofuran is a particularly nasty insecticide that first gained notoriety more than a decade ago, when it was blamed for widespread bird deaths in Kenya. It's illegal in Europe but is available over-the-counter in Kenya. Exposure to the chemical interferes with the nervous system, causing blurred vision, confusion, and general muscular weakness; in high doses, it results in cardiorespiratory paralysis and death. In early 2008, it killed five hippos and paralyzed four lions that fed on tainted carcasses. Following this event, conservationists have been lobbying to ban the insecticide (sold in Kenya as Furadan), which is sprayed directly onto soil and plants. Many believe that, should the use of the chemical persist, not only will specific lion prides be at risk, but there's every chance many scavenging species will be endangered. At least two different species of vulture in Kenya could become extinct within a decade if the use of Carbofuran persists.

Ol Tukai Lodge **Value** Overtly geared toward the mass safari market, Ol Tukai is a sprawling 2-hectare (5-acre) property that benefits from beautifully designed elegant public spaces that open to appealing vistas. Wood walkways through well-maintained gardens and manicured lawns lead to massive reception areas. The contemporary, African-themed lounge and open-fronted dining area feature local artwork, and designers opted for an eclectic, eye-catching look, studiously throwing together old travel boxes and African artifacts with red faux-leather armchairs and leopard-print sofas that anywhere else might look kitsch. Here, though, with a wide frontage that gives spectacular views of the vast acacia-dotted plains backed by the stupendous frame of Mount Kili, it all works rather well. With such a gushing sense of sophistication, you may for a moment forget that this is essentially a budget-oriented lodge and has been up and running since the mid-1990s. It's a pity, then, that the stone and slate chalets where guests are accommodated (a short distance from the main lodge) don't quite live up to expectations set by the ostentatious public areas. Although some of the same design elements—animal prints and African design fabrics—are picked up here, rooms feel poky and cluttered. And if the lodge is full, you'll find yourself surrounded by crowds—certainly not what you came to Amboseli for.

A great deal better is the more chic and exclusive—not to mention remotely situated—**Kibo Villa** ★. Tucked away from view, this undisturbed three-bedroom log-and-stone cabin has its own entrance; the house includes a spacious lounge, dining area, and full kitchen—your meals are served here, too, so you need never see the crowds back at the main lodge. The upstairs master bedroom opens onto a terrace with Jacuzzi from which—if conditions are in your favor—you can spy Kili. Rates for Kibo run $1,188 to $1,650 per night for up to six people—this includes all meals, champagne breakfast, and entertainment in the form of Maasai dancing.

P.O. Box 45403, 00100 Nairobi. ✆ **020/444-5514,** or 0456/22-275 lodge. Fax 020/444-8493. www.oltukai lodge.com. 81 units. Package rates are nonseasonal. $500 double for 1–night flying packager. Children 2–11 pay 70%; under 2 free. Rates include all meals, local airstrip transfers, return flight from Nairobi, and 2 game drives per day. AE, MC, V. **Amenities:** Restaurant; bar; babysitting; pool; chapel; clinic; currency exchange.

Intimate Camps Outside the Park

In addition to the options reviewed below, **Amboseli Porini** (✆ **20/712-3129;** www.porini.com) is a recommended traditional tented camp (the first in the Porini stable of four camps around the country) with all necessary comforts and an emphasis on simplicity and consistent standards rather than luxury. The camp is on the well-established, community-owned Selenkay Conservation Area, and local Maasai are employed here. The price per person is $800 to $1,090 for a 2-night stay, including road transfers from Nairobi, all park fees, meals, drinks, and game-viewing activities, as well as a visit to a Maasai homestead. The same 2-night deal, with return flights rather than overland transfers between Nairobi and Amboseli, costs an additional $75 (one-way) per person.

Ol Kanjau ★★ The most intimate of Amboseli's camps, Ol Kanjau (Camp of the Elephant) has just six tents and occupies a site leased from members of the pastoral Ilkisongo Maasai community—as a group, they are the main landowners of greater Amboseli. They're also hands-on stakeholders in this eco-friendly safari operation and commune with guests on a level that you won't experience anywhere else in Southern Kenya. Working alongside the Maasai are seasoned ecologists Mike and Judy Rainy, whose enthusiasm for animal and environmental conservation is infectious—Mike learned to speak Maa when a Samburu family took him under their wing in the '60s. The couple has been interacting with the elephants here for several decades, so the opportunity to get a more personal perspective on some of Africa's best-studied pachyderms is high on the agenda for most guests. Accommodations—for no more than 12 guests—are in neat, compact canvas tents. Simply laid out, they have metal-frame beds, rugs, and some practical furniture (bedside table, dresser, hanging space). Basic safari-style bathrooms are supplied with bucket showers (hot water is provided on demand) and short-drop toilets. There is no electricity, but at night lanterns light the tents. This is a real leave-no-trace experience, where you know your stay will have little impact on the environment and, because you're so far away from the maddening crowds and as detached from modernity as possible, you come away with a real taste of life in the bush. If you don't mind forgoing some of the luxuries of home, this is a pleasant space to return to at the end of an action-packed day, during which you have a wide range of activities to choose from, including animal tracking with Maasai warriors, mountain-biking, or expert-guided bird-spotting—at least 274 African species have been identified in the immediate vicinity of the camp. ***Note:*** Ol Kanjau is closed April, May, and November.

www.olkanjau.com. Reservations mjrainy@africaonline.co.ke. 6 units. Midseason $1,060 double, $265 per child under 12; high season $1,220 double, $305 per child. Rates include all meals, soft drinks, wine, beer, game-viewing activities, cultural visits, mountain biking, local airstrip transfers, and laundry. No credit cards. **Amenities:** Bar; airstrip transfers.

Satao Elerai ★ Value A series of tents—sheltered by large thatch roofs and ranged along the edge of a rocky hill—provide what is undoubtedly the most full-on view of Mount Kilimanjaro anywhere in Kenya. The scene on moon-drenched nights is staggeringly beautiful—you'll feel as though you could reach out and touch the white-glowing peak. Situated on the edge of a 2,000-hectare (4,940-acre) private conservancy that's owned by the local Maasai, Elerai is a 40-minute drive from Amboseli's Kimana Gate, far from the minibuses and crowds within the park. The tents—which are larger than those at Tortilis (below) and about three times the size of the rooms at Serena (above)—are a combination of canvas and lava rock, built on raised wooden plinths with huge stone-floor bathrooms and rainfall showers. Interiors include furniture made from locally sourced yellow acacia wood, honey-colored curtains in natural fibers, and an earthy color palette. Comfy duvet-covered king-size beds face Mount Kili directly, as do the large private verandas (and the cleverly positioned toilets), meaning you can wake up to an instant encounter with one of Africa's showstopper scenes—when your steward arrives with morning coffee, ask him to fold away the tent flaps.

Apart from the nine Kili-facing tents, there are five thatched cottages; they're smart and have bathtubs and sliding doors that open onto wooden decks that, rather than facing Kili, overlook the plains below and, in the distance, Amboseli National Park. Though good for anyone opposed to canvas, they lack the exquisite Kili views and the breeziness of the tents. Between game drives, gorge walks, or visits to a local Maasai *enkang,* slink into one of the wicker armchairs in the lounge/bar designed around massive volcanic boulders that seem to burst through the walls—or relax on the upstairs viewing deck with a predinner G&T. Given a choice for sundowner cocktails, have staff take you out on a bush walk culminating on a nearby hill just 10km (6¼ miles) from the Tanzanian border—ask for a *dawa,* served with a mixing stick and blob of honey.

Animals in the conservancy are steadily becoming habituated to the presence of humans and vehicles; because you're on private land, you can drive after-hours to try glimpsing nocturnal beasts, and off-road exploration is also permitted. At press time, a pool and spa were being planned.

P.O. Box 90653, Mombasa. ✆ **020/243-4600** through -4603. Fax 020/243-4610. www.sataoelerai.com or www.southerncrosssafaris.com. 14 units. Peak season $820 tent double, $1,070 suite double; high season $700 tent double, $920 suite double; low season $584 tent double, $770 suite double. Children 2–12 pay 50% if sharing with 2 adults. Rates include all meals, most drinks, most game-viewing activities, local transfers, sundowners, and laundry. AE, MC, V. **Amenities:** Restaurant; bar; airstrip transfers.

Tortilis Camp ★★ This chic, rustic, tented property has earned myriad accolades—appearing on *Condé Nast Traveller*'s Gold List and being among *Travel+Leisure*'s top hotel picks for 2008. Despite its international reputation and legions of celebrity guests, Tortilis is a far more relaxed, no-frills kind of place than you'd expect. The setting—on a private 12,120-hectare (29,936-acre) concession, amid a grove of flat-topped *tortilis* acacias (umbrella thorn trees)—emphasizes remoteness and a rugged wilderness experience. Add

Eric the Maasai Elder

Eric, a Maasai elder who works at Tortilis, is one of the best-informed guides I've met in Kenya. He previously worked for Amboseli's world-class elephant research center, under Cynthia Moss. And although Maasai custom dictates that Eric is known as an elder—and, therefore, a leader within his community—have no doubt that he's as young and strapping as any image conjured by the Maasai warrior class. Ask your travel agent to put him on your list of requests when making your reservation there.

to that a busy water hole—permanently besieged by awkward-looking marabou storks—and spectacular views across the plains toward Mount Kilimanjaro (which all the tents face, too), and you have the ingredients for a memorable stay. The camp is set into a natural terrace with long, sandy pathways leading down to 17 simple, moderately sized beige canvas tents set on raised stripwood plinths under large thatch roofs; each one has a slate porch where you can recline on your Lamu daybed and stare into the bush, which begins right at your "doorstep."

In the big open-air lounge, the look is decidedly old school, with traditional safari color schemes, a mélange of wood, big comfy sofas, leather poufs, chunky candles, old wood traveling trunks, and piles of photographic tomes, all under a massive *makuti* roof. With the floodlit waterhole on one side and cocktail bar on the other, it's a great place to imbibe the early evening air before sitting down to a dinner of authentic northern Italian fare, made with ingredients from the camp's organic garden—there's usually a pasta station at lunchtime.

At night, the way home is lit by paraffin lamps, but the tents have 'round-the-clock lighting and hot water. While arranged to provide relative privacy, tents are not really far enough apart to prevent noise from seeping in from neighboring digs. Potentially loud neighbors aside, tent nos. 1 to 8 have the best views (and are closest to the communal areas)—1 and 2 are stand-outs, so request these first. In the morning, you'll awake to overwhelming birdsong, and throughout the day you should spot monkeys and large monitor lizards cruising between the tents and among the trees. Keen to upgrade? Book the exquisite **family tent** ★★★, consisting of two en suite bedrooms (a double and a twin with two beds) that share a gorgeously decorated open-air lounge. It's totally private from the rest of the camp, and you can even choose to have all your meals here.

Dry as this region is, the camp has access to a natural spring with water so pure it's bottled and sold to other camps (and this is one of the few places in the country with drinkable tap water)—it also feeds the pool, a welcome spot to stave off the intense heat. In the late afternoon, hike with a Maasai warrior across the desolate Amboseli landscape to reach Kitirua Hill in time to watch the sun disappear behind the Ol Donyo Erok hills—if you're lucky, your sundowners will be accompanied by close-up views of Mount Kili.

Cheli & Peacock, P.O. Box 743, 00517 Uhuru Gardens, Nairobi. ✆ **020/60-4054** or -4053, or 020/60-3090/1. Fax 020/60-4050. www.tortilis.com. 18 units. High season $970 double, $365 per child 5–16 sharing with 2 adults, $2,530 family tent (up to 4 people); midseason $800 double, $305 per child, $1,995 family tent; low season $620 double, $230 per child, $1,500 family tent. Children under 5 free. Rates include all meals, most drinks, game-viewing activities, laundry, local transfers, and sundowners. MC, V. **Amenities:** Bar; pool; spa. *In room:* Minibar.

2 CHYULU HILLS

190km (118 miles) SE of Nairobi

Said to be the setting for Ernest Hemingway's *Green Hills of Africa,* the Chyulu Hills—hundreds of small, voluptuous green mounds composed of ash cones and craters—are among the most recently formed geological phenomena on Earth, clocking in at around 400 or 500 years. Ranged between Amboseli to the north and Tsavo farther south, the hills divide the southern extremes of Maasailand from the traditional lands of the Wakamba people. Volcanic vents, deep ash craters, and dark lava flows punctuate the rounded domes, and valleys of lush green forest spread between the hills to form a landscape of startling beauty, backed by drop-dead views of Kilimanjaro in the near distance.

Little-known and still undeveloped, the Chyulus remain blissfully remote—even the national park here lacks serious infrastructure. Nutrient-rich volcanic soil and rock from the last eruptions here—two of the cones, Shetani and Chainu, blew their lids as recently as the mid–19th century—support a dense forest that spreads through the seemingly endless surrounding plains. Volcanic activity here has left some intriguing geographic phenomena, too, including **Leviathan,** the world's longest lava tube.

Despite the absence of permanent surface water, the Chyulu ecosystem has evolved into some of Kenya's most picturesque terrain. Rough grassland and thicket give way to patches of montane forest along the spine of the hills, while mature flat-topped acacia woodland covers the area immediately below, with impenetrably thick bush growing from the nutrient-rich lava flows beneath. It's Mt. Kili, though, that's largely responsible for sustaining the vibrant ecology here. Rainwater and snowmelt running off Africa's highest mountain percolate through the Chyulu's porous lava-rock underbed to form deep, fast-flowing subterranean rivers that not only feed the hills, keeping them green and lush throughout the year, but are believed to feed many permanent freshwater sources in the surrounding plains, notably the Mzima springs (Mombasa's principal water source) in Tsavo West (p. 122) and both the Tsavo and Galana rivers.

Along with some intriguing geographic phenomena that are a result of volcanic activity here, the hills are a good place to search for 37 species of orchids, most of which are epiphytes supported by the heavy mists. And all around the Chyulu Hills, a densely forested environment and more fantastic rock-studded hills and mountains provide shelter for a brilliant variety of animal life. Buffalo, zebra, giraffe, lion, leopard, and cheetah are regularly spotted, along with rarer species such as fringe-eared oryx, klipspringer, and gerenuk. Birdlife is abundant, too. It's here that some of Kenya's last truly wild black rhinoceros may, with extreme patience, be found. Although you may not experience the density of animal numbers easily spotted on the wide-open plains of the Masai Mara, for example, your encounters will be personal, intimate, and exciting—unimpeded by crowds and safari traffic.

ESSENTIALS

VISITOR INFORMATION Management at either of the two lodges available in the area is your best bet for reliable, up-to-the-minute info on the Chyulu region.

GETTING THERE There are scheduled flights from Nairobi to Amboseli National Park and Tsavo National Park. From either park, it's a short hop to private airstrips at either Campi ya Kanzi or Ol Donyo Wuas, the only two recommended places to stay in the region, both of which have private airstrips. You could also arrange an overland transfer from either of the national parks, but be prepared for a bumpy ride. The direct flight from Nairobi to either Campi ya Kanzi or Ol Donyo Wuas takes approximately 1 hour and will be organized by the lodge or operator or via the lodge's in-house plane (such as Ol Donyo Wuas). By way of example, the cost of a seat on a plane from Nairobi's Wilson Airport to Campi ya Kanzi is $300 one-way.

WHERE TO STAY

There are two superb places to stay here. Ol Donyo Wuas is the arguably the most luxurious safari lodge in Kenya, while Campi ya Kanzi is among the country's most eco-friendly camps. The latter is set on Maasai community land, the Kuku Group Ranch, which spreads over 1,150 sq. km (449 sq. miles, two-thirds the size of the Mara National Reserve) and is green all year round, thanks to immense lava flows that support a rich, lush vegetation.

Campi ya Kanzi ★ As a boy growing up in Italy and visiting Africa with his hunter father, Luca Belpietro fell in love with Kenya and always dreamed of settling here. Having completed his doctorate in sustainable conservation using Kenya as a model, he convinced his wife, Antonella, to literally set up camp here. This they did in a remote and beautiful spot near the southern fringes of the Chyulu Hills, among the least spoiled and most perennially lush parts of Kenya. With a strong emphasis on ecological sensitivity, the camp—whose name means "Hidden Jewel"—was built using local materials and strives to be 100% eco-friendly. Water (collected during the rains or fetched from the nearest spring) is recycled for the organic garden, and most power (which is available around-the-clock, unlike in most other camps) is generated by solar panels, which also heat water for washing. Antonella decorated the shared lounge and dining room (built on split levels "because that's the surface that nature provided," she says) with African artworks, locally made furniture, and pieces she inherited from her grandmother in Italy—the result feels very much like a space in someone's home, only this one faces a scene that is surreal and beautiful in equal measure.

There are six camo-colored tents set on wood decks with stone bathrooms at the back (these have a shower, twin basins, a flush toilet, and a bidet) and a big grass roof above. Each tent has a private veranda with a unique view—most are completely private, although it's from the Hemingway tent that you have the most direct view of Mount Kilimanjaro (but also of your neighbor's porch). Accommodations are simple, neat, and functional—a large four-poster bed made with local wood, wicker furniture, and plenty of insect-proof screen "windows" to let in extra light. Frankly, the standard "luxury" tents are a bit small—far better to opt for one of the two suites (Hemingway or Simba), which have much better bathrooms, too (although the uptick in price is considerable). There's also a private five-bedroom house with its own Jacuzzi and 18m (59-ft.) swimming pool.

Meals—impressively authentic Italian, with superb pastas and homemade ice cream—happen around a communal table (although bush meals are available, too), and are usually accompanied by talk of Luca's conservation efforts (he established the Maasai Conservation Trust) and ongoing plans to preserve the Chyulu Hills ecosystem. Campi Ya Kanzi is an especially good place for walkers; you'll be taken out by a Maasai guide and tracker to explore some extraordinary terrain—sundowners atop a granite hill called Koikuma are especially memorable, with soaring Mt. Kili on one side and the undulating Chyulus on the other.

Caving Adventure

Besides its wildlife and scenic attractions, the Chyulus shelter Leviathan, believed to be the world's longest lava tube, a geographic phenomenon formed by hot lava flowing under a crust that has already cooled. Here, at some point on the hillside, part of the surface crust collapsed, allowing air to enter and causing a tube to be excavated just beneath the surface—the resultant hollow is a fascinating draw for anyone looking for a serious caving adventure. In global terms, lava tubes are relatively rare; they form only under specific conditions with lava of a specific type and viscosity. **Savage Wilderness Safaris** (✆ **020/712-1590;** www.whitewaterkenya.com), one of Kenya's top adventure activity operators, runs 3- to 4-day trekking and caving expeditions, which include time spent exploring sections of Leviathan; besides typical cave phenomena such as stalactites and stalagmites, you see elements associated with volcanic activity, such as lava ropes and sinkholes. It's not just about geology, though. You'll also walk the crest of the hills, taking in phenomenal views of the plains below and, weather permitting, glimpsing mighty Kili in the background—it's just 50km (31 miles) away. Encounters with any of the Big Five are a distinct possibility; plains game will often be spotted. Tents and sleeping mats are provided, as is all food and cooking equipment. Porters, however, are not provided, so you'll be responsible for carrying your own equipment (including a share of food and tentage), meaning you'll want to travel ultralight.

P.O. Box 236, 90128, Mito Andei. ✆ **0720/461-300.** ✆/fax 020/60-5450 or 020/802-9542. www.maasai.com. Reservations: Uncharted Outposts, 9 Village Lane, Santa Fe, NM 87505, USA. ✆ **505/795-7710** or 888/995-0909. Fax 505/795-7714. www.unchartedoutposts.com. 8 units. Luxury tents: $1,190 double, $300 per child under 12. Hemingway & Simba suites: $1,600 double, $900 per child under 12. Kanzi House: $1,190 double, $300 per child under 12. Substantial discount on stays of 4 nights or more. Rates include all meals, most drinks, most activities, and laundry; suite and Kanzi House rates include exclusive vehicle use. AE, V. **Amenities:** Bar; airstrip transfers.

Ol Donyo Wuas ★★★ Overlooking a humbling, quintessential African landscape and backed by the elegant Chyulu Hills, Ol Donyo Wuas stands out as an obvious contender for the title of Kenya's most luxurious safari lodge. Reopened in July 2008 after a complete rebuild, this is a contemporary reincarnation of what started out as a sidebar to safari operator Richard Bonham's brilliantly sited private home in the bush. Bonham, who is one of Kenya's most sought-after wilderness guides, is a stalwart conservationist who has long worked for the creation of a vital wildlife corridor that will ultimately preserve the Chyulu ecosystem. By partnering with a major international conservation donor, he's taken his formerly rustic, simple lodge to new level of sophistication.

While there's an enormous menu of activities and endless variety of ways to view wildlife—on horseback, by mountain bike, from the air, on foot, and even while charging through the bush at night—you'd be forgiven for wanting to devote some of your time to simply idling in your expansive suite. Accommodations are fantastic. Ranged along a low ridge that affords far-reaching views, each thatch-roof cottage comes with a stylishly furnished lounge and bedroom, each of which is completely open-fronted,

Moments Africa's Green Hills on Horseback

African safaris are popular and also big business. There's every danger in some spots of discovering yourself caught up among a cluster of frantically reversing Land Cruisers while the predator you're supposedly tracking has long since legged it back into the bush, far from curious humans. The Chyulu Hills are among the best places in Kenya to visit for a complete escape from the crowds. This is a true wilderness, with almost none of the development seen in the country's most popular parks and reserves. And the landscape is particularly unspoiled. The Chyulus are also where some of Kenya's prime horse-riding safaris are conducted. If you stay at Ol Donyo Wuas (above), you'll have ample opportunity to explore the region on horseback and at night return to some of the most comfortable quarters imaginable. Award-winning U.K.–based travel outfit **Black Tomato** (© **207/426-9888;** www.blacktomato.co.uk) arranges smart, all-inclusive saddle-safaris guided by experts who will take you cantering with large herds and hopefully put you on the trail on some of the more elusive predators—it's not uncommon to spot cheetah while out riding. At night, in contrast with the sturdy walls and leather-and-wood luxury of Ol Donyo Wuas, you'll bed down in canvas in a luxury mobile tented camp with all the trimmings. Each trip is tailor-made, so costs, duration, and routing will depend largely on your interests.

framing the awesome, cinemascope view of the vast plains that disappear into the horizon down below. High-off-the-ground beds with gossamer mosquito netting draped from the ceiling, oversize pillows, and sumptuous linens heighten the sense of luxury—rough, textured walls; smart finishes; and elegant combinations of clubby wicker, leather, and wood furniture up the sense of cosseting. Each suite comes with a private outdoor infinity plunge pool, an alfresco shower, and a rooftop deck for sunbathing, stargazing, or game viewing.

Although lunch is served in a communal dining room, staff ensure that each dinner is an entirely unique experience, so you might find yourself shuttled off to a clearing in the bush for a lantern-lit barbecue with full bar and Maasai singing and dancing (you'll even get a chance to compare your jumping skills with the warriors'). Quite frankly, you can do just about anything you want here—nothing is too much for your hosts, and there's an emphasis on fun so that no part of your vacation ever needs to turn into an animal-chasing routine. ***Tip:*** If you are planning to head home with your suitcases stuffed with beautiful African crafts, have your credit card handy and visit the in-house boutique, Chyulu Chic, which stocks fine Kenyan designer wear and local crafts.

www.bonhamsafaris.com. Reservations: Uncharted Outposts, 9 Village Lane, Santa Fe, NM 87505, USA. © **505/795-7710** or 888/995-0909. Fax 505/795-7714. www.unchartedoutposts.com. Local contact: Bush&Beyond, P.O. Box 56923, 00200, Nairobi. © **020/60-0457,** 020/60-5108, or 020/60-5980. Fax 020/60-5008. www.bush-and-beyond.com. 9 units. Midseason $1,060 double; high season $1,220 double. Children under 12 pay 50% of rate if sharing with 2 adults. Rates include all meals, most drinks, game-viewing activities, horseback riding, cultural visits, and laundry. MC, V. **Amenities:** Restaurant; bar; free Internet; pool; room service; spa. *In room:* Hair dryer (on request).

3 TSAVO NATIONAL PARK

200km (124 miles) SE of Nairobi

Notoriously remembered as the scene of bloody massacre inflicted by the Hollywood-immortalized man-eating lions of Tsavo, it's hardly surprising that Kenya's largest wildlife preserve isn't the country's most popular destination. Occupying a whopping 3% of the country's land area, Tsavo is comparable in size to Michigan, Jamaica, Wales, or Israel, and large enough to have been split into two separately managed parks—Tsavo East and Tsavo West—sadly divided up by the country's busiest highway, an ill-considered death-trap for animals instinctively roaming between the unfenced reserves. With the constant roar of traffic chasing between Nairobi and Mombasa, were it not for the frequent scenes of roadkill that includes rarely spotted animals, you'd hardly suspect that each of the adjacent parks shelters an overwhelming abundance of wildlife, including a third of Kenya's total elephant population—just more than 11,000 of the beasts roam this eco-system. If you have any say in the matter, ask your driver to slow down while driving between Nairobi and Mombasa.

Transformed into a wildlife preserve by pioneering warden David Sheldrick, the arid Tsavo was, until the 1940s, unchartered, completely undeveloped, and known simply as the Taru Desert. As with so many officially protected parks, Tsavo became a protected area because of its unsuitability for agriculture—a tsetse fly infestation and lack of water kept this great swath of land from human exploitation. Previously, it served as hunting grounds for the Waliangulu and Kamba tribes, and it also saw some Anglo-German conflict during World War I. More recently, its outer extremities and northern reaches have been sites of bitter conflict between poachers and conservationists too ill equipped and understaffed to adequately police such a vast terrain. Nevertheless, authorities claim that they're winning the war on elephant and rhino poachers, and game numbers are on the increase.

There are only two permanent rivers in this vast area. The Tsavo begins its life as snowmelt on Kilimanjaro and is greatly supplemented by a huge underground river flowing toward the famed **Mzima Springs,** a veritable oasis in Tsavo West. Meanwhile, the Athi River, in Tsavo East, begins near Nairobi. With the exception of small pockets of oasislike vegetation—doum palms and Tana poplars that line the rivers and shelter the springs—Tsavo's terrain can be extremely dry, dusty, and inhospitable, its miragelike plains broken by volcanic remnants and immense lava flows. Still, it's a landscape of unusual beauty and distinctive contrasts; the type of vegetation, in fact, varies so markedly that you'll notice distinct changes in the microclimate—the temperature, even—as you move around. One minute you might be watching hippos and crocodiles on a wide beach along the river, and the next observing the Tsavo's famous "red elephants" stomping in the dust. And with so much space in which to maneuver, it's not much of a challenge to steer clear of fellow visitors.

ESSENTIALS

VISITOR INFORMATION The two Tsavo parks are separately managed. For information or assistance, however, you're best off contacting the senior warden at Tsavo West (P.O. Box 14, Voi; © **43/30-049** or 43/31-011; www.kws.org; travowestnp@kws.go.ke).

GETTING THERE **By Air** Tsavo is close to both the Malindi/Mombasa coast and the Chyulu Hills, which by private charter takes approximately 35 minutes. A 50-minute flight will get you from Nairobi to Tsavo West; **Safarilink** (www.safarilink-kenya.com) has daily flights departing the capital at 7:30am ($150–$161 one-way, $237–$260 round-trip). Note that the return flight takes 70 to 80 minutes. Mombasa Air Safari (www.mombasaairsafari.com) flies from the coast to the private airstrip at Finch Hattons in Tsavo West. There are no scheduled flights to Tsavo East, but 6 airstrips in the southern part of the park and 13 in the northern part are available for charter flights—your ground operator will make arrangements for you to be dropped at the one nearest your lodge or camp, and land transfers will be organized, too.

By Road Thanks to the Mombasa-Nairobi highway and its proximity to the coast, many people visiting Tsavo do so as a sidebar to seaside holidays. By road, Tsavo East is 3½ hours from Mombasa and 4½ hours from Nairobi—of course, traffic can be scary if you have no control over the speed at which your driver decides to tear along the highway. Coming from Nairobi, Tsavo East is accessed via the town of Voi (where KWS has its headquarters) through either of two gates: Voi or Manyani. From Mombasa, entry is via Bachuma Gate, whereas if you're on the road from Malindi, you'll arrive via Sala Gate. Such details aren't likely to affect you, though, as your driver and ground operator will conspire to make sure you get there in the quickest possible time—in fact, better to request a more modestly paced drive, if you can. For **Tsavo West,** the main access points are Chyulu Gate, if coming from Amboseli, or Mtito Andei Gate if approaching via the highway from either Nairobi (240km/149 miles) or Mombasa. Visitors from Mombasa also use Tsavo Gate near Manyani.

PARK FEES Entry to either park is $50 per day for adults and $25 for children ages 3 to 18; if you want to see both parks in a single day (although, given the enormity of each of them, you should have no reason to do this), you will need to pay twice. Access to either park is by means of a KWS Smartcard, which your ground operator can purchase and load for you in advance of your arrival; don't arrive without a prepaid card, as this will mean making a time-consuming detour to park headquarters to pick up a new card.

TSAVO EAST NATIONAL PARK

Established in 1948, Tsavo East is the larger of the two parks, covering nearly 12,000 sq. km (more than 4,680 sq. miles) of harsh, rugged terrain. Considerably flatter, more arid, and a good deal bushier than neighboring Tsavo West, it's also the less-visited park. Its vast expanses of thornbrush scrubland are cut through by the impressive spine of the **Yatta Plateau**—at about 290km (180 miles) long, it's the world's longest lava flow (also the oldest fossilized lava flow on Earth), reaching up to 10km (6¼ miles) wide and 300m (984 ft.) high in places. For many years, the northern reaches beyond the Yatta Plateau have been closed to general tourist traffic, thanks to poachers who cross the border from Somalia, threatening the security of animals, visitors, and park employees alike. But park rangers have been putting up a solid fight. In 2006, five poachers were killed in two separate incidents, and rhino horns and AK-47 rifles were recovered; in 2007, conflict resulted in three rangers losing their lives. There have been no such incidences since, and officials are hopeful that the war on poaching is being won. Authorities even have plans to open this lesser-explored part of the park in the very near future, hopefully with a focus on exclusive, low-impact tourism.

Those who do take the time to explore this vast and, in parts, extraordinary terrain are rewarded with an intriguing mix of habitats; the rugged, varied landscape comprises

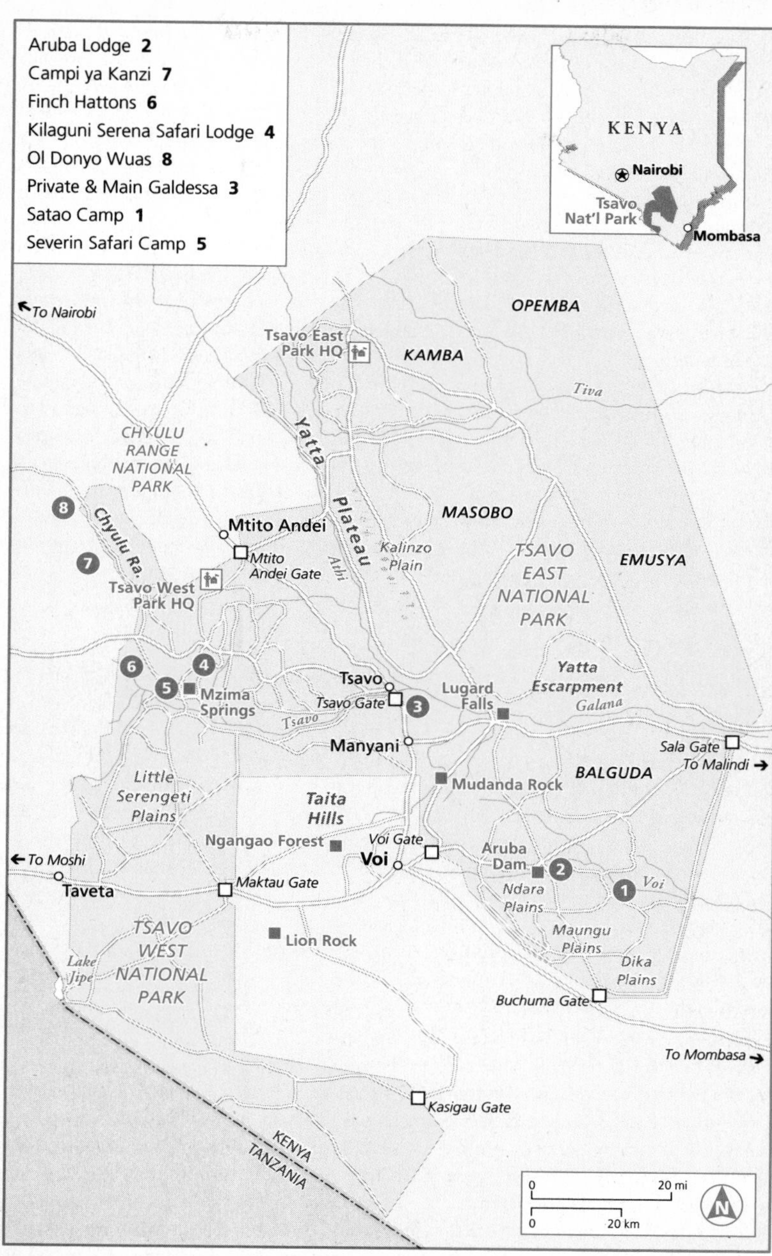
Aruba Lodge 2
Campi ya Kanzi 7
Finch Hattons 6
Kilaguni Serena Safari Lodge 4
Ol Donyo Wuas 8
Private & Main Galdessa 3
Satao Camp 1
Severin Safari Camp 5
KENYA
Nairobi
Tsavo Nat'l Park
Mombasa
To Nairobi
OPEMBA
Tsavo East Park HQ
KAMBA
Tiva
Yatta Plateau
CHYULU RANGE NATIONAL PARK
MASOBO
Mtito Andei
Mtito Andei Gate
Chyulu Ra.
Kalinzo Plain
Athi
TSAVO EAST NATIONAL PARK
EMUSYA
Tsavo West Park HQ
Yatta Escarpment
Tsavo
Tsavo Gate
Lugard Falls
Galana
Mzima Springs
Tsavo
Manyani
Sala Gate
To Malindi
BALGUDA
Mudanda Rock
Little Serengeti Plains
Taita Hills
Ngangao Forest
Voi Gate
Aruba Dam
To Moshi
Voi
Taveta
Maktau Gate
Ndara Plains
Voi
Maungu Plains
Lion Rock
TSAVO WEST NATIONAL PARK
Lake Jipe
Dika Plains
Buchuma Gate
To Mombasa
Kasigau Gate
KENYA
TANZANIA
0 20 mi
0 20 km

brown, dust-strewn arid plains; thick scrubland; and volcanic lava fields. Rugged, untamed, and often harsh, Tsavo East's vast, unpredictable expanses are stomping ground for large herds of fairly aggressive elephants—there are more here, in fact, than in Tsavo West, as well as a tiny population of one of the world's rarest antelopes—the hirola, or Hunter's hartebeest. Other uncommon species regularly spotted here include lesser kudu, gerenuk, fringed-eared oryx, and Peter's gazelle. The park also supports Africa's largest unfenced black rhino population; at least 50 of the endangered animals roam the area around Galdessa (see "Where to Stay," later in this chapter). The park also serves as a temporary refuge for birds migrating from Oman, Malawi, Iran, Germany, and Russia.

A good opportunity for visitors from the coastal resorts to make a quick game-viewing getaway, Tsavo East is a relatively easy overland trip from Mombasa, yet the park remains one of the lesser-explored wildlife destinations in Kenya, its prospects often marred by its reputation for severe drought, which creates the impression of a hostile wilderness. In the past, even the 85-hectare (210-acre) Aruba Dam, built across the Voi River in 1952, has succumbed to the heat and dried up completely. The park's salvation is the lush vegetation along its permanent and seasonal rivers. Snaking its way through the parched terrain is the doum palm-flanked **Athi River,** which at one boulder-strewn section forms the **Lugard Falls** ★★★, a tremendous, invigorating stretch of gushing white-water cataracts where it's possible to follow a riverside route on foot as you search for sunbathing crocodiles. Not true falls, but a series of rapids, the waters here gush through a tiny fissure before dropping to **Crocodile Point,** where the river merges with the **Tsavo.** Here it becomes the **Galana River,** which supports lush vegetation and is bounded by several sandy beaches—good for spotting hippos, crocs, and all kinds of animals that come down to drink.

WHERE TO STAY IN TSAVO EAST

Tsavo East's northern reaches have long been closed to general tourist traffic—at the time of writing, there were plans to introduce a number of small camps and lodges, with a total of 200 beds, into this region. Presently, most accommodations within the park are situated between the Galana River and the main highway. Of these, Private Galdessa (below) is far and away the most attractive option, with two camps in one, giving you different budgetary options. If both Private Galdessa and the cheaper, more laid-back option Satao (below) seem expensive, you may find solace at the lifeless, concrete-and-canvas **Aruba Lodge** (www.ashnilhotels.com/aruba.html), which opened in April 2008 and has space for around 100 guests. Rates are the main selling point here—you pay just $174 to $240 double, with all meals included, and a pool takes the edge off Tsavo's intense heat. Most accommodations are in small, drab brick-and-mortar rooms, but there are a handful of beige metal-frame tents with stone floors, built-in bathrooms, and a small porch that are better suited to the safari experience—but are still behind the ugly fence that secures the lodge perimeter. Aruba may be affordable, but bear in mind that none of your game-viewing activities are included in the room rate.

Private Galdessa ★★★ Hovering at the banks of the magnificent Galana River, with hippos and crocodiles permanently in your sights, nonstop entertainment by a troop of gallivanting baboons gorging on doum palm fruit, and regular visits from an ill-tempered elephant named Mugabe(!), Galdessa is not only astonishingly beautiful, but is one of those privileged spots where you hardly need to leave your veranda to enjoy an endless parade of animal life. Little Galdessa—just three wood-and-canvas *bandas* with gloriously breezy bedrooms and great big stone bathrooms, all capped by a swooping

Weird, Wonderful, and Nearly Gone

Known as the "four-eyed antelope" because of the eyelike appearance of their large pre-orbital glands, the hirola (also known as the Hunter's hartebeest) is Africa's—probably the world's—most endangered antelope and endemic to the dry Kenya–Somalia border region. Fears for the survival of the species back in 1963 prompted the Kenya Wildlife Service to undertake a translocation of about 50 hirola to Tsavo East, a move that was strongly opposed by local communities. Censuses undertaken in the 1970s counted around 14,000 animals, but competition with domestic cattle and drought, which continues to plague the region, has severely impacted their numbers. These factors, exacerbated by the escalating conflict in Somalia in the 1990s, saw a continuous decrease in population numbers and urged a second translocation in 1996—again fiercely opposed. The move has, however, resulted in an isolated and viable *ex situ* population of an estimated 100 hirola antelope in Tsavo East, while the total population is now thought to be between 500 and 1,200 animals in the wild, as well as a single female in captivity.

Critically endangered and on the brink of extinction, the hirola was identified as one of the top 10 "focal species" in 2007 by the Evolutionary Distinct and Globally Endangered (EDGE) project, a conservation program launched by the Zoological Society of London to help ensure the survival of the world's most unusual creatures. EDGE identifies species, particularly those that have few close relatives and have been otherwise ignored by prevailing conservation schemes, but that are in dire need of better protection to prevent extinction.

Spend a day or two in Tsavo East, and there's a very strong chance you'll spot hirola. Even if you've had your mind firmly set on Big Five sightings, it's worth making the effort to see these antelope. When looking for hirola, the extra set of "eyes" is a dead give-away; the animals have lyre-shaped, conspicuously ringed horns and a sandy brown coat (males are somewhat grayer), with a slightly paler underbelly and, over the bridge of the nose, a small white strip. They're diurnal, so out and about in the day, when they can be seen grazing or appearing to march in single file in herds of between 2 and 40 females led by a single territorial male. Small bachelor herds of about five hirola may also occur. Because the males are very territorial, they tend to stick to certain pockets of land, a factor that may have impacted their diminishing numbers.

upturned banana boat–style thatched roof—is perfectly intimate and thoughtfully designed with the environment in mind. Elegant and simple, there's a pleasing use of natural fabrics, textures, and colors, which makes these structures really feel like they belong here. A disarming staff waits on you hand and foot—to serve you drinks, walk you to and from your bedroom, help plan your day, and fill your safari shower with hot water when you want it—and the enthusiastic guides are extremely knowledgeable. Galdessa's game drives are the best in Tsavo East, but you can also enjoy an invigorating walk along Lugard's Falls or—for memorable photo ops—sundowners atop a chunky riverside boulder.

The Bald Maneaters of Tsavo

A harrowing primer for a visit to Tsavo is Hollywood's 1996 nail-biter *The Ghost and the Darkness* (starring Michael Douglas and Val Kilmer). The period thriller is loosely based on the book *The Maneaters of Tsavo,* a firsthand, true-life account by Lt. Colonel John Patterson, who killed an infamous pair of lions who ate almost 140 railway workers during the construction of a railway bridge here in 1898. The Nairobi-Mombasa railway, which divides Tsavo East and West, became known as the Lunatic Line, so grueling and dangerous was the construction process, which reached its mad apotheosis when the British reached the Tsavo River and over a 9-month period lost epic numbers of Indian workers to two large male lions. Despite all efforts, using campfires and thorn fences, nothing seemed to stop the lions' seemingly relentless hunt for human flesh. Building came to a halt when hundreds of terrified workers fled the scene.

Patterson, the project's chief engineer, became responsible for getting rid of the lions, which he shot and killed within 3 weeks of one another. We will never know for sure why the Tsavo lions became man-eaters, but two factors may have contributed to their unusual diet. In the 1890s, a rinderpest outbreak killed millions of zebras, gazelles, and other African wildlife, forcing predators to look elsewhere for food. Attacks by lions on humans increased across the continent. In Tsavo, it may have been poor burial practices that also contributed to the tragedy. Railroad workers who died of injury or disease were often poorly buried, if at all. Scavenging lions finding such easy meat may reasonably have developed a taste for human flesh and started going after living specimens.

After completing the railroad, Patterson became chief game warden in Kenya and later served with the British Army in World War I. He published four books and lectured widely on his adventure. After speaking at The Field Museum in Chicago in 1924, Patterson sold the museum the lion skins and skulls for the princely sum of $5,000. The two lions were stuffed and are now one of the museum's most popular displays.

Neighboring Private Galdessa is the less exclusive, but no less beautiful, **Main Galdessa** ★★ camp, with 12 similarly designed tents all quite closely packed together. Bedrooms here are marginally smaller, but if you're traveling with children, there's the option of reserving a large family tent. The chief drawback at Main Galdessa is the less intimate atmosphere, thanks to the number of guests that can be accommodated—and it's worth remembering that it's often booked up by groups who drive in from the coast.

Still, whichever part of Galdessa you find yourself in, you're assured of excellent food, warm treatment by a friendly staff, and a thoroughly enchanting environment, including a lounge where palm trees grow straight through the walls, floors, and roof. Even if you decide not to put a foot outside the camp, the animals you've traveled so far to observe will be coming to visit you.

Reservations: Intra Safaris, P.O. Box 454, Ukunda 80400, Kenya. ✆ **040/320-2630** or 040/320-2431/2. Fax 040/320-3466. www.intrasafaris.com. Contact in the U.S.: Sarah Fazendin, The Fazendin Portfolio.

Anyone seeing the stuffed lions is likely to note that although both of them are male, neither has much of a mane—and you'll note the same thing among lions living in Tsavo today. Lion manes vary considerably from place to place in terms of color and thickness; Tsavo lions, however, are typically maneless, a novel trait that is believed to be a defining familial characteristic among the lions of this region. These animals represent the world's only well-documented population of maneless lions—some have suggested that the Tsavo lions are a distinct species, but this is unsubstantiated. Scientists believe that lions evolved manes for a range of reasons; they attract females, may deter and intimidate nomadic, trespassing males, give a visual sign of a territorial male's control, and protect the vital head and neck regions during fights. Manes serve similar functions as antlers in deer. Recent research indicates that Tsavo's maneless lions have evolved over many generations, perhaps because of the difficulty posed to a mane in the hot, dry Tsavo landscape—having a mane here would be like continually wearing winter clothes in summer. A mane would also make it more difficult to negotiate the thorns and bramble of Tsavo's thick undergrowth. Another theory links manelessness to elevated testosterone levels. Testosterone causes balding among genetically predisposed humans and is thought to have a similar effect on lions. Testosterone is also known to raise levels of aggression among male lions and is found in higher levels among territorial males than in nonterritorial males. Tsavo lions are extremely territorial and enjoy a unique social system—in fact, they are the only lions known to live in large groups of females dominated by a single male. Typical lion prides elsewhere are ruled by a coalition of two to four males.

If you saw the movie, though, you'd be forgiven for wondering if the producers set the action in the wrong place entirely. Since manes are so inextricably associated with male lions, filmmakers used maned animals to represent the two man-eaters on screen. Fortunately, though, such heightened testosterone levels have yet to trigger a repeat of the violent killing spree witnessed here 110 years ago.

✆ **303/993-7906.** www.FazendinPortfolio.com. Private Galdessa: 3 units. Main Galdessa: 12 units. High season $1,000 double Private Galdessa, $700 double Main Galdessa; green season $840 double Private Galdessa, $540 double Main Galdessa. Rates include all meals, nonalcoholic drinks, local airstrip transfers, game-viewing activities, and laundry. MC, V. **Amenities:** Bar; airstrip transfers.

Satao Camp **Value** A never-ending parade of animals around the large amphitheater watering hole at this good-value safari camp makes Satao one of Kenya's best-loved places to spot animals. Baboons, highly habituated vervet monkeys, families of mongoose, impala, monitor lizards, waterbuck, elephants, silver-back foxes, giraffe, hippo, and lions hang out here; you could easily spend your entire stay parked on your veranda or up in the viewing tower with a pair of binoculars. The tents—set in a large, scruffy encampment—all face the water hole, arranged to take advantage of the ongoing spectacle. Unexceptional, rather densely arranged, green canvas accommodations are raised on permanent plinths, with a stone bathroom (bucket showers with hot water at night and cold water around the clock) at the back and a decent little porch out front. Best-positioned and a whole lot larger and more attractive than the standard tents are the four suites (definitely book one of these)—these are also the only units with double beds. Satao has a budget resort feel (a crowd gathers at the bar after dinner, and lunch is a tired-looking alfresco buffet), making it very popular with European package groups and also with younger travelers, so the vibe is very laid-back. Here you can happily slop around in a pair of boardshorts, even at dinner time, but the casualness of the experience (I once waited more than 30 min. for an *askari* to escort me to dinner) is usually compensated for by the abundance of the game.

www.sataocamp.com. Reservations: Southern Cross Safaris, ✆ **020/243-4600** through -4603. Fax 020/243-4610. www.southerncrosssafaris.com. 24 units. Peak season $620 double, $750 suite; high season $580 double, $650 suite; low season $480 double, $540 suite. Children 2–12 pay 50% if sharing with 2 adults. Rates include all meals, 2 game drives per day, most drinks and sundowners, local airstrip transfers, and laundry. AE, MC, V. **Amenities:** Restaurant; bar; airstrip transfers. *In room:* Minibar (in suites).

TSAVO WEST NATIONAL PARK

More visited than its sibling across the highway, Tsavo West is a better-developed park with well-signposted roads and a more closely monitored infrastructure. It also has a more varied topography and a greater diversity of habitats; it's notably hillier and shot through with impressive volcanic lava flows and large tracts of thick woodland. There's also more visual variety here, not to mention possible glimpses of Mount Kilimanjaro and epic runaway vistas from special points such as **Poacher's Lookout**—a fine spot for sundowners accompanied by majestic views of the surrounding landscape. Much of the northern sector is acacia bushland, and you'll also see Africa's famous "upside-down tree"—the baobab, which is reputed to live for 1,000 years—scattered here. The permanent Tsavo River runs through the northern part of the park, fringed by riverine acacia woodland. As you move farther south, expect to see more open grassy plains alternating with savannah bush and semidesert scrub.

A near-mandatory stop-off within the park is the **Mzima Springs,** where 220 million liters (58 million gallons) of water, filtered to crystal-clear purity by the Chyulu Hills lava massif, gush out into a series of pristine pools, forming a spectacular oasis where hippos swim, crocs bask, and birds and monkeys gather en masse. Despite being a true Eden in the midst of an otherwise dry landscape, Mzima can feel like a bit of a commercial experience—there's even an underwater observation tank (where you can count yourself extremely lucky if you happen to spot a submerged hippo), and you need to be escorted around the water (by an ill-informed, armed park ranger)—but it's nevertheless a haven for a rich wildlife pageant and makes an ideal spot for a picnic, provided there aren't too many other people around.

Apart from the famous red elephants, there are numerous lions, some perhaps directly descended from the infamous "Maneaters of Tsavo" (see box below), and other predators, including serval cats, hyenas, leopards, cheetahs, and caracals. For those interested in seeing rarer beasts, the park shelters less commonly spotted animals such as fringed-eared oryx, gerenuk, and lesser kudu. But that doesn't mean it's particularly easy to spot animals—thanks to the nature of the terrain, game viewing here requires patience and is more time intensive than in, say, the Masai Mara.

WHERE TO STAY IN TSAVO WEST

With more development than Tsavo East, you'll find that this park is more saturated with humans, often spilling out of the larger lodges and tearing around in minibuses commandeered by scattershot drivers; by any means, try to avoid this kind of experience. Fortunately, the frenzy is offset by some attempt at careful planning—no lodge within the park may be within 18km (11 miles) of another, so it is possible to veer off in search of less-traversed terrain. And the relatively smaller camps—Finch Hattons and Severin (both reviewed below)—provide *relative* exclusivity at a markedly better price than you'll pay almost anywhere else in the country.

Finch Hattons ★★ Value Set way up in the far north of Tsavo West, its tents arranged around a permanent freshwater spring that's inhabited by hippos, turtles, crocodiles, and untold numbers of birds, this unfenced permanent tented camp affords the best stay in Tsavo West. It's also the first choice if you want to avoid bumping into other vehicles during game drives. Named for the adventurer and lover (of Karen Blixen) who was immortalized in Hollywood's *Out of Africa* by Robert Redford, this professionally managed camp—owned and personally run by Peter and Cornelia Frank—exudes great style and character and, in many ways, pays tribute to a bygone era (especially in the formal dining room).

This camp is a stand-out favorite not only for its excellent value, but for its enchanting setting and warm, gracious staff, not to mention some of Kenya's most carefully prepared meals—dinner is a multicourse feast served on Bavarian china with all the trimmings you'd expect from a five-star hotel.

Sheltered by large papyrus-thatch roofs, the canvas tents are set on raised wooden platforms with screen window flaps and attached bathrooms made of local lava rock—they're mostly comfortable, with small, pleasing details such as antique-style brass lamps and framed portrait prints. Several of the tents have recently been upgraded to a far more luxurious (and spacious) design (reproduction antique furnishings, leather-and-wood beds, leather armchairs, and an overhead fan), making them well worth the additional $100 per night. On your porch, you're just inches from a tremendous flurry of activity that goes on in and around the spring—recline on your daybed watching pied kingfishers dive-bombing for fish, and try to make sense of the hippos' daily social rituals. If you don't want to pay extra for a superior tent, ask specifically for tent 31, which is larger than the standard tents but comes at the standard price. It's more elegantly put together (it was an unsuccessful model for a new design concept) and enjoys a great view over the water—you'll spot crocs basking on the opposite shore from your porch.

Finch Hattons, P.O. Box 24423, 00502, Nairobi. ✆ **020/357-7500** or 0735/83-2453. Fax 020/55-3245. www.finchhattons.com. Contact in the USA: Andrea Hugo Associates. 305 Booty Lane, Virginia Beach, VA. ✆ 757/428-1166. www.andreahugo.com. 30 units. High season $540 double; low season $380 double. Rates include all meals. AE, MC, V. **Amenities:** Restaurant; bar; airstrip transfers; pool; spa. *In room:* Minibar, hair dryer, Wi-Fi.

Kilaguni Serena Safari Lodge Value Kenya's first safari lodge, Kilaguni kicked off the country's long-lasting affair with mass tourism when it was opened by the Duke of Gloucester in the early 1960s. In 1999, the lodge was acquired by the Aga Khan's prolific,

Fun Facts **Red Elephants**

Tsavo's famous red elephants are not, as the mythical-sounding name suggests, red at all. In fact, they're normally pigmented pachyderms but wear a coat of red Tsavo soil—rich in iron—from time spent dusting and mudding themselves as part of their daily routine to keep cool under the heavy sun.

upmarket Serena hotel group—despite serious attempts at improving the design and bringing the property into the 21st century, it's difficult to escape the hotel-like atmosphere and the sheer number of guests. What you will enjoy here is the fantastic vista from the open-fronted lounge and dining area—you'll be entertained all day by a parade of animals around the water hole out front—elephants, hippos, buffalo, ostriches, marabou storks, and occasionally lions and leopards all find their way here, and there's often action in the form of minor altercations or even a full-scale kill; bring binoculars.

Accommodations are adequate but feel dated. Rooms are in two distinct blocks. Those in the thatched cottage-style New Wing (units 1–12) have lava-stone walls, exposed wooden ceiling beams, and clay floor tiles; they're a little dark and dowdy, with extremely tiny tiled bathrooms (shower only), but the views across the plains (units 1–9 only) make up for this. In the Old Block, rooms are even more hotel-like, with odd-shaped configurations (*très* 1960s) and similarly dowdy interiors—upstairs units nevertheless have great views. All these rooms were being upgraded in 2009; each room will be enlarged with sliding doors opening to expansive views of the plains below, and interiors are also being slightly modernized. When you're not out on game drives ($80 per person per drive, or $90 for a night drive) or watching the spectacle down by the busy water hole, you can head to the pool, shaded by a humungous mahogany tree, where, even if you can't beat the crowds, you can escape the heat.

Serena Sales Centre, 4th Floor Willliamson House, 4th Ngong Ave., Nairobi. ✆ **020/284-2333** or 0733/284-200. Fax 020/271-8102. www.serenahotels.com. Lodge: ✆ 045/34-0000 or 0734/699-865. Fax 045/62-2470. 56 units. Peak season $305 double, $700 suite; high season $550 double, $700 suite; mid-season $194 double, $700 suite; low season $155 double, $575 suite. Children 2–12 pay 50% if sharing with 2 adults; 13–17 pay 75%; under 2 free. Rates include all meals. AE, MC, V. **Amenities:** Restaurant; bar; babysitting; pool; room service; spa; nurse; Wi-Fi. *In room:* TV, minibar, phone (all in suites only).

Severin Safari Camp ★ Value Unfenced and set in what feels like a vast, uninterrupted arid wilderness, Severin is a down-to-earth German-owned permanent camp with particularly vibrant nocturnal activity around its floodlit water hole—at night you'll see bat-eared foxes scampering by as you dine alfresco on the porch. You'll also observe all kinds of plains game from your private veranda, making this a tempting place to attempt an all-night vigil; staff here can even tell you how a lion was once found sleeping on one of the sofas near the bar. Facing out onto those massive plains, accommodations are either in large octagonal tents (all with solid bathrooms, including bidets and the most powerful showers in Kenya) or, if you prefer real luxury, one of the smart tented suites (these are huge and attractively appointed, with bathtubs and a private upstairs sun terrace). Alternatively, if you really can't be bothered with canvas, reserve one of four new thatched-roof cottages (junior suites), which have stone-and-mortar walls, outdoor showers, kitchenettes, and smart furniture crafted from natural wood. Another classy addition at Severin is the recently built spa and its circular infinity pool. Knowledgeable Maasai and Akamba guides take you on entertaining walks to explore the finer details of the surrounding bush (in the immediate vicinity of the camp only), Poachers' Lookout is close at hand for sundowners, and the enthusiastic German managers work hard at evoking an interest in even the smallest creatures in the bush.

P.O. Box 82169, 80100 Mombasa. ✆ **041/548-5001** or -5005. Fax 041/548-5443. www.severin-kenya.com. 27 units. Peak season $340 double tent, $440 junior suite double, $530 suite double; high season $320 double tent, $400 junior suite double, $480 suite double; low season $250 tent double, $310 junior suite double, $390 suite double. Children under 2 stay free; children 2–12 pay 50% if sharing with 2 adults. Rates include all meals. MC, V. **Amenities:** Restaurant; bar; pool; spa; Wi-Fi. *In room:* Hair dryer; minibar (in junior suites).

7

The Central Highlands

by Keith Bain

Bestriding the equator, this region is not only the geographic heartland of the country, but the great twin-peaked mountain at the center of it all—the arresting Mount Kenya massif—is for many a spiritual place, believed to be where God himself resides. Even if you don't feel the call of heaven from its jagged summits, you're sure to be struck by the sheer, undeniable, majestic beauty of it, standing sentinel amid the steady encroachment of cultivated lands and sprawling communities on its foothills.

The Highlands incorporate a massive sweep of territory, ranged between the southern fringe of the Northern Frontier District and the eastern wall of the Great Rift Valley. Besides the hulking silhouette of Mount Kenya, which dominates the region like an ancient heavenward-surging rock temple, the Highlands' other important mountains are the Aberdares, a range that forms the spine of the thickly wooded **Aberdare National Park,** famous as the place where Elizabeth II became Queen of the British Empire.

The Highlands were for some time known as the "White Highlands," when most of the country's most fertile land was apportioned off to colonial settlers who established major coffee, wheat, pineapple, and livestock farms and turned this into yet another locus of Imperial wealth. The Highlands' main town, Nanyuki, was founded in 1907 by white colonial settlers and remains a hub for the region—not to mention a jumping-off point for the great ranches and wildlife preserves of the Laikipia Plateau (see chapter 10). Among other things, Nanyuki, at the foot of Mount Kenya, is famous as the home of the Mount Kenya Safari Club, started by Hollywood heartthrob William Holden and once graced by such illustrious figures as Winston Churchill and Bing Crosby.

But that era of apartheid-style white sovereignty was not to last, and given the extent of the foreign takeover here, it's little wonder that this was also the heart of the Mau Mau resistance, which took flame under the Kikuyu and kicked off the overwhelming changes that would lead directly to Kenya's independence. Kenya's largest and most economically (and politically) successful tribe, the Kikuyu—following their robust and violent campaign against colonial landowners—became the dominant group in the Highlands, their farms standing cheek-by-jowl with a number of large game sanctuaries and preserves. One of the best among these is Ol Pejeta, a wildlife conservancy where you're not only assured of spotting rhino—either on foot or on a game drive—but you also can visit the country's only chimpanzee sanctuary.

For a complete change of pace and scenery, head for **Meru National Park,** once the home of *Born Free* authoress Joy Adamson. Here, some distance east of Mount Kenya and quite a bit off the beaten track, is a beautifully untamed wilderness finally recovering from a prolonged period of siege by AK-47–wielding Somali poachers. Now restocked with wildlife that was virtually decimated by ruthless bandits, Meru benefits from an overwhelming lack of visitors, meaning it's an ideal place to escape the crowds. Its isolation has also ensured that it remains one of Kenya's most physically enchanting protected areas.

1 MOUNT KENYA

245km (152 miles) NE of Nairobi

Mount Kenya is an extinct volcano known to the Kikuyu people as Kirinyaga, the "Place of Light." When through its veil of mistlike clouds you first see the imposing mountain silhouetted against the African sky, you'll understand why the people of this region believe that at its uppermost reaches resides their god, N'gai. Just north of the equator, smack dab in the center of the country, the venerated mountain rises majestically from a vast, broad base some 80km (50 miles) in diameter. From afar, it's distinguished by its rugged glacier-clad twin peaks, Batian (5,199m/17,053 ft.) and Nelion (not far behind, at 5,188m/17,017 ft.). The truth is that Africa's second-highest mountain is worthy of up-close exploration. Its Afro-alpine moorlands and bamboo forests are shot through with glacial moraines and ice-blue tarns, and its slopes' diverse ecosystems support a rich variety of wildlife, not to mention some of the most unusual plant life you've ever laid eyes on. The mountain may be Kenya's spiritual and physical heartland, but it possesses good looks and fascinating details to match.

Europeans first heard about Mount Kenya as recently as 1833, when it was reported by a German missionary. Baffled by the possibility of a snow-capped mountain just 16km (10 miles) south of the equator, experts denounced his claim. Officially, Mount Kenya has existed only since 1849, when the missionary's accounts were finally confirmed. Considered one of the most treacherous climbs in the world, nobody managed it until 1899, when Sir Halford Mackinder made the summit ascent. Since then, it has become increasingly popular among seasoned climbers and was used for high-altitude training by Reinhold Messner, the first man to ascend Everest without oxygen. You need to be a hardcore technical climber to get to the uppermost peaks, but treks to the lower summits, while strenuous, throw up some truly impressive scenery.

While many visitors come here solely to climb the mountain (an expedition not to be taken lightly), the lower reaches of the mountain shelter an array of wildlife, and many find the salubrious, mountain air conditions more conducive to unharried game viewing than the semi-arid parks in the Kenyan lowlands. Below the imposing rocky peaks, the lushly covered slopes are inhabited by bands of cheeky Sykes' and colobus monkeys, and it's common to spot elephants, rhinos, and buffalos while out on a hike—more than good reason to take ample precautions and a knowledgeable guide when trekking this formidable mountain.

ESSENTIALS

VISITOR INFORMATION For updated news about the mountain, contact the senior warden of Mt. Kenya National Park (© **020/356 8763;** reservations@kws.go.ke). A far better option is to contact **The Mountain Club of Kenya** (© **020/60-2330;** www.mck.or.ke; MCKenya@iname.com); their website was being updated at press time.

GETTING THERE Mt. Kenya is accessible from Nairobi via the busy A2 highway; if you are in any way nervous on the road (and when traveling on any public roads in Kenya, you really should be), you might be better off going by air, despite the fact the road to Nanyuki is considered one of the more manageable, well-maintained routes in the country, and the journey takes as little as 2½ hours. The advantage of being driven is that you'll have easy access to your own vehicle while in the Highlands—useful if you're planning to cover a lot of ground, less so if you're coming purely to go trekking or are

Where to Stay in Mt. Kenya, Aberdare National Park & Nanyuki

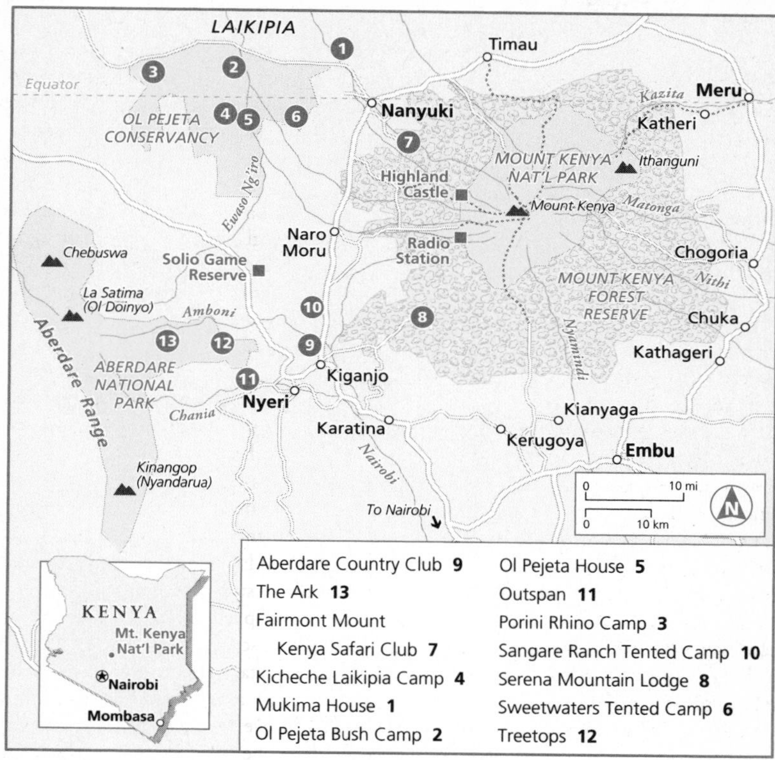

about to check in at a safari lodge for the duration of your stay. The more elegant way of reaching Mt. Kenya is to land at Nanyuki's commercial airstrip. **AirKenya** (www.airkenya.com) has one daily flight from Nairobi's Wilson Airport to Nanyuki (9:15am), and **Safarilink** (www.safarilink-kenya.com) flies the same route each day at 8 and 10:20am.

GETTING AROUND As mentioned, if you're planning to move extensively around this region, you'd do well to arrive under your own steam with a 4×4 and driver who knows the area well; your ground operator will organize this for you or fix the details of any local pick-ups that need arranging. Most of the safari lodges and camps will pick you up from Nanyuki's little airport.

HIKING & CLIMBING MT. KENYA Ascending Africa's second-highest mountain requires proper planning and preferably the services of an expert trekking and climbing company. It's possible to pick up freelance guides (locals who are, by and large, sufficiently skilled and familiar with the mountain), but you'll feel a good deal more secure if you go the route of hiring real professionals with solid credentials (see the box "Ascending Africa's Everest," on p. 128). If you do decide to take on casual guides, make sure they're

Ascending Africa's Everest

Mount Kenya's two main peaks—Batian and Nelion—are tough technical climbs and should be attempted only by experienced climbers. This is a distinction you need to bear in mind when deciding whether to tackle Kilimanjaro—for which technical experience is not required—or Mt. Kenya, which may not be quite as high but is certainly the more difficult option. You'll need ropes, crampons, and ice axes—not to mention nerves of steel and ice-climbing experience. It's here that professionals come to prepare for epic ascents, such as those to the top of Everest.

The third-highest peak, **Point Lenana** (4,985m/16,351 ft.), is a workable option that may tempt less serious climbers and is a good choice for fit trekkers and anyone with doubts about the loftier twin peaks. However, don't think that the hike is, by any stretch of the imagination, easy. There are three principal tracks to Lenana. **Naro Moru,** on the western slopes, is touted as the easiest and is consequently the most popular (it's also the most accessible for anyone coming from Nairobi). **Sirimon** is longer and requires a higher degree of fitness and stamina. **Chogoria,** on the eastern slopes, is another slightly more challenging option and is considered the most picturesque. There is a fourth and more remote trail, **Burguret,** which is a good option if you're up for a real wilderness adventure.

To make the most of your time and actually enjoy your experience of the mountain, I strongly recommend venturing onto the mountain only if you've hired the services of a professional—there's no point risking getting lost or having to carry weighty equipment. Recommended U.K.–based trekking operator **IntoAfrica** (✆ **114/255-5610** in the U.K.; www.intoafrica.co.uk) runs a 7-day trip combining Burguret with Chogoria for the most fascinating, unhurried, and challenging exploration of the mountain. The trip, which commences and finishes in Nairobi and includes 4 nights of tented camping, costs $1,800 per person for a party of two, and as little as $1,235 if you're part of a much larger group. If you want to go directly through a Kenyan operator, IntoAfrica also does bookings for **Mountain Rock Safaris & Camps** (www.mountainrockkenya.com), which has a variety of treks ranging between 3 and 8 days, rated with telling sobriquets such as "Mt. Kenya's Coca-Cola Route," "The Senior Citizen's Choice," and "A Precocious Option." Their longer packages are geared toward climbers and those looking to reach the summit rather than simply take in the scenery. **KG Mountain Expeditions** (✆ **020/203-3874;** www.kenyaexpeditions.com) is run by James Kagambi ("KG"), a local mountaineer with

card-carrying—and the license must be one issued by the Kenya Wildlife Service (KWS); local guiding associations may also issue membership cards, but only the KWS card really stands up to some kind of scrutiny. The most popular place to solicit guides (or put together an all-inclusive trek or climb) is **Mountain Rock Lodge** (www.mountainrockkenya.com), not too far from Naro Moru, at the foot of the mountain. The lodge is often loads of experience on mountains worldwide. He's based in Naro Moru at the foot of Mt. Kenya and puts together tailormade treks and technical climbs adapted to cater to different budgets.

Overzealous climbers, take heed: It's possible to gain altitude quite rapidly, and high-altitude sickness is a real risk here. A huge percentage of the world's pulmonary edema cases (a potentially fatal form of high-altitude sickness) happen on the slopes of Mt. Kenya, and the only deterrent is to tackle the slopes slowly and sensibly. This is no hardship, as the routes are all imbued with quite magnificent scenery, dominated by belts of Afro-alpine vegetation. Beautiful gnarl-wooded, feathery-leaved, red-bloom hagenia trees; giant lobelias; and huge groundsels (with flowers resembling cabbages) are some of the specially adapted plants that flourish here, and there's no end to the unusual flora you'll encounter right up to the snowline, from where lichen and moss takes over. For many, the highlights on the way up are the crystal-clear tarns, and there are 13 glaciers below the peaks, too (they're all receding pretty rapidly, though, thanks to climate change).

Solo hiking and climbing is not permitted, and you need to watch your timing on the slopes. Because it's practically on the equator, night descends with surprising rapidity (around 30 min. after sunset) and often catches climbers and hikers unawares. You need to have struck camp *before* the sun disappears.

Make no mistake, Mount Kenya can be forbidding and dangerous, with injuries and deaths every year. Make no attempt at the mountain if you aren't in good health, and don't skimp on gear, provisions, and adequate warm clothing. You're required to register with the Kenya Wildlife Service upon arrival at the mountain and must sign out on departure. KWS fees for entry to Mount Kenya are $55 per adult (children $20), and there's a 3-day package for $150 (although, strangely, children pay $70). Be sure that no fires are lit on the mountain and that you leave no trace of your visit.

Before considering any Mount Kenya hike or climb, contact **The Mountain Club of Kenya** (✆ **020/60-2330;** www.mck.or.ke; MCKenya@gmail.com), which has been operating for 60 years and owns four huts on the mountain. Besides providing information on how to go about using the huts, they've published their own *Guide to Mount Kenya and Kilimanjaro* (edited by Iain Allan), which features information of flora and fauna, as well as climbing and hiking routes. Whatever information you've stocked up on, you'll want to tackle Mount Kenya with a professional operator—failing that, though, the Mountain Club can advise on how to go about choosing guides and porters.

where climbing and trekking parties start and end their expeditions—there are basic, slightly disheveled rooms (Ksh5,500–Ksh6,600 double, including all meals) and a great big garden with close-up views of the mountain in question. But the real allure is having access to expert mountain guides and staff who can provide you with intimate, hands-on knowledge of the mountain.

WHERE TO STAY

Your choice of where to bed down in the immediate vicinity of Mount Kenya will come down to a matter of personal taste. The options reviewed below are not necessarily useful if you're primarily concerned with trekking or climbing the mountain (in which case, you'll inevitably be staying in tents or huts on the slopes themselves; see "Ascending Africa's Everest" box, p. 128). But if you want a comfortable bed, elegantly prepared meals, and at least a few of the amenities and services you can expect from a hotel, then your best options are the ones described here. Of the three choices, Mukima House offers the most intimate experience—a private colonial mansion rented for your personal use, albeit with a full staff and all the trimmings laid on. If you're mainly concerned with seeing lots of animals without setting foot outside your lodge, then the Serena Mountain Lodge is the obvious choice (although you may also want to consider weighing up this experience with a night at The Ark, in the Aberdare National Park; see p. 134). If you're unwilling to forgo the luxuries you'd expect at just about any world-class resort and, in fact, desire all the cosseting money can buy, then the Fairmont Mount Kenya Safari Club will keep you in the style to which you're accustomed.

Fairmont Mount Kenya Safari Club ★★ Built in 1959 as the private retreat of movie star William Holden, the Safari Club has near-legendary status and is now in the hands of the Fairmont hotel group. Over the last 2 years, the Club's heyday grandeur has been restored to the tune of $50 million, with all kinds of luxurious and innovative flourishes—elegant bars, themed gardens, fish-filled ponds, and posh in-room features—to enhance the value of time spent here. The sprawling, resortlike hotel is right on Mount Kenya's doorstep, with majestic views of its peaks and quick access to its scenic national park. Upon arrival, you walk along the equator right on your way to the check-in desk. There are 40 hectares (99 acres) of immaculately tended gardens spread on either side of the equator; in fact, it's something of a novelty to reserve the gimmicky Equator Suite, built so that the bed actually lies on the imaginary dividing line between north and south.

The Club's main building dates back to the 1930s, and there's a fair mix of period-style furniture and Old World reproduction items that gives the rooms and public areas a sophisticated, glamorous look. The tone here is very much about reliving an era of colonial splendor. Depending on your personal preferences, some of the Club's "rules" can be a little intrusive; there's an evening dress code, for example, which doesn't exactly equate with roughing it in the bush. Nevertheless, during the day, you have every opportunity to arrange all kinds of game-viewing experiences, and there are animals on the grounds, too. Guest accommodations come in a variety of sizes and configurations, with escalations in price to match. Unless you don't mind feeling a bit like you're in a hotel, you're best off in one of the cottages or suites with a private garden (but you'll pay handsomely for these). Irritatingly, even though Safari Club is now part of a large American chain, you still can't easily reserve a room online, and rates fluctuate according to demand. However, this means that you can score a good deal here—as little as $159 for a double room (taxes, meals, and all activities are extra), so it may be worthwhile to put in the effort to hunt down an agreeable price.

P.O. Box 35, Nanyuki. ✆ **020/226-5000.** Fax 020/221-6796. www.fairmont.com. kenya.reservations@fairmont.com. 120 units. Peak season $476 double, $536 deluxe double, $556 deluxe view double, $626 suite, $726 cottage, $776 signature room; high season $446 double, $506 deluxe double, $526 deluxe view double, $596 suite, $696 cottage, $746 signature room; low season $308 double, $368 deluxe double, $388 deluxe view double, $458 suite, $558 cottage, $608 signature room. Rates include taxes and all meals. AE, DC, MC, V. **Amenities:** 2 restaurants; 4 bars; 9-hole golf course; pool; room service; tennis; currency exchange. *In room:* Fireplace, hair dryer, minibar.

Moments **View from Above**

For those who don't fancy the chill and hardcore exertions of a climb up one of Africa's toughest mountains, the most invigorating way to see Mount Kenya is from the cockpit of a modern biplane. Will Craig, owner of Lewa Wilderness, flies a bright yellow WACO biplane built to the same specs as those used during the 1930s, when flying was, first and foremost, about thrills, spills, fun, and excitement. The joyride from Lewa lasts between 30 minutes and an hour, and takes you as much as 4,200m (13,776 ft.) above sea level, flying over scenes ranging from forest and desert to mountain slopes and snowy peaks. You'll spot large animals that look like ants on the ground below, but your sense of perspective and bird's-eye view of the scene is riveting, and having the wind on your face (you're given a scarf and nice big leather bomber jacket to stave off the cold) is exhilarating. Flights can be arranged directly through **Lewa Wilderness** (✆ **0721/970-340;** p. 218).

Mukima House ★ Set amid tropical flowerbeds and surrounded by well-tended lawns, this double-story grand colonial farmhouse was built in the 1940s. A mere 15 minutes outside Nanyuki, it occupies a 146-hectare (361-acre) estate, and the sturdy, handsome house overlooks a pretty dam (where you'll spot a diversity of waterfowl) and affords views of Mount Kenya's peaks. It was recently salvaged from disaster thanks to a large-scale renovation. Restored to echo its days as a grand colonial house, it's been tastefully decorated with African and Eastern accents that set a formal tone. Yet the place is homey and intimate enough that you can't help but relax—you're attended to by a dedicated staff, have full run of the estate (it's rented on an exclusive basis), and have the option of visiting various local parks and sanctuaries as you please. There are six bedrooms, all en suite and all comfortably, tastefully kitted out with furniture sourced from Lamu and as far away as Java. Get up early to witness the first rays lighting up Mount Kenya; take a long, languid breakfast on the wraparound veranda; and then spend your day loafing by the pool, saddling up for rides on a nearby ranch, or fishing for rainbow trout on the slopes of Mount Kenya—or even spend a couple of nights on the mountain in a log cabin ($200 per night for six people).

P.O. Box 102, 00502 Karen, Nairobi. ✆ **020/88-2755** or 0726/332-399. Fax 020/88-4497. www.mukimakenya.com. 6 units. The house is rented on an exclusive basis at a rate of $325 per person per night. 4-person, 3-night minimum. Rates include all meals, drinks, most activities, laundry, and Nanyuki airport transfers. No credit cards. **Amenities:** Bar; exercise and massage room; Internet; golf (by arrangement); pool and children's pool; sauna; tennis court; TV lounge w/DVD.

Serena Mountain Lodge ★ The biggest thrill of staying at this lodge, tucked into the lush rainforest-covered slopes of Mount Kenya, is the nonstop animal traffic around the large water hole over which the lodge looms. There's nothing spectacular about the accommodations, and if you're in any way susceptible to claustrophobia, you may feel the onset of panic as you realize that, come nightfall, you're confined to the bosom of this hulking treehouse-style hotel built nearly 40 years ago and feeling its age. The whole place creaks and groans quite a bit (understandably, since it's built of wood) when anybody moves around—and you're just as likely to hear snoring from the room next door as the steady all-night chorus of the bush. Bedrooms—which are entirely wood paneled, carpeted, and outfitted with furniture that's attached to the walls—are quite compact (beds are small, too, and the miniscule bathrooms have only the teensiest of shower cubicles). Rooms on the lowest level (there are three floors of accommodations) don't have balconies, so avoid them.

But if you don't sweat the small details, you'll get a kick out of the ongoing interaction with nature. Curious Sykes' monkeys scamper through the trees as you walk the wooden path to the little reception, and if you leave your balcony door open, you'll soon have curious primates looking for food in your room (not a good idea). Each night after dinner (meals are another highlight here), one of the in-house naturalists presents an amateurish slideshow on the lodge and the local wildlife—skip it and instead devote your time to the scene around the water hole, or get to bed early and set off the next morning on a 5-hour moorland walk that culminates with a picnic at around 3,600m (11,808 ft.). At dinner, you're also asked to decide if you'd like to be woken in the middle of the night should any special wildlife be spotted in front of the lodge—it does add a dose of excitement to the proceedings—and you simply must ask for an early-morning wake-up to see how Mt. Kenya is touched by dawn's early light. The breakfast spread is particularly lavish (and includes sparkling wine), although you're forced to put up with some quirky old-fashioned ideas, such as assigned seating (heaven forbid you sit at the wrong table!), and the fact that the restaurant doesn't benefit from many views.

Reservations: 4th Floor, Williamson House, 4th Ng'ong' Ave., P.O. Box 48690, 00100, Nairobi. ✆ **020/271-1077** or -1078. Fax 020/271-8102/3. www.serenahotels.com. 42 units. Peak season $435 double; high season $360 double; midseason $310 double; low season $285 double. Rates include all meals. AE, MC, V. **Amenities:** Restaurant; bar; massage & beauty treatments. *In room:* Wi-Fi.

2 ABERDARE NATIONAL PARK

160km (99 miles) NE of Nairobi

Famous as the place where, in 1952, Elizabeth II learned that she had inherited the English throne, Aberdare National Park takes its name from a magnificent volcanic mountain range that forms part of the eastern wall of the Rift Valley. The Aberdare Mountains make up the backbone of the park and run for roughly 100km (63 miles) between Nairobi and the famed **Thomson's Falls** (where the waters of the Ewaso Narok River fall some 72m/236 ft.).

Topographically diverse, the park is cut through with deep ravines that make for splendid vistas—wide valleys and vast slopes are carpeted by extremely dense forest and watered by icy, crystal-clear streams where trout fishing is possible. Covering 767 sq. km (299 sq. miles), the park ranges between two major peaks, Kinangop (3,905m/12,808 ft.) in the south and Ol Doinyo Satima (3,995m/13,104 ft.) to the north. Between these two summits stretch beautiful alpine moorlands that in places bear an uncanny resemblance to parts of the Scottish highlands, complete with bogs, spectacular waterfalls, and a salubrious clime. During the time of the Mau Mau uprising, freedom fighters took shelter in certain caves in these hills, spawning many modern local legends.

Even before independence, the park had earned a reputation for its famous **Treetops** hotel, where Elizabeth was staying when she became queen. Today there are two such "tree hotels," where guests find themselves ensconced in what feel like specially built gigantic viewing capsules, their sights poised on an endless array of animals that turn up—like kids in a candy store—to gorge on the mineral-rich salt licks that are constantly topped up by the hotels. For many, staying up all night and watching the nocturnal action from the viewing areas of these hotels is a Kenyan highlight; for others, it's like being on the wrong side of the cage at a zoo. Besides seeing large herds of African elephant and buffalo at close range, you might just glimpse one or two of the park's rare and endangered species, including black rhino (there are around seven in the entire park), giant forest hog, wild dog, and—should hell freeze over—bongo.

If you've made the effort to see the Aberdares and haven't managed to see rhino, you might also like to check out the fenced confines of the nearby **Solio Game Reserve,** a 6,868-hectare (16,964-acre) private sanctuary ranged between Mount Kenya and the Aberdares. With more than 200 black and white rhino, among other animals, it is considered Kenya's most successful rhino sanctuary, with the world's highest-density rhino population—although without the sense of true wilderness that you'll find in the national park.

ESSENTIALS

ORIENTATION & VISITOR INFORMATION The park is basically divvied up into two zones. The western part is dense forest and mostly interesting for the beauty of its terrain; here, on the Aberdare slopes, is where hikers and climbers may set out on foot accompanied by an armed ranger. Most visitors, however, stick to the developed Salient region, which occupies the eastern part of the park and is where the two lodges, Treetops and The Ark (see "Where to Stay," below), are located and where there's far greater opportunity to spot animals. For current details on the park, contact the senior warden (aberdare@wanachi.com), who has his headquarters between Mweiga and Nyeri, on the B5 (the same road that provides access to the park through any of the eastern gates). Aberdare National Park is open daily from 6am till 6pm.

GETTING THERE You can either drive to the Aberdares on paved roads all the way from Nairobi, or fly to Nanyuki and then drive via Nyeri (154km/95 miles from Nairobi) or Naro Moru to get to the park's eastern entrances; your ground operator can make all such arrangements for you. Smaller, less commercial airstrips (Mweiga and Nyeri) are also available for charter flights to points much closer to the park. There's a road that wends its way across the park, linking the eastern boundary with entrances to the west, where you can drive in from Naivasha (87km/54 miles from Nairobi) in the Rift Valley; this requires tremendous stamina, however, as the roads that cut through the park's mountain regions are tricky and seemingly endless—although not without great vistas.

GETTING AROUND If you stay inside the park, it'll be at either The Ark or Treetops (see "Where to Stay," later in this chapter), and you'll be shuttled there as part of the package. Once you arrive, there's seldom any reason to move on or around until departure. If, however, you're staying for 2 nights or more (for most, an unlikely event), you can arrange for daytime game drives at an extra cost. These days, it's also possible to explore the park under your own steam—a 4×4 is essential, and you will definitely need to get up-to-the-minute details on road accessibility, particularly following any rain.

PARK FEES Adults pay $50 and children $25 to enter **Aberdare National Park** (euros and sterling are also accepted); entry is by Safaricard only, which can be purchased and recharged at park headquarters not far from The Ark Gate near Nyeri. Note that shuttle buses going to the lodges inside the park will stop at park headquarters first—so that guests can load sufficient credit onto their cards—before proceeding to the gates. This can be a time-consuming and infuriating ordeal, and the fewer people who need to charge their cards, the shorter the wait will be. Visitors to **Solio Game Reserve** pay $40 each, plus there's a Ksh800 charge per vehicle and you'll pay a Ksh500 entry fee for your driver and/or guide.

WHERE TO STAY

Perhaps Kenya's most famous lodge, **Treetops** (which began in 1929 as a two-room house in a fig tree) was burned to the ground by Mau Mau guerillas in the mid-1950s. Its replacement is now one of two "tree hotels" within the Aberdare National Park. A large hotel (there are 50 guestrooms)—with tiny bedrooms and shared bathrooms—it has never been as intimate as the original, and its proximity to the perimeter of the park means that you don't get the same sense of being deep in the forest experienced at its similarly conceived competitor, a slightly more elegant hotel on stilts called The Ark (reviewed below). Still, if you prefer nostalgia over comfort, you can investigate Treetops at www.aberdaresafarihotels.com. There are four viewing decks, as well as a rooftop platform from which to watch the animals at the water hole, and special hides on the ground level make close-up photography possible. If you do end up staying here, it's worth paying a little extra for one of the two suites ($294–$473 double); standard doubles cost $248 to $383, depending on the season. Guests staying at Treetops assemble at **Outspan,** a hotel just outside the park, and are then shuttled to the lodge in the afternoon.

For something of a wilderness experience *outside* the national park, there's good value to be had at **Sangare Ranch Tented Camp** ★ (✆ **020/272-2451** through -2457, or 728/607-597; www.sangaretentedcamp.com), where you bed down in large canvas tents on the edge of a lake on a 2,626-hectare (6,500-acre) private wildlife conservancy. It's located adjacent the Solio Game Reserve, and the surrounding terrain is home to elephants, buffalos, and leopards, among others. Set on concrete plinths, the 12 camo-tents have attached, plumbed-in bathrooms (with hot water 24/7) and shaded verandas facing the water; the doubles feature king-size four-poster beds made in a rustic, comfortable style that's in keeping with the African bush setting. Instead of any overblown, over-the-top luxury, the emphasis is on down-to-earth comfort. Prices are incredibly fair—$395 is the rate for a double, including all meals and a daily conservation fee.

The Ark ★ **Moments** Yes, it's designed to be a hotel version of *that* Ark. Only here, it's not the animals that go in two-by-two, but the paying customers. Of course, the animals are just outside and virtually always visible. Open since 1969 and understandably dated, The Ark doesn't really provide much by way of comfort (and just about zero luxury), but

Fun Facts **What's in a Name?**

Exotic as their name might sound, the Aberdares were christened by Victorian explorer Joseph Thomson, who first laid eyes on them in 1884 (while walking from Mombasa to Lake Victoria) and obligingly named them after the president of the Royal Geographic Society, Lord Aberdare. The Kikuyu people who have farmed the mountain slopes for centuries have a less sycophantic name for them—Nyandarua, which means "The Drying Hide" and refers to the fact that, seen from a distance, they resemble an animal skin that's been stretched out to dry. They also call the mountains Thimbira (The Place of Gloomy Mist) and believe them to be an alternative resting place for N'gai (God), who usually inhabits Mount Kenya.

it's a good deal better than its only other rival, Treetops, and since its acquisition by the Fairmont hotel chain, it has been targeted for far-reaching overhaul. Until then, cabins are small and, well, cabinlike, with dinky bathrooms (and low water pressure), narrow beds, and a touch of drab. Your best bet is a cabin near the front, from where it's quicker to get to the animal-viewing areas when your alarm-buzzer sounds at night to tell you what animals are doing the rounds. Those on Deck A are slightly larger, and units A17 and A19 have some of the only double beds in The Ark. They also benefit from partial front views. (Most of the cabins have views only out to the side, into the forest, rather than over the salt lick.)

The prow of The Ark faces onto the Yasabara water hole, which is probably the largest natural mineral lick in the Aberdares and consequently attracts an incessant flurry of creatures—and they put on quite a spectacular performance that more than makes up for the claustrophobia-inducing rooms. At times, it's like watching a schoolyard punch-up as the young bull elephants start to tussle, locking tusks and trumpeting wildly, or ganging up on smaller buffalo. And when the hyenas become desperate enough to hunt rather than simply scavenge, you can watch for hours as they plot and plan to try bagging an off-guard buffalo.

Be warned that the check-in procedure for The Ark can be a long-winded affair: You arrive and sign in at the **Aberdare Country Club,** a lovely cluster of colonial-era stone cottages set on a game sanctuary not far from the national park gate. You're graciously served a generous lunch (on a deep colonial-era veranda with expansive views across the plains). Then you're shuttled off by bus—first to park headquarters and then to the lodge. If you're lucky, you'll spot a giant forest hog or two en route to the lodge, but even if you don't, you'll find all resistance crumbles when you arrive at The Ark to find hordes of ellies and buffalo greedily guzzling the salt that's been laid out for them.

P.O. Box 449, GPO, Nyeri. ✆ **020/214-4215,** 020/214-4216, or 0724/478-058. Fax 061/55-224. www.fairmont.com. 60 units. Peak season $310 double; high season $290 double; low season $204 double. Rates include all meals, local transfer, and taxes. MC, V. **Amenities:** Restaurant; bar.

3 OL PEJETA

15km (9¼ miles) W of Nanyuki

Once the private playground of tycoon arms dealer Ashnan Kashoggi, the 36,360-hectare (89,809-acre) Ol Pejeta Conservancy is situated more or less on the equator, between the Aberdare foothills and snow-capped **Mount Kenya.** Today it's a fence-protected preserve known for its successful integration of cattle ranching and wildlife management, and it has the highest animal-to-area ratio of any park or reserve in Kenya. The ranch was rescued just weeks before it was due to be sold off to be burned for charcoal—today it incorporates the **Sweetwaters Game Reserve,** making it the largest rhino sanctuary in East Africa. Among the large numbers of game, and helping to make the ranch financially viable, are approximately 6,500 Boran beef cattle, as well as a small herd of Ugandan Ankole cattle—their spectacular horns make them almost as popular to photograph as the rhinos and elephants here.

More than anything else, Ol Pejeta is known for its successful rhino program. At last count, 81 of Kenya's 500-or-so black rhino were concentrated in this relatively small area. There are always one or two tame orphans being rehabilitated by watchful rangers, and it's possible to set out on foot to track rhino with an armed ranger—the tracking program is so stringent, in fact, that each and every rhino must be spotted once every 5 days. Ol Pejeta is also home to Kenya's only chimpanzee refuge; opened in 1993 as a project of the Jane Goodall Institute, the **Sweetwaters Chimpanzee Sanctuary** rehabilitates orphaned and abused chimps, and guests on the conservancy are able to see the good work being done with them. It's also possible to observe researchers tracking radio-collared lions and learn how the rangers keep track of other animals, including elephants.

Because there are so many projects happening here, and the conservancy is so easily accessible from Nairobi (it's the closest conservancy to the capital where the Big Five can be spotted), Ol Pejeta can feel slightly more developed than you might want—however, despite the presence of minibuses (particularly around Sweetwaters Tented Camp), it's quite possible to escape the masses and experience an untouched wilderness. Be sure to stay at one of the smaller camps if it's an intimate bush experience you're after (and it should be).

ESSENTIALS

VISITOR INFORMATION Marketed as part of the Laikipia Plateau (most of which is covered in chapter 10), there's plenty of information about Ol Pejeta available from the **Laikipia Wildlife Forum** (www.laikipia.org). You can also go directly to the **Ol Pejeta** website (www.olpejetaconservancy.org) to find out about the latest developments here and to read up on new accommodations prospects within the conservancy. To find out about adopting Sweetwaters chimpanzees, go to www.careforthewild.com.

GETTING THERE & AROUND There are daily scheduled flights from Nairobi to Nanyuki. From Nanyuki's airport, it's a 45-minute drive to Ol Pejeta; if you're staying at any of the camps recommended below, you can arrange for them to pick you up (your ground operator will usually make all such arrangements). It's also possible to charter a flight directly into one of the two airstrips within the Ol Pejeta Conservancy.

WHERE TO STAY

The best-known lodging in Ol Pejeta—and, in fact, the busiest "hotel" in Kenya—is **Sweetwaters Tented Camp** (www.serenahotels.com). Despite the smart tents and availability of myriad amenities and luxuries (all at extra cost), it all feels a bit at odds with the setting—its 40 tents are packed so tightly that the overall effect is borderline grotesque. Sure, they're all facing the large, active water hole, but by the time you set foot on the concrete pathways that lead to the tents (made of green canvas and set on concrete plinths beneath pitched thatch), you're already feeling a bit of the wilderness spell being broken. Tent interiors are luxurious enough, but designed in such a way that they might just as well be standard hotel bedrooms. The main lodge building features parquet flooring, the rich scent of freshly polished wood, decor that can only be described as "colonial modernism," and—just about everywhere you look—price lists advertising the charges for game drives ($140 per person for a full day), nature walks, camel rides, sundowners ($50), bush dinners, lion tracking, and what not. Still, if you stay here outside of peak season (Feb, July–Oct, and the Christmas/New Year period), you can strike a fairly good-value rate ($230–$335 double, including all meals), and many like the fact that there's a pool and long list of hotel amenities at their disposal. But if you have to pay the premium rate ($575), it's simply not worth it because all those extras will add up pretty quickly to a not-inconsiderable sum.

On the other end of the scale is the intimate **Kicheche Laikipia Camp** (www.kicheche.com), the latest addition to Ol Pejeta's accommodation scene, with six tents overlooking a water hole. If Kicheche's bush camp in the Masai Mara is anything to go by, this promises to be a good bet for anyone looking for an authentic camping experience, with an emphasis on game-viewing (day and night game drives and guided bush walks are offered) and good opportunities to observe and participate in some of Ol Pejeta's conservation activities. Doubles range from $630 to $770 per night.

Ol Pejeta Bush Camp ★★ Value This attractive, unobtrusive camp is located on the banks of a river that forms a natural amphitheater where animals come to drink and the plains stretch out to distant hills. With such a tranquil ambience that it's possible to feel totally at one with the surrounding bush, this is an ideal place to get to grips with the ebb and flow of bush life. In contrast with the obvious in-room luxuries and stifling development at the oversized Sweetwaters Tented Camp, here it's the combination of pretty simplicity and a genuine back-to-basics experience that satisfies.

There are just six traditional safari tents, each with an attached canvas bathroom with a flushable toilet and bucket shower (filled with hot water on request). The safari-style metal-frame beds are covered with soothing linens and vividly colored fabrics that brighten up the tents. There is no electricity, no fence around the camp, and very few of the accoutrements taken for granted in the urbanized world. The only soundtrack you'll hear is that of the ongoing bush chorus, and at night you'll make do with glimmering lanterns and torch-bearing Maasai escorts to find your way around. In the morning you'll be awakened with tea or coffee, and in good time a polite call will announce that your "Shower is ready!"—in many ways, this is precisely the experience you've come to Africa for, with plenty of reminders that you're in the rugged wilds.

Alex and Diana Hunter, who own and run the camp, have great flare in the bush—Alex has been a walking safari guide for 2 decades, and Diana trained as a horse whisperer. There's substantial emphasis here on conservation, and the Hunters encourage guests to take away some knowledge of how Ol Pejeta manages wildlife. They also occasionally offer safari skills and other courses, including wildlife photography. And there's novelty, too—because there's so much wide open space here, this is one of the few places in the Kenyan bush where you can go jogging in the wild, accompanied by a 4×4 just in case you should, literally, run into anything four-legged. ***Note:*** Ol Pejeta Bush Camp is closed for the rains in April, May, and November.

Ol Pejeta Conservancy, 10400, Nanyuki. ✆ **0734/445-283.** www.insidersafrica.com. 6 units. $790–$990 double. Children $280–$370 if sharing with 2 adults. Rate includes all meals and drinks, all listed activities, Nanyuki airstrip transfers, and laundry. No credit cards. **Amenities:** Bar; airstrip transfers.

Ol Pejeta House ★ Like Sweetwaters Tented Camp, this house—once the personal abode of arms dealer Ashnan Kashoggi—is now managed by the Serena Hotel group. Much of the original furniture and decor remains, and, architecturally, the house is something of an oddity (described by some as "a 1970s porn palace") where decadent opulence (swaths of expensive, often-trashy framed artworks), over-the-top comfort (Kashoggi's personal bed sleeps nine people), and a propensity for bad taste (during its heyday, a gondola bearing an air hostess—naked and covered in fruit—would be lowered from the ceiling over the dining table at the end of the meal) is all expressed in a package that has been cleaned up rather neatly and is now available to paying guests, many of whom come simply out of curiosity. If you're coming to Ol Pejeta and can't see yourself bedding down under canvas, then this is the best choice—and a chance to ogle some eyebrow-raising African excess. You can stay in one of three bedrooms in the main mansion or opt for the cottage in the garden. There are plenty of interesting, comfortable spaces in which to relax, dine, or take the edge off between game drives, and everywhere you turn, there's another hint of the millionaire playboy's lavish lifestyle. All the standard game-viewing activities (and other amenities) on offer at Sweetwaters Tented Camp are available here—although, as at all Serena properties, these are at additional cost.

Serena Hotels, Williamson House 4th Floor, 4th Ngong Ave.; P.O. Box 48690, 00100 Nairobi. ✆ **045/62-2361** or 735/52-2361. Fax 045/62-2430. www.serenahotels.com. 6 units. June–Mar $695 double; Apr–May $495 double. Rates include all meals. MC, V. **Amenities:** Bar; 2 pools; beauty treatments and massage (at Sweetwaters).

Porini Rhino Camp ★★ Tucked into an acacia grove on the banks of a seasonal river, this relative newcomer (opened in 2007) is intimate and luxurious, and—like Ol Pejeta Bush Camp—places considerable emphasis on an ecologically conscious experience, so your impact on the environment is minimal. Tents are spacious (larger than those at Bush Camp) and handsomely outfitted with bush-appropriate furniture—each one with a double and single bed—and all have attached bathrooms with safari bucket showers and flush toilets. There's plenty of emphasis on in-camp comfort and cosseting, too—cushioned wrought-iron chairs and tabled lounge areas are available for those times between extended game drives or walks through the bush with Maasai guides. You can head off to track rhino (by vehicle or on foot) or simply pass the time staring across the plains from your personal veranda. Porini does tend to run its camps according to a schedule determined by its 2-night packages (and, really, you don't want to stay anywhere on safari for a single night), which can be frustrating if you value your independence—however, such packages are designed to help you make the most of your time; if it doesn't suit you, let your hosts know what you'd prefer.

P.O. Box 388, 00621 Village Market, Nairobi. ✆ **020/712-3129,** 020/712-2504, or 0722/509-200. www.porini.com. 6 units. Standard 2-night fly-in package: Dec 20–Jan 2 $1,165 per person, $510 per extra night; Jan 3–Mar 31 $915 per person, $395 per extra night; Apr 1–15, June and Nov–Dec 15 $855 per person, $365 per extra night; July–Oct $1,080 per person, $465 per extra night. Kids 8–16 pay 60% if sharing with 2 adults. Rates include 2 nights' accommodation, all meals, house drinks, return flights from Nairobi, airstrip transfers, Ol Pejeta Conservancy fees, all game drives, bush walks, and sundowners. MC, V. **Amenities:** Bar; airstrip transfers.

4 MERU NATIONAL PARK

348km (216 miles) NE of Nairobi

Meru is a classic savannah wilderness and a refreshing antidote to the overdeveloped preserves such as Masai Mara and Samburu. If getting away from it all is a priority, you'll find your poison here. Wild, rugged, and remote—and still recovering from a protracted period during the '80s and '90s when Somali poachers decimated entire animal populations here—Meru sees comparatively few visitors. Attacks by poachers were so brutal, in fact, that more than 3,000 elephants were killed, and white rhino, initially introduced here from South Africa, were completely wiped out, killed alongside the people employed to care for them. But the brutality of the past seems to have abated, and Meru has been recovering steadily, thanks to foreign funding that has supported the relocation of animals, including elephant and rhino, and the much-needed repair of roads. Still, Meru's reputation as a hotbed of poaching has meant that it has yet to suffer the onslaught of safari tourism and remains marvelously unspoiled.

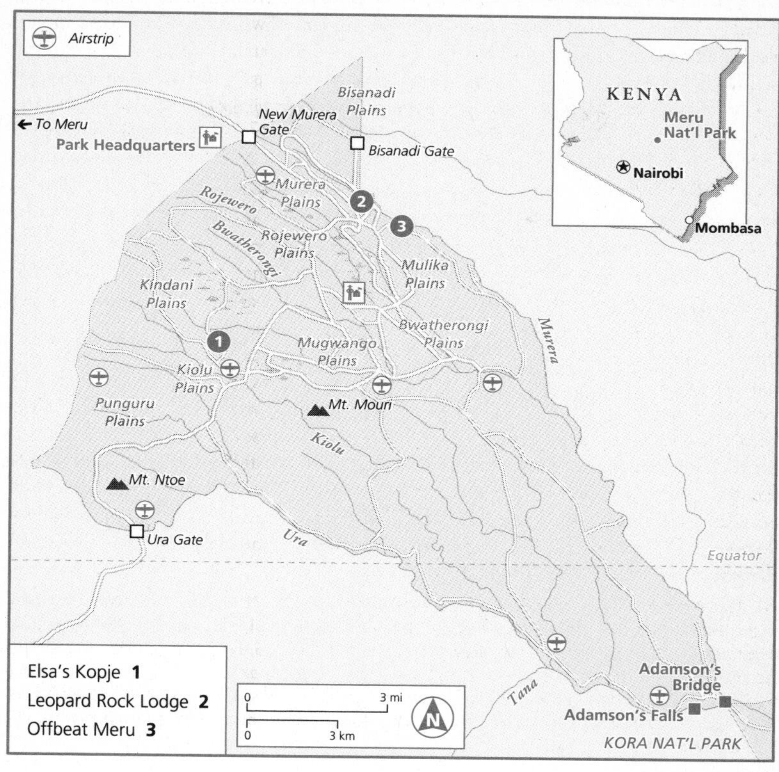

Aside from the devastation of the '80s, Meru's best-known associations are with Joy Adamson, who penned *Born Free* after hand-rearing and rehabilitating a lioness named Elsa. Also within Meru is the grave of Pippa, a cheetah that Adamson reared here and wrote about in *The Spotted Sphynx.* Meru is really the only developed part of a complex of protected wildlife areas, including several national reserves, none of which is in any way equipped for visitors—there simply are no accommodations. The adjacent Kora National Reserve, which, at 1,270 sq. km (495 sq. miles), is considerably larger than Meru, is where George Adamson lived and rehabilitated lions until his murder by Somali poachers in 1989.

Lying directly on the equator, just an hour's flight from Nairobi (an extremely scenic flight, with hulking Mount Kenya in your sights for much of the way), Meru's landscape is spectacularly scenic, which makes the search for the park's still shy, slightly elusive predators a real pleasure. Wildlife sightings are fairly good, although animals might seem a little more skittish than in the better established parks where they're habituated to vehicles. The park is bounded by a number of rivers—the Tana to the south (a great place to watch hippos and crocs), the Bisanadi to the north, and the Rojewero running through the center of the park. These, together with 14 permanent streams that run off from the Nyambeni Hills, are lined with doum palms, tamarind trees, and acacias.

Part of Meru's attractiveness is its diversity of habitats. Surrounded by hills and mountains shimmering in the distance, its terrain includes jungle and riverine forest, swampland, and vast grassland plains studded with rocky outcrops—also called inselbergs or kopjes—which are where you might spot leopards lurking among the boulders. The varied terrain provides shelter for a great diversity of animals—elephant, reticulated giraffe, Kirk's dik-dik, eland, greater and lesser kudu, and Grant's gazelle are found here—and sightings of lion and cheetah are fairly good, as are glimpses of rarer specimens such as gerenuk, oryx, hartebeest, and the endangered Grevy's zebra. Around swampier areas, you'll spot defassa waterbuck and large herds of buffalo. But wherever you are in the park, you'll never lack for incredible vistas in a wilderness that's stuffed with splendor.

ESSENTIALS

VISITOR INFORMATION You can contact the Kenya Wildlife Service for up-to-the-minute information about the park (www.kws.go.ke), or contact the senior warden (✆ **0164/20-613** or 0721/860-285; merupark@kws.go.ke). The park is open from 6am till 7pm; last admission through any of the gates is at 6:15pm.

GETTING THERE It's a long and winding road from Nairobi to Meru National Park, and the journey will probably take several years off your life (as does most open-road travel in Kenya). **AirKenya** (✆ **020/60-6535;** www.airkenya.com) flies to Meru from the capital each day at 9:15am; the trip takes 70 minutes and the airfare is $174 one-way. There are three airstrips within the park that can be used for charters flying into Meru.

GETTING AROUND As with just about every wildlife preserve in Kenya, you'll be happier in a 4×4. This is especially true during the rainy seasons, when any other vehicle will get you stuck.

PARK FEES Adults pay $50 and children $25. Pay in cash and carry foreign currency (sterling and euros are also accepted), or a miserable exchange rate will be applied.

WHERE TO STAY

Elsa's Kopje, my favorite place to stay within Meru National Park, is reviewed below. It benefits from such a dazzling location and so much imaginative design that it cannot help but take your breath away. It also benefits from a special license that enables you to go on walks and night game drives and to fish Meru's rivers and streams. The only other option inside the park itself is **Leopard Rock Lodge** ★★ (✆ **020/60-0031** or 0733/333-100; www.leopardmico.com), a smart and fabulous place with 15 antique-stocked, thatch-roofed cottages on the edge of the Murera, a tropical, meandering river. One highlight here is the river's edge swimming pool where you can stare down crocs and hippos while floating in safer waters. The cottages are suavely appointed—with massive private terraces, double bathrooms, stylish teak furniture, polished slate floors, Persian rugs, and high ceilings—but they lack the organic rusticity and spectacular bird's-eye views of Elsa's Kopje (where you can't help but feel as though accommodations are thoroughly integrated into the natural rock setting). Game package rates at Leopard Rock are low season $1,100 double and high season $1,300, but you should also bear in mind that drinks aren't included in the rate at Leopard Rock, and that might crank up your final bill substantially.

Elsa's Kopje ★★ Secreted away betwixt the rocky crags of Mughwango Hill, its cottages built directly into the huge stone boulders overlooking Meru's wide-open plains, Elsa's Kopje is nothing short of enchanting. You can hardly detect the presence of the lodge until you're up close, and this sense of being a part of the landscape rather than an intruder is part of the magic. Designed by Mark Glen, the near-legendary Kenyan architect known for creating "experimental" lodges that harmonize with the natural contours and textures of the terrain, it has picked up a string of awards and is featured on numerous hot accommodation lists (*Tatler* put it on its top 101 hotels list in 2007). Still, it's difficult to translate the rustic bliss you'll experience here into mere words or accolades.

Each cottage is unique and completely organic in its design. Each has its own special features, intriguing quirks, and, without fail, devastating views of the African plains that stretch out from the boulders below. At night you'll be aware of the surrounding wilderness—leopards are frequently heard, and there's a constant scuttle of rock hyraxes, monkeys, and baboons playing on the rocks and launching themselves through the trees. Most of the time, you're up close and at eye level with the bush because the bedrooms and rock-encrusted bathrooms are built into the kopje, with trees and branches growing around—and through—the manmade spaces. Some are built on different levels, with bedrooms below the bathrooms and great big wooden balconies stretched out in front. My favorite (and an obvious choice for honeymooners) is Bisanadi, which has an alfresco bathtub built into the rock, perched on what feels like the edge of a cliff. Bisanadi is reached via a swing bridge and, like all the cottages, is a voluminous space, sheltered by thatch, with gorgeous views from private verandas and out large picture windows.

If the weathered wood and organic, twisting design of Elsa's cottages sound a little too experimental for you, there's also a two-bedroom family suite—Elsa's Private House—with en suite bathrooms, huge living areas, a private garden, and a central infinity pool that you'll have all to yourself. The design here is more conventional, but it's a good choice if you want total privacy—you can even have your meals served here.

I could go on about the fabulous architecture, but you're really here to go out and experience the wildlife, and the guides here are well-weathered experts who'll introduce you to a superb natural Eden.

www.elsaskopje.com. Reservations: Cheli & Peacock, P.O. Box 743, 00517 Uhuru Gardens, Nairobi. ✆ **020/60-4053-4** or 020/60-3090-1. Fax 020/60-4050 or 020/60-3066. www.chelipeacock.com. 11 units. High season $1,190 double, $440 per child 3–16 sharing with 2 adults, $1,275 honeymoon suite, $2,640 private house (4 persons); midseason $990 double, $365 per child, $1,070 suite, $2,100 house; green season $740 double, $270 per child, $820 suite, $1,600 house. Children under 5 stay free. Discounts for stays of 4 nights or more. Rates include all meals, most drinks, night and day game drives, bush walks, fishing, sundowners, local airstrip transfers, and laundry. MC, V. **Amenities:** Bar; airstrip transfers; pool.

Offbeat Meru ★★ **Value** This is an excellent choice if you're looking for a more affordable alternative to the two lodges—it's a seasonal luxury camp slightly north of Meru, in the Bisanandi National Reserve. There are just six tents, making it the most intimate of Meru's accommodations, and although you're sheltered by canvas, you bed down on large, comfortable, iron-frame beds. Each simple-but-pretty tent has an en suite bathroom with traditional safari bucket shower and proper flushing toilet. Tents are lighted by solar power (and they work around the clock), and at night the campsite is lit with traditional lanterns. There's a lounge–cum–dining tent with a bar, but evening meals are often taken around the campfire, under the stars. A full range of game-viewing activities is offered, and there's a pool to come home to at the end of it all; it's a most laid-back spot from which to observe the animals gathered to drink at the Bisanadi River over which the camp looks. Rates include just about everything, making this an exceptional value (with only marginal price fluctuations in high season), not to mention the closest you'll get to a true wilderness experience in this region. ***Note:*** Offbeat Meru is closed from April through mid-June and November through mid-December.

Offbeat Safaris, P.O. Box 1146, 10400 Nanyuki. ✆ **062/31-081.** www.offbeatsafaris.com. 6 units. High season $760 double; midseason $650 double; green season $570 double. Children 12–17 $215–$285; under 12 $145–$195. Rates include all meals, drinks, game drives and other activities (including fly-fishing and walking safaris with an armed guide), laundry, and National Reserve fees. No credit cards. **Amenities:** Bar; airstrip transfers; pool.

8

The Rift Valley

By Keith Bain

Stretching across Africa like a gigantic wound, the Rift Valley is more than 6,430km (3,987 miles) long and in places up to 1,520m (4,986 ft.) deep. It cuts through the continent from Jordan all the way down to Mozambique and, when viewed from outer space, is apparently the single most identifiable geographic landmark on the face of the planet. Geologists believe that it's the result of violent subterranean forces that literally ripped Earth's crust apart, causing massive chunks of crust to sink between parallel fault lines. In return, molten rock was forced up to the surface in a series of volcanic eruptions. It was here, some 40 million years ago, that Africa began splitting apart along monstrous parallel fault lines—and the land between slipped down, creating the Rift's distinctive valleylike appearance. This process—called rifting—is still underway, evidenced in the active and semi-active volcanoes that simmer and bubble throughout the Rift Valley. When you see a boiling hot spring or hissing geyserlike steam vent, or hear the irritable rumbling of a volcano, it's evidence that Earth is still furiously at work trying to tear Africa apart.

Millions of years of tectonic movement and volcanic activity have not only literally ripped the land apart, but also divided the Rift into two separate branches. The widest and longest of these is the Eastern Rift, which splits Kenya from north to south in a series of fault lines that give spectacular shape to the landscape. In Kenya, this Eastern Rift (sometimes called the Gregory Rift, after the man who first described the Rift in the 1890s) is synonymous with magnificent escarpments, volcanic cones (more than 30 of which are still active or dormant), lava fields, and a smattering of lakes, most of which are soda. This part of the Rift is up to 100km (62 miles) wide and reaches its narrowest point just north of Nairobi, where it's a mere 45km (28 miles) across. The valley floor is at its shallowest near Lake Turkana, in the far north of the country, where there is virtually no distinction between the Great Rift and the surrounding desert. Farther south, though, the valley walls form sheer cliffs rising to 1,800m (5,904 ft.) at **Lake Naivasha,** the highest lake in the Rift system and one of the few freshwater lakes in the Valley. South of Naivasha, the Rift descends again to 580m (1,902 ft.) at the Tanzanian border.

Boiling, steam-spurting geysers are found throughout the Great Rift. You'll see them dotted around many of the lakes that are, in turn, speckled with the slender, pink-feathered bodies of thousands of flamingoes. If you're brave enough to explore **Lake Magadi** in the southern part of Kenya's Rift, you'll witness extraordinary, hellishly hot conditions where almost no living thing—save the specialized avifauna—can bear to survive. Conditions are much calmer at **Lake Nakuru,** where the bitter, alkaline-rich waters create a peculiar habitat for specially adapted organisms, such as special algae and small shrimplike creatures, which are the reason greater and lesser flamingoes are attracted to these soda lakes in the first place. Lake Nakuru is now at the center of one of the

Touring the Great Rift

If you want to get as much out of this region as possible, you'll be best off arranging a 4×4 with a driver (and perhaps an expert guide as well) through your tour operator. This part of Kenya can be traveled as a round-trip commencing in Nairobi. Spend a night or two at either Lake Naivasha or Lake Nakuru (or both), and finish off with several relaxing days on one of Lake Baringo's remote islands. From there, you can either drive or fly back to Nairobi, or head over the Rift's western escarpment, descending to the Kakamega Forest (see chapter 9) for a totally different sort of wildlife experience. You'll pay approximately $275 per day for the hire of a vehicle plus driver (including up to 200km/124 miles travel per day)—all accommodation costs and sightseeing will be extra. Your best bet for seeing this region is **Sunworld Safaris** (✆ **020/444-5669** or 020/444-5850; www.sunworldsafaris.com); you can contact them in the U.S. through Siggi Hosenfeld (9011 Mira Mesa Blvd. #226, San Diego, CA 92126; ✆ **619/254-2096;** siggi@kenyatravelideas.com), or have your Kenyan ground operator make all the arrangements.

most popular wildlife preserves in the country, packed with rhino, plains game, and assorted predators.

Of Kenya's Rift Valley lakes, Naivasha and Nakuru are the most accessible and, together with **Lake Baringo,** make up a pretty decent road circuit manageable in a couple of days out of Nairobi. The eerie, mesmeric **Lake Bogoria**—its surface capped by a flotilla of uneasy flamingoes and its slightly apocalyptic shores dotted with steam-spurting hot springs and scalding geysers—is an easy side trip from Baringo. Lake Magadi lies just south of the capital and is best seen as an outing from the beautiful Shompole lodge, tucked into the spectacular Nguruman Escarpment, which is also within striking distance of Tanzania's **Lake Natron.**

Lake Turkana, in the far north of the country, also forms part of the Rift Valley system and sits amid one of the most inhospitable regions in East Africa in a tortured desert landscape that's endlessly punished by heat and high winds (see chapter 10).

1 LAKE NAIVASHA

86km (53 miles) NW of Nairobi

Its proximity to Nairobi means that Naivasha has long been a popular getaway destination, whether for weekend jaunts or long-term colonial-era soirees. Naivasha's most tantalizing associations are probably with its sordid social goings-on—the area around salubrious Lake Naivasha was once a playground for the rich and famous who lived out a debauched and scandalous existence based in their ranches and lakeshore mansions. Notoriously known as the "Happy Valley" set, their antics were sufficiently attention-grabbing to inspire a blushing page-turner of *White Mischief,* a racy novel about a 1940s criminal investigation, during which Sir Henry "Jock" Delves Broughton was tried for the murder of the Earl of Erroll, exposing all kinds of social shenanigans in the process.

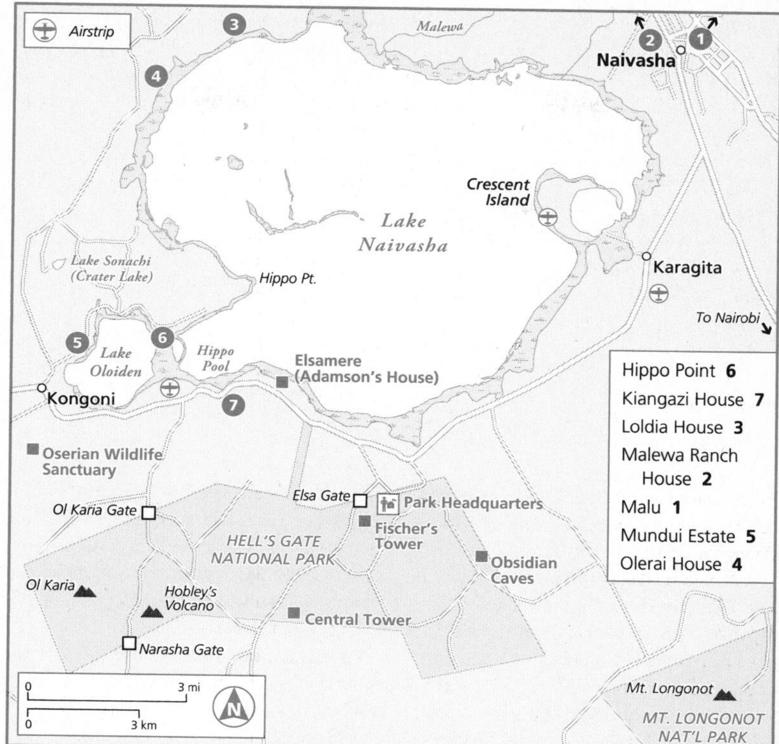

The book went on to become a mildly erotic late-'80s movie starring Greta Scacchi, Charles Dance, and a young, innocent Hugh Grant.

The lake was also, at the time, Kenya's busiest "airport" and served as a touch-down point for flying boats from the U.K. and South Africa. The region remains renowned for its huge private ranches, some of them still functioning farms—with names such as Delamere still turning a profit in dairy—and others now converted to guesthouses for well-to-do travelers. However, Naivasha today stands out as the center of Kenya's massive flower industry, which has deflated the visual appeal of the area considerably—rather than spotting herds of game around the lake's shores, you're likely to blanch at the rather unromantic evidence of the sizeable flower industry that flourishes here. With millions of blooms finding their way from here to European markets every day, Naivasha's horticultural output means big business, but the downside is that the area is inundated with ugly hothouses and appalling concrete living quarters hastily erected for the large migrant labor force that's arrived to serve the industry. Unfortunately, although the flower farms make extensive use of Naivasha's fresh water, it's been something of a controversial issue that, in return, they are feeding the lake with enough toxic effluent to impact the ecology negatively.

The Beautiful South

Perched on the edge of the Nguruman Escarpment, overlooking the volcanic hills and breathtaking plains of the Great Rift Valley, **Shompole** ★★★ is an enchanting, innovatively designed, eco-friendly designer lodge built on a cliff in one of the haziest, hottest parts of Kenya. It's one place where you're sure to find escape from Kenya's mass-market parks and reserves.

Based on a 14,140-hectare (34,926-acre) conservancy with a further 56,560 hectares (139,703 acres) to explore, Shompole is in the southernmost part of Kenya's Rift system, not far from the Tanzanian border, and near two of the Rift's flamingo-rich soda lakes, Magadi (in Kenya) and Natron (in Tanzania). Called the Lake of Fire by the Maasai, Lake Natron is especially breathtaking because it shimmers a deep crimson color, thanks to the special salt-loving algae that grows in the hyper-saline water, and attracts around 2½ million lesser flamingoes, which feed on the red pigmented algae blooms. The caustic waters also keep predators away, which reduces the threat posed to flamingo chicks, making Natron an important breeding ground for the birds.

As beautiful as the lake is—especially when seen from above—its muddied waters can reach ammonia-level alkalinity with temperatures, thanks to underground heating, of up to 50°C (122°F). One of the other highlights in this part of the Rift Valley (for archaeology buffs, at least) is the **Olorgesailie Prehistoric Site,** situated 60km (37 miles) south of Nairobi. Marked by two extinct volcanoes set amid the Rift's arid expanse, it's where excavations have turned up one of the best collections of prehistoric hand axes in Africa, most of them fashioned by humans living between 500,000 and 1 million years ago. Regularly referred to as the Cradle of Mankind, researchers link Olorgesailie to the theory that it was here—in the Rift Valley—that humankind first walked on two legs and also where we first became intelligent tool users.

Shompole's six beautiful tents—raised on stilts beneath high, undulating thatch roofs—curve around the contours of the escarpment. Each has a lounge, bathroom (shower only), and sleeping area. Simply, elegantly configured, with

On a local level, the flower farms are a lucrative source of jobs for laborers, meaning that this is a pretty populous area, with many workers filling the compounds you'll pass as you drive around the lake. This, in turn, does not bode well for resident wildlife—there are fewer and fewer wild-roaming species to be seen around the lake, with most game viewing happening within protected private sanctuaries.

Still, there are pockets of civility and beauty, mostly evident when you're sequestered at any of the upmarket ranches and lodges that continue to work for the preservation of wildlife numbers. Aside from enjoying the easy life on the lake and checking out some of the protected wilderness areas for their game, Naivasha has two worthy outings close at hand. The gorge that rips through **Hell's Gate National Park** is one of the most interesting places in the country to explore on foot, and views from the volcanic rim of adjacent **Mount Longonot** are unbeatable.

lots of white, the part-canvas, part-stone rooms are open to the elements with water flowing through them and into the plunge pool on the private verandas. Each minimalist space is bright, light, breezy, and beautiful, a theme that continues into the main lounge beneath a thatch canopy that architecturally mimics the shape of Mount Shompole, onto which it faces.

A plethora of activities are available here—day and night game drives, guided bush walks, fly-camping, mountain biking, gentle canoeing down the Ewaso Nyiro River, and excursions to see the flamingoes on the lakes. The local landowners—members of the Maasai tribe more specifically known as the Loodokiloni—are traditional pastoralists and (unlike the majority of Maasai in the Mara) still practice seasonal nomadism, regularly relocating their livestock (cattle, sheep, and goats) to new grazing pastures and water. You'll meet and be guided by these tough people as you explore the harsh environment in which they survive; the head gamekeeper here is a former poacher, so he really knows his game. And when guests finish their adventures, there are pools to laze by and massages on offer in the small spa, too. A full gamut of inspiring views is complemented by quality food and service, and the fact that the lodge has been recognized for being environmentally sound. If you're feeling particularly decadent, you can up the level of privacy at **Little Shompole** (added in mid-2008), a two-bedroom unit that's rented—with all the bells and whistles and a private staff—on an exclusive basis.

Shompole is a 30-minute hop from Nairobi (or the Mara or Amboseli) by charter plane (a shared charter is sometimes available, bringing costs down). The drive from Nairobi is 3½ hours, although it's unlikely that anybody would be tempted to go by land. To reserve your stay, contact **The Art of Ventures** (P.O. Box 10665, Nairobi; ✆/fax **20/884-135** or 20/48-610; www.shompole.com); a night's stay runs $990 to $1,110 double and includes all game-viewing activities, meals, and drinks. Little Shompole costs $1,330 to $1,650 double. There's an additional $45 conservation fee per person, per night. Shompole is closed in May.

ESSENTIALS

GETTING THERE & AWAY By Air Naivasha is a mere 15-minute flight from Nairobi. **Safarilink** (www.safarilink-kenya.com) has daily scheduled flights at 3pm ($116 one-way), and the region is also well supplied with private airstrips (serving the ranches) served by charter flights. From Naivasha, Safarilink flights continue on to the Masai Mara (40 min.).

By Road The drive from Nairobi on the hectically busy A104 Uplands road takes 1½ hours; the route is fairly scenic, winding down the Rift Valley escarpment (where there are a number of places to stop and take in majestic Valley views and browse at kitsch roadside craft stalls), heading past the black Longonot volcano, and finally skirting the picturesque shore of Lake Naivasha. You'll also get a glimpse of Kenya's predilection for

Naivasha's National Parks: Hell's Gate & Longonot Crater

For a break from watery Naivasha and a chance to check out a more varied topography, ask your hosts to pack a picnic for a visit to the nearby **Hell's Gate National Park** ★★ (✆ **050/50-407;** www.kws.go.ke; $25 adults, $10 children), where there are hot springs and spectacular gorges. Although there are some seldom-seen predators, one of the attractions at Hell's Gate is being able to hike through the park and walk among the zebra, impala, gazelle, and other plains game. If you're exceedingly lucky, you can even spot Rüppell's griffons or lammergeyer vultures amid the park's basaltic cliffs. It's also possible to bike through the park, and the red cliffs of Njorowa gorge are good for climbing—however, you need to avoid any strenuous activity in Hell's Gate (including excessive walking) during the inevitable midday heat, so aim for a morning visit. With temperatures in the bowels of Earth beneath Hell's Gate bubbling at more than 300 °C (572°F), this is one of the world's hottest natural sources of water and cleverly supplies a geothermal power plant.

Adjacent Hell's Gate is **Mount Longonot National Park** (✆ **050/50-407;** $20 adults, $10 children), centered on a mighty dormant volcano that takes its name, appropriately enough, from the Maasai word for Mountain of Many Spurs—*Oloonong'ot.* The sides of the volcano feature numerous V-shaped valleys formed by the erosion of the soft volcanic soil. You can ascend to the crater rim in about an hour (you must be accompanied by an armed ranger); with stunning vistas in every direction, you'll quickly discover why it's such a popular hiking destination. Circumnavigate the crater rim to take it all in—you'll see Lake Naivasha stretching out from the foot of the volcano and the Rift itself clearly bounded by the Mau escarpment to the west and the Aberdare mountain range to the east. You'll need a couple of hours to complete the route around the rim, and definitely avoid any urge to descend into the impenetrable forest in the crater itself.

quick-fix development—hundreds of small shanty-style structures (many of them painted in the vivid colors of local mobile phone operators) are ranged along the side of the highway where, until just a few years ago, there was little but wilderness.

GETTING AROUND As with just about everywhere in Kenya, you'll need a 4×4 to negotiate some of the deeply rutted dirt roads that run around the lake. Appropriate vehicles (with a driver) are available at any of the accommodations recommended here, and your hosts can also organize boating, horseback riding, mountain bikes, and even charter planes, should you wish to explore farther afield.

WHERE TO STAY

Lake Naivasha is most developed around its southern shore, with often ugly developments all along Moi South Lake Road where much of the horticultural industry is based—understandably, it's not a particularly pretty area.

The best accommodation options (reviewed below) come with a sense of intimacy, are relatively private, and are tucked away from the potential crowds. In the case of Malu, in fact, you'll be a considerable distance from the lake itself, which for many might be a key selling point. If you'd like to enjoy something akin to a homestay or have a lavish estate all to yourself, check out the box entitled "Colonial Farmstays, Kenya Style," below.

Another option—although this one's a little less intimate, with the ambience of a very small colonial-era hotel—is **Kiangazi House** ★ (✆ **050/202-0792;** www.oserian wildlife.com), another favorite weekend getaway for Nairobi's elite and where you'll catch embassy and United Nations staff guzzling bottles of beer and late-afternoon G&Ts on the deep veranda. A guard salutes you as you drive through the gate to this pretty throwback to an era synonymous with gracious hospitality. The five simple, spacious guestrooms are comfortable, if not necessarily luxurious—you'll probably find yourself spending most of your time here relaxing by the pool or at the bar, or reclining under shade at the edge of the lawn watching baboons romping on the lawn and animals drinking at one of the waterholes. However, it's the proximity of a wildlife corridor, connecting the lake with Hell's Gate National Park and distant Maasailand, that makes this an attractive base. The corridor sits adjacent to the 8,080-hectare (20,000-acre) **Oserian Wildlife Sanctuary,** which protects a diversity of animals, including rhino, leopard, cheetah, hyena, and a great many antelope—guests have direct access. Rates here run $630 to $850 double and include most everything—except entry fees to the nearby national parks. Otherwise, all meals, drinks, game drives (night or day) and bush walks, boating trips, and even a visit to the Oserian flower farm are part of the deal. Make reservations through **East African Treasures** (P.O. Box 63437, 00619 Nairobi; ✆ **020/712-3300** through -3302; fax 020/712-3303; www.eatreasures.co.ke).

Hippo Point ★★★ Set on a 242-hectare (598-acre) game sanctuary forming an isthmus between Lake Naivasha and Lake Oloiden, this is probably the most elegant and stylish lodge in Kenya. Large mammals—hippo, giraffe, zebra, and buffalo—roam the grounds, and huge flocks of flamingoes usually carpet the lake.

Accommodations comprise two separate entities. Set in a colorful English garden, **Hippo Point House** is an adorable 1920s triple-gabled, mock-Tudor farmhouse, which—thanks to painstaking renovation—feels every bit like the quirky, utterly luxurious colonial bolthole it once was. Part European design fantasy, part tribute to high-end colonial Africa, the attention to detail is thrilling. There are eight bedrooms, each one immaculate, dutifully restored, and decorated with wooden floors and unique turn-of-the-20th-century English and French furniture and fabrics, large four-poster beds, framed artworks, chunky antiques, and eye-catching pieces crafted by local artisans. Plenty of clean lines and a glamorous simplicity lend an aristocratic ambience—but there are baroque and rococo elements in the mix, too.

During the 1940s, Hippo Point was the Kenyan home of the Earl of Mountbatten; it now belongs to his nephew, Michael Cunningham-Reid. Michael's German-born wife, Dodo, is an interior designer and has personally reinvigorated the lavish spaces in the house and also designed the fantastical 35m (115 ft.) **Dodo Tower,** a magnificent folly near the lake's shore. The tower is quite unlike any dwelling you've ever seen—something out of a fairytale: a wood tower on five floors (with five different bedrooms—each with a unique view—and four separate balconies), reaching as high as Nelson's Column in Trafalgar Square. Views become increasingly majestic as you venture upward, spiraling up increasingly narrow stairways. Built using cedar, cypress, mahogany, ebony, and black granite, the interior (which, typical of towers, does involve *lots* of stair-climbing) is like a treasure trove of artfully arranged collectors' pieces—ebony-inlaid Biedermeier dining chairs, curtains sourced from European auctions, luxury silverware and crystal, and even

Maasai handicrafts for a hint of local flavor. The only trouble with the tower is that it isn't suitable for anyone with weak knees.

Although there's plenty of pretty decor to admire and swoon over, it's the scene by the lake that you've really come for; pink flamingoes in their thousands and half-submerged hippos are usually visible. The most relaxing way to take it all in is with a massage under the lakeside gazebo. There's a staff of at least 25 people to take care of you, and they're able to arrange just about any activity, outing, or bit of luxurious pampering you can imagine. Among other things, they grow vegetables in the on-site organic garden and source foodstuffs from neighboring farms that find their way onto your plate at mealtimes. ***Note:*** Hippo Point is closed in May.

P.O. Box 1852, Naivasha. ✆ **0733/333-014.** Fax 0311/21-295. www.hippo-pointkenya.com. 8 units at Hippo Point House, plus 5-bedroom Dodo's Tower. Peak season $1,380 double, $350 per child under 10 sharing with 2 adults; high season $1,200 double, $300 per child; low season $1,100 double, $270 per child. Rates include all meals, most drinks, most activities, local airstrip transfers, and laundry. MC, V. **Amenities:** Bar; airstrip transfers; pool; spa treatments. *In room:* Fireplace (in some), Wi-Fi.

Loldia House ★ One of Kenya's oldest farms, Loldia—run as a guesthouse even during the early 1900s—retains loads of colonial-era charm with several quaint cottages dotted around mature gardens that stretch all the way down to the lake's edge. Built by Italian POWs with timber and lava rock, the buildings are maintained and decorated in a homey, relaxed way that's more about casual comfort than any overt luxury. The main house and three satellite cottages are bright, light-filled, and breezy, and nothing at all like hotel lodgings—they feature authentic antiques, original bathrooms, thick old-fashioned drapes, and floorboards that creak underfoot. Verandas are deep, fireplaces large, and ceilings high, and the lounge features chunky, comfortable, old-fashioned furniture with bronzes and wildlife paintings by resident artist Michael Ghaui. Unless you prefer romantic candle-lit private dinners (easily arranged), meals are taken communally, and it's something of this sociable buzz that is half the pleasure of being here.

Bedrooms are a mixed bag—if size and views matter, ask for room no. 1, which features handsome antique furniture and has a big bathroom with ball-and-claw tub and even a bidet. If you want more privacy, opt for the family (or honeymoon) cottage. It's a short walk (escorted, as there are many buffalo about) from the main house and was built in 1990; it has three bedrooms (two en suite), its own kitchen, lounge with fireplace, and great views (particularly from the upstairs bedroom).

Besides venturing onto the surface of Lake Naivasha—onto which the farmhouse looks—by boat, you can explore the 3,232-hectare (7,983-acre) property on horseback or on foot, and trips to the various game parks—Hell's Gate, Mount Longonot, and Lake Nakuru—are easily arranged, along with a picnic breakfast or lunch. Even if you don't set foot off the property, you'll spot waterbuck, eland, buffalo, dik-dik, hippos, and fish eagles; with some luck, you may also see leopard, bat-eared foxes, and the elusive nocturnal aardvark. Taking care of you is the affable Peter Njoroge, a butler-manager with years of experience; he arranges meals in just about any imaginable location, lays out freshly cut roses to keep things homey, and constantly offers his special brand of cheerful, interactive attentiveness.

P.O. Box 48217, Nairobi 00100. ✆ **020/273-4000.** Fax 020/273-4023. www.governorscamp.com. 9 units. Green season $492 double; midseason $758 double; high season $872 double. Children under 12 pay about 65%. Rates include all meals, local activities, and local airstrip transfers. AE, MC, V. **Amenities:** Bar; airstrip transfers; golf nearby; tennis.

Malu ★★ Kids Situated quite far from Naivasha, Malu sits within a 727-hectare (1,796-acre) forest some 30 to 45 minutes north of the lake. Malu was formerly an Italian-owned fishing camp. Its new owners, Tim and Sophie Farrell, added beautifully decorated guest cottages packed with enough creature comforts to keep Nairobi-based Kenyans returning for regular weekend getaways. There are also two big family villas (each with a lounge and two en suite double bedrooms), and there's one massive treehouse for adventure-prone guests. Decor is simple yet beautiful; accommodations have high ceilings, four-poster beds, feather duvets and pillows, good-quality cane and wicker furniture, and bathrooms with a separate tub and shower. There's a restaurant and bar at the clubhouse, which is a 10-minute walk from the cottages. After feasting on fine Italian cuisine (prepared from locally sourced ingredients), you can stretch out on the sheepskin rugs in front of your personal fireplace, lit each evening while you're away at dinner. Cottage verandas have distant views of Lake Naivasha, but the estate has many of its own surprises, including a naturally heated spring-fed plunge pool. There are stabled horses for rides around the estate, and even a zebra, Bob, that seems to have adopted the horses as his herd. If you're not one for saddling up, mountain bikes are available, and it's also possible to hike on the estate; it's a 20-minute walk to the waterfall set in a lovely gorge. As you walk along the river, there are usually black-and-white colobus and blue Sykes' monkeys playing in the trees overhead.

P.O. Box 536, 20117 Naivasha. ✆ **050/203-0181** or 0734/666-674. www.malu-kenya.com. 2 villas, 6 cottages, 1 treehouse. Cottage or villa: Ksh16,110–Ksh17,900 full-board double; children 2–12 Ksh4,700. Treehouse (4 adults and 4 children on self-catering basis): Ksh14,850–Ksh16,500. Mahindu Cottages (2 adults on self-catering basis): Ksh8,100–Ksh9,000; children 2–12 Ksh500. MC, V. **Amenities:** Restaurant; bar; pool. *In room:* Fireplace, kitchen (in treehouse and 2 cottages).

Olerai House ★★★ A warning sign reads BEWARE OF BUFFALO at the entrance to this, our favorite Rift Valley hideaway, and tells you instantly that this is precisely the kind of place you've come to Africa to experience. This is perhaps the ultimate soft landing for anyone traveling from abroad and arriving in Kenya for the first time. Set on 81 hectares (200 acres) of lakefront property, Olerai's simple cottages are surrounded by sprawling, beautiful gardens. Stretch out on one of the vividly colored loungers on the lawn, and you'll catch a magical view of Mount Longonot, while all kinds of animals graze in the near distance. At night you'll probably see the shadows of hippos shuffling across the lawn or hear them outside your bedroom walls as you sleep (I've woken in the middle of the night to find a hippo snuffling right outside my window). Beautiful, exotic, and cosseting, Olerai has an upbeat, distinctly boho ambience. Oria Douglas-Hamilton, who grew up in a nearby house, has used bright, cheerful colors on the walls, sourced fabulous textiles, and done all sorts of artful things with recycled bottles and wood offcuts to achieve a look that is exciting and comforting in equal measure. Multicultural iconography and all sorts of *objets d'art* fill the spaces, and there are thoughtful touches everywhere. Among the tomes in the library, you'll find great photographic works personally signed by their creators, such as Leni Riefenstahl and Mirella Ricciardi (Oria's sister).

Some of the rooms have walk-in wardrobes and bathrooms with tubs and bidets. The Barbar room is especially for families (it has its own separate lounge area), and there's a gorgeous upstairs honeymoon suite, too. My favorite room, though, is the one in which Oria and her husband, Ian, penned two of their books about Africa's elephants. It's detailed with fresh floral bouquets, decorative bowls and calabashes, interesting books, Indian blockprint linens, wicker and cane armchairs, straw mats, elephant sculptures,

Colonial Farmstays, Kenya Style

If you fancy a sampling of colonial-style Kenya with an entire house and massive spread all to yourself, consider **Malewa Ranch House** ★, P.O. Box 446, 20117 Naivasha (✆ **020/353-5878** or 020/351-0720; www.malewaranch.com), a large farmstead located around 30 minutes north of Naivasha that's rented only on an exclusive basis. The house—a stone-walled structure hidden in a valley—accommodates up to five couples, with rates starting at 384€ double, including all meals, game drives, ranch activities, and drinks except champagne (the price improves as your group's size increases: It's 1,350€ for 10 people, and children under 12 pay just 95€). Decor is quaint enough—busy floral fabrics and exposed wooden beams give the lounge and dining areas a smart, old-fashioned look, whereas bedrooms are mostly large, homey, and comfortable rather than lavish or luxurious—and most of the bedrooms are twins and share bathrooms. Your hosts can arrange excursions to Naivasha, including boat trips, and the ranch makes a number of activities possible, too, including fly-fishing, abseiling, mountain biking, horseback riding, and swimming in pretty Kasuki Gorge.

If you want to be nearer the lake, though, consider **Mundui Estate** ★ (✆ **050/202-1050**), a 469-hectare (1,158-acre) property on the shore of Lake Oloiden. Comprising acacia woodland and dry savannah, the estate is home to all kinds of wildlife, and a short drive around the property is all you need to spot a good selection of plains game. Dik-dik, buffalo, giraffe, eland, and hartebeest are regularly seen, and at night, hippos emerge from the lake to graze on the lawn right in front of the farmhouse. Cormorants, egrets, and pelicans nest in the trees above the shore, a few hundred feet from your front door. The estate has its own private airstrip, sturdy off-road vehicles for game drives around the estate, and a swimming pool nestled among palm trees and bougainvilleas in an enclosed courtyard. Accommodations are in a massive cottage—built in 1933 as a hunting lodge—alongside the main farmhouse; it's suitable for a family or small group because it's rented on an exclusive basis. There are two spacious bedrooms and a smaller single bedroom (or dressing room) that share a bathroom on the first floor above an enormous whitewashed reception hall where you have your own private lounge, library, bar, and huge fireplace. The cottage was where a certain Yugoslavian prince was exiled during World War II. Much of the furniture is original, as are the creaking floors and tattered hunting trophies. This is an opportunity for something akin to a homestay, where you feel like the personal guests of your hosts—in fact, meals are taken in the main house with Andrew and Sarah Enniskillen, the Kenyans who ranch here. You can plan a day trip to Hell's Gate and Longonot, or even go as far as Lake Nakuru or the Aberdare National Park—they'll happily oblige and pack a picnic basket, too (there's a $200 daily charge per vehicle for such excursions). You can book for Mundui through **Bush Homes of East Africa** (✆ **020/60-0457** or 020/60-5980; www.bush-homes.co.ke); you'll pay $900 double, including all meals, drinks, laundry, and local activities.

and useful goodies in the bathroom (including headache tablets, stomach salts, and a nailbrush for stubborn African grime).

At night you take predinner drinks (from a help-yourself bar) and drape yourself on big, plump cushioned loungers around the campfire; meals are prepared with fresh ingredients grown on Oria's farm, and breakfast is usually served on the lawn with views of animals grazing in the near distance. You can explore the lake extensively by boat—Oria's African gondola rides are highly recommended. If you're looking for a venue for a big family getaway or special function, consider renting out **Sirocco** ★★★, Oria's original family home, which is available for paying guests; it has six double bedrooms and costs $6,500 per night, including all meals, drinks, and household staff.

P.O. Box 54667, Nairobi. ✆ **020/89-1112.** www.olerai.com. 5 units. High season $640 double, children under 12 pay $200 if sharing with 2 adults; green season $600 double; children $180. Rates include all meals, drinks with dinner, bird walks and hikes, cooking classes, and laundry. **Amenities:** Bar; pool (at Sirocco, when available). *In room:* Hair dryer.

2 LAKE NAKURU

160km (99 miles) NW of Nairobi

Famous for its flamingoes and rhinos, Lake Nakuru—a shallow alkaline lake measuring around 60 sq. km (23 sq. miles)—is the main focus of one of Kenya's most accessible and popular state-run parks. Declared a UNESCO World Heritage Site in 2002, Nakuru (the name is a Maasai term for Swallowing Wind, referring to a dust storm, or Dusty Place) was the first park in Africa dedicated to the preservation of bird life. Since 1987, it has also been a sanctuary for rhinoceros—nowhere else are you guaranteed to get a photo of a rhino against a backdrop of thousands of pink flamingoes sifting food from a shimmering lake.

Nakuru's huge flamingo population—an estimated one million of them cover the lake's fringes—has long attracted visitors and compelled photographers to capture the velvety pink carpet that ebbs and shifts over the water. The birds are here because the soda lake is a potent breeding ground for spirulina, the algae upon which the flamingoes feed. When conditions are good, an acre of lake produces as much as 8 tons of the algae in a year.

In addition to the flamingoes, the lake draws more than 450 other bird species—Egyptian geese, pied kingfishers, fish eagles, herons, egrets, grebes, secretary birds, and around half a million great white pelicans flock around the lake's shore. The latter come to dine on the alkaline-resistant fish that were introduced here to feed on mosquito larvae in the 1950s. Most curious of the birds here are the grisly looking marabou storks—often referred to as the "undertakers" of the wild—which feed on the intestines of freshly dead flamingoes, often competing with the scavenging hyenas that skulk around the shoreline.

Just north of the park is Nakuru town, which today has the fourth-biggest urban population in Kenya. If you view the park from high enough up, it's startling to witness how close human settlements have encroached upon Lake Nakuru—as a result, there is a 74km (46-mile) electric fence around the park, making this the only completely fenced national park in Kenya. The lake's proximity to such a dense human population has some serious drawbacks, and pollution from the town has taken its toll on the water—and, accordingly, also on the numbers of flamingoes that are seen here; at one point, they all seemed to have disappeared.

Park authorities claim that there are now strict controls on the effluent flowing into the Njoro River, one of three rivers that feed the lake, and it is hoped that this, together with grand schemes initiated by the World Wildlife Fund, will eventually restore the lake to its former glory. Sadly though, not all problems are so easily overcome. In late 2007, a bushfire completely eradicated the Euphorbia Forest to the east of the lake, wiping out a unique habitat, and the numbers of monkeys in the Colobus Forest have inexplicably thinned out, too.

Because of the fence around Nakuru, there are no elephants in the park, but the other Big Five species are regularly spotted; if you're exceptionally lucky, you may even see one of the park's legendary tree-climbing lions (apparently, they prefer the acacias). The park also functions as a sanctuary for around 85 Rothschild giraffe, relocated here from Western Kenya where agriculture has impinged on their natural habitat. Nakuru is also the best place in Kenya to see mountain reedbuck—they have long, soft, woolly coats and live on rocky slopes, stone ridges, and escarpments. Although it gets pretty crowded, it's worthwhile making your way up to **Baboon Cliff,** where there's a lookout point and picnic spot overlooking the entire lake—seen from up here, Nakuru looks like a well-formed upside-down map of Africa.

For scenic variety, visitors with time on their hands set off to visit the dormant, dull-looking **Menengai Crater,** which borders Nakuru town, to the north. Views from the top are incredible—crusts of solidified black lava spread outward against the red cliffs below you, and you can gaze into the chasm of the crater pit within the volcanic cone itself.

ESSENTIALS

VISITOR INFORMATION Fenced off in an attempt to protect its increasing rhino population, **Lake Nakuru National Park** (P.O. Box 539, Nakuru; ✆ **051/221-7151;** www.kws.go.ke) is spread over 188 sq. km (73 sq. miles) and is strictly managed—this hasn't, however, prevented cases of poaching, instances of park staff being killed by lions, and rampant littering at some of the park's overcrowded viewing points. If you require information about the park in advance, try contacting the senior warden at lakenakurunationalpark@kws.go.ke.

GETTING THERE The quickest way to get in and out of Lake Nakuru National Park is to charter a plane to the Naisha airstrip, which is inside the park and operated by the Kenya Wildlife Service; this can be arranged through your tour operator. Charter arrangements can also be made through **Sunworld Safaris** (✆ **020/444-5669** or 020/444-5850; www.sunworldsafaris.com), which also conducts personalized overland packages. **Offbeat Safaris,** the owners of Deloraine House (see "Where to Stay," below), will also make all travel arrangements if you are using their accommodations, although you'll be based some distance from the park itself. The drive from Nairobi to Nakuru takes around 2 hours; the main gate and park headquarters is 4km (2½ miles) south of Nakuru town. If you're driving from Naivasha, you can bypass the town by entering Nderit Gate in the southeastern corner of the park—however, you will not be able to obtain a Safaricard here, so make sure you have one (usually organized through your tour operator).

GETTING AROUND You'll be most comfortable exploring the park in a 4×4, although standard cars and taxis do manage on the decently maintained roads here. If you don't arrive in a chauffeured 4×4, you'll be able to sign up for guided drives around the park through the Sarova Lion Hill Game Lodge (see "Where to Stay," below).

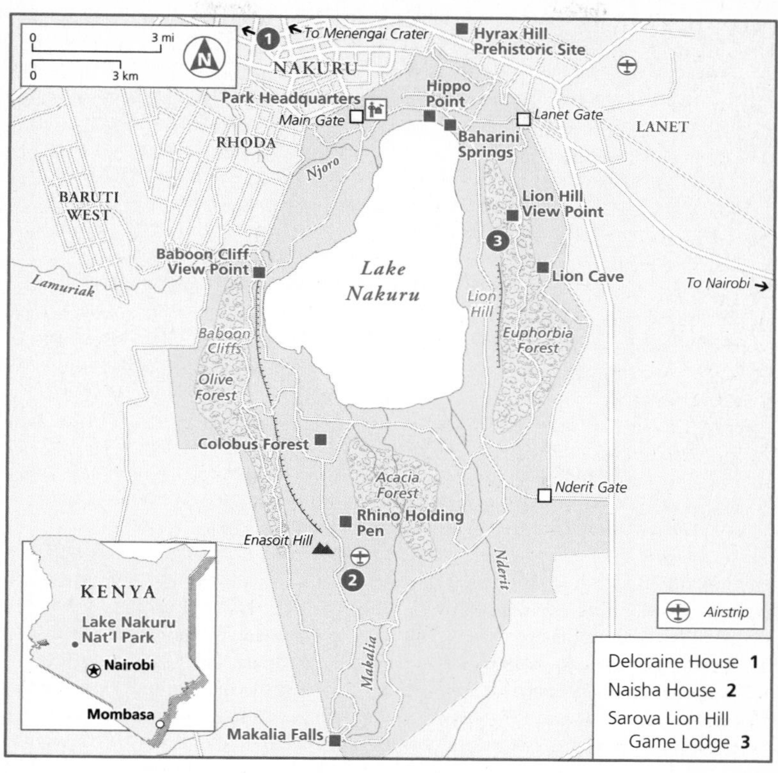

WHEN TO VISIT If you want to see the flamingoes, avoid coming in March, April, or May, when the majority of the large birds head to Lake Natron in Tanzania. It's also worth noting that flamingo numbers can be unpredictable and depend on specific conditions in the lake. If seeing the birds is a priority, confirm their presence ahead of your arrival.

PARK FORMALITIES Entry to Lake Nakuru National Park is by Safaricard (if you don't have one, you can obtain one at the park's main entrance); as one of the country's most popular state-run parks, it's also one of the two costliest (the other is Amboseli), with adult admission a hefty $60 ($35 for each re-entry) and children paying $30 ($23 for re-entry). The park is open from 6am to 6pm. There are three entry gates; **Main Gate** (where Safaricards can be obtained) is near the edge of sprawling Nakuru town and is where you'll also be able to pick up freelance guides (their knowledge is hardly worth the effort, though). There are designated tracks for vehicular access, but areas exist along the lake's shore where it's permissible to drive off-track and even get out of your vehicle in order to better photograph the scene on the water; this should obviously be done only with extreme caution.

Fun Facts Flaming Flamingoes

Derived from the Spanish word *flamenco,* via a Latin word meaning "flaming," the name *flamingo* is directly linked to the striking appearance and unusual habitat of the pink—or flame-colored—bird. Living on volcanic lakes, some of which continue to pump up hot steam and sulphur, the flamingo strongly recalls the ancient myth of the phoenix, which occurs in a number of different cultures. The story describes an immortal—and, by all accounts, majestic—bird that's consumed by flames, only to rise again from the ashes. Add to this the reddish hue of the long, slender flamingo, and it's no coincidence that the flamingo is associated with fire. It's their specialized diet, in fact, consisting of the blue-green algae, spirulina, that gives them their flaming, pink-tinted appearance. Particularly abundant in the alkaline lakes of the Rift Valley, spirulina makes up the entire diet of the lesser flamingo. Greater flamingoes are slightly paler because they get their pigmentation second-hand by dining on other, larger organisms that feed on the algae.

The flamingo is pretty fabulous in its design and is one of few creatures that has evolved to specifically survive the caustic volcanic lake environment. The secret lies in their beaks, which are equipped with a unique filter-feeding system that enables them to skim the microscopic algae from the water's surface. They swing their upside-down heads from side to side or swish the water with their fat tongues and siphon the lake water through their filters to trap algae, separating the minute organisms from the deadly soup in which they grow. They can filter as many as 20 beakfuls of algae-rich water in a single second. This unique feeding system gives flamingoes a certain security: While they must watch out for predators such as jackals or eagles, they compete with no other animals for food. Flamingoes are, however, preyed upon by Maribou storks and also by fish eagles, and around Lake Bogoria, migrant Steppe eagles from Eastern Europe and Russia have even learned to pirate flamingoes from the fish eagles.

Flamingoes have yet another behavior that sets them apart, and it's one that is as hard to explain as it is interesting to watch: They dance. The birds will posture and signal with their wings, bow and bend their necks, run back and forth in a group, and then suddenly take flight, wheeling around the edges of the lake in a mass formation. It's one of the more peculiar scenes in the natural world, and scientists remain uncertain of whether it's a mating ritual, a means of burning up excess energy, or simply an exercise in fun.

WHERE TO STAY

Catering mostly to resident Kenyans who prefer their independence but don't necessarily want to put up with the inherent inconveniences and lack of amenities that go hand-in-hand with camping, the Kenya Wildlife Service rents out some of its former wardens' digs as self-catering holiday homes. One of the best that I've seen is Lake Naivasha's **Naisha House** (reservations through the park warden, lakenakurunationalpark@kws.

go.ke, or through KWS headquarters in Nairobi, www.kws.org). This simple stone house is set among acacia trees in a grove right near the park's airstrip—you'll be visited by buffalo, baboons, and all kinds of plains game, and you may even be lucky enough to spot predators from your front porch. The rental comprises a main house with two bedrooms (each with a double and single bed), full kitchen (with gas stove, fridge, crockery, and cutlery), dining area, lounge with fireplace, a single bathroom (with tub and shower), and barbecue area. A small annex with two single rooms and a long-drop toilet is ideal to accommodate a driver and a guide. Electricity is available for 4 hours every evening; there's kerosene lighting and hot water; and the house comes with a pair of housekeepers, Irene and Geoffrey, who keep things tidy and can supply you with firewood. The biggest drawback might very well be the overwhelming popularity of the house; you'll need to reserve your place anywhere between 2 months and 1 year in advance. You also need to be aware that there is some KWS staff housing nearby, so things can get a tad noisy. The cottage costs $200 to $250 per night on a self-catering basis—besides supplying your own food, you'll need to bring bottled drinking water, and park fees are not included.

Deloraine House ★★ Although it's a good 45 minutes from Nakuru, this is definitely one of the smarter and more romantic places to stay within striking distance of the national park. Built in 1920 by a prominent settler, Lord Francis Scott, it's a big colonial house set on a 1,414-hectare (3,493-acre) farm where many British aristocrats—including the late Queen Mother—stayed during Kenya's years under the empire. Considered to be among the finest examples of colonial architecture in Kenya, Deloraine is a lofty stone mansion, with deep verandas and large, immaculately maintained interiors, all sumptuously decorated and furnished in keeping with the elegant setting. You'll want for few comforts here.

Surrounding the house are immaculate grounds with manicured lawns, mature tropical gardens, a croquet lawn, and a tennis court. There's also a cottage adjacent to the main house with three additional double en suite bedrooms. Deloraine is primarily a base for horseback riding—horses and ponies are available for polo matches and cross-country rides, and at least 80 horses are stabled at any one time. Many of the guests here are at the tail end of a multiday riding expedition organized by Deloraine's owners, Tristan and Cindy Voorspuy—their company, Offbeat Safaris, is one of Kenya's most successful horse safari operations (for more on these safaris, see p. 209, or visit their website).

Offbeat Safaris, P.O. Box 1146, 10400 Nanyuki. ✆ **062/31-081.** www.offbeatsafaris.com. 8 units. $700 double; $170 per child under 12. Rates include all meals, drinks, game-viewing activities, daily conservation fee, local airstrip transfers, horseback riding, and laundry. No credit cards. **Amenities:** Bar; airstrip transfers; pool; tennis court.

Sarova Lion Hill Game Lodge With nearly 70 old-fashioned chalets sorely in need of a face-lift, you need to know that the main reason to stay here is that it's the *only* relatively "luxurious" place to stay within the park itself. It gets busy and feels crowded at times, but you can at least be distracted by baboons and monkeys playing on the lawn, and you'll inevitably want to spend most of your time exploring the park and the lake, so the lodge (with its dated resort ambience) will largely serve as a place to dine and retire at night. Bedrooms are, frankly, a bit cell-like—they're not tiny, but they're bare-bones basic, poorly lighted, and rather ungraciously cluttered together in unattractive stone cottages. Really, if you want to feel a lot less hemmed in during your stay (no matter how brief), opt for one of the three suites—these are more private and infinitely more stylish and spacious, with polished timber floors, soft linens, decent-sized bathrooms, sliding glass windows to let in plenty of light (the standard rooms have dinky louver windows), and lovely views across the lake. Although Sarova piles on the usual mass-market undertakings—predictable buffet meals, inauthentic nighttime entertainment, and a children's entertainer—it's worth knowing that staff here are pretty knowledgeable about the park. Manager Robert Kimani is especially well informed about what's happening in and around the lake.

P.O. Box 72493, Nairobi. © **020/276-7000.** Fax 020/271-5566. www.sarovahotels.com. 67 units. High season $515 standard double, $540 1-bedroom suite, $1,135 2-bedroom suite; midseason $410 double, $445 1-bedroom suite, $900 2-bedroom suite; low season $260 double, $320 1-bedroom suite, $550 2-bedroom suite. Rates include all meals. MC, V. **Amenities:** Restaurant; 2 bars; babysitting; children's activities; pool; room service; sauna; spa treatments; clinic; currency exchange. *In room:* Hair dryer (in suites), minibar (in 1 suite).

3 LAKE BARINGO & LAKE BOGORIA

280km (174 miles) NW of Nairobi, 114km (71 miles) N of Nakuru

Ninety minutes north of Nakuru is the beautiful freshwater Lake Baringo, its water the color of tea. Fished by Njemps tribespeople—cousins of the Maasai—who set out each day in their simple canoes, Baringo is dotted with 13 small islands—sometimes referred to by locals as Devil Islands because of the hot springs and fumaroles that still cough up enough steam and boiling water to make them useful as public baths. Baringo's largest island is Ol Kokwe (The Meeting Place), an extinct volcano with several especially noticeable hot springs, small bubbling pools, and steam jets along the northeastern shoreline. Some of the springs in the lake's northern reaches are believed to have curative properties and are used to treat skin diseases.

Besides the Njemps fishing communities, Baringo is populated with crocodiles that have supposedly lost their appetite for mammalian flesh, thanks to an abundance of fish. Locals actively encourage swimming and watersports in the lake, although the lodges will certainly have you sign an indemnity form before letting you dive in. Hippos are fairly active in and around the lake, and you'll probably spot them emerging from the water to graze at night. Because it's a freshwater lake, Baringo doesn't attract flamingoes. It is nevertheless one of East Africa's prime birding destinations, with nearly 500 species recorded here, some of them extremely rare or otherwise endemic to this area. Fish eagles are plentiful, and you'll inevitably be treated to a close-up view of them swooping down to catch fish thrown out for them by local boatmen—the majestic birds have become so accustomed to this perk, in fact, that they respond to human whistles. The rocky isle of Gibraltar, at the eastern shore, is blessed with the largest Goliath heron population in East Africa. No one lives on the island, but many locals believe it to be where the spirits of the dead reside.

Captivating in its beauty as a peaceful oasis under big African skies and surrounded by cliff-edged escarpments, Baringo is nevertheless subject to staggering climactic mood swings. Dramatic winds kick up unexpectedly, a decidedly good thing when conditions are hot (which they usually are). Epic rains fall and winds sweep up the milky brown surface, making Baringo seem all the more glorious—a high-energy display of nature in one of its most beautifully tempestuous, splendid dramas.

Great beauty surrounds Baringo as well. The lake lies in a vast bowl flanked by rocky mountains and spectacular escarpments, reaching more than 1,500m (4,920 ft.) above the Rift Valley floor. To the east, beyond the low plains that border the lake, a series of steep hills and gorge-indented ridges climb to the top of the Laikipia escarpment, stretching off as far as the eye can see. On the other side of the lake, just a few miles from the

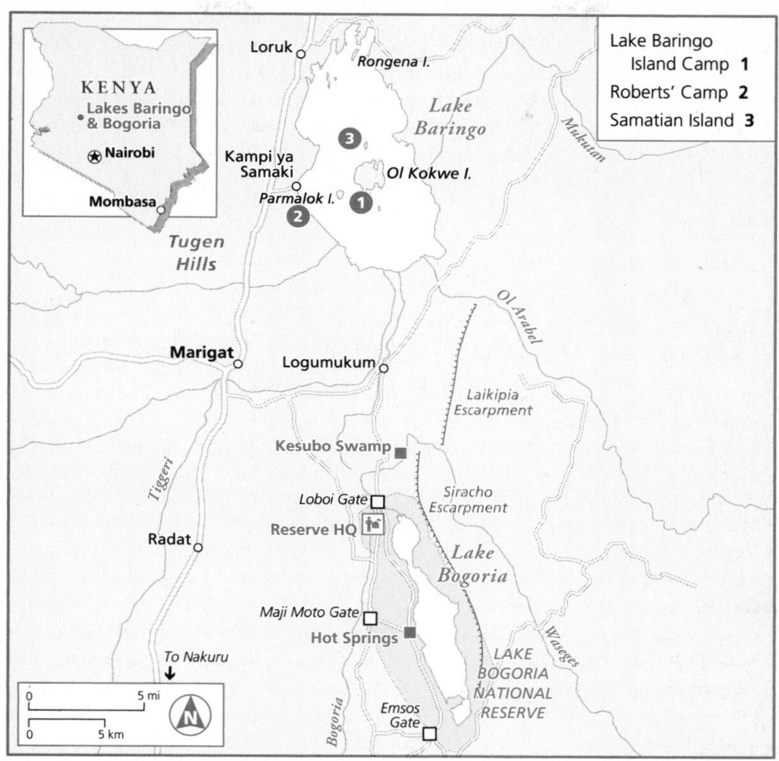

shore, the land rises suddenly in sheer basalt cliffs, some 100m (328 ft.) high. These distinctive cliffs, split by vertical cracks and fissures, but flat on top, are the most recent major structural development in the physicality of the Rift Valley, probably the result of solidified lava flow spewed out by the Karosi volcano—which lies to the north of the lake—some 10,000 years ago. At a distance, the cliffs appear black and include fascinating basaltic features such as gigantic natural towers; if you do set out to explore them, look out for Verreaux's eagles, which nest in the cliffs.

Fascinatingly, scientists have yet to confirm where exactly the outlet for Lake Baringo's water is. Geologists theorize that it's at Kapedo, a gorgeous spring situated some 60km (37 miles) north of Baringo in the Suguta Valley. Here, in one of the hottest places on the planet, boiling, crystal-clear water gushes out of the ground and passes through a series of waterfalls to join the crocodile-rich Suguta River, which flows toward Lake Turkana. It's possible to arrange outings to this remote area, where you can fish the river or picnic under the doum palms that line its banks.

About an hour south of Baringo is **Lake Bogoria**—once known as Lake Hannington—the most eerie of the Rift lakes, with bubbling hot springs and seething geysers marking its shores, while the scattered remains of dead birds create a decidedly ominous apocalyptic atmosphere. Bogoria is 18km (11 miles) long and 4.5km (2¾ miles) at its widest point. Some locals believe that people—members of the Lost Tribe of Bogoria—actually live beneath the lake, although it's widely known that the original people of the Bogoria region are now extinct. The high alkalinity of the lake water means that nothing lives in the water other than blue-green nutrient-rich spirulina algae, on which the lesser flamingo feeds. The spirulina also gives the lake its dark green color.

The sense of visiting a haunted, forgotten realm is underscored by the shocking state of the dusty track (which was, until quite recently, a decent paved road) that runs south along the lakeshore from the entrance. Besides its population of around one million migratory flamingoes, Bogoria has at least 373 species of other birds, a high population of greater kudu, a small number of Patas monkeys, and more species of dragonfly than are found throughout the entire British Isles.

In drought-like conditions, the lake can turn coppery brown—or even blood red—and foul smelling. Superstitious locals believe that this is a sign that the devil has entered the lake and regard it as an omen of death. Tradition dictates that a cleansing ceremony be performed—at the Loburu Hot Springs—during which a goat is slaughtered and milk, millet, and beer is poured into the boiling water. If all goes according to plan, the ceremony should bring rain, which also returns the lake to its natural green color. In reality, the color change is a simple result of evaporation, which causes the spirulina to die and decompose, releasing iron compounds that cause the brown discoloration; scientists believe that the pinkish-reddish color is a result of the bacteria blooming in the water.

ESSENTIALS

VISITOR INFORMATION A modest website with information about Lake Baringo is www.lake-baringo.com. To access Lake Baringo by road, you need to pay a toll at the entrance to the lakeside "village" of Campi ya Samaki; at press time, this was Ksh200 per person, plus Ksh100 per car, but it does vary unexpectedly and the payment of fees depends on whether someone is posted at the checkpoint (also known as Lake Baringo Statistical Information & Boating Centre). For information on Baringo, you're best off contacting someone from the lodge or camp where you intend to stay. Bogoria is part of Lake Bogoria National Reserve and is managed (very poorly) by the Baringo and Koibatek county councils (P.O. Box 64, Marigat); they charge Ksh2,000 entry per adult, Ksh500 per child, and Ksh200 per vehicle (your Kenyan driver will probably be charged

Fun Facts A Rose by Any Other Name

Called *mdiga* in Swahili, the desert rose (found in the northern, arid parts of Kenya's Rift Valley) is not a rose, but a shrub that looks suspiciously like a miniature baobab tree. As the name suggests, these handsome, hardy plants can survive in hot, arid conditions—when in bloom, their pretty pink flowers are particularly striking. As beautiful as this "rose" can be, however, be warned that such looks are deceiving—its sap is deadly and is traditionally used by African tribespeople as a poison for their arrows. Unfortunately, such knowledge has not been wasted on poachers, who have been known to use the poisonous roots to kill elephants. In a less threatening context, the plant has been used traditionally to detick cattle.

Fun Facts The People with the Swimming Cows

The Njemps—also known as the Il Chamus—are the smallest tribe living in the immediate vicinity of Lake Baringo. They've been based here, on the lake's eastern shore, since the 1700s. Since then, their proximity to such an abundance of fish has meant that they've changed from being purely pastoralists into fishermen. They use *ambatch* (balsa wood) to make their small, simple boats, known as *gadich,* and are a familiar sight upon the lake surface, although the best time to meet them out on the water is in the early morning, since they usually spend all night fishing.

Traditionally, during times of drought, they take their livestock to the islands, where they'll have at least some access to grazing. They ferry their sheep and goats by boat, but their cows must swim there. To make sure the bovine beasts know where they're going, they're led to their destination by the "head cow," a special, privileged animal that, perhaps for its navigational prowess and instinctive leadership ability, is never slaughtered for meat.

It's possible to arrange a visit to a Njemps homestead, based at any of the camps or island lodges on or around Baringo. The people you meet can demonstrate how they build their boats, construct their simple dwellings, and smoke the fish they catch. And, of course, you'll see where they keep those very special swimming cows.

Ksh500). If you wish to speak to someone about conditions around the lake or want more details about entry, the current state of the roads (which were dire at the time of researching), or camping within the reserve (Ksh500 per person), contact the senior warden (✆ **0721/343-808**).

GETTING THERE If you want to fly to **Baringo,** you'll need to charter a plane; the flight from Nairobi will take around 45 minutes. If you drive directly from Nairobi, you'll be on the road for at least 4 to 5 hours, although you're more likely to break up the trip with a night (at least) at Naivasha or Nakuru, or both. If you're staying at either of the two island "resorts," you'll be transferred by boat from the mainland—if weather conditions are bad, this part of your trip might be delayed, so it's a good idea to have some flexibility time-wise. There are parking facilities on the mainland, and your driver will be able to find accommodations in Campi ya Samaki while you're staying on the island. The most convenient way to see **Bogoria** is as a day-trip from Baringo—if you don't arrive with your own vehicle, the outing can be arranged through your accommodation. Alternatively, if you're covering the whole Rift Valley region and are looking to save time, it's possible see Bogoria as a stop-off en route from Nakuru to Baringo.

GETTING AROUND Once on the shores of Lake Baringo, much of your sightseeing will be by boat. You'll need a 4×4 to get to Bogoria or to explore any of the offbeat destinations north of Baringo. Boat trips, as well as excursions to any outlying locations, can be arranged through your lodge or camp.

Animal-Spotting at Bogoria

Surrounded by thick, impenetrable thorn bush that makes animal-spotting difficult, Bogoria is not recognized as a place of great mammalian diversity. The main reason to visit is to check out the flamingoes and witness eerie evidence of the ongoing tumult beneath Earth's surface. There are times, particularly in the early morning, when the steam coming from Bogoria's geysers forms a misty, cloudy blanket, amplifying the primal drama of the lake. You're allowed to get out of your vehicle and investigate the lake at fairly close quarters, but pay heed to the warning signs and stay away from the edge of the lake, where boiling water, hot mud, and strange underground conditions can make walking here tricky and dangerous. One animal that is abundant around Bogoria and can be quite rare elsewhere is the greater kudu. A beautiful antelope characterized by wide ears, a body vertically striped in white, and a tell-tale white chevron between the eyes, it is identified most quickly by the grandeur of the males' large spiral horns and hairy fringe on the throat. The greater kudu population, once quite large, was severely affected by rinderpest transmitted by cattle during the 19th century. Patience in the reserve will also reward you with sightings of buffalo, baboon, Grant's gazelle, Kirk's dik-dik, and, at the rocky slopes south and east of the lake, klipspringer.

WHERE TO STAY

A cluster of lodges and camping facilities along the lakeshore make up the tiny community of Kampi ya Samaki, built on the back of a fish factory established in the 1950s by the pioneering Roberts family, David and Betty. Offering the most variety in terms of accommodation is Roberts' Camp (reviewed below), where you can stay in an atmospheric lakeshore house, bunk down in a simple two-bed *banda,* or set up camp under the trees and listen through the canvas as hippos munch their way across the lawn each night. Besides the two options reviewed below, one other option worth investigating is **Lake Baringo Island Camp** (P.O. Box 1141, Nakuru; ✆ **051/85-0858;** www.eihr.com/baringo), which has long occupied a prime position on Ol Kokwe, Baringo's largest island. Although its tents are now a bit long in the tooth, new management stepped in recently, and there's been some overhaul of facilities—the complete renovation has been put on hold due to the prevailing economic situation, however. In the past, guests have slept in large green canvas tents with attached bathrooms; they're comfy, but nowhere near as romantic as the solid, open-fronted cottages you stay in at Samatian (the other island resort, reviewed below). New owner Perrie Hennessy intends to replace the tents with large, breezy thatch-roofed cottages with whitewashed walls and simple wooden furniture. Twin tents go for $400 (including meals, afternoon tea, and boat transfers to and from the mainland), but if you're looking for a touch of romance, with a hint more luxury, upgrade to the new superior cottage (at press time, just one was complete), which currently costs $440 double per night—an absolute bargain. In the future, all the tents will be replaced by just 10 of these swanky cottages, each of which will have a private plunge pool on the veranda. Rates will increase considerably, though, when Island Camp becomes an all-inclusive operation. It will also start to take environmental concerns more seriously by stepping up its reliance on solar power.

Roberts' Camp ★ With noisy hippos interrupting your slumber and the sound of snapping crocodile jaws alerting you to the fact that a new day has dawned, time spent in the **Hammerkop Roost** ★★★—a big, rustic wooden cottage on the very edge of the lake—will be romantic, exciting, and memorable. Sure, the big wooden two-floor house may creak and groan as you explore its multiple views, but you'll never forget this wonderful place. One guest back in 2004 called the experience "as marvelous as the first day of the world." Others who've stayed here have referred to it as "paradise."

Roberts' Camp sprawls over a fairly large chunk of lakeside real estate with four different cottages, all with a kitchen, plenty of space to lounge, and terrace areas for taking it easy—if you wish, you can hire the services of a butler who will assist with everything from making tea to cooking and cleaning. The cottages all have a weather-worn, slightly ramshackle ambience, but they're imaginatively designed and fit in with the laidback lakeshore vibe—rustic-but-gorgeous Hammerkop, the nearest to the water, is my favorite, but each one has its particular charm. If budget is a major concern, there are a handful of simple *bandas*—basic, thatch-roofed rondawels with a wardrobe, a table, two beds, and an armchair—that share one kitchen. There's a wide-open, tree-shaded area for camping; it's Ksh500 per person if you bring your own tent, or you can use the large dome tents provided (from Ksh2,000 if you're self-catering, Ksh3,100 full board). You can also opt for a luxury tent with bedding for up to four people (Ksh2,600 if you're self-catering, Ksh3,400 full board).

P.O. Box 13953, Nakuru 20100. ✆ **0733/207-775.** www.robertscamp.com. 4 cottages, 4 *bandas,* plus various camping arrangements. Cottages: Ksh12,000 full board double; self-catering rates are seasonal, Ksh7,000–Ksh9,500 for up to 4 people. *Bandas:* Ksh7,900 full board double; Ksh3,400 self-catering double. No credit cards at press time; MC, V expected soon. **Amenities:** Restaurant; bar; massage and beauty treatments. *In room:* Kitchen (in cottages).

Samatian Island ★★ For a chance to put your feet up and soak up some of Africa's most blissfully laidback rhythms, Samatian Island is the ultimate away-from-it-all experience. As you pull away from the mainland on a 20-minute boat ride from Robert's Camp (above) and take in the breathtaking views—massive escarpments under a big African sky, an expanding shoreline, volcanic islands, and tribal fishermen in their simple canoes—it feels like you're slipping away for a taste of paradise. With the entire island (albeit a smallish one) to itself, this pretty, rustic, completely solar-powered resort, imbued with just a handful of individually designed rock cottages teetering on the water's edge, is a thrilling retreat. Ensconced in your open-fronted cottage, perhaps relaxing in a bath built into the rocks, there are few more heart-stoppingly beautiful experiences than watching the weather approach the island—as the wind picks up, storm clouds brew, and waves begin to heave, you'll have a sense of being consumed by the tempest, yet you'll be totally protected by large thatch roofs and waterproof blinds, free to observe from what feels like the eye of the storm.

Decor is a couple of steps up from castaway chic—neat, imaginative bedrooms with gorgeous bathrooms; furniture made from wicker, cane, and various natural pieces of wood; artifacts collected from around the continent; piles of *National Geographic;* rough concrete floors; and drop-away balconies. Room nos. 2 and 3 (this latter is the family-sized chalet, with two sleeping areas and a rooftop terrace for star-gazing or sunbathing) are the most comfortable, although neither of their bathrooms have views (a fact that's more than made up for by the view across the lake from the bedrooms).

Hippos and crocs do come onto Samatian, but only at the other end of the island, and most of your adventures here will involve a dreamy boat ride. As you cruise around from island to island in *sesse* canoes, you'll have brief encounters with Njemp fishermen, spot crocodiles basking on the island shores, see geyserlike hot springs, and witness a rich diversity of birdlife, including fish eagles that have learned to swoop down for fish thrown to them by lodge guides (it sounds cheesy, but it's a thrilling encounter—and photo op—with these majestic birds). You can also arrange a trip to a Pokot homestead where you can meet a people who are quite unchanged by Kenya's modernization. And, of course, if that all sounds like too much effort, there's nothing wrong with giving in to the simple thrill of just lazing at the side of Samatian's small infinity pool—but be prepared for some fierce sun and heat. When you're offered sundowners out on the lake, though, jump at the opportunity to witness the effects of the changing light on the water, the sky, and the birdlife, which is staggering, no matter where you look for it.

P.O. Box 13953, Nakuru 20100. ✆ **020/211-5453** or 0722/464-413. www.samatianislandlodge.com. Reservations: The Safari and Conservation Company, P.O. Box 24576, 00502 Nairobi. ✆ 020/211-5453, 020/219-4995, 0735/57-9999, or 0712/57-9999. www.thesafariandconservationcompany.com. reservations@scckenya.com. 5 units. High season $950 double, $285 per child under 16 when sharing with 2 adults; midseason $780 double, $240 per child. Rates include conservation fees, all meals, most drinks, boat rides, bush walks, boat transfers, and laundry. No credit cards at press time; MC, V expected soon. **Amenities:** Bar; pool; room service.

9

The Masai Mara & Western Kenya

by Keith Bain

Kenya's premier safari destination, the **Masai Mara,** is an iconic savannah wilderness alive with prolific numbers of resident and migrating wildlife. Add to this the fact that this is principal stomping ground for Africa's best-known tribe, the Maasai—traditional pastoralists who have become landlords in control of this enormously important ecosystem—and you have the makings of one of Africa's must-see destinations.

While the Mara has long been a priority on tourist itineraries, the rest of Western Kenya—a major crop-bearing region with shimmering tea-carpeted hills and a bustling sugar industry—has remained well off the beaten track. With almost half the entire Kenyan population squeezed into this part of the country and with agriculture its core business, there have been few legitimate attempts to develop a tourist infrastructure. Consequently, relatively few foreign visitors bother to venture this far from the major wildlife parks. But there are rewards for more intrepid travelers, and, as the ancestral home of the U.S. president, it's assumed that Kenya's far west will soon be welcoming a new generation of curious visitors on cult-like "Obama Roots" tours.

Here, on Kenya's far-flung western border with Tanzania and Uganda, is the country's tiny sliver of **Lake Victoria,** the second-largest freshwater lake on Earth after North America's Lake Superior. Kenya claims a mere 6% of the lake as its own, but that's still a generous area to sample island-style Africa and get to know the friendly Luo people—Kenya's second-largest tribal group—who settled these shores several centuries ago, substituting raising cows for fishing.

From all along the shores of Lake Victoria and its islands, fishermen set sail in mahogany dhows and canoes—or, increasingly, their motorized boats—to cast their nets for much-sought-after, shark-sized Nile perch. And in a small village near the lakeside city of Kisumu, everything from beer to schools has, in the aftermath of the most recent American election, been rebranded to celebrate "Obamania," since the laid-back region suddenly became famous as the home of the American president's grandmother and extended "family."

And just a few hours' drive—albeit along often shocking roads—from where Obama's father grew up is **Kakamega,** one of Kenya's lesser-known treasures and the country's last remaining natural rainforest, a wet, dense jungle full of exotic monkeys and a fascinating diversity of birdlife. After days of bounding along in a safari vehicle stalking predators and witnessing the dramatic abundance of wildlife grazing the plains of the Mara, this is an idyllic place to stretch your legs for a day or two. Set out on foot beneath the dense forest canopy, and you'll soon be caught up in an intimate encounter with a fast-disappearing African paradise.

1 THE MASAI MARA ★★★

275km (171 miles) SW of Nairobi

Cynics will tell you that the Mara has been spoiled by years of overdevelopment, that its reputation as one of the richest game-viewing regions in Africa—in the world, in fact—is overblown. While its detractors revile the heavy tourist numbers and corrupt management of the National Reserve at the Mara's core, none of that can really take away from the startling reality—an iconic African wilderness teeming with game, prowled by predators, and plump with impossible-to-miss Big Five action; this is epic animal-viewing terrain. Come during its busiest seasons, particularly when the thrilling Great Migration, widely considered the largest terrestrial wildlife spectacle on Earth, hits Kenya, and you'll be spotting camera-clicking *homo sapiens* almost as readily as the breathtaking teams of wildebeest, zebra, impala, topi, and gazelle being stalked and hunted by extraordinary numbers of lion.

And with regularly spotted cheetah, loping hyena, and shyer carnivores also out to up their protein intake, the Mara is a priority destination for observing animated and furious interactions between predators and their prey. If lion kills and cheetah chases aren't your thing, there's always plenty of mellower hippo and croc action down at the river. Or simply take in the endlessly compelling sight of elephant herds cruising the wilderness, tan-colored topi standing sentinel atop termite mounds, or groups of sullen-faced buffalo giving you the once-over. And backing up all this animal magic is an enduring, ever-enchanting landscape. With its vast acacia-dotted plains cut by the life-giving waters of the Mara and Talek rivers and its western flank overlooked by the spectacular Siria Escarpment, the Mara's classic vistas are the stuff that *Out of Africa* dreams are made of. This is Hollywood's African idyll—grass plains interspersed with *migunga* and croton thickets, rolling hills and small islandlike kopjes.

Thrown into the mix is the opportunity to rub shoulders with the Maasai. Kenya's most famous group of people is a tribe of tall, elegant pastoralists who—despite encroaching modernity—have somehow managed to sustain many of their traditional ways. You'll see young Maasai boys herding hundreds of cattle or shepherding goats across the land, or come across the legendary Maasai warriors *(morani)*—dressed in their bright red *shukas* and long-lasting sandals made from recycled rubber tires—who have long stirred the imagination of visitors to East Africa. If you're lucky, these men will be the guides and drivers assigned to take you through the Mara wilderness.

Established in 1961 on lands owned by the Maasai and once hunted by wealthy Brits, the Mara is part of a huge conservation area that stretches into neighboring Tanzania and that, thanks to the establishment of new community-owned conservancies around the edges of the Mara National Reserve, is actually expanding. A promising sign, one would hope . . .

Yet, as with so many of the world's great wonders, there are disturbing consequences, too, and the Mara's fame is not without its drawbacks. Many consider the park—the Mara's core area, under the control of local Maasai councils—overexploited, poorly managed, and simply too packed with tourists, many of them charging around in ubiquitous white minibuses that environmentalists generally consider the scourge of the Mara's thriving safari market. A *National Geographic* report recently confirmed that mass tourism is degrading the area. Having long run the risk of overdeveloping, authorities claim there are new plans in place to try to prevent the damage that's been caused by poorly

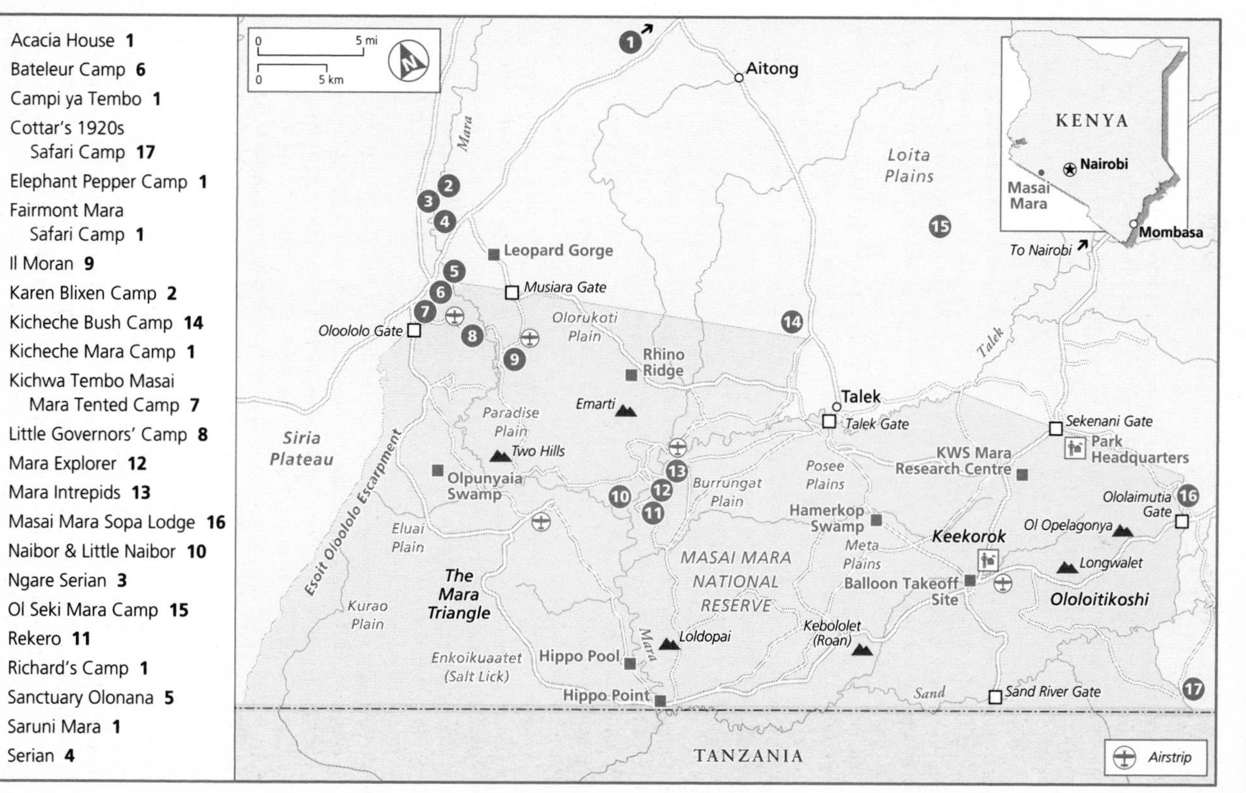

Acacia House 1
Bateleur Camp 6
Campi ya Tembo 1
Cottar's 1920s Safari Camp 17
Elephant Pepper Camp 1
Fairmont Mara Safari Camp 1
Il Moran 9
Karen Blixen Camp 2
Kicheche Bush Camp 14
Kicheche Mara Camp 1
Kichwa Tembo Masai Mara Tented Camp 7
Little Governors' Camp 8
Mara Explorer 12
Mara Intrepids 13
Masai Mara Sopa Lodge 16
Naibor & Little Naibor 10
Ngare Serian 3
Ol Seki Mara Camp 15
Rekero 11
Richard's Camp 1
Sanctuary Olonana 5
Saruni Mara 1
Serian 4
0 5 mi
0 5 km
KENYA
Nairobi
Masai Mara
Mombasa
To Nairobi
Aitong
Loita Plains
Talek
Talek Gate
Sekenani Gate
Park Headquarters
Ololaimutia Gate
KWS Mara Research Centre
Keekorok
Ol Opelagonya
Longwalet
Ololoitikoshi
Balloon Takeoff Site
Sand River Gate
Sand
Posee Plains
Hamerkop Swamp
Meta Plains
Kebololet (Roan)
MASAI MARA NATIONAL RESERVE
Burrungat Plain
Loldopai
TANZANIA
Rhino Ridge
Emarti
Mara
Hippo Pool
Hippo Point
Leopard Gorge
Musiara Gate
Olorukoti Plain
Paradise Plain
Two Hills
Olpunyaia Swamp
The Mara Triangle
Enkoikuaatet (Salt Lick)
Ololoolo Gate
Eluai Plain
Kurao Plain
Esoit Oloololo Escarpment
Siria Plateau
Airstrip

Africa's Lost Tribe, Part I

They're among Africa's most celebrated, fabled, romanticized tribes, a tall, slim, dark-skinned, proud, and, by all accounts, handsome people who make up a mere 2% of the Kenyan population. Despite relatively scant numbers, the Maasai inhabit the popular imagination as a near-mythical race. Having stirred a cult-like curiosity from European adventurers who first met them in the 19th century, they still stoke the flames of untold love affairs with the African wilderness with which they are so intimately associated. Many Maasai—those who have embraced some of the most romantic theories created around their origins—will tell you that they are directly descended from one of Israel's biblical lost tribes. Another theory pegs them as the offspring of a band of Roman infantrymen who drifted south from Sudan while defending the southern borders of the empire. There's no getting away from the close resemblance Maasai warriors bear to some images of ancient Roman soldiers—a brightly colored shawl, or *shuka,* wrapped over a red tunic bearing, and always with a dagger at their hip. Add to this that classic image of Maasai men loping through the wilderness, unshackled by material possessions, save perhaps their beloved cattle, and you have a definite case for a people whose eternal wandering conjures a lost tribe fantasy.

In reality, though, today's Maasai increasingly find themselves under pressure to conform to the strictures of contemporary development. Kenya recognizes around 50 tribes, but because of their traditional relationship with the land—one that includes nonownership and semi-nomadic pastoralism—the Maasai are struggling to stand their ground and sustain their cultural identity.

For many, the truly humbling reward of visiting the Mara is encountering *morans* (warriors) striding across the plains, young boys herding goats, or elders grouped under a tree discussing matters of the day. Today most of your encounters with the Maasai, however, will be in the context of their new role as game lodge guides and animal trackers, playing cultural hosts and ambassadors, or performing their traditional dances and haunting songs to the applause and camera-clicking of enthralled tourists. In modern Kenya, the Maasai are especially visible in the immediate vicinity of the Masai Mara—part of a greater region known as Maasailand, which was essentially a portion of colonial-era East Africa that nobody wanted. Colonial history effectively compelled them to be here, and the ongoing struggle for land still threatens their survival.

At the beginning of the 20th century, the Maasai were the dominant tribe in Kenya, but their role changed significantly with the arrival of European weapons, technology, and colonizers. Until the British settlers arrived, fierce Maasai tribes occupied Kenya's most fertile lands. At the height of their power in the mid–19th century, their lands stretched as far as the fertile Laikipia Plateau and Central Highlands. Rinderpest, an infectious virus-borne febrile disease, apparently accompanied the white settlers (who else?) and decimated the Maasai cattle herds that have always been an essential part of their diet and way of life. Famine followed the rinderpest outbreak, as did another colonial disease—smallpox.

As in much of Africa, Maasai society began its slow absorption of foreign concepts (such as landownership) when the Europeans began to redistribute the best land among themselves. Despite initial attempts to fight back against the new rulers, a disease-weakened Maasai fell victim to some tricky political maneuvering. They tried to preserve their territory, but their spears were no match for British troops armed with guns, and their lawyers never had a fair chance in British courtrooms. In 1911, a small group of Maasai gave up their lands to British settlers, perhaps ignorant of the consequences of the settlement treaty. The Maasai lost about two-thirds of their land, and by 1913 the British government had relocated most of them to southern Kenya and northern Tanzania. Their own pastoral lands were turned over to foreign farmers, some of whose descendants still maintain large ranches there. But farther south, on lands the colonizers did not want (except to use for colonial-era hunting), the Maasai were forced to eek out a devalued existence. In Kenya, the creation of wildlife preserves on some of this land has meant that a handful of Maasai, those who have become suit-wearing politicians and modern businessmen, have grown fat, flying high on the backs of their no-less-impoverished kinsmen. Theirs is very much the story of post-colonial Africa, with most ordinary Maasai finding themselves in bitter competition with the wildlife and tourists for scarce resources. It's been an ongoing struggle since the game reserve was established in the early 1960s, and much communal pastoral land was suddenly off-limits and pressure for grazing intensified.

Nowadays, as the cash economy impacts increasingly on their lives, visitors will witness the influence of the West throughout the greater Mara region—tin-roof homes, concrete schools and clinics surrounded by fences, garishly signposted shops, and "hotels" (bars) where Maasai elders drink themselves in and out of despair. Instinctively, most visitors are quick to judge the brutalizing impact these "modern" edifices have on the landscape. The obvious reaction to the ugly architecture and unchecked development is outrage. It's a common Western response to blame these people for desecrating the unspoiled landscape. There's no denying that, as the Maasai construct their equivalent of villages and towns—however ramshackle and simple they are—they are steadily ruining the environment that sustains the local tourist industry and serves as the economic lifeblood of the region. Some argue that it's only fair that these people be allowed to develop alongside the rest of Kenya, but it's difficult not to feel personally affronted by the mushrooming of unsightly, ill-fitting structures—particularly when seeing the situation through the eyes of the developed world. Outsiders are quick to react to tribal Africans attempting to shift with the times, struggling to make ends meet in a dispensation that shrugs off a culture it overtly perceives to be primitive. More worrying, perhaps, is that some Maasai have turned to self-exploitation as a means of subsidizing their meager resources. While many Maasai are putting their skills as wilderness experts to good use as guides, others devote themselves to inauthentic *faux*-village experiences where the sole aim of the exercise seems to be taking money off unsuspecting (and quickly frustrated) tourists.

But don't be guilty of making your mind up too quickly—throughout the Mara, you'll find hard-thinking Maasai ready to share their personal thoughts on the matter; speak to them while they're still around.

Fun Facts What's in a Name?

The Mara—a Maa (or Maasai) word meaning "Mottled"—is a visually evocative reference to the patchy landscape in this region. Not only does the Mara's acacia-speckled terrain make sense of this name, but when the land fills up with wildlife, the name is surely imbued with new meaning, as the plains are suddenly speckled with living beasts. You'll hear different explanations for the name, depending on who you talk to, so it's often a useful point of departure for conversation.

managed game-drive vehicles and excessive numbers of lodges and tented camps. But by all reasonable accounts—despite claims that the Mara is entering a period of renaissance with a more considerate form of low-impact and sustainable tourism emerging—the building of new, large lodges continues apace.

That's no reason to be put off, though. For the first-time traveler to East Africa, the Mara—a comparatively tiny portion of the expansive game-rich wilds known as the Serengeti just across the border in Tanzania—is indispensable, considered the ultimate opportunity to view wildlife in all its untamed, theatrical glory. If the literature is to be believed, the Mara boasts the highest concentration of terrestrial wildlife on Earth. And, yes, the Great Migration—an awesome, rollicking natural cycle when hundreds of thousands of wildebeest attempt dangerous, frequently foolhardy river crossings as part of their annual biorhythmic round-trip exodus from Tanzania into Kenya—really is as spectacular and mesmerizing as the wildlife documentaries would have you believe. Those astounding images of thousands of seemingly hypnotized animals flopping, diving, and tripping into crocodile-infested rivers are the stuff of every wildlife enthusiast's dreams, and it is reckoned that this particular migration—one of numerous animal treks that happen around the world throughout the year—is best witnessed here in the Masai Mara, where the massive animal numbers are compressed into a relatively small area. Imagine 2½ million visiting animals cluttering the plains and clogging the rivers as they squeeze into an area that covers just more than 1,500 sq. km (585 sq. miles). It's one of nature's must-see dramas—although, with its high death toll, not necessarily for the squeamish (and the sight of Bambi being mauled to death by lions is sure to traumatize the kids).

Even if you don't make it in time to see the Migration, you'll be treated to one of the richest and most diverse animal kingdoms in the world. And if you choose carefully, you'll be staying in intimate, luxurious surrounds, far from the maddening crowd (the best of these are among my top choices, reviewed in this chapter).

ESSENTIALS

ORIENTATION Situated in the southwest of Kenya along its border with Tanzania, the Masai Mara National Reserve consists of 1,510 sq. km (589 sq. miles) made up of three group ranches—the Mara Triangle, Musiara, and Sekenani—under the control of local county councils. All around the National Reserve, the wildlife dispersal area continues into several other community-owned ranches, unfenced Maasai-owned ancestral lands where free-roaming wildlife commingle with semi-permanent human settlements. Here, too, concessions have been granted for the establishment of private game lodges and tented camps where it's possible to experience a safari without the crowds. Within the conservancy areas, however, the Maasai are entitled to graze their cattle (which is illegal within the National Reserve), so don't be alarmed to find herdsmen, their cows (often with tinkling cowbells audible for miles around), and various other signs of human habitation.

VISITOR INFORMATION The most reliable online source for information about the Mara is **www.maasaimara.com**. You will find maps of the area at most of the entrance gates, but don't always expect to find accurate, up-to-date, or English information at these entry points. The Mara—its size, shape, rules, and development—is constantly changing, and it's best to be cautious when accepting information from anyone.

GETTING THERE **By Road** Most visitors come to the Masai Mara as part of an all-inclusive safari package, commencing with a cramped drive in a minibus from Nairobi. If you want to get there by road, opt to be driven in a 4×4 (preferably a Land Cruiser), which will then be used as your game-drive vehicle throughout your stay; count on spending around $250 to $350 per day for the privilege. Narok is the main point of access to this region and is a 3-hour drive from Nairobi; from Narok, the transfer to your lodge will take between 2 and 4 hours, depending on which part of the park you're staying in and also on weather conditions. If you're counting your shillings, you might want to know that regular buses and *matatus* arrive in Narok from Nairobi and other destinations.

By Air A far better option—and the only one if time and comfort are of any consequence—is to fly directly into the Mara. Most lodges and camps are within 45 minutes of the nearest landing site (there are several), and a few places have private airstrips, too. There are daily scheduled flights from Nairobi (AirKenya and Safarilink have two flights each), the coast, and Nanyuki (for connections from Laikipia). Private charters also use these strips. Most lodges will provide transfers from the airstrip, meaning that your game drive begins shortly after you touch down. Generally speaking, your tour operator, who will book all your accommodations, will reserve your flights and ensure that you touch down at the correct landing strip.

GETTING AROUND The reserve has an extensive network of dirt roads that are maintained by park authorities. You will hopefully be driven around by experienced guides trained to look for clues telling them where animals are most likely to be found. It is also possible to sign up for hot air balloon safaris (p. 183), horse safaris (p. 188), bush walks, and scenic flights. Several safari operators can arrange specialized tours, treks, or hikes in this area.

WHEN TO GO The migration of wildebeest from the Serengeti commences in July and continues through to October; it's when accommodations are at a premium and when the Mara is most crowded with visitors. Many camps close during the rainy seasons; the "short rains" happen in November, while the "long rains" fall in April and May. The rainy season is the best time to come if you prefer the solitude and verdant green of the quiet season. The birthing season—known as "Toto Time"—starts in December and continues into February; it's a popular time for visitors (accommodations are again at a premium) who come to witness infant wildlife staggering to their feet and skittering as they take their first steps—it's a magnificent scene, often accompanied by thunderous storms. March and October tend to be the hottest times of the year, but the Mara is seldom oppressively hot, and some of the higher-altitude lodges can get cold at night.

Moments The Great Migration

Time your Mara visit accordingly, and you can prepare for one of the world's great wildlife dramas—a hoofed mob of a million-plus gnu (known here as wildebeest) moving en masse across grass-filled plains, over hills, and through rivers besieged by hungry crocs and watched by salivating lions and excitable hyenas. Pounding up the dirt in a splendid display of obedience to some powerful biorhythmic clock, it's a riot of wild, unbridled energy and fierce determination as hordes of wildebeest and other, less clunky hangers-on—some 360,000 Thomson's gazelle and 191,000 zebra—move across the border from Tanzania, filling the Mara with the primordial sounds, smells, and lumbering charm of their bovine feeding frenzy. So what's the story?

After the long rains in April and May, the Mara's sweet, tall, red ort grass, much loved by wildebeest, starts to grow, and, having exhausted the pastures of the Serengeti National Park, two million animals respond to some inexplicable instinct that ultimately brings them together into what looks like a single massive herd and steadily drift northward. Visually it's breathtaking, although it's a myth that these animals come bounding along as though this were some kind of goal-driven marathon—in fact, this "annual" migration is an ongoing circuitous event with no real start or end point. Sheer force of numbers creates the spectacular effect of a single surging column of life that stretches across the horizon. With little more than grass (and an inkling of survival) on their minds, they continue to pour across the border, and as they fill the Mara, the ensuing action is relentless. Lurking by the wayside, prides of magnificent Mara lion—some numbering up to 40 strong—prepare to ambush their lumbering victims. And like kids in a candy store, Nile crocodiles wait along the rivers that will prove the undoing of tens of thousands. Leopards, cheetahs, and hyenas pick off unfortunate stragglers. The gruesome sight of predators pulling a struggling wildebeest apart is not for the faint of heart, but for those who can stomach the savagery, it's a thrilling open-air lesson in survival of the fittest.

PARK FEES At press time, Masai Mara National Reserve fees were $80 per person (ages 12 and older) or $40 per child per day. Always ask whether these fees are included in any accommodations package and, if so, ensure that you have evidence of having prepaid these fees with you when you travel into and around the park. Fees for overnighting in the conservancies are often higher but may include access to the main Reserve—often if you stay in one of the conservancies, you'll have little need to enter the crowded National Reserve at all. If you're traveling with a tour operator, your park fees may have been added to your account in advance; alternatively, you'll need to pay in cash either on arrival or when you pass through one of the entry gates. ***Note:*** Discussions are afoot to potentially divide the Mara into zones, with cheaper admission to areas that will be set aside for budget and package tourists and higher levies for more exclusive zones where visitor numbers will be more strictly controlled.

Navigating by instinct and memory, the beasts—in their eagerness to reach the long grass that covers the northerly plains—must cross the swirling waters of the Mara and Talek, rivers encountered along their circular route. It's an awesome, inexplicable sight. One animal will raise its head as if testing the air and bound into the water, only to immediately be followed by thousands more. Diving and dashing into the waters with marauding predators waiting to pounce, these river crossings give visitors the chance to witness nature at its most brutal and bloody. Thousands of the animals drown, and the body pile-ups attract a motley assortment of scavengers. Instinctively—as if part of a natural ritual culling process that will weed out the weak and make room for future generations—the migrating herds inevitably choose terrifically dangerous fording points and attempt to cross near-impossible points in the river. The result is a mass drowning coupled with attacks by ravenous jubilant crocs and other predators. These grotesque and spectacular migration pile-ups may easily see up to 1,000 wildebeest dead at any particular point—but freak events, where the frenzied lemming-like wildebeest surge into fording points that are dangerously steep, or where the river current proves too fierce, can see the death toll rise to several times this number.

But the Migration is really not about death, but part of an endless, ongoing cycle of life. Drive into the midst of the herds, and you are immediately aware of the constant movement and ceaseless activity, and at night there's a veritable concert of grunting gnus, barking zebras, roaring lions, and laughing hyenas against a backtrack of chorusing cicadas.

Finally, having grazed their way across the Mara over a 3- or 4-month period, the survivors steadily return south, usually before the onset of the short rains in November. By December or January, they will have reached the Ngorongoro highlands in time for their calving season that sees as many as 8,000 wildebeest calves dropped each day. Six months later, these newborn wildebeest will be strong enough to tackle the long march back toward the Mara. Such is the constant theater of primal, primordial Africa.

WHERE TO STAY

To the northwest, the Mara ecosystem is bounded by the Esoit Oloololo Escarpment, and here—in a part of the park watered by the Mara River—is the Mara's most scenic and game-rich terrain. This area can be difficult to traverse during the rainy seasons (Apr–May and Nov), and the swampy ground generally becomes impassable after heavy showers. Many of the upmarket lodges are located here, too. Because of its accessibility from Nairobi, the eastern part of the Mara is generally associated with mass tourism lodges, meaning that it's where you see a considerable number of crammed minibuses. The most remote and unhindered part of the region is the southeastern corner of the Reserve (and beyond its borders), where the Sand River prevents minibuses from venturing at all.

Tips Maa 101

The language of the Maasai, Maa, is a Nilotic language that can be written using the Latin alphabet; *q* and *z* don't feature. However, while you may quickly discover a fondness for the lilting, sing-song flow of a Maa conversation—there's a discernible rhythm in the backward and forward exchange of statement and response that will remind you a bit of an orthodox sung prayer—you've got practically zero chance of ever joining in. With an unprecedented number of *r*'s rolling off the tongue, and no recognizable pauses to indicate phrases, clauses, or sentence breaks, learning to speak Maa if you weren't brought up with it is devilishly difficult. However, don't let that stop you from impressing your hosts and guides with a few easy-to-remember one-word basics: *Sopa* means "Hello"; *Sopa, olleng?* is "How are you?"; and one you'll be using frequently is *Ashé,* meaning "Thank you." Be warned, though, that an extremely important feature of Maa is the use of tone (or pitch), which is used to alter the meaning of individual words—get the stress on one syllable wrong, and you could be barking up the wrong tree. The sad fact, however, is that tribal languages such as Maa inevitably have a limited lifespan. In a country with dozens of different tribes, each with a different language or dialect, only English and Swahili are taught at schools. Coupled with the swift embrace of modernity and the pressure on all children to be state educated, the chance of long-term survival for these highly individual languages is slim.

Shameless development in and around the Mara has meant that there's an ongoing rise in the number of available beds. Although this means there is more to choose from, it also means that there are more vehicles within the Reserve and an ever-growing number of off-road tracks grafted into the landscape by undisciplined drivers. Depending on your priorities, your first concern may very well be finding lodging as far from the masses as possible—although, with the exception of Cottar's (reviewed below) in the far south of the Mara and a few more isolated spots in the private concessions, you have very little chance of not meeting up with other vehicles while out on game drives. That might be one problem you'll battle to overcome (unless you insist that your driver steers you far away from the maddening crowds), but you can stave off the effect of crowded lodgings by selecting smaller, more intimate accommodations (the best of which are reviewed below). With no fences or manmade barriers, wildlife can move freely throughout this "dispersal area"—essential for sustaining a vast transnational conservation zone—so game viewing is pretty good no matter where you choose to bed down.

Accommodations range from too-basic-to-recommend campsites with zero facilities to palatial tents with all the trimmings and tip-top service straight out of some fantasy colonial heyday. If you're after a peaceful bush experience that leaves the crowds behind, then you'll definitely consider the significance of staying in an eight-tent camp as opposed to a lodge with 70 or 80 bedrooms. You came here to commune with nature and wildlife, but it's inevitable that at the larger, blander, resort-style lodges you'll be inundated by *homo sapiens.* If you value privacy and a true wilderness experience, don't think twice about paying a little extra for more exclusive accommodations—you'll be rewarded with memories that are unforgettable for the right reasons (as opposed to wishing your fellow guests would quiet down). Also, be aware that "exclusivity" out in the bush doesn't always translate to luxury in the same sense of a city hotel or resort. If non-stop power, permanent hot water, and a full-on spa are requisites when you go on holiday, here you may find yourself sharing those "luxuries" with large groups. However, this doesn't mean that some of the intimate camps don't pull out all the stops, too.

Just about every lodge and tented camp organizes game drives in the early morning and late afternoon—traditionally the cooler times of the day when the wildlife is most active—but at the larger establishments, this pattern can quickly become a numbing routine. Many of the smaller places emphasize individually tailored programs so you can determine not only when you wish to go game viewing, but also what format you'd prefer this to take. So rather than spend each and every day bouncing along in a 4×4, there'll be opportunities for bush walks, too. Or, during the Migration, you can happily pack a picnic and stay out for the entire day.

Northern Mara

Acacia House ★★★ **Value** It's neither a lodge nor a camp. There are no other guests—you have a small Maasai staff all to yourself, and a 4×4 (with expert guide) is at your disposal around the clock. It's tucked away deep in the bush, and your nearest neighbors are miles away. Nestled in the Ol Chorro Losoit valley, this big, beautiful three-bedroom house is situated at the foot of Kipileo Hill within the 1,414-hectare (3,493-acre) Rekero Conservancy, owned and run by the same conservation-minded people who operate Rekero, arguably the finest tented camp within the Mara Reserve (p. 192). Built for a Londoner who wanted a family escape in the heart of Africa, it's now available for visitors looking for much the same personal, individual experience of the Mara that's prized by Kenyans who've grown up in the bush but don't necessarily appreciate the crowds.

It's a fully kitted house with plush beds, quality linens, and just the right amount of natural wood to suggest a space inspired by the untamed landscape that surrounds you. Large picture windows frame live-action images of the bush—don't be surprised to find a buffalo staring back at you (as I did one morning while looking up from checking e-mails) or an elephant trundling past. Delicious, simple meals are prepared in your kitchen by your personal staff—ultra-efficient Maasai gentlemen who cook, clean, pour drinks, and chew the fat with you—so you soon feel at home in this private paradise. Acacia has two ground-floor double bedrooms—both en suite—and another loft-style bedroom upstairs; the ground floor also houses a TV room, lounge with open fireplace, and open-plan dining area. Take breakfast on the veranda, and then spend the day checking out the drama around the watering hole. Or head out early with a packed lunch and spend the day exploring the varied bush terrain that stretches for miles in every direction.

For first-timers, the experience might feel a little too isolated from the action (the cottage is a good hour from the Reserve at the northernmost tip of the greater Mara region), but for others, this will be the perfect escape and a chance to cultivate a truly intimate love affair with Africa. In fact, the remote location is likely to ensure that you avoid catching sight of *any* other vehicles or tourists *ever.* ***Note:*** A swimming pool was completed in spring 2009, and at press time a second cottage, Leleshwa House, was in the works.

Reservations: Uncharted Outposts, 9 Village Lane, Santa Fe, NM 87505, USA. ✆ **505/795-7710.** Fax 505/795-7714. www.unchartedoutposts.com. Local contact: Bush&Beyond, P.O. Box 56923, Nairobi, 00200. ✆ **20/60-0457,** 20/60-5108, or 20/60-5980. Fax 020/60-5008. www.bush-and-beyond.com or www.rekero.com. Cottage with 3 bedrooms $700 double; $950 for up to 4 guests; $1,200 for 6 guests. Rates include all meals, most drinks, and all safari activities. No credit cards. **Amenities:** Bar; Wi-Fi.

Bateleur Camp ★★★ A strong contender as one of Kenya's most lavish and cosseting camp experiences, Bateleur scores high marks for its sumptuous style, top-notch guides, and sweeping views of a quintessential African landscape, which stretches out into the distance from drop-dead luxury tented accommodations. Although the tent count—18 units in all—sounds steep, these are divided into two separate-but-identical neighboring camps, so privacy, peace, and quiet are much enhanced (especially when compared to the very large Kichwa Tembo, right next door). Each large, beautiful tent (made of canvas, but you'd hardly know it) is draped beneath a pitched wooden roof with gleaming hardwood underfoot. Stone-and-glass bathrooms, plenty of dark-wood furniture, built-in wardrobes, overhead fans, and wooden blinds for extra privacy all contribute to the sneaky suspicion that this isn't a tent after all. And the pampered excess continues with all kinds of luxuries—linen dressing gowns, footstools upholstered in rare Maasai beaded leather, Egyptian cotton linens on massive king-size beds, silver candelabras, his-and-hers *kikois* (an African sarong) for use during your stay, and a pile of *National Geographic.*

Time your evening game drives appropriately, and you'll return to glowing torches, flickering candles, and open fireplaces—before dinner, there's time to slink into the leather armchairs on your private veranda on the edge of the plains. Or investigate the richly ornamented library lounge—chic colonial antiques (shiny brass compasses, framed maps, leather-bound books, and leather trunks piled high) work well alongside elegant African artifacts (cowhides, ostrich eggs, clay pots, and hunting spears) to produce a beautiful safari baroque look that's both elegant and fun. Cushy sofas and polished leather chairs tip the balance in favor of a homey atmosphere, while fine china, crystal, and polished silver remind you that you're in the arms of luxury. A butler is on hand to handle everything from doing laundry to mixing a great G&T.

For some, the ultraluxurious surrounds might contradict the spirit of the bush, but if you like it classy, you'll want for nothing here. Rent *Out of Africa,* and prepare yourself for sundowners atop the very hill where some of the movie's most enduring images were captured. During the Great Migration, the parade happens right beyond your veranda.

Private Bag X27, Benmore, Johannesburg 2010, South Africa. ✆ **11/809-4441.** Fax 11/809-4400. www.andbeyond.com. In the U.S. ✆ 888/882-3742 toll-free. Fax 305/221-3223. 18 units. Low season $1,030 double; midseason $1,250 double; high season $1,880 double. Rates include all meals, most drinks, scheduled safari activities, airstrip transfers, emergency medical evacuation insurance, and laundry. MC, V. **Amenities:** 2 bars; airstrip transfers; babysitting; pool. *In room:* Hair dryer.

Elephant Pepper Camp ★ Camouflaged by thick forest, this intimate camp is packed with class and run by people with genuine enthusiasm for the bush. Occupying this site for 12 years now, the camp is named for the medicinal trees—with fiery-tasting leaves much loved by pachyderms—which shade its eight simple tents. With clear views of the plains at the edge of the tree line, the tents are raised on sandbox-style plinths and have attached bathrooms (bucket showers and eco-toilets), wrought-iron furniture, hand-woven rugs, and a little porch. By day you can watch zebra grazing at the edge of the lawn just steps from your bedroom, and at night, when hurricane lamps light the way home, you're sure to hear elephants trundling between the trees, their intimate sighs and shudders penetrating the canvas walls. Much of the functional gear inside the tent—wash basins, water jug, light fittings—is crafted from recycled glass and prettified with colorful Maasai beadwork. For a marginal uptick in price, it's worth booking the **honeymoon tent** ★★★—about twice the size of the others (and easily converted into a family room), it gets terrific morning sun, has its own fireplace, and is especially well positioned for privacy, set in a part of the forest much favored by a certain family of elephants.

Within the Reserve, or Without?

Baffling bureaucracy plagues the Mara's management, such that it's virtually impossible for mere visitors to figure out when they are inside the National Reserve (which, notoriously, is under the control of corrupt county councils) or have crossed the boundary and entered a privately managed conservancy where different park fees (and rules) apply. The one noticeable difference within the Reserve itself is the absence of Maasai cattle herding, and the only signs of human development should be the safari lodges and camps (and a handful of airstrip). The Reserve also attracts the lion's share of visitors, so when you hear bad press about overcrowding in the Mara, this is where it's actually happening. If you stay in a camp or lodge outside the Reserve, you'll probably have little cause to ever venture away from the private concession on which you're based. Generally, the conservancies offer a more exclusive experience, since vehicles based in the Reserve won't have traversing rights for the private lands where numbers tend to be limited. It's also worth noting that the conservation fees paid while staying in areas outside the Reserve go directly to the landowners and local communities. By contrast, park fees paid within the Reserve go to the county councils, and that inevitably means that the money goes directly into the pockets of a few well-placed politicians. So it's actually a lot more community-friendly to stay in areas outside the National Reserve.

Game drives are conducted in brand-new Land Rovers; during the Migration, request a full-day outing—you'll get a picnic breakfast and lunch. The guides here are real characters, too—ask for Stanley, and discover how he earned his sobriquet "The King." Meals, when you choose to dine in camp rather than in the bush, are taken communally (though private dinner at your own tent is also doable) in a lovely mess tent with sectional walls that can be taken down entirely to give a greater sense of being in the midst of it all. For added sustenance, a help-yourself drinks cabinet means the bar is always open. ***Note:*** Elephant Pepper is closed April, May, and the first half of June.

Cheli & Peacock, P.O. Box 743, 00517 Uhuru Gardens, Nairobi. ✆ **020/60-4053** or -4054, or 020/60-3090/1. Fax 020/60-4050. www.elephantpeppercamp.com. Lodge: ✆ 0735/33-7630. epc@chelipeacock.co.ke. 8 units. High season $1,090 double, $400 per child 5–16 sharing with 2 adults, $1,300 honeymoon suite; midseason $880 double, $325 per child, $1,030 honeymoon suite. Discounted rates for stays of 4 nights or more. Rates include all meals, most beverages, day and night game drives, bush walks, laundry, airstrip transfers, bush breakfasts. No credit cards. **Amenities:** Bar; airstrip transfers.

Fairmont Mara Safari Club ★★ If you'd prefer to have a fence and a river between yourself and those hungrier animals, then the Fairmont—unavoidably on the large side and with an atmosphere that's more plush resort than true bush experience—may be right for you. Extensively overhauled in 2007 when the luxury-oriented Fairmont group took over, this now feels a lot like a big, smart, thoroughly contemporary hotel in the bush—even if your walls are canvas and "rooms" are linked by stone pathways rather than passages.

Set on 8 hectares (20 acres) of well-tended gardens on one side of the Mara River, there are more than 50 well-equipped, ultrasmart stone-floor tents, which are surprisingly spacious inside and, despite being irritatingly close together, offer a sense of privacy and exclusivity; for the best views, choose tent 12 or 12A. Each one is identically decorated,

You Say "Manyatta," I Say "Rip-Off"

Although you'll frequently be hearing about opportunities to visit a Maasai *manyatta,* it's worth knowing that this name is a bit of a cultural misnomer. Maasai villages are not, in fact, called *manyattas,* but are actually *enkangs.* A *manyatta*—or *i-manyat*—is something quite different, in that it's a place of temporary encampment established specifically for warriors (*morani*) to live during the *eunoto* period, during which they pass into elderhood. The *manyatta* may comprise about 50 huts, and all the members of one age group in a district live there. Living together as they learn about the new social hierarchy into which they've entered, these men are taught their responsibilities as future husbands and tribal leaders. The *enkang* is a semi-permanent settlement (although it may exist in one place for many years) and consists of 10 to 20 huts (which are built by the women) with several families who communally care for their livestock. The settlement is surrounded by a thorn fence, which serves both to keep cattle in and unwelcome visitors out.

There are also cultural villages—also known as fake *manyattas*—built exclusively as tourist attractions and staffed by Maasai who dress up purely as spectacle (and for your photos, of course), as well as *enkangs* that have become so commercialized that they might just as well be billed as Maasai souvenir stalls; costs to visit these places run anywhere from $10 to $40, with much of this being pocketed by unscrupulous guides, drivers, and tour operators. And then you'll spend much of your visit being cajoled into purchasing handicrafts at criminally inflated prices—the experience is unpleasant, at best.

If you would like to visit an authentic Maasai *enkang,* talk with the manager of your camp or lodge about the kind of experience you'd prefer, and insist on being accompanied by a Maasai guide who can not only explain the rhythms and complexities of the daily life of the people you are visiting, but also act as a translator so you can engage your hosts in meaningful conversation. Once there, crouching down inside the dark, smoky interior of a dung-smeared Maasai hut or witnessing the poverty and relative filth (by Western standards, at least) and the simplicity of these people's lives, it's unlikely that you will not be moved. At some point, bags of handmade crafts will be hauled out; making a donation by buying something is a gracious way of thanking your hosts for an eye-opening interaction. And don't forget to honor any promises to mail any photographs taken of the people you meet.

with elegant, mass-produced furniture and lots of "African" design details. With colorful rugs on the floor, soft white linens and red suede comforters on large wooden beds, leather-framed mirrors, bead curtains, practical wardrobes with basket-style drawers, and a cupboard disguised as an antique leather trunk, the overall effect is pleasing enough, and you're spoiled with an array of amenities. They're kept secure from most of the wildlife (baboons are exempt) by electric fence, but you'll spot plenty of hippos and crocs in the river right below your private porch. So-called "deluxe" units don't differ from the better-value standard tents—what they do offer for the extra $35 per person is a more exclusive location (at the far end of the property) and an outside shower.

The contemporary African theme is even more overt in the public lounge and bar areas—world music is piped into a vast space with enormous fireplaces, hand-carved Congolese stools, leather sofas, and cowhides spread across the walls. Trading on its swanky good looks and cosseting luxury, this is one place you'll feel safe and comfortable, definitely—but just a touch put out by the impersonal service; not only is much of the staff alien to the Mara, but their knowledge of the bush leaves much to be desired.

P.O. Box 58581, Nairobi 00200. ✆ **020/221-6940** or 050/22-170. Fax 020/221-6796. www.fairmont.com. 51 units. Best Available Rate policy applies. $159–$449 double; $229–$519 deluxe double. AE, MC, V. **Amenities:** Restaurant; 2 bars; Internet; pool; room service; transfers; in-house doctor. *In room:* Hair dryer, minibar.

Il Moran ★★ The most upmarket of the growing empire of Governors' Camps (which have achieved legendary status thanks to their part in the BBC's *Big Cat Diary* series and now include a property in Rwanda—a good choice if you want to add gorilla-spotting to your African experience), Il Moran is situated high on a sheer-drop bank of an S-bend in the Mara River. All day and night, hippos grunt, snigger, and snort as they pop in and out of the water down below. Tucked into a thick grove of shade-providing trees, the unfenced camp comprises 10 huge tents with possibly the largest bathrooms in the Mara (each with double showers, twin basins, ball-and-claw baths, and bidets). They've also got enormous beds (with wonderful Egyptian cotton linens), crafted—along with the other furniture—from natural pieces of olive wood. With animal-print bedspreads, ancient travel cases for decorative effect, and slightly dark interiors lit by large kerosene lamps, designers have made few concessions to contemporary style, but accommodations are no less comfortable or functional as a result. There's a place to sit and a desk to write at, you can even charge your appliances (albeit using a socket in the bathroom), and a private veranda provides ample space to recuperate after a game drive or replay the excitement of a thrilling early-morning balloon safari (which launches from neighboring Little Governors'). Despite all the snatches of luxury (most evident at mealtimes, when silver service and inventive cuisine set Il Moran apart from most Mara camps), it's hard to ignore the fact that Il Moran's best attribute is its prime location in what is considered the finest part of the Mara for game viewing. You can opt for three game drives a day, or ask the camp's manager to take you walking—he's been leading clients through the bush for almost 2 decades.

P.O. Box 48217, 00100 Nairobi. ✆ **20/273-4000.** Fax 20/273-4023 or -24. www.governorscamp.com. 10 units. Green season $640 double; midseason $984 double; high season $1,130 double. Children under 16 pay about 65% of the adult rate. Rates include all meals, most drinks, game-viewing activities, local airstrip transfers, and laundry. AE, MC, V. **Amenities:** Bar; airstrip transfers.

Karen Blixen Camp ★ (Value) Many of the Mara's accommodations are in either extremely large lodges or very pricey intimate camps. Until recently, there's been a bit of a gap in the middle, with only a handful of medium-size properties (with Little Governors', reviewed later in this chapter, probably pick of the bunch). Since mid-2007, this Danish-owned tented camp, facing the Oloololo Escarpment on the edge of the Mara River, has been a strong contender as one of best in this neglected category. Tents are elegant, spacious, and tastefully designed, and from the big, breezy, thatched mess area, you get nonstop views of hippos wallowing in the river where all sorts of animals come down to drink. Named after the Danish author whose East African exploits continue to make hearts flutter, the camp comprises 22 wheat-colored tents set on large mahogany platforms with attached, furnished verandas facing the nearby river. Interiors are spruce and minimalist, with white curtains (rather than mere zip-up flaps), plump duvets, and just enough detailing to hint at the safari style Blixen herself might have enjoyed in the 1920s. Bathrooms feature twin metal basins and flush toilets, but the highlight for many is an outdoor shower screened off from the outside world by thatch grass walls—there's nonstop hot water, thanks to an automated gas heating system.

Comfortable as your sleeping quarters are, don't expect to have the same kind of intense bush experience you'll have at, say, Rekero or Kicheche—tents are very close together, and there's a definite hotel-like ambience in the public areas (even if they're attractive, breezy, and imaginatively styled). It's also less intimate than the smaller camps (there are set mealtimes and a reception-like check-in desk, and a limited number of game-drive vehicles means it's anyone's guess who'll end up guiding you and who you'll share the experience with), but you're unlikely to miss any animals. And for those moments between game drives, there's a small kidney-shaped pool, a resident masseuse, and a menu that explores various culinary styles with a Kenyan theme—Indian one night, Swahili another, for example.

Bruce House 7th Floor, Standard St., Nairobi. ✆ **020/221-1496** or 0737/49-9706. Fax 020/221-1981. www.karenblixencamp.com. 22 units. Green season $590 double; high season $730 double; peak season $790 double. Children under 12 pay $205–$255 if sharing with parents. Rates include all meals, tea and coffee, 2 game drives per day, and airstrip transfers. MC, V. **Amenities:** Restaurant; bar; airstrip transfers; pool. *In room:* Minibar.

Kicheche Mara Camp With no fences and a general sense of impacting the natural environment as little as possible (thus earning it a bronze eco-rating from the Eco Tourism Society of Kenya), Kicheche offers a pleasant synthesis of real bush camping experience (with bucket showers and personal verandas that look right out into the heart of the wilderness) and many of the creature comforts that you might miss at an ordinary campsite ('round-the-clock electricity, a smartly decorated lounge, serviced accommodations, and delicious meals three times a day). Set in a beautiful, secluded spot in a grove of African olive and Euclea trees, this neatly shaded camp—just 12 large canvas tents set on raised plinths, a dining tent, an open-air library/bar, and safari chairs around the campfire—specializes in photography packages. This means there's an emphasis on providing access to the animals, and one way of ensuring that seems to be making the animals feel welcome to stroll into camp. Don't be alarmed to hear elephant and buffalo grazing outside your tent at night, while through the day you're guaranteed to have zebra on your front lawn and giraffe in the near distance—climb aboard your personal hammock and take it all in. With room for 22 guests, this may not be the most intimate camp in the Mara, but the tents provide a good sense of privacy—especially if you insist on one of the outward-facing tents ranged around the outer perimeter of the camp (these afford tantalizing views of the surrounding plains)—and most are a decent distance apart (some are closer together for families). If you're likely to panic at the first sign of a "whooping" leopard, let it be known that you want an inner-perimeter tent. For the best tent in camp, ask for Ngiri (Warthog), which is traditionally reserved for honeymooners; it is the most private and has impressive views of the plains. ***Note:*** Kicheche Mara Camp is closed April and May.

P.O. Box 1013, Nairobi 00502, Kenya. ✆ **020/89-0541** or 020/89-0358. Fax 020/89-1379. www.kicheche.com. 12 units. Green season $600 double; shoulder season $660 double; peak season $730 double. Rates include all meals, most drinks, game drives, bush walks, airstrip transfers, and laundry. No credit cards. **Amenities:** Bar; airstrip transfers.

Fun Facts Bovine Banking

Cattle—hump-backed zebu, originally bred in India—are highly revered by the Maasai and are believed to have been granted to them by their god, *Engai*. Maasai believe *Engai* created them, bestowed upon them all the cattle in the world, and only later made other human beings. It's a convenient excuse for traditional cattle-rustling, which has always been one of the Maasai warriors' favorite activities—not to mention a good reason for a little tribal warfare. So blasé are the Maasai about their relationship with their cattle that they call neighboring tribes of farmers and hunter-gatherers *Ndorobo,* a derogatory term meaning Poor Folk. Maasai measure wealth by the quantity of cattle that you own, so people without cows are considered poor—you might hear it said that their cattle are like a bank deposit kept in perpetuity, while goats (which the Maasai also own) are like a moveable ATM, easily exchanged for quick cash. Interestingly, just as you'd probably consider it rude if someone asked you how much you earn, it's considered impolite to ask a Maasai man how many cows he owns. Cattle are also the primary nutritional source, providing milk, blood, and, in certain circumstances, meat and hides. Cows are not commonly slaughtered, but are kept instead for important ceremonies; for protein, the Maasai traditionally drink cow blood as part of the diet, especially when milk is scarce (and it's sometimes mixed with milk, too). Blood is usually tapped from a vein in the living animal's neck using a tiny puncture wound that is then sealed with cow dung so it can heal, and the animal can be tapped again in the future. And just when you thought you'd heard every imaginable mad cow story, one Maasai elder told me that he was once asked to produce photographs of all his cows as part of his application for an American tourist visa.

Kichwa Tembo Masai Mara Tented Camp ★ Value Long-established Kichwa Tembo—the name translates as Head of the Elephant—might not be the most exclusive camp in the Mara (there are 40 rather tightly packed-together tents), but it makes up for its shortcomings with good value, affable service, and top-quality safari guides (the type of guides other guides follow around the park). Owned by South Africa's top-ranking safari company, &Beyond, this is a great base if you've come to see wildlife and don't mind sharing the experience with many like-minded individuals. Situated on a private concession—meaning that bush walks and night game drives are possible—these permanent tents are built on raised concrete platforms amid the trees of a dense riverine forest on the Sabaringo River. Choose between "classic" or "luxury" tents; your choice will probably come down to budget, but the upgraded luxury tents are considerably smarter, raised off the ground on stilts, and accessed via wooden bridges over the river—if you opt for one of these, 37 to 40 are slightly more exclusive, with fewer tents clustered together (and 40 is the most private of all). They also have in-room power points, so you can recharge your batteries in your tent, but there's an abiding lack of in-room character. The best-positioned tents are actually the "classic" tents arranged along edge of the forest facing a wide lawn and the vast plains beyond (there are 14 of these and worth requesting). The drawbacks here have much to do with the age and size of the property—tents (especially those tucked into the thickest part of the forest) tend to be a bit gloomy, and noise from neighboring tents can be extremely intrusive.

There's something of an '80s resort ambience here, and if you're up for a bit of a party atmosphere, that's doable, too. Although the property is fenced off (largely to prevent elephants from destroying the forest), warthogs graze nonstop and exotic monkeys clamber in the branches overhead—take time to look for them. Laze at the pool, caught up in the views across the plains, or join fellow guests for post–game drive barbecue lunches served alfresco on the lawn. Evening meals can be pretty lavish—fresh seafood from the coast, salads tossed to order, and a repertoire of recipes garnered from &Beyond's experienced chefs. When the Migration makes its meandering way across the Kichwa Tembo concession, you can fill the entire day with a single, prolonged game drive (a picnic lunch will be packed for you).

Private Bag X27, Benmore, Johannesburg 2010, South Africa. ✆ **11/809-4441.** Fax 11/809-4400. In the U.S.: ✆ 888/882-3742 toll-free. Fax 305/221-3223. www.andbeyond.com. 40 units. Low season $400 classic double, $600 luxury double; midseason $570 classic double, $770 luxury double; high season $780 classic double, $950 luxury double. Rates include all meals and game-viewing activities. MC, V. **Amenities:** Restaurant; bar; Internet; pool. *In room:* Hair dryer (in luxury tents).

Little Governors' Camp ★★ (Value) The adventure begins before you arrive—a ferryman pulls you across the Mara River in a small boat, and once on the other side, you're constantly aware of the presence of wildlife. Unfenced and untamed, despite the sprawling permanent encampment of comfortable tents, justifiably famous Little Governors' is ranged at the edge of a permanent swamp that draws a remarkable variety and intensity of animals. Near-tame warthogs perpetually trim the lawns, and I've had a family of elephants tearing up the swamp grass right in front of my tent's veranda (guest security is a priority, so you should have little need to fret). Folks who own and run the Governors' properties—the Grammaticus dynasty—are perhaps a little snooty about their privileged location, in the center of some of the best game-viewing terrain in the Mara (they've got all kinds of exclusive rights, thanks to a longstanding arrangement with a local Maasai landowner); truth is, they can probably afford to have attitude, because their camps are consistently voted among the best places to stay in the world (although if you prefer a sense of exclusivity, you'll be better off at Il Moran, next door). The BBC filmed its *Big Cat Diary* series nearby (which can mean having to put up with endless conversations obsessing over intimate details of the show), and Little Governors' is the launch site of the best balloon safari outfit in the Mara (see "Up, Up & Away," on p. 183).

P.O. Box 48217, 00100 Nairobi. ✆ **020/273-4000.** Fax 020/273-4023 or -24. www.governorscamp.com. 17 units. Green season $574 double; midseason $882 double; high season $1,014 double. Children under 16 pay about 65% of the adult rate. Rates include all meals, local airstrip transfers, and 3 game drives per day. AE, MC, V. **Amenities:** Bar; airstrip transfers.

Ngare Serian ★★★ Across the river from his longer-established Serian Camp (reviewed later in this chapter), legendary safari guide Alex Walker has upped the ante with this smart four-tent waterside camp that oozes charm and delivers luxury on top of an incredibly intimate bush experience. Unless you arrive by helicopter, access is either via a one-person-at-a-time swing bridge or (for anyone who's the least bit nervous) by boat. Either way, you arrive at one of the most tastefully presented tented camps in the Mara—simple, laid-back, beautiful, and arranged to take maximum advantage of the riverside setting, hippos popping in and out of view all day. Accommodations are in large, pale canvas tents draped over multilevel wooden platforms that extend toward the

Moments **Up, Up & Away . . .**

Soaring across the savannah, sometimes so close to the ground that you swear you could reach out and touch the trees and animals below, a **balloon safari** ★★★ is the ultimate predawn adrenaline rush. Floating over the plains and above the forest that straddles the Mara River, you get an entirely unexpected perspective on this animal-rich world, particularly enchanting during the Great Migration, when sightings of lion, hyena, and other predators are all but guaranteed. Taking off as the sun starts to rise, check-in time is 5:30am, and that means making a *very* early start—particularly if you're traveling from a faraway lodge or camp. Based at Little Governors', **Governors' Balloon Safaris** ★★★ (✆ **020/273-4000;** www.governorscamp.com) offer the finest balloon trip. Flight time is usually 1 hour, culminating with a champagne breakfast in the open grassland, complete with Maasai chefs preparing pancakes to order. The all-inclusive cost (with transfers that include a game drive en route back to your lodge) is between $394 and $435 (highest during the Migration and Christmas/New Year period) per person; kids under 12 pay $207 to $218.

Note: Be warned that, during the Migration, you should reserve your place when you book your accommodations because demand frequently outstrips availability—in 2007, when a record 10,000 people were flown above the Mara River, the company turned away hundreds of disappointed would-be passengers.

river's edge; from your bedroom, you step down into an open-plan bathroom area with shower *and* a tub just a few feet from the river. Your large, private lounge deck is furnished with sofas and rugs so you can lean back and take in the unfathomable soap opera orchestrated by the sociable families of honking and snorting hippos down below. When you feel like engaging in a bit of socializing yourself, relax in the breezy mess tent—theatrically designed like someone's posh lounge, it's decorated with sought-after David Schaefer animal bronzes and completely open to the elements. Recline on comfy armchairs, help yourself at the bar, or engage the strikingly attired, disarming Maasai butlers in conversation. All this, and you haven't yet been out on a game drive or bush walk; all of the adventure activities available at Serian are on offer here, too, only you are always guaranteed exclusive use of a game vehicle.

2A Convent Dr., Lavington, P.O. Box 76677, 00508 Nairobi. ✆ **020/386-4565** or 020/386-4566. Fax 20/386-4567. www.serian.net. 4 units. $1,500 double; $375 per child 3–15 sharing. Rates include all meals, most drinks, park and conservation fees, all game-viewing activities, fly-camping, and laundry. No credit cards. **Amenities:** Bar; babysitting; clinic.

Richard's Camp ★ **Value** With a private airstrip right on your doorstep and the wild African bush all around you, it's pretty difficult not to imagine that you've stepped into the ultimate adventure as you settle in at this simple-but-elegant camp in the northern part of the Mara ecosystem. The eight green army-style tents—arranged around an open, tree-studded lawn—rest directly on the straw-covered ground; the plumbed-in basin, flush toilet, and safari bucket shower (you simply ask when you want hot water delivered) are built into a stone-floor bathroom, and there's 'round-the-clock solar-powered lighting. If you want to secure the only king-size bed in camp, book the honeymoon tent (no. 8).

The simplicity of the bedrooms (with small red-cedar beds, metal-frame tables, and a couple of rugs on the canvas floors) is offset by elegant, homey touches—soothing white linens, Indian block-print throws, mirror-embroidered scatter cushions—so the ambience never detracts from the fact that you're in the bush with wildlife for neighbors (another reminder will be the tracks of hippo and buffalo that you'll find in camp each morning).

Simplicity reigns in the mess tent, too—sofas are draped with white fabric, there's an open stone fireplace, and when screens are rolled up, the big, open picture "windows" frame idyllic views of the African bush. Evening meals are like dinner parties—everyone gathers to share tales of their day in the bush—usually under the stars or, when it's chilly, alongside that wonderful open fire. And for romantics, there's the chance to enjoy an open-air Victorian bath tucked away in the forest, surrounded by flickering candles and the sounds of the bush. ***Note:*** Richard's Camp is closed in May.

P.O. Box 24513, Nairobi 00502. ✆ **020/211-5453** or 0722/43-4413. www.richardscamp.com. 8 units. Reservations: The Safari and Conservation Company, P.O. Box 24576, 00502 Nairobi. ✆ 020/211-5453, 020/219-4995, 073/557-9999, or 071/257-9999. www.thesafariandconservationcompany.com. reservations@scckenya.com. High season $1,220 double, $460 per child 5–16; midseason $1,040 double, $385 per child. Under 5 free. Rates include all meals, nonpremium drinks, bush meals, day and night game drives, guided bush walks, sundowners, local airstrip transfers, laundry. AE, MC, V. **Amenities:** Bar; airstrip transfers.

Sanctuary Olonana ★ Just 10 minutes from the Oloololo Gate, beneath the Siria Escarpment, Olonana has its 14 massive tents ranged along the edge of the Mara River. Named for an important Maasai spiritual leader, the camp occupies the site of a cultural center first established here by the famed South African explorer Kingsley Holgate; it has since been transformed into a luxury establishment where guests are ensconced in vast, beautiful bedrooms; fed lavish meals; and handled with kid gloves. At one end of a long stone footpath, you're met and then led for a "briefing" (on security, animals, hot water, mealtimes) inside the mud- and dung-clad lounge. Here you'll notice a modern approximation of traditional Maasai building technique—with faux-traditional decorative paintings, large fireplaces, a library of Africana tomes, all-day bar service, and board games to pass the time. While the hippos (and occasionally crocs and even leopard) are never far away, the camp is completely fenced off, so there's little danger of an unexpected encounter.

Tents are private, with big rectangular army-style spaces set under thatch on hardwood floors and attached stone-wall bathrooms (shower only) at one end. Each one has a pair of queen-size beds; you can view the river and the opposite bank with your head on the pillow, and there's a shaded terrace out front, right over the water's edge. Hot water and electricity are available between 6 and 10am and 6 and 10pm, and there's 'round-the-clock lighting. Olonana has traditionally prided itself on being eco-friendly; all water (pumped from the Mara River to service the camp) is returned after being treated—however, drinking water is still the plastic bottle variety. Game drives explore the adjacent Mara Triangle conservancy, and sightings are usually excellent, but Olonana is also a great spot from which to stretch your legs on a bush walk (with an armed Maasai warrior for protection). Guests also get priority at the nearby Olonana-funded Maasai cultural village.

Dorland House, 4th Floor, 20 Regent St., London, U.K. ✆ **0207/190-7749.** Fax 0207/190-7751. www.sanctuaryretreats.com. 14 units. Low season $778 double; high season $1,078 double; peak season $1,556 double. Children under 12 pay 50% if sharing with at least 1 adult. Rates include all meals, all game-viewing activities, Maasai village visit, laundry, emergency medical evacuation, most beverages, and airstrip transfers. AE, MC, V. **Amenities:** Bar; airstrip transfers; pool. *In room:* Hair dryer.

Saruni Mara ★★ Living out his fantasy of exchanging a high-paced career for a life in the bush—with Maasai neighbors and daily visits by elephant and African buffalo—Italian writer–turned–lodge owner Riccardo Orizio enjoys an enviable position. He traded his life as a journalist and CNN correspondent (who's interviewed some of the world's most powerful dictators) for the enchanting, mystical rhythms of the African outback. Chat with Riccardo, and it's hard not to pick up on his enthusiasm for this rugged wilderness, particularly evident in his love for the secluded spot he chose here in the northern Mara. His luxurious six-cottage lodge clings to the gentle slope of a remote hill—a hand-picked location on a 2,000-hectare (4,940-acre) private concession above a forest of olive and cedar trees—and beneath you are sweeping views over the vast plains beneath Mount Kilileoni.

Saruni's enormous thatched cottages have a slightly experimental look that mixes locally found materials—rocks and wood felled by the elephants—with timber floors and tough, pale canvas used to create the front walls and large screen "windows" and "doors" that open onto large private terraces. Stretch out on your hammock, and you'll soon lose yourself in a view that disappears way into the distance. Or roll up the entire front "wall" and take in the scene from your huge cedar poster bed. Individually styled, bedrooms have big antique wardrobes, proper writing desks, and a chic, rustic mix of colonial antiques, Persian rugs, and African art. Bathrooms, too, are massive, stone-clad spaces with rainfall showers (water is solar-heated and fire-warmed in the morning and evening), twin basins, Italian fittings, and bidets. Reserve cottage 6 for the most secluded and romantic stay—it also has the most impressive view (2 is another favorite, but it gets some noise from staff quarters), while room 1 is best if you want to be right in the forest (which means forgoing the views).

When you're not off hunting for game, you can curl up with a book from Riccardo's well-stocked, dedicated library (the best in the Kenyan bush) or foist your gaze on the distance and watch the setting sun. Or find your way to the Maasai Wellbeing Space, a spa in the forest where imported Italian treatments have been adapted to incorporate traditional Maasai knowledge of natural therapies, resulting in some memorable original treatments. Meals—accurate interpretations of Italian dishes made from fresh, local ingredients (with Parmesan, olive oil, and balsamic vinegar always on the table)—are served at a massive dining table (crafted by the architect from disused railway sleepers) in Kuro House, where you can take predinner drinks in front of the huge open fireplace or on the deck, lording it over that mesmerising view.

P.O. Box 304, Narok, Kenya. ✆ **050/22-424** or 0734/76-4616. www.sarunicamp.com. Reservations: Cheli & Peacock, P.O. Box 743, 00517 Uhuru Gardens, Nairobi. ✆ 020/60-4054 or -4053, or 20/60-3090/91. Fax 20/60-4050. 6 units. High season $1,190 double, $440 per child 5–16 sharing; midseason $990 double, $365 per child; green season $740 double, $270 per child. Discounted rates for stays of 4 nights or more. Rates include all meals, most beverages, game-viewing activities, laundry, local airstrip transfers, 1 massage per room. AE, MC, V. **Amenities:** Bar; airstrip transfers; spa.

Serian ★★ In the Mara, Alex Walker is a bit of a legend—a filmmaker and safari guide whose knowledge of the wild is matched only by the infectious way in which he shares his love of the bush with his guests. At this intimate, rustic-chic camp, eight marquee-style tents nestle under huge walburgia and oleadendra trees along a hippo-filled stretch of the Mara River in a valley beneath the Siria escarpment. Bedrooms—furnished in comfortable colonial style with metal-frame beds and swaths of billowing cotton, white fabrics, and textured linens—have a faintly Moroccan flavor; they're set on grass-covered hardwood decks with private verandas and rugged open-to-the-elements

Moments Deep in the Bush

An appendix to Saruni's luxurious lodge is its satellite bush camp, **Campi ya Tembo** ★ ($640–$990 double, all-inclusive), some 14km (8¾ miles) away. Secreted away in a peaceful acacia grove, here's where the emphasis shifts away from luxury to the genuine thrill of being right in the thick of things—at this secluded camp, you're quite literally in the bush. With just three big beige, no-frills canvas tents, this is a good base for anyone looking to experience the African bush on more or less its own terms. I say "no-frills," but you actually get plenty of in-room comfort, including indoor plumbing (with hot and cold running water and flush toilets) and excellent handcrafted cedar beds. Guests share a common mess tent furnished with a couple of comfy sofas, small dining area, and full bar—but little else. Poke your head out of your tent, and you're eye level with the bush—although game drives and bush walks are thrilling (taking in valley, forest, and mountain scenery), you can just as easily stay in camp, pondering the busy world that's all around you—elephants and buffalo are among Campi ya Tembo's frequent visitors. This is also an ideal place to spy animals that prefer making their appearance at night—leopard, genets, white-tailed mongoose, and greater galago are all regulars in and around the camp. You're certain to be awakened in the middle of the night by the very sounds you've come to Africa to experience. By day, one of the special attractions here is the chance to skip a game drive and instead practice bush survival skills with a Maasai, or learn the art of animal tracking. Booking details are the same as those for Saruni Mara (reviewed earlier in this chapter).

bathrooms with showers and sunken bathtubs. There's a tremendous sense of being at one with nature here—in fact, if you're the slightest bit squeamish, you may have difficulty imagining that you won't find animals sharing your bed, and it seems that no matter where you are in the camp, you'll be aware of the river rushing by; one of the tents (no. 6) sits right on the lip of the water, in fact, affording eye-level views of the hippos not only from your private deck, but from every part of the bathroom.

Nights (and days) here are exhilarating; sand pathways amid knee-high grass make this a perfect location for leopard, and with candle-lit lanterns instead of electrical lighting, there's a magical ambience once the sun goes down. Days can be packed with quality game drives or the chance to walk in the bush with Maasai warriors who will even teach you to work with a bow and arrow—or you can opt to overnight in the wild on a fly-camping excursion. You could even choose to sleep under the stars on a specially built deck on the escarpment across the river.

Walker also operates a mobile camp consisting of five "Selous-style" tents with simple furnishings and en suite long-drop toilets and bucket showers; rented on an exclusive basis, the camp can travel to just about anywhere in Kenya.

2A Convent Dr., Lavington. P.O. Box 76677, 00508 Nairobi. ✆ **020/386-4565** or 020/386-4566. Fax 020/386-4567. www.serian.net. 8 units. $1,580 double; $280 per child 3–15 if sharing with 2 adults. Rates include all meals, most drinks, park and conservation fees, all game-viewing activities, fly-camping, and laundry. No credit cards. **Amenities:** Bar; airstrip and local transfers; babysitting; Internet; on-call clinic.

Central Mara

Although far less exclusive, the larger lodges in and around the Mara Reserve will definitely put a smaller dent in your wallet. If you can overlook the potential intrusiveness of having up to 200 fellow guests sharing your interaction with the wilderness, then by all means consider the sprawling **Masai Mara Sopa Lodge** (✆ **020/375-0235;** www.sopalodges.com), which consists of rondawels designed in approximation of a rural village. The drawback, of course, is that there will inevitably be more guests than you'll find in a typical Kenyan village. Nestling in the not-too-shabby Oloolaimutia Valley, not too far from the Ngama Hills where some of the Mara's best rhino sightings happen, there are 100 rooms, a pool, and three different bars, making it feel more like a budget resort than a safari getaway. Still, if you cleverly redirect your expenditure toward renting a private vehicle and skilled driver-guide, you could get away from the human traffic for most of your stay. Doubles here start at $245, including all meals (everything else is extra, including all safari activities), and you're usually able to secure one of the family-size suites at no additional cost. Considering that the property is fenced in, this can be a very good option if you're traveling with children. (There are no restrictions on age here, which may not be the case at many of the more intimate camps.)

Kicheche Bush Camp ★ **Value** Privacy really makes all the difference at this fantastically remote camp in the Olare Orok Conservancy. Human visitor numbers are strictly controlled, so you won't see quite so many vehicles careening around here. By contrast, wildlife numbers are good and resultant sightings can be extraordinary. Generously spread out, Kicheche's six enormous canvas tents occupy an exposed acacia grove, each one facing into the bush so as to take full advantage of potential sightings (which you'll experience not only from your private veranda, but from the attached bathrooms, too). Something about Kicheche makes it particularly easy to get caught up in a reverie as you're struck by the immediacy of the bush and the intimacy of the experience. For the city dweller, time here can be powerful and overwhelming; it's the kind of place where, should you leave your shoes outside on the porch, they'll likely be stolen by lions! In fact, a large lion pride lives nearby, and there are regular sightings of kills both in camp and in the immediate vicinity.

But there's plenty to take the edge off, too. Amiable, bush-savvy hosts look after you like guests in their own home, and the camp's chefs ensure that you're well fed; dining is around a communal table—often alfresco, and with a chance to sample African dishes (just ask if you'd like to steer away from straight-laced European cuisine)—or opt for a completely private mealtime experience; say the word, and a secluded spot in the bush becomes your dining room. ***Note:*** Kicheche Bush Camp closes in April and May and for around 2 weeks in November.

P.O. Box 1013, Nairobi 00502, Kenya. ✆ **020/89-0541** or 020/89-0358. Fax 020/89-1379. www.kicheche.com. 6 units. Green season $680 double; shoulder season $750 double; peak season $830 double. Rates include all meals, most drinks, game drives, bush walks, airstrip transfers, and laundry. No credit cards. **Amenities:** Bar; airstrip transfers.

Mara Explorer ★★ Ranged along the banks of the Talek, this attractive, straight-laced, unfenced camp feels pretty much as though it's on an island—the river snakes its way almost entirely around the property. Taking full advantage of the river's-edge location, each tent has a different view of its sandy beaches, rock pools, and flowing waters. Designers of the 10 well-secluded tents—on hardwood floors and backed by brick-and-mortar bathrooms—have opted for "African chic" interiors with mahogany furniture,

Moments The Mara from the Saddle

With a reputation as one of Kenya's top safari operators, Tristan Voorspuy, once a rider with the British Cavalry, runs expeditions for riders keen to encounter African wildlife on horseback. With action-packed 10-day itineraries that include more than a week in the Mara, these are highly recommended, but only for saddle-fit, relatively experienced riders. The journey includes morning and evening rides, and one marathon day in which you travel 50km (31 miles) on approach to the Mara ecosystem. Accommodations are in different mobile tented camps, some of them on the banks of the Mara, and the journey ends with 2 nights at Deloraine, the Voorspuy's posh colonial mansion where royalty were once entertained and where their 80-or-so horses are stabled. While there, you can take a day-trip to see rhino and flamingoes at Lake Nakuru or to see the steaming geysers at Lake Bogoria, and cap off the day with more horseback exploration. Come prepared for a backside-challenging adventure—but know that the discomfort is offset by the prospect of galloping among herds of zebra, eyeball-to-eyeball encounters with giraffe, and the epic vistas as you reach the top of the escarpments. Add to that a couple of optional game drives—for better views of elephant, buffalo, lion, and other predators best not encountered at close quarters on horseback—and you have the makings of an unforgettable wilderness experience (certainly, your butt and thighs won't forget). A 10-day Mara safari, which includes 8 days in the Mara and 2 nights at Deloraine, as well as transfers at either end of your trip, costs £3,600; there are just nine departures per year (Jan–Oct), so it's worth signing up as early as possible. Or, if you'd prefer to go your own way, you can organize a customized horse safari, and there are a handful of trips that cover other animal-rich parts of Kenya. To book, contact **Offbeat Safaris** (P.O. Box 1146, Nanyuki 10400; ✆ **054/623-1081;** www.offbeatsafaris.com).

hand-woven rugs, and faux-antique ornaments, all in sober shades of brown and orange with plenty of geometric patterns. A king-size bed, writing desk, wicker-and-wood planter's chairs, and bedside tables fashioned from tree stumps complete the ensemble. Have the butler prepare your open-air Victorian-design bath while you're out on a game drive and return for a relaxing soak on your private deck while watching submerged hippos wallowing beneath your feet; for the best sightings, book tent 4 (Ne'e). Tents are supplied with books on Kenyan wildlife and *kikois.* Meals are usually taken on the large deck (also over the edge of the river) that extends from the open-fronted library/lounge and bar area, also with an Africana theme. But do insist on at least one meal out in the bush, where you have every chance of spotting a different beast with each course that's laid on.

Heritage Management Ltd., P.O. Box 74888, Nairobi 00200. ✆ **020/444-6651** or 020/444-4585. Fax 020/444-6600. www.heritage-eastafrica.com. 10 units. Low season $952 double; high season $1,187 double; peak season $1,327 double. Rates include all meals, 3 game drives per day, airstrip transfers, bush breakfast and dinner, bush walk, laundry, most drinks. MC, V. **Amenities:** Restaurant; bar; airstrip transfers; pool (at Mara Intrepids); currency exchange; on-site doctor.

Mara Intrepids Value With decent-sized tents and little private balconies facing the Talek River, there are plenty of allusions to luxury here. The neat, comfortable, simple canvas spaces are sleek and kitted out with wood floors, back-supporting beds, indoor plumbing, hot running water, wardrobes, dressing tables, writing desks, plenty of mirrors, and power outlets (frustratingly absent in many of the Mara's tented camps). Intrepids ultimately provides a sensation of cosseted bush life (albeit behind an ugly, unhidden electric fence) rather than the real thing, but that won't necessarily detract from the chance to appreciate the scene by the river (reserve tents 1–12 for the best views), shake your shoulders in rhythm to the evening Maasai warrior performances, or spend most of your day out in the Reserve witnessing the ongoing drama on the plains. The downside here—potentially forgivable, given the relatively bargain prices on offer—is that it's hard to get away from the buzz of fellow guests; whether you can hear them in the (very) nearby neighboring tent, or amassed around the breakfast buffet, or view them tanning at the pool while trying to enjoy your lunch. And it's hard not to be offended by some of the tackiness here—a shop cluttered with cheap souvenirs and evidence everywhere (starting in the unkempt reception office) that, despite overhauled accommodations, the property (running since 1985) has seen better days.

Heritage Management Ltd., P.O. Box 74888, Nairobi 00200. ✆ **020/444-6651** or 020/444-4585. Fax 20/444-6600. www.heritage-eastafrica.com. 30 units. Low season $566 double, $140 per child under 13 when sharing with 2 adults; high season $941 double, $235 per child; peak season $1,053 double, $263 per child. Rates include all meals, 3 game drives per day, airstrip transfers, bush meals, bush walks, laundry, most drinks. MC, V. **Amenities:** Restaurant; bar; airstrip transfers; pool; in-house doctor.

Naibor & Little Naibor ★★ Kiswahili for Space and Simplicity, Naibor is stylish and elegant enough to suggest that its creators took inspiration from both meanings of the word. The brainchild of Anthony Russell—whose first such project, Shompole (p. 146), is among Kenya's most prestigious—this tented camp owes much of its charm to a striking position in a riverine grove of yellow-bark acacias along the edge of the Talek. In addition to being just a short drive from one of the Mara's famed Migration river crossings, you need not budge from your shaded veranda as you take in the wildlife action. Animals perpetually come down to the river to drink and, in the case of elephants, shower themselves with water slurped up with their trunks. Feeling super lazy? Thanks to "walls" that you can zip open entirely, you can watch the scene without putting a foot outside your spacious, earth-toned bedroom. Location aside, the eye-catching, easy design of the camp and the breezy, spacious tents also work their magic—it's a traditional camp experience with a decidedly up-to-date ambience with huge fig-wood beds, soft quilts, sofas with plumped bolster cushions, and a decidedly uncluttered look; so what if you can't plug in your hair dryer or need to ask when you want hot water for your safari shower?

Although you'll never forget that you're in the bush—and in the wilds (the chorus of birdsong and the scene at the river will never let you forget)—you can enhance the experience with a game-drive picnic or by choosing to dine under the stars at night. Unlike experiences at many of the big, impersonal lodges, there's plenty here to break the monotony of daily routine—the camp's intimacy is complemented by the convivial, laid-back atmosphere—and you're perfectly fine taking time away from game viewing for a rejuvenating massage, or simply kicking back in your hammock, listening for baboons as they try to raid the kitchen, or getting active on a mountain bike excursion.

Looking for complete escape from humanity? **Little Naibor** is a private camp with just two tents and your own lounge, dining area, bar, and dedicated staffers. All your game drives will be thoroughly exclusive, with your own vehicle, guide, and made-to-order

Africa's Lost Tribe, Part II

Perceptions about the Maasai abound in the Western imagination, possibly because, as a people, they fit so readily into the role of the exoticized other. Dark, mysterious, eccentrically costumed, and defiantly adhering to strange customs and primitive superstitions, they're a people who legitimize foreign interpretations of who and what Africans are. Regarding the Maasai as "noble savages" has long been the outsiders' approach to a people who for so long clung to ancient ways even in the face of rapidly encroaching modernity. Hemingway accorded the Maasai a kind of "ignorant" dignity, referring to them in his *Green Hills of Africa as* "the tallest, best-built, handsomest people I had ever seen and the first truly light-hearted people I had seen in Africa"—despite his overt bigotry toward native Africans, he was undeniably awed by the people of Maasailand. Another Western observer, the Danish author Karen Blixen (Isak Dinesen), positively fell over herself in praise of the Maasai in her famous novel, *Out of Africa*. "A Maasai warrior is a fine sight," she wrote. "Those young men have, to the utmost extent, that particular form of intelligence which we call chic; daring and wildly fantastical as they seem, they are still unswervingly true to their own nature, and to an immanent ideal. Their style is not an assumed manner, nor an imitation of a foreign perfection; it has grown from the inside, and is an expression of the race and its history, and their weapons and finery are as much a part of their being as are a stag's antlers." Yes, outsiders are quick to idealize and romanticize.

Their physicality aside, it's difficult to pinpoint the source of their attraction. Perhaps it's their elegant simplicity—as pastoralists, they have traditionally wanted for little and have measured wealth in terms of their cattle and children. There's always been a certain grace with which the Maasai tread upon the earth—their semi-nomadic lifestyle has meant that they frown upon agriculture, and by eschewing individual land ownership, they have tended toward a zero-impact lifestyle, leaving little trace of their presence when they relocated their semi-permanent *enkang* (a corral of dung and clay huts) to new grounds. Until recently, Maasai did not have villages with permanent buildings, but would periodically abandon their *enkang* and construct a new, equally biodegradable one with better water and grazing. These days, the nomadic life is increasingly substituted with tin-roof houses and small villages centered on schools, clinics, and shops.

Modernity has brought attempts to impose external law and order on this tenacious, clannish, traditionally war-mongering tribe. When they first arrived in Kenya, it was their ferocity and skill in battle that marked them out as a superior race—not only thwarting their enemies, but rustling cattle with remarkable skill, establishing their reputation as a people not to be trifled with. But contemporary legislation has banned the warring, illegalized cattle theft and, as far as possible, tried to prevent customary social practices. Until quite recently, part of the ritual by which a Maasai boy would achieve warrior *(moran)* status was to single-handedly kill a lion with his spear—it was as essential as circumcision. But the Kenyan government has put an end to that, not to mention making warriorhood illegal. Already the classic *moran* is under threat; these days they're often "warriors" in name and appearance only, posing for photographs and dressing the part to satisfy expectations at safari lodges.

Maasai males are rigidly classed by age into categories defining them as boys, warriors, or elders, and they must pass through various intricate rituals in order to move up through the ranks. Despite the horror imagined by outsiders at the thought of the male circumcision ceremony—during which the boys are forbidden from showing one jot of pain, lest they be labeled cowards and their family disgraced—it's rite of passage that many young boys eagerly anticipate, so keen are they to enjoy the rewards and status that go with becoming a *moran*. Later, when their warriorhood expires, they will undergo another ceremony as they become elders, during which their mothers will shave off their long locks of hair—ironically, it is during this ritual stripping of one kind of privileged lifestyle (warriors are the pride and joy of the community and, by many accounts, carry on like playboys) that makes many men break down in tears.

Experts claim that the system of age grades that is at the core of Maasai culture won't endure. Many traditional practices will disappear long before this century is up, they say. To outsiders, of course, some of these practices are intrinsically barbaric. Many are quick to squirm when they learn of the Maasai practice of leaving the dead (and the very old) to be devoured by hyenas rather than buried. And the discourse around female circumcision (derided by Westerners as "female genital mutilation") remains one of Africa's biggest human rights battles. Maasai girls are summarily forced to endure this painful, anesthetic-free procedure—before being married off to a much older man, usually while they themselves have barely hit puberty. Some would argue that these women (who are responsible for most of the work, including the building of homes), never attain any rights whatsoever, and there's a deep sense of patriarchal dominance in a polygamous society where the men are virtually always the ones seen enjoying life—notably in the company of other men. In fact, one of the Maasai's more pusillanimous superstitions is that it's bad luck for women to witness men eating meat. Yet when it comes to pregnant women, even one of the strongest Maasai taboos—a ban on eating wild animal flesh—may be broken in order to ensure that mother and child are adequately nourished.

The Maasai have slowly adapted some of their ways to meet the challenges of a life increasingly regulated by a central government that is overtly dismissive of tribal ways and eager to modernize, even at the expense of cultural identity. Nevertheless, they remain fiercely bound by their traditions—as one Maasai elder who has toured the U.S. and been to the U.K. told me of his experiences there: "At least now I know why they come here . . . they have lost their culture." This from one of the most gentle, civil, and honorable men I've ever known—yet James, who is never without his red tunic, tartan-design *shuka,* and short dagger, wears a wristwatch, dotes upon his mobile phone, and consults his notebook computer virtually every night. It remains to be seen how much of his culture will be left by the time his children are old enough to appreciate the significance of their unique heritage.

itineraries. ***Note:*** Naibor is closed April, May, and November, and a minimum 2-night stay is required.

The Art of Ventures, P.O. Box 10665, 00100 Nairobi. ✆ **020/204-8610** or -8621. Fax 020/88-4135. www.shompole.com. Naibor: 6 units. Little Naibor: 2 units. Naibor: Peak season $1,100 double; high season $870. Little Naibor: Peak season $1,380 double; high season $1,150 double. Children 8–12 pay 35% when sharing with 2 adults; 50% discount for under 8. Rates include all meals, most drinks, game-viewing activities, bush meals and sundowners, local airstrip transfers, and laundry. MC, V. **Amenities:** Bar; airstrip transfers; babysitting; Internet; spa.

Ol Seki Mara Camp ★★★ Perched high on rocky cliffs with epic views over vast plains cut through by the Il Supukiai River, Ol Seki (appropriately named after a Maasai symbol of peace, the sandpaper tree) occupies one of the Mara's most dazzling locations. Built on sound eco-friendly principles by veteran safari operators who understand the fragile balance between tourism and environment, the camp blends neatly into the surrounding bush, shot through with dazzling plant, bird, and animal life. Modern, cosseting spaces set among acacia and cordia trees, the tents don't get much lovelier or light filled than the voluptuous cream-colored structures erected here—each 12-sided unit is raised on a large wooden platform that extends around your living quarters like a floating veranda. Simply, elegantly furnished, your living space includes a large sleeping area (a double bed plus extra sofa bed suitable for a small child), a dressing area with ample packing space, and a handsome bathroom. With a sleek, streamlined finish in predominantly neutral tones, the design is fairly contemporary—crisp white linens, brown throws and matching cushions, an antique-style trunk, a pair of foldable director's chairs, and large drapes against canvas walls that can be zipped open entirely to allow better access to the expansive views.

By day, you have the chance to explore the wilds with one of Kenya's few female guides, or ask to be guided on foot in the Bardamat Hills—a boon for anyone with botanical interests. Or pay your respects to a cave once used by members of the Il Ndorobo tribe, an outing sure to deepen your cultural awareness as much as a visit to a nearby Maasai *enkang,* surprisingly unspoiled by modern tourism. And if all that sounds like simply too much hard work, stop by the massage tent and tune into the call of the wild as your muscles are given a restorative going-over. Before slinking off to dinner, hit the library/lounge for sundowners and catch 360-degree views as the sun sinks below the horizon. ***Note:*** Ol Seki's new owners, Cathy and Leo Giovando, are planning to install a pool in 2010 and have recently added two family tents, each with two double rooms and a private dining deck.

Reservations: Uncharted Outposts, 9 Village Lane, Santa Fe, NM 87505, USA. ✆ **505/795-7710.** Fax 505/795-7714. www.unchartedoutposts.com. Local contact: Bush&Beyond, P.O. Box 56923, Nairobi, 00200. ✆ **020/60-0457** or 020/60-5980. Fax 020/60-5008. www.bush-and-beyond.com or www.olseki.com. 6 units. Regular season $1,600 double, $1,300 suite, $200–$325 per child under 12 when sharing with 2 adults; premium season $1,220 double, 1,520 suite, $305–380 per child. Rates include all meals, soft drinks, beer, house wine, shared game drives, shared night game drives, guided walks, cultural visits, laundry, and local airstrip transfers. No credit cards. **Amenities:** Bar; airstrip transfers.

Rekero ★★★ As you approach this riverside camp in the center of the Mara, you can just make out the tips of one of the discreetly tucked away beige tents. Born of a line of pioneering conservationists whose family arrived in Kenya in 1889, Gerard Beaton—along with his Maasai business partner, Saigilu Ole "Jackson" Looseyia—has selected what is possibly the prime campsite in the entire Mara. Here, instead of driving around after the migrating herds, you watch the animals tackle a key river crossing point while enjoying your breakfast on a verge overlooking the Talek. The same shallow stretch of river—forming rocky pools in the riverbed of quartz and mica—completes the view for each of the secluded, utterly private tents. Accommodations are in simple, authentic bush canvas with few frills or urban excesses. But that doesn't mean you forgo comfort. There's on-demand hot water for safari showers, throne-like bush toilets, and jugs of water for brushing teeth (with eco-friendly spittoons)—but other than the spruce beds and neatly maintained space, the only concessions to luxury reside in the exceptional location, impeccable service, and unbeatable guiding. For a top-class wildlife interaction—along with unabashed insight into Maasai culture—request Tuleto "James" Sengeny as your guide; he's as fabulous a gentleman as he is a skilled interpreter of all that happens in the bush (with a cool wit and humbling manner that doesn't hurt, either).

Rekero is not for the squeamish—nor those who'd prefer to be surrounded by concrete walls—as there is no fence, animals come and go at will, and the intoxicating (and, for some, frightening) sensation of being in the wilds is an ongoing reality. And with only solar lanterns and kerosene lamps to light them at night, the tents retain a true sense of what being in the bush is all about. However, with three superb meals each day and effortless attention from your hosts, it's a far cry from "roughing it," and there's excellent 'round-the-clock camp security. ***Note:*** Rekero is closed April, May, and November.

Reservations: Uncharted Outposts, 9 Village Lane, Santa Fe, NM 87505, USA. © **505/795-7710.** Fax 505/795-7714. www.unchartedoutposts.com. Local contact: Bush&Beyond, P.O. Box 56923, Nairobi, 00200. © 020/60-0457 or 020/60-5980. Fax 020/60-5008. www.bush-and-beyond.com or www.rekero camp.com. 8 units. Regular season $1,060 double, $265 per child under 12; premium season $1,220 double, $305 per child; green season $800 double, $200 per child. Rates include all meals, soft drinks, beer, house wine, shared game drives, laundry, and local airstrip transfers. No credit cards. **Amenities:** Bar; airstrip transfers; Internet.

Southern Mara

Cottar's 1920s Safari Camp ★★★ Kids If you want to track the safari bloodline, it's said, you go to Cottar's. Twenties' trailblazers, the Cottar clan has been referred to as the First Family of the safari business—they were among the first to import safari cars to Kenya and started the first fixed camps in the country. A pioneering American who became a wildlife cinematographer, Charles Cottar moved to Kenya in 1911, inspired by the hunting exploits of Teddy Roosevelt. He established Cottar's Safari Service in 1919 and was later killed while filming rhinos—such are the danger-in-the-wilds safari tales you're likely to hear around the dinner table here, where you're reminded at every turn of a bygone era. Drinks around the campfire and candlelit dinners are served by waiters kitted out in elegant costume—a smart waistcoat over a full-length *kanzu* (Swahili tunic), finished off with a crimson fez—designed to nostalgically recall the colonial past. Fourth-generation Calvin Cottar, who set up the current camp in 1996, raided the family stores and dug out loads of beautiful vintage pieces. The main mess tent is adorned with family portraits, North African rugs, silver hipflasks, yesteryear hunting trophies, telescopes, binoculars, ancient typewriters, tapestry cushions, original safari traveling gear, and all kinds of eccentric colonial bric-a-brac arranged to create a homey, vintage ambience.

The tented accommodations are beautiful and private—families with children have an entire wing of two-bedroom suites to themselves, while couples get large, lovely white canvas tents. Each one has an attached stone-wall bathroom with antique toilet and dressing area. Billowing mosquito nets are draped over the huge four-poster beds and sumptuous linens, more for effect than anything else, since the bloodsuckers don't survive at this altitude. When you're not off exploring the wilderness, pull up a rocking chair on your private porch, help yourself from a decanter of port, and watch as animals graze their way across the lawn. During a 2007 safari-themed *Vogue* fashion shoot, actress Keira Knightley wrote that "Cottar's is like something out of a fairytale." Never more so than at night, when the entire camp is lit up with candles and lanterns, transformed into its most romantic avatar.

Reservations: Cheli & Peacock, P.O. Box 743, 00517 Uhuru Gardens, Nairobi. ✆ **020/60-4054** or 020/60-3090. Fax 020/60-4050. www.chelipeacock.com or www.cottars.com. 10 units. High season $1,560 double, $550 per child 3–12 sharing with 2 adults, $2,800 suite; midseason $1,340 double, $480 per child, $2,400 suite; green season $980 double, $280 per child, $1,600 suite. Rates include all meals, most drinks, 1 massage per tent, night and day game drives, bush walks, laundry, fishing, bush meals, and sundowners, Cottar's airstrip transfers. MC, V. **Amenities:** Bar; airstrip transfers; pool; spa.

2 LAKE VICTORIA

130km (80 miles) NW of Masai Mara

On approach to Lake Victoria, flying in over the Mau Escarpment or from the nearby Masai Mara, the view from above is exhilarating, a series of undulating topographical features evolved over millions of years and, in recent times, greatly impacted by humanity. Keep your eyes trained on the scene below, and you could witness vast swaths of tea-covered hills around Kericho, a gigantic archaeological site resembling the stone fortress of Great Zimbabwe, the almost perfectly circular crater lake of Simbi not far from the lakeshore village of Kendu Bay, ancient plugged-up volcanic cones piercing the vast green landscape, and the predictably ugly, smoke-spewing sugar mills that never quite succeed in blighting the scene. But nothing quite prepares you for the sheer vastness of the lake itself, its calm, flat surface melting into the distant horizon.

When the Luo people who settled these parts arrived some 500 years ago, Africa's largest freshwater lake was called Ukerewe. It was "discovered" by Europeans only in 1858, by John Hanning Speke (on one of those epic quests to find the source of the Nile), who immediately renamed it in honor of his queen. Although Kenya's portion of the 70,000-sq.-km (27,300-sq.-mile) lake is negligible, it was here, on Rusinga Island in 1948, that Mary Leakey caused a global stir when she unearthed the last common ancestor of the great apes and humans, *Proconsul Heseloni,* then one of the world's most significant archaeological discoveries. Meanwhile, on larger, little-visited Mfangano Island, prehistoric cave paintings are just one distraction, in addition to watching fish eagles, monkeys, and dog-paddling monitor lizards.

In this corner of the lake, there's room enough to sample the type of languid tropical lifestyle that you might have thought existed only in postcards and movies. Cruise the waters, and you'll be inundated with scenes of bucolic island activity. Uninhibited children wave as they cast a line from the rocks, stark-naked villagers bathe at the water's edge, and fishermen work their nets from their dhows and canoes. The latter are on the hunt for enormous Nile perch—in extreme cases, reaching up to 250kg (550 lbs.)—an introduced species that sustains the lake's lucrative fishing industry but has been responsible for the extinction of countless smaller, more beautiful tropical fish that had evolved here over many millennia. The lake has had its fair share of problems—prolonged drought from 2002 through 2005 caused the water level to drop considerably, a crisis much compounded by the construction of an artificial lake in Uganda. In a positive turnaround, the lake has risen some 15cm (6 in.) since 2006.

Ecological doom and gloom aside, there's every chance that, during your visit to the lake, you'll have the opportunity to sample freshly caught perch, as well as the local specialty, tilapia, also a favorite among the Luo fishermen. Stare across the water at night, witnessing the surface lit by twinkling lights of these fishermen, and it's hard not to be won over. Easily, you could wile away the days simply counting off the inestimable numbers of birds—from majestic fish eagles to tiny iridescent sunbirds and lightning-fast kingfishers—many not found elsewhere in Kenya. With so much focus on big game action in other parts of the country and the relative absence of tourists on these shores, this is a fitting place to experience a very different sort of Kenya.

ESSENTIALS

ORIENTATION Kenya's wedge of Lake Victoria—shaped a bit like a fallen T—stretches from its unmarked border with Uganda, which cuts through the water in the west, to the lakeside town of Kisumu (Kenya's third-largest city) on the far eastern shore of Winam Gulf. The principal points of interest—Mfangano and Rusinga islands—are to the west, close to the Ugandan border. These islands offer the best opportunity in

Tips Luo Basics

There's no hardship raising a smile from Lake Victoria's friendly Luo population—they're an open people who seem happy to share their knowledge, history, and political opinions (perhaps more so now that they have a man in the White House). The Luo people you speak to here are descendents of a migrating group that settled on Victoria's shores after driving away or overwhelming the Bantu-speaking groups and primitive hunter-gatherers who had been living here—that was around 500 years ago. They absorbed many of the cultural influences of the people they encountered, invaded, and married, ultimately giving up their nomadic cattle-rustling for a more settled life of fishing and farming. During the 20th century, they endured what can only be described as a period of enforced development during which heavy-handed tactics were used to encourage colonial-style education and "progressive" behavior. Their language (and many of their traditions) is strongly related to those of the people of southern Sudan, from whence the Luo's ancestors migrated several centuries ago. Armed with just a few basic words (to demonstrate your keen interest), you'll easily strike up a conversation (which will hopefully quickly revert to English) that'll help you more readily get under the skin of the culture. Use these to get started:

Hello	*Naadé*	(nay-day)
Good morning	*Oyawre*	(oh-yah-ray)
Good evening	*Oimore*	(oh-eem-oh-ray)
How are you?	*Musawa*	(moo-sah-wa)
Goodbye	*Oriti*	(oh-ri-tee)
Thank you	*Erokamano*	(eh-ro-koman-oh)

One word of caution, though. Given the fierce rivalry between the Luo and Kenya's dominant tribe, the Kikuyu, you'd do well to refrain from using Luo to address the wrong person—at best, you'll be snubbed for your awkward cultural assumptions.

Kenya to appreciate Victoria's mellow charms. By contrast, Kisumu (the main point of arrival for the region) is a strange mixture of heady market town and dull civility, and most of the villages around the lakeshore have little to recommend them—most noticeably, a lack of decent accommodations.

GETTING THERE **By Air** Visitors destined for Mfangano Island Camp get priority on the private Governors' air charters from the Masai Mara direct to the eponymous island; from the airstrip, a waiting motorized boat transports you to the camp (owned by the well-established Governors' group). Alternatively, you can access either of the two lake lodges by private air charter, commencing in Nairobi (80 min.), the Masai Mara (35 min.), or Kisumu (20 min.); your lodge or tour operator will arrange all the details, since there's a good deal of logistical planning. Kenya Airways has daily flights between Nairobi and Kisumu, from where your lodge can organize your onward transfer (by either light aircraft, boat, road, or a combination of these).

By Train From Nairobi, you could catch a slow train to Kisumu, and while this is definitely not the most time-efficient option, it's an overnight trip (supposedly with three departures per week; 13 hr.) and is a great deal cheaper than flying. You'll still require an onward transfer to get to either of the islands, of course.

GETTING AROUND Your lodge will arrange any boat transfers you require in the immediate vicinity of Mfangano and Rusinga islands; they are unlikely to help with madcap attempts to explore vast stretches of the lake because weather conditions are highly changeable and there's every chance of being caught up in an unexpected, unpredictable storm while you're out on the water. A boat transfer from Mbita to Mfangano takes about 1 hour.

DAY TRIPS You can see the islands of Lake Victoria on a day-trip fishing package from the Masai Mara (inquire through your lodge or camp there, or visit www.governorscamp.com). These cost $473 to $496 per person and include air transfers from the Mara to Mfangano Island and boat transfers from the airstrip to Mfangano Island Camp, where, after you've been out fishing, a generous alfresco lunch is served (both tilapia and perch are usually part of the spread). This can be arranged through virtually any of the lodges, although guests staying at any of the Governors' camps have priority. While a good deal of the outing is devoted to traveling to and from the island, the flights are scenic enough to make the whole experience worthwhile, and the day makes a good break from the monotony of land-bound game drives. The same excursion without the fishing is $100 less.

WHAT TO SEE & DO

With its near-tropical clime, affable Luo fishing communities, and alternative biodiversity, Lake Victoria presents an opportunity to take in Western Kenya at a tranquil pace. At this ornithologist's dream, you don't need to make any effort here to witness the antics of waterfowl—cormorants, egrets, sandpipers, herons, sacred ibises, and all kinds of kingfishers (it won't be long before you're able to distinguish among malachite, pied, pygmy, and giant) are everywhere. Pelicans, too, are spotted between the islands, and fish eagles regularly swoop down over the surface to pluck out their catch.

Most remote and idyllic of the islands is **Mfangano,** where, over and above its radiant, twittering birdlife, you can watch spotted-neck otters dashing around the rocks, monkeys zipping through the green canopy above, and monitor lizards swimming through the shallow waters or basking in the sun. Mfangano is widely inhabited by members of the Abasuba community, descendents of a Bantu tribe, greatly assimilated through intermarriage by the invading Luo. Unlike the Luo, the Suba (whose name means People Who

Warning! **Snail Alert**

No matter how inviting Lake Victoria's water may seem, and despite the regular sight of locals bathing or swimming in it, you'd do well to stay clear. Bilharzia—a highly invasive parasite—is rife among the freshwater snails that inhabit the grassy shores here, and you wouldn't want to tempt fate. The bilharzia's flukes carried by the snails migrate to the human host directly through the skin and then make for the bowel or bladder, where they can cause serious organ damage, not to mention setting off a cycle of water contamination.

Obamania

Son of a woman in whose veins flows the blood
of ancient Ireland and dark Africa's plains.
You are Obama, nick-named the standing king
You are Barack, oh, son born to deceive
The suffering hoards of Africa look up to you,
See a black saviour where nought but a Judas strides.
—Credo Mutwa

Kenya's tourism planners have for some time been preparing for a slew of Obama-obsessed travelers to touch down in cities such as Kisumu, on the northeastern shore of Lake Victoria. Apparently, there's been a surge of interest in this region from visitors hoping to touch base with the American president's African roots. It wasn't too far from Kisumu, in the tiny village of Nyangoma-Kogelo, that Obama's Kenyan father, Hussein, once herded goats—that, of course, was before heading to the U.S. to study economics and meet Barack's mother. Obama Senior died in 1982, but the president's step-grandmother, Sarah Obama, still lives in her tin-roof bungalow in Kogelo, which Barack visited during his very brief Kenyan tour in 2006. He met with Mama Sarah but was unable to speak to her because she didn't know a word of English—perhaps emblematic of the great distance traveled by African Americans. Meanwhile, many of Barack's "relatives" in Kogelo remain impoverished and socially immobile.

Nevertheless, Luoland locals are wildly obsessed with Obama's rise as the leader of the free world. A brand of beer produced here celebrates their hero—it was originally called Senator but is commonly known as Obama—and even the local school has been renamed in Obama's honor. If you want to get locals excited, simply mention Barack Obama, and you'll get a positive reaction—just

Are Always Wandering) have traditionally included male circumcision among their rites of passage. The largest of Victoria's Kenyan islands—all the more alluring for its lack of development (until recently, there wasn't a single private car here; now, in addition to a truck and couple of tractors, there's one car parked permanently near the airstrip)—Mfangano is also where you can climb to the summit of Mount Kwitutu or hire a guide (Ksh500) for a hike to see the **rock paintings** (admission Ksh200) of Kwitone and Mawanga. Believed to be the work of the ancient Twaa people who were the island's first inhabitants, these red and white concentric circles, spirals, and sunbursts continue to hold the local population in awe, and visitation is governed by various superstitions; for more information, contact the **Abasuba Community Peace Museum** (Mfangano Island; **© 723/898-406;** www.abasuba.museum).

More easily accessible—and joined to the nearby lakeside village of **Mbita** by a causeway that's negated any sense of isolation—is **Rusinga Island,** rich with fossils dating back 18 million years and once the epicenter of an archaeological dig that turned up fragments of one of the great links in human evolution. Not only is Rusinga well-placed for exploring the lake, with plenty of activities on offer, but it's also within striking distance of one looking slightly American these days will be cause for onlookers to break into celebration, and the typical casual, heartfelt greeting you're most likely to get from strangers in the street will not be "Hello," but a cheerful "Obama!"—or perhaps, "Obama?"

By all accounts many Luo are expecting nothing short of miracles from the man—he is Africa's new hope, with songs written in his honor and a public holiday declared to celebrate his electoral victory. Rumor has it that soon after the election, hundreds of Luo arrived at the airport demanding that they immediately be taken to America—the land where their brother is president—despite the fact that most Kenyans can expect to wait years before being granted American tourist visas. Following Obama's victory, in fact, the U.S. embassy in Nairobi shut up shop rather than face the onslaught of demands from people wanting to emigrate to their new homeland. And while officials in Kogelo have proposed setting up an Obama Cultural Home—with a museum, gallery, library, and leadership center—in an ironic twist on democracy, the Kenyan government has placed an embargo on members of Obama's extended family, preventing them from freely talking to the media.

It's certain that life in the tiny village of Kogelo will never be the same. Roads leading there have been graded, and the Kenya Power and Lighting Company has hooked the once-sleepy village to the national power grid. Land value in Kogelo has skyrocketed following speculation among investors planning new hotels for the flood of tourists envisaged to hop aboard the Presidential Heritage Tourism Circuit; at press time, tour operators had begun rolling out "Obama Package" tours, but these tend to include only a brief, fairly aimless stop in tiny Kogelo.

of Kenya's less-visited animal preserves, **Ruma National Park,** undiscovered and undisturbed by the masses. Existing almost exclusively for the preservation of Kenya's last surviving roan antelope, Ruma is a short drive from Mbita, the main point of access to Rusinga, and has been spared agricultural development due to a tsetse fly infestation. Large, rare antelope with ridged backward-curving horns averaging 70cm (27 in.) and beautiful black and white clownlike facial markings, the roan exist alongside some other special species, including the Jackson's hartebeest, small fawn-colored oribi, Rothschild's giraffe, Bohor reedbuck, and topi. Unlike the Mara, Ruma is not teeming with large predators, but with some considerable luck, you may see leopard. The real thrill, though, is the park's remoteness—this is one wildlife sanctuary where you could find yourself entirely alone with the beasts.

Understandably, the principal activity around the islands, and from many of the towns and villages around the lake's shore, is **fishing;** you can trawl for Nile perch along the shores or cast for tilapia in the evenings. Your lodge will make all the necessary arrangements (and there's even a deal that allows guests to fish outside the permitted season).

Fun Facts A Hole in My Head, Please, Doctor

Kenya's second-largest tribal group (after the Kikuyu, who are most prevalent in the Central Highlands), the Luo have stood out in Africa as one of the few tribes that have historically not included ritual circumcision as one of the initiation practices marking the transition from childhood to adulthood. Before breathing a sigh of collective relief on their behalf, it's worth knowing that, instead of circumcision, young men (boys, really) were traditionally subjected to the removal of six teeth from the lower jaw—without anesthetic. As in the case of tribes practicing circumcision, during this horrendous procedure, the initiate was not permitted to show even the slightest inkling of pain. Mercifully, the ceremony is no longer common practice.

The Kisii (or Gusii) are another tribe found in Western Kenya whose people have long been renowned sculptors, working principally in soapstone. Their sensitive use of their fine-boned hands meant that, for centuries, traditional Kisii medicine men practiced a form of brain surgery using primitive tools and—you guessed it—no anesthetic. Apparently, these traditional healers tapped a small hole in the skull with much the same precision as modern surgeons. It's anyone's guess, however, what they got up to once the hole had been drilled.

WHERE TO STAY

The best way to experience Kenya's smidgen of Lake Victoria is to stay on one of its islands, where you are truly away from the crowds and the bother. The luxurious choices hereabouts are intimate island "resorts" set on the water's edge. Of these, Mfangano is more remote and benefits from being relatively cut off from the "mainland" (there isn't even a telephone at the camp); however, Rusinga offers more in the way of easily accessible activities.

If both of these options sound steeply priced (and they are), the more affordable option by a long stretch is **Lake Victoria Safari Village** (© **0721/91-2120;** www.safarikenya.net), with accommodations in attractive thatched cottages near the water's edge just 3km (1¾ miles) from the lakeshore village of Mbita. Simply furnished, with mosquito nets draped over the beds, all the units have en suite bathrooms, too. Full board costs $150 double; add $35 to this, and you get to stay in the romantic Lighthouse Suite, billed as the resort's honeymoon accommodations and, by all accounts, a more memorable option.

Mfangano Island Camp ★★ In a secluded bay on the large, relatively remote island of the same name, this dreamy little sunset-facing resort is right on the water. The especially fabulous **Achiel,** or honeymoon suite ★★★, hangs right over the lake edge; the bed is set in a semi-circular open-to-the-elements room built on the rocks—weaver birds construct their hanging nests from the lip of the overhanging thatch, framing an idyllic 270-degree view as you stare off across the horizon. "Shabby chic" probably best describes the ambience here—the multilevel space has a walk-down bathroom with built-in sunken tub, and part of the wall looks like exploded volcanic rock. Achiel is more secluded than the other five cottages, and also has a private wooden deck under an enormous fig tree—vervet monkeys bounce around in the branches up above, and there's a nonstop chorus of birds (pack your binoculars). While charming, the other rondawel-style chalets aren't quite so marvelous—although, being farther from the water, they don't see quite so bad an infestation of lake flies in the rainy season (yet they still have lake views).

Seasonal streams flow through a lush garden where long, languid meals are served near the shore—it's the kind of place where staff has enough time on their hands to decorate dining tables with marigolds and origami napkins. Accessible only by boat or by plane and then boat, the camp offers a complete break from the rigors of up-at-dawn game viewing. This doesn't mean you'll have nothing to hunt for here—fishing is perhaps the *raison d'être* to visit (you can happily spend all day on a boat with a rod in your hand, and if nothing's biting, you can buy directly from passing Luo boatmen—a perfect opportunity to interact with the islanders). ***Note:*** Mfangano is closed in April and May.

The Governors' Camps, Musiara Limited, P.O. Box 48217, Nairobi 00100. ✆ **020/273-4000** or -4005. Fax 020/273-4023. www.governorscamp.com. 6 units. High season $678 double; midseason $588 double. Children under 12 pay about 65% of the adult rate. Rates include all meals, airstrip transfers, local activities, and laundry. No credit cards. **Amenities:** Bar; airstrip and boat transfers; pool; limited room service.

Rusinga Island Lodge ★★ Capped by high, toadstool-shaped thatched roofs and fronted by deep verandas, Rusinga's seven large stone-and-wood cottages afford gorgeous views over pretty gardens and the lake itself. It's an idyllic sort of place, manned by a doting staff and possessed of a casual, carefree atmosphere that does justice to the lake's

Fun Facts Rainmaking & Goat Slaughtering

Not far from Mfangano is a sacred island known to its guardians (members of the Wasamo clan) as Nzenze, also known as the "Moving Island," since Nzenze apparently followed the Wasamo here when they migrated from Uganda. No one other than Wasamo clan members is permitted on the island, and bizarre obstacles supposedly meet anyone who dares test this superstition. Wasamo elders have long used the island as their magical weather control center, engineering rain for Mfangano by conducting a sacred ceremony there. Elders would despond to the island and slaughter a black goat. Slicing the animal in half (while still alive), they would leave half the sacrifice on the island (presumably to be consumed by the large python that guards the island's sacred shrine), and take the other half home with them, where they'd roast and feast on the meat. Apparently, this would appease the gods and bring rain. Cleverly, when the elders wished to replace incessant rain with sunshine, they'd perform the same ritual using a white goat instead. Other myths reveal that the island was also a place where, when famine and drought faced Mfangano's people, food would miraculously present itself—often in the form of a humungous goat, large enough to feed the entire clan. Times have definitely changed, and the rainmaking ceremony no longer happens, although the Wasamo have started cultivating crops on the island. For visitors, it remains one of the few islands in the area where hippos and crocs can still be spotted, although if you attempt to land on its shores, you'll be at the mercy of the gods.

laidback rhythm. While the emphasis at Mfangano's smart little resort tends to be on fishing, Rusinga's attractions are a touch more varied, with water sports, cultural excursions, and the chance to visit Ruma National Park. At Rusinga, you're also likely to have greater contact with humanity because, unlike at Mfangano, here you're literally attached to the mainland, and the island itself is more heavily populated, with roads and traffic. That doesn't necessarily undermine the lodge's exclusivity, though, and the lovely accommodations emphasize tranquility. The elegant wood-furnished spaces feature king-size beds made up with fabrics in natural, earthy tones and a large net canopy to protect guests from mosquitoes; the attached bathrooms have exposed wood-beam ceilings, twin basins, and stone-walled showers. As at Mfangano, you'll get your fill of tilapia and Nile perch—ask if the chef will prepare your fish Zanzibar style, with coriander, lime, and coconut. And try to have at least one meal on the jetty.

Reservations: Chronicle Tours & Travel, I&M Bank Towers, 4th Floor, Kenyatta Ave., P.O. Box 49722, 00100 Nairobi. ✆ **020/224-6112** or 020/31-1786/7. Fax 020/31-6933. www.chronicletourskenya.com or www.rusinga.com. 8 units. High season $1,050 double, $365 per child under 12 when sharing with 2 adults; midseason $880 double, $330 per child; green season $560 double, $140 per child. Rates include all meals, most drinks, all activities except air excursions, and laundry. No credit cards. **Amenities:** Bar; pool; spa.

3 KAKAMEGA FOREST

45km (28 miles) N of Kisumu

Boasting a unique biodiversity, little-visited Kakamega Forest is the only natural tropical rainforest left in Kenya—once a contiguous part of the Guineo-Congolian forest ecosystem, which stretched from the equatorial rainforests of West Africa. Thick foliage, towering trees, and a light-filtering canopy of tangled vines create an exquisitely wet, dense habitat that supports all kinds of rare and endangered birds and animals. That Kakamega exists at all is something of a miracle because its trees have long been valued for timber, and gold discovered in the area in 1923 set off a brief mining frenzy that, mercifully, quickly came to naught. But commercial tree-felling continued until the late 1980s—native trees such as the precious Elgon teak, Elgon olive, *mukomari,* and African satinwood have been heavily exploited. Conservation efforts continue to be hampered by illegal tree-felling, and one of the heart-breaking sights hereabouts is of poor villagers carrying bundles of wood destined to fuel their home fires. Kakamega supports a sizeable population—the densest rural population on Earth, in fact, and the Luhya people who live around the forest rely heavily on it for fuelwood, charcoal, and timber. Authorities are faced with a real moral bind, given the plight of impoverished local communities who have nowhere else to turn for their basic needs. The forest also continues to play a central role in some of their traditional practices—certain clans carry out male circumcision ceremonies at sacred *mugumu* trees within the forest. Evidently, the race to save the forest is on, but that hasn't stopped the tidal wave of abuse. As a self-sustaining ecosystem, the rainforest is especially fragile—even the removal of organic matter from the ground poses a threat to soil fertility and the very existence of the forest. Doomsayers observing the forest's steady decline predict that its disappearance is inevitable, making a visit to this sodden paradise not only an attractive off-the-beaten-track adventure, but an urgent detour.

ESSENTIALS

ORIENTATION Kakamega Forest occupies an area along the northeastern edge of the Lake Victoria basin. Along its eastern edge rises the partially forested Nandi Escarpment, which runs along the western edge of the Rift Valley. The northern part of the forest is a small protected area (Kakamega Forest National Reserve), with its main entrance some 15km (9¼ miles) from the ramshackle town of the same name.

GETTING THERE One of the main reasons Kakamega remains so far off the beaten track is the relative complexity of getting there. There is no airstrip in or near the forest, and roads in the immediate vicinity of Kakamega are horrid, a problem that's continually exacerbated by the heavy daily rainfall that also makes this such a special ecosystem. The direct drive from Nairobi can be anywhere between 6 and 8 hours, and the road journey from the Masai Mara isn't any quicker. With the roads in highly variable condition, your best bet for visiting Kakamega is to catch a flight to Kisumu, having arranged with your tour operator to have a 4×4 and driver with local experience meet you and transfer you to the forest (allow 1–2 hr. for the road trip); this vehicle will have a better chance against the perpetually wet roads, and you'll need local experience to navigate the poorly signposted region. Flying in not only will cut down on traveling time, but is a more comfortable introduction to the region.

You can also get to this part of Western Kenya on a touring circuit that commences in Nairobi and first takes in the lakes of the Great Rift Valley (see chapter 8). From Lake Baringo, there's a scenically spectacular (if, depending on the current state of the roads, excruciating) drive across the Kerio Valley and up to the cool mountaintop town of Iten (where you should overnight at Kerio View; see below), before descending into the west and heading through the towns of Eldoret and Kapsabet en route to the Kakamega Forest. You'll need plenty of time and, when the roads are in poor condition, nerves of steel and a level-headed driver to complete the road journey.

PRACTICALITIES Confusingly, Kakamega is divided into two separate management schemes. The northern part of the forest (the National Reserve) is managed by the **Kenya Wildlife Service** (The Warden, Kakamega Forest National Reserve, P.O. Box 879, Kakamega; ✆ **056/20-425** or 056/30-603), while the southern section (known as the Forest Reserve) is run by the **Forestry Department** (✆ **0722/61-9150**). Needless to say, such bureaucratic confusion does not bode well for the security and welfare of the forest, which is permanently under threat from loggers, as well as local villagers looking for firewood. Entry to Kakamega Forest National Reserve is $20 per adult and $10 per child under 18; there's an additional fee of Ksh300 per vehicle. Alternatively, entry to the Forest Reserve, which lacks the diversity of habitats, costs just Ksh20 (Ksh5 for children and students). Driving is permitted on roads within the National Reserve, but this is a complete waste of time because the bush is so thick that it's impossible to catch a glimpse of any wildlife for more than a moment before it'll be startled by your engine noise and disappear back into the vegetation. Far better to leave the car in one of the designated areas (where there are also KWS-managed campsites and *bandas*—useful if you're up for a self-catering experience with limited comfort and few amenities) and set out on foot. You can wander through the forest unaided, as long as you stick to those trails that are marked, but if you want to get the most from the experience, learning about the flora and fauna you encounter along the way, a local guide is highly recommended. Without such assistance, you'll easily miss out on half the birdlife.

Tips Over the Top

Given sufficient time, you can reach Kakamega as part of a road trip that traverses the lush Kerio Valley and the steep incline of the Elgeyo Escarpment by way of the Rift Valley (see chapter 8). As you head out of the Rift and over its immense "side-wall" escarpments, you'll need to take a break from what will otherwise feel like an arduous journey. With its staggering views across the Kerio Valley, and even Mt. Kenya (some 220km/136 miles away) occasionally visible beyond the Tugen Escarpment, you could do a whole lot worse than to bed down at pleasant, upbeat **Kerio View** (P.O. Box 51, Iten; ✆ **053/42-206** or 728/102-991; www.kerioview.com; 64€ double, including breakfast). Built and run by a fascinating Liverpudlian named John Williams (who came to Kenya in 1972 but retains his distinctive accent), it's located on the edge of the escarpment just outside the shambolic little market town of Iten, which has a distinctly Afro-Alpine atmosphere. It won't take you long to figure out how Kerio View gets its name or why this has become a secret haven for paragliders. Between January and March each year, these extreme sports enthusiasts arrive here from Europe to take advantage of the thermal winds that make for exquisite gliding conditions. It's possible to ride the currents for up to 3 or 4 hours, with some gliders landing many miles away. Iten is also where Kenya's superstar athletes are cultivated under fairly stiff conditions (it's 2,300m/7,544 ft. above sea level) at the High Altitude Training Academy. The presence of athletes and adventure-seekers gives Kerio View quite a convivial atmosphere, and there's usually some pleasant socializing in the fire-warmed bar and restaurant—although food takes forever to arrive, the kitchen prepares a number of Kenyan dishes, so the menu is worth investigating. Accommodations are passable, too—you stay in simple, wood-paneled chalet bedrooms with tile floors; big, hard foam mattresses; and kitschy '70s fabrics. When there isn't a thick cloud of mist or fog, views from the little balconies are staggering.

GUIDES Local community tour guides are available via the KWS office upon entry to the northern part of the forest. Freelance guides hang around the southern entry point near Isecheno (a short distance from Rondo Retreat; see "Where to Stay," below) and offer their services for walks through the forest. One reliable fellow is **Moses Livasia** (✆ **0723/029-329**), who has been guiding in Kakamega for 14 years; in addition to his standard 2-hour guided walk (Ksh300 per person), Moses conducts specialized sunrise (5–8am) and evening (5–8pm) walks for Ksh500 per person. You can also hire a guide directly through Rondo Retreat (Ksh300). The forest, which is best experienced on foot, includes a number of self-guiding nature trails for those looking to explore *sans* guide.

ANIMAL-SPOTTING IN THE KAKAMEGA FOREST

Around 10% to 20% of all the mammals, reptiles, and birds found in Kakamega are found nowhere else in the country. Among the 330 species of bird here, those you don't want to miss include the great blue turaco (often seen trotting around in a most ungainly manner in groups of up to 12), the black-and-white casqued hornbill (surely the noisiest creature in the forest), and the gray parrot, which is under severe threat here. Monkey lovers will thrill at the sight of the black-and-white colobus—which looks a bit like it's permanently wearing a shaggy woolen shawl—catapulting itself between the trees; or search a little harder to find more elusive creatures, such as tree pangolins, rare De Brazza's monkeys (also known as swamp monkeys, of which there are a mere 30 or so left in Kakamega—found exclusively in the isolated Kisere Forest Reserve, which is part of the larger Kakamega Forest), or the unusual potto, a large-eyed nocturnal primate said to be the world's slowest-moving mammal. If you're sufficiently quiet and keen-eyed, you'll also catch a glimpse of the smaller antelope—tiny dik-dik, duikers, and forest buck are also at home within the forest. When the flowers bloom in October, butterflies fill the air (there are more than 400 species here), while at night, fruit bats and scaly tailed flying squirrels take to the air.

The forest also harbors quite a rich snake population—27 species, including the arboreal Gold's cobra—but apparently no one has been bitten here since the park first opened. Nevertheless, I strongly recommend a pair of closed shoes, as much for the potentially slushy, muddy ground as for any creepy-crawlies. And always have something on standby to fight off the rain—the heavens open virtually every day of the year (hence the term *rainforest*), and the downpour can be relentless. Finally, while traipsing through the forest, even if your focus is on spotting animals and birdlife, don't miss out on the chance to see the 60 different types of orchid that grow here (9 of them are endemic to Kakamega, so you won't see them anywhere else on Earth), and there are 62 different fern species, too. Ask your guide to point out the popular local aphrodisiac plant, *mkombero.*

WHERE TO STAY

Rondo Retreat ★ Value Owned by the Trinity Fellowship Mission, and first established in the southern part of the Kakamega Forest in 1948, Rondo is a delightful colonial throwback with large, homey, old-fashioned accommodations and a spectacular setting. Today, although very much a preserve of traditional good values (it bills itself as "a Christian sanctuary for nature lovers" with even a chapel in the garden), it's also a haven for birders and monkey lovers who trek to this little-visited Western Kenyan enclave to experience the most jungle-esque part of the country. Stupendous, vast gardens surround the Main House and the guest cottages, and a number of fabulous forest walks (some of which require a guide) start at the edge of the property, which is a very good place to start scanning the forest canopy for shaggy-haired colobus monkeys. Traditional home-style meals (spaghetti bolognaise, roast chicken, and steamed vegetables) are served at set mealtimes in a casual-but-formal dining room where alcohol is taboo and animated conversation about the day's bird sightings usually predominates; afternoon tea is served on the veranda. Accommodations—in a former family home in the clapboard and corrugated iron tradition—are a mixed bag and individually styled, but each room will remind you of an earlier era (in this case, Kenya's colonial period) when windows were large, verandas were deep, furniture was crafted by hand, and open stone fireplaces kept the evening chill at bay. For the most authentic experience, bag a room in the main house (the three garden cottages are '80s additions)—of these, only Bob & Betty's Room has a private en suite bathroom, while the other three rooms share facilities down the hall. Be warned, though, that beds are short, and you'll probably need to ask for an extra blanket before retiring, as it gets pretty chilly here.

P.O. Box 2153, Kakamega. ✆ **056/30-268.** Fax 056/31-057. www.rondoretreat.com. 18 units. Ksh9,372 full-board double; Ksh8,520 half-board double; Ksh2,556 per child 4–11 sharing; no charge for children under 4. No credit cards.

10

Laikipia & Kenya's Northern Frontier District

by Keith Bain

If the Masai Mara is Kenya's commercial wildlife hotspot, then its expansive northern frontier—virtually everything above the equator—must represent the opposite end of the spectrum. A Holy Grail for seasoned purveyors of African game and adventurers seeking forgotten worlds, the vastly untamed north makes up more than half the country. Much of this has a reputation as harsh, waterless desert populated by quarrelsome tribes, its meager roads roughshod, rutted, and historically plagued by heavily armed Somalis known as *shifta,* classic gun-toting highwaymen. But to those looking for unsentimental beauty and haunting images of classic, unspoiled Africa, the forbidding expanses of its sweltering deserts—the Chalbi and the Dida Galgalu (Plains of Darkness)—are mystifying and magnificent.

By contrast, at the southern fringes of this immense northern zone are some of Kenya's best-managed game-viewing regions. The wide, central **Laikipia Plateau** is where prime agricultural lands have been co-opted for hugely successful environmental management programs, juxtaposing areas of human habitation, cattle husbandry, crop production, and zones of wildlife habitat. And the successes are everywhere. Ranches where livestock farming, conservation, and low-impact tourism run concurrently have been developed to benefit both animals and local communities. Laikipia's patchwork of wilderness preserves and private game parks represents the more sustainable future of Kenya's conservation industry and a welcome alternative to the heavily touristed government-run parks that see much higher visitor numbers. The result is a genuine—if cosseted—safari experience that's perfect for visitors looking to get away from the overburdened mass tourist circuit. It's also where you'll discover some of the most intimate and authentic places to stay in all East Africa—each one enviably positioned. Many are personally managed and hosted by the very people who've dedicated their lives to these conservation projects.

And right in the center of the country, just north of Mount Kenya, **Samburu National Reserve**—practically indistinguishable from two neighboring parks, **Shaba** and **Buffalo Springs**—is another of Kenya's most important wildlife sanctuaries, not only popular with tourists, but also where one of the world's great animal research projects, Save the Elephant, is based. In fact, there are about 5,400 elephants living within the combined Samburu-Laikipia ecosystem, and you're likely to be inundated with sightings of large multigenerational herds, many of them thoroughly habituated to vehicles and their human passengers.

But if you're after an adventure that feels on the edge of reality, then you might consider setting aside time for the untamed far north—one of the most remote and isolated regions on Earth. In contrast with Samburu, the area north of Laikipia and

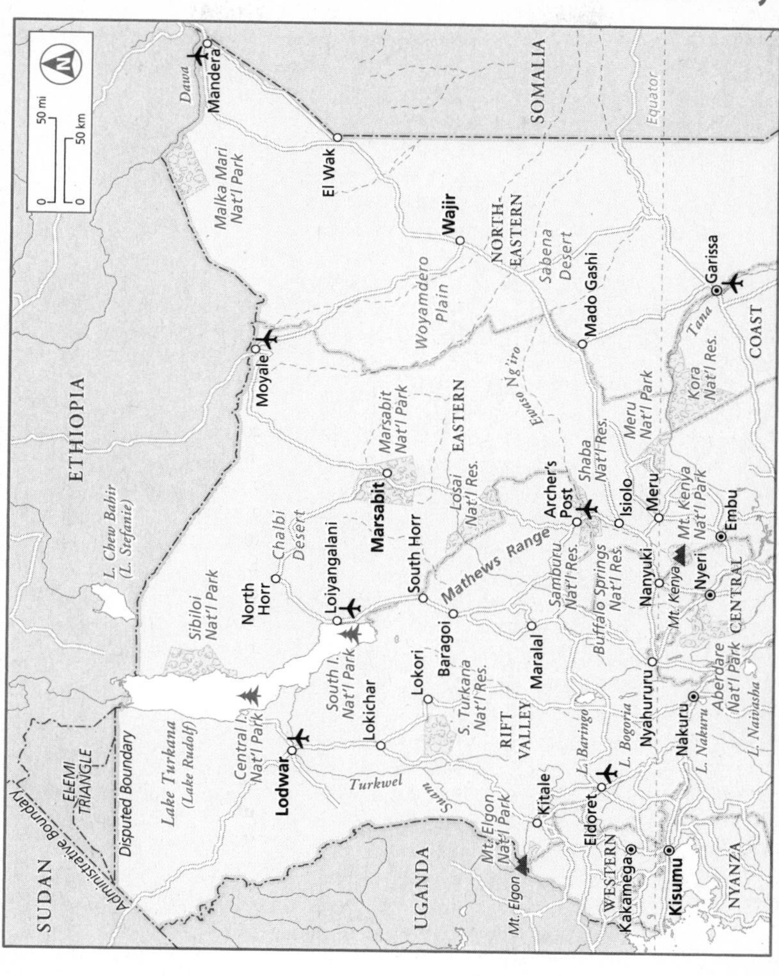

Shaba, stretching all the way to the Ethiopian border, is hardly seen by travelers. Here, where little grows (except, perhaps, UN and NGO funding) and common sense tells us that nothing should exist at all, beautiful tribes survive against all odds, and the immense **Lake Turkana**—breathtaking enough to be called the Jade Sea, its shore longer than the entire Kenyan coast—shimmers like a gigantic diamond in the rough. To visit the far-flung north, you'll need to join either an utterly exclusive and expensive fly-in excursion or an overland journey during which you'll see some of the world's hardiest tribespeople—the Turkana, Rendille, Boran, Gabbra, and Samburu—eking out the ultimate minimalist existence, hunting crocodiles and surviving the harsh, barren nothingness of the inhospitable desert, often with

Safari Adventures in Kenya's North

Safari companies are a dime a dozen in Kenya, and you'll come across numerous touts pushing many of these on the streets of Nairobi. Here's a selection of the more exclusive safari companies that run tours in Kenya's north. If you have the stamina and yearn for an experience that will feel like true adventure, consider one of the multiday camel safaris offered by several companies; more specific details of these are discussed in the box on p. 214.

Abercrombie & Kent Extreme Adventure ★★★ (www.akextremeadventures.com) offers an 11-day whirlwind tour led by top East African guide Toby Fenwick-Wilson. On his tour, you'll sample the best of Kenya's north, sinking your teeth into some of its most exciting activities, with relative luxury always in the foreground. You'll get to ride horses, go mountain-biking, ride in a replica vintage 1920s biplane, and even take a helicopter to the remote, beautifully located Desert Rose lodge. In the Chalbi Desert, you'll walk with camels and meet all kinds of tribespeople along the way. There are only six departures per year, so it's worth investigating way ahead of schedule.

Horseback in Kenya (✆ **0727/532-091;** www.horsebackinkenya.com)—the name says it all. El Karama is a 5,665-hectare (13,993-acre) cattle and wildlife ranch between Mt. Kenya and the Great Rift Valley, and folks here offer horseback-riding safaris for intimate groups. Camels come along to carry supplies for the temporary camping sites, which are set at new locations every second day. Each day, riders set off just after breakfast and settle in around 4pm, with a midday break for a picnic lunch.

Karisia Walking Safaris (www.karisia.com) is based on a 1,215-hectare (3,001-acre) ranch called Tumaren. Your hosts specialize in luxury walking safaris with a strong eco-friendly emphasis. Guests (never more than 12) are accompanied by local tribespeople trained as guides, and nights are spent in classic safari tents. You can also opt to combine walking safaris with game drives, or ask to put together a specialist trip (from ornithology to local culture). Rates for Samburu-led walks start at $612 double per day. Karisia also acts as a booking service and can arrange for other parts of your East Africa itinerary.

Charlie Wheeler's **Northern Frontier Ventures** ★★★ (www.laikipia.org) is based on Laikipia's renowned Lewa Wildlife Conservancy and offers exciting walking safaris (with camels to assist by carrying the heavy loads) into the wild, little-traversed terrain of Kenya's far north. With professional guides, you'll follow old elephant migration routes and trek to some of the region's high-altitude oases, including the Mathews Mountains and Mount Marsabit. Each safari is tailor-made, lasts between 3 and 14 days, and takes on no more than six guests. You can also opt to climb the sacred mountain, or do what only a handful of foreigners have ever dared do—slaughter a goat and drink the blood with your tribal guides. You can end your camel experience at one of the luxurious Laikipia community-owned lodges, Tassia being the best located, to tie in with Charlie's safaris. A 2-night camel safari commencing from Lewa Airstrip and culminating at Tassia costs $400 per person, plus $150 in conservation fees for the three different conservancies (Lewa, Il N'gwesi, and Lekurruki) you'll traverse along the way.

Offbeat Safaris (www.offbeatsafaris.com) offers horseback-riding safaris for small groups of relatively experienced riders. Days in the saddle are long, but nights are spent in luxury mobile tented camps set up by a support team that travels ahead by Land Rover. Either join a prearranged safari or have Offbeat design one to meet your needs and interests.

John and Amanda Perrett's **Ol Maisor Camels** (www.laikipia.org; olmaisor@africaonline.co.ke) is based on their family-run ranch, where they have more than 60 working camels available to accompany you on walking trips as far as Lake Turkana. If time is limited, they'll put together 1- or 2-day taster safaris; all their safaris are designed to order, and it's best to go for an all-inclusive deal so you never need worry about a thing. If you're limited by budget, this is perhaps the most attractive option—costs are Ksh7,000 per person, per day (covering your camels and their handlers, full catering, tents, and equipment—although you pay for bottled water, drinks, and any camping on private or community-owned ranches). Safaris take about 3 days to organize, so this is also a good bet for relatively last-minute arrangements.

If you want to overland through the north in style, your best bet is **Robert & William Carr-Hartley Safaris** ★★ (✆ **722/510-673** or 722/510-556; www.carrhartley.com). The Carr-Hartleys have years of experience in various destinations around Africa, and they focus on luxury camping—not only do you sleep in large, comfortable, insect-proof tents, often with attached bathrooms, but, of course, you always have the option of staying in Laikipia's intimate, upmarket lodges. You can also design your own itinerary or go with suggestions made by experienced guides.

Ol Siruai Horseback Safaris (www.laikipia.org) operates horseback and photographic safaris (or combinations of both), with trips to just about anywhere in Kenya. Tailor-made to meet your needs, there's plenty of flexibility to your program, but with an emphasis on the type of luxury that goes with meeting local (white Kenyan) landowners, dining with them, and soaking up the decidedly neocolonial vibe.

Riding Wild ★★★ (www.borana.co.ke) is one of Kenya's finest horse safari operators; see the box on p. 215.

Robin Hurt Safaris ★★★ (✆ **020/88-2826,** 020/88-4068, or 0722/644-131; www.robinhurtphotosafaris.com) are specialists in photographic safaris, with luxury-minded trips that combine bivouac-style camping; nights in private, established camps; and camel-assisted on-foot trekking. They're not cheap—their 12-day African Bush safari costs anywhere between $6,840 and $12,935, depending on the level of exclusivity and time of year—but you get a quality experience in return.

Owned by Helen Douglas-Dufresne and Pete Isley, **Wild Frontiers** ★★★ (www.wildfrontierskenya.com) organizes custom-designed camel-assisted walking safaris around the Mathews and Ndoto ranges; look at spending at least 6 days to get a genuine feel for the region. You'll be walking between 8km and 20 km (5–13 miles) a day, guided by a Samburu crew, and sleeping in netted tents or right beneath the stars.

camels at their side. Although there are isolated towns and backwater outposts here—African versions of Wild West settlements slogging it out under dire conditions—and even a handful of wildlife reserves where specialized habitats and pockets of lesser-known animals are protected, for the most part, Kenya's north is one of Africa's final frontiers—little explored, more than a touch surreal, and startling to behold.

1 LAIKIPIA

190km (118 miles) NW of Nairobi

Steadily gaining ground as Kenya's hottest game-viewing destination, with a reputation among savvy wildlife enthusiasts as the future hope for conservation management in East Africa, the Laikipia Plateau incorporates some of the richest lands and most impressive wildlife numbers in the country. Thrown into the mix of mesmerizing landscapes—jagged hills, river-torn gorges, sweeping plains—and rare and exotic animal species are traditional communities of tribal people—the Laikipiak Maasai and the Samburu—whose ability to survive against all odds in often harsh and inhospitable conditions will astound and inspire you. For many, the real draw here is the profusion of highly individual, intimate, and blissfully uncrowded safari lodges that have transformed this region into a blueprint for how nature tourism *should* work. Pioneering projects in sustainable land use allow domestic animal ranching and wildlife conservation to coexist, in turn producing a viable responsible ecotourism model that helps service and sustain local communities. Endangered beasts (including more than half of Kenya's black rhino population), and rare, unusual animals—such as the endangered Grevy's zebra (which are found only north of the equator)—traverse well-managed lands that are grazed upon by cattle. Reared in ultimate free-range fashion, these domestic livestock thrive on lands cohabited by the highest diversity of large mammals anywhere in the country. Besides bringing responsible tourism and sound eco-friendly principles to the region, these lodges and camps also involve local communities, hopefully ensuring the continued survival of tribal groups and their coexistence alongside the animals with which they have long shared the land that they have defended for generations. And because you'll inevitably be on private land for much of your visit, there's plenty of opportunity for alternative experiences—horseback riding, camel safaris, mountain biking, and limitless game-viewing opportunities within environments where there are fewer restrictions and rules (and far fewer human visitors) than the government-run parks. Much like the wildlife that roams this terrain, you'll have a lot of freedom to do what you want, when you want, and while money spent at the government-run parks notoriously ends up in back pockets and spent on dubious bureaucracy, conservancy fees in the Laikipia go toward fostering community development and sustaining some of Africa's most important wildlife projects. The Lewa conservancy, for example, holds 12% of Kenya's black rhino population and the largest single population of Grevy's zebras in the world. Little wonder it has become Kenya's leading model for private conservation, ensuring Laikipia's emergence as a leading destination for low-impact tourism.

ESSENTIALS

ORIENTATION The vast Laikipia Plateau stretches from Mount Kenya in the east to the Great Rift Valley in the west; it encompasses a vast, diverse terrain of around 808,000 hectares (2 million acres) ranged more or less between the colonial-era frontier town of

Nanyuki in the south and the remote wilderness town of Maralal in the north. The plains of Laikipia stretch from the Great Rift Valley to the escarpments descending down toward the Northern Frontier District. The region is largely comprised of enormous wildlife conservancies, huge cattle ranches, and community-owned lands—many of these have been developed to receive visitors in small-scale tourist operations that offer high-end experiences intended to impact as little as possible on the environment.

VISITOR INFORMATION For the lowdown on anything and everything Laikipia-related, you can contact the **Laikipia Wildlife Forum,** based in Nanyuki, where it has an office at the tiny airport (✆/fax **020/216-6626;** www.laikipia.org).

GETTING THERE By Air Because the majority of accommodations within the Laikipia region are in relatively remote camps and lodges, most visitors choose to fly, as chartered flights don't necessarily imply a considerable uptick in price. There are plenty of scheduled trips, too, with Nanyuki the most obvious regional gateway. There are several other scheduled touch-downs across the region, with short-hop light aircraft dropping and collecting passengers on demand. Scheduled flights to Nanyuki, as well as other airstrips around Laikipia, are operated by **AirKenya** (www.airkenya.com) and **Safarilink** (www.safarilink-kenya.com); these typically arrive in the morning and also connect Nanyuki with Lewa Downs and Loisaba (both popular jumping-off points in Laikipia), as well as the Samburu and Shaba reserves and the Masai Mara. The best charter companies are **Tropic Air** (www.tropicairkenya.com), for trips commencing at or destined for Nanyuki, and **Boskovic Air Charters** (www.boskovicaircharters.com), if you're departing from Nairobi. Both companies will transport you from destinations farther afield, but remember that charter flights are priced to account for both legs of a journey (even if you're not onboard, you'll pay for the "dead leg" of the trip). ***Note:*** If you are catching a scheduled flight, remember that you may need to factor in your ground transfer costs—in some cases, this might add another $200 or even more to the cost of getting there (although the road transfer is typically charged per transfer rather than per person).

By Road The road trip from Nairobi to Nanyuki (also a major hub for Mount Kenya; see chapter 7) takes around 3 hours (although this is always quoted at about 2 hr.) without pit stops. From Nanyuki, some of the onward journeys to lodges and camps in the Laikipia are likely to fill up what's left of your day. Although getting to Lewa Conservancy is an additional 45 to 60 minutes from Nanyuki, it'll take a total of 6 hours on the (often-harrowing) road getting from Nairobi to Tassia (see "Where to Stay," below) on the Lekurruki Conservancy. Though overland travel may cut down on costs, it's most likely that you'll be thoroughly exhausted upon arrival; bear in mind that the quality of driving in Kenya is nerve-wracking, at best.

GETTING AROUND The great thing about game viewing in Laikipia is that once you've arrived, you don't need to plan, plot, or organize anything. You'll be asked what you want to do but shouldn't have to make any arrangements yourself. Roads within the conservancies are suitable only for 4×4s, but horses and camels are popular for alternative, leisurely exploration. All the lodges offer walking safaris, too, and some have mountain bikes and even quad bikes.

PARK FEES Daily conservancy fees vary from lodge to lodge, ranging from around $40 to $80 per adult. The good news is that this money—unlike what you would have paid at the gates of state-run parks—is more likely to go directly toward conserving the environment and enhancing its wildlife, not to mention contributing to the livelihood of local communities.

WHERE TO STAY

Laikipia has the greatest concentration of intimate, luxury lodges in Kenya. Privately owned and managed, they come with a sense of style, inimitable charm, and personal reward that is likely to provide you with some of your favorite memories of Kenya. Each of the lodges reviewed below has individual character and a superb location that sets it apart from the next, and while you could quite easily make one of these your home for your entire visit, it'll be worth your while to mix and match your choices to create an itinerary that takes you to different parts of the Laikipia Plateau and enables you to meet the different personalities who operate each of the properties—engage them at the dinner table, and you'll hear mind-blowing tales. One thing is certain: Each of the Laikipia lodges is remote and very private; no matter where you are, you'll have a sense of being somewhere very special, a place that's far, far away from the crowds. Most of these places offer a wide assortment of game-viewing possibilities over and above the usual vehicle safari, so you can strike out on foot (with a guide who knows what he's doing) or explore the terrain on horseback or with camels.

Lewa, home of the world-famous Lewa Wildlife Conservancy, which first spearheaded the conversion of cattle ranches into wildlife sanctuaries, is one of Laikipia's best-known destinations, with an assortment of accommodations options, including exclusive-hire lodges, a tented camp, and the excellent Lewa Wilderness (reviewed below), where you're made to feel like a part of the family. Lewa and neighboring Borana occupy the eastern part of Laikipia and provide a buffer between the farming areas to the south and the wild rangelands farther north. Immediately north of here are two attractive community-owned properties, Il N'gwesi and Tassia, both staggeringly situated on mountain bluffs (both reviewed later in this chapter). Tassia is possibly my top choice as one of the most exciting places to stay in Kenya.

In many respects, northern Laikipia is even more wild and exciting than down south. Ranch fences (and cattle) have largely been removed, so not only does wildlife flourish, but animals are starting to follow old migration patterns once more. Loisaba (reviewed below) is among the more famed of the north Laikipia lodges; previously known as Colcecchio, it's one of the ranches that features in Kuki Gallman's memoir, *I Dreamed of Africa.* Loisaba is a sprawling property where cattle and wildlife commingle, and—like Lewa—it has a variety of accommodation types to choose from. Many lodges in the north tend to take advantage of the Ewaso Nyiro, which serves as the region's principal

Moments Aboard the Flying "Squirrel"

The quickest way to see Northern Kenya—and, for many, the most exhilarating—is by chartered helicopter. With the great advantage of being able to explore otherwise difficult-to-access regions and touch down in remote, untouched spots that don't have the advantage of runways or roads, nothing really comes close to the possibilities posed by helicopter flight. **Tropic Air** (© **20/203-3032** or -3033, or 734/333-044; www.tropicairkenya.com) offers on-demand flights in its turbine-engine Eurocopter Squirrel (apparently the quietest helicopter on Earth), with space for up to five passengers for a princely sum of $2,050 for an hour (2 hr. minimum). Bookings can be made through your lodge, from where you'll also be picked up.

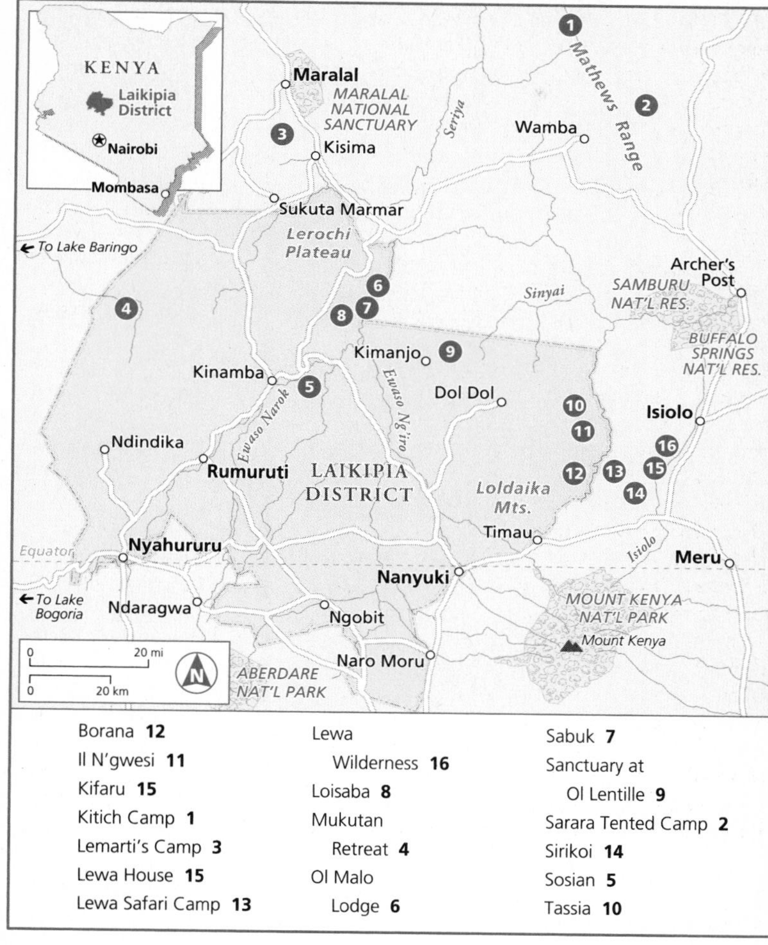

game corridor. Some, like Sabuk (reviewed later in this chapter), afford stunning views over the river, with bedrooms built fabulously close to the water.

And then there are impeccably remote and secluded spots on Laikipia's northernmost frontiers. Visitors to Ol Malo are welcomed as personal guests into the gorgeous home of Colin and Rocky Francombe (who also get a mention in Gallman's book), while the far-flung Sanctuary at Ol Lentille is a fabulous oasislike luxury boutique-style resort bounded by spectacular vistas of the arid north. More a retreat for all the senses, Ol Lentille doesn't yet see the kind of game numbers you might expect, but it is nonetheless Kenya's most fabulous inland lodging option, with utterly chic accommodations and personally assigned Maasai guides. Both Ol Malo and Ol Lentille are reviewed in the following pages.

Moments Trekking with the Ships of the Desert

They're big-eyed, ever-so-slightly dopey-looking beasts, but when it comes to padding it across the arid, open plains, there's none as elegant as a camel, and the sight of them is one of Northern Kenya's eternal, iconic images. While camel riding does happen, it is by all accounts a real drag and hard-going on the backside. Rather than ride them, local tribespeople tend to use them as beasts of burden, for milk, and even for meat, rather than for personal transport. **Camel safaris** ★★★ are perhaps the most authentic way of experiencing the vast open territories of Northern Kenya. Camels are used for carrying supplies and camping equipment, a bit like pack mules, only with greater carrying capacity and less likelihood of suffering dehydration. You'll be accompanied by local tribespeople who set up camp, prepare meals, provide protection, and alert you to many of the wonders of the bush you mightn't notice until your senses became more accustomed to your surroundings. The details of each day and the route you take to get to your next camp is never the same and ultimately depends as much on you and your team as it does on the vagaries of the wildlife and terrain. There are usually elephant and buffalo on these walks.

Safaris such as these typically last 3 to 4 days, with nights in attractive, unspoiled locations, often near a river. At the end of a pretty grueling morning—3- to 4-hour's trekking once you set off at 8am—afternoons are spent recuperating and escaping the heat. Meals are prepared over an open fire while you're off exploring or enjoying sundowners. You return to camp for a good feed before bedding down, usually in shade-netted tents. Comfortable bedrolls, hot showers, and portable ablution facilities should also come standard, but check before signing up. It's not always fancy (although the price you pay will determine the level of luxury you can expect), but it is perhaps precisely the experience you came to Kenya for.

Traveling on foot in desertlike conditions under blazing sun and intense heat can be physically and mentally challenging. You'll need to be fit and have sufficient stamina to withstand the heat; spare camels are usually available if someone falls ill. While you're not necessarily signing up for a pampered, lazy sojourn, you'll be rewarded with a real sense of accomplishment, traversing little-explored terrain with hardy warrior-class Africans. For contact details of selected camel safari operators, see the box on p. 208.

Borana ★★★ Perched on a steep-sided ridge overlooking the Samangua Valley and affording views of Mount Kenya, the Ngare Ndare Forest, and the sweeping Borana plains, this rugged cattle and wildlife ranch has been owned and managed by the Dyer family for three generations. The transformation of 12,928-hectare (31,932-acre) Borana into Kenya's first boutique safari lodge, dovetailing conservation and high-end tourism, has been an immense project for Michael and Nicky Dyer, who have built eight beautiful cottages, each one evolving organically with the shape and contour of the cliff edge to which it clings. That's in addition to farming with the humped boran cattle that give the farm its name and starting a leather workshop that employs blind and disabled members of the community.

The first stone cottages, all individually designed, have huge glass walls and beds, bathtubs, and showers perfectly poised to take advantage of the mesmeric views. They're styled with natural timber, eye-catching boran cowhide, leather armchairs, lamps crafted from oversized calabashes and chunky earthenware pots, recycled glass bottles, and grass mats. But it's the more recently built units (7 and 8) that will take your breath away. Moroccan-influenced design, with open-to-the-elements rooms, lime-washed floors, and views framed by arches and natural wooden beams, these spaces are built directly into the rocks, forcing you to rethink everything you thought you knew about architecture. Cottage 8 is the most fantastical—chic, yet not without an appealing rusticity, its cool, stylish spaces are enlivened with subtly lit nooks, shimmering panels of blue glass, and stairways carved into the rock substrate. The bathroom, in fact, is virtually the same size as the bedroom, and there are fantastic views directly from the shower—glass doors open onto a little private lawn and wooden decks (perfect spot for romantic dinners, easily arranged) that stretch down to your private plunge pool.

Borana is well known for its congeniality. Creative meals are served around a large communal dining table each night, after which you retire to the cozy lounge, with armchairs and sofas in front of an enormous open fire, for more drinks and conversation. There's some poignant popular contemporary history here, too; Borana is where the artists who designed the world imagined for Hollywood's *The Lion King* stayed even before the lodge opened, taking much of their inspiration from the local environment.

Borana Ranch also has its own private house, **Laragai** ★★★, rented out on an exclusive basis. With more than a hint of glamour, it's convincingly cosseting. Huge gold-framed mirrors hang above massive fireplaces, deep leather sofas are plumped with cushions, and oversized lamps, eye-catching African *objets d'art,* and intriguing fossils and animal bones are on display straight from the bush. This elegant, cushy mansion isn't literally on the edge of a cliff like Borana's suites, and the property isn't as exposed, meaning that access to views of the surrounding wilderness are never as in-your-face as you'll experience at the main lodge (although there is a spectacular viewing platform from which to take in the vistas), but with its eight chic bedrooms, splendid lounge and dining

Out on the Range

Borana is well known as a horseback-riding destination and has a stable of hardy breeds—Ethiopian, Arab, and thoroughbred horses—available for multiday safaris across the Laikipia wilderness. Some decent riding experience is essential, as you won't be dealing with pushover ponies here, and you'll spend long days out in the saddle (although horses especially bred for beginners are also available for shorter rides). You have a choice of fly-camping out in the bush at night (with decent, comfortable tents and hot-water showers, as well as three-course meals served around a camp fire) or returning to one of the luxe eco-lodges in the neighborhood; either way, you'll spend your days discovering a wonderfully untamed terrain where you'll encounter wildlife on a whole new level. To arrange your horse safari, inquire through Borana (see above), or write to Michael and Nicky Dyer at ridingwild@borana.co.ke.

areas, private pool, tennis court, immaculate gardens, and private airstrip, it's certainly a place to escape to with a group of close friends. It's charged at a minimum of $3,200 to $3,700 per night (for up to six guests; each additional person is charged extra), plus daily conservation fees of $80 per head.

Note: Both Laragai and Borana close for the November rains.

© **722/464-413.** www.borana.com. Reservations: The Safari and Conservation Company, P.O. Box 24576, 00502 Nairobi. © 020/211-5453, 020/219-4995, 073/557-9999, or 071/257-9999. www.thesafariandconservationcompany.com. reservations@scckenya.com. 8 units. Mid-season $1,120 double, $430 per child 5–16 sharing with 2 adults; high season $1,280 double, $375 per child. Rates include all meals, most drinks, game-viewing activities, local airstrip transfers, horseback riding, mountain biking, cultural excursions, conservation fees, and laundry. MC, V. **Amenities:** Bar; airstrip transfers; pool. *In room:* Fireplace.

Il N'gwesi ★ A community project in the extreme northeastern part of Laikipia, Il N'gwesi was Kenya's first safari lodge to be built, owned, and managed directly by local tribal landowners; everyone you meet here is a member of the 6,666-hectare (16,465-acre) group ranch, 80% of which is given over to conservation. In turn, the lodge helps support 634 households, or around 6,000 people. Its location, alongside the Mukogodo Escarpment, is spectacular. Each of its six open-fronted, thatched *bandas* overlooks the Ngare Ndare River, with tough-climbing Olmaroroi Hill opposite and panoramic 180-degree-plus views spreading out across the infinite expanse of Kenya's rugged northern terrain; in the foreground, you can watch activity at the nearby watering hole. Constructed with local materials—a combination of sand, cement, and deadwood—the spaces are organically conceived and take on intriguing shapes, with gnarled, naturally crooked tree trunks erupting through the red-cedar floors. Built with loads of ingenuity and imagination, raised high on wooden beams, their elevation emphasizes the bird's-eye perspective; alfresco stone-wall showers are attached, and some of the rooms are reached via wooden footbridges. Two *bandas* have extended platform balconies where you can roll out the double bed and spend the night under the stars.

Although the rusticity might appeal to youngsters, I'd be hesitant to bring small children because the balconies (with a massive drop below) are protected by just a few low railings. Everything is run on solar power, which also heats the water, all of which is sourced from a natural spring. While the majority of lodges in Laikipia serve primarily Western food, you can be assured of sampling Kenya's national dish, *nyama choma* (roast meat), and if you've an inquiring culinary mind, this is a good place to probe your hosts for details of the Maasai predilection for blood and milk. Bear in mind, though, that getting beyond the hurdle of cultural difference isn't always easy, and service can be iffy. Riding on the back of early success, the lodge has been struggling to meet expectations, and when times are tough, your hosts may too easily let you feel their despair.

© **20/203-3122.** www.ilngwesi.com. Reservations: Uncharted Outposts, 9 Village Lane, Santa Fe, NM 87505, USA. © **888/995-0909** or 505/795-7710. Fax 505/795-7714. www.unchartedoutposts.com. travel@unchartedoutposts.com. 6 units. High season $690 double; rest of the year $600. Children 2–12 pay 50%. Rates include all meals, drinks, game viewing, and other activities. No credit cards. **Amenities:** Restaurant; bar; pool.

Lewa Safari Camp ★★ Value Having inherited his family's ranch, third-generation Kenyan Ian Craig set about transforming this expansive property, located where Mount Kenya's fertile escarpment plunges into the dust and gloom of the Northern Frontier, into one of the continent's biggest biodiversity conservation success stories. Within a decade, Ian had also encouraged local Samburu and Maasai tribal elders to create their

Exclusively Yours: Lewa's Glam-Pad Hideaways

In addition to its Safari Camp (reviewed above), Lewa Wildlife Conservancy has two lodges designed for unabashed privacy and more suitable for anyone who's disinclined toward bedding down in a canvas tent, no matter how stylish it may be. Both of these can be rented only on an exclusive basis, so they're not suitable if you actually wish to fraternize with strangers.

The shameless choice of celebrities, visiting royalty, and Lewa's well-to-do patrons (many of whom *are* aristocrats and Hollywood stars) is **Kifaru** ★★ (meaning Rhinoceros), a six-*banda* property with views stretching all the way to Mount Kenya. Of the two lodges, it's the more contemporary and emphasizes full-blown luxury. Accommodations are massive, with timber floors, big four-poster beds, colonial-style furniture, huge tiled bathrooms, and elegant, sweeping roofs made from swamp reeds. There's a pool (with superb views), beautiful lounge and dining areas, and fine-tuned gardens, not to mention a choice of just about any imaginable game-viewing activity, including horse riding.

No less exclusive, but with a less-ostentatious atmosphere and a touch more charm, **Lewa House** ★★ has six double rooms, a dedicated staff, and facilities for your use only. Between game drives and bush walks, you can watch weaver birds noisily construct their nests, laze around the pool, or learn about the intricacies of Maasai culture from your personal guide. Accommodations are also stone-wall cottages with heavily sloping thatch roofs, but the decor is a little more in keeping with the bush safari experience.

Each of the "houses" costs a minimum of $2,400 to $3,700 per night (for up to six guests). Additional guests pay $400 to $610 per night ($200–$305 per child), with a maximum of 12 guests. Rates include all meals, most drinks, game-viewing activities, local airstrip transfers, horseback riding, camel treks, cultural excursions, conservation fees, and laundry. Reservations can be made through U.S.–based Uncharted Outposts (9 Village Lane, Santa Fe, NM 87505, USA; ✆ **888/995-0909** or 505/795-7710; fax 505/795-7714; www.unchartedoutposts.com).

own community reserves as a way of restoring the land and supplementing their income with ecotourism—404,690 hectares (more than a million additional acres) where pastoralists had previously eked out a meager living on drought-ravaged and overgrazed Samburu communal land. The camp is located on the site of the former Rhino Sanctuary headquarters; in fact, the horned beasts still gather at the watering hole right in front of the main veranda, so there's animal viewing whether you're cruising around in a 4×4, walking with an armed ranger, or relaxing in camp with an early evening G&T. The thrill, though, for most city-slickers, is soaking up the back-to-nature atmosphere; rather than sleeping in a stone-wall cottage or luxury villa (as you do at the other Lewa Conservancy lodgings), guests stay in a big, sturdy tent capped by a thatch roof. However, that doesn't mean you want for basic luxuries. Inside, guests have attached bathrooms, proper beds, and plenty of furniture, including a writing desk and comfy chairs on the private veranda. Given the extent of Lewa's commitment to improving animal numbers—particularly of those species under threat—you'll be inundated with good sightings.

www.lewasafaricamp.com. Reservations: Cheli & Peacock, P.O. Box 743, 00517 Uhuru Gardens, Nairobi. ✆ **020/60-4054/53** or 020/60-3090 or -91. Fax 020/60-4050. P.O. Box 56923, Nairobi 00200. ✆ 020/60-0457 or 020/60-5980. Fax 020/60-5008. 9 units. High season $960 double, $240 per child 5–16 sharing with 2 adults; mid-season $820 double, $205 per child; green season $620 double, $150 per child. Rates include all meals, most drinks, game-viewing activities, local airstrip transfers, choice of 1 horseback ride or camel walk per stay, conservation fees, and laundry. AE, MC, V. **Amenities:** Bar; airstrip transfers.

Lewa Wilderness ★★★ High above a twisting river that runs through a fantastic gorge, the setting of what is really the expansive family home of Will and Emma Craig is breathtaking. It's perched at the edge of a drop-away cliff with drop-dead views that are reason enough to stay here. Mature bougainvilleas tumble over beautiful thatched cottages, squirrels and rock hyraxes clamber over the rockface on which the lodge is built, and everywhere there's a real sense of being at a lived-in home, with well-worn, comfy furniture and a homey buzz—there's a help-yourself bar amid the sofas, armchairs, and chaise lounges, piles of well-thumbed books, and even a guitar and electric piano. Your hosts dine with you, inspire you with their love of Kenya, and share tales of high adventure. The only formality here seems to be the care taken to help you decide how you wish to spend your time. With so much to keep you occupied and so many ways to interact with the environment, it helps to have some guidance—although you'll just as easily spot elephant down by the river from the cliff-edge pool or the open-fronted dining room, with its massive communal table and endless supply of food, drink, and stimulating conversation. Game drives are rewarding, too, but this is a great place to vary the daily routine. You can saddle up on any of 30 horses and—at a pace of your choosing—ride out onto the plains to really eyeball the game (many animals are sufficiently horse-habituated for you to get fantastically close), visit a local Maasai homestead and join your hosts for a barbecue goat feast, check out a weaving workshop, track rhino with a masterful Maasai warrior (who took me within 20m/66 ft. of three hefty adults, not to mention thrillingly close to the biggest bull elephant I've ever laid eyes on), and—perhaps the most exhilarating experience in all Kenya—get a bird's-eye view of Laikipia and its four-legged inhabitants in a replica 1930s open-cockpit Waco biplane.

At the end of the day, you have your visually striking and utterly cozy guest suite to come home to. Each one is a high-ceilinged thatched cottage with mountains of space, deep verandas, and plenty of variety in terms of where you can stretch out, put your feet up, or catch the views. The better cottages are the newer models, designed and decorated by Emma (a few of the older ones look out across the lawn instead of off the edge of the cliff); she's injected the interiors with more than a dash of pizzazz—beautiful stone floors; huge, high poster beds; gorgeous big bathrooms (most with tub *and* shower); open stone fireplaces; furniture made from local wood; a personal bar; and—in the fantastic family unit (no. 8)—a great loft created especially for children.

Reservations: Uncharted Outposts, 9 Village Lane, Santa Fe, NM 87505, USA. ✆ **505/795-7710.** Fax 505/795-7714. www.unchartedoutposts.com. Local contact: Bush&Beyond, P.O. Box 56923, Nairobi, 00200. ✆ 020/60-0457 or 020/60-5980. Fax 020/60-5008. www.bush-and-beyond.com. 11 units. Regular season $1,060 double, $265 per child under 12; premium season $1,220 double, $305 per child; green season $800 double, $200 per child. Rates include all meals, most drinks, game-viewing activities, local airstrip transfers, horseback riding, camel rides, cultural excursions, conservation fees, and laundry. AE, MC, V. **Amenities:** Bar; airstrip transfers; pool; tennis. *In room:* Bar, fireplace.

Loisaba ★★★ Bestriding Laikipia on the edge of the punishing arid expanse of the Northern Frontier District, Loisaba is a private game ranch of some 24,644 hectares (61,000 acres), a thriving symbiosis of foreign investment and conservation-minded

Still Dreaming of Africa?

There's a good chance that if it's a book that's inspired you to come to Africa—to Kenya, specifically—then your heart was led here by a phrase, a paragraph, or a chapter in Kuki Gallman's bestselling memoir, *I Dreamed of Africa* (which was made into a movie with Kim Basinger in 2000). In it, the Italian-born writer recalls her intimate relationship with the continent that became her home; many of her heart-stopping memories were created on the northwestern fringes of Laikipia, where she famously created a home for herself and her family on Ol Ari Nyiro Ranch. **Mukutan Retreat** ★★ (✆ **020/52-0799;** www.gallmannkenya.org) is Gallman's lodge, where guests have a choice of just three stone-and-papyrus cottages, each with a fireplace and private veranda overlooking the Mukutan Gorge. Here, from the edge of the Great Rift Valley, you not only have access to Laikipia's abundant, well-managed wildlife, but also magnificent views of two of the Rift's prominent lakes, Baringo and Bogoria. While you'll enjoy all the luxurious comforts associated with Laikipia's best lodges, there's a good chance you'll get to meet Gallman herself, always a highlight for anyone who takes the time to visit this unique part of the country.

locals (where all profits are ploughed directly back into protecting the environment). Set on the escarpment with panoramic views extending hundreds of miles toward Mount Kenya, the Loldaiga Hills, and the Mathews Range, the main **Loisaba Lodge** ★ has ample luxury amenities—pool, tennis court, spa, classy lounges, an excellent library, and a host of game-viewing opportunities. Its bedrooms, however, while adequate, are fairly small and unexciting, completely outclassed by the exclusive-hire accommodations available in Loisaba's two private cottage-mansions (where you also get your own cook, driver-guide, and house staff); with rates starting from $1,800 for up to four people in low season, they're quite a good deal, too.

The real magic, however, happens at Loisaba's celebrated **Star Beds.** The first of their kind in Kenya, these rustic-but-wonderful accommodations are where you get to experience the bush in an unforgettable way. You stay in simple high-off-the-ground bedroom-platforms under a thatch canopy; they have bathrooms with flush toilets and safari showers like many of the camps, but the clever innovation here is that the high, four-poster beds are on large wooden carts with wheels, so it's simple to roll them onto your private, open terrace before you get into them at night (a large mosquito net protects you). Two separate projects—Kiboko and Koija—run independently, each with a small Samburu staff attending to you, guarding the remote camps day and night, and—if you're feeling ultra-adventurous—giving you a first-hand look (and taste) of local culture (and cuisine). Of the two, **Koija Starbeds** ★★★ (which is community-owned and more remote) is my pick. To get there, you first cross a 30m (98 ft.) swing bridge over the Ewaso Nyiro along whose banks the stilted accommodations are arranged; with your terrace-bedroom virtually hanging over the water's edge, you're practically guaranteed to see animals drinking here. **Kiboko**'s bedrooms overlook a dam—from a bit of a distance—and while they do have fantastic views of the hills beyond, much of the special atmosphere I find at Koija is mysteriously lacking. Wherever you choose to bed down on Loisaba, one thing is guaranteed, and that's extraordinary game viewing. It's the kind of place where you're more than likely going to be held up by elephants who've commandeered the roads. Always set off early if you need to catch a flight.

www.loisaba.com. Reservations: Cheli & Peacock, P.O. Box 743, 00517 Uhuru Gardens, Nairobi. ✆ **020/60-4054** or 020/60-3090. Fax 020/60-4050. www.chelipeacock.com. Main lodge: 7 units. Kiboko & Kioja Starbeds: 3 units each. 2 private houses. High season $1,190 lodge or Starbeds double, $440 per child 5–16 sharing with 2 adults, $2,640 Loisaba Cottage (4 people), $3,280 Loisaba House (5 people); midseason $990 double, $365 per child, $2,100 Cottage, $2,910 House; green season $740 double, $270 per child, $1,600 Cottage, $2,910 house. Children under 5 stay free. Discounted rates for stays of 4 nights or more in mid- and green seasons. Rates include all meals, most beverages, game-viewing activities, local airstrip transfers, cultural visits, and laundry. MC, V. **Amenities:** Bar; airstrip transfers; pool; spa; tennis court; Wi-Fi. ***Note:*** Most amenities are at the Main Lodge but are available to all Loisaba guests.

Ol Malo Lodge ★★★ Four individual, totally private rock cottages stand watch along the edge of a broad lava ridge made of black stone spewed up when the Rift Valley was being ripped through Africa. Imaginative, detailed, and, at the same time, utterly groundbreaking, the stone and wood constructions are the work of Colin and Rocky Francombe, who came to this northernmost outpost of Laikipia in the early 1990s (long after cutting their teeth as ranch managers elsewhere in the region) and brought a groundbreaking trend to tourism: small, private, intimate bush experiences. Each cottage has high papyrus ceilings, stone walls and floors, handmade cedar furniture made from trees felled by elephants, and huge picture windows framing an expansive view of the valley down below. Each room also has an enclosed open-fronted pavilion, always with the emphasis on the sweeping view of the valley below. Arrange your wake-up tea or coffee for just before sunrise, and you can watch the African sky turn a dozen shades of orange, gold, and red as the sun's disc ascends from behind the hills and mountains in the distance. Right below you, hyraxes, leopard, myriad birds, and elephants roam, play, and mingle. The Francombes—gracious and welcoming—make you feel like you're a guest in their home. Always sharing a story or revealing fascinating details of local culture or local wildlife, Colin pours drinks, offers canapés, and mixes a mean ginger and honey tea before bedtime. And then he's up at dawn ready to accompany you for an on-foot safari adventure.

If you're after a totally exclusive experience, or perhaps want to host a private party (or bring the kids) in the African outback, check out **Ol Malo House ★★★**, an imaginatively designed retreat with six huge, high-ceilinged en suite bedrooms crafted from local materials and decorated with a personal touch. The house, which has its own pool, massive entertainment areas with a mix of African and Indian antiques, and cliff-edge views over the plains below, is rented out as a single unit; although it's totally private, you still enjoy hands-on service and—according to your preferences—the company of the Francombes. ***Note:*** Ol Malo is closed April, May, and November.

www.olmalo.org. Reservations: Uncharted Outposts, 9 Village Lane, Santa Fe, NM 87505, USA. ✆ **888/995-0909** or 505/795-7710. Fax 505/795-7714. www.unchartedoutposts.com. Local contact: Bush&Beyond, P.O. Box 56923, Nairobi, 00200. ✆ 020/60-0457 or 020/60-5980. Fax 020/60-5008. www.bush-and-beyond.com. 6 units. Regular season $1,060 double, $265 per child under 12; high season $1,220 double, $305 per child; green season $800 double, $200 per child. Rates include all meals, most drinks, game-viewing activities, local airstrip transfers, horseback riding, camel treks, cultural excursions, conservation fees, and laundry. MC, V. **Amenities:** Bar; airstrip transfers; Internet; pool.

Sabuk ★ (Kids) Ranged along a bluff above a particularly attention-grabbing twist in the Ewaso Nyiro River, Sabuk's dramatic setting is especially blissful if you fancy being lulled to sleep by the nonstop murmur and quiet roar of water; here it is forever gushing by, just below your cottage. Completely open to the elements on the side facing the river, the stone-and-thatch cottages (and the big, meandering mess lounge) are meant to blend harmoniously with the environment. Step out through your front door, and you're pretty much in the bush, making this a decidedly more intimate and less commercial option than the main lodge on the neighboring Loisaba wilderness. Each cottage has its own unique architectural features—a child's loft bedroom, a cliff-edge bathtub, or a rope-strung daybed on your private sun terrace hanging right over the water. Bathrooms are built into the thick rock boulders, and beds are covered in bright fabrics under large, billowing mosquito nets—it's pure "rustic chic," offset by that dazzling bird's-eye view of the river. Accommodations are perfectly private, but for a dash more exclusivity, choose the Eagle's Cottage, a two-bedroom suite with its own dining area and swimming pool; perfect for families, it's also a little more contemporary-looking (it's a more recent addition), with smart-rustic decor, walk-in wardrobe, and fabulously designed bathrooms, including his 'n' hers basins.

Wherever you are, there's plenty to look at. Views stretch toward the Karissia Mountains and the Mathews Range, and all around you is an animal-rich wilderness. Verity Williams is one of the hands-on owners and will arrange alternative ways of exploring the terrain—camel safaris, nature walks, sundowners, or full-blown meals in the bush. When the river cooperates, there's the chance to swim or go tubing along its surface. If you crave a more hardcore adventure, Verity will put together a bivouac-style excursion—you set out on foot with camels carrying your gear, and at night you strike camp in various remote spots, your Laikipiak Maasai guides keeping guard over your tent through the night.

www.sabuklodge.com. Reservations: Cheli & Peacock, P.O. Box 743, 00517 Uhuru Gardens, Nairobi. ✆ **020/60-4054** or 020/60-3090/91. Fax 020/60-4050. www.chelipeacock.com. 7 units. High season $1,190 double, $440 children 5–16 sharing with 2 adults, $2,640 Eagles' Cottage (up to 4 people); midseason $990 double, $365 per child, $2,100 Eagle's Cottage; green season $740 double, $270 per child, $1,600 Eagle's Cottage. Discounts for stays of 4 nights or more in mid- and green seasons. Rates include all meals, most drinks, all game-viewing activities, camel safaris, most other activities, sundowners, local airstrip transfers, and laundry. No credit cards. **Amenities:** Bar; airstrip transfers; pool.

The Sanctuary at Ol Lentille ★★★ Among the most luxurious accommodations in Africa, award-winning Ol Lentille sits like a fancy mirage atop a rocky ridge in one of the more mountainous bits of the Laikipia plateau. On land belonging to the Laikipiak Maasai community of the Kijabe and Nkiloriti Group Ranches, the Ol Lentille conservancy covers 2,600 hectares (6,422 acres) of beautiful hills and valleys. The site was chosen by the African Wildlife Foundation because it's an important corridor for the migration of elephant and endangered Grevy's zebra—it was also the poorest part of Laikipia and most in need of a financial boost. It's also the driest, hottest part of Laikipia, a fact that's inspired the cool, chic design: breezy, open spaces that create an oasis amid semi-arid surrounds. It's not quite desert, but the rock-strewn landscape, giant termite mounds, and dust down below emphasize a sense of seclusion. Its location not only ensures total privacy (making it the choice of world-class movers, shakers, and superstars looking to escape the limelight), but also secures stunning views from just about anywhere on the expansive property—on a clear morning, these stretch to the jagged peaks of Mount Kenya, and from the deck of the amoeboid pool, you can make out the Matthew's Range to the north. It's like being on an island in the middle of a sea of African wilderness.

Moments Rites of Passage

An inspired and inspiring pairing is the marriage of Nairobi-based fashion designer Anna Trzebinski and her Samburu husband, Loyapan Lemarti. While their union has all the earmarks of a silver screen romance—they met on safari where he was her guide—their relationship has also resulted in a remarkable business venture. In 2007, they opened their own dream camp, a synthesis of beautiful location and stunning design. Not far from the Laikipia Plateau, in an oasis of palm and fig trees, their camp is a very personal enterprise. Anna personally stitches the tents using locally loomed cotton in the same workshop where she creates beaded tunics and accessories inspired by indigenous Kenyan designs. The couple run **Lemarti's Camp** ★★★ (✆ **20/894325;** www.lemartiscamp.com) personally, and either Anna or Loyapan is always on hand to host you.

Set on platforms above a river bend, the camp's tents are furnished with tables and beds built with wood from disused dhows and decorated with locally found objects: crocodile skulls, elephant shoulder blades, beaded walking sticks, and traditional clubs. Anna's preference is for tents that don't intrude on your interaction with the bush, more like a veiled than a walled space in which you can still smell, hear, and sense the wilds outside. Add to that a comfortable bed and sufficient comfort to justify the hefty price-tag ($1,360 double, including everything except champagne), and you have one of Kenya's finest, most authentic tented camps.

They've also developed two less-permanent (but no less lovely) nearby camps. **Nomadic Camp** is pitched seasonally, and the romantic **Stargazing Camp** is by a river. And if you're the braver, more adventurous sort, you should take Loyapan up on his fabulous Rites of Passage safari—it's an unstinting (and, for some, unnerving) interaction with the wilderness, during which you head out into the bush on foot with a Samburu warrior to guide you (and only his traditional weapons to protect you, should danger arise). The aim is to give you a sense of how these tribespeople attune with the environment and hopefully give you some pointers. To reserve your stay at Lemarti's (or either of the satellite camps), contact U.S.-based **Uncharted Outposts** (✆ **888/995-0909;** www.uncharted outposts.com).

Ol Lentille's four eye-catching villas bring together imaginative architecture, great interior design, and luxurious finishes. Each house is unique but comes standard with its own butler, safari guide, elegant dining and sitting areas, lavishly designed bedrooms, and plenty of quirk: The thatch-roofed Sultan's House has low-slung Moorish sofas and a distinctive Swahili theme; the Colonel's House features campaign desks, Persian rugs, antique telescopes, and English scroll armchairs; the three-bedroom Chief's House has a West African decor with a soothing limewash finish; and the contemporary-retro Eyrie might as well have been called The Austin Power's Shagadelic Suite.

You're hosted by an expat couple, John and Gill Elias, and attended to by a gracious, professional Kenyan staff. You'll get an intimate cultural perspective direct from local Maasai warriors who are assigned to be your link with the Laikipia outback and will drive you in search of game, walk you through the bush, share cultural knowledge with you, and even take you jogging in the wilds. When you're worn out from exploring, stretch out on a massage table in the smart little spa (ask for a hot stone massage). A great place to end your time in Kenya, Ol Lentille is every bit the sanctuary it claims to be. You can do just about anything here, eat where and when you desire, and set your own rhythm, just as a vacation should be, without the frantic emphasis on charging around in search of animals. And as if the product weren't proof enough of its own success, it's gratifying to know that within the first 2 years of Ol Lentile's existence, the Kijabe group ranch has become one of the wealthiest in Laikipia.

www.ol-lentille.com. Reservations: Uncharted Outposts, 9 Village Lane, Santa Fe, NM 87505, USA. ✆ **888/995-0909** or 505/795-7710. Fax 505/795-7714. www.unchartedoutposts.com. Local contact: Bush&Beyond, P.O. Box 56923, Nairobi, 00200. ✆ 020/60-0457 or 020/60-5980. Fax 020/60-5008. www.bush-and-beyond.com. 4 private houses. Chief's House (sleeps 6): $12,700 for 3 nights, $3,400 extra night; $24,300 for 7 nights. Sultan's House (sleeping 4 or 2): $6,400 or $4,300 for 3 nights, $1,750 or $1,150 extra night; $13,100 or $8,100 for 7 nights. The Colonel's House (sleeps 4): $8,550 for 3 nights; $2,250 extra night; $16,200 for 7 nights. The Eyrie (sleeps 2): $4,300 for 3 nights; $1,150 extra night; $8,100 for 7 nights. Entire property (sleeps 14–16): $22,300 for 3 nights; $6,750 extra night; $45,600 for 7 nights. Minimum 3-night stay. Standby rate booked and paid within 14 days of arrival attracts 50% discount (certain activities charged extra). Rates include all food, most drinks, game-viewing activities, spa treatments, and other activities. MC, V. **Amenities:** Bar; pool; spa; Wi-Fi. *In room:* Bar, iPod docking station, fireplace, hair dryer.

Sirikoi ★★★ A superb addition to the properties on the expansive Lewa conservation area, Sirikoi—the name means Place Where the Animals Come to Water—is personally operated by Willie and Sue Roberts, a Kenyan couple known for their classy safari operations. Their latest creation breaks new ground with its beautifully designed tents and attractive setting in a shaded grove of acacia tortilis trees overlooking a busy waterhole. Although Lewa is plump with game, you could do worse than to plant yourself on your deep veranda and just watch the unfolding scene around camp.

There's been no corner-cutting here. Each of the six tents is vast and infinitely stylish, with wood floors covered with hand-woven rugs and impeccably detailed with chunky wood furniture, hurricane lanterns, and freshly cut flowers—draw back the curtains to reveal huge screen "windows" with views into the bush. Most of the tents have Victorian baths and built-in fireplaces, as well as verandas overlooking the waterhole. In the attached bathrooms, you'll find ball-and-claw tubs, showers, and twin basins with antique-style faucets (dispensing filtered spring water). Those looking for more privacy—and space—can opt for the two-bedroom family cottage; its large deck and location in the wetlands make it a good spot to view elephant and buffalo.

Much of the socializing happens on the alfresco deck with cushioned wrought-iron sofas and a raging log fire; sit back and let the animals come to you, as they regularly do. Taking advantage of the magical setting, most meals are served outdoors, shaded by the trees or under a canopy of stars. And much of what you'll eat is grown in the camp's own organic garden.

✆ **727/232-445.** Reservations: African Explorations, P.O. Box 24513, 00502 Nairobi. ✆ 0720/774-208 or 0722/522-542. www.sirikoi.com. wroberts@africaonline.co.ke. 6 units. High season $1,500 double, $460 per child under 16; midseason $1,380, $420 per child. Rates include all meals, drinks, transfers, game-viewing activities, sundowners, and laundry. No credit cards at press time. **Amenities:** Bar; airstrip transfers; on-call masseuse; pool. *In room:* Hair dryer.

Sosian ★ (Value) This 9,696-hectare (23,949-acre) unfenced wildlife conservancy is centered on an original 1920s ranch house. You'd never suspect that, before its lengthy transformation into a guest lodge, it had fallen into disrepair and its grounds were infested with goats. A firm guiding hand—and serious injection of cash—has resulted in another of Laikipia's high-end conservation projects. While some cattle ranching continues here, supplying Sosian's kitchen with its top-grade beef (not to mention home-grown lamb, duck, and vegetables), the focus has shifted almost exclusively to wildlife tourism; the land is well stocked with animals. The ranch boasts a resident pack of wild dogs, and the lodge is frequently visited by larger beasts; don't be surprised to see elephants watching you on the tennis court or by the pool. Horseback-riding safaris are a specialty here, and there are also opportunities for camel-trekking and excellent walks—including multiday excursions with overnight fly-camping—into the wilderness; beyond Sosian's unfenced border, you have access to a further 30,300 hectares (74,841 acres) of conservation lands. Besides indulging in the sybaritic pleasures around the house, you can try your hand at ranching for a bit (ever taken cattle for a dip?) or visit a nearby Pokot village for some cultural interaction. After dark, use the night-vision camera to spot bat-eared foxes, leopards, zorillas, and aardwolf.

Accommodations are in sizeable cottages arranged at the edge of the sprawling garden. Each unit has a personal terrace (with great view across the grounds) and wonderfully big bathroom, and all are generously, handsomely furnished without being over-the-top luxurious. The only drawback, perhaps, is that they're all side by side and fairly close together. The exception is the fabulous Italian Cottage on the other side of the property; what it lacks in views, it makes up for in privacy and colonial elegance (there are plenty of original fittings here, including the ball-and-claw tub in the sumptuous bathroom). Considering all the luxury pampering, the price here feels really good, too.

Offbeat Safaris, P.O. Box 1146, 10400 Nanyuki. ✆ **62/31-081.** www.offbeatsafaris.com. 7 units. High season $840 double, $315 per teen 12–17, $210 per child under 12; mid season $720 double, $270 per teen, $185 per child. Rates include all meals, most drinks, game-viewing activities, and laundry. AE, MC, V. **Amenities:** Bar; pool; tennis court.

Tassia ★★★ Kids Value With an exquisite cliff-edge location, imaginative architecture that takes every advantage of the extraordinary surrounding vistas, and enough adventure to pack a lifetime's worth of safaris, Tassia stands out as one of Kenya's most fabulous little lodges. Community-owned and managed by hands-on business partners Antonia Hall and Martin Wheeler, Tassia will leave you feeling like you've made a very personal connection with Africa. It's built on a rocky bluff protruding from the Mokogodo Escarpment; down below spreads a seemingly endless valley rich with elephants that come to dine on their favorite Loimugi trees and snack on salt that's put out for them just below the lodge. Named for the mountains that they face, the open-fronted cottages are extraordinary, designed around the naturally occurring rocks, boulders, and vegetation and then given a creative spin. Not a single tree was felled for construction, and only low-impact materials were used, so that each suite works like an extension of the natural environment. Although each space is unique, they all enjoy magnificent unimpeded views (most are positively cinemascopic)—in reality, the only walls are those necessary for privacy and to support the thatched roofs.

While the lodge looks out over the Northern Frontier District toward Samburu National Reserve and the sacred Ol Lolokwe Mountain, the surrounding terrain is packed with diversity. You can set off with Martin to explore caves once used by local Maasai hunter-warriors, or head out on foot to reach the top of Blood Hill. There's no queuing up for early-morning game drives here, and when you want to spy elephants up close, you hide behind a gigantic rock just meters from the daily-visited salt lick. The entire lodge works off solar power, and there are no phones, mobile reception, or Internet connections (any communication happens under a tree down near the airstrip). However many nights you've set aside for Tassia, add another two, and prepare to be captivated—better still, opt to walk to Tassia on a multiday camel safari (led by Martin's father, Charlie Wheeler; see the "Trekking with the Ships of the Desert" box on p. 214) starting at Lewa; after slogging it out through the wilderness on foot, there's little to beat Tassia's effortless charms.

www.tassiasafaris.com. Reservations: Let's Go Travel, ABC Place, Waiyaki Way, Westlands, Nairobi. ✆ **020/444-7151** or 020/444-1030. www.lets-go-travel.net. 5 units. $800 double; children 2–12 pay 50% if sharing with 2 adults. Rates include all meals and game-viewing activities. No credit cards. **Amenities:** Bar; pool.

2 SAMBURU, BUFFALO SPRINGS & SHABA

Samburu is 347km (215 miles) N of Nairobi, Buffalo Springs is 300km (186 miles) N of Nairobi, Shaba is 343km (213 miles) N of Nairobi

These three reserves, remote and isolated to the north of Mount Kenya, form a big block of vital conservation area. Bare granite inselbergs rise from the semi-desert like marooned tombstones in endless seas of bush and scrub. Volcanic mountains add drama to the skyline, and through the heart of it all runs the Ewaso Nyiro (River of Brown Waters), a ribbon of life graced by tall doum palms and shade-giving acacias. Here, in addition to the more formidable predators, live the beautiful dry-country animals of Northern Kenya that make up the Samburu "Special Five"—gerenuk, oryx, reticulated giraffe, Somali ostrich, and the endangered Grevy's zebra, characterized by its big round ears and designer pinstripe coat.

The busiest of the three reserves, Samburu covers a relatively small area of 165 sq. km (64 sq. miles) and is mostly semi-arid savannah, rough highlands, *luggas* (or dry washes), and riparian forests. As a wildlife preserve, it doesn't disappoint—sightings of the Big Five (elephant, lion, leopard, buffalo, and rhino) are prodigious, and you have a remote chance of seeing packs of wild dog and the critically endangered pancake tortoise—two rare species besides the Grevy's. Cheetah sightings are particularly good, too, and do look out for those fabulously unwieldy-looking kori bustards (the largest flying birds on Earth). Above all, though, Samburu is known as elephant country.

Elephants—large, busy herds of them that have grown particularly accustomed to the presence of humans—are dominant and the focus of a massively important study project, Save the Elephants, under Iain Douglas-Hamilton, a Scottish biologist who first came to Kenya with an eye on being in the bush in the early 1960s. They're especially active in and around the muddy waters of the Ewaso Nyiro River, where they're regularly spotted bathing and drinking in the morning, and you're likely to encounter them along the roads as you explore the reserve.

The downside, as with all things that have earned a reputation for magnificence, is the relative onslaught of visitors. Charging around the limited confines of Samburu and its adjoined neighbor, Buffalo Springs National Reserve, are ubiquitous minibuses stuffed with camera-toting travelers, often under the guidance of ill-mannered, uninformed drivers who lack the skill or patience to deliver a positive impression of the African bush. If you have any influence over your game drives, request that your driver respect the sanctity of the park and its animals. Keep your distance when observing any living creature, don't interfere with predators engaged in the hunt, and, for heaven's sake, don't stalk or pursue any wildlife in an undignified, off-putting manner.

Sexual Freedom in Samburuland

You'll hear a lot said about the sexism inherent in tribal patriarchies. You'll hear how women do most of the work, raise the children, endure beatings and painful circumcision, and put up with drunk, violent husbands. But it's worth noting that there are some concessions when it comes to the sexual liberty of people like the Samburu. According to tradition, Samburu girls may have boyfriends (as long as they are *boys,* not men) before they are circumcised and—as long as they do not fall pregnant—their relative promiscuity is, by Western standards, accepted. Once married, however, it's widely known that women continue to have lovers, usually younger men (mostly handsome, virile warriors). By all accounts, one of the prime motivations for female circumcision is to prevent married women from sleeping with anyone except their husbands, since the removal of the external sex organs prevents the woman from experiencing any sexual pleasure. Oddly, though, women continue to take younger lovers, and this behavior is common enough for it to be regarded as inherent social practice, largely ignored as long as their much older husbands aren't overtly aware or made to feel cuckolded. Secretly, such adultery seems to be a taboo that can be legitimately broken, with an unspoken shared understanding within the community. After all, men have multiple wives, and some observers believe that this sexual liberty helps retain a sense of cohesion within the community (not to mention a high prevalence of STDs).

If you really want to escape the crowds, be sure to choose one of the more intimate camps outside Samburu's confines, or escape to seldom-visited Shaba National Reserve, a mere 9km (5½ miles) east of Buffalo Springs, but somehow worlds apart and with only a fraction of the safari traffic. Although it's part of the Samburu ecosystem, Shaba has a number of springs and swampland areas, not to mention a distinctive topography (starkly beautiful landscape dotted with rocky kopjes and dominated by Shaba hill, a massive volcanic rock cone that rises above a rugged landscape with steep ravines). On Shaba's remote eastern boundary, you can stay in one of the classiest tented camps in Kenya, and—given how few people actually visit Shaba—probably the best antidote to Samburu's dense visitor numbers. The camp is also where conservationist Joy Adamson—who was murdered here in the 1980s under mysterious circumstances—kept leopard and lion orphans, and where *Born Free* was filmed. Admittedly, the game is often thinner in Shaba, but there are rewards that come with the solitude and pristine landscape. Try to find time for a hike along the river, a surefire way to imagine yourself in an absolute, personal Eden.

ESSENTIALS

ORIENTATION Samburu National Reserve is in the southern corner of Samburu District in Kenya's Rift Valley Province. The region is often referred to as the Northern Frontier District, a colonial-era hangover denoting its untamable remoteness. The Ewaso Nyiro River forms its southern border, separating it from neighboring Buffalo Springs National Reserve which, in turn, connects to Shaba National Reserve that lies farther east. Together the three reserves make up the Samburu ecosystem.

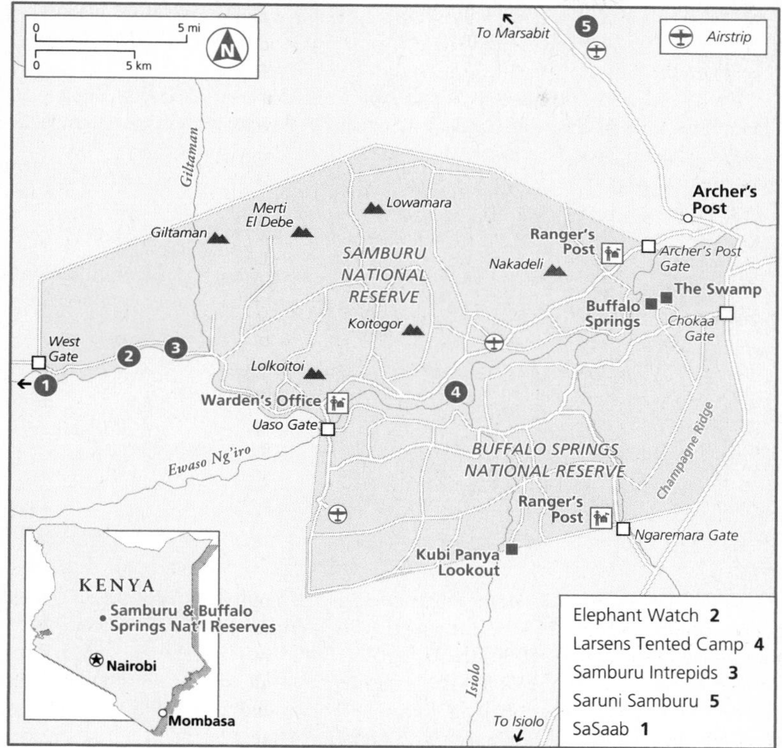

VISITOR INFORMATION Samburu National Reserve is managed by the Samburu County Council; limited (and sometimes confusing) information is available directly from these authorities (P.O. Box 519, Isiolo; © **65/22-83;** www.samburucouncil.com), but don't expect a swift or particularly helpful response. A better contact—particularly if you have a serious interest in conservation issues—is **Save the Elephants** (P.O. Box 54667, 00200 Nairobi; © **020/89-1673** or 720/44-1178; www.savetheelephants.org), one of the world's most respected conservation projects, operated by Ian and Oria Douglas-Hamilton and based in Samburu. Shaba and Buffalo Springs are managed by the County Council of Isiolo (© **064/52-519**), so there's little hope of getting anything useful out of them.

GETTING THERE **By Road** It's a hard but doable 6-hour drive from Nairobi, crossing the equator and bypassing Mount Kenya on the A2 (Isiolo–Marsabit main road) before reaching Kenya's Northern Frontier District. The main point of entry for travelers driving from Nairobi to Samburu is Archer's Gate (354km/220 miles).

By Air A far more convenient and time-saving option is to fly. **AirKenya** (www.airkenya.com) flies to Buffalo Springs and Samburu twice daily; the flight from Nairobi takes between 45 minutes and an hour (depending on whether it's direct). Private charters are also easily organized and can be handled directly by your travel operator or lodge; the best operator out of Nairobi is **Boskovic Air** (© **020/60-6364;** www.boskovicaircharters.com). Or, if you're arriving from Laikipia or Nanyuki, use **Tropic Air** (www.tropicair-kenya.com).

GETTING AROUND Samburu's road network is fairly extensive and well maintained, although it's not unknown to be held up by ill-equipped larger vehicles getting stuck in the sand while trying to cross *luggas* (dry river beds).

PARK FEES Daily fees for Samburu are $40 per adult, $20 per child; the same fee applies to Shaba and Buffalo Springs, but tickets are interchangeable for these two reserves.

WHEN TO GO The Northern Frontier District is generally hot and dry. April through October is a marginally cooler period, with some rain, and may be more comfortable.

WHERE TO STAY

Despite its remoteness, Samburu probably has the highest guest bed density of any game park in East Africa. Sadly, Samburu's fame as an elephant stronghold has made it immensely popular, and the majority of accommodations here are large compounds—impersonal (and often unattractive) lodges where the game-viewing experience is drastically inferior to the smaller, pricier places. Fortunately, the better lodges are adept at working their areas with enough grace and savvy to steer you away from the worst of the traffic. If you want to be inside the reserve itself, there's none better than the infinitely stylish Elephant Watch (see box later in this chapter); otherwise, the two super-chic concessions (SaSaab and Saruni Samburu) on community-owned lands adjacent the park are among the finest lodgings in the country. In Shaba, Joy's Camp (reviewed below) provides a singularly luxurious tented experience with other safari vehicles unlikely to be seen at all, while those seeking an intrepid escape head much farther north—too far to visit the reserves by road, in fact—to the remote, little-known Mathews Mountains, where there are two luxury camps with access to a massive untouched forest.

Private Concessions Near Samburu Reserve

Two of the most exciting accommodations projects in the country occupy private concessions on community-owned land beyond the borders of Samburu National Reserve. Of course, you also have direct access to Samburu and Buffalo Springs, neither of which is fenced. However, staying here you have the distinct advantage of access to huge additional tracts of land that will feel like your own private wilderness—they're entirely off-limits to the minibuses, so you can effortlessly escape the crowds when you've had your fill of Samburu's dense game viewing.

SaSaab ★★★ A beautiful location poised over the edge of the Ewaso Nyiro River and facing the distant Lekurukki Mountains, SaSaab, like Saruni (below), is at the cutting edge of a new generation of safari lodges where the cool, contemporary design is much enhanced by harmony with the surrounding terrain. Set just above a twist in the Ewaso Nyiro River, in the arid heart of Samburuland, SaSaab comprises nine fabulous thatch-roofed living spaces. Shot through with onion-dome motifs and other Moroccan-influenced design details, each fabulous suite is more than 100 sq. m (1,076 sq. ft.), with an airy, open-fronted bedroom, sitting area, full bathroom, personal garden, and private plunge pool—each also enjoys a stupendous view. Suites are handsomely styled, with

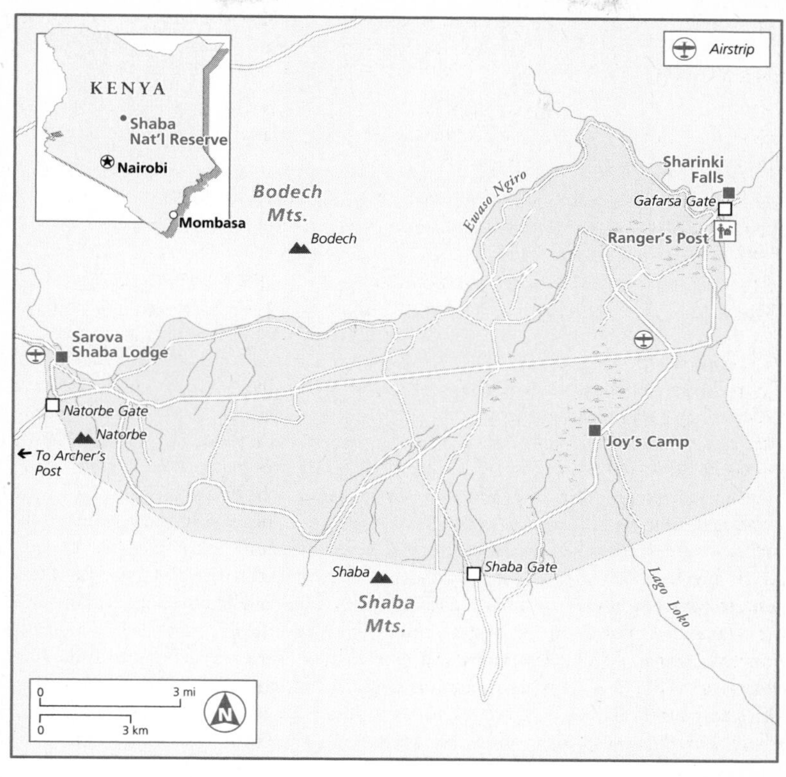

whitewashed walls, canvas, and plenty of space, and luxuriously furnished with antique four-poster beds brought from the coast, palm trees in giant clay pots, stacks of wicker baskets, and an eclectic range of materials ranging from beaded coat hangers and straw lampshades to wicker baskets and old hurricane lanterns. For the most privacy, reserve tent 1. Tent 2 is closer to the river, its rushing waters always audible, and affords spectacular views upstream.

You dine either in the large, breezy, open-fronted mess with its Moorish and Balinese arches, Indian pillars, brass lanterns, and views over the river and the plains beyond, or on a remote rocky promontory reached on camel back. Meals, too, are Moroccan inspired—light and fresh, to counteract the heat—and accompanied by a selection of Italian wines. There's much to do and see here—mountain bikes and camels are available when you grow tired of exploring the Samburu ecosystem in some of the country's best-equipped game vehicles—or simply take in the gorgeous views from the infinity pool, which sits on the lip of the river. Game drives (note that there's some distance to be covered before reaching the Samburu Reserve) are tremendously professional, with a proper briefing before setting off and every effort made to accommodate your special requests. Note: SaSaab is closed May and November.

Changing Their Ways, Cementing Their Doom?

To outsiders, encounters with the unfamiliar, strange, and often unfathomable traditions of African people can be immensely unsettling, occasionally challenging personal notions of morality. Much Western understanding of African tribal practices comes in the form of human rights reports. They tell chilling tales of teenagers subjected to circumcision, complain about medieval practices such as forced marriage and polygamy, and scream in horror about many other cruel, inhumane practices that run contrary to "civilized" ideas of existence. But there's another side of the coin, a version of the saga that's almost completely ignored because it doesn't fit in with the thinking favored by Western morality and modes of existence. Much of the north—particularly in the foothills of Mt. Kenya (around Laikipia and Samburu National Reserve) and as far north as Lake Turkana—is stomping ground of the Samburu, a Maasai splinter group who, like their cousins, are cattle-owning pastoralists who speak a dialect of Maa. Amongst other tribes of Kenya, the Samburu are known as *loibor kineji,* People of the White Goats, and they refer to themselves simply as White Goats, a relatively sparse group now numbering around 110,000. While the Samburu have shown some inclination to give up their traditional ways—besides tending their goats and cattle, exchanging raids against their enemies and neighbors, they take tribal fashion to rather elaborate levels, costuming themselves with gorgeous accessories and incorporating all kinds of beads and baubles and feathers in their finery—they've adhered to a traditional way of life far more vehemently than their cousins in Maasailand.

Yet there are facets of modernity, encroaching Western civilization, and a changing way of life that, as with the Maasai, threaten the Samburu's very existence. One frightening development is that some Samburu are buying AK-47s from Somalis and Ethiopians in order to protect themselves in raids from other tribes—or, indeed, to arm themselves when raiding others. As a means of dealing with increasingly harsh, arid, dry, and waterless conditions—a result of both global warming and encroaching modernity—many Samburu have exchanged their cattle for camels (which fare better under harsh desertlike conditions) and taken to crop-growing, which might sound like social evolution to some, but it is riddled with inestimable problems.

Many of the solutions offered by institutionalized charities sound promising, and the media is rife with tales of humanitarian aid schemes involving NGO and World Bank bailouts for starving tribes. They build schools where children need education, operate where people are sick, and dig water holes where there is drought. But, according to some, such tried-and-tested Western aid—generous handouts coupled with heavy-handed social change—isn't necessarily helpful in the long run. While we may take delight in "helping" to settle these traditionally nomadic people, there may be dire consequences to changing centuries-old norms.

A few Kenyans contest that some blame for the changes in lifestyle should be placed at the feet of humanitarian aid workers. "Oftentimes they fail to recognize the consequences of their interference," says Julia Francombe, who works closely with her Samburu neighbors to help them develop sustainable projects. She argues that the problem lies with *how* outsiders sometimes go about implementing change. "When we simply dig water holes, putting water where water shouldn't be, for example, it disrupts the environment, compelling people to settle in one particular area, which leads to overstocking, overgrazing, and ultimately erosion. Quickly, the balance tips, so by interfering with these people's nomadicism, we're not only helping destroy the environment, we're causing a situation by which, in 5 or 10 year's time, they won't be able to survive."

Consider, for example, the scourge of female circumcision, derided by foreigners as well as most modern Kenyans. Where there are reports of teenage girls being prepared for circumcision, the standard reaction may be to have them dragged from their communities and placed in orphanages while their fathers are imprisoned for conspiring to break Kenyan law. Lobbying against clitoridectomy—also known as female genital mutilation—is always a headline-grabber. Yet Samburu tradition dictates that all girls between 14 and 16 be circumcised before they are married off to much older men. An uncircumcised woman, however, has almost zero chance of being married to a traditional, rural Samburu man and will spend her life alone and on the fringes of society. As much as the outsider might struggle to deal with the very notion of female circumcision—an excruciatingly painful, dangerous procedure—there are problems resulting from outside interference. In one incident, a nurse reported a father's intention to marry off his teenage daughter. The girl was taken into state custody and placed in boarding school, while the father was arrested. After his release, the father was bound to honor his agreement with his future son-in-law, but because his older daughter was no longer available, he was forced to marry off his 10-year-old instead. Without delay, the girl was circumcised and married, and when authorities got wind, the father was imprisoned and the child-bride placed in an orphanage with her sister. Cut off from their community, their family, their customs, and their way of life, both girls are almost certainly destined for a life of prostitution as they try to eek out an existence in towns and settlements that are completely out of sync with the world they were born into. Parents are circumcising younger girls to avoid government intervention or potential defiance from more savvy, older girls.

Adding to the dilemma is Kenya's education system. It not only fails to offer learning in any of the tribal languages, but it teaches nothing connected with tribal culture or traditional way of life. For most, the classroom is an alien world where strange, irrelevant ideas are foisted on a people who are being made strangers in their own land.

If you want to get involved in a nonintrusive way, contact Julia Francombe (julia@olmalo.org), who has established a series of self-empowerment programs for Samburu women and children without treading on cultural toes.

P.O. Box 15565, 00503 Nairobi. ✆ **020/89-2234** or 733/960-202. Fax 20/89-2234. www.sasaab.com. 9 units. $1,240 double; children under 12 $424 sharing with 2 adults. Rates include all meals, most drinks, game-viewing activities, airstrip transfers, and laundry. No credit cards. **Amenities:** Restaurant; airstrip transfers; bar; pool; spa and beauty treatments. *In room:* Wi-Fi.

Saruni Samburu ★★★ Italian author Riccardo Orizio's second Kenyan camp—co-created by the country's most prolific designer-architect, Mark Glen—is a triumph of the imagination. Inspired by the arid, rock-strewn surrounds, with a look that's a mix of Moroccan Moorish and nomadic Samburu homestead, they've come up with a fittingly minimalist design. Smart and contemporary, the beautiful, simple structures interface seamlessly with the rugged, cliff-edge, middle-of-nowhere terrain. Approached via a broad rockface driveway (you won't believe your eyes as you ascend), you'll know immediately that you've arrived at one of Kenya's freshest properties. Each massive, airy, light-filled cottage—a combination of canvas, stripped wood, and locally quarried rock—is organically designed, inspired by its unique position. There are just four cottages; two are family-sized suites with enormous open-fronted living areas, two attractively attired bedrooms, walk-in dressing areas, and spacious bathrooms, again with show-stopping views from alfresco showers. Artfully furnished, with luxurious beds and sensuous linens, the interiors are shot through with artifacts collected from exotic locations; unfussy, clean-lined, and simple, they're dreamy spaces to return to at the end of a busy day of game drives or bush walks. To the accompaniment of flickering candles, a dense canvas of stars, and the ongoing cacophony from the surrounding bush, evenings commence with drinks in the open-to-the-elements lounge, where you're served by gentle Samburu men (who are slowly getting accustomed to the odd predilections of Western guests) dressed in chic traditional gear. The experience is elegant and faintly colonial, without being overly Europeanized; staff approach their duties with a charmed naïveté, pulled off with a humbling desire to do well. For those in-between moments during the day, you can laze by the pool or summon up a muscle-tingling massage, or spend some time getting to know the locals—hardy, bush-savvy warriors—a little better.

P.O. Box 304, Narok, Kenya. ✆ **050/22-424** or 0734/76-4616. www.sarunisamburu.com. Reservations: Cheli & Peacock, P.O. Box 743, 00517 Uhuru Gardens, Nairobi. ✆ **020/60-4054** or 020/60-3090/91. Fax 020/60-4050. www.chelipeacock.com. 4 units. High season $1,190 double, $2,640 family cottage (up to 4 people), $440 children 5–16 sharing with 2 adults; midseason $990 double, $2,100 family cottage, $365 per child; green season $740 double, $1,600 family cottage, $270 per child. Discounted rates for stays of 4 nights or more in mid- and green seasons. Rates include all meals, most beverages, game-viewing activities, local airstrip transfers, 1 massage per room, and laundry. AE, MC, V. **Amenities:** Bar; airstrip transfers; pool; spa.

Samburu National Reserve

The best—and, by a long stretch, most exclusive—place to stay inside Samburu National Reserve is Elephant Watch (see "At Home with the Elephants" box below), which operates in conjunction with Save the Elephants, the labor of love of world-famous conservationist Ian Douglas-Hamilton and his design-conscious wife, Oria. Their handsome seasonal camp is not only the most ecologically sound place to stay, but it's also the least crowded and the only one where the animals are accorded the respect and dignity they deserve and where you also have every chance of savoring a personal moment with the reserve's wild elephants. Exclusivity such as you'll find at Elephant Watch doesn't come cheap, though, so you may find yourself looking into staying at one of the less intimate camps—not necessarily a disastrous option if you're keeping your visit very short. Tread with caution, however, because there are a handful of total duds, with prison compound–like accommodations worth avoiding.

Fun Facts **The Samburu Miracle**

One of the most extraordinary and endearing wildlife events ever witnessed on camera occurred in Samburu National Reserve. A lioness named Kamunyak adopted an orphaned baby oryx and nurtured it for several days while a BBC film crew observed and astounded locals and tourists watched in fascination. While the oryx suffered increasing malnutrition as it was unable to suckle, the lioness also started to waste away as she traded hunting for instinct-driven mothering. Although the tale could not have ended any other way, the oryx was finally killed and eaten by other lions—and if the film footage is anything to go on, the loss of her adopted baby broke the lioness's heart. The event proved so strange, surreal, and suggestive of the inexplicable wonders of the animal kingdom that Kamunyak was dubbed "the miracle lioness" and thousands believe her action to have truly been an act of God.

There are two midsize, relatively acceptable options that you may want to investigate: One is Larsens Tented Camp (reviewed below), and the other is **Samburu Intrepids** (✆ **20/444-6651;** www.heritage-eastafrica.com; $515–$963 double, including all meals and two game drives per day), a slightly tired, old-fashioned place with cluttered public areas set on large wooden stilts under a high thatched ceiling. Reached via stone and concrete pathways, the tented accommodations are raised on sturdy plinths beneath straw-pitched roofs; neatly refurbished, with dark strip-wood floors and mass-produced furniture, they're pretty dull. They're well-shaded, though, and each room also has a ceiling fan—although nights are coolish, daytime temperatures tend to be around 33°C (91°F); you also have a personal terrace with views toward the Ewaso Nyiro River. Whereas sleeping quarters are tidy, maintenance in some of the public areas is sorely lacking, especially around the pool (where monkeys come to drink) and in the dark, dinky massage room and adjacent gift shop. As you'll soon pick up from the price lists stuck up all over the public spaces here, most activities cost extra; these include camel safaris, visits to Samburu homesteads, and overnight fly-camping on sacred Mount Ololokwe.

Larsens Tented Camp ★ A member of Small Luxury Hotels of the World, Larsen's is the best of the larger Samburu camps with big, widely spaced tents ranged among tall doum palm, acacia, and fig trees about 30m (98 ft.) back from the Ewaso Nyiro River. Decorated in hushed, neutral tones, tents are made up to convey a faintly colonial-era safari theme (wardrobes disguised as old-fashioned leather traveling trunks and hurricane lanterns as bedside lamps), with billowing, foldaway drapes, hand-woven rugs, and welcome extras such as in-room slippers and fluffy bathrobes. They're more spacious (and private) than those at Intrepids, with larger bathrooms (although similarly tiled and dull) and a look that's decidedly less mass produced. Although the camp *askaris* are burdened with constantly chasing away the monkeys, half the pleasure at Larsens is having at least some animals in the camp with you, although you definitely need to keep your tent zipped up to prevent them from pillaging your valuables. The tented central areas are perhaps a little bland, with a certain old-fashioned stiffness, but if you like your meals served on candlelit tables with silver and china, you might not feel too put out by the

Moments At Home with the Elephants

In conservation circles, the Douglas-Hamiltons—Ian and Oria—are global crusaders. They launched their trendsetting pachyderm-tracking program, Save the Elephants, right here in Samburu National Reserve. Besides initiating the first all-Africa elephant census, conducting a major study on the ivory trade, monitoring the movements of elephants around the continent, and authoring ellie-centric books (for grown-ups and children), they've brought global attention to the plight of these creatures and shared their enthusiasm (and fund-raising know-how) with everyone from politicians and celebs to ordinary travelers.

For several years, Oria has also been hosting privileged guests (including celebs) at her intimate, personally styled, semi-permanent tented camp inside the Reserve. **Elephant Watch** ★★★ is without question the best place in Kenya to get up close and personal with the eponymous big beasts, many of which pass the time hanging around the camp and are known individually—by name—to Oria and her Samburu staff; you'll easily spend entire days watching and listening as they wander into camp, ripping up the grass as they feed, mudding in the river, or picking pods beside the tents—don't panic, there are Samburu warriors to protect you. As you witness them going about their business, you'll notice a range of behaviors that bear an uncanny resemblance to human emotional and social patterns.

An ecologically sound camp ("no waste, no pollution, and no noise") with just six large desert-style tents under thatch, Elephant Watch is dotted along a winding sandy bank of the Ewaso Nyiro River and barely visible beneath the broad-spreading trees. Everything is solar powered, and even your hand-washed laundry is pressed using irons powered with hot coals; during the rainy season, the entire camp is dismantled to allow the environment to recover fully. Oria's got "shabby chic" down to a fine art—her tents are simple, rustic,

river-facing dining tent (which is open on three sides) or meals taken under the trees. It may not be perfect (and doesn't share nearly the same intimacy as Elephant Watch or the sexiness of SaSaab or Saruni), but Larsens is sufficiently light on the pocket (although you pay extra for game drives) and—with such proximity to Samburu's wildlife—doesn't leave you feeling short-changed.

Wilderness Lodges, P.O. Box 42788, 00100 Nairobi. ✆ **020/53-2329.** Fax 020/65-0384. www.discoverwilderness.com. 20 units. $815 double. Children 3–12 sharing with 2 adults pay 50%; under 3 free. Rate includes all meals and limited alcoholic and nonalcoholic beverages. AE, MC, V. **Amenities:** Restaurant; bar; Jacuzzi; pool; spa; Wi-Fi; clinical officer/nurse on standby; currency exchange. *In room:* Hair dryer, minibar, Wi-Fi.

Shaba National Reserve

Joy's Camp ★★★ One of Kenya's new breed of impeccably stylish tented camps, Joy's is far away from tourist traffic, situated amid captivating Shaba scenery—compared with Samburu, this is a virtual backwater. Whether you plant yourself on your private veranda, on a lounger at the pool, or on a sofa in the breezy open-air lounge/bar, you'll fabulous creations with hessian-covered sand floors and outdoor bathrooms. Yet, thanks to her compulsion for glamour, they're pretty, feminine, and eye-catching, with hand-painted four-poster beds; swathes of bright, colorful cotton fanning in the breeze; huge cushioned sofas; handcrafted furniture made from elephant-felled trees; and locally woven palm mats. Built around a tree, the simple bathrooms provide a touch of novelty—under the gaze of cheeky monkeys, you wash using sun-heated water (from the camp well) provided in hand-painted buckets.

The eye-catching use of vividly colored fabrics—made by Samburu and Turkana tribespeople—continues into the mess tent, furnished with padded daybeds and handcrafted chairs made from gnarled and twisting acacia branches. Besides the usual game drives, guests are encouraged to take away intimate knowledge of the ellies; staff introduce you to the families, and you can visit Ian's elephant research facility nearby. Go on guided bird walks, hike Ololokwe, the sacred mountain of God, or choose a remote spot for a sundowner. For the culturally inclined, you can learn to milk goats, throw spears, and make jewelry on a visit to a Samburu homestead. The kitchen uses fresh ingredients directly from Oria's farm in the Rift Valley, and every meal might be served in a different location, depending on the position of the moon and the seasons—and the well-stocked bar is always open.

Reserve your tent well ahead through Elephant Watch Safaris (P.O. Box 54667, Nairobi; ✆ **20/89-0596;** www.elephantwatchsafaris.com). Doubles run $1,100 to $1,230 and include all meals, drinks (excluding champagne and special wines), game-viewing activities, elephant interactions, visits to Samburu villages, local transfers, and laundry. A portion of your payment also helps support Save the Elephants.

get a good sense of being in the midst of a beautiful landscape with volcanic hills on all sides and breathtaking, iconic African wilderness stretching off into the distance. It was here that the famous conservationist and author Joy Adamson lived with her animals until her death in the mid-1980s, where she reintroduced Penny the leopard to the wild, and where she penned her last book, *Queen of Shaba,* based on that story. Approximating an elegant Bedouin camp, the utterly gorgeous tents here are reached via neat white gravel pathways—each one is a massively proportioned (100 sq. m (1,076 sq. ft.) chic space set on a solid concrete platform with polished whitewashed floors, onion-dome archways, Boran and Somali textiles, and locally made furniture. Bedrooms are done out in pale, natural tones, offset by sparing use of brightly colored beads, recycled-glass baubles, and amber lights laid into the floor. Each tent has its own private deck, and clever design means you have an outdoor view from the indoor shower through a Moorish arched space in the wall. (Less-intelligent design means your clothes hang in the bedroom, some distance from the bathroom—small crisis this because walking through the bedroom to get to your dressing rack is about the only exercise you'll get here unless you request to go on a bush walk or spend some time in the pool.)

At night, the camp is lit with hurricane lamps and Moroccan candle lanterns flicker throughout the lounge and dining area. Large sheets of elegant canvas are strung up to create attractive shaded areas around the pool. The camp overlooks a large natural spring where animals jostle for watering rights, while elephant and buffalo graze just beyond the fence and are often visible from your tent. Most of the staff here are Boran tribespeople and most of them Muslim, shedding an alternate light on the Kenyan cultural experience.

www.joyscamp.com. Reservations: Cheli & Peacock, P.O. Box 743, 00517 Uhuru Gardens, Nairobi. ✆ **020/60-4053/4** or 020/60-3090/1. Fax 020/60-4050. www.chelipeacock.com. 10 units. High season $1,190 double, $440 per child 5–16 sharing with 2 adults; midseason $990 double, $365 per child; green season $740 double, $270 per child. Children under 5 stay free. Discounted rates for stays of 4 nights or more in mid- and green seasons. Rates include all meals, most beverages, game-viewing activities, local airstrip transfers, cultural visits, and laundry. MC, V. **Amenities:** Restaurant; bar; airstrip transfers; babysitting; pool.

Mathews Range

The farther north you suggest traveling in Kenya, the more confounded locals become, often hinting at the "adventure" that lies in store, always warning of the potential dangers, and, more often than not, utterly unable to imagine where you intend to stay. As you dip off the Laikipia Plateau and enter the badlands of the Northern Frontier District and beyond, you, too, may start to suspect that you're leaving all contact with the civilized world behind. Don't fall for the doomsayers' gloom. If you want to penetrate north, moving beyond Samburu National Reserve, it's certainly possible to do so in style. The **Mathews Mountain Range,** midway between the Samburu and Marsabit preserves, is a thickly forested, untamed mountain park covering approximately 1,000 sq. km (390 sq. miles) that rises majestically out of the arid surrounds; at its highest point (Mathew Peak), it reaches 2,375m (7,790 ft.). The forest is home to elephant, melanistic leopard, bushbuck, giant forest hog, rhino, and buffalo, as well as ancient cycads, wild orchids, spectacular butterflies, and turacos—bulky, colorful birds you'll spot scrambling around the forest floor. There are black-and-white colobus monkeys in the forest, too.

Here, beside the Ngeng River, beneath towering fig trees, is **Kitich Camp** ★ (www.kitichcamp.com; $800 double, including all meals and most drinks, airstrip transfers, activities, laundry, and daily conservation fees). Kitich is one of two upmarket camps in the region—relative luxury in one of four safari-style twin tents (each with a private alfresco stone bathroom) is accompanied by infinite solitude in the unspoiled bush. Based here, you basically have the whole mountain range and forest to yourself. Walk along forest paths guided by the Samburu and Ndorobo people, swim in natural rock pools of the crystal-clear mountain streams, or idle away the hours in the fire-warmed lounge overlooking the river glade. Reservations are through Cheli&Peacock (✆ **20/60-3090/1** or 20/60-4053/4; www.chelipeacock.com).

Even better than Kitich is **Sarara Tented Camp** ★★ (www.lewa.com; all-inclusive doubles $960–$1,380), located on the Namunyak (Place of Peace) conservancy, a 343,400-hectare (848,198-acre) tribal community-owned wilderness area with five guest tents situated just below Warges peak to the north of Ol Donyo Sabache (also known as Ol Lolokwe, the sacred mountain). The setting affords unrivalled views of the Mathews Range, and since the camp isn't in the mountains themselves, Sarara can offer game drives through the Namunyak wilderness, where guests have a better chance of seeing lion, leopard, and two separate groups of African wild dog—one pack here numbers more than 30 individuals, making this Kenya's most significant wild dog habitat. Now that once-furious poaching has been stopped—much thanks to the Sarara community initiative—Namunyak also attracts large herds of elephant. The emphasis here is mainly on walking excursions—you can head across to the Mathews forest for a walk with a Samburu scout. Sarara tents each have an open-air bush shower, veranda, and comfortable beds, and quality bed linen, bathrobes, towels, and other essentials are provided. The lounge and dining *banda* overlooks a natural pool (for swimming) and a waterhole (where animals drink). Don't miss a chance to check out the Sarara Singing Wells, where Samburu warriors water their herds during the dry season. Since some of these wells are as much as 10m (33 ft.) deep, the men strip off and climb into the pits, forming a human chain. For several hours each day, they'll chant traditional tunes as they haul out the water, passing it up by hand for the cattle.

You have to make an effort to get to Sarara Camp, but the journey is completely worth the time and expense. It is approximately 5 hours from Nanyuki to Sarara by road, so it is recommended to go by air; Boskovic Air Charters (out of Nairobi) or Tropic Air (from Nanyuki) are your best bets for private air charters directly to Namunyak airstrip. Reservations for Sarara Camp are through Bush & Beyond (© **020/60-0457;** www.bush-and-beyond.com).

3 LAKE TURKANA & THE FAR NORTH

750km (465 miles) N of Nairobi

> "The north is not Kenya," an African told me in Nanyuki. "It is not Somalia or Ethiopia. It is another country. The Kenyan government does nothing for it. It is a place run by foreigners—they manage everything, the schools, hospitals, churches. They are run by charities and aid agencies and NGOs, not by us."
>
> —*Dark Star Safari,* Paul Theroux

Remote, untamed, untamable—the heat-drenched deserts that stretch north toward the Ethiopian border are rough and inhospitable. The roads north of dusty Maralal and Archer's Post—considered by most to be Kenya's final frontiers—represent instability, danger, and unpredictable trouble. Whether it's the *shifta* bandits; the harsh, sudden climate; or the savage pitted roads, this is a part of the world not to be taken lightly. Nor is it necessarily the Kenya of postcards and tourist brochures. Despite its patches of magnificence—well-watered oases, densely vegetated wildlife preserves, and the immense green-tinged shock of water that is Lake Turkana—Kenyans themselves remain immensely wary of this far-flung zone. Although the goal is often to reach Turkana, the world's largest desert lake—splendidly isolated and surrounded by volcanic hills, lava flows, fierce winds, and a formidable mix of hardy tribespeople—there's plenty of interest along the way, particularly for anyone searching for an alternative look at paradise. Here, in the deserts, topographical contrasts are all the more striking, and images of human survival will burn deeply into your memory. The going can be extremely tough, but there's adventure to be had along the way; which is why the north is a popular overland safari circuit favored by rough 'n' ready backpackers.

FLY-IN SAFARIS

There are no scheduled flights to Lake Turkana, but if time and comfort are of any concern, the only reasonable way of visiting the far-flung north is on an exclusive and expensive fly-in excursion. You'll need to charter a plane, with costs well upward of

$2,000 just for the one-way air transfer (from Nairobi)—which doesn't account for the fact that you'll pay again to be collected if you wish to spend a couple of days. Given sufficient warning, a few of the Laikipia lodges will arrange a 1-day or multiday outing, during which you'll camp in relative luxury, receive five-star service, and get personal insight into local tribal customs and culture. One of the best options for a comparatively upmarket, quality fly-in adventure is through Oria Douglas-Hamilton's boutique safari operation (which includes her fantastic Elephant Watch tented camp in the Samburu National Reserve). Oria and her team put together bespoke itineraries with chartered flights to Lake Turkana, where you'll enjoy exclusive camping on its shores and islands. You'll get to meet local tribespeople in a totally noncommercial way and be treated with the reverence of a visiting dignitary. Contact Oria by writing to elephantwatch@africa-online.co.ke.

OVERLAND SAFARIS

The vast expanse north of Samburu and Shaba was never inhabited by European settlers or ranchers and has always enjoyed a high degree of isolation from the rest of Kenya. Still referred to by old, white Kenyans by its colonial-era name—the Northern Frontier District, implying a strong degree of insecurity and danger—Samburuland is a combination of upland plateaus created by the same tectonic movements that created the Rift Valley and immense deserts of varying degrees of aridity. Many consider it the most visually astonishing part of Kenya. Die-hard adventure-seekers are quick to point out that the wild, empty, harsh, untamable north is where you just might find your very perception of the term *civilization* takes on an altered meaning. Here, closer to Kenya's borders with Somalia and Ethiopia, desertlike conditions and a harsh climate prevail.

These flat, dry expanses are speckled with microclimatic pockets, such as lush, green Marsabit—a mountainous forest that rises high above the surrounding Dida Galgalu Desert—and the Kalacha oasis, where water unexpectedly flows from beneath parched, cracked soil. If you travel overland toward Turkana, you'll inevitably be stopping off at these bases.

If you choose to travel overland, you'll be facing all kinds of challenges—your mettle will be tested by the long, difficult, unkempt roads and the frustrations that will come with vehicle breakdowns or getting stuck in the mud (if it should rain) or deep sand (at any given time), not to mention an overwhelming lack of infrastructure, basic amenities

The Ugly Irony

Kenya's ban on hunting hasn't necessarily thrown up the kind of animal-saving goodwill one might expect. Prior to the ban in the 1970s, the north was rich in wildlife—Burchells' and Grevy zebra, Reisa oryx, topi, rhino, ostrich, cheetah, lion, hyena, leopards, elephant, reticulated giraffe, and numerous gazelle species were seen here in good numbers. But the hunting ban kicked off a dramatic rise in poaching, since there were no longer hunters and wardens keeping an eye out, and economically there was no longer any reason to protect the animals. So many were slaughtered, in fact, that the north has become relatively barren, its larger animals particularly affected. It's up to tourism now to remedy the situation, since travelers' dollars might be the only motivation to start providing better protection for the animals.

most of us take for granted, and the inevitable disquiet that comes with traveling into the unknown with a group of strangers. For much of your journey, your overland safari company will also need to enlist a **police escort** (included in the cost of your trip), mandatory practice in these uncertain parts where bandits are believed to pose a legitimate threat to the safety of travelers. Happily, hold-ups are increasingly rare, but there's little point taking any chances hereabouts.

The Journey

There is more than one routing for overland trips to Lake Turkana, but in each case, it's worth remembering that the journey is as much part of the experience as the destination. This might sound like a travel cliché, but you'll not only see remarkable sights along the way—camel-herding tribespeople, strange mirages, phenomenal volcanic remnants—but you'll have the chance to overnight in miniature Edens, even more beautiful thanks to the vastness of the stark, lunar desert that you'll travel through to reach them. Described below is just one of the overland routes, but it's the most obvious and fruitful one, commencing in the vicinity of Samburu National Reserve and doing a U-turn in the vicinity of Turkana. Most safari companies also do a similar trip in reverse, and there's the option of chartering a flight (at enormous cost) to any of the stop-off points mentioned along the way, but you'll need to ensure that you've properly arranged onward 4×4 through one of the travel companies mentioned here or through your tour operator. Bear in mind that (for a reasonable uptick in price) you can create a personal itinerary through any of these overland operators—you can hire their services on an exclusive basis, specify how long you wish to overnight at any point along the way, upgrade to a better vehicle, and decide whether you'd prefer to camp in portable tents or stay in privately owned lodges where, indeed, these are available. (The few that do exist are mentioned below.)

Isiolo to Marsabit

A true frontier town, Isiolo is at the edge of the desert and feels almost like the last chance to consider turning back before heading deep into the unknown. If you've driven all the way from Nairobi or Nanyuki, you're sure to stop here for fuel and to pick up supplies (if there's anything you're likely to crave farther down the line, this may be your last chance to stock up). You'll also get your first real look of the type of disheveled cosmopolitanism that's evident throughout the north—a heady blend of Somalis plus tribespeople in traditional attire. Isiolo is south of Samburu National Reserve and attracts foreigners being transported to their lodges there, which means that locals are familiar with tourists and are likely to try hawking bargain-priced curios. (Much of what's available isn't quite as authentic as what you'll find on offer later in the trip.)

Between Isiolo and Archer's Post, the muddy roads and rain-soaked fields turn to dry dust and desert. You'll leave behind the pastures, cornfields, wooded valleys, and hills scored with furrows of cultivation. No more the tufted green copses on the banks of little creeks when you reach Archer's Post—about an hour away from Isiolo (in a fast car)—you'll have a real sense of being in a tiny, dust-blown sprawl that's pretty much in the middle of nowhere. If you stop, you'll be pestered by young boys—as much out of curiosity as out of need.

North of here exists a landscape that's unequivocally beautiful; hardly settled, it's a stretch of the imagination to assume that it's a part of the Kenya you've left behind. Passing Samburu game reserve, you cross the Ewaso Nyiro River and head—along the famous A2 northern highway—into the stark wilderness of Samburuland and across wide-open country inhabited by members of the Rendille tribe. Unearthly, even

Tales of the Jade Sea

Exotically nicknamed thanks to the effect of light glinting off the green algae in its undrinkable alkaline waters, Lake Turkana (called *Ka'alakol,* meaning The Sea of Many Fish, by the Turkana people) is romanticized and idealized by many as the most beautiful destination in all of Kenya. Its isolation, formidable size (up to 290km/180 miles long and 32km/20 miles wide), and startling location—betwixt coarse, black sandy shores and striking volcanic cones—no doubt account for much of the hype. But beauty comes with a price. By all accounts, it's a grueling, forbidding destination, with sparse vegetation—mostly wind-ravaged acacias—and furious temperatures. Besides the intense year-round heat—impacted little by sporadic rains—the lake is besieged by unpleasant winds and never appears at rest. Unpredictable squalls and full-blown storms can transform the water into a vicious tempest. It's been the undoing of many a fisherman, and a handful of ill-fated explorers, too.

The first European "discovery" of the lake was in 1888 by the Austrian duo Count Teleki and Lieutenant von Hohnel, who named it after their archduke, Rudolph—the name stuck until well after independence. The world's largest desert lake is also where some of the most important traces of our prehuman ancestors continue to be unearthed by scientists following in the footsteps of Richard Leakey, who found hominid fossils here in 1968.

The lake also sustains the world's largest population of Nile crocodiles, sizeable hippo pods, exotic birdlife, and tribespeople who have managed to survive the unimaginably harsh conditions. There are three reserves here—two are on islands within the lake itself, and the third, **Sibiloi National Park** (✆ **54/21-223;** admission $25 adults, $10 children), on the northeastern shore, surrounds Koobi Fora, a remote archaeological site that partially explains Turkana's other nickname, the Cradle of Mankind. Fossils dating back millions of years have been found here. A near-complete *homo erectus* skeleton—known as the Turkana Boy—was discovered here in 1984, while in 1999, a 3½ million-year-old skull was found by Richard Leakey's wife, Meave, and has become known as *Kenyanthropus platyops* (The Flat-Faced Man of Kenya).

Arguably the most rewarding place to visit is **Central Island National Park** (✆ **054/21-223;** admission $25 adults, $10 children), a relatively barren vapor-spewing trio of volcanoes with crater lakes and multitudinous reptiles—this is breeding ground for most of the lake's crocodiles, and there are cobras, puff

enchanted, the plains that stretch out before you are mostly flat and gravelly, but studded with sudden and stupendous volcanic outcrops that poke out of the barren wilderness. Some of the massive, broad, tall mountains, with 1,524 to 1,828m (4,999–5,996 ft.) rounded summits, are brilliantly rounded by millennia of harsh winds coursing through the desert. Most of these are *sans* vegetation or sparsely tufted with clumps of ragged bush. But then there are patches signifying nature at its most paradoxical, such as in Marsabit.

adders, and saw-scaled vipers. Traversing the lake to get to its islands can be treacherous (and not necessarily cheap), however, and is always subject to unpredictable weather conditions (the lake can be stirred up into a tempest in no time at all) and whether there's an available boat (although, if you're on a well-outfitted safari, such matters will be pre-arranged).

Near-extinct tribes are found around the lake, too, making this prime territory for cultural voyeurs—the El Molo, Kenya's smallest ethnic group, dwell in dwindling numbers (now around 250) around the eastern shore. On islands in the mouth of a bay just north of Loiyangalani, they live simple lives in doum palm-frond huts, hunting crocodiles and sometimes hippo; by some accounts, there are a further 500 El Molo living on difficult-to-access South Island. On a visit to Turkana, you are also certain to make contact with the Turkana, who inhabit the lake's western and southern shores and as far as Loiyangalani, on the eastern side. Renowned for their fighting prowess and recently purported to be the oldest tribal society in the world, legend has it that some 200 to 300 years ago, the tribe started to move east from the Dodoth escarpment in northeast Uganda. Of this powerful and influential people, who number more than a quarter of a million, the majority live on the western flank of the great Lake Turkana. Some, however, have migrated to make their home on the eastern shore, living among the Samburu, El Molo, Rendille, and Gabbra peoples clustered around the meager water resources.

Unusual for this part of the world, the Turkana have shunned circumcision as a practice and instead usher their male children into their age set by means of an alternative rite known as *Athapan* (a ritual dance). Fine craftsmen, the Turkana make use of leather, shells, seeds, bones, ivory, and horns to fabricate fine jewelry and clothing (they produce particularly striking triangular leather aprons, known as *arrac,* worn by unmarried women). Distinctive earrings of beaten metal hang in rows from the top to the bottom of each ear, and women are still often seen wearing the copper lip plugs of old. While you may come across completely naked, bead-wearing Turkana men, you'll notice that they always carry with them a highly decorated head rest, designed to prevent their elaborate coiffure, heavily decorated with ostrich feathers, from touching the ground when they sleep. If you are planning on picking up tribal curios, these are the people you want to bargain with to get your hands on the real thing.

Marsabit

Accessible only by 4×4 (along tough dirt roads, 260km/161 miles from Isiolo) or by chartered plane (it's a 2½ hr. flight from Nairobi, which is some 560km/347 miles south), Marsabit exists because of its high elevation in the midst of the desert plains. It is an anomaly, a lush, thick-vegetation mountain with a climate resembling that of a rainforest. Buzzing Marsabit town draws all kinds of traders and tribespeople from as far as Ethiopia, and it's an eye-opener for anyone looking to get a taste of a colorful mix of local

A Rose Among the Thorns

Currently, the only luxury accommodation anywhere north of the Mathews Range or even remotely near Lake Turkana is the sumptuous, beautifully designed **Desert Rose** ★★ (✆ **722/638-774,** or satellite phone 162/110-7002; www.desertrosekenya.com), a remote and exquisite lodge in the vicinity of Baragoi. Pleasingly, it's off the track regularly beaten by overland trucks and highway traffic, a hidden jewel on the slopes of Ol Donyo Nyiro. The lodge consists of private individually designed cottages that seem to erupt from the natural contours of the landscape. There are five in all, each with an open-air bathroom (with a tub) and jaw-dropping vistas. Besides lazing at the pool taking in the scenery, there's a long list of activities to keep you occupied, whether your interest is predominantly in tribal culture or simply exploring the terrain (you may even spot the occasional wild beast, although—as with much of the far north—this is certainly not a serious wildlife destination). Rates are $1,000 double and include all meals, most drinks, transfers, and activities. Reservations and transport arrangements should be made through **New African Territories** (✆ **020/386-4831** or -4832; www.africanterritories.co.ke). Baragoi is a 5-hour drive from Loiyangalani and some 90km (56 miles) north of Maralal, which translates into yet another 4 or 5 hours along a terrible rock-strewn track. If you can't face the thought of any more driving, Desert Rose has its own Cessna 206, available for transfers to and from the lodge or for scenic flights over Lake Turkana and the Suguta Valley.

cultures. The town is just .5km (⅓ miles) from the entrance to **Marsabit National Reserve** (✆ **69/2028;** kwsmarsabit@yahoo.com; admission $25 adults, $10 children), a dense and untamed forest where there's reasonable, inexpensive accommodation at **Marsabit Lodge** (✆ **735/555-747**). The only alternative to camping, the lodge is best remembered for its views (the little bungalows are arranged around one of the cliff-lined crater lakes), and although the 24 basic guestrooms are nowhere near ideal, they do have attached bathrooms, relatively decent beds, and views of the waterhole (although you'll probably want to head for the lounge, where the seating is more comfortable). There's a swimming pool, and the lodge's location overlooking the water makes it one of the few places in the reserve that's often teeming with game. Although there's a good mix of wildlife in the forest—including elephants known for their oversize tusks—game viewing isn't always easy because of the density of vegetation. You'll need a bit of patience and may have to wait out the heavy rains that slick the roads. If you do make it to Marsabit, though, make every effort to check out the more beautiful of the crater lakes, aptly named Paradise Lake (Gof Sokorte Gud).

Kalacha

Heading north out of Marsabit, it's only a matter of minutes before the wet and green is replaced by desert once again; it's a long, hot, tiring journey—140km (87 miles) through the Chalbi Desert to the next vaguely hospitable stop, **Kalacha,** situated on the edge of an oasis in the Chalbi Desert between Maikona and North Horr, and 65km (40 miles) south of the Ethiopian border. **Kalacha** is the main stomping ground for the people of the Gabbra tribe who live alongside the lesser-known Kosso, a dedicated tribe of blacksmiths. Custom dictates that the Gabbra are forbidden from forging their own weapons, so they must rely on the Kosso to supply them. The Chalbi—a Gabbra word meaning Salt—is named for the white salt patches that cover the dry sand here, but Kalacha itself really is an oasis, with water flowing from beneath the parched, cracked ground and serving as a watering hole for local communities. It's also a place of incredibly fierce winds that are known to lift people right off the ground. **Kalacha Camp** (✆ **020/33-032** or 0722/207-300; www.kalacha.org) was built as a Gabbra community project by the owner of Tropic Air and comprises just four *bandas* designed with desert-inspired Moroccan-influenced architecture using local palm trees. Facilities are basic, although you do get a flush toilet and shower (no hot water, though), but the experience is more about gaining insight into Gabbra tradition and getting to grips, however slightly, with their way of life. In Kalacha town, there is even a little Catholic church with some striking interior murals. And you can be entertained by Gabbra dancers and performances, with your hosts even acting out traditional ceremonies. Kalacha is famous for sand-grouse shooting, with two main seasons, February through March and July through October.

Loiyangalani & Lake Turkana

Out of Kalacha, the road continues west to North Horr and then turns south to Lake Turkana's seemingly desolate shore, where the principle town is **Loiyangalani.** This hodge-podge desert town features as a backdrop to some of the action in John le Carre's political thriller, *The Constant Gardener.* Here, too, are natural hot springs, unusual lava formations, and doum palms that provide shade and building materials for the Turkana and El Molo tribespeople based in the area. It's not at all the idyllic, isolated experience you might expect, however, and much of the tribal way of life has been upended by the promise of financial rewards the impoverished locals can expect from camera-wielding tourists. In this respect, Loiyangalani—and any of the "larger" settlements in the north—can feel a little disillusioning and commercial. Still, the assortment of tribes represented here imbues the place with a ramshackle cosmopolitan flavor, offset by Christian missions, aid workers, and awestruck visitors.

Loiyangalani is an obvious base from which to explore Lake Turkana's eastern shores. It's also where safari companies usually make use of **Oasis Lodge** (✆ **729/954-672;** www.oasis-lodge.com; $240 full-board double), traditionally the only half-decent permanent accommodations situated anywhere near the lake (and your best—and only—chance to grab a cold beer). Guestrooms—there are 24, so it's hardly built for exclusivity—are basic-but-bearable and have attached bathrooms, and there are swimming pools and the chance to hire chauffeured vehicles, take boat trips to sample Turkana's excellent fishing or to visit South Island, and drive to an El Molo village. Management at Oasis Lodge has become a bit hit-and-miss in recent times (when tourism slows, it seriously impacts the will to go on in such an isolated spot), so you might want to arrange a back-up plan through your tour operator before your arrival. If you choose to travel overland with Gametrackers (see below), you'll be staying outside Loiyangalani, either in tents or in a simple, semi-permanent beach village comprising huts in the style traditionally used by the Turkana people.

Maralal

From Loiyangalani, the road takes you south toward South Horr and Tuum, to the east of the Suguta Valley. Suguta is a huge sector of the Rift Valley between Lake Baringo and Lake Turkana. At the north end, the valley floor is only a few hundred meters above sea level, making it one of the lowest parts of the Rift Valley. It is also one of the hottest parts of Kenya, with deserts, volcanic cones, salt lakes, and uneven lava fields. Some safari companies use Tuum as a stop for guided camel walks, usually ending at a campsite at the foothills of Mount Nyiro. Encircled by desert, Mount Nyiro is heavily forested, thanks to underground springs that feed the many small settlements hereabouts. The drive south from Turkana is scenic but incredibly rough, taking you through lava flows to the edge of the Kaisut desert. The area is sliced through by bottomless ravines, which are regularly dry but become soaked with sudden flash floods after rain. If you want to inject a dash of class into the whole experience, arrange to break this sector of your journey with a couple of nights at the superb Desert Rose (p. 242).

The road trip back to civilization inevitably takes you through disheveled and dusty **Maralal,** a sad-looking town that's famous as the location of the International Camel Derby, held in August each year. In Maralal (if you're not camping), you'll probably need to break the journey with a night at the **Maralal Safari Lodge** (✆ **065/62-060,** or reservations 020/21-1124; $196–$245 double, including all meals). Again, it's the only (and, consequently, overpriced) reasonable option besides camping. The lodge is 2.5km (1½ miles) from the town and is somewhat redeemed by the fact that it overlooks a waterhole attracting a fair share of animals—zebra, buffalo, elephant—from the adjacent Maralal National Sanctuary. Guestrooms are in huge chalet-type cottages built with cedar wood; each one has a private bathroom, and most have a veranda and additional sleeping space in a loft. It's not luxury, but a great deal better than any of the dives in town, and there's a pool and poolside bar—a welcome antidote to the grueling desert drive you've just endured. Maralal, like many of the towns of the north, is a melting pot of different tribes and so is another opportunity to observe and photograph the local color.

Choosing the Safari That's Right for You

Deciding how, and with whom, to venture into the badlands of the north is extremely important. Known as the experts in overland trucking safaris in Northern Kenya, **Gametrackers** (5th Floor, Nginyo Towers, Moktar Daddah St., Nairobi; ✆ **020/222-2703** or 020/221-4568; fax 020/31-3619; www.gametrackersafaris.com) is a well-established operator that has been covering the Lake Turkana circuit for years. Standard Turkana packages include 8- and 10-day overland shared-truck safaris (the type Theroux so vehemently despises), with up to five departures per month. Costs are between 540€ and 665€ per person, excluding park fees, which must be paid in cash at the various park gates. Gametrackers will do upgraded versions of the same tours, should you wish to tackle the route in a more exclusive way—the 8-day Chalbi Desert safari in a 4×4 vehicle, and with no other passengers, will cost $3,760 double. On request, you could ask to also swap tented accommodations for nights in the lodges for a corresponding uptick in price. Gametrackers also offers a 10-day camel safari led by Rendille tribesmen, and there's a 2-week Jade Sea Journey (with 8 days spent on foot with Rendille tribesmen and their camels), available through their sister company Wild Horizons (www.wildhorizonsafaris.com; $5,040–$7,356 double). Don't even begin to contemplate any of these desert walking safaris unless you are in excellent health and physically (and emotionally) fit—conditions are harsh. Note that none of Gametrackers' rates include any beverages (you even need to bring your own water), toilet paper, cultural activities, or the hire of sleeping bags.

The other option—particularly if you outright shun the idea of camping—is **Origins Safaris** ★★★ (✆ **20/22-9009;** www.originsafaris.info), which offers all-inclusive airport-to-airport packages with a strong focus on meeting members of tribal communities. The itinerary is not as time-and-travel-intensive as the completely overland schedule of, say, Gametrackers; instead, Origins combines chartered flights with limited driving (around Lake Turkana and across the Chalbi Desert), but you'll fly between Nairobi and

Loiyangalani, and, after 2 nights in each of three lodges (Oasis, Kalacha, and Marsabit), fly from Marsabit back to Nairobi. You'll travel in relative luxury, too—solid 4×4s rather than bulky overland trucks shared with sweating, slightly nervous, always frustrated budgeters. Costs are considerably higher than you can expect on a purely overland safari; you're looking at around $1,000 per person, per night, depending on the size of the group that makes the trip. You can't book directly through Origins, but should instead contact Tom LaRock of U.S.-based **Safari Professionals** (© **800/779-2146;** www.safari professionals.com).

11

The Kenyan Coast

by Keith Bain

The East African coast—known to early Arabian traders as the Land of Zanj—boasts a fierce and fascinating history. It's a tale of high sea adventure; international trade in slaves, ivory, rhino horn, and coconut; myriad intermingling cultures, including violent escapades by vicious Portuguese invaders and rampaging cannibals; and a furious struggle for control of ports that served as gateways connecting Africa, Asia, the Middle East, and Europe. Coastal Zanj was also a battleground for the hearts, minds, and souls of local Swahili people as Christianity met its bitter rival in Islam, which had arrived with Shirazi and Omani settlers several centuries earlier. It was these business-minded Arabs who had established ports and trade routes and prospered on the back of slave labor.

This long history has had a profound impact on the region, which stretches from the war-ravaged Somali capital of Mogadishu to Mozambique in the south, and to this day, Swahili (an Arabic word meaning "People of the Coast") culture is more discernible and vibrant here than it is inland. Here, it's not only language that serves as a common bond between people of disparate ethnicities, but often also identification with a common faith, adherence to a unifying architectural style, dress, cuisine, and sense of community. Unlike the Indonesians, who forgot their original homeland after migrating to Madagascar (known as the Waqwaqs, these ancient immigrants had initially brought bananas to the Swahili Coast, but found the Zanj mainland too hostile and so ended up on Madagascar), the settlers who had come from Arabia and Persia always looked back to the great Middle Eastern cities that helped define their identity, bowing to Mecca in their mosques, where they listened to readings from the Koran and thereby sustained a unifying faith. Meanwhile, ancient cultural links with Islam were maintained by the movement of dhows that continued to sail between Arabia and the African coast.

Today commercial ships outnumber the Swahili Coast's traditional dhows, and the once-great sultanate of **Mombasa** has become a grimy industrial port. Tourists regularly pile onto the beaches north of Mombasa, but they're relatively sordid, crowded, and unappealing stretches that may be good for the mass-market resort set but are no place for the discerning traveler. South of Mombasa, though, the coast holds some beautiful surprises, with immaculate beaches, such as **Tiwi** and **Diani,** stretching all the way to Tanzania. Interrupted only by gorgeous coves, coral islands, and fabulous mangrove waterways, this is a genuine Swahili paradise offering great snorkeling, spectacular deep-sea fishing, and a handful of exclusive hideaways for a memorable post-safari de-stress.

North of Mombasa, the enclave of **Malindi** is an ancient Swahili town that's fallen victim to foreign colonizing instincts. It's overflowing with Italians who've set up shop here and is an unexpectedly garish cultural melting pot where

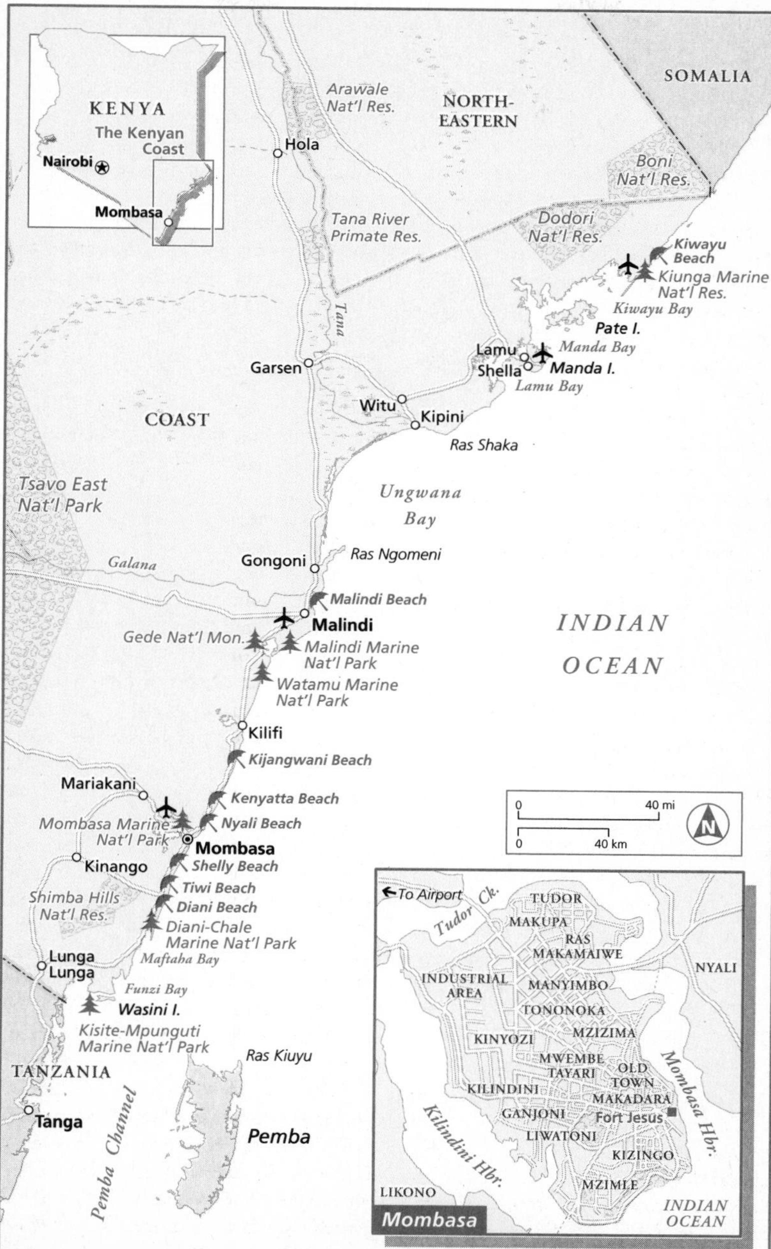
KENYA
The Kenyan Coast
Nairobi
Mombasa
SOMALIA
Arawale Nat'l Res.
NORTH-EASTERN
Hola
Boni Nat'l Res.
Tana River Primate Res.
Dodori Nat'l Res.
Kiwayu Beach
Kiunga Marine Nat'l Res.
Kiwayu Bay
Tana
Pate I.
Lamu
Manda Bay
Garsen
Shella
Manda I.
Lamu Bay
Witu
Kipini
COAST
Ras Shaka
Tsavo East Nat'l Park
Ungwana Bay
Galana
Gongoni
Ras Ngomeni
Malindi Beach
Malindi
INDIAN OCEAN
Gede Nat'l Mon.
Malindi Marine Nat'l Park
Watamu Marine Nat'l Park
Kilifi
Kijangwani Beach
Mariakani
Kenyatta Beach
Nyali Beach
Mombasa Marine Nat'l Park
Mombasa
Kinango
Shelly Beach
Tiwi Beach
Shimba Hills Nat'l Res.
Diani Beach
Diani-Chale Marine Nat'l Park
Maftaha Bay
Lunga Lunga
Funzi Bay
Wasini I.
Kisite-Mpunguti Marine Nat'l Park
Ras Kiuyu
TANZANIA
Tanga
Pemba Channel
Pemba
0
40 mi
0
40 km
N
To Airport
Tudor Ck.
TUDOR
MAKUPA
RAS MAKAMAIWE
NYALI
INDUSTRIAL AREA
MANYIMBO
TONONOKA
MZIZIMA
KINYOZI
MWEMBE TAYARI
OLD TOWN
KILINDINI
MAKADARA
Mombasa Hbr.
Kilindini Hbr.
GANJONI
Fort Jesus
LIWATONI
KIZINGO
MZIMLE
LIKONO
INDIAN OCEAN
Mombasa

The Taste of the Swahili Coast

Abundant fresh seafood, an endless supply of coconut, a love of spices that sailed in from the East, and various influences from successions of colonizers and settlers (Arab, Persian, Indian, and European) make Swahili cuisine wonderfully wholesome and exotic without being overblown or too complex. The use of tropical fruits such as tamarinds and passion fruit means that getting a piquant flavor—often a wonderful accompaniment to fresh, tasty, line-caught fish—is easy, and *samaki paka* (fish of the day) will often be prepared with coconut. The influences of Arabian and Indian kitchens are also evident; you'll find curries, often prepared with coconut, served with rice or chapati. Other dishes and snacks to look out for include:

Achari: Dried mango dipped in a sugary chili paste

Bajias: Deep-fried balls made with beans, onion, coriander, and spinach

Guvaji: Sweet potato; often accompanies a meat dish

Kachumbari: Traditional salad of tomato and onion that's found on most tables and is often used to add flavor to other dishes or temper a spicier dish or curry

Labania: A sweet made with milk, sugar, and ground nuts

Maandazi: Deep-fried, donutlike flour triangle

Mabuyu: Flavored baobab seeds

Maharagwe: Kidney beans with onion, tomato, and coconut cream

Makai: Roasted corn

Mishikaki: Barbecued kebabs, usually made with lamb and chicken

Mkate wa mayai: Swahili pizza made with vegetables and potato

Muhogo: Cassava; often accompanies a meat dish

Pojo: Concoction of green gram lentils with onion, tomato, coconut cream, and lentils

Samosas: Triangular parcels of slightly spicy vegetables, meat, or fish

Wali wa nazi: Coconut rice

bronzed Europeans hog the sun, snorkel among the most sublime coral reefs at nearby **Watamu,** and explore the mysterious **Gede ruins.**

But for a combination of cultural insight and a chance to unfurl your beach towel on a secluded beach—or set sail aboard a weather-bruised dhow cruising between virtually unexplored islands—there's no better destination than Kenya's far northern **Lamu Archipelago.** Lamu has acquired a raffish reputation as the most charmed of the Swahili coast's antique settlements, a place to lose yourself in an ancient culture and sink full force into an islander's life. It's the oldest living Swahili town in Kenya, and much-appreciated for its narrow labyrinthine laneways shaded by high stone walls. Although there's now an ATM and a bright pink motorized three-wheeler serves as the ambulance (besides one official car, the town's only other transport is waterborne or donkey powered), the town—and the entire seven-island archipelago—feels like a time-embalmed place, a soothing, mellow escape from the world.

You might have come to Kenya dreaming of nothing other than lions and leopards, but chances, are you'll lose your heart along the Swahili coast, a 530km (329-mile) stretch of impeccable, white sandy beaches dotted with laid-back villages and an improving number of idyllic intimate places to rest your safari-ravaged bones.

"Pole pole" ("Slowly, slowly"), they tell you at the coast, but be warned that the insidious charm of the Swahili Coast is addictive. Warmly referred to as the "Coastal Flops," the tendency to find yourself horizontal sets in quickly, the accumulated result of the sultry climate and the laid-back approach of the people who'll receive you. A few days here, exploring the long stretches of perfect white beaches, investigating an ancient and intriguing culture, or perfecting the art of unfurling in a hammock dangling from your private terrace, and you could end up beached here for eternity.

1 MOMBASA

Kenya's most tangibly heady, lively city, Mombasa—originally *Manbasa* in Arabic, and known as Kisiwa Cha Mvita, or "Island of War," in Kiswahili—certainly boasts a more intriguing history than the almost wholly modern landlocked capital. It's a cultural stew of African, Middle Eastern, and Asian influences, spiced by vague remnants of Portuguese and British colonial periods, although the latter perhaps is still evident only in some surviving architecture. It's a city where palm trees grow from the sidewalks and mosques vie, along with churches, Hindu temples, and Sikh gurdwaras, with modern industrial monsters. The city's indomitable spirit is strongly defined by its coastal location. As an island, it has always relied heavily on its natural harbor, which has sustained centuries of contact with the outside world and a steady stream of visitors, traders, invaders, and exotic rulers who have left their mark and impacted strongly on local culture. It is, in many respects, a deeply cosmopolitan city—or, as less enthused visitors might remark, a hodgepodge of diverse ethnicities competing for space, business, and your attention.

Mombasa has the distinction of being one of the oldest settlements in East Africa. A town has existed on the island for more than 700 years, and some proof dates Mombasa to a much earlier period. The real intrigue, however, began with the arrival of Vasco de Gama in 1498. Denied entry to the port, the Portuguese adventurer went on to Malindi, where he was greeted with open arms. From then on, the island city became a target of Portuguese fury, which escalated into all-out destruction on several occasions. So brutal were the Portuguese that contemporaneous historians report that when they attacked, they massacred every living soul, including women, children, and animals, hacked down palm trees and orchards, and set fire to any towns they had targeted. During their reign of tyranny along the coast, they became increasingly hated, to the extent that tyrannical harassment of the Swahili coast became cause enough in the 1580s for local sultans to request the intervention of the Turkish buccaneer Amir Ali Bey; the unstoppable Bey arrived in Mombasa and began building substantial fortifications. Bey might have gained control over the entire Swahili Coast, had it not been for the arrival of a cannibal horde—the Zimba tribe—which had been eating its way up the African coast, having already defeated the powerful and ancient island city-state of Kilwa (in what is now southern

Tanzania). While Bey was preparing for the inevitable Portuguese attack that would come from the sea, the Zimba amassed on the mainland and besieged the island city. The Portuguese took this as an opportunity to attack, sailing from Goa and arriving in sight of Mombasa on March 5, 1589, and prepared to take advantage of the fact that the Turks had enemies on two fronts. The Portuguese took Mombasa and even allowed the man-eating Zimbas to massacre and eat surviving Swahilis left hiding on the island. The Portuguese installed the sultan of Malindi as a puppet ruler acting on orders from Lisbon. Keen to hang on to strategically situated Mombasa, the Portuguese began building their still-standing Fort Jesus here in 1593, and they remained until the Omanis ousted them in 1698 after an epic siege that lasted more than 2 years. When Fort Jesus finally fell to the Omanis, it pretty much marked the end of Portuguese involvement in the affairs of East Africa. While they still controlled only a sprinkling of insignificant ports in Mozambique (where their influence is still evident today), the power and influence of the Omani (and, later, Zanzibari) Arabs was set to continue with only brief interruptions until the British leased the coast from the Zanzibaris. They made Mombasa the capital of the British East Africa Protectorate from 1887 to 1907.

Sadly, while the city's cultural history is wrapped up in the contours of the architecture and in the nature of its neighborhoods—particularly in Old Town and around Fort Jesus—the city itself is widely considered a stinking industrial sprawl, and beyond the relatively tiny historic enclave, there is virtually nothing that is likely to hold your attention for very long.

Bounded by water and linked to the mainland by several causeways and a ferry service, Mombasa certainly possesses something of a time warp sensibility—and that's despite the office towers, incessant traffic, and gigantic full-color advertising hoardings. Head on to the coastal mainland immediately north of here, however, and the sense of being in an evolving modern world is instantly apparent. It's here, starting with the upmarket suburb of Nyali, that the massive luxury plots, tight security, and, with a handful of exceptions, largely hideous beachfront resorts set the tone. By all means, spend a few hours exploring the old Swahili quarter and visit the infamous Fort Jesus, but if you have any say in the matter and are gagging for a genuine holiday experience, push south to the coastal playgrounds around Diani Beach or head north to Lamu.

ESSENTIALS

GETTING THERE **By Air** The flight from Nairobi to Mombasa takes around 45 minutes. These flights, as well as other domestic services and a handful of international flights, arrive at Moi International Airport, situated on the mainland around 10km (6¼ miles) west of central Mombasa, which, in case you'd forgotten, is an island. **Kenya Airways** connects Mombasa with Nairobi and has flights to and from Zanzibar on certain days of the week. The low-cost airline **Fly540** connects Mombasa with Nairobi, Malindi (north of Mombasa), Zanzibar, Kisumu (in Western Kenya), and the Masai Mara. **AirKenya** also flies here from the capital and connects Mombasa to a number of safari and coastal destinations. Offering a more limited number of connections is locally based **Mombasa Air Safari,** which flies to Diani Beach, Lamu, Malindi, Amboseli and Tsavo West, and the Masai Mara. Local taxis at the airport have fixed prices for most imaginable destinations in and around Mombasa, as well as for destinations all along the coast. If you'd prefer not to face a fairly insistent mob at the terminal entrance, prebook your transfer with **Southern Cross Safaris** (✆ **041/243-4600** through -4603; www.southerncrosssafaris.com), which covers the gamut of destinations at a reasonable rate, but also offers a pricier VIP service, which goes a long way toward taking the edge off. By way of example, they charge $25 ($40 VIP) per person to hotels on Mombasa's north coast, and $40 ($60 VIP) per person to Diani Beach. Transfers from the airport to the center take around 30 minutes, although traffic can choke things up considerably.

By Road I do not recommend driving between Nairobi and Mombasa; although the trip takes as little as 5½ hours, it feels genuinely hazardous. It's not that the road itself is particularly nasty, but the traffic can be a little overwhelming, and my impression of many drivers (including those at the helm of large-capacity buses) is that they have cowboy tendencies that are somehow exaggerated by what is perceived to be Kenya's best stretch of uninterrupted asphalt. If you're arriving in Mombasa from the south-coast beaches (also known as Diani Beach) or even from Tanzania, you'll need to take the **Likoni Ferry** to get onto the island; drivers are well versed in the procedure, but you're advised to take extra security precautions (to prevent pickpocketing and muggings) if you get out of the vehicle (the windows of which should be fully closed whether you're in it or not). The ferry inevitably involves a short wait, but crossing time is a mere 5 minutes. If you do arrive in the city by **bus,** you'll get off right in the center of the island; most of the bus companies have their offices on Jomo Kenyatta Avenue, where it shouldn't take more than a few seconds for a mob of taxi drivers to try for your business.

By Train Increasingly unreliable and virtually always delayed, the overnight train service (which theoretically runs three times a week) between Nairobi and Mombasa can no longer be recommended.

VISITOR INFORMATION The Mombasa & Coast Tourist Information Bureau (✆ 041/222-5428) on Moi Avenue doesn't so much provide assistance as try to sell you some of the region's most touristy products (including ugly resorts and crowded tours).

GETTING AROUND There's plenty of transport available in Mombasa, and you'll be able to flag down a taxi or *tuk-tuk* just about anywhere. *Tuk-tuks* are theoretically cheaper than taxis, but that doesn't mean you're not going to get ripped off.

Kenatco Taxis (✆ **041/222-7503;** www.kenatco.co.ke) offers 'round-the-clock service at fixed rates; they will dispatch a vehicle to take you just about anywhere up or down the coast or within the city. You can also hire a car and driver for the day (Ksh10,000) or half a day (Ksh6,000), with unlimited travel within a 100km (62 mile) radius of the city.

TOUR OPERATORS & GUIDED TOURS Award-winning **Southern Cross Safaris** (✆ **041/243-4600** through -4603; www.southerncrosssafaris.com) is very reliable and offers a broad range of services, from airport transfers to full-blown safaris around the country, including trips up and down the length and breadth of the Kenyan coast. They also run half-day city tours if you're really keen to take in the Fort and the Old Town, and they have a number of options for dhow cruises and snorkeling trips should you prefer to get away from the city. Southern Cross is personally managed by founders Mike Kirkland and Torben Rune, who are both passionate about their country.

Fast Facts Mombasa

Airlines **Kenya Airways,** Electricity House, Nkrumah Avenue (✆ **041/212-5000,** 041/222-7613 through -7616, 041/212-5529, or 041/212-5251 through -5254), **AirKenya** (✆ **020/391-6000,** 020/60-5745, or 020/60-1727; www.airkenya.com), **Safarilink** (✆ **020/60-0777** or -0787, 072/088-8111, or 073/433-8888; www.safarilink-kenya.com), **Fly540** (✆ **0**20/445-3252 through -3256, 073/354-0540, or 072/254-0540; www.fly540.com), **Mombasa Air Safari** (✆ **073/440-0400,** 073/450-0500, 072/279-1509, or 072/220-2559; www.mombasaairsafari.com).

Ambulances & Hospitals A reliable choice with emergency ambulance service is **Pandya Memorial Hospital,** Dedan Kimathi Street (✆ **041/231-3577,** -4140, or -4141, 072/220-6424, or 073/360-0663; www.pandyahospital.org).

Area Code The dialing code for Mombasa is ✆ **041.**

ATMs & Banks ATMs are ubiquitous in Mombasa, both on the island and on the north coast. You'll find numerous banks along Nkrumah Road in the vicinity of Treasury Square (not far from Fort Jesus).

Emergencies If calling from a mobile phone, dial ✆ **112** to report any emergency. To reach the **Mombasa Central Police Station,** dial ✆ **041/22-5501.**

Safety On the whole, Mombasa is a safer city than Nairobi, but you'd do well to remain vigilant and read our general safety briefing on p. 74. People tend to be active on the streets of central Mombasa well into the night, but there are some areas that feel deserted after dark. In general, you probably have little to fear, but stick to busier areas just to be on the safe side.

Taxis See "Getting Around," above.

Weather Kenya's coastal region has a balmy, tropical climate and tends to be hot and humid, with average temperatures ranging from 26° to 32°C (79°–90°F). Nights are warm, averaging 22°C (72°F). Rains typically fall in May, June, October, and November.

WHAT TO SEE & DO

Frankly, there isn't all that much to see in Mombasa. If you're into old architecture, focus on seeing the famed Fort Jesus, and then spend time wandering through the narrow and sociable streets of Old Town, the perfect place to get a feel for the social glue holding this neighborhood together.

Mombasa Island & Old Town

Most visitors might spend some time strolling down **Moi Avenue.** The colonial-era **Castle Royal Hotel** here has a veranda that's still a popular spot for a drink, and everyone seems interested in the so-called **Tusks Monument,** elephant tusk–shape archways incongruously perched above the street in tribute to Princess Elizabeth for her visit here in 1952. Today the tusks have become a symbol of the city, but they're really of zero interest. A short stroll through Mombasa will give you some idea of the intermingling cultural layers. The gigantic ocher walls of **Fort Jesus** (see below) constitute the main tourist attraction, but unless you have a particular interest, there's every likelihood this will be a massive disappointment—the exterior really trumps what you get to see on the inside and, frankly, the history far outweighs its stature as a modest museum today. Still, the fort is not without its fair share of disturbing ghost stories, and given the decimation of human life that has gone on within and around its walls, you should probably make a point of asking your guide to share some of the more blood-curdling reports. But really, the best part of a visit to Mombasa is the chance to explore the narrow, convoluted streets of its **Old Town** ★, with its mélange of Arab, British, and Indian architectural influences. Passing beneath the overhanging timber balconies and admiring the carved doors, it's a good place—although a little tacky and rundown in parts—to experience the ebb and flow of Swahili-Arab culture. There are more than 20 mosques in this compact area, muddled together among the vibrant bazaars, antiques stores, ice cream parlors, car-repair workshops, and hole-in-the-wall food vendors. Interest in preserving and restoring some of the older buildings has come rather late, and there's little sign of the type of gentrification you'll see in fashionably redeveloping Lamu.

While wandering through the old streets, be sure to stop for an ice cream or fruit juice. There are a number of parlors dispensing delicious freshly squeezed concoctions (the most brilliant of which is **Equatorial Fruit Parlour;** see the box "Avocado with a Straw," on p. 257).

Fort Jesus Looking out over the harbor from which it was so often bombarded, this solid pile on the edge of the sea was built by the Portuguese over many years, commencing in 1593, and is the only genuine sight in Mombasa. Ironically, while the fortress was meant to symbolize Portuguese dominion over the Indian Ocean, it was built at a time when a Spaniard, Philip II, sat on the Portuguese throne, and it was designed by an Italian military architect named Cairati (working under his Portuguese nom de plume, João Batista Cairato).

His final commission, this was undoubtedly Cairati's finest achievement, incorporating High Renaissance ideas about the link between architecture and the symmetrical unity of the human form. Built directly onto a coral rock platform, the shape of the fort can be compared to a torso (the central portion) with four limbs (the bastions) and a seaward-facing head (the outworks). The design anticipated a shortage of manpower and was meant to disguise any evidence of this from potential attackers. The inherent simplicity of the classical form thus served to make the fort look a lot more imposing and indestructible than might have been the case.

Quite impenetrable by cannon fire, the fort left Portuguese control only after a 33-month siege by Omani forces; by the end of a brutal, long-winded struggle, an estimated 6,500 men, women, and children had lost their lives either in combat or to disease. At one stage, when reinforcements arrived, it was found that the fort had been under the defense of a young sheikh with a small band of Swahili soldiers and a mob of 50 women who had been trained to use muskets. When the British protectorate was proclaimed in July 1895, the fort was converted into a prison. It's been a national monument since 1958. Across the street is the Mazrui Graveyard, where the sheikhs who lived in the Fort and ruled the town autonomously from 1741 to 1837 are buried.

Old Town end of Nkrumah Rd. No phone. www.museum.org.ke. Ksh800 adults, Ksh400 children under 18. Mon–Sun 9:30am–6pm.

Greater Mombasa

To coincide with the resort frenzy that stretches along the mainland on Mombasa's north coast, there are a number of touristy spots offering distractions that vary from downright tacky to just plain weird. Frankly, I'd skip most of them in favor of one of the crafts workshops, such as **Bombolulu,** 4km (2½ miles) north of Nyali Bridge (✆ **041/47-1704,** 073/381-1603, or 072/356-0933; www.apdkbombolulu.com), where you might pick up one or two interesting souvenirs. Founded in 1969, Bombolulu is a cultural center where handicrafts—from jewelry to screenprinted *kikois* to carvings—are produced by more than 150 people with disabilities who work here. **Ngomongo Cultural Village,** Shanzu (✆ **041/548-7063** or 072/494-2395; www.ngomongo.com), is a slightly gimmicky cultural diversion where around 10 tribal groups are represented in a sort of African multi-ethnic Disneyland. There are living members of the represented tribes demonstrating aspects of their daily life; examples of their huts, cultivated crops, and domestic and wild animals (for the El Molo man from Lake Turkana, there are even crocodiles) are on display, and there's even a village witch doctor.

If you'd prefer to see a more restrained side of Swahili culture—particularly if you're not going to make it up to Malindi to see Gede (p. 275)—then you might want to visit **Jumba la Mtwana,** the sedate-looking ruins of a town otherwise known as the "Large House of the Slave" (www.museums.org.ke). The site is situated some 15km (9¼ miles) north of Mombasa on and above the beach, about 1km (½ miles) from the mouth of Mtwapa Creek. Still in recognizable condition are a tomb, four houses, and four mosques, including the Great Mosque. Excavated ceramics found here suggest that the town was established in the 14th century and abandoned soon afterward.

WHERE TO STAY

For some strange reason, Mombasa is frequently sold as a beach destination with the added convenience of a few cultural attractions thrown in. Don't be fooled. The beaches here—stretching along the coast on the mainland north of Mombasa island—have been overdeveloped and are cluttered with vacationers looking for a cheap deal. In truth, you shouldn't stay in Mombasa unless you really want to take your time exploring the city. And, as I've mentioned, there isn't all that much to explore.

On Mombasa Island

There are no luxurious options in the city center, but there are two reasonably comfortable hotels that work out to be fairly good value and are pretty convenient if you simply need a bed for the night and would like to spend whatever time you have here checking out the Old Town.

Castle Royal Hotel Scores of travelers are drawn to the deep, sociable veranda that separates this cheap half-decent hotel from the sidewalk. Apart from the whitewashed colonial exterior, it's hard to imagine that this was built in 1919; inside it's much like any rambling, pieced-together hotel. About 1km (½ mile) from Fort Jesus, it's one of Mombasa's favorite time-passing venues, but that in no way makes up for the very average rooms. In all respects, you'll be far better off at Tamarind Village (reviewed below). Prepare to find yourself stuck behind the world's slowest bellhop, who'll seem more surprised (and impressed) by the rooms than you. Though they're ordinary spaces with gray walls, linoleum-covered furniture, tiled floors, and metal-frame beds, they're comfortable enough. I still can't figure out why the executive rooms are more expensive (perhaps they're slightly more "up-to-date" looks-wise), since it's far more appealing to have a standard room that opens directly on to the rooftop terrace (ask for this).

Moi Avenue., P.O. Box 82326, 80100 Mombasa. ✆ **041/222-8780,** -2682, or -0628; 073/533-9920; or 072/084-3072. Reservations: P.O. Box 43436, 00100 Nairobi. ✆ **072/220-7361** or 073/385-2083. Fax 020/34-3875 or 020/221-8314. www.sentrim-hotels.com. 68 units. Ks5,100 standard double; Ksh6,200 executive double. MC, V (credit card use incurs 5% surcharge). **Amenities:** 2 restaurants; ice cream parlor; bar; airport transfers (Ksh1,000 one-way); room service. *In room:* A/C, TV, Internet (cable provided; Ksh750 per day), minibar.

Royal Court Hotel Despite its ugly exterior, this modern edifice does have the neatest guestrooms on Mombasa island—although that's not saying much. In contrast with the Castle Royal (see above), this feels like a far better value, but the slightly alienating midcity location counts against it. The lobby is a big, hollow space decorated with modern African artworks; it's a characterless hotel populated by a strange mix of people, some of whom you can't help suspect are eyeballing you from behind their dark glasses. On Sundays you'll encounter one of the church groups that gathers here for services. Although it lacks the Castle Royal's sociable veranda, at least you can hide away in your room—they're bland spaces, but neat, very clean, and light-filled. Most important, in contrast with the Castle Royal, you get a proper mattress.

Haile Selassie Rd., P.O. Box 41247, 80100 Mombasa. ✆ **041/222-3379,** 041/223-0932, 041/231-2317, or 041/231-2389. Fax 041/231-2398. www.royalcourtmombasa.co.ke. 92 units. Ksh5,500 double; Ksh6,850 executive double; Ksh11,000 executive suite. Rates include breakfast and all taxes. AE, MC, V. **Amenities:** Restaurant; pool bar; airport transfers (Ksh1,000 one-way); health club; pool; room service; casino. *In room:* A/C, TV, Internet (Ksh354 per hr., Ksh1,180 per day), minibar (in most).

Mombasa's North Coast

I wouldn't recommend this stretch of coastline as a true beach destination, but the places here are a good alternative to the soulless hotels in the city center. Ranged along the beach are numerous large resort-style hotels, and many of them are truly deplorable. Closest to Mombasa island, but without actual beach access, **Tamarind Village** (reviewed below) is strides ahead of the competition, and although it lacks a beach of its own, the views from its rooms, the famous restaurant, and its poolside terraces are the most interesting for miles—they look onto Mombasa island itself, providing the most vivid understanding of how the city might have looked a few hundred years ago. Don't be fooled by the upbeat marketing of places such as **Voyager Beach Resort** and **Sarova Whitesands Hotel,** which both have more in common with sardine factories than places to rest and have a relaxing time. If you do favor the crowds, however, and must choose between the two, you'll probably be better off at Whitesands (✆ **041/212-8000;** www.sarovahotels.com), where there's every chance (I'm told) of sharing the pool with African royalty, such as Swaziland's King Mswati III.

Serena Beach Hotel & Spa ★ With a strip of seedy hotels behind it, some truly ugly neighbors, and a beach filled with overbearing beach boys out front, this imaginatively designed hotel looks and feels like a safe haven. In a way, it's like a getaway from pirates on both fronts, and it's no hardship to kick back here. If you are able to dodge the snipers trying to sell you something on the beach, you might manage a dip in the ocean. If you don't manage to move beyond the bougainvillea-filled grounds, there's always plenty of space poolside, with all kinds of resort-style distractions, including a first-class spa and evening entertainment. All things considered, this isn't a bad hotel, but you should opt for one of the refurbished Village rooms, which have a slick finish with plasma TVs and decently sized bathrooms with modern glass showers. The Serena lays on the best breakfast spread in town, complete with avocado juice, sparkling wine, and divine minicroissants.

Shanzu Beach, P.O. Box 90352, 80100 Mombasa. ✆ **041/548-5721** through -5724. Fax 041/548-5453. www.serenahotels.com.com. Reservations: Williamson House, 4th Floor, 4th Ngong Ave., Nairobi. ✆ **020/284-2333** or 020/271-1077. Fax 020/271-8102. cro@serena.co.ke. 164 units. High season $385 double, $475 village/seaview and garden wing double, $510–$700 suite, $100–$135 extra bed; midseason $295 double, $375 village/seaview and garden wing double, $420–$650 suite, $125–$165 extra bed; low season $255 double, $325 village/seaview and garden wing double, $310–$580 suite, $150–$195 extra bed. AE, DC, MC, V. **Amenities:** 3 restaurants; coffee shop; ice cream parlor; 2 lounges; 2 bars; airport transfers (Ksh2,200); babysitting; concierge; health club and spa; pool; room service; 2 squash courts; 2 tennis courts; watersports. *In room:* A/C, TV, hair dryer, minibar, Wi-Fi (Ksh300 per hr.; Ksh1,000 per day).

Tamarind Village ★★ Seen from this cliffside position at the edge of the harbor channel, Mombasa is magically transformed into something beautiful. Views from here—with dhows and fishing boats gliding across the water and palm trees rising from between the coral outcrops—might even transport you back to an earlier time. It's just 10 minutes by car from central Mombasa, yet far from the mayhem and mugginess of the island city, with lovely views across Mombasa Harbor toward Old Town, giving you perhaps the most definitive view you'll get of Mombasa. Catering to high rollers who seem to jet in and out of Mombasa without wanting to deal with any of its inconveniences, this "village" offers fully serviced apartments (with up to three bedrooms), all with impressive views of the harbor and fully kitted kitchens. Laze on the poolside lawn, sunbathing at the edge of the harbor, or curl up on your huge private terrace, where you can survey the tropical scene before dozing off to the sounds of competing calls to prayer that drift across the water from a dozen or so mosques on the island. Two boats for deep-sea fishing operate from here, and staff are happy to arrange golf at the nearby Nyali Golf Club or book all kinds of watersports, including kitesurfing and scuba diving.

Silos Rd., Nyali, P.O. Box 95805, Mombasa 80106. ✆ **041/47-4600** through -4602. Fax 041/47-3073. www.tamarind.co.ke. 55 units. Ksh10,500 1-bedroom apartment, Ksh16,500 2-bedroom apartment, Ksh22,000 3-bedroom apartment. AE, DC, MC, V. **Amenities:** 3 restaurants, including **Tamarind & Tamarind Dhow** (see "Where to Dine," below; guests get 15% off their food at Tamarind Restaurant); bar; babysitting; health club; 2 pools; room service; squash court; casino. *In room:* A/C, TV/DVD, hair dryer (on request), kitchen, free Wi-Fi.

WHERE TO DINE

Aiming to revive the coffee house tradition, **Jahazi ★**, Ndia Kuu, Old Town (✆ **072/383-5492;** www.jahazicoffeehouse.com), is a cozy space in Old Town. Stylishly furnished, with low seating and elegant decor that celebrates the local history, it's a great place to stop off for delicious homemade Swahili snacks or to try a cup of invigorating ginger-infused Swahili coffee. Also served are set lunch and dinner menus (Ksh800–Ksh1,500) with typical Swahili dishes and snacks, freshly squeezed juices, coconut milk, *samosas,* kebabs, Swahili-style prawns, *biriyani, tandoori*-baked bread, chapatis, and traditional puddings. Less intimate and without Jahazi's good looks is **Swahililand,** Ndia Kuu Road (✆ **072/344-0666;** swahililandheritage@gmail.com; daily 8am–5:30pm), a restaurant that opened on the ground floor of Leven House, one of the most important historic buildings in Old Town. Although I don't think it's quite matured into the full-fledged restaurant it wants to be, it does benefit from a pleasant location next to the water. Like Jahazi, it's open for all-day dining and snacking, but if you want dinner, you need to order in advance. Swahili cuisine is also the specialty at **Island Dishes,** Kibikoni Street (✆ **072/088-7311** or 041/231-7019; daily 7am–midnight), an Old Town institution that is especially good for just sitting and watching as the neighborhood breezes by. Sip your way through a large mug of tamarind juice while local people stop off to say their *"salaams"* to the proprietors. For views, besides the obvious (and expensive) choice—**Tamarind** (reviewed below)—you might want to head over to the sociable after-work mainland drinks venue, **jd's** (also known as Just Drinks; ✆ **072/137-2456**), which also has a reasonably priced restaurant that's much loved by residents. Located at The Creek Marina, it's owned by a pleasant guy named Sonny, opens at 5pm, and stays open till very late.

Misono ★★ JAPANESE This highly respected sushi and teppanyaki eatery is one of Mombasa's best bets (there's a branch in Nairobi), with a loyal following among locals in-the-know and visitors after something a little more elegant. Instead of the pared, minimalist look, they've gone for a more imaginative Kabuki style, with hibachi tables and a big gong that sounds as you enter. When it's busy, the place can be plenty of fun, and the exquisitely fresh sushi elevates it to one of the city's best. The chili prawns are excellent, but sashimi lovers should not pass up the yellow-fin tuna.

Links Rd., adjacent Bob's Bar, Nyali. ✆ **041/47-1454** or -1455, or 072/253-0204. 8-course set menu around Ksh1,600. MC, V. Mon–Sun noon–3pm and 6–11pm.

Tamarind & Tamarind Dhow ★★★ SEAFOOD With its clifftop setting above Mombasa's tropical harbor, Kenya's most famous seafood restaurant is perhaps the most obvious dining recommendation—a bit touristy, slightly overpriced, and definitely overhyped, but worthwhile for that one-off meal in a city you're unlikely to hang around in for very long. Arrive early, install yourself at one of the seaview tables (reserve in advance), and give in to the moment. Despite the gimmicky decor (Moorish lanterns hang above the bar, waiters wear Arabic robes, and there's even an indoor coral waterfall), you'll understand why this has long been one of Kenya's most celebrated restaurants. The visitor's book reads like a who's who (Barack Obama dined at the Nairobi branch when he visited in 2007, and Kenya's President Kibaki dines here a few times a year).

The local tropical lobster, properly known as *langouste* (or "spiny rock lobster"), is a highlight (but not cheap, at around Ksh2,500 for a small portion) and can be enjoyed either charcoal-grilled (and brandy flambéed), thermidore style, or in the Swahili tradition (sautéed in garlic, saffron, tomatoes, and coconut cream). They also do amazing things with crab, whether you prefer it steamed or lightly fried in garlic, ginger, olive oil,

Moments Avocado with a Straw

Swaleh Abdallah Altamimi's sweet and simple **Equatorial Fruit Parlour** (✆ **073/655-5568**) is my favorite stop in the city's atmospheric Old Town and just 200m (656 ft.) from Fort Jesus. Swaleh—one of Old Town's true characters—prepares masterful juices, whipped up while you wait, from fruit procured daily at the market. His flavors range from passion fruit, orange, mango, and watermelon to the more unusual tamarind, tangerine, masterfelly (custard apple), and *bungo* (a Kenyan coastal fruit). Don't leave Mombasa without sampling the delicious avocado shake, blended with sugar and milk (and ice cream, if you want); kids go bonkers for his "Scud," a combination of mixed fruit and ice cream. Swaleh will mix up just about any combination you desire, as long as what you're after is in season and freshly available; there's even cucumber juice for the ultra health conscious. As it's situated in a residential neighborhood, this is a great place to rub shoulders with locals. The shop is on Nyeri Street, just off Kibokoni Road (there isn't a soul in Old Town who doesn't know where it is, so just ask), opens at 4pm (once people have started returning from work and school), and stays open till midnight.

and chili (delicious). Prawns are straight from the Indian Ocean; the garlic beach prawns are wonderfully simple, and the prawns piripiri is legendary. If you're not a fan of seafood, there are some excellent meat dishes (including superb ostrich filet with wild berry sauce), and there's a separate vegetarian menu (just ask for it). For dessert, it's a toss-up between the tree tomato teardrop and the trio of crème brûlée, so you may want to opt for the dessert sampler. There's live jazz at night.

If you want the full tourist experience, then reserve the Tamarind Dhow. There are two such dhows—not unlike what you might expect a genuine medieval pirate boat to look like—both topped by gigantic white sails. The food—with choices from a set menu—is less memorable than the experience (you sail past Fort Jesus and up Tudor Creek), and I'd rather have the sound of the lapping waves than the onboard cover band.

Tamarind Village, Nyali. ✆ **041/47-4600** through -4602. www.tamarind.co.ke. Reservations essential. Restaurant: Main courses Ksh1,150–Ksh2,250. AE, MC, V. Daily noon–2:30/3pm and 7pm–midnight. Dhow: Mon–Sat 1–3pm and 6:30–9pm. Lunch $40 per person; dinner $70 per person.

2 THE SOUTH COAST

Diani is 35km (22 miles) S of Mombasa and 500km (310 miles) SE of Nairobi

Creamy white beaches protected by an immense coral reef. A warm, cobalt-blue sea dotted with pretty islands. Large scimitar-shaped sails drifting across a shimmering surface. If you're looking for that endless succession of postcard-perfect images, you'll find them here, stretching south from Mombasa toward the Tanzanian border. At the center of the South Coast action is **Diani Beach,** a pretty and extensively developed resort that's managed to retain its celebrity good looks (and, thanks to the exclusivity offered by captivating places such as the Alfajiri villas, remains a bolthole for the likes of Africa-mad icons such as Brad and Angelina). Easily one of Kenya's best beaches, it's possible to walk for 8km (5 miles) in either direction. You'll find a couple of caparisoned camels trundling across the beach, and bevies of beach boys planning their assault strategy as they aim to sell anything from safaris to sexual adventures to the unsuspecting (or terribly keen) tourists. Yes, there's a sleazier side to Diani's easily romanticized charms, but it's one that's easily avoided. Instead of falling for the pesky hustlers on the beach, there's plenty to keep you active between mealtimes. Numerous companies offer all kinds of waterborne adventures and activities, including snorkeling and diving in the **Kisite-Mpunguti Marine National Park** and big-game fishing out of Shimoni, a village just north of the Tanzanian border. The coral-rich marine reserve is also a good place for dolphin-spotting and whale-watching. It's also possible to explore some of the offshore islands. **Wasini** is a forested island with old Arabic ruins and is a popular luncheon venue, while at the northern edge of the marine park, a maze of water channels spreads between a patchwork of pretty mangroves and forested islands, one of which has been transformed into a paradisiacal castaway resort, **Funzi Keys,** which ranks among the most relaxing and atypical beach spots in Kenya. And close by are the **Shimba Hills National Reserve** and the **Mwaluganje Elephant Sanctuary,** decent enough outings if you haven't yet had your fill of safari.

ESSENTIALS

GETTING THERE & AWAY Mombasa's airport is a mere 1½ hours away, and daily scheduled flights also arrive at Ukunda airstrip, which is a 5-minute taxi drive from the nearest beach. **Safarilink** began flying to Diani's Ukanda airstrip in July 2009, and

Mombasa Air Safari flies you here for $20 one-way (less than the cost of a road transfer). Contact details for any of these airlines are found in the Mombasa "Fast Facts" on p. 252. For information on arranging transfers or taxis from Mombasa to the South Coast, see the "Essentials" section for Mombasa, earlier in this chapter.

GETTING AROUND Based in Diani, you can get just about anywhere by marching up and down the beach in either direction. At night, if you want to try out the local restaurants or look for nightlife away from your hotel, hire a taxi (best organized through your hotel); some of the restaurants offer free pick-ups. If you want to explore by bike, contact **Diani Bikes** (✆ **071/395-9668;** www.dianibikes.com), an eco-tourism initiative where you can rent bikes or join a guided tour, including one that cycles along the beach and one to a local village.

VISITOR INFORMATION The resorts and guesthouses along this strip are well versed in all things tourist-oriented; stick to our recommended accommodations, and you'll also hear about less touristy options from your host. Shops, banks, travel agencies, tour operators, drugstores, cybercafes, and restaurants can all be found in the increasing number of shopping centers on Diani Beach Road, most of them in the vicinity of the junction for the road leading to Ukunda.

FISHING, SNORKELING & DIVE CHARTERS Pat Hemphill and his son Simon own and operate **Sea Adventures** (✆ **072/148-5365** or 072/279-6198; www.biggame.com) and are known as the country's top fishermen, with record numbers of marlin landed by boats that they've skippered, mostly in the Pemba Channel, where they take their charter clients on exclusive fishing adventures. Broadbill swordfish are abundant here, as are world-record-size giant trevally and huge sharks, including mako, tiger, and hammerheads; you could also spend time landing tuna, wahoo, narrow-barred mackerel, and barracuda. Tag and release is the general practice. They run two boats, the 14m (46-ft.) *Broadbill* and the newer 13m (43-ft.) *Kamara II,* and operate full-day excursions for $550 to $700, depending on the season. November through March is prime billfish season, while tuna fishing is best from July to October. They also offer nightfishing (4pm–9am; $1,000–$1,400). Incidentally, the Hemphills also run multiday fishing safaris to the northern Kenyan coast, where you can fish the abundant waters around the Lamu archipelago.

Steve and Sally Mullens of **Wasini Island Dhow Tours & Scuba Diving** (✆ **072/229-0514,** 072/241-0599, or 040/52-410) offer exclusive hire of a dhow or speedboat for snorkeling and scuba diving; for the latter, proof of PADI certification is required. You'll pay $115 per dive, or $150 for a double dive session, while snorkeling is $70; hire of the boat is extra ($200 per day). If you fancy diving or snorkeling but don't mind sharing a boat with other travelers, there are a couple of operators offering a day out on the water; the best of these is Pilli Pipa Dhow Safaris (p. 270), which provides a relaxing day out with an exquisite lunch.

THE TOP ATTRACTIONS

Kisite Mpunguti Marine National Park ★★★ This 39-sq.-km (15-sq.-mile) marine reserve shelters some of Kenya's best diving and snorkeling—there are some staggering coral gardens beneath the shallow waters and visibility is generally excellent. The park, surrounded by coral reef, is home to four small islands, including Wasini, known for its volcanic landscapes and sprinkling of old Arabic settlements. Unless you can afford to charter a private boat, your best bet for diving or snorkeling in the park is with

Warning! Beachwise

The biggest irritation along any of the East African beaches that are popular vacationing resorts is the abundance of so-called **"beach boys."** They're basically anyone who makes a living out of hustling people—you—on the beach and range from men trying to sell dhow trips or outings with fishermen (which could be quite enjoyable but might just as easily turn out to be complete disasters) to guys hawking their bodies with promises of sex, companionship, or whatever. There are many stories of women heading back to Europe with lovers found this way, but for the most part, these guys are simply a nuisance, insinuating themselves into your space and often refusing to stop hassling you until you've agreed to buy something or finally, out of complete desperation, handed over some cash. Logic would dictate that your first course of action should be to ignore any advances, not even responding to a simple "Hello." This seldom works, however, and you might find yourself a victim of verbal harassment implying that you're rude or even racist. Try being polite, by all means, but make every effort to clarify from the get-go that you (a) have no intention of purchasing anything, (b) have no money, and (c) have no interest in what's being offered. Typically, none of these will exempt you from having to put up with the prolonged sales pitch, but you may just score enough time to walk to a nearby bar or restaurant or back to your hotel. Never suggest that you may—in any manner whatsoever—be interested later, as this will result in being stalked for the remainder of your vacation. Really, these guys want your money, and they'll go to unusual lengths to get it from you. Bear in mind that beach boys are illegal, so it really doesn't make any sense to encourage them.

Also note that **nude and topless sunbathing** is illegal in Kenya and will offend many local cultures. Don't approach single women or girls on the beach, and carefully note that the word *malayas* means "hookers" in Swahili. Finally, be aware that the **export of shells and coral** from Kenya is illegal; do not buy anything made from either of these, as trade in shells increases poaching through demand. Do not touch, damage, or remove any coral, which is a living organism and takes years to develop; besides killing the coral, touching or breaking it interferes with the living environment of many rare and endangered species. It's illegal to remove shells, starfish, or any other marine life, plant or animal, as the disruption to the ecosystem can be severe.

super-efficient **Pilli Pipa,** a well-organized and long-established company that throws in lunch on Wasini—it's one of the most sumptuous meals you'll have on the coast.

Main access is from Shimoni, 85km (53 miles) S of Mombasa; the park is 6km (3¾ miles) off the Kenyan coast, and 8km (5 miles) N of Tanzania; KWS HQ is 200m (656 ft.) S of main Shimoni pier. ✆ **040/52-027.** www.kws.org. Admission $20 adults, $10 children and students.

Shimba Hills National Reserve ★ Said to be home to Kenya's last breeding herd of sable antelope, this is one of the country's lesser-known parks with a diverse ecosystem that incorporates belts of coastal rainforest and good animal diversity. Particularly healthy pachyderm numbers have spawned the creation of the community-owned **Mwaluganje Elephant Sanctuary,** where you're guaranteed to see plentiful herds among the gorgeous cycad forests; it is currently home to the highest density of elephants in the country, and probably all of Africa. The Reserve is a good bet if you want to see animals but are no longer interested in feeling the great strain to chase down lion, leopard, or cheetah and are looking for a more laid-back interaction with nature.

Near Kwale, 33km (20 miles) S of Mombasa. © **040/4159** or 040/4166. www.kws.org. Admission $20 adults, $10 children and students. Daily 6am–6pm.

WHERE TO STAY & DINE

Try to stay away from the larger resorts—you'll enjoy a more memorable interaction with the coast if you're based at one of the intimate retreats.

Pungu

Just 6km (3¾ miles) south of bustling Mombasa and just moments beyond the mayhem of the Likoni ferry crossing, quiet and isolated Pungu—basically a wilderness stretching between the highway and the beach, with a few villages and small holdings—comes as a real surprise and a genuinely humbling alternative to the more developed parts of the south coast.

Tijara Beach ★★★ (Finds) One of the coast's most impressive finds, this fabulous 2-year-old property lies at the end of an unmarked dirt road that leads through what looks and feels like totally uncharted territory. You'll arrive at a wall made of coral rock with bougainvilleas spilling over the top. On the other side of the wall is a vast beachside property with lawns rolling down toward a series of sandy coves. There are four gorgeous individual cottages built from coral stone with *makuti* roofing; superb, tasteful furnishings; and lovely views. Each one has a sea-facing terrace with chill-out sofas and Lamu-style beds canopied by gigantic mosquito nets; interiors are very pretty, with stone floors and fabrics in dazzling colors. There are no distractions from the peace and quiet, and sumptuous views (no phones, TVs, music, or air-conditioning), but the rooms (and bathrooms) get plenty of light and a gorgeous breeze. Your hosts do as much as possible to ensure you're left to relax at your own pace, making this as far removed from any typical resort experience as you could possibly imagine. Out front there's a fantastic reef sheltering starfish, beautiful coral, and moray eels—the water gets low enough to walk all the way out there, and there's beautiful snorkeling. When the tide is out, the water-dappled coral rock looks like some kind of blue-green marble.

P.O. Box 99982, 80107 Kilindini, Mombasa. © **020/205-7701** or 072/270-1701. www.tijarabeach.com. 4 units, 1 with tub. High season $870 double; midseason $740 double; low season $630 double. Rates include all meals, most drinks, and transfers. No credit cards. **Amenities:** Restaurant; bar; free airport transfers; free Wi-Fi (in restaurant). *In room:* No phone.

Tiwi Beach

Not nearly as developed as Diani Beach, Tiwi's only substantially sized Tiwi Beach Hotel suffered a devastating fire in 2009 and was closed at press time. **Shéshé Baharini,** the miniature-resort style hotel next door, is a good (and well-priced) alternative. The advantages at Tiwi include the promise of tranquillity and true escape from the crowds—this place has simply never seen the development of Diani, nor is that likely to change in the near future. There's also a relative lack of infrastructure. It's not an area you go wandering around in; stick to the beach and you'll be fine. If you like the idea of a self-catering cottage but want something a little more modern (and "luxurious") than what's available at **Sand Island Beach Cottages** (reviewed below), then you might consider one of the executive cottages offered at **Maweni & Capricho Beach Cottages** (© **040/33-0012** or

-0040, or 072/232-8365; www.maweniheach.com), a little farther south. It's a muddled development of different types of accommodation; be sure to avoid their hotel "suites" and standard cottages. There's nothing here that can match the accessibility or magnificence of the beach at Sand Island, and, in fact, the Maweni/Capricho beach is a bit on the tiny side, more like a coral cove than a full-on beach, and it's quite a steep climb to get down there. They charge from Ksh15,000 for a two-bedroom cottage to Ksh35,000 for the sumptuous four-bedroom Angelina's House, which overlooks the sea from a high cliff near the beach. There's the advantage of restaurants and bars here, but the place is marred by some ill-planned construction and worrying neglect in some areas. Note, too, that some of the cottages are actually functional gray blocks, and some are far away from anything resembling a sea view.

Sand Island Beach Cottages ★★ **Value** It takes great effort to tear your eyes away from the hypnotic scene along the oceanfront of this remote and rustic hideaway at the northernmost end of Tiwi Beach. The sea is a magnificent cobalt-green, and the water bounces and tumbles to form a natural Jacuzzi around the sand island that forms with the tides just offshore. Built in the 1940s, this is the stuff of castaway dreams—backed by a citrus plantation that helps hide it from the world, the area is teeming with birdlife, butterflies, and tiny dik-dik antelope. There are just seven cottages—from basic bedsitters to simple three-bedroom units suitable for a family—each with a gas-fitted kitchenette, stone floors, wood furniture, dining area, and solar-heated water all under a *makuti* roof. In many ways, they're perfectly timeless beach cottages, although each has its benefits and quirks. Tewa is the one to go for; it has a large kitchen, a big dining area, and a sizeable terrace. Cottages are serviced every 4 days, but you can take on the services of a dedicated chef (Ksh450 per day), and it's easy to buy fresh seafood from local fishermen. It may be rustic and a little rough around the edges, but it's hard to suggest a more genuinely "Kenyan" experience—and that Jacuzzi in the sea is one of the most romantic spots in Africa.

Tiwi Beach, P.O. Box 5516, 80401 Diani Beach. ✆ **073/366-0554** or 072/239-5005. www.sandislandbeach.com. 7 self-catering cottages, most with shower only. $55–$70 bedsitter (2–4 people), $70–$105 2-bedroom cottage (4–5 people), $105–$115 3-bedroom cottage (6 people); $20–$25 extra person. No credit cards. **Amenities:** Airport transfers (Ksh3,000 from Mombasa, including supermarket stopover). *In room:* No phone, kitchenette.

Shéshé Baharini Beach Hotel Laid-back and a fine value, this small beachfront hotel has everything you'll need for a peaceful time at the ocean. Consisting of 10 separate cottages—each with a pair of standard rooms and one deluxe unit—the hotel offers simple, compact accommodations, all very neat and agreeable, with poster beds and lots of white to celebrate the beach theme. Sliding-glass doors open onto a small porch overlooking the pool. Don't bother with the standard units, as these have miniature bathrooms (with a very macabre color scheme); deluxe rooms have much more space (there's even an extra bed) and handsome, locally produced, Lamu-style furniture. It's not the most modern or slick place, but access to the beach is all you truly want (try to reserve room 1B or 2B, which both face directly onto the beach). There's a small fishing community right next door, and a glorious strand, unfettered by beach boys, stretches out in either direction in front of you.

Tiwi Beach. ✆ **073/551-1436** or 071/753-5333. Reservations: P.O. Box 6320, 00619 Nairobi. ✆/fax **020/856-2025.** www.sheshebeach.com. 30 units. Ksh11,000 standard double; Ksh12,400 deluxe double; Ksh13,800 seafront double; Ksh15,200 superior seafront double. Children under 12 pay 50% if sharing with 2 adults; under 3 free. Rates include all meals and taxes. MC, V. **Amenities:** Restaurant; 2 bars; airport transfers (Ksh4,000 from Mombasa); pool; room service. *In room:* A/C.

Diani Beach

This is the main resort strip along the Kenyan Coast, and when it comes to lodging choices, Diani has something for everyone.

Afrochic ★ This house by the beach is packed with African artifacts and decor, a reasonable mix of classy and kitsch. It's not exactly chic, but it does prove to be a very friendly, familial environment (there's even a good-natured house dog) and certainly feels lived in. You have plenty of places to lounge around the pool or on the sand at the edge of the beach, and you can get 'round-the-clock bar service. All the rooms are different but feel a bit hotel-like and are just a touch unkempt (and some a little stuffy). Definitely insist on a room that faces the beach; those on the other side face an ugly hotel and a garden. The in-house restaurant has a long and varied menu with some good Swahili dishes and plenty of seafood.

Diani Beach. ✆ **073/364-5564.** www.elewana.com. Reservations: P.O. Box 72630, 00200 Nairobi. ✆ **020/375-0183,** or 027/250-0630 or -0639. reservations@elewana.com. 10 units, half with tubs. Peak season 460€ deluxe double, 576€ junior suite, 700€ executive suite, 40€ extra child, 70€ extra adult; high season 380€ deluxe double, 470€ junior suite, 576€ executive suite, 35€ extra child, 65€ extra adult; low season 284€ deluxe double, 400€ junior suite, 470€ executive suite, 30€ extra child, 60€ extra adult. MC, V. **Amenities:** Restaurant; bar; airport transfers (Mombasa Ksh3,000–Ksh4,000 one-way; Ukunda free); babysitting; pool; room service; spa treatments. *In room:* A/C, TV/DVD, hair dryer, Jacuzzi (in suites), minibar, free Wi-Fi.

Almanara ★★★ This classy villa-style option vies with Alfijiri (p. 267) for top honors in Diani. It's luxurious, and each house comes with plenty of pampering and the full attention of a dedicated staff. The immense and immaculate villas each have three en suite bedrooms, a large outdoor lounge, and a fab rooftop terrace, plus a chef who'll prepare almost anything you desire (most ingredients are fresh from the sea or from Almanara's own farm). The main drawback is that the standard villas don't overlook the sea; if you happen to score the main house, however, you have a spectacular five-bedroom mansion that not only overlooks the beach, but has its own private pool as well. Decor is stylish and inspired by traditional Swahili elements, although the overall look is somehow entirely modern. It'll suit you especially well if you're looking for only the faintest hint of being in Africa and don't want to forgo the luxuries of home.

Diani Beach Rd., P.O. Box 5468, 80401 Diani Beach. ✆ **020/213-8501** through -8503. Fax 020/213-8504. www.almanararesort.com. Reservations: www.bush-and-beyond.com. 7 units. Premium season $420 per person; regular season $275 per person; green season $200 per person. Children under 12 pay 50% with 2 adults, under 2 free. Rates include all meals, most drinks, transfers, laundry, household staff, spa treatments, and access to watersports equipment. MC, V. 3-night minimum stay. **Amenities:** Restaurant; bar; free airport transfers; Jacuzzi; pool; watersports center. *In room:* A/C, TV/DVD, hair dryer, computer and free Wi-Fi.

Diani Reef Beach Resort & Spa ★ **Overrated** This is meant to be the best resort in Diani, but frankly, it's an immense let-down, with overambitious decor (and lots of bulk-produced furniture) and really poor service (even when they're almost completely empty, they make new arrivals wait in the lobby for an obscene amount of time). It's a resort in every sense of the word—spread over 12 hectares (30 acres) with theme nights by the beach (you've got to traverse all sorts of bars, lounges, steps, and an immense coral rockery before you hit the sand) and all kinds of activities laid on, including a team dedicated to keeping children entertained. Sure, the public areas are impressive, but what's most disappointing is the ordinary feel of the accommodations. They typify hotel rooms just about anywhere, and while comfortable enough (and prettied up with flowers, decent cane furniture, and lots of white paint), they hardly offer a satisfying excuse to leave your beach lounger, and bathrooms are small.

Diani Beach Rd., Diani, P.O. Box 35, 80400 Ukunda. ✆ **040/320-2723** or -3308, 072/378-6301 through -6305, or 073/478-6301 through -6305. Fax 040/320-2196 or -3067. www.dianireef.com. 143 units. Ksh14,970–Ksh25,700 standard garden-facing double; Ksh6,690–Ksh28,740 standard ocean-facing double; Ksh19,735–Ksh31,790 deluxe ocean-facing double; Ksh21,460–Ksh48,000 junior suite. Children 5–11 Ksh1,790–Ksh4,400 with 2 adults; under 5 free. Rates include breakfast, dinner, taxes, and service charge. 4- to 7-night minimum stay. AE, MC, V. **Amenities:** 3 restaurants; 4 bars (including 1 w/dancing); night club; airport transfers (Ksh4,500); babysitting; children's activity center; health club and spa; 2 pools; room service; squash court; 2 floodlit tennis courts; casino. *In room:* A/C, TV, hair dryer, minibar; Wi-Fi (cable; Ksh900 per hr.).

Jacaranda Indian Ocean Beach Club ★ As resorts go, this is one of the least overwhelming, with an unusual layout and strange combination of laidback luxury and indifference (starting with a receptionist who couldn't be bothered to say hello). The breezy, open-sided lobby showcases the resort's eclectic approach to design—a mix of whitewashed Moorish design, country/Western music, and a solitary crystal chandelier. Slate pathways lead you past a pair of ancient baobabs to the pretty *makuti*-topped cottages where accommodations are neat, functional, and smart, with stone floors, wood-beam ceilings, and large, comfortable beds. Decently proportioned minimalist interiors translate into breathing space, making things feel less cluttered than at many of the other large resorts. The spice coast theme pervades the public areas, and there are plenty of nooks and lounges to hide from the crowds, although you might find the profusion of beach boys between the hotel and the sea a little off-putting.

P.O. Box 73, 80400 Ukunda, Diani Beach. ✆ **040/320-3730,** 072/167-2111, or 073/460-0922. Fax 040/320-3557. www.jacarandahotels.com. Reservations: ✆ **020/444-8713,** 072/220-5486, or 073/360-1613. Fax 020/444-5818. 100 units. July 15–Apr 5 $468–$568 club room double, $496–$596 ocean-front double; Apr 6–July 14 $174 club room double, $188 ocean-front double. Rates include all meals. AE, MC, V. **Amenities:** 3 restaurants; 3 bars; airport transfers ($28 per person round-trip); babysitting; children's activities; pool and plunge pool; room service; 2 tennis courts. *In room:* A/C, hair dryer, minifridge, Wi-Fi (Ksh500 per hr.; Ksh2,000 per day).

Leopard Beach Resort & Spa ★ This award-winning resort—like many of those along the coast—doesn't fully live up to its reputation but is nonetheless one of the better deals amongst the big beach hotels. You start your holiday in a big lobby full of the continent's art and artifacts (cushions bedecked with cowrie shells, portraits of tribal people, wildlife paintings), which is eye-catching but feels a little dated, as do the concrete blocks in which most of the standard accommodations are located. Nevertheless, things are fairly well spread out, and you can definitely escape the sense of being hemmed in if you bag a sea-facing room; they're large, with tiled floors, wicker furniture, and bright, beachy pastel color schemes, and they all have an outdoor seating area or small terrace. Better still, there are two villas right on the beach and seven very beautiful and spacious honeymoon suites with gigantic double showers. The resort is closed April 27 to June 25.

Diani Beach Rd., P.O. Box 34, Ukunda, 80400 South Coast. ✆ **040/320-2721** or -2110. Fax 040/320-3424. www.leopardbeachresortandspa.com. 157 units. Festive season 300€ standard double, 360€ garden-facing superior double, 390€ sea-facing superior double, 500€ seaview cottage double, 625€–1,100€ suites and villas, 100€ extra bed; high season 175€ standard double, 210€ garden-facing superior double, 228€ sea-facing superior double, 295€ seaview cottage double, 385€–680€ suites and villas, 55€ extra bed; midseason 150€ standard double, 180€ garden-facing superior double, 195€ sea-facing superior double, 250€ seaview cottage double, 335€–575€ suites and villas, 50€ extra bed; low season 120€ standard double, 145€ garden-facing superior double, 155€ sea-facing superior double, 200€ seaview cottage double, 275€–465€ suites and villas, 40€ extra bed. Rates include breakfast and lunch or dinner, all taxes, and service charge. AE, MC, V. **Amenities:** 2 restaurants; 5 bars; airport transfers (40€ per adult, 20€ per child round-trip); babysitting; health club and spa; 2 pools; room service; 2 floodlit tennis courts. *In room:* A/C, TV, DVD (in suites and villas), minibar.

Pinewood Village Beach Resort (Value) At the far southern end of Diani, where it officially transforms into Galu Beach, this 2009 TripAdvisor Traveler's Choice Award–winner looks a bit like a low-slung condominium. The lobby feels small and intimate and smells a bit like a spa, but there's a large sprawl of neatly paved development behind all that, culminating with a big, mellow beachside area filled with Europeans roasting under the African sun or chilling beneath the *makuti* umbrellas. Accommodations are in rows of cottages, each one with a suite downstairs and two deluxe units above. Unless you plan properly and reserve one of the sea-facing rooms (there are only a couple—191 and 192 are standard rooms, and 190 and 200 are sea-facing suites—so move quickly), you'll have a view into the garden (which isn't bad and gets colobus monkeys), as well as a wire security fence. Living quarters are quite spacious, with neat wood furniture, tiled floors, and a bright, bleached, beachy look that's completely inoffensive, quite relaxing, even faintly elegant. Because it's quite far from the main strip, the beachfront here sees much less of beach boy bother, and there's a well-managed watersports facility here. Unlike the other, bigger resorts, there's emphasis on creating a peaceful, relaxing environment, so there are no over-the-top entertainments, and the lower-than-average room count means you've a better chance of unwinding.

Diani Beach Rd., P.O. Box 90, Ukunda. ✆ **020/208-0981** through -8093, 072/395-7080, or 073/469-9723. Fax 040/330-0045. www.pinewood-village.com. 58 units (2 with tubs). Festive season $340 deluxe double, $400 executive double, $432 suite, $512 executive suite; high season $230 deluxe double, $290 executive double, $338 suite, $418 executive suite; midseason $208 deluxe double, $268 executive double, $314 suite, $394 executive suite; $168 deluxe double, $228 executive double, $276 suite, $356 executive suite. Rates include breakfast, dinner, and afternoon tea. AE, MC, V. **Amenities:** 3 restaurants; 3 bars; airport transfers (Ksh4,500); health club and spa; pool; room service; squash court; tennis court. *In room:* A/C, hair dyer (in suites; on request in deluxe rooms), free Internet (cable), kitchen (in suites), minibar.

The Sands at Nomad ★★ You'll probably spot colobus monkeys darting through the treetop canopy as you pass beneath the gigantic baobabs that mark the entrance to this formidable little resort. Known for its proliferation of hand-carved woodwork (even the oversize clothes hangers have been whittled specially), this is a very handsome setup consisting of comfortable standard rooms in a block tucked into the forest where the pool, reception, and spa are located, and a collection of stunning cottages and suites right on the beach. If possible, aim at least for an oceanview unit—really the size of a suite, with a sitting room, four-poster bed, canopied ceiling to create a romantic atmosphere, private outdoor seating area, and wonderful bathroom—and if you're after the best deal, insist on beach cottage no. 33, which features a Jacuzzi in the alfresco bathroom and its own mini-waterfall. These beachfront cottages have stupendous *makuti* roofs that reach all the way down to the ground; the ceilings are unimaginably high, and beneath them there's good Lamu-style furniture. They open onto a private terrace and lawn, and then a fabulously wide stretch of sand. Up against lesser competition than Water Lovers (see below), this boutique resort might be a strong contender for the title of Diani's finest. What bugs me about this place is the cluttered atmosphere around the pool (where diving lessons also take place), which really feels a bit tacky when it's busy, and the lobby area is truly claustrophobic (probably left over from the days when this was a budget resort).

Beach Rd., P.O. Box 5066, 80401 Diani Beach. ✆ **040/320-3643** through -3647, 072/537-3888, or 073/337-3888. Fax 040/320-3648. www.thesandsatnomad.com. 37 units, some with tub. Festive season $372 forest-view double, $420 sea breeze double, $608 oceanview and beach cottage double, $700 junior suite, $915–$1,140 suite; high season $243 forest-view double, $324 sea breeze double, $446 oceanview double, $518 junior suite, $527 beach cottage double, $548–$965 suite; midseason $210 forest-view double, $243 sea breeze double, $372 oceanview double, $458 junior suite, $446 beach cottage, $482–$875 suite. Children under 12 pay 50% with 2 adults, children under 2 free. Rates include breakfast, taxes, and service charge. AE, MC, V. **Amenities:** 2 restaurants; ice cream parlor; 2 bars; airport transfers ($60 per person round-trip); small exercise room; Internet cafe; pool; spa; dive school. *In room:* A/C, TV, hair dryer, Jacuzzi (in some), minibar.

Shaanti Holistic Health Retreat Intimate and relatively private, this is one of Diani's more relaxing resorts, which blends some unusual design with a focus on offering an alternative to the more obvious and hectic entertainment routines presented at the bigger places. Room nos. 105 to 108 are slightly superior, with a slightly Zen-retro look that's helped along by some curved walls, built-in concrete beds, and great big bathrooms, but their full potential isn't realized and there've been some unfortunate—and slightly cheap—choices when it comes to some of the finishes.

With two yoga sessions and two meditation sessions a day, not to mention candle-gazing, it's hard not to relax here. And, of course, you could simply focus all your energies on the beach. It's not nearly as luxurious or slick as some of the places along this stretch of beach, but it's small, intimate, and imaginatively put together. Perhaps if it were in better hands, it would amount to more than just a peaceful place to hide away after a safari.

Diani Beach, P.O. Box 80, Ukunda. ✆ **040/320-2064,** 072/220-550, 072/278-6841, or 073/322-7381. Fax 040/320-2263. www.shaantihhr.com. 8 units. $500–$600 double; $100 extra bed. Rates include all meals and full-day yoga program. AE, MC, V. **Amenities:** Restaurant; bar; airport transfers ($100 round-trip). *In room:* A/C, free Wi-Fi.

Water Lovers ★★★ **Value** The name says it all. This is a gorgeous place to indulge in a true barefoot holiday, where the sand pathway that leads to your front door continues on to the glistening white beach. It's a sexy, chic place with impeccable grounds and wonderful integration with the environment onto which it opens. Built and managed by a creative young Italian couple, the resort is also a work of art, designed and executed with real flair and attention to detail. There are just eight rooms—one up, one down—occupying four handsome whitewashed cottages. Riccardo is a genius with woodwork, having designed and made much of the furniture himself, while Valentina put her skill as a painter and potter to good use; she created the ceramic handbasins and even hand-painted the bedside lampshades and the drapes. All the rooms have enormous picture windows, the biggest of which faces onto your private veranda, the pool, and the beach just beyond it. The Swahili-style beds, big and high off the ground, have been specially made. Next to the gorgeous infinity pool, the beach bar features stools designed like a whale's tail, and daydreaming happens either in one of the grass pod hanging chairs, the swingbeds, or the fat cushioned sofas that fill out the big, sexy beach lounge. They've thought of clever, useful details that will make your holiday that much easier, such as providing each room with a local mobile phone SIM card. There's also one villa with a big terrace, private bar, dining area, lounge, and views toward the sea. It's airy and filled with light, and has a loft-style breeze-cooled upstairs bedroom that is perfect for children. A chef can be hired for 40€ per day.

Diani Beach Rd., Diani Beach. ✆ **073/579-0535** or 072/700-8840. www.waterlovers.it. 9 units, including 1 villa, none with tub. High season 310€ cottage double, 100€ extra bed, 500€ villa (4 people); rest of year 180€–200€ cottage double, 60€–65€ extra bed, 320€–350€ villa (4 people). Children 2–4 pay 50% with 2

Diani's Best Villa

Condé Nast Traveler called it "one of the most beautiful villas in the world," *Harpers and Queen* called it "the most glamorous house on the Indian Ocean," and I like to think of **Alfijiri** ★★★ (✆ **073/363-0491** or 072/272-7876; www.alfajirivillas.com) as the ultimate in "rock 'n' roll, modern, African chic." Little wonder it's the celebrities' choice—a place where privacy is guaranteed, yet a creamy beach lies just beyond the deep verandas that invite you to stretch out horizontally on oversized sofas. Inspired by Africa and filled with African objects and artworks, it's nevertheless an international, innovative aesthetic that holds all the pieces together, producing living spaces that are novel, exciting, sexy, and totally ballsy. Every piece of furniture and decoration—the thickly hand-woven rugs and bold Zimbabwean cloth against ivory-white Danish floors, implements turned into ornaments, copper urns, Maasai antiques, beadwork, geometric patterning, and piles of cushions—looks and feels like an invention of the imagination. The design is the work of Marika Molinara, former fashion designer and now one of Kenya's top interior designers, who owns Alfajiri with husband Fabrizio. Two of the villas (Garden and Beach) are a dreamer's take on an African-inspired palace, effervescently decorated with African and Eastern artifacts, while the third (Cliff Villa) has Caribbean overtones. All are capped with high *makuti* roofs with floor-to-ceiling glass walls to let in the views, surrounded by magnificent gardens with lily ponds, and have a scene-stealing infinity pool, lengths of fabric rippling in the wind, relaxing barazas, and comfortable sofas piled with pillows. Throw in traditional Lamu doors, hand-carved wood beams, and driftwood sculptures, and there's more than a hint of drama in the design of each. Two ayahs (nannies), who both speak English, are available 24 hours a day, and there are plenty of games, a TV, and movies, if needed. Villa rates depend on the number of guests ($1,100–$1,400 double in high season; $2,000–$2,500 for four people, and so on up to eight guests; children 16 and up 50%, under 2 free) and include all meals—exquisite and prepared by your personal chef—and all drinks (except French champagne), a vehicle for local use, and all kinds of activities, should you choose to give up the blissful embrace of your decadent beachfront palace, your eager-to-please butler, and attentions of around two dozen staff. Prices go up substantially over the Christmas/New Year's period.

adults; under 2 free. Rates include breakfast; half-board and full-board rates available. MC, V. **Amenities:** Restaurant (**Tides;** see "Where to Dine," below); bar; airport transfers (Mombasa 40€ one-way; Ukunda 10€); pool. *In room:* A/C.

Farther South: Kinondo, Msambweni & Funzi

Of my three favorite options south of Diani, two are on the mainland, while the third, **The Funzi Keys,** occupies a finger-shaped island just offshore. You can fly directly to Funzi Keys (which has a private airstrip)—a one-way charter (for up to five people) costs $450—or arrange for a boat to pick you up from the jetty.

The Funzi Keys ★★★ **Kids** This "Lazy Island" is heaven on Earth. One of a patchwork of keys, it's a privately owned mangrove island that's been painstakingly transformed into a tropical-looking paradise, with palm trees and handsome *makuti*-roofed bungalows ranged along a private beach. Everything here—from the spectacularly oversize bungalows (each one designed and built by Allesandro Torriani, the Swiss owner, and gorgeously decorated by Claudia, his South American wife) to the custom-engineered sofas (with their back legs cut down so you're absolutely forced to recline in them)—is designed to help you relax. Come here to do nothing, feast on spectacularly fresh seafood, meditate on the tide, have breakfast on a sand island that appears and disappears with the rhythm of the ocean, lie idle by the pool (where you may spot the resident monitor lizard doing laps across the water), or watch for dolphins.

What began as the Torrianis' single-cottage home has transformed into one of East Africa's most sought-after hideaways, a place that offers a refreshing spin on luxury. Each of the bungalows is fashioned from local materials. Walls are clad with bamboo and held together with grass roping, mats are made by women from the local village, and the natural straw hues are brought to life with beautiful color fabrics, furniture made from bits of old *ngalawa* boats, pretty Swahili chests, and ornamental fossilized coral. The best—which are seaview bungalows—have what feels like their own private beach area, with sunbeds stationed under the palm trees, and there are huge glass windows framing the close-up views of the beach and the water. A magnificent lounge and bar (with upstairs restaurant) is built around an enormous mangrove tree, with a retired dhow and plentiful antiques and well-cushioned sitting areas for decor. It's fine to simply laze here, but there's plenty for adventurous types, too. The deep-sea fishing in this part of the world is legendary, and you can set off to explore the Ramisi River, checking out the mangrove swamps, crocodiles, monkeys, birdlife, and local fishermen. You can also visit the neighboring village, an unspoiled Swahili community that still seems untouched by tourism. You'll quickly come to know the thrill of discovering a place that's so remote and unspoiled that your hosts had to convince the Kenyan government of its existence in the first place—there was a time not too long ago when Funzi wasn't even charted on any map.

Funzi Island. ✆ **073/390-0446** or 073/390-0582. www.thefunzikeys.com. Reservations: About Africa Ltd., The Priory, Syresham Gardens, Haywards Heath, West Sussex RH16 3LB. ✆ **1444/46-6400** in the U.K. Fax 1444/45-7400 in the U.K. info@thefunzikeys.com. 17 units. Dec 23–Jan 6 $840–$1,040 seaview double, $1,200–$1,400 deluxe beachfront double, $1,380–$1,580 deluxe family beachfront double; Jan 7–Feb, July 16–Oct, and Dec 16–Dec 22 $640 seaview double, $920 deluxe beachfront double, $1,100 deluxe family beachfront double; Mar–Apr 10, July 1–15 $480 seaview double, $700 deluxe beachfront double, $830 deluxe family beachfront double. Rates include all meals, most drinks, and local airstrip or boat transfers. AE, MC, V. **Amenities:** Restaurant; bar; airport transfers ($100 one-way from Mombasa; $50 one-way from Ukunda); pool. *In room:* Cooler box/minibar, Jacuzzi (in most).

Kinondo Kwetu ★★★ **Kids** A place that feels more like a home than a business, this is among East Africa's most magical beachside retreats, elegantly put together, stylishly operated, and packed with character and good energy. Totally unpretentious, it's situated on a tranquil, virtually private bay some 20 minutes south of Diani Beach. Owned by a vivacious and beautiful Swedish couple, Ida and Filip Andersson, this place lends itself to the dreamiest of holidays, with plenty of things to do (horses, spa treatments, watersports) but just as much opportunity to do absolutely nothing. They've thought of everything, executed it all with passion and finesse, and are blessed with the loveliest staff. In a way, this was destined to be a special place; at least two baobab trees on the grounds are sacred, believed by the local people to be the dwelling place of their ancestral spirits, and religious rituals are performed at another sacred spot on the coral crags by the sea, where every now and then a cow is ritualistically drowned as part of a fascinating traditional ceremony.

Accommodations are very special—there are no locks, and the transition between outdoor and indoor is effortless, with big shuttered windows and doors that fold away to reveal a view and a terrace. Interiors are a lively mix of African art and crafts, Swahili and colonial furniture, and stylishly carved wood; four-poster beds are topped with fat mattresses. Candles and lanterns are lit at night, transforming your room and the surrounding gardens. My favorite is Ubani, an upstairs unit close to the sea that gets an awesome breeze and has a perfectly positioned balcony accessed through large foldaway doors that you can leave open at night. Before dinner, enjoy drinks at the bar, and be sure to try the brie *samosas.* Parents will feel especially privileged here; the place works very well for families, and there are nannies with first-aid training and plenty of games and toys for kids to use in the pool. All this, and they run a number of authentic community projects, too. It's just perfect.

Galukinondo Beach Rd., P.O. Box 5445, Diani Beach. ✆ **070/578-2885,** 071/025-1565, or 040/330- 0031. www.kinondo-kwetu.com. 12 units. High season \$870–\$970 double; midseason \$760–\$860 double. Children 5–16 pay 35% with 2 adults; under 5 free. Rates include all meals, most drinks, nonmotorized watersports, village outing, and limited laundry. MC, V. Closed May–July 15. **Amenities:** Restaurant; bar; free airport transfers; babysitting; 2 pools; spa treatments; spa; tennis court; free Wi-Fi; scuba diving and dive school; snorkeling. *In room:* No phone, hair dryer (on request).

Msambweni Beach House ★★★ Painted from head to toe in the off-white color of coral, this fabulous contemporary approximation of a Swahili mansion is one of Kenya's best guesthouses. Accommodations are large and very pretty, and feature wonderful balconies with views toward the gently crashing waves. You can stay in the main house, in one of the freestanding Swahili villas, or even in the novel tented cottage. Accommodations have an exclusive, charming ambience—built-in beds and cushioned corners are dressed in white, with metallic gold fabrics bringing the spaces to life. A raised wooden walkway and some steep steps lead to a beautiful alfresco beachside "lounge" and bar where you can spend all day doing as little as possible or thinking about where to have your next meal. Dinner can be served alongside the pool (among the prettiest in Kenya), in dedicated honeymoon spots at the beach, or even on your private terrace. Water is intimately connected with this dreamy house with an infinity pool that emerges from the lounge of the main house and the gentle, ever-present roar of nearby waves. Occasionally, the attentive staff put together miniature musical recitals, entertaining guests before or after dinner. The Belgian owners are heavily committed to community projects, and you can tour the local village with a guide or find out how to contribute to a development project.

P.O. Box 51, 80404 Msambweni. ✆ **020/357-7093** or 072/369-7346. Fax 020/213-7599. www.msambweni-house.com. 8 units. Festive season 640€ main house double, 830€ Lamu villa double; high season 370€–390€ main house double, 490€–530€ Lamu villa double. Rates include all meals, most drinks, introductory massage, local snorkeling, and certain activities. V (credit card payment incurs 5% surcharge). Closed Apr 20–June 1. **Amenities:** Bar service; beach bar; airport transfers (Mombasa 120€ return; up to 4 people). *In room:* A/C, TV/DVD, hair dryer, minibar, free Wi-Fi, private pool and Jacuzzi (in Lamu villas only).

Moments **Dive In . . . Then Tuck In**

Several companies offer dhow cruise packages that usually combine snorkeling, the possibility of diving, potentially dolphin-spotting and whale-watching, and then lunch. The best of these is **Pilli Pipa Dhow Safari** ★★ (✆ **040/320-2401,** 072/444-2555, or 040/320-3559; www.pillipipa.com), which runs—if you'll excuse the pun—a very tight ship and is owned by a Dutch dive instructor and his marine biologist wife. You need to be up fairly early for the transfer to Shimoni in the far south of the Kenyan Coast. There you'll board one of the dhows and set sail (although usually it's an engine that powers the cruise) for the action-packed reef beds that make the **Kisite Mpunguti Marine National Park** one of the best experiences along the coast, with some extraordinarily colorful specimens among the 350-plus species that dwell in the coral beds (although the coral itself is not quite as colorful as you might find elsewhere). You'll get two chances to jump in—at two marginally different reef points, with variations in the kind of marine life you're likely to spot—with quality snorkeling equipment and a number of good-humored guides to watch your back and point out interesting undersea phenomena; each session lasts between 30 minutes and an hour. Bring waterproof sunscreen, and protect yourself front and back. If humpback whales and whale sharks are spotted, you'll spend some time trying to move closer for a better look—you may even get a chance to jump in with curious dolphins. And if you'd prefer to dive with scuba gear, be sure to arrange this in advance.

No matter how spectacular the diving is, you'll be blown away by the delicious Swahili spread that's laid on at the Pilli Pipa base on Wasini Island. There, gazing out over the water, back toward the mainland, you're served by an enchanting team of ladies from the island who've cooked up delicious mangrove crab and plenty of local specialties. The food is ceremoniously carried in on baskets accompanied by singing before being explained by one of your gentle servers. The crab shells are cracked open for you at the table, and you can eat until you're completely satisfied.

On the way back to the mainland, you have the chance to make a brief visit to the Shimoni Caves, immense coral grottos once used to inter slaves before they were trundled onto dhows and shipped off to Pemba and Zanzibar. The short tour of the caves is pretty dull, and the caves and the resident bats do little to evoke the unimaginable horrors that were wrought upon thousands of innocent people here. Still, taking the tour is a chance to contribute to the local economy, something that you could also do by picking up a few random trinkets from the stalls near the cave entrance. The full excursion will last the entire day, with crack-of-dawn pick-ups from hotels all along the coast and drop-off in the early evening.

WHERE TO DINE

There are three beachfront restaurants attached to small resorts that are worth a mention and where you'll have a wonderful meal. **Tides** ★★, adjacent the pretty pool and alfresco lounge at Water Lovers (✆ **073/579-0535;** daily 12:30–2:30pm and 7:30–9:30pm), is one of my favorites, especially appealing for the fresh, healthful ingredients and focus on home-style cooking; the owners are Italian, so the small menu features Mediterranean-inspired dishes. The menu changes daily according to what's available and what's fresh—the emphasis is on healthy, organic food—and everything is scrupulously homemade. There are typically seafood, meat, and vegetarian choices, so lunch (15€) might be grilled fish skewers or risotto with pumpkin and parmesan, while for dinner (19€) you could get deep-fried crab claws followed by homemade brown-flour fettuccine with pesto and prawns. Reservations for mealtimes are essential and should probably be made a day ahead; you can also drop by during the day for snack, salads, and sandwiches (Ksh350–Ksh750). They serve great homemade ice cream here, too.

One of the busiest and best resort restaurants, with a lively lounge/bar atmosphere, is the **Beach Bar** ★ (✆ **040/320-3643;** daily 7am–11pm), which is literally right on the beach in front of The Sands at Nomad. The food is reliable, and there's a very large selection, including authentic-tasting pizzas and a lunchtime buffet (Ksh1,800). For an even breezier ambience, head to one of the slickest spots along the beach, **Sails** ★★ (✆ **020/213-8501;** daily 10am–11pm or later) at Almanara, toward the southern end of Diani. It's a beachfront alfresco restaurant and bar with a handful of tables and cushioned armchairs under large canvas sailcloth, and some sea-facing sun loungers where you can sip premeal cocktails; it's wonderfully sociable, without the potential tackiness (and crowds) of the large resorts (and definitely the place to be if you're trying to get away from buffet tables). The menu—which includes daily specials—is perfect beach vacation fare. Fresh seafood is bought directly from the local fishermen, and salads and vegetables are grown in Almanara's own gardens at Villa Malaika. Salads are a mainstay here (try the octopus salad), best enjoyed with a serving of king fish or yellowfin tuna *carpaccio,* marinated with lemon juice and ginger. There's plenty of tasty comfort food, such as grilled rosemary chicken and thick-cut pepper steak, too.

If you're looking for a memorable experience, then what you really want is a private beach barbecue. Quite a number of fishermen in and around Diani will put on a fine spread for you, preparing straight-off-the-boat fish over the coals, but I suggest you contact Mohammed (✆ **072/620-4862**); he and his team will set up an adorable makeshift dining area on the beach and treat you to a sumptuous meal for around Ksh1,500 per person (feel free to give something extra).

You'll hear about it frequently while you're in Diani, so it's worth warning you *not* to try **Ali Barbour's Cave Restaurant,** probably one of the most overhyped dining experiences in Kenya. What's marketed is the supposedly romantic thrill of feasting inside a genuine grotto, but reports of lackluster food (and, in some cases, illness) and the prospect of having to jostle for space with just about every other tourist in Diani makes this a wholly unsavory option.

3 THE NORTH COAST

Watamu is 120km (74 miles) N of Mombasa, Malindi is 24km (15 miles) N of Watamu

In the streets of Malindi, you're as likely to hear locals greeting you with *"Ciao!"* as *"Jambo!"*, a sign of the influx of Italian tourists and long-term visitors who've fallen in love with the place and established homes here. Malindi is one of the Swahili coast's oldest towns, founded in the 7th century, apparently on the site of a more ancient village that may have had trade links with India as much as 2,000 years ago. The Chinese were trading here in the 12th century, and the Arabs in the 13th century. Malindi was, in fact, regarded by Arab documenters as the "capital of the Land of Zanj" and was known for its sorcerers and its links with Persia. Because it was less than a month's sea voyage from the Indian port of Calicut, it was an important Indian Ocean *entrepôt* with which the Chinese had the greatest contact. It was the sultan of Malindi, in fact, who sent as a gift the first giraffe ever seen in China. Europeans turned up only late in the 15th century when Vasco da Gama was warmly welcomed following a hostile reception in Mombasa. Rivalry between Malindi and Mombasa meant that the Malindi king was keen to score points with the Portuguese, so Malindi became Portugal's main base along this coast until Mombasa was finally conquered a century later. After Fort Jesus was built, the Portuguese invited the ruling family to relocate to Mombasa, which meant that Malindi spiraled into decline. By 1669, Malindi lay in ruins, and accounts observe that nomads had occupied what was left of its houses and mosques.

Today, however, it's the enormous Italian population that gives the town its special atmosphere. Designer hotels are a dime a dozen; delis sell locally produced pecorino, scamorza, and mozzarella; and the scene is painted with bronzed glamour girls soaking up the sun in crocheted bikinis and loud, flapping men clamoring for attention. Meanwhile, developers scramble to create glitzier resorts or set themselves up in the most glam villas. Most recent among these is The Lion in the Sun, built in 2008 by Flavio Briatore, the ultrawealthy Italian businessman (and lover of a long list of high-profile models) whose most recent intrigues included being banned from Formula 1. At night, after pasta, pizza, and real-deal espresso, there's casino action and gossip turns to the latest mafia-in-hiding sensation.

This shouldn't put you off, however. Ernest Hemingway caught a big sailfish here in the 1930s (the top hotel is named after him), and the area is still renowned for its full-day deep-sea excursions. Snorkeling the coral reef here is an unmitigated highlight of any visit to this part of the Swahili coast; if you simply want a fabulous beach without the overblown Il Familia scene, then head slightly south to less-developed Watamu. It's well known for entertaining some of the world's greatest sport fishing, while the gorgeousness of its beach, divided into three distinct coves by large coral outcrops, is reason enough to settle in for a few days. Watamu, too, caters overtly to a foreign market, but it's still possible here to escape the crowds and find a patch of sand that feels virtually private. It's also worth knowing that Malindi and Watamu are a mere 90 minutes from Tsavo National Park, which means you can mix it up with a bit of bush, beach, and undersea adventure. (Note, however, that Watamu's beaches are usually covered with seaweed from May to mid-Oct.)

If you have a true yen for a sense of being in a remote and unfettered corner of the world, there's no better place than **Delta Dunes** (see "Where to Stay," below), perched atop the dunes high above the **Tana River Delta.** It's unquestioningly one of my favorite spots in East Africa—wild and unencumbered by the weight of modernity, these tranquil wetlands are unique in East Africa, with marvelous creeks and waterways stocked full of aquatic species, incredible birdlife, and large numbers of hippos and crocodiles that somehow exist in the semi-saline waters close to the ocean. And getting there is an adventure all on its own.

ESSENTIALS

GETTING THERE The drive from Mombasa to Malindi is relatively hassle-free and takes up to 2 hours, depending on traffic getting out of Mombasa. Daily flights connect

Malindi with Nairobi, Mombasa, and Lamu. Both **Kenya Airways** (✆ **042/20-237,** -574, or -192, or 072/378-6314) and **AirKenya** (✆ **042/30-636** or -411) have offices at Malindi Airport, just 3km (1¾ miles) from town on Mombasa Road. **Fly540** also flies here; book online at www.fly540.com. For onward travel to Watamu, you can grab a taxi or even a *tuk-tuk* (see below), or pre-arrange a transfer through your hotel or with ever-reliable **Southern Cross Safaris** (✆ **041/243-4600** through -4603; www.southerncross safaris.com).

GETTING AROUND You'll probably spend a lot of time simply ambling along empty beaches. In order to get to many of the attractions, or between your hotel and the towns, you should make use of a *tuk-tuk.* These are fairly ubiquitous, and all you need to do to signal one is look as though you need a lift—or wave your hand slightly. In Malindi, I make use of only one *tuk-tuk* driver, a pleasant young man named **Charles,** who is worth the little effort of calling for (✆ **071/442-1747**). He quotes prices that are almost ridiculously fair, so add a good tip. If you want to get a bit of exercise while exploring, consider sightseeing by bicycle. Steve Curtis (✆ **073/389-7661;** steve@diveinkenya.com), who owns the Aqua Ventures dive center, is well versed in getting off the beaten track and offers a number of **bush bike tours** to explore some of the points of interest, including cycling on Malindi beach and exploring the Sokoke Forest and Mida Creek.

VISITOR INFORMATION The Watamu Marine Association runs a useful, well-maintained website (**www.watamu.biz**) with handy links and advice.

WHAT TO SEE & DO

Known throughout Kenya as a place where the locals incongruously speak Italian, at the heart of **Malindi** is actually a vibrant Muslim town with a distinctive culture all its own. It's a small heartland, however, and doesn't have quite the same punch as Lamu or Zanzibar's Stone Town. If you're taking a break from the beach and the ocean, you may want to devote an hour to it, perhaps investigating some of the shops that are so obviously geared toward the tastes of European visitors. For the rest, Malindi is a bit of a dusty, dirty town and its beach far from spectacular, although it gets better south of the jetty, which is where you'll see the totally uninteresting **Vasco da Gama Pillar,** apparently one of the oldest remaining European monuments in Africa, set up when the Portuguese arrived in 1498.

None of this, though, is likely to lure you to Malindi. If you're here, it should be for the chance to explore the mesmeric underwater universe of the **Malindi & Watamu Marine National Parks** ★★★ ($15 adults, $10 children and students), where a profusion of beautiful coral gardens teeming with Technicolor fish have been protected since 1968. These parks—now managed as a single entity covering 261 sq. km (102 sq. miles)—were the first of their kind in Africa and are easily accessible from either Malindi or Watamu. The only marine park in the world with a larger number of fish species is the Great Barrier Reef, which is several thousand kilometers long—the reef here is a mere 7km (4¼ miles). Snorkeling—or "goggling," as it's known locally—is the best way to experience the reef. Forget about the glass-bottom boat trips unless you're seriously aquaphobic, as you'll soon end up resenting the glass that separates you from what you're admiring. In these magical kingdoms, you'll spot masses of multicolored fish—angelfish, butterfly fish, triggerfish—ducking in and out of the coral beds, and there are moray eels, fantastic clams, and pretty sea urchins. Snorkeling trips can be arranged through any of the hotels or at the Marine Park entrance. If you're feeling more adventurous, you can

Kites, Tanks, Tackle: Staying Active in Malindi & Watamu

Snorkeling above the sublime coral reefs in the Marine Park will satisfy most travelers' fascination with the azure waters off the Malindi–Watamu coast. This can be arranged through any of the hotels in Watamu, or you can contact Saidi through **Driftwood Beach Club** (✆ **042/212-0155,** 073/474-7133, or 071/664-7530) in Malindi; he charges $37 (including transfers and park entry fees) for 2 hours of snorkeling in Malindi Marine Park. Going underwater also offers the chance to swim with whale sharks, a big highlight here. **Scuba diving** is offered by well-established PADI operation **Aqua Ventures** (✆ **042/32-420;** www.diveinkenya.com), based at the Ocean Sports hotel in Watamu and run by Steve and Helen Curtis, who've been here since 1990. The dive sites are all a 10- to 20-minute boat ride from shore; there are around 18 buoyed dive sites, as well as a few seldom-dived, unbuoyed sites. A Watamu reef dive costs 30€, night dives are 40€, and a full-day diving safari with cave and reef diving costs 120€; they also have a number of dive packages, rent equipment, and offer courses all the way up to divemaster. You need to be aware that diving and snorkeling are greatly marred by river silt from March through June, with visibility usually poor enough to keep you out the water entirely. If you're in Malindi, you can contact **Upinde Diving** (✆ **073/541-8570** or 072/396-2123), which charges 70€ for two dives in a single morning or 320€ for 10 dives over 5 mornings.

A good place to be when you can't go beneath the surface is flying above it. Widely considered prime **kitesurfing** territory, the wind here lures pro-kiters

also scuba-dive here, and there's the opportunity to scope out a wreck and venture into underwater caves (see box above). If you want to see whale sharks, come here in November. The main fishing season runs from December through March, but there are also good-size tuna caught between April and November.

At the far southern end of Watamu's long, empty beach is the mouth of **Mida Creek,** another beautiful waterway composed of mudflats and mangrove forests that attract a wide variety of flora and fauna; bird-watching is especially rewarding between March and May.

En route to Malindi, at the mouth of the **Sabaki River,** it's a tremendous sight to spot the hippos that can frequently be seen gamboling in the surf where the river enters the sea.

Arabuko-Sokoke Forest ★★ Small but beautiful probably best sums up this astonishing swath of green. Declared a UN Biosphere Reserve, this 420-sq.-km (164-sq.-mile) protected forest is all that remains of a once-huge coastal forest that stretched from Somalia all the way to Mozambique; there are more than 230 species of birds, 240 types of butterfly, and 40 mammal species, including elephant. A substantial number of these species are found nowhere else on Earth, including the regularly spotted golden-rumped elephant shrew, the largest of its kind in Africa, growing to the size of a small rabbit and capable of reaching speeds of up to 25kmph (16 mph). You may also be lucky enough to and kite pioneers to the beach north of Malindi. They come as much for the sense of wild, open space—at Che Shale (p. 280), where **Kitesurf Kenya** operates, there are 5km (3 miles) of deserted beach—as they do for the dependable winds. Averaging 16 knots (and reaching up to 25 knots) and with around 300 days of wind per year, it's a formidable destination for the sport. There's an 8-month season, with cross-shore and on-shore winds from July through September and January through May. Kitesurf Kenya offers everything from beginner's instruction (with 2–4 hr. of action per day; 300€, including all equipment) to refresher courses and equipment rental.

Finally, some of the country's finest **game fishing** takes place out of Watamu and Malindi; in fact, the Malindi Coast is among the finest fishing locations on Earth, and game fishing has been truly spectacular in recent years. Wahoo, barracuda, dorado, giant trevally, yellowfin tuna, and kingfish are caught daily. Most hotels will help with arrangements, and Hemingways in Watamu is particularly geared toward deep-sea fishing, but the **Malindi Sea Fishing Club** is one of Kenya's great hangouts for sport fishing enthusiasts. It's a bit of a social hangout, with lots of focus on the pub (you need to pay for daily membership if you're not signed up; Ksh100 for the day). Midafternoon you can spot the fishermen coming in and weighing their catch. **Kingfisher** (www.kenyasportfishing.net) is a reliable deep-sea company that has operated from Malindi for more than 4 decades and holds some of the country's most impressive catch titles. Besides daytime fishing trips, they do all-nighters and longer fishing expeditions.

catch sight of one of the world's smallest owls, the Sokoke Scops, which is both endangered and rare.

Malindi Rd., Watamu. ✆ **042/32-462.** $20 adults, $10 children; additional Ksh200–Ksh500 per vehicle. Daily 6am–6pm.

Bio-Ken Laboratory and Snake Farm Just outside Watamu, this place has the biggest collection of snakes in Africa, with around 200 belonging to 30 different species. The farm was established to breed snakes for use in research, and the snakes here are milked for medical research and for the preparation of antivenom. And if looking at the caged beasts isn't enough for you, they also organize a couple of snake safaris showing off snakes and reptiles in their natural habitat.

2km (1¼ miles) north of Watamu. ✆ **042/32-303** or 073/329-0324. www.bio-ken.com. Ksh700 adults, children under 12 free but must be accompanied by an adult. Daily 10am–noon and 2–5pm.

Gede Ruins ★★ Dating back to the late 13th century and abandoned in the early 1600s, this is yet another mysteriously little-recorded medieval ruin, considered by many to be the best example of its kind in East Africa. We're not talking Pompeii here, but there is some clear semblance of a profoundly organized and efficient society that built a proper town and went to pains to establish at least seven mosques and some very decent toilets.

Why precisely the town was abandoned is uncertain, although, given the circumstances of the entire East African coast during the 17th century, it can almost be assumed that the city was attacked and plundered, leaving the forest to take hold and create the evocative site that remains today. What is known is that the people—who followed an adapted form of Islam—had trade links with China, Phoenicia, and Europe, evident from the types of artifacts unearthed here (these can be seen in the little museum). Today Sykes' monkeys live in the trees around the ruins, and it's possible to see other small animals here, including the golden-rumped elephant shrew.

Gede, Watamu, 16km (10 miles) S of Malindi. ✆ **042/32-065.** www.museums.org.ke. Ksh500 adults, Ksh250 children under 16. Daily 7am–6pm.

WHERE TO STAY & DINE

As if preparing for Malindi's much-anticipated return as an Indian Ocean superpower, the development of resorts, villas, and holiday villages for wealthy Europeans has meant that pickings are particularly rich for anyone looking for a place to stay close to the beach. Price and quality both tend to be considerably higher that you might expect.

Watamu

Besides Ocean Sports (reviewed below), **Turtle Bay** (✆ **042/32-003** or 042/32-226; www.turtlebay.co.ke) offers good-value accommodations and has earned a silver eco rating from the Eco Tourism Society of Kenya.

If you've grown tired of the buffet spreads or simply want a change of scenery, head for **Savannah** ★ (✆ **072/628-7637** or 072/184-5446; main courses Ksh500–Ksh1,000; Tues–Sat 4pm–midnight and Sun noon–midnight), where Mike Carr and Jackie Couch operate the best-loved restaurant in Watamu. It's geared toward families, with a games area, pool table, and dartboard, so you can spend a long, unhurried afternoon or evening here. The setting is very inviting, with sumptuous gardens and a laid-back, pub-style vibe. Start with the smoked sailfish, and follow with king prawns in brandy and chili sauce. There's also an excellent crab salad and plenty of comfort food—burgers, fish and chips, pasta, steak, and chicken.

Hemingways Resort ★★ Deep-sea fishing and excellent snorkeling are the *raisons d'être* for this smart, if old-fashioned, resort set on a prime location along Watamu's best-looking beach. From here you can walk for miles till you reach the mouth of Mida Creek to the south, or head north to meet the crowds on the busier coves nearer Watamu village. Or, if you prefer, you can take things at a gentler pace and sip *dawa* cocktails on a dhow sunset cruise. This is also a resort of lazy days around the pools and long sessions at the sociable bar; at night, guests dress up (no jeans or shorts) for the fancy buffet dinner, and everyone loses themselves to the nostalgia and sentiment that's conjured up by a five-piece band doing popular covers. Accommodations are very appealing, especially

> **Tips** **Mind the Weeds**
>
> If your main reason for visiting Watamu is to sprawl out on its beach, you need to know that strong winds prevail between May and August, and during this period—which includes the rainy season, when most places shut down anyway—the beach is littered with seaweed.

A House to "Dhow" For

In Watamu, with direct access to the world-class coral-white sandy shore of Turtle Beach, the magnificent **Dhow House** ★★★ (www.dhowhousekenya.com) is one of Kenya's most riveting villas. A brooding clay-colored fortress-castle on the outside—it's a contemporary take on traditional Swahili-Lamu design—once you move inside, everything about this place screams convivial party palace. There's space galore, with ultra-high ceilings and, everywhere, evidence of scrupulous good taste and enormous attention to detail. It's built on three levels and comfortably sleeps 10 people (at around 300£ per night). Done in a sumptuous blend of Swahili and Moroccan styles, the house has all sorts of elegant lounge and relaxation spaces, tied together by an orderly mix of beautiful fabrics and textiles, handsome furniture, and appealing decor, including beautifully romantic nighttime lighting. There's no air-conditioning, but fans and a reliable breeze ensure that you're comfortable, or simply plunge into the magnificent pool on the first floor. The cook throws together spectacular meals, and your butler will help you with grocery purchases or negotiate with the local fishermen for the freshest possible catch. When you're bored with lazing by the pool or drifting into a reverie on the spectacular beach out front, there are all kinds of activities to get the blood pumping (snorkeling, deep-sea fishing, dhow cruising, kitesurfing, cycling in the Arabuko forest, yoga, Pilates, and massages on the rooftop terrace). You could even charter a flight to the Masai Mara, where you could catch a glimpse of the Great Migration and be back in time for sundowners on the rooftop terrace.

in the year-old North Wing, where the deluxe rooms face the beach directly; these units have tiled floors, big beds, furniture made with mango and jacaranda wood, and a slightly Deco design. Drawbacks include the sniffy service from the folks at the fishing center, a slightly formal dress code, and the obsession with rules—the signs warning you of all the dos and don'ts can get up your nose.

Mida Creek Rd., P.O. Box 267, 80202 Watamu. ✆ **042/32-624** or -724, 072/220-5917, or 073/341-1112. Fax 042/32-256, -181, or -255. www.hemingways.co.ke. 76 units. $210–$470 superior double; $250–$520 deluxe double; $280–$590 junior suite; $480–$1,500 executive suite. Rates include breakfast, dinner, afternoon tea, taxes, and service charge. AE, MC, V. Closed May–Jun 14. **Amenities:** Restaurant; bar; airport transfers (Malindi free; Mombasa £75 one-way, up to 6 people); babysitting; health club and spa; 2 pools; room service; floodlit tennis court. *In room:* A/C, TV, hair dryer, minibar, free Wi-Fi (unreliable).

Ocean Sports (Value) Right next door to Hemingways, the Ocean Sports hotel is a more reasonably priced alternative but a far less luxurious option, with fewer rooms and variable service. In the bar there's a boat with an inscription informing you that the hotel's founder arrived in it from Mombasa, while behind the reception, large broadbill swordfish key you in to the hotel's obsession with the sea. This place is especially popular with Kenyans looking to mix their own brand of mayhem with a bit of ocean-going adventure. The full-blown party vibe might also have something to do with the wonderful—and hugely sociable—beachfront terrace where you can eat and drink to the accompaniment of an awesome view. There's also a good dive school here (p. 277), and in a way, this feels a bit like a clubhouse for watersports enthusiasts, with the added benefit of a room for the night. Arranged around the edge of a garden built up with coral stone, accommodations are in an agglomeration of rooms in variously sized whitewashed cottages with *makuti* roofs. They're basic but cheerful, done out in white and offset by dark-stone flooring and a dash of color; each unit has a little private outdoor seating area. There's also a self-catering cottage that sleeps eight and comes with its own chef, housekeeper, and beach entrance.

Mida Creek Rd., P.O. Box 208, 80202 Watamu. ✆ **042/233-2288** or -2008. Fax 042/32-266. www.oceansports.net. 30 units. Dec 20–Jan 4 $300 double, $120 extra bed; Jan 5–Apr $220–$230 double, $90 extra bed; July 21–Dec 19 $200, $80 extra bed; May–July 20 $170 double, $70 extra bed. Rates include breakfast and lunch or dinner. Children 2–12 pay about 50%; under 2 free. Holiday supplement during Christmas and New Year's. AE, MC, V. **Amenities:** Restaurant; bar; airport transfers (Ksh2,500); 2 pools; squash court; tennis court; free Wi-Fi (in public areas). *In room:* A/C, hair dryer (on request).

Malindi

Driftwood Beach Club ★ Value Kids Probably the most relaxed and relaxing spot in Malindi, this is a pleasant place to watch a wide variety of travelers drifting in and out, whether on their way to the beach, passing through the very sociable bar, or preparing for more rigorous pursuits on or under water. You'll hear all kinds of accents here—South Africa, Zambia, New Zealand, Nairobi, the U.K., and the U.S.—making this feel like a refuge from the full-blown Italian takeover that's happened elsewhere in Malindi. Driftwood has comfortably avoided all pretenses of modernizing or smartening up and, by retaining a laid-back, inscrutably barefoot holiday attitude, comes up trumps, even if accommodations are quite simple and functional rather than attractive. Rooms are all in simple thatch-topped *bandas* and have only the most basic amenities and nothing resembling decor. A low coral rock wall divides the hotel's palm-filled grounds from the beach, but it's an easy walk from your room (or the bar or the pool) straight into the ocean. You'll be inclined to spend most of your time around the pool, on the beach, or—and this is a big attraction here—soaking up the vibe in the big, open-plan bar (it's a great place from which to watch the moon rise over the ocean) before heading to the adjacent restaurant, which is the most consistent in town.

Set a little away from the beach, but with access to semiprivate pools in their own gardens, there are handful of cottages and villas suited to families; they're all simply but brightly decorated with a lounge and terrace area, and the villas have their own kitchen. Nannies are provided if you need help with the children, and they can arrange special activities for youngsters, too.

Silversands Rd., off Casuarina Rd., P.O. Box 63, 80200 Malindi. ✆ **042/212-0155,** 073/474-7133, or 071/664-7530. Fax 042/213-0712. www.driftwoodclub.com. 39 units, including 2 cottages and 3 villas. $196 double, $560 cottage/villa (4 people). Children under 12 $35; under 5 free. Rates include breakfast; half-board rates available. MC, V. **Amenities:** Restaurant; 2 bars; airport transfers (Ksh750 one-way); babysitting; pool; free Wi-Fi (in bar). *In room:* A/C.

Kilili Baharini Resort & Spa ★★★ The name means "Bed in the Water," and that sums up the persistent love affair with all things aqua at this totally sexy resort in Malindi's upmarket quarter. If it weren't for the extensive use of African art and artifacts, you'd forget where you are and imagine yourself perhaps in some kind of tropical version of the Italian Riviera. Slate pathways glide between the wonderfully tailored gardens leading to clusters of thatched cottages with some very swanky accommodations. Ask for a room close to the beach, as the property is quite large and the alternative is a long walk to the shore. The rooms are spacious and tidy, with a fresh, classy ambience (white stone floors with large, simple beds and furniture made from muriki wood with glass-inlay panels); each room has a little dressing room and slickly finished bathroom with big

Tips My Own Private Africa

Situated on a coral bluff overlooking Silversands Beach, **Himaya House** ★★ (www.himayahouse.com) is one of Malindi's loveliest, breeziest, and most laid-back villas. The focus is on providing matchless privacy, scintillating views, and easy beach access—the most important prerequisites for maximizing your enjoyment of this coastal town. The main house features a big lounge–cum–living area, with the main bedroom upstairs, two bedrooms (also both en suite) in the guest wing, and, if you're traveling in a large group, space on the veranda for children to curl up on a couple of extra beds. There's no air-conditioning, but plenty of fans and a good breeze keep things cool. You'll enjoy the services of a small, dedicated staff, including an excellent cook who will even help you sort out your grocery shopping—although you'd do well to buy fresh seafood directly from the fishermen who turn up at the gate with lobster, fish, prawns, and crab. Linen and towels are provided and laundry is included. The owner, Lissa Ruben (✆ **072/270-2351**), lives on-site most of the year but will give you total privacy, making an appearance only to ensure that everything is going smoothly and to give advice and make recommendations. Best of all, this place is an absolute bargain, at 150€ per night in low season and 200€ in busier periods.

shower. Superior rooms have more space, with bigger beds, deeper verandas (which have their own daybeds), and prettier bathrooms. There's a huge, very enticing beach area with Lamu beds transformed into sofas, and big swaths of fabric billowing in the breeze. Be sure to make a date with the celebrity-grade spa.

Casuarina Rd., P.O. Box 93, Malindi. ✆ **042/212-0169.** Fax 042/212-0634. www.kililibaharini.com. 35 units. Peak season 366€ standard double, 448€ superior double, 614€ junior suite, 638€ suite; high season 272€ standard double, 306€ superior double, 400€ junior suite, 424€ suite; regular season 224€ standard double, 260€ superior double, 348€ junior suite, 372€ suite. Rates include all meals; B&B and half-board rates available in high and regular seasons. AE, MC, V. **Amenities:** 2 restaurants; 2 bars; free airport transfers; exercise center and spa; 5 pools; room service; Wi-Fi (in lobby; Ksh10 per min.). *In room:* A/C, TV (suites and junior suites only), fridge, hair dryer.

Lion in the Sun ★ Sure, this place was created by celebrities (Naomi Campbell is a partner with Italian playboy millionaire and ex-fraudster Flavio Briatore) for celebrities, and it looks like a million bucks. There's tight, slightly officious security at the gate, and the whiff of glamour has gone completely to the heads of the people working the front office. The rooms and suites are palatial, and the state-of-the-art spa is arranged around fake-rock waterfalls, four saltwater pools, various ultra-sexy lounges (indoor and out), a snazzy gym, and look-at-me sunbeds. Rooms—all individually styled and packed with refreshingly original furniture and lots of art—have a decadent, richly textured look, with anything from Indian paintings and giraffe-skin rugs to tribal artifacts and slightly risqué photographs. However, in the details there lurk some big errors, such as the ultra-ordinary linen covering the big four-poster beds, and the hotel's location, almost conspicuously away from the beach (in a manmade oasis across the road from the entrance to Malindi Marine Park), which usually requires guests to be ferried, first by road and then by boat, to a more-or-less private beach where they can avoid mingling with the masses.

Let the Wind Take You . . .

If you prefer to be surrounded by wood and thatch rather than concrete and favor a natural breeze over air-conditioning, then head north of Malindi to **Che Shale** ★★ (✆ **072/223-0931;** www.cheshale.com; 180€–260€ double, including all meals), best known as the headquarters of Kenya's slickest kitesurfing operation (p. 274), where riders-in-the-know return year after year to enjoy the excellent wind conditions. The five open-to-the-elements thatch *bandas* are lovely, breezy spaces with a crisp Robinson Crusoe look. Renovated by Milanese designer Marzia Chicherretti, known for her "tropical contemporary" style—big, bouncy cushions, simple mango and cedar wood furniture, and earthy colors echoing the natural surrounds—the cottages all have alfresco showers and personal verandas. The food is excellent, too. They cook interesting specialties such as battered seaweed, Zanzibar-style calamari, and crab and coconut soup, and also bake their own bread. They also offer a handful of budget-oriented accommodations in their **Kajama Beach Bandas,** which are rustic (no electricity, shared bath facilities) and utterly relaxed, and share the same superb beach as Che Shale (85€ double, with all meals included). Kajama consists of five *bandas* that are built on stilts with a palm-thatched roof, wood floor, and private veranda; there's a communal dining and barbecue area. Each *banda* is set in a peaceful tropical garden facing miles and miles of empty beaches and the ocean, and can sleep up to three people.

Marine Park Rd., Causarina, P.O. Box 1056, 80200 Malindi. ✆ **042/30-066,** 072/590-6044, or 073/363-4766. www.lioninthesun.net. 16 units. 330€ superior double; 550€ suite. Rates include breakfast, taxes, and service charge. AE, MC, V. **Amenities:** Restaurant; 2 bars; free airport transfers; health club and spa; free Internet (in business center); 4 pools (including 2 saltwater); room service. *In room:* A/C, minibar.

Scorpio Villas ★ (Value) (Kids) There's a bit of a party atmosphere at this neatly laid-out resort centered on a loungey restaurant and two sociable bars (unless you fancy listening to rather loud R&B each time you arrive at the hotel, you might want to consider staying elsewhere). You also need to know that these aren't villas at all, but rather multiple clusters of rooms set around pleasant grounds with a variety of open-to-the-elements public spaces; it's a design that takes full advantage of the tropical climate, while there are the usual clichés (*makuti* roofs, coral stone walls) and a few unexpected ones in the garden (statues of African warriors with oversize lampshades on their heads, little wooden bridges). Guest rooms are spacious and attractive, with exposed wood-beam ceilings, gleaming white floors, and four-poster beds. The setup is simple, yet stylish, making this an extremely good value. Best of all, you have direct access to the beach, and there's the obligatory designated beach area for guests.

Mnarani Rd., P.O. Box 368, Malindi. ✆ **042/20-892** or -194. Fax 042/21-250. www.scorpio-villas.com. 25 units. Ksh4,400–Ksh7,600 double. Rates include breakfast, taxes, service charge, and training levy. Minimum stay may apply. MC, V. **Amenities:** Restaurant; 2 bars; airport transfers (Ksh1,000); 2 pools; Wi-Fi (in public areas; Ksh200 per day). *In room:* A/C, TV, plunge pool (in 1 suite).

Around the World on a Plate: Malindi's Culinary Mélange

Perhaps it's the abundance of Italians supposedly obsessed with excellent food, but Malindi has a disproportionate number of worthy places to eat. Top of everybody's list is **The Old Man and the Sea** ★★ (✆ **042/31-106**), which is, in Malindi at least, almost as much of a classic as Hemingway's novel. Moorish arches and *kikoi* tablecloths set the scene, but it's the seafood, as you might suspect from the waterfront location—it's right near the fishing boat dock and is where freshly caught game fish is weighed—that'll make you a fan. Incidentally, it was this place that sparked Malindi's love affair with smoked sailfish, now a local specialty. Another decent choice (from the same owners) near the jetty is **I Love Pizza** (✆ **042/212-0672** or -0879), which is a lot better than it sounds and serves a lot more than just pasta and pizza. It's also right next door to another, even better, choice, **Tangeri** ★, Sea Front Road (✆ **042/212-0414**), a Moroccan-theme restaurant with an Italian menu, hookah, and cappuccino-flavored *shisha*.

Baby Marrow ★★, Silversands Road (✆ **073/380-1238**), is widely exalted as the finest eatery in town, with a stunning lounge/bar in the garden adjacent the partially-open-to-the-elements restaurant. The atmosphere and cuisine are top-notch, even if the hostess is totally offputting. Try one of the seafood pasta dishes, served in the pan.

Driftwood Beach Club ★ (p. 278) has a friendly, highly sociable vibe and a very eclectic menu—it's also a great venue from which to watch the moon rising over the ocean. Start the evening at the bar, which feels like the beachside version of a bush pub, decorated with sturdy lengths of driftwood and spirit bottles arranged around the branches of a tree. They serve just about everything, from pizzas and pasta to quality seafood, including piripiri crab claws and the catch of the day, prepared to your taste.

Tana River Delta

There is only one place to stay here, and it enjoys one of the most breathtaking locations—especially for anyone who loves the outdoors—on the East African coast. If you need to feel the throb of people and a sense of an ongoing bustle, then stick to Malindi or Watamu, but if peace and unfettered nature are what you crave, this is where you want to be. The lodge works closely with the local community, who will manage a 60,700-hectare (149,929-acre) conservancy that's been set aside. As part of the privilege of staying here, a conservation fee is paid to the local people for every guest that stays at the lodge.

Delta Dunes ★★★ *Moments* "You've got to be mad to build on sand dunes," is what any sane person would say, but here the near-impossible has been achieved, and the result is one of the most spectacularly located lodges in East Africa. The large, open-sided *bandas* are spread over different levels across the tops of a number of high dunes looking down on epic scenes that take in the river, the ocean, and the tops of yet more dunes.

The Crusoe-style bungalows are completely open to the elements, with extraordinary views; the absence of doors and windows means that they're kept fresh by a cooling breeze that circulates. They're beautifully decorated using mostly shells, sculptural pieces of wood, and lovely Swahili fabrics. Large chunks of driftwood have been fashioned into pillars and furniture, with shells for decoration and cushions for sprawling on. This is a magical place to come if you favor a more active beach holiday; you can venture along the beach for miles, chancing upon local fishermen (you may even spot lion paws in the sand or see yellow baboons hunting for crabs on the shore), or cruise the waterways by boat looking for game and birds, watching crocs practically dive into the water from the river banks while bulbous hippos wallow in the brackish river fringes. If you're very lucky, you might get to see elephants crossing the river below the lodge. In the lounge bar at night before dinner, genet cats and bushbabies come, as if tame, to take food from your hands, or if the wind is calm, you can dine under the stars beside the pool, watching as the dunes glow under the moonlight.

Tana River Delta. ✆ **071/130-7911.** www.tanadelta.org. Reservations: African Territories, P.O. Box 76677, 00508 Nairobi. ✆ **020/386-4830** through -4832, 072/240-9869, or 072/132-2745. www.africanterritories.co.ke. 7 units. $1,120 double; children 3–16 $280. Rates include conservation fee, all meals, all drinks, airstrip transfers, laundry, and taxes. MC, V. Closed Jun. **Amenities:** Restaurant; 2 bars; airport transfers (from Malindi $40 per person one-way); pool. *In room:* No phone.

4 LAMU ARCHIPELAGO

260km (161 miles) N of Mombasa

Sometimes compared with an earlier, more intimate, less-developed Zanzibar, Lamu (to the north of Malindi) is an old Arabic trading town on an island of the same name. Mentioned in a Greek seafarer's manual as early as the 2nd century A.D., the Lamu Archipelago, incorporating the island of **Kiwayu** some 60km (37 miles) from the Somali border, is sufficiently far north along the Kenyan Coast to have avoided mainstream tourism. Still, Lamu is hardly a travel secret. Princess Caroline of Monaco and Prince Ernst of Hanover "discovered" this place many years ago and still spend time each winter in their restored house in fashionable **Shela,** Lamu's second village and a fine place to explore once you've had your fill of the main town, which is busier and comparatively crowded. While Caroline and Ernst are hardly the only savvy Europeans who've invested in the restoration of old Arab houses here, development has been slow, and in many ways the relative isolation has drawn a more elite crowd—certainly more discerning than those who swarm into the resorts along Mombasa's north coast. For many years, Lamu has offered a hideaway for aristocrats and celebs. They've established summer retreats in restored Arabic mansions, retaining the medina-style architecture and injecting them with a posh, contemporary sensibility. While the local population has tried to avoid outside influence, it's hard to say that Lamu is not affected by the arrival of foreign money and the slow gentrification that's happened along many of its narrow lanes.

Kenya's oldest living town—claimed by some to predate Islam—Lamu is a UNESCO World Heritage Site. In its heyday it was a major Indian Ocean trading post and an important stop-off for Arabia's ocean-going dhows blown in by the southbound monsoon in winter. Arriving laden with exotic goods from the Middle East, they would wait for the northbound *kusi* winds, which would send them home, laden with ivory and rhino horn, concubines, and slaves. The golden days of the dhow trade routes are long gone, and Lamu's slippage into relative obscurity has spared it from modernization seen in busier ports such as Mombasa. Having sunk into genteel decay, the towns of Lamu and Shela became hippie magnets in the 1960s, and the archipelago has since unexpectedly evolved into a bolt-hole hideaway for the privileged set, with tourism steadily prodding it back to life. Its discreet popularity seems in some ways inexplicable—Lamu town and Shela village are dusty, labyrinthine muddles where losing your way between the crumbling, towering coral houses is a whole lot simpler than avoiding the splattered donkey droppings, and the shoulder-width laneways are as atmospheric as they can be disconcerting. Yet the sense of stepping back in time, and of being in a place that's a true cultural anomaly with a unique and auspicious identity, is very real indeed. And once you step beyond the confines of the meager settlements—high up on the dunes, on a vast palm-backed beach on the islands of **Manda** or **Kiwayu,** or on the southern tip of Lamu at **Kipungani**—the sense of being on an island paradise, where the rhythm of life is determined by the tides and the phases of the moon, is very real, too.

If ever there was a place for a prolonged, hassle-free holiday with as little as possible to do—yet with plenty of options (from kitesurfing to low-flying air safaris) to make you feel alive—then this is it. And the time to visit is now. If ever there was a scheme set to challenge Lamu's languid cultural soul, it's the much-anticipated heavy-duty port planned on the mainland facing the far northern end of Manda Island. Although work on the port is yet to begin, many believe it will spell the end of Lamu's romantic entanglement with timelessness.

ESSENTIALS

GETTING THERE & AWAY Lamu can be reached by air from Nairobi, Mombasa, and Malindi. **Air Kenya** (**© 042/463-3445;** www.airkenya.com), **Safarilink** (www.safailink kenya.com), and **Fly540** (www.fly540.com) all have daily services. All flights land on Manda Island, just across the channel from Lamu; from the quaint and slightly surreal little airport, it's a short walk (with porters from your hotel waiting to carry your luggage) to the jetty, where a boat will be waiting to whisk you off to your hotel. Some of the flights also stop at Kiwayu's little airstrip, but this is happens only by demand.

If you choose to travel here by car or bus, it's around 3 hours from Malindi on variable roads. You arrive at the Mokowe jetty and wait for the ferry, which regularly transfers people to Lamu town; you can also arrange for your hotel to send a boat.

GETTING AROUND Part of the enormous charm on Lamu Island is the near-total absence of motorized transport. With the exception of two hospital vehicles (one of which is a *tuk-tuk*) and the District Commissioner's seldom-seen Jeep, only a few tractors and the odd motorbike account for any sort of land-going, engine-driven transport. For the most part, locals and visitors must rely on boats (wind-powered dhows being the more traditional choice), donkeys, and shank's pony. I don't personally recommend using a donkey, as these poor beasts are overburdened enough as it is—they are, however, astoundingly tough. Walking around the villages is mandatory, while cruising between the islands by boat is part of the great adventure of being in Lamu in the first place. It can also be a source of great frustration, given the number of "local fishermen" willing to sell you all kinds of trips on their motorized dhows. Travel between the islands can be tide-dependent; although it's a 10-minute boat hop between Lamu and southern Manda, getting to Kiwayu is best achieved by private air charter (15 min.), by speedboat (100 min.), or, more romantically, by dhow, which may take 8 hours or more. Finally, as much as it sounds like an ecologically unfriendly activity, there is simply nothing to beat a scenic flight over the archipelago. Studying the patchwork of blue and green from the sky is mesmerizing. You fly for miles passing above nothing but water, mangroves, palm trees, and acacias, and in the water, occasional sandbars and sand islands dotted throughout the marblelike blue, green, and indigo water channels. Waves break over the reef banks farther out to sea, and dhows and fishing boats motor by—then suddenly you're passing over white-and-green mosques, their minarets towering above the *makuti* roofs of tiny waterside fishing villages. Both **Manda Bay** and **Majlis** (see "Where to Stay," below) have their own light aircraft and can offer scenic flights, not to mention transfers between the islands.

VISITOR INFORMATION Culturally, the most interesting time to visit Lamu is during **Maulidi,** a festival celebrating Mohammed's birth. Events range from donkey races to dhow sailing events and swimming competitions, but there are also literary performances and displays of traditional dance. The festival, which happens in the spring, draws religious pilgrims, so you should secure accommodation well in advance. A more recently introduced celebration, the **Lamu Cultural Festival** is held for 1 weekend in November. Information about both these festivals and Lamu can be found at **http://lamuheritage.org**, a fairly comprehensive website operated by Kenya's National Museums authority. If you're interested in the developments around Lamu's fragile marine ecology, check out postings on **http://lamumarine.wildlifedirect.org**. If you need cash, the **KCB ATM** directly opposite the main jetty in Lamu town accepts Visa and MasterCard credit cards, but you need to know that if electricity goes down, so will your chance to withdraw money; the same problem is likely if and when the machine runs out of cash.

WHAT TO SEE & DO

Lamu, with 20,000 people, 6,000 donkeys, and 2 cars, seems like some kind of East African Venice. It's not just the absence of vehicular traffic, the narrow lanes, and the reliance on water to get around and get things done, but a kind of cultural autonomy that makes this place look and feel like it was made to be admired, studied, and loved.

Even if you're sequestered in total tranquillity on Kiwayu or on the far end of Manda (both of which are superb island destinations in their own right), arrange a day trip to Lamu town (the donkey-clogged lanes alone are worth a few hours of your time, preferably in the cooler morning or early evening). Life here revolves around the numerous mosques and along the seafront, tethered with weather-beaten dhows. Day begins with the first hour of daylight—*saa moja*—when you'll spot fishing dhows navigating through the gap in the reefs that leads to the open sea. Back in town, men go about their business (which is often doing very little at all) in cheerful *kikois* or full-length *djellabas,* while many women remain shrouded in black *bui buis,* their expressive eyes the only point of contact with passing strangers. And, as everywhere on the coast, the young men of today strut the waterfront in their boardshorts and oversized Manchester United shirts, and while they feign and mimic city-slicker attitudes, this is still a devout Muslim community with around 30 mosques and a faithful devotion to regular worship.

Here you'll hear the *muezzin* calling for prayers and the less melodic calls of hustlers urging you to use their guide services or to climb aboard their boat for the day. For guides, use the recommendations of your hotel (the men and boys who hang around the jetty are a serious nuisance), and then ask them to show you anything other than the museums and obvious "attractions." Lamu's pulse is best felt in the cool, labyrinthine streets, shaded by multistory Swahili houses, many of which are now enjoying a second life as the winter retreat for fashionable Europeans. Make an effort to chat with people in the streets or visit with the storekeepers; you'll soon get the knack for telling the hustlers from the genuine souls, and when you bump shoulders with ordinary people who have no interest in selling you a guided tour, you'll find the interaction refreshing and agreeable. Don't be afraid of trying out the local, seedy-looking eateries and juice shops—the food may be served in grimy surrounds, but it's generally delicious, and the juices thirst-quenching. If you'd prefer to snack and dine in more salubrious surrounds, you can find respite from the heat (which can be furious as the day marches on, prompting the afternoon closure of most stores) on the balcony of **Lamu House** or in the garden courtyards at **Whispers Café** or **Bustani** (see "Where to Dine," below).

Tiny as it is, Lamu town consists of more than 40 *mitaa* (or areas), the main focus of which is now the **Usita wa Mui**—or main business street (Harambee St.)—which separates the old stone town (the World Heritage–listed area) from the 19th-century **seafront.** A few laps along either of these vibrant, always-bustling stretches will key you in to the exotic scents and images that will burn into your memory. Whether you're watching the dhows being loaded and offloaded, seeing artisans chisel away at a chunk of wood, or simply observing as the children splash in the water or the donkeys huddle for shade beneath the boats marooned by low tide, there's always something extraordinary, yet simple, to see.

If you'd prefer a more formal introduction to Swahili culture, you could visit the **Lamu Museum** (no phone; Ksh500 adults, Ksh200 children; daily 8am–6pm), initially established as the residence of the last English governor. There's a collection of exhibits meant to reflect the history and cultural life of Lamu Island and the surrounding Swahili towns, and there's some focus given to the tribes of Kenya's northern coastal areas. Sadly, despite the beautifully restored facade, the museum conceals a lackluster exhibition space and in places looks as if it's been ransacked. Still, if you have the patience, you might pick up a few insights.

One good reason to be in Lamu is to get better acquainted with **Swahili architecture.** The historic houses are generally built according to the same traditional style—typically, they're two- or three-storied, flat-roofed, oblong structures built around a small open courtyard—with elements designed to defend against the elements (you'll notice how the rooms stay cool despite the temperatures outside). Rooms are usually long and narrow, which—together with lots of small open windows—helps with air circulation. Walls are coated in a lime paste known as *neru* made from coral, which also works as a natural coolant. You'll see these and other architectural quirks in a number of the restored houses now serving as guesthouses and hotels, but you'll also get a good look at such details at the **Swahili House Museum** (near Juma Mosque, Old Town; no phone; www.museums.or.ke; Ksh500; daily 8am–6pm), occupying a restored upper-class home dating from the 18th century. It's worth noting the wells or pools in the gardens and courtyards of the traditional houses; these are known as *birika* and were used to store water for bathing. Water was drawn from the pools using a coconut-shell ladle—small fish are traditionally kept in the *birika* and help keep the water clean, while controlling mosquito numbers by feeding on any mosquito larvae. Inside you may notice that Swahili beds are quite high off the ground—apparently servants and slaves would sleep under here.

Another historic landmark—quite imposing from the outside and something of a geographic and social landmark—is **Lamu Fort** (admission Ksh200, or free with Lamu Museum ticket), built by the last sultan of Lamu between 1813 and 1821 after Lamu defeated Pate and Mombasa in the Battle of Shela. Sadly, as an attraction, it's a total letdown, used these days as a conference venue and municipal offices, with not a single jot of useful information or exhibition material to help you make sense of it as part of the town's history. Views of the town from the upper bulwarks are pretty good, but not necessarily worth the ticket fee. Frankly, there's a lot more going on in the square in front of the Fort. Here you'll usually spot men playing *bao,* said to be the oldest game in recorded history, while the **market,** tucked off to one side of the fort, is a good place to sample a bit of local color.

But Lamu is more than just an ancient, labyrinthine town of narrow streets packed with secrets. The islands of Lamu, Manda, and Pate are a mix of deep-blue channels and coral reef with protected bays and broad, sandy beaches with sand dunes and mangroves; there's plenty to explore once you get out of town. Lamu's most obvious beach is the unbroken 13km (8-mile) crescent-shaped stretch that runs southwest from the edge of Shela village to the steadily evolving collection of holiday villas around unspoiled Kipungani. Backed by sand hills and palm trees, it's a gloriously secluded place to unfurl your beach towel (bring lots of sunscreen), and you could spend hours simply gathering shells and watching crabs scuttle over the shore.

Shela village, at the foot of some high dunes, can be reached easily by a short boat trip or a pleasant 45-minute walk from Lamu town (it's 4km/2½ miles away) and is another must-see. A bit of a hippie stronghold during the 1960s, it continues to serve as a popular retreat for foreigners who've invested in Lamu. While the beach is a big attraction, the village itself is also a more placid place than Lamu, and locals are even more willing to interact. There are also one or two prestigious-looking boutiques and galleries (see "Shopping," later in this chapter) tucked between the renovated mansions. Now considered the wealthy neighbor to Lamu, it's ironic that Shela was originally established as a colony for the people who had fled Manda when their water supply dried up. Best known of the buildings here is **Peponi Hotel,** Shela's unchallenged landmark and society hub; the beautiful colonnaded villa on the edge of the water was built by the English governor in the 1930s. A sunset drink on the terrace is considered one of the quintessential Lamu experiences, although some find the busy bar a bit too much of a scene.

Immediately behind Peponi's is the **Jumaa Mosque** (or **Friday Mosque**), probably the most interesting and unusual-looking building in all of Lamu, especially loved by photographers because of its pepper-pot minaret.

No trip to Lamu would be complete without a full and proper **dhow trip** ★★★, preferably powered by wind rather than diesel (see the "Dhow Days" box, below), while a visit to the **Takwa Ruins** at the end of the mangrove-lined creek on Manda Island makes for an intriguing visit. For snorkeling, your best bet is a day trip to **Manda Toto,** a tiny island near the northern end of Manda (the season runs Dec–Apr, when the water clears up), and intrepid divers will potentially find enormous sharks if you're brave enough to drop in beyond the reef that protects the archipelago. You could combine any of these activities with dhow sailing, and if you have the time, you could also set off on a daytrip to **Kipungani,** a laid-back town with two eco-friendly resorts and a gorgeous beach on the southern end of Lamu Island.

Northernmost of the islands is **Kiwayu,** a narrow strip of beach rising to a high ridge with dense bush-covered dunes. The island, with just two small villages, shelters a beautiful bay and lies at the heart of a marine reserve with more great snorkeling.

And between Manda and Kiwayu lies the virtually unexplored island of **Pate,** where archaeologists have found evidence of mud mosques dating back to the 8th century at a place called **Shanga,** and you can visit the impressive **Siyu Fort,** built around the same time as the fortress in Lamu. If you want to visit this seldom-seen island, you'll need to organize a boat and a guide and go prepared for a full day's adventure.

WHERE TO STAY

Considering its remoteness—and the relative lack of infrastructure—Lamu has a disproportionate number of places to stay. Lamu town itself can be noisy, but based here for a few days, you get a real feel for the rhythm of the town. Shela, a smaller village that's a half-hour walk (or 10-min. boat ride) from Lamu, has a wider range of accommodations and, being the A-list choice, has many great villas (see box below) over and above the three pretty hotels worth considering. Then, if you want to be far away from any potential crowds, there are plenty of no-news, no-shoes places to stay, where you'll have instant access to multiple deserted stretches of strand.

Lamu Town

Cats, chickens, and donkeys. *Bui bui*-clad women marching through extremely narrow lanes; men congregating to discuss the latest gossip, plying *samosas* and selling boat trips, or skulking in grass hats and boardshorts tucked beneath their *kikois*. Along the seafront, provisions are constantly being loaded and offloaded from heavily laden boats, and passengers are constantly assembling around the jetty. If you want to get caught up in, or simply observe, the constant ebb and flow of Lamu's distinctive way of life, then spend a couple of nights here before moving on to one of the relaxed and tranquil islands where your chances of interacting with locals will be limited to dealing with staff who are paid to fuss over you.

Baytil Ajaib ★★ This "House of Wonders" is a beautifully restored patrician house with great character and immaculate interiors, all done in a pale sepia finish that underscores the ancient influence on its design. There are two apartments and two suites gorgeously furnished with a mix of authentic Swahili antiques and appropriate reproductions (ask for the suite with a bed similar to that belonging to the sultan of Kilwa). Much of the life of the house happens in the sunlight-dappled central courtyard, with its palm trees and ferns, and in the nearby original well, still stocked with fish that serve as a natural control against mosquitoes. There's been great respect for the house's original design elements, and the result is a thoroughly peaceful abode and a true Swahili experience, affording simple, appealing luxury that emphasizes the functionalism of the Swahili home. There are also as a variety of nooks and spaces for you to lose yourself in silence, and a rooftop terrace from where you can peer down into the heart of Lamu's intriguing laneways. Step outside and you're in the heart of the town, instantly part of an ancient culture that's changed little over the centuries.

P.O. Box 328, Lamu. ✆ **042/463-2033.** www.baytilajaib.com. Reservations: Chic Retreats. ✆ **20/7307-2797** in the U.K. www.chicretreats.com. 4 units. $234 apartment double; $346 suite double. Rates include breakfast. MC, V. **Amenities:** Free airport transfers. *In room:* No phone, hair dryer.

Jannat House This dilapidated old house has seen better days. It feels like a rundown backpackers' haunt, with lackluster service and almost zero attention to detail (broken chairs are simply left lying around, and they really need to get a handyman in soon). Reasonable rates ensure that it draws a crowd during high season, and as unspectacular as it is, it gets by on the notion that it's probably the best budget option in Lamu's old town, although I find it a bit claustrophobic and a far cry from the comparably palatial rooms at Baital Aman Guest House in Shela (reviewed below). There's a small pool in the

Lamu's Magical Villas

If you'd like to join the ranks of the high-profile jet-setters who station themselves in Lamu for prolonged doses of sun, sand, and respite from the paparazzi, then consider renting a villa rather than checking into a hotel. That way, you'll have a better shot at blending in with the locals—in theory, at least.

With the biggest range of rental houses, **Lamu Homes** (www.lamuhomes.com) is possibly the first place you should look to get a good idea of the types of villas available—the variety and level of comfort are quite extraordinary.

Built in the Balinese style, with foldaway wooden screen doors, appropriately named **Manda Dream** ★★★ (✆ **073/567-1732;** www.mandadream.com) is a superb choice, with two gorgeous houses right at the edge of the beach on Manda Island. **Blue Empire House** has three double bedrooms and goes for 300€ per day on a self-catering basis (or 600€ with all meals and drinks); neighboring **Equator House** has four bedrooms (400€–800€ per night), which can also be rented individually (150€–250€ per room). There's a private boat launch and the services of a full, well-trained staff.

Also on Manda is **La Marelle House** ★★ (marcella.anselmetti@gmail.com), right on the beach. Built in the colonial style, with verandas, an internal patio garden, arched French doors and windows, wooden floors, and a spacious interior, it overlooks a lawn shaded by acacias and gigantic baobabs. It, too, has a full staff, as well as a boat with a captain who will transport you to Shela and Lamu, or take you to a pretty nearby beach—a great spot for snorkeling. The self-catering rates are about 600€ a night for high season, including the boat, and 500€ a night in the off season.

Shela House Management (✆ **042/463-3419** or 020/240-5808; www.shelahouse.com) has four gorgeous homes for rent in Shela village. Each is a beautiful restoration of an old house, now exquisitely transformed and immaculately decorated in a cool, upbeat revival of Swahili style. Facing the water directly, the sexy **Beach House** ★★★ is the most expensive (700€–2,000€) of the four but is the most popular, thanks to its dramatically gorgeous infinity pool, a surreal spectacle against the backdrop of dhows drifting by. Views are epic, whether from one of your terraces or from your bedroom. The other three houses may not share the same majestic position, but they're equally beautiful, with cool interiors, alfresco terraces, comfortable *barazas,* and a keen sense of barefoot, laid-back glamour that fuels the desire for a lazy holiday. If you want something a little more affordable, the other villas run 225€ to 450€ and 350€ to 1,000€, respectively. The houses are all done in simple, elegant Swahili style, with appropriate furniture and bright, eye-catching fabrics to set off the white adobe walls; a CD player is the only possible intrusion. You'll probably spend much of your waking time on the rooftop terrace or trying to pick up tips in the kitchen from your cook, who bakes fresh bread and whips up fabulous Swahili and international meals. If you want three meals a day included in the price, it's

50€ per person extra. As with most of Lamu's villas, there's a 3-night minimum stay in the low season and 7-night minimum in summer (and 14 nights over Christmas/New Year's). Remember that while beer and soft drinks are readily available in Lamu, you might want to bring your own wine and spirits, as local suppliers may not necessarily have what you're looking for.

Another option in Shela is bougainvillea-bedecked **Kisimani House** ★★ (www.kisimanihouse.com), a restored property that was first built for the caliph of Zanzibar in the 18th century. Comfortably sleeping eight people in four double bedrooms, it's another glorious villa with carved *zidaka* niches and a wonderful courtyard garden. The house goes for 200€ to 800€ per day, excluding meals (add 60€ per person for full board).

On the southernmost tip of Lamu Island, separated from Shela by a fantastic 12km (7½-mile) stretch of beach, seven gorgeous, innovatively designed houses—part of Leslie Duckworth's **Kizingoni Beach** ★★★ (www.kizingoni beach.com)—are spread across 10 hectares (25 acres) of perfectly wild, pristine coastal land near the unspoiled village of Kipungani. Designed to take maximum advantage of the setting sun, with impeccable views framed by coco-palms and bush, each house is set within its own large forested grounds and is completely independent and self-sufficient. With imaginative design and hints of architectural innovation, the houses blend colonial Arab Swahili style with high-end materials sourced from exotic locations. There's no air-conditioning, but there are plenty of fans and the design ensures great circulation of natural air. You'll have your own big freshwater swimming pool, with outdoor showers and a day bed suspended beneath the veranda. Each house also has its own 23m (75-ft.) speedboat and skipper, and you have a choice of full-size or small dhows for excursions, too. Rates run 2,600€ to 10,800€ per week for up to 8 people; add 65€ per person, per day for full board, including drinks (your live-in cook makes everything from ice cream to international cuisine).

For more intimately proportioned, modestly sized houses, **www.lamu holiday.com** (✆ **072/304-3754**) is a good option. This new company had just two available houses at press time, with a third scheduled to launch by 2010. The houses are new constructions but follow Swahili architectural rules to some extent and combine the convenience of Western influences on the design, too. Four-story **Bembea House** (145€–395€ per night for up to four people) is next to the dunes on the edge of Shela village, close to Peponi Hotel and its famous bar. Done out in natural textures and fabrics, its bedrooms feature four-poster Lamu beds; the dining and living rooms are above these, on the third floor, where there's a small library and sound system. And, of course, you'll find great views from the rooftop terrace, its *barazas* ideal for daytime sunbathing, nighttime stargazing, or luxuriating in the spell of a silvery moon.

internal courtyard and panoramic views of Lamu from the upstairs sitting areas scattered over various bits of rooftop, but the rooms are tired and uninspiring. While the six-bedded "family" room sounds like a good deal, be warned that it relies on natural ventilation and has a cubbyhole-size bathroom, and mattresses are threadbare.

Lamu Old Town, P.O. Box 195, Lamu. ✆ **042/463-3414** or 072/028-9897. www.jannathouse.com. jannathouse@gmail.com 16 units. High season $105 double, $38 budget room; regular season $92 double, $33 budget room; low season $60 double, $26 budget room. MC, V. **Amenities:** Restaurant; bar; free airport transfers; pool. *In room:* No phone.

Lamu House ★★★ This is the best place to stay in Lamu proper. A wonderful modification of a pair of waterfront houses (known respectively as Azania and Salama), it has an awesome position facing the harbor and is an extremely sociable and stylish space centered on a pool courtyard with shaded open-to-the-elements sitting areas. Owners Frank and Marian, originally from Belgium, love the property so much that they live here, too, and provide more of a warm, personable guesthouse experience than a mere hotel stay. In fact, they'll go to exceptional lengths to ensure you have a superb time—not just at Lamu House, but in Lamu. Frank arranges donkey rides, introduces you to the best shopkeepers in town, sets you up for a town tour with one of his neighbors, and takes you sailing on one of his very own dhows. The guesthouse is a fabulous arrangement of beautiful rooms, elegant *barazas,* and two very relaxing courtyards with swimming pools and space to lounge. Mixing African artifacts, contemporary art, traditional wood ornaments, colorful fabrics, overflowing bougainvilleas, and coconut palms in the whitewashed courtyards, Frank and Marian have transformed this into a homey, vibrant retreat from Lamu's bustling, narrow lanes. Ask for a seafront room—these have superb views through Moorish arched windows. A couple of the rooms in Salama, on the other hand, are especially good for looking in on the neighborhood action.

Lamu seafront, P.O. Box 471, Lamu. ✆ **042/463-3491.** Fax 042/463-3492. www.lamuworld.com. 11 units. 175€–200€ double; 200€–225€ superior double. $30 supplement over Festive Season. Rates include breakfast. MC, V. **Amenities:** Restaurant (**Moonrise;** see "Where to Dine," below); bar; airport transfers; 2 pools. *In room:* No phone, minibar, free Wi-Fi.

Shela

For those in the know, this has long been an increasingly gentrified pocket of island life with millionaires and aristocrats renovating houses for personal use, hotels, and guesthouses, the first and most famous of which is **Peponi's,** which still draws a crowd to its sociable bar.

Baitil Aman Guest House ★★ **Value** Originally a royal family house built in the 18th century, this is an awesome find in the heart of Shela's narrow laneways. The name means "House of Peace," and it's situated adjacent a mosque and a bird-filled garden. It's a tall house with many steps, which is worth knowing if you're averse to climbing, in which case you should book a room with a low number. Inside there's plenty of space and all kinds of sitting areas and lounges on different floors. Unusual plants and pretty flowers decorate the stairways and terraces, and there's a sense of being in a place that's fresh and unaffected—it really pulls off the shabby chic look well. Staff look dashing in white shirts with *kikois,* and their laid-back, affable approach is infectious. The antique-style rooms have whitewashed walls, shuttered windows, and plenty of respect for the original architectural elements. Cracked wall effects and signs of natural aging add to the minimalist look—bedrooms are huge, with big beds and lovely attached bathrooms; light

Moments Dhow Days

Picking up a dhow cruise is straightforward enough, as you can make arrangements through your hotel (usually a very good idea, given the amount of bargaining that you'll otherwise be subjected to by the myriad fishermen offering this service). Alternatively, there's the totally upmarket and exclusive ***Tusitiri* Dhow** (✆ **073/364-9833;** www.enasoit.com), which offers a unique opportunity to sail around the Lamu archipelago aboard a traditional Swahili ship with an 11-man crew and evocative decor. The boat is available for sundowner cruises (10–20 adults at $70 per person, with 3 hr. of music, drinks, and canapés) or dinner (8–12 people for 6 hr. at $140 per head for a three-course meal with soft drinks, wine, and beer), but the ultimate is a 3-night safari where you stay on board. There are below-deck bathrooms, and your hosts provide linen, bathrobes, and towels, ensuring that this is a truly hassle-free experience. You sleep on deck under the stars on comfortable roll-up beds that are unfurled after dinner; there's space on board for up to 10 guests. By day, besides the incessant wining and dining (mostly fresh seafood, huge mangrove crabs, lobster, prawns, and the catch of the day), there's a range of activities (snorkeling, fishing, waterskiing, windsurfing, and other watersports) for when you tire of the languid exploration of the inland waters, deserted beaches, and island hideaways. Although there's a motor, when conditions allow, *Tusitiri* raises her sails and the wind powers you around in time-honored tradition. The cost is $3,000 per night for the hire of the boat, plus $80 per person full board, which includes accommodation, wine, beer, soft drinks, certain spirits, boat transfer, deep-sea and creek fishing, watersports, sundowners, and travel between the islands.

pours in through arched, unglassed windows with straw mats that can be rolled down. Some details may be lacking, but the whole is definitely greater than its parts, and there's something unforgettably engaging and memorable about sitting on the cushioned ledge of your terrace watching the action in the tiny lanes below.

Shela, P.O. Box 179, 80500 Lamu. ✆ **042/463-3022,** 073/337-5380, 077/257-6669, or 071/357-6669. Fax 042/463-3584. www.baitilaman.com. 8 units. High season $180 double; regular season $120 double; low season $100 double. Rates include breakfast. No credit cards. **Amenities:** Restaurant; free airport transfers. *In room:* No phone.

Kijani House Hotel ★ This hotel is set in what looks like a secret garden, hidden from the world by a high wall, stocked with kunazi trees, palms, bougainvilleas, frangipanis, flamboyants, and yellow oleander. The garden, grounds, and rooms are decorated with beautiful antiques and reproduction artifacts recalling the long history of this coast. Don't hesitate to splurge for a suite—they have loads more space and you'll have your very own rooftop terrace. Bedrooms are pretty and, in keeping with local style, have mustard-colored walls, stone floors, exposed wood-beam ceilings, straw mats, high beds, and antique-style furniture. Recline in your harbor-facing planter's chair and spend a lazy afternoon watching the action on the water just beyond your balcony. The garden-facing, open-to-the-elements restaurant serves wonderful grilled fish and dishes that are fresh and homemade; don't miss the honey and poppyseed ice cream.

Shela, P.O. Box 266, Lamu. ✆ **042/463-3235** through -3237, 072/554-5264, or 073/554-5264. Fax 042/463-3374. www.kijani-lamu.com. 11 units. 160€–180€ double; 200€–220€ suite. Children 3–11 30€; under 3 free. Rates include breakfast, taxes, service charge, and boat transfers. Half-board and full-board rates available. Holiday supplements during Christmas and New Year's. MC, V. Closed May–June. **Amenities:** Restaurant; bar; free airport transfers; 2 pools. *In room:* No phone.

Peponi Hotel ★★★ With its social epicenter bar, enchanted waterfront garden, secret nooks, and sun-soaked terraces, Peponi's has long been the most distinguished and lovely place for travelers and locals to meet up over a drink, while a handful of the fortunate get to bunk down in some truly gracious digs. Built like a fortress against the sea, this water's edge hotel was first constructed in the 1920s, when it was the district commissioner's house. It was later bought by a Danish family and transformed into one of Kenya's most celebrated lodging experiences—and it remains a quintessential East African trip highlight, with all of Shela at your fingertips and easy access to any of Lamu's top sites. Spread along the Shela waterfront, guest rooms are variously arranged and give focus to the gorgeous views over the channel between Lamu and Manda islands. Rooms come in a variety of configurations and with different views and varying ambience, but they all feature the signature Old World colonial style, with just enough local design influence to remind you where you are. If you're traveling with children, opt for rooms in the Palm Garden. If you prefer to just plonk down on the beach, it's a fairly easy walk, or you can sign up for adrenaline-inducing pursuits, set off to explore the Takwa ruins, or check out the Siyu Fort on the island of Pate; for true romantics, there's a moonlight dhow trip. Service is swish and professional, starting with the effortless pick-up from the airport and the personal introduction to the facilities, the island, and your room. There's a courtesy dhow trip to Lamu town every morning, and the owners will set you up with the very best guides to maximize your time here.

Shela, P.O. Box 24, 80500 Lamu. ✆ **042/463-3421** through -3423 or -3154, 072/220-3082, or 073/420-3082. Fax 042/463-3029. www.peponi-lamu.com. 24 units. 300€ standard double; 360€ superior double; 10€–80€ extra bed. Rates include breakfast, taxes, service charge, and training levy. Full-board rates available. AE, MC, V. Closed May–June. **Amenities:** Restaurant; bar; free airport transfers (by boat); pool; room service. *In room:* No phone, hair dryer, Wi-Fi (network card for hire; Ksh300 per 1/2 hr.).

Manda

The Majlis ★★★ Seen from across the water in Shela, this new hotel is an incongruous sight, an architectural mélange that ignores all the rules. Get closer, however, and you discover a fascinating hideaway with posh digs set right on the beach. From an Arabic term meaning "Meeting Room," this hotel represents probably the largest investment of capital in the region—ever. The whole place has been put together like some kind of rock

Moments An Unforgettable Dawn

During your stay at Manda Bay, be sure to schedule at least one early-morning scenic flight, checking out Manda's coral reefs, the Takwa ruins, and Lamu town from the sky before spotting game on the mainland and flying above the villages of the Orma people who graze their cattle along the banks of the Tana River. Having flown over the Tana River Delta's enormous dunes, potentially spotting crocodiles at close quarters, you'll be back in time for a fabulous breakfast.

star's pleasure palace, divided into three villas, each with a number of suite-size rooms and even sexier suites filled with an incredible collection of artwork (some commissioned, some collected), artifacts (from antiques to African crafts), and eye-catching furniture. However, they've stuck to the spirit and charm of East African coastal design while including contemporary elements and all the comforts you'd expect from a top-end luxury pad such as gracious lounges, a relaxing bar, meandering water features, and all manner of exciting activities to keep things interesting—don't pass up a chance to visit the Takwa ruins and then cycle back, stopping at the Timboni coral rock mines along the way.

Manda Island, P.O. 502, 80500 Lamu. ✆ **071/819-5499** or 071/819-5498. www.themajlisresorts.com. Reservations: ✆ **020/88-2028,** -2598, or 7979/90-3006 in the U.K. Fax 020/88-2868. 25 units. 480€ superior double; 580€ deluxe double; 680€ junior suite; 1,044€ family room; 1,600€ royal suite; 140€ extra bed. Rates include all meals and nonmotorized watersports. V. **Amenities:** Restaurant; 2 bars; free airport transfers; 3 pools; room service; Ayurvedic spa. *In room:* A/C, free Wi-Fi.

Manda Bay ★★★ A smooth wind-in-your-hair boat trip delivers you from Lamu's miniature airport to this amazingly private beachfront paradise, sheltered by coconut palms, acacias, and tamarind trees, on a mainland-facing corner of Manda Island's northernmost peninsula. With the 18m (59-ft.) *Utamaduni* dhow anchored in the bay out front, this looks a bit like an ultrahip pirate cove, a playground for celebrities and scenesters, not to mention ordinary folks who fancy the matchless solitude. Your sociable hosts—Andy and Caragh Roberts and Fuzz and Bimbi Dyer—are stalwarts of the Kenyan hospitality industry and take care of you with unflinching kindness; prepare to be offered impromptu game drives after dinner, and expect habituated bushbabies to take banana slices from your hands in the lounge/bar as you sip cocktails before dinner. Manda Bay is filled with surprises, including abundant animals, which serve as a foil for the diverse watersports on offer. The deep-sea fishing is a highlight, and there's fabulous snorkeling at nearby Manda Toto Island. At night, when the sandy pathways between the waterfront *bandas* are lit up with storm lanterns, the moon casts an incredible glow over the glass-flat water, and dinner is served beneath the stars. You sleep in enormous, beautifully laid-out and totally relaxing bungalows—leave the big picture "windows" open and wake up before sunrise to witness dawn breaking over a silvery white sea and the gold disc of sun peeking through the cracks in the clouds behind Manda Toto. Then slip into the water—just meters from your personal terrace—or slink around to the tony outdoor lounge around the pool. It's the type of place where you forget where you last left your shoes, but will rarely wear them anyway.

Manda Island. ✆ **073/420-3109.** www.mandabay.com. Reservations: The Safari and Conservation Company, P.O. Box 24576, 00502 Nairobi. ✆ **020/211-5453,** 020/219-4995, 073/557-9999, or 071/257-9999. www.thesafariandconservationcompany.com. 16 units, all with shower only. Festive season $1,500 double; rest of year $1,140. Children under 16 $440–$450; under 5 free. Rates include all meals, wine with meals, afternoon tea, sundowners, and laundry. MC, V (credit card payments incur surcharge). Closed May–June. **Amenities:** Restaurant; bar; airport transfers (Lamu $85 one-way; local airstrip free); pool; spa treatments. *In room:* No phone, hair dryer, minibar.

Kipungani

On the far southern end side of Lamu island, Kipungani has long been considered the remote and thoroughly unspoiled half-sister to Lamu and Shela. There's some skillful development going on here, however, with plush villas (p. 288) and beautiful private homes. The first hotel, **Kipungani Explorer ★** (www.heritage-eastafrica.com), is still

Moments **Baobabs of Kitangani ★★★**

Tucked into a tranquil patch of Kiwayu Island, the **Baobabs of Kitangani** is a private idyll offering the ultimate luxury castaway experience, with exclusivity, awesome views, and enough romantic thrill to kick-start a few epic novels. Consisting of two thatch-covered, treehouse-style, open-to-the-elements areas—one for sleeping and one for lazing—this is a chance to hole up beneath the stars and lose yourself in a prolonged moment. A night under these baobabs doesn't come cheap (rates per couple start at $1,065 low season, $1,600 high season Oct–Feb), but everything—from luscious linens to superb private dining and your very own *askari*—is laid on, and you can explore the island or drape yourself over a pile of cushions and do nothing but stare back toward the mainland, watching as dhows cruise through the channel. Bookings are through Kiwayu Safari Village (see below), which gives you an idea just how fabulous the food will be.

here and remains a pleasant, still-remote getaway with 16 luxurious-yet-rustic thatch-roofed beach huts that open to ocean-facing verandas. Featuring locally made furniture, with lots of *mkeka* matting, shells, and driftwood branches for decor, they're very comfortable and retain an intimate relationship with their natural surrounds. Nightly rates run $588 to $721 double, including all meals. But for real tranquillity, you need to get in on the class-act villa action offered by **Kizingoni Beach** (p. 289), or experience true barefoot beachcombing at **Kizingo** (reviewed below).

Kizingo ★★ This is an eco-adventurer's getaway, with few signs of modernity and an escape-from-it-all vibe that's emphasized by its empty stretch of beach and abundance of crabs scuttling over the sand. Prepare to lose all track of time and all sense of direction. If you can handle staying in a simple, eco-conscious beach *banda* with eco-flush toilet, solar-heated water, a natural breeze for ventilation, and minimal electricity, then you'll be thrilled here, waking up in your king-size bed to the sight of dhows sailing by. It's a tough call, deciding whether to venture out at all, when you can simply lounge about on your large veranda, swinging on your hammock. The area is still wild and untamed—some dislike the unkempt, totally natural look, and a few are freaked out by the crabs, the rough sea, and the back-to-basics ethos—so if you're squeamish, go elsewhere. Set among the dunes not far from the sea, all the palm-thatched *bandas* have ocean views but little else. Take a sunset sailing trip on a dhow; try kayaking, deep-sea fishing, windsurfing, and snorkeling; or explore little-visited islands such as Pate. However, the big thrill here is the chance to swim with dolphins (Nov–Apr), which are more or less habituated to human interaction. Lodge owners Louis and Mary Jo van Aardt are real eco-warriors (the lodge is built on land rented from Kipungani village, the power is solar, and shower water is recycled to grow plants and stabilize the dunes) and have done much to invest in the local community. Besides providing work for villagers, buying fish and vegetables from local farmers, and supporting two island schools and other community projects, they'll take you on a cycling excursion to visit the local village.

Southern tip of Lamu Island, 15 (9¼ miles) S of Shela, P.O. Box 138, 80500 Lamu. ✆ **073/395-4770,** 071/257-5261, or 072/290-1544. www.kizingo.com. 8 units, all with shower only. $390 double. Children under 12 $70 with 2 adults; children 12–18 $90. Rates include all meals and airport transfers by boat. MC, V. Closed May–Jun. **Amenities:** Restaurant; bar; airport transfers (by boat). *In room:* No phone.

Kiwayu

The island of Kiwayu lies within the Kiunga Marine National Reserve, established in part to protect the dugong—the seal-like creature once thought to be the mermaid of ancient legend—and brimming with amazing coral and brilliant tropical fish. It's a thoroughly peaceful and remote corner of Kenya and looks and feels undiscovered, although there are regular flights to its makeshift airstrip just behind the stylish **Kiwayu Safari Village** (reviewed below), which is actually on the mainland, facing the northern end of Kiwayu from across the channel. On the island are two small villages, and for the rest it's rugged bush, an endless untamed beach, wonderful surf, and the eco-friendly **Munira Island Camp** (reviewed below), spread across the top of the dunes and providing a genuine barefoot castaway experience. Superbly isolated, it can take up to 3 days by dhow to get from Lamu to Kiwayu (although it's a 15-min. flight). Once you're here, there are awesome waves for bodysurfing, and then you can explore some wonderful coves and bays along the mainland shore, either heading out on foot or hopping aboard one of the boats (there are motorized and wind-powered cruisers). Reef fishing (Nov to mid-Apr), deep-sea fishing (mid-Oct to mid-Apr), and creek fishing are all possible; you can take a boat to Lamu (or fly there for around $900 round-trip), water-ski or windsurf, explore the mangroves in a motorized canoe, enjoy sundowners on a working dhow, or head up the coast for a private picnic or to discover uninhabited islands.

Kiwayu Safari Village ★★★ This is one of the world's most enchanting beachfront hideouts, overflowing with suggestions that you kick off your shoes and forget the world you left back home. Tucked into the foot of sheltering dunes, this beach kingdom looks onto the sheltered lagoon and the northern end of Kiwayu island. The gorgeous beach bungalows are built entirely of natural materials (there's virtually no concrete here); they're chic, huge, doorless sanctuaries with fine views out onto the beach (in fact, you're always on the beach here). A family-run lodge, Kiwayu Safari Village was started in 1973 by Alfredo Pelizzoli, a pioneer in the safari business. The idea was to create a place for friends and family to cool off in the ocean after long, hot game-viewing safaris; his vision has grown and evolved over 3½ decades. It's now arrived in its most handsome, fresh-hued, and vibrant incarnation—pretty *kanga* brilliantly sets off the natural tones of palm matting and off-white coral—but the fabulous setting remains as gorgeous and memorable as ever, with the turquoise-blue ocean, dunes and coastal bush, clusters of date palms, a handful of villagers passing through, and vervet monkeys scrumming for the high tea buffet (who can blame them?).

Around 48km (30 miles) N of Lamu. ✆ **073/559-8858.** Reservations: P.O. Box 55343, City Square, 00200 Nairobi. ✆ **020/60-0107,** -0891, or -6906. Fax 020/60-6990. www.kiwayu.com. 18 units. Dec 20–Jan 6 $1,250 double; Oct–Dec 19 and Jan 7–Feb $1,050 double; Jul 23–Sept $850 double; Mar–Apr $700 double. Children 5–16 pay 75% with 2 adults; under 5 free. Rates include all meals (including private lunches), most activities, airstrip transfers, laundry, and taxes. AE (incurs 8% surcharge), MC, V. **Amenities:** Restaurant; bar; free airstrip transfers; free Wi-Fi (in office). *In room:* No phone, cooler box.

Munira Island Camp ★★ **Moments** Mike Kennedy is an impassioned innovator, having created the ultimate Crusoe-style bungalows spread over a high ridge on one part of Kiwayu's 14km (8¾-mile) spine. Since the island is only ever ½km (⅓ miles) wide, you get great views front and back, with the azure blue calm of the channel and the dense bush of the mainland on one side, and the mild crash of waves on the ocean side. With a wild, untamed beach (where turtles nest and local fishermen roam) to explore and play on all day (unusually for this coastline), waves that can be tackled with a boogie board, a sumptuous starscape at night, villagers for neighbors, and a totally relaxed vibe, this is a marvelous place to escape, complete with eco-warrior instincts (not one tree was felled to create this place). The supersize *bandas* are rustic, back-to-basics creations, swathed head to toe in woven palm matting with dozens of open "windows" that can (and should) be rolled up to let in the views. You're asked to tether your doors only so that the donkeys that roam the island don't come inside and steal your water. The entire lodge is powered using wind and solar energy (your shower water is heated directly by the sun), and fresh water is carried in by donkey (and your bucket shower isn't the only bathroom appliance that must be filled manually). Besides offering his company at the bar, Mike (who's a bit of a Kenyan cowboy, known for letting his hair down and letting guests let theirs down, too) can key you in on some of the region's undiscovered snorkeling locations—he knows loads of secret spots between here and the Somali border and can take you to some fabulous islands—and will also interpret the blanket of stars for you. And for the rest, well, it's all about lazing in hammocks, reclining on daybeds, and finding yourself free to do absolutely nothing at all.

Kiwayu Island. Reservations: P.O. Box 40088, G.P.O., Nairobi 00100. ✆ **071/800-49200.** www.mikescampkiwayu.com. 7 units. $500 double. Rates include all meals, nonmotorized watersports, and laundry. AE, MC, V. **Amenities:** Restaurant; 24-hr. bar; airport transfers (Kiwayu airstrip $50; Lamu airport $400). *In room:* No phone.

WHERE TO DINE

For the ultimate indulgence, you can catch a speedboat—or even fly by charter plane—to **Kiwayu Safari Village** ★★★ (p. 295) for lunch. The food is exceptional—the best I've had in the archipelago—and the view and the setting idyllic. Expect plenty (and I mean plenty) of fresh fish with great accompaniments—crab mayonnaise to start, crunchy salads, and a wonderful cheeseboard, topped off with a sensational citrusy dessert. Arrive early to spend some time on the beach, or arrange to go snorkeling in the Kiunga Marine Reserve, then make yourself comfortable at the bar and put back a few cocktails before sitting down to a well-dressed table decked out with freshly baked bread, soft butter, olive oil, balsamic vinegar, and fine finger salt. It's one of Lamu's most magical dining experiences and one that's likely to make you wish you were spending the night here. Lunch will cost around $40 per head, and advance reservations (at least a day before) are essential.

Lamu Town

Hidden deep in Lamu's back lanes, with its own little bookstore, **Bustani Café** (✆ **072/285-9594;** www.lamucafe.com; daily 8am–7pm or later) is a peaceful, relaxing garden courtyard worth visiting for delicious Lamu shakes, made with fruit, milk, and mangrove honey. They also serve decent coffee, smoothies, and *madafu* (fresh, tender coconut), and they bake their own cakes. There's an excellent mango salad, or try the island seafood soup or pasta with creamy prawns. With some advance notice, you can arrange for a full-on Swahili lunch or dinner.

Moonrise ★★★ SWAHILI/MEDITERRANEAN This is not only the best place to dine in Lamu town, but the only decent place to have a drink (including cocktails and a selection of mainly South African and Chilean wines). Set on a raised terrace (thoughtfully designed so that local Muslims won't have to witness alcohol consumption when they walk by), the restaurant gets a wonderful cooling breeze. Tables are wrapped in white linen, with pretty *kikoi*-covered cushions, and the staff are delightful. Order the crab bisque to start—it's spectacular—and then follow with fish, steamed in a banana leaf, seared with soya and lime glaze, or pan-fried with tamarind (all are exceptionally tender and delicious). If available, order the tuna steak, very lightly pan-seared to perfection.

Lamu House, Lamu seafront, Lamu. ✆ **042/463-3491.** Main courses Ksh500–Ksh2,500. MC, V. Daily dawn until last guest leaves.

Whispers Café ★ LIGHT FARE/DELI You can sit here for hours, enjoying the laid-back ambience and listening to fresh African tunes in the garden courtyard or indoors under gently turning fans, your senses tantalized by the aroma of fresh-baked breads and all kinds of delicious-looking treats. Whispers has the best tea, coffee, and juice selection in Lamu. Although it's not a restaurant in the full sense of the word, and tends to focus on comfort dishes such as pastas, pizzas, burgers, and healthy sandwiches, they also serve more substantial fare such as grilled Lamu Bay prawns and *moussaka,* and even do a seafood platter—or catch of the day prepared any way you want. They also try out various African recipes, such as Ghanaian chicken palava, to keep things interesting. Their breakfasts are highly recommended (they do proper muesli with fresh yogurt and natural honey), and they also make delicious homemade ice cream (in wonderful flavors, including ginger nut, coconut, and lime cream).

Harambee Ave., Lamu. ✆ **042/463-2024** or 071/732-0299. Main courses Ksh300–Ksh950; snack menu Ksh160–Ksh500. No credit cards. Daily 8am–6pm.

Shela

Peponi's ★★★ INTERNATIONAL/SWAHILI With its X-factor location and constant sloshing of water down below, this stalwart of the Lamu social scene offers excellent variety. Start with some *samosas* followed by excellent seafood ranging from tasty mangrove crabs steamed with ginger and garlic and warm calamari salad, to piripiri prawns and a seafood risotto. You can also sample some of the more exotic tastes from the delicious Swahili selection, including *mchuzi wa kamba,* prawns done in local spices with either tamarind or *siki* (coconut vinegar). In the evenings, there's a special chef's menu.

Peponi Hotel, Shela. ✆ **042/463-3421** through -3423, -3154, 072/220-3082, or 073/420-3082. www.peponi-lamu.com. Reservations essential. Main courses Ksh750–Ksh3,950. AE, MC, V. Daily noon–3pm and 7:30–9:30pm.

Manda

The Majlis ★★★ INTERNATIONAL With gorgeous views across the channel toward Lamu island, this is the most spacious and sumptuously designed restaurant in the archipelago, with a chichi upstairs terrace-style bar and an excellent, varied menu featuring fresh seafood, salads, pasta, wood-fired pizzas, and a range of international dishes. Expect an ever-changing menu: Catalan-style lobster with roasted vegetables, spaghetti with seafood, tempura of jumbo prawns with ginger and tamarind sauce, tagliata of tender sirloin steak. A free boat shuttle operates from Shela jetty so you won't need to worry about getting back to your hotel.

The Majlis, Manda Island. ✆ **071/819-5499** or 071/819-5498. www.themajlisresorts.com. Main courses 12€–25€. V. Daily 7:30–10am, 12:30–2:30pm, and 7:30–10:30pm.

SHOPPING

There's a branch of **MagicGrace** ★★★ (✆ **042/463-3228** or 072/673-2804), one of the country's best places to shop for well-made, artfully designed souvenirs and curios, in Lamu town. The all-white boutique/gallery features jewelry, cool cotton dresses and blouses, and brilliantly comfortable Maasai Treads sandals for men (these go for Ksh3,500).

Bear in mind that most stores in Lamu are closed between 12:30 and 4pm.

Aalyshah Designs Value Pick up *kikois,* beachwear, and beaded jewelry from this home-grown shop just behind Peponi Hotel. Shela. ✆ **042/463-3268.** aalyshahdesigns@hotmail.com.

Aman ★★★ A gorgeous clothing and accessories boutique that comes as a total surprise in the in the maze of Shela's narrow lanes. Sadly, they're not always open when they're supposed to be. Shela.

Blue Rhino ★ This shop carries an eclectic mix that includes door frames, bathrobes, and cushion covers. Lamu. ✆ **071/069-1950.**

Gallery Baraka ★★ Lamu's best-known arts and crafts store, with a wide range of handsome items, from handmade slippers to beautiful homeware. Don't forget to remove your shoes upon entering, or you'll be barked at by one of the assistants. Harambee Avenue, Lamu. ✆ **042/463-3399** or 072/261-1282.

Mariam's Shop ★★ Exquisitely comfortable men's sandals (made in Malindi), a great rage of *kikois,* and beautiful ladies' blouses are stocked in this shop at the back of Lamu House. Mariam is a fashionista formerly based in Antwerp. Lamu. ✆ **071/257-5371.**

My Eye ★★★ Daniela Bateleur has created one of East Africa's loveliest galleries, featuring some amazing art created from recycled materials and many intriguing canvases by prolific local artist Ali Lamu, a fisherman "discovered" by Daniela. You're sure to walk away clutching beautiful reminders of your stay here; besides Daniela's own photographs of scenes from around the Lamu archipelago, there are some hardy, handsome bags made from reconditioned dhow sails. This store—not too far from Batil Aman Guest House and opposite Kisimani House—is not to be confused with a copycat gallery occupying the original location of My Eye, and now cheekily calling itself My Blue Eye. Shela. ✆ **072/270-2510.** www.alilamu.com.

Ogres Beads Workshop ★★ Making unique beaded jewelry, this small home-grown operation is a wonderful find not too far from Lamu House. It was established by Kagiri "Ogre" Murathimi and his wife, and now they have a team of seven local designers who produce an original range and will also prepare necklace and earring designs especially for you—as they did for Sienna Miller. Lamu. ✆ **072/226-1917** or 042/63-2061. kmurathimi@yahoo.com.

Slim Silver Smith ★ Step inside his shop, and Mbarak O. Slim will proudly inform you that he's the best silversmith in Lamu and boast on and on about his work—which is a good opportunity for you to chat intimately with this local artisan. Mbarak's specialty is making rings and pendants using what he believes to be bits of Chinese porcelain left in the archipelago by a Chinese ship heavily laden with treasure that passed this way (and may well have sunk) back in 1415. He also does Lamu henna rings—unusual and beautiful silver jewelry pieces—which can be commissioned. Harambee Road, Lamu. ✆ **072/247-8876.** slimsilversmith@yahoo.com.

12

Dar es Salaam & the Tanzanian Coast

by Keith Bain

It's a rare commodity, an endless, unblemished beach. With 1,424km (883 miles) of Indian Ocean shoreline and relatively few urban blips along the way, Tanzania's coastline is a revelation. Beyond Dar es Salaam, the country's economic workhorse, there's precious little development and, apart from a handful of towns and villages, nothing resembling the concrete claustrophobia and human overcrowding that afflicts better-marketed tropical destinations such as Zanzibar and Mombasa.

An exotic jumble of beautiful palm-lined beaches and a steamy industrial port, Dar es Salaam—the "House of Peace"—is a confluence of striking contrasts. Wrapped in Swahili kangas, village women on their way to market bump shoulders with citified ladies tucked into Western office suits; men in traditional Omani-style koffias walk alongside lads in board-shorts and T-shirts bearing images of Barack Obama; and teens in hip-hop get-ups sit next to their sisters modestly tucked away in black bui-bui. You're as likely to hear the call to prayer ringing out from the mosques as you are to see crowds congregating outside steepled churches, and the sleek mirror-glass business blocks stand cheek-by-jowl with crumbling monstrosities. Everywhere there are visual tableaux that leave you scratching your head, trying to remember where in the world you are. In parts this is unquestionably a part of Africa, but there are pockets of Asia, Europe, and the Middle East here, too. For better or worse, the city represents an exotic cosmopolitan blend that is a reflection of a multifangled, albeit compact, history.

If you have absolutely no interest in seeing Dar es Salaam (or, simply, Dar), chances are, you're here just for a night, either preparing for your trip into the bush or about to head home. Or perhaps you've set your sights on Zanzibar's fabled beaches and haven't even considered the mainland coast. But instead of going with the flow, it may be seriously worth considering the path less traveled, with the chance to locate yourself on a paradisiacal stretch where the tour buses just don't go.

Here, along the coast, you could also choose to combine the best of both worlds at Sadaani National Park, where one of the country's loveliest lodges abuts both beach and bush, with a rare chance to witness pachyderms frolicking on the shore, watch hippos and crocs wallowing in the river, and even swim with dolphins and turtles in the warm, blue sea. Or, if you'd like to balance your safari with a look at an enchanting undersea world, you can sign up for some exceptional diving at little-known places such as Mikindani (a time-warped Swahili town in the far, far south) or Ushongo (a remote haven on the epic beach that stretches virtually unimpeded between Dar and Kenya).

Along this coast, too, there are still remnants and ruins signaling an ancient

Staying Active on the Tanzanian Coast—Above & Below the Surface

One of the best reasons to visit the coast of mainland Tanzania is to recharge your batteries after an inland safari, where often you're up before dawn each day and careening around in a Land Rover for most of your waking hours. Many vacationers simply want to be left in peace after such an inherently "stressful" form of sightseeing, and the emptiness of the beaches north and south of Dar can be especially seductive if your fantasies are of seaside cocktail bars shaded by coco palms and lazy days with your toes in the sand. At worst, you might imagine yourself bobbing in the gentle surf or floating on the surface staring down at tropical fish through a pair of goggles. If you're less than thrilled by the idea of lying idle on impossibly white sandy beaches bronzing your body under a vast African sky, you'll be glad to know that there are usually plenty of waterborne activities such as snorkeling, boating, and fishing, offered at the various beach resorts. But for specialized pursuits such as diving and kitesurfing, you need to choose your destination carefully.

Kitesurfing Relatively new to Tanzania, kitesurfing relies on the Swahili Coast's seasonal winds: Between December and April, the Kaskazi brings speeds of between 15 and 30 knots, while the Kuzi blows from June to mid-September at about 15 to 35 knots. Either way, **Dar es Salaam's South Beach** area is ideal and easily accessible, and the relative lack of human clutter makes flying here a tidy prospect. Toby Mayers' **TZ Kite Surfing** (✆ **075/399-9001;** www.tzkitesurfing.com) offers a variety of courses, from taster sessions to level 3 beginner courses, and also rents equipment.

Diving A wonderful place to dive—sans crowds—is at **Ushongo Beach** (p. 329); besides the tranquillity of a little-discovered piece of paradise, Ushongo provides access to Maziwe Island Marine Reserve, which has been spared the destruction caused by dynamite fishing that's too common in Tanzania. Dives are operated by small, personal, and conservation-minded **Kasa Divers** (www.kasadivers.com)—the only professional dive operation between Dar and Kenya—which focuses on the spectacular coral garden in the reefs around the island. The diving here has been compared favorably with that in Zanzibar

history of interaction with the outside world. Many of these reminders, clustered around little-developed Swahili towns such as Pangani and Bagamoyo, point to dark times when slavery and colonial exploitation were legitimate commercial enterprises. While the beach and the ocean are surely where you'll be focusing your attention, you can easily diversify your holiday with a short visit to these time-ravaged former Arab trade centers.

Dar may strike most as little more than a transit point between ill-timed flight connections, but there are some fabulous beaches within easy reach of the city, and whether you're a barefoot beachcomber or sun-worshipping snob, there's a patch of paradise earmarked just for you.

and Mafia, but the advantage here is the near-total absence of human activity, and the area is protected from fishing by a local community project. You're very likely to spot green turtles, and sightings of humpback whales and bottlenose dolphins actually increased in 2009. Owners Wim and Kerstin are experienced PADI instructors and offer a range of courses, from kids' level up to divemaster.

There's also fantastic, virtually undiscovered diving in the far southern town of **Mikindani,** near the Mozambican border. The marine park here, comprising Mnazi Bay and the Rumuva Estuary, protects a unique ecosystem, thanks to the movement of the Southern Equatorial current. Some of the most abundant and extraordinary marine life from across the Indian Ocean is found here, providing perhaps the best diving in East Africa—more than 400 fish species and 258 types of coral have been recorded. Large pelagic fish, turtles, and giant groupers are common. Divers also regularly report seeing octopus, not to mention unusual specimens such as striped frogfish, ghost pipefish, crocodile fish, stonefish, and sea moth, and even varieties of seahorse that aren't easily identifiable. The excellent PADI center here was started in 2004 by Martin Guard, a marine biologist with years of dive experience who was drawn to the healthy and relatively undiscovered reefs. The focus is on low-impact dives, and his **eco2 dive center** (www.eco2tz.com) also functions as a marine research and education facility. The best place to stay in Mkindani is **The Old Boma Hotel** ★ (✆ **075/636-0110;** www.mkindani.com; £70–£110 double), a fine restoration of a century-old fort on a hill overlooking the ocean. The laid-back hospitality comes with a colonial, time-warp atmosphere, and there's a good pool in the garden where you can relax after exploring the marine park. Keen divers on a limited budget will find cheaper digs at **Ten Degrees South Lodge** (www.tendegreessouth.com), with just eight fan-cooled rooms, half of which have attached bathrooms. Mikindani—accessed via daily scheduled flights to nearby Mtwara—is a typical Swahili town, with idiosyncratic architecture, narrow streets overhung by first-floor balconies, and handsomely carved wooden doors. The town turns out to be a great place to imbibe some local culture between dives.

1 DAR ES SALAAM

The youngest city along the Swahili coast, Dar—which doesn't register a blip in pre-19th-century history—has grown into Tanzania's economic powerhouse. Although no longer the capital, Dar remains Tanzania's largest city and its financial hub. Although it's almost impossible to get a grip on the size of the population, estimates stand somewhere between 3 million and 3½ million, and Dar is the third-fastest-growing city in Africa (after Bamako and Lagos) and the ninth-fastest-growing city on the planet, its office blocks going up as quickly as its periphery is expanding outward. Today it is a regional economic fulcrum, with clusters of high-rise buildings, traffic jams, and an ever-burgeoning surfeit of international hotels and fine restaurants, not to mention a huge expatriate population. Despite its cumulatively busy and chaotic atmosphere, Dar never feels too dense or overpopulated—shambolic, perhaps, but not really crowded. This has much to do with the sprawl, and despite having what feels like a relatively compact center, it can take forever to get from one end of Dar to the other—or, indeed, to figure out where the city begins and ends.

Still today, though, the sight of weather-beaten dhows remains as a clue that, some 150 years ago, Dar was still a measly fishing village, hardly an alluring prospect in the global economy. Although the first European, a German named Albert Roscher, arrived here as recently as 1859, it was this foreign presence that would later revive the fledgling port town, which had immediately gone into decline after the death in 1870 of founding ruler Sultan Seyyid Majid, a man evidently hypnotized by Dar's magical setting. Before the Zanzibari sultan's infatuation with the port town, Dar had been little more than a simple fishing village. Even today, behind the veneer of rapid modernization, that fishing culture lives on—check out the fishing market at dawn for a sense of Dar's relationship with the ocean's bounty, or head up or down the coast where village after village is sustained by daily toils of fishermen who set out on their simple mashua dugout canes or small ngalawa catamarans powered by tanga sails. Dar might, in fact, have looked a bit like that today had it not been resuscitated from the ashes to become an economic and administrative center servicing the East German Africa Company. Today you'll see more remnants of European influence—particularly in the photogenic colonial structures in the immediate vicinity of the Kivukoni seafront—than buildings built in the Arab-influenced medina style that typifies Swahili architecture.

If you do want to get into the swing of things, there's little harm in meandering through the center and bumping shoulders with Dar's interesting cosmopolitan hodge podge—thrown into the mix of Swahili coastal people and Africans from diverse tribes who've come to seek their fortunes from the interior of the country are sizeable Asian and a Western expatriate communities. A few Tanzanians of European extraction—many of them German—cling to the land of their birth. People say that, despite the prevalence of crime and the overt corruption, life in Dar is good. Indeed, if you're here for a few hours or in transit for a day, you'll probably feel the same way.

For my money, though, it's the beaches north and south of Dar that make a stop-off here truly worthwhile. Head an hour south of Dar's heady traffic, and you'll be traveling over dirt roads past increasingly remote, ridiculously small villages on your way to some epic coastline. It's like disappearing into a virtually undiscovered paradise where every single person you pass will look up and stare. Here you can experience the simple joy of watching fishermen put out to sea or watching the ocean turn many shades of gold, silver, and blue as the sun rises over the horizon; or examine a glittering starscape as the moonlight turns the sea's mirrorlike surface silver.

GETTING THERE & AWAY

BY AIR Situated 12km (7½ miles) southwest of Dar es Salaam, **Julius Nyerere International Airport** (✆ **022/284-4212,** -4371, -4372, or -4224; www.jnia.aero) is served by flights from Europe, Asia, the Middle East and all across Africa. Upon arrival at Terminal 2 (used for most international and domestic flights), you will first pass through an unsophisticated health screening point where you'll fill in a form relating to the H1N1 virus; if

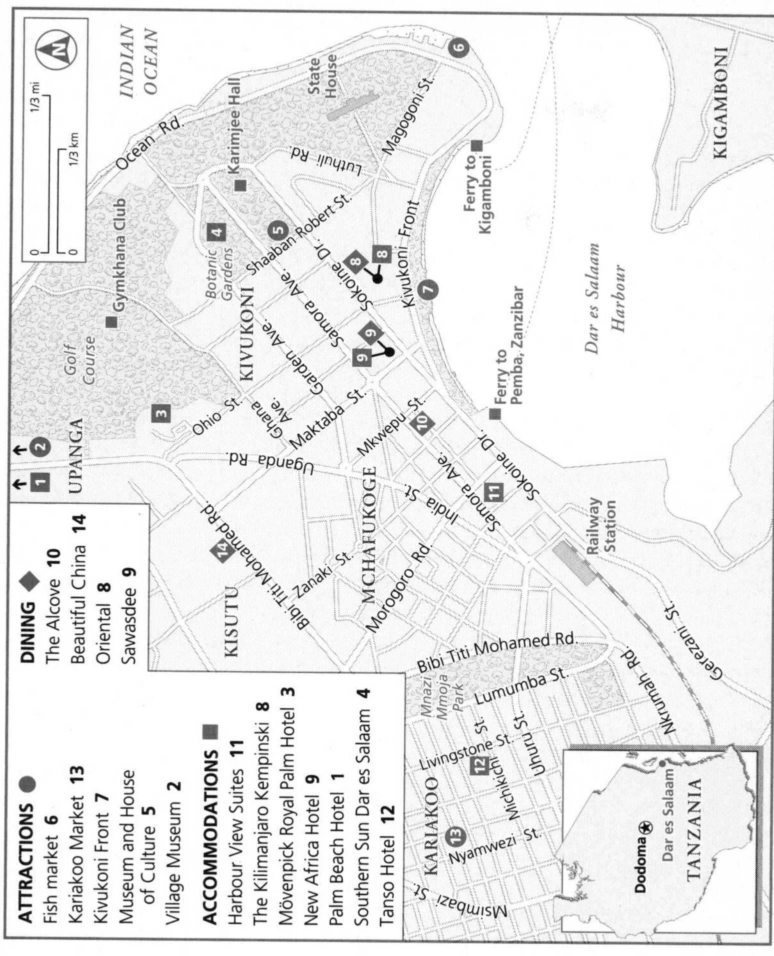

you're arriving from Kenya, you'll be required to produce your yellow fever vaccination certificate (have this ready). If you haven't arranged your entry visa in advance, you must fill in a form and hand this in, together with your passport and $50. Visa processing time is usually quite speedy, but it does help if you can arrive ahead of everyone else on your plane, so don't dally. Once you have your visa, it's a swift march through baggage claim and into the arrivals hall. A taxi into the city from the airport costs Tsh25,000; if you're going to the expensive hotels in town, you'll be charged $25, while a trip to any of the hotels on the Msasani Peninsula is $35. A taxi directly to Bagamoyo will cost $120. If you can't be bothered putting up with the slightly seedy attitude of the drivers who congregate around the airport arrivals doors, a number of transport companies will do the same transfer for more or less the same price—simply arrange this in advance, and a driver will be waiting for you at the arrivals terminal. If you have the good fortune to be staying at the Oyster Bay Hotel, your transfer will be waiting with a nameboard in hand and drinks in the car.

There are several ATMs that accept Visa credit cards on the concourse outside the terminal; remember that one U.S. dollar is the equivalent of around 1,300 Tanzanian shillings (Tsh), so don't be afraid to withdraw 100,000 or even half a million shillings for incidental expenses. Remember that when you pay in foreign currency, you'll inevitably be given a poor rate of exchange, so it's useful to have some local cash in hand. Terminal 1, which serves as the main base for charter flights, is located some .8km (½ mile) from Terminal 2.

Any local tour or travel agency (including any of those recommended in chapter 3) will book onward flights for you within Tanzania or farther afield. There have been reports of travelers having difficulties using online booking services (even for large, reputable airlines) for flights out of Tanzania, so (as always) it's advisable to make your international flight arrangements well ahead of schedule so that you can turn to an agency if you have difficulties online. If you wish to book your internal flights without the aid of an agency or tour operator, **Coastal Aviation** (✆ **022/284-3033** or -3170; www.coastal.cc) is the first choice, with a wide range of scheduled services to prime safari and beach destinations (including Zanzibar and Pemba and Mafia islands) within Tanzania, and also offers **private charters.** Note that some of their flights operate only if there are sufficient passengers to cover costs. Coastal Aviation has offices at J. K. Nyerere International (Terminal 1), at The Slipway, and in the city center. **Indigo Aviation** (www.indigoair.co.tz) is a new airline servicing Dar, Zanzibar, Selous Game Reserve, and Mafia Island. See "Fast Facts," below, for local contact details of both airlines.

BY BOAT There are seven to eight daily ferries between Dar es Salaam and Zanzibar; these depart every hour or two and take anywhere between 90 minutes and 4 hours (in the case of the late-night "overnight" boat). Tickets costs $20 to $40, depending on speed and level of comfort. The Zanzibar ferry launch is on Sokoine Drive, near the Old Boma; do not confuse this with the Kigamboni ferry (Tsh200 per pedestrian), which does the 5-minute hop across the mouth of the Kurusini Creek, linking Dar with its southern beaches.

BY ROAD Any of the travel agents or ground operators mentioned below can arrange chauffeured overland transport to Dar from just about any other part of Tanzania; some may even be able to make arrangements for you to travel from Kenya, although this is seldom recommended. Road transfers from Dar to any of the coastal destinations recommended in this chapter can also be arranged directly when booking your accommodation.

CITY LAYOUT

As with many coastal cities, Dar isn't planned so much as fanned out around its port. Most points of interest in the city—a beak-shaped spit of land that hooks around to form a natural harbor—are within easy striking distance of the **Kivukoni Front,** a waterfront boulevard that culminates in the **ferry launch** for boats to **South Beach** and the nearby **fish market,** both key sites in a town that owes its existence to its people's relationship with the sea. Kivukoni itself is where many of Dar's colonial-era buildings—now mostly government and administrative offices—as well as the National Museum and Botanical Gardens, are located. West of here, moving inland, sprawls the **city center,** a bustling

Tips Moving to a Local Rhythm

There's a special language defining the various modes of transport used by the locals and available to you at a fraction of the cost of any taxi or pre-arranged transfer. A *dala-dala* is the ubiquitous minibus taxi (known as a *matatu* in Kenya) that is the principal mode of transport for ordinary people. These potentially hazardous and inevitably claustrophobic vehicles are everywhere. Those servicing the city tend to be well organized and operate without squashing in as many passengers as possible, but once you journey beyond the city limits, all bets are off and you've as much chance of standing as you have of practically sitting on someone's lap (don't, though, as that would be considered impolite). Your incredible proximity to fellow passengers makes this sardinelike environment an excellent place to strike up conversation, but be warned that your life is always in the hands of the driver—and the Divine. In spirit more akin to a private taxi, the *tuk-tuk* is a three-wheel cross between a scooter and a miniature car; if you're been to Asia, you'll be familiar with them, although they're not nearly as popular here in East Africa just yet. You should ask for a helmet when climbing on the back of a *pika-pika,* the cute name for a "motorbike taxi." These are usually stationed at major *dala-dala* drop-off points, ready to take passengers to more specific destinations; they're very useful along the coast, where public transport works only along main roads and the motorbikes do all the side-road transfers. The *pika-pika* drivers will happily adjust their speed according to your comfort level, and most will take two passengers. Finally, if you're in no particular hurry, the *boda-boda* is a bicycle taxi, mostly useful for very short distances (the name derives from the fact that they were originally used to ferry people across borders) or if you're simply too lazy, or lethargic, to walk.

muddle of congestion incorporating all kinds of exotic styles, sights, and smells that may entice more adventurous travelers. Deep into this colorful stew is where you'll find Kariakoo Market—at the heart of the lively, down-home **Kariakoo** neighborhood—where locals go to buy just about anything.

Running in a roughly northwesterly direction from the Kivukoni ferry launch is **Ocean Drive,** a broad boulevard that follows the coastline (and a wide swath of beach) toward the **Msasani Peninsula.** Msasani, heavily concentrated with foreign embassies, expatriates, and white Tanzanians, is Dar's most prestigious finger of real estate. Although it's located just a few kilometers north of the city center, it feels like a destination in its own right, closer in spirit to the beaches of **Dar's north coast** (such as Kawe, Jangwazi, and Kunduchi, which have been developed with a string of resorts) than the downtown business district; Msasani, with its members-only Yacht Club and expansive high-security mansions, represents the other end of Dar's social spectrum, where the best shopping centers are found and where the small, excellent **Oyster Bay Hotel** and some wonderful restaurants serve as social magnets for the privileged classes.

Back in the city, ferries regularly make the 5- to 10-minute crossing from Kivukoni to **Kigamboni** at the southern end of the harbor into which the Kurusini Creek flows. From Kigamboni, the road (the first part of which is sealed) stretches south, leading to vast tracts of virgin beaches—locals refer to this as South Beach, although the luxury retreats of **Ras Kutani** and **Amani Beach** are nearly an hour's car drive away (or a 10-min. hop in a light aircraft).

GETTING AROUND

To get between the city and the beaches north or south of Dar, or to explore the Msasani Peninsula, you'll need to hire a cab or get a car and driver for the day. Dar's **taxis** are white with a thin stripe (usually green) and are ubiquitous; if you don't see one when you need one, you can be pretty sure that a taxi driver will make himself known to you (even when you don't need one). Traffic within the city can be a little hectic, so consider self-driving there only if you've plenty of patience and are accustomed to a chaotic driving culture. With good directions (and a decent map), you should be able to negotiate the coastal roads north and south of the city, but you'll want off-road capability for inevitable stretches of dirt road when you venture off the main highway. A novel way of seeing the city—if you can deal with the traffic fumes—is by ***tuk-tuk,*** the motorized three-wheeler that's ubiquitous in Asia; they're officially banned in the city center, but **Afric'Aventure** (**© 022/270-0606;** www.africaventure.net) offers a tour of the city's main attractions using a specially designated *tuk-tuk.* Although you can wander about the city's central hub with little difficulty (apart from incessant offers of a taxi ride), Dar tends to feel very spread out, and if you're in any way nervous about being here, you'd do well to hire a car and driver for the day or join a tour (see "Travel Agents & Ground Operators," below).

VISITOR INFORMATION

Your concierge or host will give you the lowdown on developments in the local scene. If you want to surf the Internet for interesting tidbits, consider the offerings at **www.my-daressalaam.com**—it's not in the least bit opinionated, but it does list forthcoming events and has Google maps for all the places listed on its pages. There are various advertorial-style publications promoting Dar's businesses and social calendar, but they're far from discriminating; you'd do well to consult a real person (in conjunction with this chapter) rather than picking through the blurb. One look at the website of the **Tanzania Tourism Board** (http://tanzaniatouristboard.com) is enough to convince you that there's no point visiting them in person; nevertheless, their **Information Centre** is on Samora Avenue, on the ground floor of the Matasalamat Building (**© 022/213-1555**)—occasionally, their enthusiasm spills over into something approaching meaningful assistance. A website worth looking at is **Kiu** (www.swahilicourses.com), a Swahili language and culture training organization—their list of do's don'ts on their "Intro to Tanzania" page is as amusing as it is enlightening.

Tips Check Your Dollar Bills

Tanzanian banks accept only U.S. dollars printed in or after the year 2000. If you are carrying any notes printed earlier than 2000, they will not be accepted for payment anywhere. Some vendors like to give you a really dirty look—as if you are a counterfeiter trying to hustle them—so best to check your notes before leaving home. You might also be interested to know that when you exchange dollar bills for Tanzanian shillings, you usually get a better rate for higher denominations; notes with a value of $50 or more attract the best rate.

TRAVEL AGENTS & GROUND OPERATORS

If you've arrived in Dar without having prearranged all your travel plans, you'll find scores of agencies looking for your business. It's worth shopping around, but for a touch of class, Dar-based **Savannah** (✆ **022/213-9277;** www.savannahtz.com) is the high-end tour company I'd recommend; Cliff D'Souza's team can put together just about any kind of itinerary you desire. Besides taking you on extended safaris, Savannah will provide transfers to any destination in the country—the level of luxury you enjoy depends on your budget, but they're fairly adept at arranging ultra-luxurious trips or having vehicles waiting for you in the bush after a charter flight. Based at the Sea Cliff Hotel on the Msasani Peninsula, **TravelMate** (www.travelmate.co.tz) can assist with flight bookings, car rentals, and bespoke safaris. Besides their flight operations, **Coastal Aviation** (see above) runs a full booking service for accommodations, transfers, and overland safaris, and can assist with itineraries and trip planning; be warned that their level of helpfulness isn't always that great when it comes to dealing with walk-in clients, so keep your options open. The other respected agency with offices in Dar is **Kearsley Travel & Tours** (www.kearsleys.com). You'll find them in the business center at the Southern Sun hotel (✆ **022/213-1652,** -1653, or 022/211-1146); while you can probably engage them for transfers and such, I've found some of their staff pretty scatty (not to mention rude), so you may need to check everything before accepting any of their arrangements. **Safari Solutions** (✆ **022/212-0892** or -0893; www.safarisolutionstz.com) is one of several travel operators offering a Dar city tour during which you get to visit what precious few sights there are with a guide; these run from 8:30am to 1pm. The same company also offers full-day tours of Bagamoyo (p. 327), as well as day trips to Zanzibar (bearing in mind that no one should visit Zanzibar for just 1 day).

Fast Facts Dar es Salaam

Airlines Local contacts for the main **international airlines** that service Dar: **Precision Air,** Nyerere/Pugu Road (✆ 022/212-1718); **British Airways,** Mövenpick Royal Palm Hotel, Ohio Street (✆ 022/211-3820 through -3822); **Swiss,** Luther House, Sokoine Drive (✆ 022/211-8870 through -8872); **Kenya Airways** (✆ 022/211-9376); **KLM** (✆ 022/211-3336 or -3337); **Emirates,** Haidry Plaza Complex, Ali Hassan Mwinyi Road (✆ 022/21-6100 through -6102); and **South African Airways** (✆ 022/211-7044 or -7047). Domestic airlines: **Coastal Aviation** (✆ 022/211-7959, -7960, 075-432-4044; or, at Dar es Salaam Airport, ✆ 022/284-2700, -2701, -71-332-5673); **Indigo Aviation,** 6 Chole Road, Masaki (✆ 022/260-0780 or 078-477-7779; www.indigoair.co.tz); **ZanAir** (✆ 022/212-4553 or, in Zanzibar, ✆ 024/223-3670).

Area Code The dialing code for Dar es Salaam is ✆ **022.** The international dialing code for Tanzania is ✆ **255.**

ATMs There are plenty of bank machines where you can withdraw cash using your credit card. Make sure you are carrying a Visa or MasterCard (with Visa the most widely accepted), as American Express and Diners Club are mostly meaningless here. Bank machines are usually located in or near most upmarket hotels and shopping centers, as well as at the airport, so you can draw cash the moment you have cleared immigration.

Banks Banking hours are Monday to Friday 8:30am to 3pm and Saturday 9:30am to noon, while some banks (such as **Barclays Bank** at The Slipway shopping center on the Msasani Peninsula) stay open until 6pm on weekdays and 3pm on Saturday. You'll have little trouble finding a bank in the city center. There's a convenient branch of **Standard Chartered Bank** adjacent the Southern Sun hotel on Garden Avenue.

Bookstores **A Novel Idea** is a small chain of book shops carrying a decent range of English titles, including books on Tanzania and African-interest literature and coffee table glossies. There are branches at The Slipway and at the Sea Cliff Shopping Centre on the Msasani Peninsula, and there's a branch on Ohio Street in the city center, next to the Steers fast food joint.

Car Hires **Just Rent A Car,** Oyster Bay Shopping Centre, Ghuba Street, Oyster Bay (✆ **022/260-1683,** 0784/88-3366, or 0715/88-3366; jrc_tz@yahoo.com), rents a range of vehicles from their small office in the shopping center just behind the Oyster Bay Hotel. **Xcar Rent a Car,** Old Bagamoyo Road, adjacent Shoppers Plaza, Mikocheni (✆ **022/277-1126;** www.xcarrentals.com), rents vehicles from as little as $45 per day; **Lucky Rent-A-Car,** Skymark Shopping Mall, Morogoro Road (✆ **022/213-5843**), is theoretically even cheaper. **Travelmate** (see "Travel Agents & Ground Operators," above) also arranges car hire.

Courier Services The best solution for getting goods sent home is to contact **TNT International Express** (✆ **022/212-4581**) or **DHL** (✆ **022/286-1000**).

Currency Exchange You can exchange your foreign notes at the airport; rates are clearly posted. If for some reason you're exchanging large amounts, you'll probably want to do this inside a bank, such as at the **Barclay Bank** at The Slipway or **NBC (National Bank of Commerce)** at the Sea Cliff Shopping Centre.

Doctors & Dentists Use the recommendations of your host or concierge (it'll usually be a healthcare professional who is well known within the expatriate community); in serious cases, a doctor can usually be summoned directly to your hotel. There's an upmarket dental office in the Mövenpick Royal Palm Hotel.

Drugstores As always, it's best to ask your host or concierge for the nearest reliable drugstore (pharmacy). On the Msasani Peninsula, you can use **Oysterbay Pharmacy** (✆ **022/260-0525** or 078/426-6654); **Premier Care** (✆ **022/266-8385** or 0784/CLINIC [254642]) is another decent option.

Embassies & Consulates U.S. Embassy, Old Bagamoyo Road, Msasani (✆ **022/266-8001**); British High Commission, Umoja House, Garden Avenue (✆ **022/211-0101**); Canadian High Commission, 38 Mirambo St. (✆ **022/216-3300**); Irish Embassy, 353 Toure Dr. (✆ **022/260-2355**). Note that Australians will find assistance at the Canadian High Commission.

Emergencies For all emergencies, you can call ✆ **112** or ✆ **999.** If you have problems getting through to these public service numbers, you can try for privately managed help: In the event of any kind of emergency (including fire, ambulance services, breakdown recovery, and even air evacuation), contact **Knight Support** (✆ **078/455-5911** or 075/477-7100).

Hospitals Oysterbay Hospital (454 Haile Selassie Rd.; ✆ **022/260-0015**); Aga Khan Medical Services (✆ **022/211-4096** or 022/211-5151 through -5153).

Internet Access Internet is available at most hotels.

Mobile Phones For a nominal amount, you can buy a SIM card, which gives you a local phone number, from any of the Tanzanian mobile network companies such as Zain and Vodacom. Scratch cards are used for air time top-up and are widely available.

Police Tanzanian police (especially traffic police) are notorious for their capacity to solicit bribes. As a general rule, and to avoid any cultural misunderstandings that might entangle you in an ugly and prolonged situation, use one of the emergency numbers given above. If you need to report an incident to the police, do so through someone at your hotel; alternatively, call ✆ **112.** Try to avoid getting into any sort of discussion, debate, or argument with anyone in uniform.

Post Office Dar's main post office is on Azikiwe Street, but avoid the trip there by asking your concierge to post any articles for you.

Restrooms Stick to restrooms in hotels, restaurants, and shopping centers. If you're out on the town, be wary of toilets in dingier clubs and bars.

Safety There are plenty of reports of after-dark muggings, not to mention daytime snatch-and-grab situations that happen on the beach or just about anywhere. The rule is to be alert, use plenty of common sense, and have your wits about you. You can also avoid being robbed by leaving your valuables at your hotel—in the safe.

Taxis See "Getting Around," above.

Weather Dar es Salaam enjoys an equatorial climate with high humidity. The rainy seasons (Mar–May and Nov–Dec) can bring dramatic torrential downpours, but these are typically short and are followed by brilliant sunshine.

WHERE TO STAY

Your choice of where to stay will depend on a combination of budget, priorities, and the amount of time you need (or want) to spend here. If you're here to unwind at the end of your safari, make for the beaches to the south of the city—or choose **The Retreat,** a sumptuous beachside hideaway just north of Dar (reviewed below). But if you want to experience the pulse of city life and are here for only a night, stick to the hotels in the center or on the Msasani Peninsula.

The Msasani Peninsula & Dar's Northern Beaches

The advantages here are pretty self-explanatory—most of the hotels either have views of the ocean or are easily accessible. The excellent value **Alexander's Hotel** (reviewed below) is tucked away in the midst of a residential neighborhood without the benefit of ocean frontage, but it more than makes up for this in other ways. Another option here, due to open at press time, is the new **Double Tree by Hilton Dar es Salaam** (http://doubletree1.hilton.com), which occupies an aesthetically worrisome building overlooking the sea, just down the road from The Slipway shopping center. Targeting business travelers, it'll offer all the usual amenities and comforts, not to mention the anonymity of a large, faceless hotel.

Very Expensive

The Oyster Bay ★★★ If money's no option, this is Dar's most spoiling choice. Set in a former colonial-era hospital next to pretty little Coco Beach, it's stylish, intimate, and exclusive, with plenty of pampering laid on hassle-free. Maretha, the gregarious manager, is passionate about Dar and will share local knowledge on bars, clubs, local dives, and once-a-month discos—it's probably the only place in Dar where you're encouraged to enjoy your time discovering the city. On the other hand, you could happily sequester yourself right here amid the relentlessly eye-catching decor. Plush with assorted textures and natural fibers—distressed wood, weathered cowhide, antique bones, twisted seed pods, colored glass, shells, feathers, and all kinds of beautiful African artifacts (sourced entirely from a South African interior design store)—it's Africa at its most contemporary, chichi, and upbeat, and looking wonderfully natural and organic. Go horizontal at the pool, or join the locals who jog along the beach, accompanied, if you wish, by your very own Maasai *askari.* And at the end of the day, you'll retire to a spectacular suite-size room—choose no. 8 if you don't mind a few stairs and want the best view and an enormous bathroom—with more designer good looks. Yes, it's outrageously overpriced—but if you can, do.

Toure Dr., Oyster Bay, Msasani Peninsula, P.O. Box 2261, Dar es Salaam. ✆ **022/260-0530.** www.theoysterbayhotel.com. 8 units, all with tub and shower. $800 double. Rate includes all meals, drinks, airport/harbor transfers, taxes, and service charge. AE, MC, V. **Amenities:** Bar service; free airport transfers; free Internet (in lounge); pool; room service. *In room:* A/C, TV, hair dryer.

Expensive

Sea Cliff Hotel ★★ After a devastating fire, this spectacularly situated hotel—set on a low-rise cliff at the northern end of the Msasani Peninsula—reopened after a 1½-year revamp that transformed it into one of Dar's finest-looking establishments. It's a brighter, more contemporary-looking place now, with smart Afro-chic accents against a pearl-hued backdrop that works quite well this close to the sea; it also offers pretty much all the on-site services (including two very good restaurants) you could want, despite the absence of a sandy beach. The slick, sumptuous bedrooms have pale-wood floors, earthy hued fabrics, leather armchairs, plasma TVs, and just enough token African art to set the right sort of mood. Rooms on the third floor give the best view of the palm trees and the sea. A big drawback might be the shambolic reception, where it seems that a bunch of clowns have assembled around the switchboard and the check-in computers; you'll need to reconfirm anything that goes through these people—and then confirm with someone else, too. Reception is so bad, in fact, that I'd opt for a room on the executive floor, where you have the benefit of private, hassle-free check-in (these open-plan rooms are more enticing, anyway—you can even watch the ocean from your glass-wall shower).

Tip: Budget-minded travelers might want to look into one of the viewless rooms at the Sea Cliff Village adjacent the hotel, where a standard room goes for $200 double and a superior unit is $220, including breakfast and taxes.

Toure Dr., Msasani Peninsula, P.O. Box 3030, Dar es Salaam. ✆ **022/260-0380** through -3887. Fax 022/260-0476 or -0419. www.hotelseacliff.com. 93 units. $330 deluxe double; $380 superior deluxe double; $430 executive double; $480 junior suite; $830 presidential suite. Rates include breakfast. MC, V. **Amenities:** 2 restaurants, including **Alcove** (reviewed on p. 319); 2 bars; airport transfers ($20 per person one-way); heath club; pool; room service; casino. *In room:* A/C, TV, hair dryer, minibar, free Wi-Fi.

Moderate

Alexander's Hotel ★★ Value On a dirt road in a residential neighborhood near the Yacht Club, this is a wonderful find in the heart of the Msasani Peninsula—stylish,

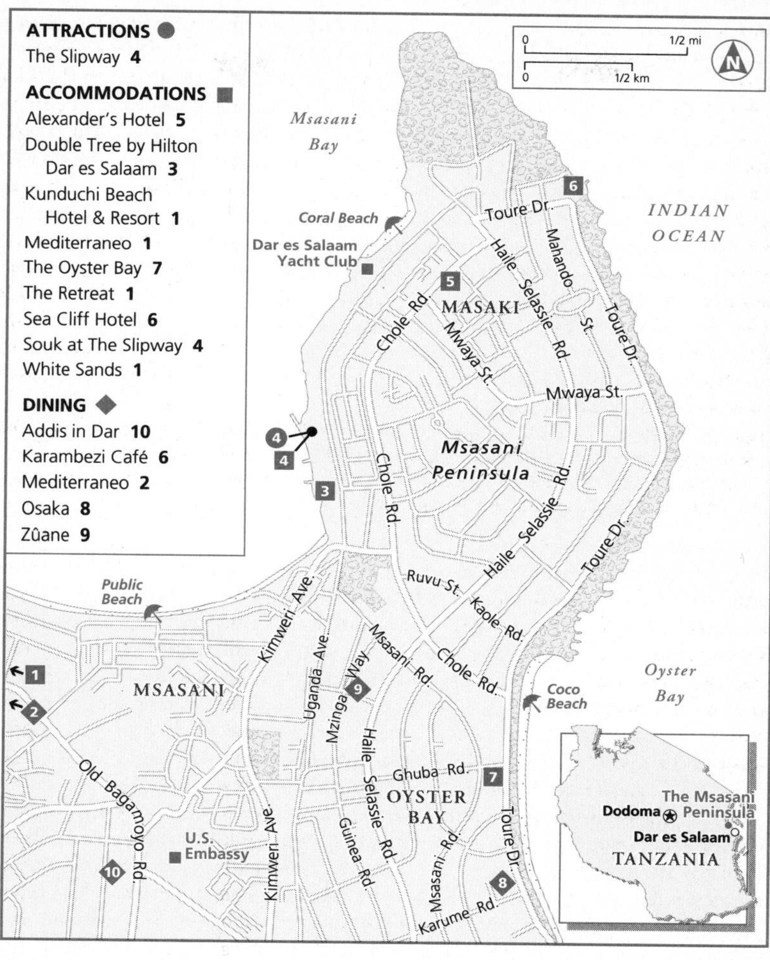

intimate, and extremely good value. With all the flair and hands-on attention you might expect from a boutique hotel (owner Gordon Alexander lives here, too), this place is warm and inviting, and there's been great care taken to create a variety of vital-looking spaces with genuine character. Accommodations are spacious and comfortably laid out, with few frills but very plush beds and smart bathrooms. The bedrooms are in two wings with arched and colonnaded open passages on either side of a pretty courtyard pool area. All this is overlooked by a stunningly designed open-sided multilevel lounge, bar, and restaurant area with twirling concrete stairways; sumptuous relaxation alcoves piled with cushions; and an underground wine cellar capped by a thick slab of glass. All in all, it feels like one of the best deals in town, where you'll be comfortable and feel pampered, and can easily transition between romantic, party, and business frames of mind.

Off Chole Rd., near the Yacht Club, Plot 1216, P.O. Box 110331, Msasani Peninsula, Dar es Salaam. © **0754/58-0225** or 0754/34-3834. www.alexanders-tz.com. 14 units. $190 double. Rate includes breakfast. MC, V. **Amenities:** Restaurant; bar; airport transfers ($30 per vehicle); pool. *In room:* A/C, no phone, TV, minibar, free Wi-Fi.

Kunduchi Beach Hotel & Resort Kids Designed to resemble a sultan's palace, this is a reasonably luxurious (but big) beach resort built to mimic the so-called "Afro-Arabic" style. The primary draw here is the fabulous beach onto which the resort edges, although if you're looking to take it easy or hoping for a romantic time alongside the Indian Ocean, I can't imagine why you wouldn't opt for The Retreat (reviewed below), which is vastly superior. Still, if you're traveling with family, the children will probably appreciate being close to the Wet 'n' Wild waterpark (owned by the hotel), especially if they've been stuck in the back of a safari vehicle for a few days.

Off Bagamoyo Rd., Kunduchi Mtongani, 24km (15 miles) north of Dar city center, P.O. Box 361, Dar es Salaam. © **022/265-0050,** 022/265-0542, or 074-506-2262. Fax 022/265-0332 or 022/212-5323. www.kunduchiresort.com. 196 units, including 48 serviced apartments. $170 superior double; $255 Jacuzzi suite double; $290 executive suite double; $325 honeymoon suite. Rates include breakfast and taxes. MC, V. **Amenities:** 2 restaurants; 3 bars; airport transfers ($25 per person one-way); babysitting; concierge; health club; pool; room service; squash courts; tennis courts. *In room:* A/C, TV, minibar.

Mediterraneo ★★ Value One of Dar's best-kept secrets, this lovely family-run hotel offers a sense of easy-going style, hassle-free beach access, and superb value. Follow a dirt detour off the main road, and you arrive at a tree-shaded clearing at the edge of the ocean. A variety of buildings are spread around the lawns and garden, centered on a deep-blue pool and a fabulous lounge/bar/restaurant overlooking the beach. Accommodations are spacious and attractive and designed with individual flair. Blue Mediterranean floor tiles set off yellow walls, and large wrought-iron beds are draped with mosquito nets; each room has a little patio with a built-in day bed. Although you'll probably find little need to do more than laze around the pool or relax in the lounge, staff can also organize trips to the Bongoyo and Mbudyo islands if you feel like stretching your legs, or you can step directly onto the beach and wade into the sea.

Tip: Note that the **once-a-month party** held here is among the biggest events on Dar's social calendar, and you are warned not to stay here on that night if you intend to sleep (if you're up for a boogie with Dar's hottest socialites, however, you'll be perfectly located to collapse into bed after a night of decadence). It's usually held on the third Saturday of the month.

Off Kawe Beach Rd., 10km (6¼ miles) N of Dar city center, P.O. Box 36110, Dar es Salaam. © **022/261-8359** or 075/481-2567. www.mediterraneotanzania.com. 19 units (15 with tubs). $125 sea-facing double; $115 garden-facing double; $30–$50 extra bed. Children under 5 free. Rates include breakfast. MC, V (credit card payment incurs 5% surcharge). **Amenities:** Restaurant; bar; airport transfers ($25 one-way); fitness room; pool; room service; tennis court; free Wi-Fi (around the lounge). *In room:* A/C, TV.

The Retreat ★★★ Value This tranquil, intimate, and luxurious boutique hotel is a godsend—a refreshing change from the larger resorts and infinitely superior to the city's comparatively bland hotels. The designers, like those at Oyster Bay, have made great efforts to imbue the place with a real sense of being in Africa, and it's also a great pleasure to have a beautiful, swimmable beach right at your front door. Rooms feature antique Zanzibar furniture and four-poster beds, while the entire house—a bit like a homey colonial villa—is decorated with African artworks and individually sourced crafts. You can choose to do absolutely nothing or make full use of your proximity to the ocean; sail off on a catamaran, dive the local islands, or charge around behind a speedboat on water skis. And to cap things off, they can feed you very well, too, with lots of organic produce and freshly caught seafood aplenty.

Mbezi Beach, off Kawe Beach Rd., P.O. Box 13757, Dar es Salaam. ✆ **078/701-3666** or 022/261-7964. www.retreat-africa.com. 6 units, half with tubs. $160 double; $200 deluxe double; $120 day room double. Rates include breakfast and taxes. No credit cards. **Amenities:** Restaurant; bar; airport transfers ($60 per vehicle); babysitting; pool; room service. *In room:* No phone, A/C, Internet (w/portable external modem; $10 per hr.), minibar.

White Sands (Kids) If you're looking for a bed by the beach, coupled with wide-ranging amenities, then this is a decent-enough option, albeit of the heavily manicured, slightly bland sort. Stretched along the beachfront, this place is vast enough to require golf carts for the journey from reception to your room. Four small en suite units are compressed into each of the thatch-roofed villas (two upstairs and one down). Considering how large the resort is and how spacious the lobby feels, it's odd that the accommodations should be so small (with *very* tiny showers)—decor is unimaginative, if inoffensively neutral, with clay-tile floors and a palm tree motif that only hint at decoration. Still, all the standard rooms have lovely views of the palm-studded beach and, in the distance across the impossibly blue water, a handful of offshore islands.

Africana Rd., Jangwazi Beach, 25km (16 miles) north of Dar, P.O. Box 3030, Dar es Salaam. ✆ **022/264-7620** through -7626. Fax 022/264-7875 or -7876. www.hotelwhitesands.com. 146 units, all with shower only; includes 28 apartments. $175 superior double; $160–$290 apartment; $190–$320 seaview apartment. Superior room rates include breakfast. MC, V (credit card payments incur 5% surcharge). **Amenities:** 2 restaurant; 2 bars; airport transfers ($30 per person one-way); babysitting; health club and spa; pool; room service. *In room:* A/C, Internet (cable; $10 per day), minibar.

Inexpensive

Souk at The Slipway (Value) Moorish arches and palm trees vie with Victorian street lamps to create a convoluted kasbah-by-the-sea atmosphere at this small hotel–cum–shopping center. As a bit of a tourist enclave, complete with an interesting waterfront location (you can occasionally watch fishermen toiling over their vessels in the old boatyard) and its own boat jetty, the Souk offers clean, comfortable (if small) rooms and access to myriad shops, several restaurants, and enough services to ensure that you never really need to leave the premises. There's even an outdoor play area for children and a cinema screening Hollywood fare. The whole place is designed like an indoor-outdoor bazaar. Accommodations weren't designed as hotel rooms, but they serve their purpose and are adequate for a night's rest (or, for $80, can be used as a day room), and there's just about enough space in the bathroom for one person to squeeze in. Service is variable, ranging from pleasant to downright hostile.

Msasani Slipway, P.O. Box 250, Msasani Peninsula, Dar es Salaam. ✆ **022/260-0893.** Fax 022/260-0908. 9 units, none with tub. $100 double. MC, V. **Amenities:** 2 restaurants (several others on-site); several bars; airport transfers ($15–$30 per person); free Wi-Fi (in 1 restaurant; but very slow). *In room:* A/C, TV, fridge.

In & Around the City Center

Very Expensive

The Kilimanjaro Kempinski ★★ Far and away Dar's smartest and most luxurious hotel (and correspondingly pricey), this is *the* ultimate hangout for anyone traveling on an expense account or with money to burn. It also offers some of the very finest facilities on mainland Tanzania and comes across as a decadent celebration of Dar's material aspirations. Difficult to imagine that this was once a sad, decaying wreck of a government-run hotel: Behind the slick tinted-glass facade (a touch severe, in the Soviet style), accommodations are sleek and up-with-the-times, with hardwood floors, dark furniture, and lots of straight lines. Big picture windows frame different aspects of the city—views obviously get better the higher up you go. Definitely ask for a harbor-facing room, but if you don't get one, be sure to pull up a sunbed at the edge of the upstairs infinity pool and, later, toast the sunset at the Level 8 bar. An executive-level floor offers perks such as free Internet and all-day beverages.

Kivukoni St., P.O. Box 9574, Dar es Salaam. ✆ **022/213-1111.** Fax 022/212-0777. www.kempinski-daressalaam.com. 180 units. 479€ deluxe double; 579€ executive double; 857€–8,571€ suite. Rates include breakfast, taxes, and service charge. AE, DC, MC, V. **Amenities:** 2 restaurants, including **Oriental** (see "Where to Dine," below); 2 bars; airport transfers (30€ one-way); babysitting; health club and spa; pool; room service; casino. *In room:* A/C, TV, DVD (in suites), hair dryer, Wi-Fi ($8 per day).

Expensive

Mövenpick Royal Palm Hotel ★ The Royal Palm was apparently Dar's best hotel until the Kempinski stepped in and yanked the crown from them. The most recent overhaul (2007) has introduced some modern gadget updates to all the rooms, but with the hotel's ongoing buzz, you'll have better things to do here than play with the interactive home cinema (like checking out the action by the sociable, palm-shaded pool). Still, the rooms are slick, smart, and comfortable, done out in dark browns with carpets, sparse bathrooms, and a couple of framed prints of the eponymous palm trees above the bed. From some of the rooms on the seventh floor, you get a bit of an ocean view in the distance beyond the adjacent golf course. All in all, despite the Swiss endeavor to mold this into a tightly run business hotel, the Royal Palm fastidiously clings to a wholeheartedly African sensibility. Behind the hulking, horrid facade, shiny-suited business types yell across the lobby while having their shoes shined, while the sprawling indoor-outdoor lunch spread draws scores of finger-clicking dealmakers to feast on the city's best-loved buffet spread. It feels, in fact, like a business *resort,* where the deal-signing lunch and pool cocktail party meld into one continuous all-day soap opera, and the executive floor comes with a butler and free Internet access.

Tip: When booking online, you're likely to score a deal roughly $100 cheaper than the rack rates given below.

Ohio St., P.O. Box 791, Dar es Salaam. ✆ **022/211-2416.** Fax 022/211-3981. www.moevenpick-daressalaam.com. 230 units. $355 standard city-view double; $375 standard garden-view double; $385 executive city-view double; $405 executive garden-view double; $575 city-view suite double; $625 garden-view suite double. Rates includes breakfast, tax, and service charge; executive room rates include Internet, executive lounge access, VIP treatment, and happy hour drinks. AE, MC, V. **Amenities:** 3 restaurants; patisserie; 2 bars; airport transfers ($20 per person one-way); concierge; health club; pool. *In room:* A/C, hairdryer, minibar, Wi-Fi ($10 per day; $20 per 24 hr.).

New Africa Hotel ★ Thoroughly off-putting from the outside, this concrete block in a slightly unappealing corner of the city (usefully close, though, to the Zanzibar ferry launch) nevertheless conceals some very decent rooms. The simplest units are larger than the standard rooms at the Southern Sun (see below), and here you have a chance of a harbor view, too, so definitely opt for a sea-facer. There's been some extensive renovation work: Bedroom interiors are actually quite appealing, and you get a definite sense of being in Africa as you amble through the public spaces. Service may be slow at times, but it's generally friendly and enthusiastic.

Corner of Azikiwe St. and Sokoine Dr., P.O. Box 9314, Dar es Salaam. ✆ **022/211-7050.** Fax 022/211-2495. www.newafricahotel.com. 196 units. $210 standard double; $220 superior sea-facing double; $320 executive suite double. AE, MC, V. **Amenities:** 2 restaurants, including **Sawasdee** (see "Where to Dine," below); 2 bars; airport transfers ($10 per person one-way); health club w/massage; pool; room service; casino. *In room:* A/C, TV, minibar, Wi-Fi ($4 per hr., $10 per day).

Southern Sun Dar es Salaam ★ This is one of Dar's most sensible options if you need to be near the city center, particularly if you're on business or simply overnighting while en route elsewhere. The former Holiday Inn offers a decent location (in a leafy part of town that doesn't feel like it's in the city at all, yet is right near the thick of things), and staff run a pretty tight ship. Accommodations aren't exactly lavish; standard rooms feel terribly small and are very overpriced, but the executive king-size units are considerably larger and better appointed—yet just $11 more. Although it caters almost exclusively to business travelers, it does have a leafy pool area that opens directly onto the botanical gardens, and staff are incredibly accessible and happily engage in conversation about practically anything.

Garden Avenue, P.O. Box 80022, Dar es Salaam. ✆ **022/213-7575.** Fax 022/213-9070. www.southernsundar.com. 152 units. $305 standard double; $316 executive double; $539 executive suite double; $759 diplomatic suite double. Rates include breakfast, taxes (20%), and service charge (5%). AE, DC, MC, V. **Amenities:** 2 restaurants; bar; airport transfers ($15–$30 one-way); babysitting; health club; pool; room service. *In room:* A/C, TV, hair dryer, free Wi-Fi.

Moderate

Harbour View Suites ★ Value An exceptional value and usefully located if you're planning to catch a ferry to Zanzibar, this "hotel" specializes in self-catering suites for business travelers. Opt for the executive king rooms, however, since these have much more space (they're the size of a suite but without the lounge area), bigger beds, and a less cluttered ambience (because there's no kitchen) and private balcony. Pricier superior king rooms face the harbor, but the city views are quite interesting, too. Sleek, no-nonsense decor makes the most of modern, inoffensive finishes—plasma TVs, fat mattresses, white linens, and plenty of natural light complete the fresh and utterly livable look. There are shops in the downstairs mall area and a handful of places to eat nearby, including the in-house Cajun-cum-Creole restaurant.

Harbour View Towers, Samora Ave., P.O. Box 9163, Dar es Salaam. ✆ **022/212-4040.** Fax 022/212-0333. www.harbourview-suites.com. 49 units. $180 standard studio double; $195 executive studio double; $210–$420 suite; $270 executive king double; $310 superior king double; $20 extra person. King room rates include breakfast. MC, V. **Amenities:** Restaurant; bar; airport transfers ($20 per person one-way); fitness room; pool. *In room:* A/C, TV, Jacuzzi (in superior king rooms), kitchenette (in self-catering units), minibar, Wi-Fi ($15 per day).

Inexpensive

Seedy, throbbing Kariakoo is where Dar's ordinary people go about their business, and this is also where the majority of the city's cheap digs are located. If you're keeping a tight harness on expenses, one place you won't feel ripped off is the **Tanso Hotel,** Livingstone Road, Kariakoo (✆ **079/728-2065** or -2001; bdc@citygardentz.com); with rooms for as little as $35 per night, it's among the cheapest places in town.

Palm Beach Hotel Value It really does feel a little bit like the African version of a cheap, half-decent Miami hotel I stayed at a few years back, and somehow the Art Deco touches aren't lost on this old but sufficiently revitalized place. Although it's not in the same league as Alexander's Hotel (see above), the great value here also means that you can get a triple room for just $120—an option if you're traveling with children. Rooms are compact and basic but very neat and clean, with wooden floors and tiled, functional bathrooms. Bring earplugs if you're a light sleeper, and set aside any expectations of frills and luxury; service, too, is pretty middling.

Ali Hassan Mwinyi Rd., P.O. Box 1520, Dar es Salaam. ✆ **022/213-0985,** 022/212-2931, or 071/322-2299. Fax 022/211-9272 or 022/260-0151. www.pbhtz.com. 32 units (all with shower only). $110 double. Rates include breakfast and taxes. MC. **Amenities:** Restaurant; bar; room service; casino. *In room:* A/C, TV, minibar.

South Coast Beaches

Also known as South Beach, the stretch of pure white sand immediately south of bustling Dar comes as a bit of a surprise, considering how close it is to a big city. Yet within a few minutes, it's possible to find yourself on a near-virgin beach backed by a tropical forest and perhaps a sparsely populated village. You can spend your day horizontal, with cocktails brought to you as you watch dhows drifting by and tune in to the gentle, endless drone of crashing waves. Or you can find all kinds of watersports to stave off the inevitable tropical narcolepsy.

Some of the loveliest beach resorts (small, intimate, beautiful, luxurious) are located about an hour south of Dar's Kigamboni ferry crossing, and getting there is a little easier these days, thanks to the recent overhaul of the dirt road that stretches south. Budget travelers need not travel far at all to check into the terribly laid-back Kipepeo Beach Village (reviewed below), while decidedly upmarket **Ras Kutani** and **Amani Beach Hotel** (both reviewed below) are a good 35km (22 miles) south of Dar. Any of these places offers a cushioning hideaway, far from the crowds.

Expensive

Amani Beach Resort ★★ Value Kids The name means "Peace," and there's plenty of it at this smart retreat comprising 10 enormous thatched cottages, all facing the ocean. They're spread over a large beachfront property with neatly tailored Swahili gardens and 32 hectares (79 acres) of indigenous forest. Although the grounds and accommodations are sumptuous (and the bar well stocked), the focus here is the beach. Hemmed in on one side by a strangely beautiful cliff outcrop, there's something infinitely seductive and engaging about the shore terrain here. However, if you're looking to surf, you may be disappointed; the lack of a strong current here means that you can swim even during high tide, although you should also take the opportunity to set sail on a dhow or snorkel around Sinda Island. Fashioned after an Afro-Arabic style, the cottages are voluminous and well poised to take advantage of the spectacular views. They feature big high-off-the-ground Zanzibari beds under huge billowing mosquito nets, locally crafted furniture, and plenty of spaces to recline and relax, including a generous private terrace. Choose a cottage close to the beach and pool if you're traveling with children, or ask for one located up on the cliff if you prefer privacy and gorgeous views. Managed by a dynamic young

Warning! Hide Your Shame

Nude or topless sunbathing is illegal in Tanzania and will offend the predominantly Muslim population found along the coast. While Western beachwear is generally tolerated in areas where there are resorts, it's only polite to respect local customs and laws.

couple with loads of energy and enthusiasm (and a real love of the location), Amani is constantly being scrutinized for improvements. Don't miss the chance to visit the local Swahili village or, if your timing's right, to witness turtles hatching on the beach.

P.O. Box 1736, South Coast, Dar es Salaam. © **075/441-0033.** www.amanibeach.com. Reservations: Hippotours, P.O. Box 13824, Nyumba Ya Sanaa, Dar es Salaam. © **022/212-8663.** Fax 022/212-8661. reservations@amanibeach.com. 10 units. $390–$440 double; $146 extra bed. Children under 12 pay 50%; under 2 free. Rates include all meals and taxes. AE, MC, V. Closed for 1 month after Easter. **Amenities:** 2 restaurants; 2 bars; babysitting; airport transfers ($95 per vehicle from Dar); tennis court. *In room:* A/C, hair dryer, fridge.

Ras Kutani ★★★ This is the chichiest resort along the Tanzanian coast, although calling it a resort is a bit of an insult. It's small, intimate, classy, and designed with such flair and imagination that you are instantly transported not only into the lap of easygoing luxury, but into a state of complete relaxation. This is where Dar's wealthier, savvier expatriates go to escape the daily grind. Accommodations—a handful of big, beautifully designed, open-plan thatched bandas—are spread among the trees at the edge of a rainforest not too far back from the beach; the low roar of the ocean is a constant reminder of where you are, and the creamy white sand is never far away. I don't imagine I have ever compressed so much relaxation into such a short stay. Designed as a place for you to kick off your shoes, there's just enough going on (you can snorkel to the offshore wreck, go sea-kayaking, or plonk around in the limited surf) to stop you from drifting into a narcoleptic coma, but mealtimes are definitely worth staying conscious for. Landlubbers can explore the virgin coastal forest on a walk that takes you around the lagoon—look out for shy colobus monkeys in the upper canopy, and listen for bush pigs foraging in the bush. You're also able to spend a couple of hours visiting a local village with which Ras Kutani has established a conservation partnership and from where most of the staff come; it's a good way to get a firmer understanding of life on the Swahili coast.

Amani, Gomvu Ward, Temeke District. © **077/473-5689.** www.raskutani.com. Reservations: Selous Safari Company, P.O. Box 1192, Dar es Salaam. © **022/213-4802** or 022/212-8485. Fax 022/211-2794. www.selous.com. 15 units. $500–$610 cottage double; $580–$700 suite double; $750–$900 family house (sleeps 4). Rates include all meals, tea, coffee, laundry, local airstrip transfers, and taxes. AE, MC, V. **Amenities:** Restaurant; bar, airport transfers ($50 per person; 2-person minimum); pool.

Moderate

Although aimed primarily at Norwegian vacationers, **Kasa Beach Hideaway** ★ (© **022/277-2766,** 0754/61-8163, or 0754/69-7408; www.kasabeach.com) is another decent option about 38km (24 miles) south of Dar. Comprising a handful of coral rock cottages ($166–$212 double, including all meals) and self-catering villas ($180 without meals) in a palm grove on the edge of a plateau overlooking the beach, it's a comfortable and totally relaxed option that lacks the luxury of Ras Kutani and Amani Beach, but is more exclusive than Kipepeo (see below), with somewhat more modern facilities and less focus on waterborne adventure.

Inexpensive

Kipepeo Beach Village ★ *Value* Right up against a glistening silvery beach, this laid-back budget resort has Robinson Crusoe atmosphere in spades. This is a great value if you're the hassle-free beachcombing sort who doesn't need air-conditioning—or, indeed, four walls—to help you relax. You have a choice here of a very basic, shared-bathroom banda on the beach, or a breezy, en suite, open-to-the-elements chalet that balances on stilts and affords views toward the ocean. Run by a mild-mannered, beach-loving Australian, the main activity here seems to be lying horizontal under the makuti thatch umbrellas. With your feet in the sand and exotic-sounding cocktails never far away, this place feels a million miles from civilization. If you're slightly more energetic, you can jump on a dhow and go hunting for mackerel and sailfish, propel yourself between the nearby islands on a sea-going kayak, or jump in the water with a pair of goggles and check out the parade of Technicolor fish. And when that lazy holiday hunger strikes, the restaurant serves a mean Swahili-style seafood curry. A fabulous choice for barefoot, no-frills Puritans.

Kipepeo Beach, Mjimwema, Kigamboni. P.O. Box 1520, Dar es Salaam. ✆ **0754/27-6178,** 071/375-7515, or 073/292-0211. www.kipepeovillage.com. 35 units, some with shared bathrooms, none with tubs. $75 chalet double; $25 *banda* double. Children 5–12 pay $15 if sharing; under 5 free. Chalet rate includes breakfast. MC, V. **Amenities:** Restaurant, bar; airport transfers ($30 per vehicle one-way); room service. *In room:* No phone.

WHERE TO DINE

Tanzanian cuisine—headlined by a carbo-rich porridge-like concoction called *ugali*—is unlikely to feature on any lists of national favorites. Basically a mix of maize, flour, and water, *ugali* is a cheap, multifunctional dish usually eaten in its more solid state, when it's typically dipped into some sort of stew. Eggs, which are always seen being punted around the markets and bus stations in their boiled form as a quick protein snack, are also popular, and the country's other favorite dish is a kind of omelet called Chips Mayai—or chips and egg—which may get topped off with a splodge of minced beef, accompanied by a greasy bottle of ketchup. You'll see the *mayai* stalls being pushed around like trolleys and served up at simple streetside makeshift diners or wrapped in newspaper as a takeaway.

Fortunately, you won't have to put up with such unimaginative dishes, and because coastal Tanzania takes its cue from the ocean, there's always good, fresh seafood on offer in the city's diverse restaurants. A great deal of this is put to excellent use in the city's two best Japanese eateries, **Oriental** and **Osaka** (both reviewed below). Exquisite seafood pastas add to the experience at **Mediterraneo** (reviewed below), my top pick for Swahili-nuanced Mediterranean and Italian cuisine—and, in fact, simply the most delightful place to eat anywhere in or around Dar es Salaam. For pure Italian, and the place most recommended by expatriates who can't survive without at least one plate of pasta per meal, try **Zûane** ★★, Oyster Bay (✆ **022/260-0118**), a trattoria that also does authentic pizza. Another lovely choice for seafood (and much more) is the **Karambezi Café** ★, at the Sea Cliff Hotel (✆ **022/260-0380;** daily 6am–1 or 2am; main courses Tsh14,000–Tsh63,000). With an open kitchen and counters made from recycled dhows, its setting overlooking the water at the northern tip of the Msasani Peninsula is a definite highlight, but the seafood platter is memorable, too.

Many of the top restaurants are located in the large, high-end hotels. One of the best (and most beautiful) eateries in the city is **Sawasdee** ★ (✆ **022/211-7050;** daily 7–11pm), widely considered the only *authentic* Thai restaurant in Dar. Catching the elevator up to this elegant, refined space comes as quite a surprise after the ugly exterior of the New Africa Hotel in which it's located. Here, on the ninth floor, there's a lovely view of the harbor.

Addis in Dar ★★ ETHIOPIAN One of Dar's most atmospheric choices, where you can dine beneath the stars and find yourself cooled by a gentle breeze even on the warmest of nights, this Ethiopian restaurant also brings home some of the cultural idiosyncrasies of its cuisine. Your hands are washed in anticipation of eating with your fingers, and you share food from a communal dish at the low Messob tables. Using pieces of pancake-like Ethiopian bread to mop and scoop the different concoctions, you tuck into a variety of dips, with different kinds of stewlike lentil, vegetable, seafood, and meat dishes prepared with exotic sauces and gravies.

35 Ursino St., off Migombani St., Msasani Peninsula. ✆ **071/326-6299** or 075/446-1167. Main courses Tsh13,000–Tsh16,000; set menu Tsh26,000. No credit cards. Mon–Sat 6–10:30pm.

The Alcove ★ INDIAN/CHINESE The two branches of this much-respected Dar institution couldn't be more different. The original eatery in the city's grubby downtown heartland looks like it hasn't changed in the 2 decades it's been there. The bland streetside entrance conceals a salmon-and-pink interior that feels a lot like a flashback. The posh new venue at the Sea Cliff Hotel on the Msasani Peninsula looks positively jewel-like by comparison and caters to a glitzier crowd. Either way, there's a long and reliable list of Indian dishes—the seafood curries, particularly the crab masala, are wonderful. Less appealing, though, are the Indianized Chinese dishes (although the ginger prawns are delicious); for authentic Chinese, try Beautiful China (reviewed below). Don't forget to let the waiter know if you need the spices tempered to a more delicate palate.

✆ **071/321-3744** or 076/721-3744. City Center: Samora Ave. ✆ **022/213-7444** or 022/213-8449. Msasani Peninsula: Hotel Seacliff. ✆ **022/260-1980** or 022/260-2390. www.alcovetz.com. Main courses Tsh5,700–Tsh25,000. MC. Mon–Sat noon–3pm; daily 7–10:30pm.

Beautiful China ★★ Value CHINESE Still known to most of Dar by its former name (Sichuan), this big, bright restaurant occupies an unlikely spot in a business park on a busy road. Step inside, however, and you leave the tackiness of downtown for a restaurant that's a dead ringer for countless Chinese eateries from Hong Kong to New York—no-nonsense, understated styling with loads of fluorescent lighting, a few essential ornaments, and an encyclopedic menu. This is a labor of love for restaurateur-cum–interior designer Jacky-Chen (pronounced "Jacky Chan"), who is usually on hand to help you decide from the compendium of options. Chef Fan (who's been in Dar some 15 years now) works with ingredients straight from the market and does some tantalizing work with fish and seafood. Try the sweet and sour fish, cooked whole, with the bones removed, or have the same fish prepared with chili and soy. *Gangbao* chicken, prepared with a sauce of peanut and dried chili, is another favorite.

Note: Jacky-Chen is planning to open a second branch of this much-loved restaurant in 2010, so call ahead, in case it's nearer to you than the original.

Mhasibu House, NBAA, Bibititi Mohamed Rd. ✆ **022/215-0548,** 078/466-8888, or 061/266-8888. Main courses Tsh7,000–Tsh20,000. No credit cards. Mon–Sat 11:30am–3pm; Mon–Sun 6–11pm.

Mediterraneo ★★★ MEDITERRANEAN/ITALIAN/FUSION The setting alone deserves three stars, but the exemplary Mediterranean food—along with inventive and subtle coastal Swahili influences—makes it perhaps my favorite restaurant in East Africa. Owned by an Italian-Somali family with a passion for design and an understanding of good food in their blood, Mediterraneo offers that rare combination of well-prepared food and seductive surrounds. There's a wood-burning oven for authentic pizzas, and they serve what is simply the best pasta (all homemade) you'll have in Tanzania. A personal favorite is the *fettuccine alla Mediterraneo,* a delicious invention: Black fettuccine (made with squid ink) is mixed with chili, lobster, and clams and cooked in garlic and white wine. Another special dish is *ravioli al cacao* and *pili pili*—the ravioli is stuffed with three kinds of cheese, chili, and an almond and cashew sauce; it's spicy, but it's a revelation. Finally, the tiramisu (traditional or strawberry-flavored) is a winner, too.

Mediterraneo Hotel, off Kawe Beach Rd., 10km (6¼ miles) north of Dar city center. © **022/261-8359** or 075/481-2567. Main courses Tsh14,500–Tsh29,500; pizza Tsh9,500–Tsh18,000. MC, V. Daily noon–11pm (last order).

Oriental ★★★ JAPANESE/THAI At the open-plan sushi kitchen, steam rises from large metal pots and *dim sum* bamboo baskets are piled high behind a team of hard-working chefs carving up fresh fish and dunking homemade noodles into boiling water. This is unquestionably Dar's slickest restaurant, representing the brave new face of a city in a state of rapid transformation. It's abuzz just about all the time—lone business executives man the counter, while the tables fill up with families, NGO groups celebrating their latest funding windfall, and gatherings of upscale locals looking to sample authentic Eastern dishes. There's no harm in mixing things up a bit, starting with impeccably fresh red-meat tuna sashimi and then proceeding to one of the spicy Thai noodle dishes. Cap off your meal with one of the unusual sorbet flavors, such as lemon grass and black pepper. Everything tastes and looks fantastic, and were the service snappier, this might well rank as a world-class restaurant—for the time being, however, it's the food alone that really warrants a visit.

The Kilimanjaro Kempinski, Kivukoni St. © **022/213-1111.** Sushi and sashimi Tsh6,000–Tsh45,000; main courses around Tsh20,000–Tsh22,000. AE, DC, MC, V. Tues–Sun 12:30–2:30pm and 7–10:30pm.

Osaka ★ JAPANESE This Korean-owned establishment in the midst of the Msasani embassy belt has a marvelously laid-back, breezy ambience. The *makuti*-roofed open-to-the-elements dining area is often packed with people digging into extensive and varied sushi platters or partying it up around the lively teppanyakki counter. It's a great place to meet people (notably members of the extensive expatriate community) and, for a quieter experience, to tuck into a good-value lunchtime set menu. Here you will find every imaginable variety of sushi and sashimi, all kinds of noodles, and tuna—lightly grilled on the coals—that is simply melt-in-the-mouth fantastic.

4/1 Chaza Lane, Oyster Bay. © **075/526-8228** or 077/787-0568. Teppanyaki Tsh7,000–Tsh35,000; sushi and sashimi Tsh2,000–Tsh80,000; set dinner menu Tsh18,000–Tsh25,000. No credit cards. Tues–Sun 12:30–2:30pm and 6:30–11pm.

EXPLORING DAR ES SALAAM

Many people arrive here with preconceived notions that it's little more than an awful stop-off en route to safari destinations inland or a terrible place to pass the time before a flight connecting them back to Europe. Although there's a relative dearth of real attractions, Dar turns out to be more about a feeling that about sightseeing, and there are a few intriguing corners to simply watch and imbibe the local life, color, and day-to-day routine. There's some mildly interesting architecture scattered around the city's colonial quarter, but nothing stands out as obviously impressive, and much of the built heritage is in a slightly tattered state. You can spend a couple of hours getting a feel for the rhythm of the city by setting off at the crack of dawn to visit the bustling **fish market,** where straight-off-the-boat merchandise is graded, sorted, and displayed in some elaborate, unfathomable system designed to catch the eye of prospective buyers—from housewives laden with plastic buckets filled with finger-size fish to restaurateurs searching for top-quality tuna that might be transformed into your lunchtime *sashimi.* You can become engrossed in the raucous parlaying that goes on as basket after basket of early morning catch makes its way up from the boats, or turn your eyes to the water to witness the action amid the colorful tangle of fishing dhows and ropes and nets. Look out, too, for the wandering *kahawa* (coffee) hawkers and fuel up with a dose of Swahili "espresso"— it's a strong, bitter black coffee best taken with a bite of the candied nut brittle provided. Don't be afraid to try out your Kiswahili here—a heartfelt *"Jambo"* (Hello) and *"Habari?"* (How are you?) goes a long way toward coaxing a smile out of even the toughest-looking fisherman, although you'd better be on standby with *"Sisema Kiswahili"* (I don't speak Kiswahili) before you confuse a friendly local into assuming that you're being rude. Although a few people don't like having their picture taken, you'll usually get a positive response if you politely ask these guys, *"Mikupige picha?"* (May I take your picture?)— you won't regret making the effort.

When you've had your fill of the fishy stench, take a stroll along the **Kivukoni Front** to experience the city as it comes to life. From here you can watch the harbor scene on one side and the confluence of modernity and colonial leftovers on the other. Between it all, the taxi drivers and shoe-shiners, hustlers and hookers, dock workers and diplomats make for their particular corners of the city. Later, if you want a sense of how modern Dar's population goes about its business, stop by **Kariakoo Market,** where the city's pulse beats hardest—its vivid sights and pungent smells and frenzied, frenetic sounds are Dar in its most concentrated form (except perhaps for the mayhem you might witness at any of the larger bus stations). Once a small village, Kariakoo takes its present-day name from the German carrier corps that resided here during the war—the name is simply a corruption of "carrier" *(karia)* and "corps" *(koo).* At Kariakoo's heart is the Eastern Bloc–style concrete hulk that comprises the main market building; I'm told that people travel from all over East Africa to shop here, and some go so far as to call it the "Dubai of Tanzania," which is perhaps a little far-fetched. Step inside for a gander at a disparate array of goods—everything from industrial fertilizers to electronic appliances can be bought, and mixed in with the high-tech gadgetry is the smell of freshly cracked coconuts, the tang of green peppers, aromatic spices, and sweet citrus juice. Outside, illegal vendors line the streets, pushing bribes into the hands of potbellied police officers who, in return, allow them to sell their fresh fruit and vegetables alongside racks flogging beautifully patterned *kangas.* And amid it all, scores of people throng in every direction— women out to shop, traders gathering their gear, pedestrians dodging traffic, and heavily loaded carts being dragged through it all by tough, bedraggled workers. ***A word of caution:*** You'd do well to leave all valuables at your hotel when exploring here (or pretty much anywhere in the city, for that matter); the crowds can be thick, and your overtly displayed jewelry or purse will be gone long before you notice.

If you're feeling particularly adventurous, hop on the **Kigamboni Ferry,** which launches not far from the fish market and transfers you—along with hundreds of fellow passengers—to Kigamboni, an eclectic mix of market stalls as colorful as they are chaotic. Here you can watch fishermen working on their boats or pick up local transport for a trip to beaches along the south coast.

If you want to get a feel for Tanzania's emerging art scene, there's no beating **Mawazo** ★★★ (at press time, searching for new premises; see "Shopping," below), which hosts exhibitions showcasing the very best in contemporary art. If there's a chance of finding collectible, exciting local work, this is it. There's also a new art gallery at the city's **national museum,** properly known as the House of Culture (reviewed below), where you can fawn over the skull of one of our earliest proto-human ancestors, unearthed by Richard Leakey in the Rift Valley.

Few people know that author Roald Dahl once lived a life of relative luxury in Dar es Salaam when he worked for the Shell Petroleum Company in the 1930s. When World

Tanzania's Signature Artists

Ubiquitous pretty much all over East Africa—especially where there's the chance of a tourist sale—the paintings that have become synonymous with modern Tanzania tread a thin line between fine art, graphic design, and cartoon. Chief among these are the naïve, childlike depictions of wide-eyed animals that comprise the famed Tinga Tinga school. Few people who head home with a handful of paintings in their luggage realize that this particular style has its roots with one man, **Eduardo Saidi Tingatinga.** Born in Southern Tanzania in 1937, Tingatinga was the original artist who inadvertently founded a movement, having found himself inspired by some Congolese paintings he had seen. With no training at all, he tried his hand at creating images of wild animals and village scenes using enamel liquid paint bought at a local hardware store. His images of simplified human figures or wild animals painted from one side with the head turned toward the viewer are two-dimensional and give the impression of almost childlike simplicity, with no background, no depth. Yet with the absence of any pretense at realism, and by cutting the subject to its bare essence, revealing only what he saw as the main elements, Tingatinga's works have been described as atmospheric and poetic, capturing the fragile spirit of his subjects. His paintings have been called "a sort of essential art" in which he uses subtle color, form, and shape to convey a charming sense of beauty, which some critics have suggested represents the artist's reality, albeit in a straightforward, graphical medium—an adult artist who managed to preserve the original and unabashed spontaneity of childhood. Sadly, Tingatinga—who probably began painting only in 1967—was accidentally killed in a police shootout in 1972. During his brief time as an artist, however, he trained members of his own family in his style, and his technique has become Tanzania's most popular art form—the Tinga Tinga School.

Other famous images that have come to epitomize the spirit (literally, in this case) of the Tanzanian art world are the quirky, cartoonesque *shetani* ("spirit" or "devil") figures realized by **George Lilanga** during his illustrious career. Widely considered to be one of the world's major contemporary artists, Lilanga was greatly influenced by the Pop movement, and the impact of Keith Haring is particularly evident in his work. Whereas Tingatinga's style teeters on the edge of the banal, Lilanga (1934–2005) explored a realm of magic and fantasy that spans the space between reality and the spirit realm. His paintings are ironic explorations of common themes in everyday life, and history, too, is

War II broke out, he captained a platoon of *askaris* and went on to serve in the Royal Air Force, with missions across North Africa. Dahl, my sources tell me, lived in the exclusive enclave of **Oyster Bay,** at the southern end of the **Msasani Peninsula,** which remains a hub of expatriate luxury living, replete with enormous mansions, 75 embassies, and real estate averaging $1 million. It's also the setting for the most sociable swimming beach in the immediate vicinity of the city; pretty **Coco Beach** is a good place for a walk or a dip, and there's a casual beach bar and restaurant with plastic chairs, cold beers, and a straightforward menu.

transformed through tongue-in-cheek juxtapositions. His paintings and sculptures have titles such as There's a World but I've Forgotten It and Wait a Minute, My Neck Is Itchy, and there's little chance of remaining a casual, uninvolved observer when trying to make sense of the fantastical scenes that he created. His figures twist and writhe on the canvas, and his carvings are alive with energy—it's a rhythm said to evoke the traditional dances of Lilanga's people, whose mythology and culture are represented in his art. Using an imaginary, graphical world populated by fantastical, grotesque characters, Lilanga draws inevitable parallels between universal psychological demons of the traditional spirit world. A member of the woodcarving Makonde tribe, Lilanga learned to sculpt wood in the traditional way, first using soft cassava root and then later working with hard black wood. He continued to carve when he moved to Dar but found his break when, while working as a security guard at the Nyerere Cultural Centre, he managed to show his creations to one of the organizers. In 1978, his work featured in an exhibition in Washington, D.C., following which he was in great demand internationally. His worldwide repute made him a living icon for Swahili art. In and around Dar and Bagamoyo today, you'll come across hundreds of artists trying to reenact Lilanga's legacy, hoping to make it big. There are countless artists throughout Africa who are destined to try flogging their canvases and carvings at streetside stalls or from curio markets where original and unique creations are always a rarity.

You can find knockoff Tinga Tinga and Lilanga paintings everywhere (imitative works in Lilanga's style will include a copy of his signature, or that of his grandson, Henrick John Lilanga). For the widest selection of canvases (of varying quality and pretty much indeterminate value) in Dar, visit the **Mwenge Craft Village** (well known to taxi drivers, it's close to the Village Museum), where you can also browse for *kangas,* masks (most of them from West Africa), drums, and some intriguing musical instruments. You'll be expected to bargain and will need to endure some pretty pushy sales talk, but the stall keepers are ultimately engaging, entertaining, and eager to show you behind the scenes, where many of the handicrafts are being manufactured by a hardworking team, most of whom taught themselves to carve at an early age. There's an established group of Tinga Tinga artists at **The Slipway** (✆ **076/274-4054**); they've been creating within this niche genre since 1982.

Finally, one of the favorite daytime pursuits for visitors to the city is a **dhow cruise to Bongoyo** ★★, a small island marine reserve close to the Msasani Peninsula. The boats set off on the ½-hour trip every 2 hours from 9:30am, returning an hour later—you can easily spend half a day exploring the island. The all-inclusive trip costs Tsh25,000; you can call Sylvester Bigona (✆ **022/260-0893** or 071/332-8126) or simply turn up at The Slipway on the northern end of Msasani. Or, better still, skip the city and head for one of the virtually untouched **beaches along the south coast** ★★★. There you will come to remember the meaning of the word *paradise* and discover hushed alternatives to the development that has occurred on popular, over-exploited Zanzibar.

The Top Attractions

Museum and House of Culture ★ Having just undergone an extensive expansion and renovation, Tanzania's flagship museum is aiming high. It originally opened in 1940 as a memorial to King George V, and over the years the collection has come to include some pretty impressive items, including fossils of some of the earliest human ancestors, unearthed during the Leakey digs at Olduvai Gorge. The world-famous *Zinjanthropus baisei* skull has, until now, been seen by the public in the form of a cast replica, but the original should be on display from early 2010. You get a good overview of Tanzanian history, with some focus on the impact of slavery and the colonial era, and the ethnographic section will help you better understand some of the customs and traditions that play so central a role in the lives of the country's many different tribes. Among the new additions to the museum is a gallery that will include contemporary art.

Shaabaan Robert St., btw. Sokoine Dr. and Samora Ave. ✆ **022/211-7508.** www.houseofculture.or.tz. Tsh6,500 adults, Tsh2,600 students. Daily 9:30am–6pm.

Village Museum Just 5 minutes from the Mwenge craft "village," this is envisioned as a sort of one-stop cultural quick fix aimed primarily at Tanzanian school children. Here the young city slickers are given a cultural overview surveying a number of the country's 120 tribes. The traditional homesteads of 20 different tribes have been re-created here, and part of the constantly changing exhibition is live appearances by representatives of tribal groups from different parts of the country. Spread over 6 hectares (15 acres), the museum incorporates a nature trail, but you'll surely be more interested in the ongoing traditional dance performances (Tsh2,000), even if these lack the intensity of dances that happen in a more authentic context.

Ali Hassan Road. ✆ **022/270-0437.** Admission $5 adults, $2 students. Daily 9:30am–6pm.

SHOPPING

If you make just one stop for local arts, make it the **Mawazo Contemporary Art Centre ★★★** (✆ **075/483-1551** or 078/478-2770; www.mawazoart.com), which hosts solo and group exhibitions with visual artists working in Tanzania today. Organizers have a definite eye for talent; apparently when Matt Damon visited the gallery, he left with half the stock. Besides several other projects, Mawazo organizes the biannual **Makutano Art & Craft Fair** (usually in May and Nov–Dec; www.makutanotz.com), and they have recently started publishing a series of books: *Black Aroma, the Story of Tanzanian Coffee* and *Climate Change in Tanzania* are their first two titles. Note that, at press time, Mawazo was on the hunt for new premises; call ahead for details.

Dar also has a few places to sift through a wide variety African arts and crafts, with the better shops over on the Msasani Peninsula. **The Slipway** shopping center is a bit like a miniature version of Cape Town's V&A Waterfront, with at least a dozen worthwhile stores catering to tourists; among these, look out for **African Dream,** where you can pick up antique Zanzibari beaded slippers, and **Yatima,** which sells handmade, hand-dyed cottons printed with traditional and modern designs that feature in hotels and safari lodges around the country. If you're fond of those candy-color *kikoi* fabrics that form an essential part of the Swahili beach experience, take a look at the selection at **One Way.** There's even an outdoor **flea market** with all kinds of crafts and curios, including the ubiquitous Tinga Tinga paintings, a few decent restaurants, a jetty for trips to the island of Bongoyo, and a bank with extended hours.

While you're in the neighborhood, you may also want to pop in to **Treasures of Africa,** 72/73 Chole Rd. (✆ **022/260-2573** or 076/215-7393; info@treasuresofafrica.co.tz), if only to check out how retired dhows have been recycled and turned into furniture. They also sell Zanzibari furniture and Swazi candles, homeware, and colorful artworks. Also on the Peninsula, there are a handful of decent shops at the **Oyster Bay Shopping Centre,** including a very respectable leather goods store called Ngozee (✆ **075/437-8108** or 022/260-1961).

For tanzanite, head for **The Tanzanite Dream** on Mataka Road, behind the fire station in Upanga (✆ **071/326-2326,** 075/467-4893, or 022/215-2100; www.tanzanites.net). They also sell other gemstones and cut gems to produce their own jewelry. You can also buy tanzanite (of dubious quality) from **African Art,** New Bagamoyo Road (✆ **022/277-3717;** www.africaart.co.tz), but I think it's a better bet for traditional African crafts, including baskets, beaded jewelry, and textiles.

Finally, of course, everyone will send you to **Mwenge Craft Village,** where you can sift through an infinite variety of carvings, Tinga Tinga paintings, and curios in every size, shape, and form. You'll need a keen eye if you want to walk away with something special.

NIGHTLIFE

Dar's biggest party night ★★★ happens once a month at the Mediterraneo Hotel and Restaurant (see "Where to Stay," above); the city's sexiest crowd—usually a good 500 or 600 people—gathers for an all-night festival of drinking, dancing, and strutting that kicks off around 11pm or midnight. Admission is Tsh15,000, and you might want to hire a taxi to wait for you all night. On nonparty nights, Mediterraneo's open-to-the-elements lounge/bar at the edge of the beach is always a splendid spot to hang out with a chilled bottle of wine and lusciously deep sofas. Owned by one of the brothers from the Mediterraneo, **Runway Lounge** ★★★, on the second floor of Shopper's Plaza on Old Bagamoyo Road, is Dar's outright hottest after-dark venue and a world-class spot to drink, lounge, and boogie side-by-side with a flamboyant crowd. For details, you can contact the venue (✆ **075/544-1922;** info@runway-lounge.com) or call Samantar himself (✆ **078/490-9095**), who'll make sure you get a good table and experience Dar's dizziest night out. Make sure you wear long pants and closed shoes.

Tips — Conscious Shopping

If you're in any way concerned about the potential environmental impact of your purchases in East Africa, it's worth considering that wood carvings obviously require trees to be felled. You may want to avoid contributing to the destruction of forests by choosing to buy gifts and souvenirs that are less environmentally impactful, such as baskets made from woven straw and grass, recycled products, stone sculptures, and certain kinds of jewelry. Also avoid anything with shells or pieces of coral, and definitely be alert when it comes to anything made from animal products—some unscrupulous types will even try to sell you ivory.

In the small shopping complex just behind The Oyster Bay Hotel, **Sweet Eazy** ★ (✆ **075/575-4074;** www.sweeteazy.com) is a vibey restaurant and bar with live music (often by cover bands such as Banana Zoro & B Band, Dar's favorite act—cheesy but fun) on Saturday nights (9pm–1am; Tsh5,000 admission). It's a safe, comfortable place to watch the easy rhythm of after-dark Dar as expats, tourists, and even a few ladies of the night trying haplessly to be discreet gather under one roof to enjoy the cold beer and cocktails.

More than a little bit seedy, **Q Bar,** off Haile Selassie Road, Oyster Bay (✆ **075/428-2474;** www.qbardar.com), is rather rough and raucous, but popular with a wide range of people (locals, expats, and backpackers), and has everything, including live music, pool tables, and squadrons of hovering prostitutes. A little less downmarket is **O'Willies Irish Pub** (✆ **022/260-1273**), located on the ground floor of a small hotel set right on the water's edge. There's trip-down-memory-lane live music on weekends—and a lot of drinking.

Finally, since Dar nightlife kicks off quite late, the best place to *start* off your evening is at **Level 8** ★★, at the Kempinski hotel (✆ **022/213-1111**), down by the waterfront. With its breezy, elegant layout and scintillating view over the port, this is arguably the best sunset spot in town, where you can watch dhows mingling with cargo ships on the gold-tinged water down below. Then suddenly the scene is silhouetted by enormous spotlights that illuminate the harbor after dark. Listen to business deals being struck and romantic deals smoothly negotiated. Every Friday night from 9pm, Tanzanian songstress and musician Carola Kinasha brings a bit of magic to the place.

2 THE NORTH COAST

As tranquil and, with few exceptions, untouched as the shores of the Tanzanian mainland seem today, the virginal coast belies centuries of turbulent and often bloody conflict that raged along this coast as Africa's tragic destiny unfolded in the hands of hostile outsiders, greedy to tap into the wealth of the largely unexplored continent. With a long history of exploitation, ports along the Tanzanian coast reached degrees of prominence during the 18th and 19th centuries, along with a growth in the international demand for ivory and slaves. Towns such as Tanga, Pangani, and Bagamoyo, on the coast north of Dar, emerged as major trade centers connecting Zanzibar with inland trade routes. Although there had long been some kind of foreign presence here, Arab traders had traditionally installed themselves on the islands off the Swahili coast—Zanzibar and Pemba (chapter 13), Mafia (chapter 14), and Kilwa (chapter 17)—because of an abiding fear of attack by the indigenous African population and as a way of preventing their slaves from escaping.

Christian missionaries and European politicians crusaded against the slave trade, gradually stamping out one form of human exploitation (at least on the mainland, where slavery was criminalized) and replacing it with their own brand of imperial control. With the decline of the trade routes and the relocation of the German Protectorate's headquarters to Dar es Salaam in 1891, Northern Tanzania's ports fell out of favor (Bagamoyo's harbor simply wasn't deep enough for the new kinds of ship), and much of the land around them was given over to cash crops destined for European markets. Today these towns live on with some poignant reminders of the past, but none is likely to hold your interest for too long; generally, they're best thought of as beach escapes with the added bonus of some off-the-beaten-track cultural add-ons (including the ancient Kaole Ruins near Bagamoyo and vestiges of an old Arab slave town at Pangani). Only Tanga, at one point a major focus for German development, retains a port of any significance, but the town itself is a lazy, cheerless place, barely worth lingering in for longer than it takes to recover for your onward journey.

In a way, the easy-going rhythm of this coastal belt is like a giant collective sigh of relief following a history of oppression by slave-trading Arabs, and, much later, the Europeans who put an end to the slave trade but made every effort to install themselves as colonial overlords. While the scimitar-shaped dhow sails billowing on the horizon may take you back to the days when waves of traders, explorers, adventurers, pirates, slavers, and invaders landed on these shores, it takes very little effort in coming to the conclusion that the true wonder of this once-harangued coastline lies in the discovery of one of the world's finest beaches.

BAGAMOYO

Most accessible and potentially enlightening of the stops you can make along the north coast (and, indeed, the only one within striking distance of Dar), this once-prosperous slave and ivory trading port comes with a pleasant mix of beach and culture. Having served as the capital of German East Africa from 1886 till 1891, today much of the town has gone to seed, but there are glimmers of its former glories, if you can see past the decay and the tumble-down facades. It's also a popular weekend getaway for the Dar crowd, so there are an inordinate number of resorts, few of them worth recommending.

Although there had earlier been a more ancient community here, it was only in the late 18th century that Omani settlers set about extracting taxes from the locals and trading in salt farmed along the town's northerly shore. At the heart of present-day Bagamoyo is a crumbling, still-inhabited **Swahili stone town** (properly known as Dunda), which—together with the chance to spot a few examples of **German colonial architecture** and a 19th-century **prison-fort** built by an Arab slaver—merits some on-foot exploration. The town feels like a place that's permanently on the cusp of some sort of minor renaissance, and there are a number of centers where local artists work and sell their paintings and sculptures. You might want to pop into **The African Modern Art Park** (opposite the Old Post Office Hotel), where Saidi Mbungu (✆ **078/284-8547**), himself a talented artist, can tell you about some of the work that's happening to teach children through art. Or perhaps visit the nearby **Bagamoyo Talent Studio** (a small room diagonally across the road from the **Old Boma**), where artists such as Emmanuel Philip Kuta (✆ **078/719-4323**) and his partner, Lucas, will tell you about the struggle to be an artist in a poor country.

Besides exploring the old town and hanging around the **dhow harbor**—a lively place to observe the fishermen in action and perhaps sample some of their catch, which they deep-fry and salt at the stalls on and around the beach—Bagamoyo's biggest draw (aside from Kaole) is the **Catholic Museum** (✆ **023/244-0010** or -0063; Tsh1,500; daily 10am–5pm). The museum is actually a group of late-19th-century church buildings, including the **Holy Ghost Church,** where David Livingstone's body spent a night before being packed off to Zanzibar and onward to Westminster. The Holy Ghost Mission—East Africa's first Christian mission—was initially established as a shelter for children rescued from slavery. The museum itself provides plenty of insight into the scourge of slavery, but besides coming face to face with some of the tools of the trade and many disheartening images, you need to work quite hard to patch the discombobulated narrative together—good enough reason to take on the services of the local guide (Tsh10,000 for a 1-hr. tour of the museum and the entire grounds).

To pick through another, much earlier layer of Bagamoyo's history, head 5km (3 miles) south along the coast to the crumbling **Kaole Ruins** (Tsh2,000; daily 8am–5pm). These are the remains of a medieval Shirazi settlement (presumed to have been built around 1250), which some believe may have been a kind of religious enclave, with a few poignant archaeological traces, including a well-preserved graveyard and a 15th-century mosque. Evocative as the overgrown site is, it's difficult to get a handle on the place without a guide, but be warned that whatever you're told will probably be highly speculative; the site is not yet fully understood by scholars trying to figure out exactly what happened here.

Essentials

GETTING THERE Bagamoyo lies about 70km (43 miles) north of Dar es Salaam. The trip takes about an hour (and up to 90 min. by bus) on good tarmac road; a taxi here from Dar should cost $130. Any of the hotels here can arrange transfers from Dar's airport. There are fairly frequent buses and *dala-dala* services between Dar and Bagamoyo.

VISITOR INFORMATION & GUIDE SERVICES Staff at Bagamoyo's **Tourism Information Office** (**© 076/444-2823;** daily 8am–5pm) can assist with most questions you might have, whether it's about securing transport or finding a guide; they can arrange tours of the town (or to specific points of interest), with or without transport. The best **guide** in town is **Peter Junior** (**© 078/486-9652**), who speaks good English and has even written a book on the town. If you're looking for someone else to make all your arrangements and plan a coastal-cultural tour, contact **Ancient Ost Afrika** (**© 075/622-7761;** www.ancientostafrika.com), a home-grown tour operator based in Bagamoyo; they can arrange multiday excursions that take in Dar, Bagamoyo, and Saadani National Park.

Where to Stay & Dine

Expensive

Lazy Lagoon ★★ Hands down the best place to stay anywhere in the vicinity of Bagamoyo, this rustic beach retreat is also the most relaxing—a great choice if you're coming to cap off your wildlife safari. The lodge occupies the very tip of a 9km-long (5½-mile) narrow peninsula; it's inaccessible by land and, consequently, feels like an island. The approach—by boat—is an unforgettable start to an unimaginably lazy holiday. While it's possible to snorkel here, go fishing on a *ngalawa* with the local fishermen, and visit Kaole and Bagamoyo on a day trip, you'd better bring a few books to read. There are just 12 split-level bungalows at the very edge of the beach, each with two additional beds in the upstairs loft (ideal if you're traveling with children). They're wonderfully private, and the design is simple, unfussy, and slightly rough around the edges. Mattresses are foam, and bathroom fittings are outdated. The new manager has promised a refurbishment (during which he'll hopefully change the curtains, too). Despite its faults, this feels like just the kind of understated design that you need on the beach—you'll probably spend half a day sprawled across the enormous swing bed on your private porch. At night, beneath a spectacular starscape, you drift off to the sound of waves lapping at the shore near your room. Wake up just before dawn to witness dozens of fishing boats zooming past your room—it's got to be one of the most magical sights along this coast. The only real downside can be the service; most of the staff are locals with minimal experience, and while they get the job done (most of the time), don't expect a whole heap of enthusiasm.

Lazy Lagoon Island, Ras Luale, opposite Mbegani Fisheries Institute, Bagamoyo. Reservations: ✆ **1452/86-2288** in the U.K. fox@tanzaniasafaris.info. In Dar es Salaam ✆ **0784/23-7422,** 0713/23-7422, or 0754/23-7422. www.tanzaniasafaris.info. 12 units. June–Oct and Dec 23–Jan 5 $330 double; Nov–Dec 22 and Jan 6–May $280 double. Children 2–12 pay 50% if sharing. Rates include all meals, tea, coffee, laundry, and boat transfers. MC, V (credit cards attract 5% surcharge). **Amenities:** Restaurant; bar; pool; airport transfers ($35 per person one-way). *In room:* No phone.

Moderate

The smartest rooms in Bagamoyo are the six suite-size executive units at the **Millennium Sea Breeze Resort** (✆ **023/244-0201;** www.millenium.co.tz). They're thoroughly modern and packed with all the amenities you could hope for—including air-conditioning and big, comfortable beds (the best ones also have terraces that face the ocean)—but the hotel itself lacks any atmosphere that might be described as relaxing. Instead, it's a very popular conference facility, and you're almost always surrounded by people conducting business in little breakaway groups around the pool. Fortunately, the beach is close at hand and once you're on it, you can walk for miles in either direction. Standard doubles cost $150 (including all meals), but the rooms are truly hideous; fork over the extra $60 for the executive suite—or, better still, make a beeline for Lazy Lagoon.

Another resort with comfy rooms but a totally inappropriate atmosphere is the **Livingstone Club** (✆ **023/244-0059;** www.livingstone.co.tz), which is the best of a generally awful cluster of beachfront hotels to the north of town. Again, this feels like a once-decent hotel that's gradually gone downhill despite some interesting architecture, amazing tropical gardens, and fair rooms (which are far better than the standard units at the Sea Breeze, and marginally cheaper).

Owned by the same people as the Sea Breeze (who, it turns out, are politically connected at the highest possible level) is Bagamoyo's first heritage property, the **Millennium Old Post Office Hotel** (same contacts), which has six vaguely characterful, comfortable bedrooms above the town's original German-built post office (which is now the bar and hotel reception area), right in the center of the old stone town. Accommodations are superficially appealing, and there's some attempt to keep with the heritage theme (despite the wall-mounted plasma TVs, ugly minifridge, and ill-fitting tile floors), but there's no attention to detail (no bedside reading lights), with sparse decor and cheap finishes. Worse still, the owners have built a new concrete block with two dozen more rooms right next door. They're planning a nightclub in the basement and currently pride themselves on having Bagamoyo's most advanced kitchen appliances. Their website cheekily claims that this is a five-star hotel—it's not, and there's no beach access, either (lots of potential noise, though). By all accounts, you'll be far happier in one of the simple, light-filled beach cottages at **Travellers Lodge** (✆ **023/244-0077** or 075/485-5485; www.travellers-lodge.com). They're all en suite, air-conditioned, and set in a vast beachfront garden—at $80 double (including breakfast), they're definitely the best deal in town, with sufficient space to escape the conference crowd, should one turn up.

USHONGO & PANGANI

Ushongo is 377km (234 miles) N of Dar es Salaam and 66km (41 miles) S of Tanga

A near-uninterrupted swath of virgin beach stretches north of Bagamoyo for nearly 322km (200 miles). Sometimes referred to as the Pangani Coast, it's the type of unspoiled, awe-inducing coastline that finds itself on lists declaiming the world's top-secret beaches. If ever there was a place to rediscover the art of doing nothing, this must be it. And along this stretch, it's **Ushongo Beach**—around 17km (11 miles) south of the

Where Bush Meets Beach: Saadani National Park

With hardly a coconut tree in sight, **Saadani Safari Lodge ★★★ (© 022/277-3294;** www.saadanilodge.com) is one of East Africa's finest bush hideaways, with the added enchantment of a spectacular—and, in all other respects, tropical—beach. This world-class retreat is situated within Tanzania's youngest wildlife preserve, **Saadani National Park,** a 1,150-sq.-km (449-sq.-mile) wilderness that's distinct from any other part of East Africa, thanks to its special confluence of habitats. Hippos and crocodiles cruise the Wami River right near the open sea, elephants have been spotted ambling along the beach, and dolphins and endangered turtles swim just offshore. In and around Saadani village, not too far from the lodge, ruins of stone houses, the old German Boma, and a few gravesites bear witness to a time when the area was firmly in the grasp of international trade—first in slaves and ivory, and later in all manner of crops desired by European overlords. There's a bit of something for all tastes here—snorkel around a tidal sand island, gawk at abundant birdlife, wait in anticipation at turtle nesting sites, or visit a thoroughly untouristy Maasai community. Shabby chic in design, the lodge melds seamlessly with nature; spread out for privacy, there are 15 elegant thatched-and-tented cottages with wood floors and sailcloth ceilings. Just because you're practically on the beach doesn't mean you have to forgo modern conveniences—there are attached bathrooms with solar-heated water, plush beds, and canopied mosquito nets. A game reserve since 1969, Saadani was officially protected only in 2005 and incorporates several distinct ecosystems. Besides the Wami River, Saadani encompasses the Zaraninge Forest, one of the very last bits of coastal forest in Tanzania, and the acacia woodland rubs shoulders with mangroves, meaning that there's diverse and interesting birding. The park itself may not be as high on the list of priorities among East African reserves as, say, Selous or the Masai Mara, but its relative obscurity means that you're likely to have a more intimate, personal interaction with the wildlife (not to mention the beach). Yes, game drives are possible, of course, as are walking

old Arab slaving town of Pangani—that is possibly the most seductive place to find yourself barefoot under a thatched umbrella. Ushongo itself is a traditional Swahili fishing village, its people little affected by tourism; theirs is a way of life apparently governed by the tides, their community spilling right out of their palm-leaf houses and onto the shore. With no riptides, no sharks, and no strong currents, the sea here is perfect for swimming. And while Crusoe-types will need no more reason to come other than the epic palm-backed seashore that spreads in either direction, there's more inspiration just offshore, in the series of reefs that protect Ushongo Bay. The **Maziwe Island Marine Reserve** is an awesome, little-known scuba-diving site, its reef bustling with multihued fish, and smaller **Fungu Island** nearer the shore provides fine snorkeling.

Pangani is considered one of the most alluring towns along Tanzania's coast—a languid and surprisingly little-developed example of Swahili coastal culture infused with glimmers of Arab and Euro-colonial history. Although its precise history is garbled, to the point that's it's not even certain who established the town (or when) in the first place, safaris and fly-camping, but Saadani is not really a first choice if game tracking is your priority (in fact, sightings are dismal compared to the vast open plains of the inland parks)—you'll probably just be happy to station yourself in the hide overlooking the waterhole behind the lodge and let the animals come to you. When the beasts do turn up, the scene has the power to transfix you—if you can't pull yourself away, staff will even provide sundowners, a magical way to toast your time in Africa. Arrange your reservation immediately by calling ✆ **071/355-5678,** or e-mail reservations@saadanilodge.com. A night here costs $720 to $920 double, including all meals, park and concession fees, local transfers, laundry, taxes, guide services, and a number of in-house activities. A night in the honeymoon suite is $1,400.

If that strikes you as too costly, another blissful option is **Tent With A View** ★★ (www.saadani.com), where the full-board rate starts at $390 double, including local airstrip transfers. Situated just outside the National Park (so you pay park fees only when you go on game drives), the lodge bumps up against a stunning driftwood-strewn beach. You can cruise through the mangroves in a canoe and spend sunset in the treehouse, listening and watching as the light fades. The "tents" in question have permanent wood frames and are extremely comfortable and neatly turned out. While there's hardly a soul for miles in either direction, you are likely to spot monkeys, civet cats, and bush babies right from your dinner table.

Charter flights take 15 minutes from Zanzibar and 30 minutes from Dar es Salaam into Saadani airstrip. By road, you're looking at around 4½ hours from Dar (via Chalinze and Mandera) and approximately 7 hours from Arusha. Typically, transfers to Saadani Safari Lodge from Dar cost $300 one-way (or $400 return) in a 4×4, but you can also arrange to be brought here by boat from either Bagamoyo or Pangani/Ushongo, and there are a number of scheduled flights and air taxi services available.

it's said to date back more than 1,000 years and to have long been a significant stop on the East African dhow route established by Arab traders. More modest accounts peg its origins to the 15th century. In any case, it grew into a prosperous port connecting the inland caravan route from Lake Tanganyika to the sea; ivory and slaves left from here, while missionaries and explorers arrived here to begin their journeys inland. It's worth having a guide with you if you intend to explore the town. The oldest building is the Old Boma (1810), built as the home of a well-to-do Omani trader who had slaves buried alive in the foundations, supposedly in order to strengthen them. Although the building was greatly modified by the Germans, it retains its original, handsomely carved wood doors. North of Pangani, about midway to Tanga, are the remains of a medieval Swahili town, known today as the **Tongoni Ruins.** If you've a specific interest in archaeological sites, you might want to take a look at the graveyard here—many of the fallen pillars are elaborately decorated.

About 1½ hours north of Pangani, **Tanga** is the second-biggest urban area along the Tanzanian coast, and although it was once a thriving port town, nowadays it feels half-asleep. All things considered, it's not a bad place, but there's really very little reason to visit and certainly holds nothing that should tear you away from your beach break. You may, however, find yourself in transit here before transferring on to Ushongo, Arusha, Pemba, or Zanzibar. Built on a natural harbor, the town revolves around industry rather than leisure, and there are no beaches here to compete with the magnificent one at Ushongo. You can, however, swim at the beach on the little island of **Toten,** which lies within the harbor—for a chance to experience a bit of local color, see if you can strike a deal with one of Tanga's fisherman to get you there and back on a traditional sail-driven boat. A walk around the island, picking through the ruined mosques, will swallow a couple of hours, after which you may want to stretch out on the beach along the **Raz Kazone Peninsula,** which is Tanga's upmarket neighborhood and the setting for the bulk of its expatriate activities (and where you'll find the most upmarket hotel in town; see below). A popular outing—although certainly not for anyone without a specific interest—is a visit to the **Amboni Caves.** Packed with outlandish tales (some of them true) about how they've served as a hideout for gangsters and are a habitat for all kinds of wild animals, the limestone caves feature the requisite stalactites, stalagmites, and bats, as well as some unusual crystal formations. One chamber serves as a sort of pilgrimage site and is known as the *Mzimuni,* or "spirit chamber," where local villagers offer gifts to the ancestors and people from all across East Africa come to ask for help. Local guides also like to tell visitors that certain passages from the caves lead to Nairobi, Mombasa, and Kilimanjaro, but the jury is definitely out on that one.

Getting There & Around

It's possible to drive from Dar (460km/285 miles) or Moshi (360km/223 miles) to Tanga (from where it's a farther 51km/32 miles along a bumpy dirt road to reach Pangani). You need to know, however, that the journey from Dar is pretty grueling and will eat into your leisure time considerably. There are daily flights from Dar, Arusha, and Zanzibar to both Tanga and Mashado (The Tides' private airstrip at Ushongo/Pangani); flights cost between $111 and $396 and are with either **Coastal Aviation** (**© 071/337-6268** or 078/481-0608; www.coastal.cc), **Regional Air** (**© 075/428-5754** and 027/250-4164; ww.regionaltanzania.com), or **Safari Airlink** (**© 077/772-3274** and 077/372-3274; www.safariaviation.info), depending on your points of departure and arrival. Transfers to Ushongo from the Mashado airstrip will be arranged by your lodge; they'll similarly organize any transfers from Tanga (around $125 per vehicle or $55 per person) if you make prior arrangements, or you can hire a taxi at the airport (make sure it's a very sturdy-looking, preferably off-road vehicle, since the road is a shocker). Note that a **public ferry** (for passengers and vehicles) is the only way of crossing the river at the southern edge of Pangani. If you're catching a taxi from Tanga to Pangani, you should probably hop out at the ferry and cross over as a pedestrian, having arranged to be picked up on the other side for the remaining 25-minute drive to Ushongo.

A far more memorable way to arrive at Ushongo (or at Mkomo Bay, just north of Pangani) is by **boat,** providing you're commencing from a point with boat launch capacity (such as Saadani Safari Lodge or Bagamoyo). The romantics' choice would probably be to catch a dhow from Zanzibar (a trip that you can also make in reverse, of course). You can usually arrange boat transfers when booking your accommodation, but be aware that boats must inevitably time their activities with the tide.

Moments **Swim with the Fishes, Dive with the Turtles, See Life Begin . . .**

With none of the frenetic activity found at better-known and more developed beach resorts, Ushongo has proven to be one of Tanzania's hugely successful rehabilitated **turtle nesting sites.** The cutting down of trees on nearby Maziwe Island has rendered it unsuitable for turtle nesting—without the trees, it's reverted to being a tidal sand bank covered by water at high tide, so any eggs buried under the sand rot before they have a chance to reach maturity. As part of a coast-wide program to protect the endangered turtles, conservation group Sea Sense relocates eggs laid on the island to reconstructed, properly protected nesting sites along the mainland beach. Several of these nests are under the watchful eye of **Kasa Divers** (www.kasadivers.com), a small, conservation-minded operation that runs dive courses, rents gear, and helps promote turtle awareness by inviting locals and visitors to watch carefully monitored hatchings.

Witnessing the turtles emerge from beneath the sand after 55 days of incubation is a rather extraordinary opportunity. During her lifetime, a female turtle lays around 7,000 eggs, yet only one in a thousand will live its full 60- to 80-year lifespan. The hatching phase is just one breathtaking hurdle in a series of unimaginably tough adventures that will determine whether a particular baby turtle will make it. Around 120 to 170 turtle eggs are laid at a time, and the eggs are deep enough that when they emerge from their shells, the hatchlings will take another 2 to 3 days before reaching the surface. Once they pop out through the sand, they instinctively head toward the water, crawling at—considering their miniscule size—breakneck speed to avoid predation by birds and reptiles. It's during this brief, momentous race to the sea that the turtles gather sensory information that will, by some profound mystery of nature, enable the females to return, some 30 years later, to the exact same beach to lay their eggs.

Of the seven marine turtle species found worldwide, five are found off the Tanzanian coast, and only the green and hawksbill turtles nest here. If you are told about a **turtle hatching** ★★★ at Kasa Divers, make sure you turn up to witness what is surely one of life's special miracles, an experience that's greatly enhanced here by the interest shown by the children from the local village. And, once you've seen the last of the tiny hatchlings off on their epic voyage, you can sign up with Kasa for some of Tanzania's best diving and a chance to swim among the very turtles that are so desperately in need of protection. They charge $80 per dive (plus $12 in park and community fees), or $470 for a 10-dive package.

Where to Stay & Dine

Ushongo

If The Tides (reviewed below) is beyond your means, take a look at nearby **Emayani Beach Lodge** ★ (✆ **027/264-0755** or 078/430-5797; www.emayanilodge.com), a simple and laid-back collection of 12 spacious *makuti*-topped *bandas* spread along the beach amid the coco palms. *Makuti* is used extensively in half the cottages—the floors, the walls, and roll-down "windows" are all created from interwoven palm leaves, and the resulting rusticity is quite charming. In fact, there's massive emphasis on using renewable local materials in the construction, and it's just about only the bathrooms (Western in style and with solar-heated water) where you'll see some concrete. Beds are large, linens white, furnishings more than adequate, and the sense of freedom to relax infinite. If you're here primarily to dive, this will be your first choice; at $160 double, including two meals a day, it's a very decent value, and the dive school is right on your doorstep. The same young Dutch couple who own and run Emayani also have the nearby **Tulia Beach Lodge** (✆ **027/264-0680** or 027/250-1741; www.tuliabeachlodge.com), which isn't quite as smart but has much the same facilities and comes in at $110 double (with breakfast and dinner).

The Tides ★★★ Value If there's one beach hideaway worth the effort of journeying this far up the Tanzanian coast, this is it. Spaced out between the coco palms and sufficiently distant from one another to ensure privacy, the handsome, high-ceiling *bandas* are big, simple, and unfettered by needless tat. Done with lots of natural fibers and shuttered windows with drapes to match the whitewashed walls, they're right near the beach and dominated by large, firm beds and gigantic mosquito nets. Step out of your cottage, and it's a few steps down a sand path to reach a pair of beachbeds beneath your very own thatched umbrella. Spend part of your day here and the rest of it swimming, snorkeling, or walking for miles in either direction along the beach. While there's all the solitude and peace you could hope for, if you want a bit of action or company, pull up a stool at the sociable little bar, laid out with plenty of cozy, cushioned nooks where you can lie back as the cocktails are shaken and cold beers dispensed. At night, after a well-prepared meal, you'll be surprised how loud the ocean can be as it dutifully lulls you to sleep.

Ushongo Beach, P.O. Box 46, Pangani. ✆ **078/422-5812** or 071/332-5812. www.thetideslodge.com. Reservations (in the U.K.): ✆ **1869/34-0887.** 11 units, none with tubs. $330 beach cottage double; $375 honeymoon suite; $550 family house (4 people); $65 extra bed. Children 6–12 pay $49, under 6 $20. Rates include all meals and taxes. All-inclusive and half-board rates available. MC, V (6% surcharge). **Amenities:** Restaurant; bar; airport transfers (local airstrip $5 per person; from Tanga $125 per vehicle); bikes; pool. *In room:* No phone.

Pangani

There are no recommendable accommodations in Pangani itself, but some 4km (2½ miles) north of the town (or 45km/28 miles south of Tanga) is the lovely **Mkoma Bay ★** (✆ **078/643-4001** or 027/263-0000; www.mkomabay.com), where efforts have been made to capture the mood of a bush safari (there are seven thatch-covered luxury en suite tents set among the trees; $180–$190 double, with breakfast and dinner), but with all the benefits of being at the coast, including direct access to the beach, a pool, and the usual water activities, such as diving and snorkeling off Maziwe Island. There's also a big four-bedroom, Swahili-style house that caters well to families ($75–$90 per person, half board) and a few budget bungalows ($105 double).

Tanga

If for some reason you find yourself stuck in Tanga and are forced to overnight there, there's only one viable option: **Mkonge Hotel** (✆ **027/264-2440** or 075/324-8611; www.mkongehotel.com). The saving grace here is the sense of space and relative tranquillity once you step out onto the vast manicured lawn that spreads from the hotel toward the edge of the harbor. Sadly, they've put a huge ugly fence right in front of the view, but there's still a decent, slightly old-world atmosphere as you sip your evening gin and tonic while listening to the call to prayer from the nearby mosque. At $75 to $80 double (with breakfast), accommodations are merely adequate—parquet floors, king-size beds, a TV, and a tiny balcony—but be prepared for mosquitoes (I found lots of them hovering in the room), painfully cramped bathrooms, and indifferent staff.

You might also want to skip the restaurant at Mkonge and instead go across the road for Tanga's best dining experience at **Pizzeria D'Amore Restaurant & Bar** ★ (✆ **078/439-5391** or 071/539-5391; Tues–Sun 11:30am–2pm and 6:30–11pm; main courses Tsh7,500–Tsh20,000), which serves wood-fired pizza as well as other comfort foods—pasta, prawn curry and rice, succulent chicken, stuffed squid, and grilled jumbo prawns—in a relaxed garden setting. The vivacious owner, Jenny Graber, who came to Tanga from Mozambique, regularly puts together special menus and goes out of her way to charm her guests, who turn out to be a crazy mix of locals, expatriates, travelers, and NGO workers.

13

Zanzibar

By Pippa de Bruyn

Zanzibar. Just saying it sounds like a warm breeze on a powder-soft beach. And the island is as it sounds: blessed with a warm, sultry climate; beaches with sand so soft in parts it feels like walking on flour; and reefs so rich with coral and tropical fish you feel as if you're swimming in a giant aquarium. Comprising two large islands fringed by many more, the archipelago vies with the Serengeti as Tanzania's most precious natural asset, able to mesmerize the most jaded traveler into meditative contemplation.

Apart from its beaches, which reach deep into the ocean, turning the shoreline into unreal shades of turquoise blue, Zanzibar offers island-hoppers a uniquely East African flavor. From the tall traditionally garbed Maasai striding across the beach (here, in sunglasses) and Swahili and Indian traders in long *salwar kameez* and embroidered skull caps, to the women harvesting seaweed, their bodies and heads chastely wrapped in colorful *kangas,* the blend of cultures is as identifiable as the cuisine. Zanzibar kitchens produce delicious flavors, a combination of Arabic and Indian influences that showcase the islands' abundance of coconut milk, freshly ground spices, and even fresher seafood.

A warm, hospitable people, the phrase you will hear most often—after the typical East African greeting of *Jambo, karibu* (Hello, welcome)—is *Pole pole!* (Slowly, slowly!). Haste and stress is so unusual that when the Zanzibari witness it in travelers, they do so with an incredulous air of concern. It is incomprehensible to them that you are on holiday with your Blackberry and expect to remain in touch, or that you should care so deeply when your breakfast order is misheard. What do these matter when you are in paradise?

Comprising two large islands, Unguja (commonly referred to as Zanzibar) and Pemba, the archipelago's strong draw is Stone Town, center of the East Coast trade during the 19th century and the best-preserved trade center of its type in Africa. For many, Stone Town is the heart of Swahili culture, home to *taraab* music and spicy tea, a labyrinth of narrow streets lined with tall crumbling buildings, minarets that resound with the sonorous call to prayer, and carved doorways through which a lifestyle unchanged for centuries can be glimpsed. While it is a popular tourist destination, Stone Town is no sanitized historical re-creation, but an inhabited sprawl, and refuse and rubble are as real as the inhabitants who scurry along, getting on with the business of daily life and, for the most part, paying little heed to the influx of tourists.

Like Lamu and Mafia, Zanzibar's beaches offer the perfect reprieve from the excitement and thrill of tracking the Big 5 on bone-jarring roads on the mainland. Here you'll find wild life drifting on the tide, a magical world unfurling beneath you; take walks on beaches as pristine as when the sultan set foot on them almost 200 years ago; and be lulled to sleep by the

Fun Facts **What's in a Name?**

Zinj ib-Bar means Land of Blacks in Arabic and probably alludes to the dark and pivotal role the island played in the 19th-century slave trade, traces of which can still be found in historical Stone Town.

rhythmic lapping of the ocean. Others come to Zanzibar or Pemba as a single destination, spending 2 weeks unwinding on the beach, mastering nothing but the instinctive urge to keep picking up their camera to capture yet another image of white sands lapped by teal-green waters and fishermen unfurling their triangle-shape sails as the dawn parade of dhows drifts across the reef. Whatever you decide, you'll leave *pole pole.*

STRATEGIES FOR SEEING THE REGION

Fringed with sandy beaches and rocky inlets, the main island of Zanzibar (Unguja) is about 97km (60 miles) in length and no than 32km (20 miles) wide, making it a very manageable size to explore. UNESCO–protected Stone Town, the capital, will be your point of entry; with any beach on the main island 45 to 90 minutes from the airport, you can choose to head straight to your beach lodgings from the airport (or sea port, if you have arrived by ferry). However, if you have an interest in the history of the island or simply want to shop for souvenirs, set aside a day or two to soak up the atmosphere of Stone Town, preferably after your safari (when a bit of history and culture wouldn't be remiss) and before your beach sojourn (after which you are likely to be blissed out by gorgeous horizons and find Stone Town's labyrinthine streets claustrophobic and dirty). Alternatively, visit Stone Town as a half-day trip from your beach resort, unless you've opted to stay on the nearby island of Pemba, in which case you will need to schedule a night in Stone Town.

With regard to choosing your beach location, most settle into one resort and stay there for the duration. However, if you are here for more than a week, consider combining a stay in either the south or the east with a few days in the north. When choosing where you wish to settle, bear in mind that the south has the least-developed coastline (other than the west, where there are very few beaches) and offers proximity to Jozani, the last remaining indigenous forest on Zanzibar, as well as the best opportunity to swim with the bottlenose and humpback dolphins of Kizimkazi. Broken into the southeast and east in "Where to Stay" (p. 362; the routes there are different though they are similar in atmosphere), the east coast has what is generally considered to be the most beautiful beaches on the island, lined with palm trees and a string of sprawling resorts and more intimate, rustic-style boutique choices. The north coast has its fair share of beautiful coastline concentrated around cosmopolitan Nungwi, which has two intimate and exclusive resorts, as well as a string of budget accommodation choices and backpacker-type travelers providing color and bustle to the beaches. Aside from the northeast, Nungwi is closest to Mnemba Atoll, generally considered the best diving and snorkeling area in Zanzibar, for which the Mnemba Island Lodge is, of course, the most ideally positioned, with Matemwe Bungalows the second choice.

1 STONE TOWN ★★

By far the largest settlement on the island, Stone Town is unlike any other African capital. Strung along a widget of the coast, the history and atmosphere of the old city surrounding the port, declared a UNESCO site in 2000, is tangible, its town planning almost medieval: a labyrinth of narrow winding lanes lined with tall crumbling buildings and virtually identical peeling facades guaranteed to confuse and disorientate. Wandering ever deeper, looking skyward for a minaret, spire, or any other recognizable landmark, you could as easily turn a corner and be dazzled by the sparkling ocean as find yourself in a courtyard, halted by the rhythmic drone of local schoolchildren intoning the Koran. African men in long dresses stride past women draped in black, their faces hidden but talking into cellphones as gold as their sandals and the embroidery on their sleeves. On the seashore, bare-backed men sweat beneath huge bags of spices as they load them onto the waiting boats, while holidaymakers sit with their feet in the sand drinking cocktails or listen to *taraab* musicians sing songs of lost love at the Serena, an aromatic meal on their plate.

Merchant traders from India, Arabia, Persia, China, Japan, and Russia have roamed the shoreline for centuries, but it was only during the 11th century that the first permanent structure, a mosque, was built at Kizimkazi in the south. After taking control of this small trading outpost, the Portuguese (who, thanks to Vasco da Gama and his crew, the first Europeans to circumnavigate Africa, ruled the entire east coast with impunity during the 16th and 17th centuries) moved the main harbor to the bay now overlooked by Stone Town. The only remnants of this era are the rather insignificant-looking archway you will see on your right as you approach old Stone Town and the cannons that guard the entrance to the House of Wonders.

Sultan Seif bin Sultan, imam of Oman, liberated Zanzibar from the Portuguese "tyranny and extortion" in 1698, but the real impact of this was felt more than a century later when the then-ruler of Oman, the pragmatic Sultan Seyyid Said, saw the obvious benefits of moving his court from the hostile and desert-harsh environment of Muscat to the benign island of Zanzibar. Not only would this position him much closer to his business interests, the slave and ivory trade, just 40km (25 miles) away on the mainland, but Zanzibar also provided the sultanate with hectares of fertile soil. Keen to promote trade with India, with its riches in cloth, jewelry, and arms, Seyyid Said invited Indian merchants from Gujarat to settle here and embarked on an ambitious clove-planting project, threatening his local subjects with eviction if they did not plant two clove trees for every existing coconut palm. At the same time, he controlled the mainland slave trade; all slaves "harvested" on the mainland had to pass through the island where a tax was extorted, turning Zanzibar into the largest slave-trading center on the East African coast.

The move to Zanzibar was astute, and as the sultanate became wealthier and the economy expanded nearly five-fold, the stone buildings housing his expansive family and the avaricious traders it attracted spread north and east of the harbor. Seyyid Said himself built two large palaces, one in Stone Town and another a few kilometers north at Mtoni (the ruins of the latter still stand), where his principal wife was said to hold court over a household of 1,000. But it was his successor, the extravagant Barghash, who despite his brief rule (1870–88) was to be Stone Town's most prolific builder, of which the most ostentatious relic is Beit el Ajaib, the House of Wonders, so called because it was the largest and tallest building in Zanzibar and the first to have electric lights and an electric lift.

Aside from the traders, the wealth generated by the sultanate attracted Indian artisans who arrived to decorate, carve, and stitch for their Arab patrons, as well as moneylenders attracted by the abundance of spice and ivory. The Indians left an indelible mark on the architectural fabric of Stone Town, as did the later arrival of the English and German colonialists, though the latter's effect was, in many cases, a synthesis of the city's existing design ethos. The colonialists approach to power rather than architecture was less subtle.

From the outset, the sultanate welcomed the colonial trading partners with a diplomacy born of necessity, but during the last 15 years of the 19th century, the colonialists appropriated most of the empire of Zanzibar for themselves. By the time Khalifa Bin Harab took over in 1911, the sultan was a constitutional monarch without powers, and

Salme: Zanzibar's Famous Princess

Memoirs of an Arabian Princess is a fascinating account written by Princess Salme of her life in the royal court of Zanzibar in the 1800s.

Women in the royal court of Oman and Zanzibar were not taught to read or write, but Salme taught herself and, as a result, was able to provide the most telling, albeit biased, insights into the practical aspects of life on the island, as well as the political intrigue of the day. The progeny of Sultan Seyyid Barghash and, according to her, one of his most beautiful concubines, Salme grew up in Mtoni Palace and later in a house in Stone Town, and was very close to her brother, Majid, the heir apparent, until she fell prey to the in-house maneuvering of the ambitious Barghash and betrayed Majid. When she repented, Barghash never fully trusted Salme again, and she made a break for a new life after falling in love with a German merchant, eloping, converting to Christianity, and taking a new name, Emily Reute. Tragically, her husband was killed in a tram accident a few years later, and Reute was left in a foreign country with two small children to raise. She longed to return to Zanzibar, but aside from a brief visit, her soured relations with Barghash and the political expediency of her quest left her in exile. The book is widely available on the island. While the insights into life of a Zanzibari princess at the close of the 19th century are intriguing, it's worth noting that Reute's opinions would today be described as somewhat bigoted.

by the 1920s, Zanzibar was an established British protectorate, which it would remain for the next 4 decades until it made a successful bid for independence in 1964.

Despite its UNESCO–protected heritage status, Stone Town is home to a real community, where locals live, work, and worship, indifferent to tourist trade. If you are expecting pristine streets and well-maintained buildings, you will be disappointed. Many historical buildings are crumbling, rotting refuse collects in corners, and the locals are unapologetic about their desire to get on with their lives without interference (and generally do not like to be photographed while doing so). Certainly, it is not a beach destination—though there are beach bars, the culture is conservative, and women are discouraged from dressing scantily—and, because it's also a bustling port, is not conducive to sunbathing and swimming. However, you could easily base yourself at one of the beach resorts located a mere 10 to 15 minutes north or south of the center.

Stone Town offers a totally different experience from the rest of Zanzibar and is ideal as an overnight stop only if, after experiencing a large dose of the wilderness on the mainland, you are ready to immerse yourself in an African destination that offers history and culture, not to mention a fair bit of shopping.

ESSENTIALS

GETTING THERE **By Plane** Zanzibar airport is connected to every major tourist destination on the mainland via scheduled twin-engine flights, though travelers in Tanzania will have to stop (and probably overnight) in Dar es Salaam or Arusha, both a short hop (20/30 min. and 60/90 min., respectively) from the main island of Zanzibar (Unguja). The principal carrier from Kenya to Zanzibar is Kenya Airways, with a transit stop in Nairobi; note that you will need $50 in cash upon arrival for your Tanzanian visa.

Other international carriers all stop in Dar es Salaam; direct international flights to Zanzibar are rare. 1Time (www.1time.co.za), the South African budget airline, flies direct from Johannesburg to Zanzibar twice weekly. During peak season, plenty of charter flights fly direct from Italy, but these are not scheduled. At any rate, facilities are so rudimentary that any international arrival turns the tiny airport into bedlam; best to get here utilizing one of the domestic airlines, the most established being Precision Air, ZanAir, and Coastal Air. If you're flying from Arusha to Zanzibar, newcomer Tanganyika Flying Company (www.tanflyco.com) offers the best experience but is the most expensive; they also do not fly Dar to Zanzibar. Coastal Air (www.coastal.cc), generally considered the most reliable of the remaining airlines listed, is your next port of call. It's worth comparing prices among all the airlines, but at press time, a one-way ticket between Dar and Zanzibar cost around $80, while a one-way "direct" ticket between Dar and Pemba cost around $120. If you choose to overnight in Stone Town, you'll spend $180 (Dar to Zanzibar $80, plus Zanzibar to Pemba $100). ***Tip:*** When departing Zanzibar, make sure that your departure airport tax of $50 is included in your airline ticket, or simply keep dollars handy, as this must be paid in cash if not included.

By Ferry There are several sea ferry companies that ply the waters between Zanzibar and Dar es Salaam daily, the largest and most efficient being Azam Marine (www.azammarine.com), which operates two daily runs with **Sea Bus.** Sea Bus takes around 90 minutes and departs daily from Dar es Salaam at 2 and 4pm (departing Zanzibar at 10am and 1pm). Economy-class tickets cost $35; first class (which is not hugely different to economy) costs $40: this must be paid in dollars, pounds, or euros. You can pay for your ticket online, which is the most cost-effective way to do so. If you wait to purchase your ticket in Dar (or Zanzibar), make sure you do so a day in advance (particularly in peak season), and don't buy tickets from street hawkers. Other reputable ferries crossing in more or less the same time are **Sea Star** (**© 024/223-4768**) and **Sea Express** (**© 024/223-3002**). **Sepideh** is also pretty reliable but takes a little longer. It's not worth booking Flying Horse or Aziza; while cheaper, you will need to spend the night on board. Note that all foreigners are required to carry their passports when traveling between the islands and mainland Tanzania.

Getting to Pemba from Zanzibar will take around 90 minutes and costs around $40. While the ferries between Dar es Salaam and Zanzibar run like clockwork, the ferry run between Pemba and Zanzibar relies on a more fair-weather approach. Ferry trips are not daily, and the schedule can change at short notice, depending on demand. Unless you have time on your hands and a flexible schedule, fly.

GETTING AROUND Getting from the airport to Stone Town (only around 10km/6¼ miles away) is pretty straightforward, as there are plenty of taxis outside; the trip will cost around Tsh10,000. If you prefer a better-looking vehicle, book a transfer with one of the recommended island operators (below) or ask your hotel to arrange a transfer. Hotels charge around $20 for airport transfers to Stone Town and around $70 for an airport transfer to the east or north coast.

If you're going to a hotel in the old part of Stone Town, note that your taxi may not be able to drop you off directly outside your hotel, as the narrow lanes make it accessible to pedestrians only; be sure to have a tip handy for your driver, who will help carry your luggage to your hotel. Once you are in Stone Town, you will not need taxis. All the sights are within walking distance of the recommended hotels; if you opt for a beachfront hotel some minutes north or south of town, make sure they include a free shuttle into town (most do).

Getting around the island is pretty straightforward; your resort will arrange your transfer direct from the airport or from your hotel. If you are the adventurous type and fancy exploring the island on your own, you can hire a jeep; the starting price is around $35 to $40 a day, with no fuel. A tank of fuel will get you around the island and will cost around Tsh60,000. You will need an international driver's license. Alternatively, hire your car through **Mohammed at Suna Tours** (© **077/741-8323;** see "Organized Tours" for more information).

WHEN TO GO Located around 6 degrees south of equator, with an average 7 to 8 hours of sunshine daily, Zanzibar is a pretty sure beach bet. That said, it can get very hot and uncomfortably humid during the peak season (Dec–Feb); make sure you book a resort along the east or north coast, which is cooled by pleasant sea breezes. The so-called rainy season is April to May; sometimes June can be rather wet, too. Showers continue to fall year-round but never last long.

FESTIVALS Ramadan, the most holy month in the Muslim calendar (when Muslims refrain from drinking, eating, smoking, and displays of affection to remind themselves what life is like for those less fortunate), affects tourists, in that everyone is expected to follow suit in public, and some of the restaurants and bars that are open to the street (or managed by Muslims) close down. Its onset and duration depends on the moon but generally runs from the end of August to September. Eid el Fitr marks the end of Ramadan, and a hugely festive atmosphere prevails everywhere, with everyone in a party mood, feasting and giving gifts, and the streets filled with kohl-eyed girls in sparkly new dresses. The Eid celebrations last for 4 days and are best experienced in Stone Town, either at the Mnazi Moja grounds across from the National Museum or at the Kariakoo fair grounds near the main post office.

EVENTS One of the most exciting events in Africa takes place during the first 2 weeks of July when Zanzibar hosts the ZIFF Festival of the Dhow Countries, encompassing the African continent, the Gulf States, Iran, India, Pakistan, and the islands of the Indian Ocean. It's a showcase for filmmakers (it's the second-biggest film festival in Africa), dancers, performers, and musicians (see "Calendar of Events" on p. 26). If you are interested in Zanzibari music, plan your visit for February, when the Swahili music and culture festival Sauti Ya Busara (Sounds of Wisdom), a 3-day cultural extravaganza of music, theater, and dance, is held.

ORGANIZED TOURS While the Zanzibar Association of Tourism Investors and Commission for Tourism have clubbed together to produce a good general-info website (www.zanzibartourism.net), there is no independent tourist bureau in Zanzibar itself, so be aware that any signs asserting as such are actually tour operators. For general information about Zanzibar history, take a look at www.zanzibarhistory.org, an independent site that isn't trying to flog anything. The following operators are all highly recommended.

The upmarket operator **Gallery Tours & Safari** (© **024/223-2088;** www.gallerytours.net) is a little more expensive but an excellent choice. Founder and managing director Javed Jafferji is very passionate about Zanzibar and, for years, has captured its beauty and intrigue in his photographs; just about every coffee-table book celebrating the island has his name on the cover. Gallery has handpicked staff offering slick service and a large range of tours, from the obvious to the more specialist (the Freddy Mercury Tour follows the boyhood experiences of the Queen lead singer, born in the heart of Stone Town). They also arrange very romantic weddings. If you're looking for a reliable operator who offers the best price-to-value ratio for his services, look no further than Mohammed at **Suna Tours.** If you want to self-drive, Mohammed can also arrange a 4WD vehicle, as well as a driver's permit ($10) if you don't have an international driver's license (this is likely to be cheaper than arranging the latter at home). Call Mohammed at © **0777/41-8323,** or find him at the south end of Forodhani Gardens. **Island Express** (© **024/223-4375** or 077/43-5866; www.zanzibarsafaris.com) is a reliable operator with excellent guides and a fleet of efficient vehicles offering the standard range of tours. **Zanzibar Unique** (www.zanzibarunique.com) is another top-notch operator that is highly recommended for their staff and vehicles.

WHAT TO SEE & DO

The only way to explore historical Stone Town is on foot, windowing through narrow lanes lined with three-story buildings, the majority of them built in the 1800s when Zanzibar was the most important trading center along the east coast of Africa. It's a relatively small area and rather pleasurable to simply wander around getting lost: This way, you get to see the unexpected, and locals are almost always willing to point you in the right direction (ask for your hotel or the seafront). Should you prefer a more organized approach, book a guide, or vaguely follow the walking tour below.

WALKING TOUR: STONE TOWN

Note that you can start anywhere on this circular route, depending on where you are staying, but for ease of reference, we start off at:

1 Forodhani Gardens

Located on the seafront and laid out in 1936 to mark the silver jubilee of Sultan Khalifa, the gardens have recently been revamped and are pleasant enough to stroll through. However, they really become one of Stone Town's main attractions in the evenings, as storeholders set up for the **night market,** lighting their fires and lacing fresh seafood onto skewers. This is both the cheapest and most convivial place to pig out on fresh lobster, prawns, fish, and Zanzibari "pizza."

Directly behind the gardens, on Mzingani Street, is the:

2 Old Fort

This is the oldest structure in Stone Town, its dark brown, windowless walls topped by castellated battlements. Built between 1698 and 1701 by Seyyid Said's grandfather into the ruins of a Portuguese chapel, the Old Fort never saw much military action. Today it is home to hawkers selling tourist tat and an open-air theater where evening performers tout for dollars, as well as a private tourism bureau run by the charming "Octopus" (so named because he has a finger in many pies).

Adjoining the fort is the:

3 House of Wonders ★★

This is the most elegant building in Stone Town, with proportions like those of a Southern plantation mansion, its facade broken by tall tiers of pillars and deep balconies, and topped by a grand clock tower. Built in 1883 by Sultan Barghash as a ceremonial palace, it is the most ostentatious of follies and impressed his subjects (aside from its grandiose architecture, it was the first building in Zanzibar to have electric lights and an electric lift), who dubbed it Beit el Ajaib (House of Wonders). Housing the Museum of History and Culture, it is still one of the largest buildings in Zanzibar, and while the displays look somewhat forlorn and more like high school projects, it is well worth a visit if only to familiarize yourself with the tale of Princess Salme, a daughter of Seyyid

Said who eloped with a German merchant in 1866 (p. 340). It contains family photographs and excerpts from her book, as well as a sample of her typical wardrobe. Also, don't miss the interesting exhibition of *kangas,* the traditional cloths the local women wrap around their bodies and heads, with Swahili slogans that are integral to the design; translations range between the amusing and the poignant, such as *Mama nipe kuishi radhi na walu kazi,* translated as "Mother, give me your blessings; living with people is really tough," referring to the practice by which a new wife moves into the homestead of her in-laws.

From the balconies of the House of Wonders, you can look into the rooftops and castellated battlements of the **Palace Museum,** which was built on the site of the first sultan's palace that Seyyid Said erected in 1832. The current building dates back to the late 1890s and housed members of the sultan's family, becoming the official residence of the sultan of Zanzibar from 1911 until the revolution of '64, when it was renamed the Peoples' Palace. It is not really necessary to enter; nothing seems to have been done since it opened as a museum in 1994, with dusty interiors and moth-eaten, haphazardly arranged furnishings doing nothing to evoke the lifestyle of this once powerful dynasty. Both Palace Museum and House of Wonders are open daily 9am to 6pm; entrance $3.

Having passed the Palace Museum, you will continue walking along Mzingani Road, looking out for the massive fig tree, known locally as "Big Tree." Just before this is:

4 Old Customs House

This is where Sultan Hamoud was proclaimed sultan in 1896. Note the solid timber door, one of the oldest in Zanzibar (as you can tell from the shape; the more modern doors are semicircular at the top). Zanzibari doors (also found in Lamu and Mombasa) are a distinctive feature of Stone Town architecture and were coded communication about the status and wealth of the people living behind them. Many of the doors have an Arabic inscription carved into the top frieze (usually from the Koran) and are richly decorated around the frame; the more ornate, the wealthier the inhabitant. Those with gold studs protruding were imported from India, where they were designed to repel the elephants that the Rajput used in battle. An inventory done some 30 years ago recorded 800 historic doors; sadly, this number has been drastically reduced by voracious antique dealers.

TAKE A BREAK
Depending on inclination or time of day, you may want to stop and have a drink at **Mercury's,** diagonally opposite the Old Customs House, one of Stone Town's most popular beachfront bars/restaurants, with great ocean views.

Alternatively, keep walking, looking out for most ornate facade in Stone Town:

5 Stone Town Cultural Centre

This is also known as the Old Dispensary and was originally commissioned by Tharia Topan (see "The Rise of Topan," on p. 348).

From here you leave the beachfront and venture into the heart of Stone Town, crossing it to reach the market. There are literally a hundred routes, but perhaps easiest is to backtrack to the Big Tree and head down Jamatani Road, looking out for signs (or asking) for:

TAKE A BREAK
Zanzibar Coffee House (p. 353), where you can stop for the best coffee in town.

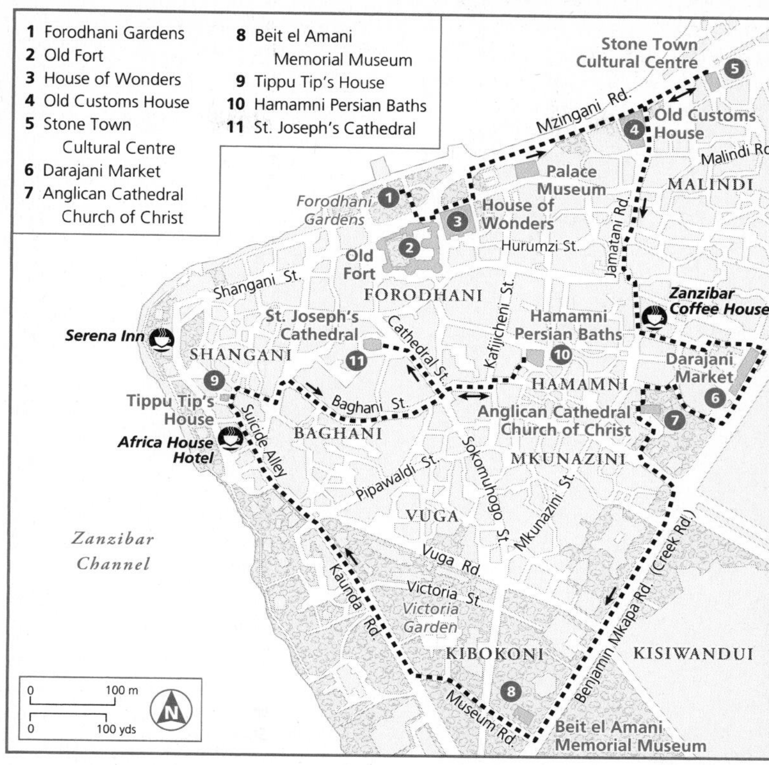

After the relative calm of the coffee house, head to the:

6 Darajani Market

The covered market is quite an assault on the senses, located in a gable-fronted building erected in 1904. There are separate markets for red meat and fish, and dozens of traders selling fruit, vegetables, spices, and grains that spill out onto Creek Road (officially Benjamin Mkapa Rd.); on Wednesday and Saturday, they are joined by antique dealers.

The market is the most vibrant place in Stone Town, bustling from 8am to 6pm (though it quiets down from 2pm) with people who travel from all over the island to trade for a variety that is unrivaled elsewhere in the archipelago. Auctions are held in the morning fish market, and everywhere there is the cacophony of people bargaining, gossiping, and touting their wares. If you are squeamish, try to come first thing in the morning before the smell of fresh meat can turn rank; even then, those with sensitive stomachs are warned to stay away from the red meat section, where the smell of raw meat and the rivulets of blood may turn even hardened carnivores vegetarian. You can always concentrate on purchasing spices (this is a good place to stock up on *masala* tea; spice sellers tend to be concentrated to the east of the main building) or a few brightly colored *kangas* (you'll find them packed out on the ground behind the *dala-dalas* on the left toward Darajani Rd.).

When you're done touring the market, head down Creek Road. A major thoroughfare, usually clogged with traffic, Creek Road denotes the end of the historical quarter and the start of Michenzani (New City), an unattractive sprawl of buildings most tourists will only pass through on their way to the coast. A few minutes' walk down Creek Road (going south from the market), you'll find the:

7 Anglican Cathedral Church of Christ

Built between 1873 and 1883 by the Universities' Mission in Central Africa (UMCA) under the auspices of Edward Steere, third bishop of Zanzibar (1874–82), the church itself is not much to write home about. Its artifacts, however, are a reminder of the most sordid aspects of Zanzibari history, and for many, a visit to the **cellars** ★, beneath the nearby St. Monica's Hostel and said to be where the slaves were kept in holding cells before being sold, are a chillingly worthwhile experience that stands in distinct contrast to the blissfully benign beach experience the island is usually associated with.

Along with missionary-explorer Dr. David Livingstone, another fierce antislavery campaigner, Steere was much resented by the sultanate for the fierce battle he fought against the slave trade, a crusade he finally won in 1877. In celebration and thanks, Steere built this church on what used to be the island's largest slave market, apparently positioning the altar over the exact location of the whipping post. He also had the Cathedral's timber cross carved from a branch that once hung over Livingstone's heart, where it is buried at Chitambo, Zambia. Several other missionaries are remembered on plaques around the cathedral wall.

You can visit the cathedral to pray, but if you are here purely as a tourist, you will have to pay the $5 entry fee, which entitles you to a visit to the cellars, as well as a guide.

After the cathedral, you have two options. If you're interested in an overview of Zanzibari history, continue south down Creek Road for about 400m (1,312 ft.) and look out for:

8 Beit el Amani Memorial Museum ★

Literally "House of Peace," Beit el Amani is a grand colonial-era building designed by J. H. Sinclair, the same architect who designed the island's High Court and a man who was, thankfully, a great fan of traditional Zanzibari architecture, incorporating much of the local style into his own. Inside is a hodge podge of displays relating to the island's history and the figures who shaped it. Along with a collection of the lithographs, maps, and photographs dating from the 19th and early-20th centuries, there are various items belonging to the sultans, slave traders, locals, colonial administrators, missionaries, and many explorers who used the island as a base. Next door is a small natural history museum that is largely missable unless you want to visit the large land tortoises that live outside; it's worth it if you're not doing a trip to Prison Island.

From here you turn right onto Kuanda Road, which becomes Kenyatta Street, one of the main shopping drags. Take the left fork into one of the narrow alleyways (ominously called Suicide Alley) to wander past:

9 Tippu Tip's House

Around 100m (328 ft.) from Serena Inn, this was once the home of a famous slave trader, and though it's a private residence, the current proprietor is often happy to show visitors the interior (which is dirty and in ruin), much to the chagrin of his family living in penury inside.

After this you could:

TAKE A BREAK

Choose to either relax at the large balcony bar of the nearby **Africa House Hotel** or head for one of the wicker chairs at the patio outside the **Serena Inn bar;** both are perfectly positioned to toast the setting sun.

Tips Shopping

The majority of shops in Stone Town are located in the western part of the historical quarter, particularly along Kenyatta Road in Shangani and Gizenga Street behind the Old Fort. Wood carvings, Tinga Tinga paintings, and jewelry abound, with many of the shops appearing to have all purchased their contents from the same Dar es Salaam or Nairobi warehouse. There are exceptions, however. **Zanzibar Curios,** on Gizenga Street (near Old Fort), is a three-story treasure-trove of hidden gems (antique clocks and other *objets* steeped in Zanzibari history); make sure you set aside at least an hour to explore the innards of this shop and ask to see the higher floors. The other discovery, at least for ladies with a sandal fetish, is **Doreen Mashika** (✆ **078/636-9777;** www.doreenmashika.com). Doreen's shoes—perfectly proportioned, elegant, strappy beauties, often incorporating Masaai beadwork—are not exactly cheap, but given that they are real one-off designer items, they are worth every cent. Zanzibari-born Mashika is slowly starting to export to international markets but is as yet a real find; don't miss her shop on Hurumzi Street. If you're shopping for kids, especially girls, it's worth popping into **Upendo** (meaning Love), a funny little shop located next to Coco de Mer, behind NBC Bank. It is a woman's cooperative, and all profits go toward paying salaries and maintaining the sewing school. And yes, the clothing is pretty cool, too (www.upendomeanslove.com). Lastly, if you've fallen in love with the Omani-influenced Zanzibari furniture so ubiquitous to all the hotels in Stone Town, pick up a few hard-wood pieces from **Classic Furniture** in Funguni (✆ **077/741-0695;** near the Noodle Market) and arrange to have them shipped home.

An alternate route after the cathedral will have you cutting across town. You will likely get lost, so ask for directions to the:

⑩ Hamamni Persian Baths ★★

Located in its namesake neighborhood in the middle of Stone Town, the baths are well worth a visit. Commissioned by Sultan Barghash in the 1880s, the Hamamni (literally Place of the Baths) offers a cool respite from the heat, as well as insight into what life for Stone Town's upper classes must have been like more than a century ago. The baths have been well preserved and are usually empty (the best time to visit; if the baths are full of people, it's worth coming again later). Upon entering, you are faced with a number of cubicles, each with a specific function, such as the area where people disrobed (incidentally, men and women had separate hours of admittance); from here, you walk deeper into the baths, into what used to be the "warm room," heated by underground hot-water aqueducts, and then into the heart: the hot baths with the cold baths adjacent and more private areas.

After the baths, you could wend your way to Cathedral Street to look at the ornate:

⑪ St. Joseph's Cathedral

A far prettier building than the Anglican church, this cathedral was built between 1886 and 1898 by French missionaries, but thanks to a dwindling congregation the doors are, sadly, almost always closed.

From here, keep heading toward the seafront Mizingani Road. Once there, turn left onto it and head for a beachfront bar to watch the harbor traffic with your feet in the sand and a cool drink in your hand, and time your return to Forodhani Gardens for around 7pm, when the barbecues will be smoking with finger-licking-good seafood snacks.

The Rise of Topan

Arriving as a penniless Gujarati trader in Zanzibar during the early years of the Sultan Seyyid Said's reign, Tharia Topan soon showed a noteworthy business acumen and rose through the ranks to become chief financial advisor to the sultan, who eventually ceded total control of the island's customs duties. Topan's skills were such that he survived the turbulent succession and was made honorary prime minister when Barghash took control. But both the sultanate and Topan's personal fortune were on the wane when he set off for India in 1885 to find the best designers and craftsmen to build his hospital, the Tharia Topan Jubilee Hospital, a legacy that would celebrate and commemorate his good fortune and name, as well as the Golden Jubilee of Queen Victoria. Topan wanted his hospital to be the most beautiful building in Stone Town and decided on the services of Bombay-based firm Gostling and Morris in 1885. Gostling and Morris prepared plans and supervised the joinery, but Topan's endeavor was undermined when he fell seriously ill while still in Bombay and was unable to return to Zanzibar. Undeterred, he sent over a crew of Indian craftsmen and masons from his native Gujarat, along with a foreman, Haji Mistry, in 1890, the same year Topan was knighted by Queen Victoria in recognition of his political and philanthropic achievements. A year later, Topan died in Bombay, having never seen a brick laid, and work on his project came temporarily to a halt. In honor of his memory, Topan's widow resumed construction, but by 1893 she had run out of funds. The building near complete, it was thankfully deemed to show "exemplary craftsmanship," according to Fredrick Pordage, consulting engineer of the British Consul, who finally helped complete the building in 1894. Despite this, the building stood empty until 1900, when it was purchased by the estate of Nasser Nur Mahomed, who turned Topan's hospital into a dispensary, with a pharmacy and a resident doctor on the ground floor and apartments above. After the 1964 revolution, the building was once again abandoned, falling into government control until 1990, when the Aga Khan Trust for Culture offered to restore the building to its former glory. Today the building plays host to various cultural events, a photographic exhibition, and offices.

WHERE TO STAY

Being a World Heritage Site, Stone Town has an active local conservation authority, and nearly all its hotels and guest houses are in renovated buildings located within the historic center. The western section is the more touristic, while the area nearest the market is the most authentic; if you want to live among the locals, the elegantly low-key Zanzibar Coffee House (p. 353) offers the best value in town. However, it's worth knowing that, given the maze of winding narrow lanes and dense concentration of shops, apartments, mosques, and temples, some visitors find being right in the center of it all claustrophobic and noisy. With most structures dating back 150 years or more, buildings are pretty porous, and the tinkling of a bell, drumming practice, crying child, beeping scooter, and *taarab* music will all mingle and drift along with the welcome breeze as it finds you on a rooftop or reclining in rooms once frequented by the long-deceased sultan and his wealthy traders. Personally, I find the proximity of real Stone Town life immensely engaging, but if you value your peace, you're probably better off booking a seafront hotel in the western part of town, where the gorgeous Serena Inn is hands-down the best hotel option. More affordable options are Beyt al Chai (opposite Serena), a small peaceful guesthouse with a great restaurant, and the new Seyyida Hotel, entering the fray with my "Classiest Newcomer" award. Of the three, only Serena Inn has a pool; if this is a prerequisite, the beachfront Tembo is an affordable option on this side of town. Alternatively, you can opt to stay at one of the beach resorts that lie a few minutes' drive north and south of the old town; of these, my favorite is Mbweni Ruins Hotel, a few clicks south but right on a gorgeous beach (all reviewed in more detail below).

Note: At the time of writing, Emerson (of Emerson and Green fame) had run into a funding logjam, but do look to see whether his hotel **Emerson Spice Inn** is operational yet. Located a stone's throw from the market in the heart of old Stone Town, it's likely to be very charming.

236 Hurumzi ★★ This American-managed guesthouse (formerly known as Emerson & Green) is a classy shabby-chic option. Staff are confident and welcoming, and the tall historic building (built more than a century ago by Topan, then the wealthiest man in Zanzibar and second in height only to House of Wonders) houses the most atmospheric rooms in town. Each room is different, with antiques (including a bed that belonged to one of the sultan's princesses) and colorful fabric off-set against similarly saturated walls that will have you grabbing your camera. However, don't expect decent water pressure, two-ply toilet paper, hot water on tap, or any of the usual luxuries you'd expect at this price. Stairs are steep and tiring, so this will not suit the elderly, the unfit, or the infirm (if you fall into any of these, you'll struggle with most options in Stone Town). This is a personal favorite despite the caveats. The toneless, early-morning chiming from the adjacent temple that drifts in through the windows (many of them open to the elements, as is traditional), toasting the setting sun at the Tower Top restaurant above or wandering down to reception as the *muezzin* calls the faithful to prayer, makes it undeniably authentic.

236 Hurumzi St., P.O. Box 3417, Zanzibar. ✆ **077/742-3266.** Fax 077/742-9266. www.236hurumzi.com. 16 rooms (plus 6 rooms in 240 Hurumzi). MC, V. $165–$185 double B&B; $225–$250 suite double B&B. Extra bed $35. **Amenities:** 2 restaurants; room service; free Wi-Fi (in lobby).

Africa House Hotel ★ Just a short stroll south of Serena Inn and Al Johari Hotel, this old Stone Town stalwart, erected by a wealthy Omani trader and later transformed into the English Club, is located (like Serena Inn) on the western coast, affording grandstand views when the sun sets over the Indian Ocean. The best thing about Africa House is the aptly named Sunset Bar, a large, sprawling balcony with lots of wicker chairs, a great place to toast the setting sun. Inside it's an eclectic mix of old-style grandeur—broad corridors with high ceilings—and old-fashioned decor that, truth be told, could do with a revamp. En suite rooms, while clean and comfortable, are nothing to write home about. "Royal deluxe" purports to grandeur but have no views. The best are the "deluxe seaview" rooms overlooking the ocean, but these do not make the most of the views, with windows a little too high, as was the style some 50 years ago. Sister outfit, the 15-room Zanzibar Hotel (www.zanzibarhotel.co.tz), located a short stroll from here, has larger rooms and better furnishings, but because it's surrounded by buildings, it has no views.

Shangani Street, Stone Town, Zanzibar. ✆ **077/443-2340.** www.theafricahouse-zanzibar.com. 15 units. High season $150–$215 double; low season $120–$170. Extra bed $30. Rates include breakfast. MC, V. **Amenities:** Restaurant; bar; room service. *In room:* A/C, TV, hair dryer, minibar, Wi-Fi.

Al Johari ★★ Another option located in the more touristic western part of Stone Town, the compact Al Johari will suit those who like their modern comforts (large flatscreen TVs, efficient air-conditioning, and showers with satisfying water pressure). Views from the rooftop lounge/bar are also a boon, and the extensive wine and whiskey list and specials such as sunset happy hour and live *taarab* music on Saturday evenings attract a bustling crowd beyond checked-in guests. Rooms are dressed in classic Zanzibar-style furnishings (carved beds swathed in mosquito netting), but most are cupboard-tiny and have no views (great as sleeping pods but not to hang around in).

116 Shangani St., Stone Town, or P.O. Box 3234, Zanzibar. ✆ **024/223-6779.** Fax 024/223-6199. www.al-johari.com. 15 units. $180 double; $200–$350 suite. Rates include breakfast. MC, V. **Amenities:** Restaurant; bar; airport transfer ($15); free Wi-Fi. *In room:* A/C, TV, hair dryer.

Beyt al Chai ★★ Also known as Stone Town Inn, this intimate guesthouse is located on shady Kelele Square (opposite Serena Inn in the touristic western section) but is one of the most peaceful guesthouses in Stone Town, with the square affording a sense of space that is lacking from the options in the historical center. Despite its small size (only five rooms), it has a highly rated restaurant (p. 355) and a comfortable lounge area (for in-house guests only). Once a teahouse (hence the name), it has been adroitly renovated, and each of the large rooms is individually decorated with typical Zanzibari pieces and style; saturated wall colors and richly colored curtains are a further nod to the 236 Hurumzi recipe. Given that there are only a couple of flights of stairs here, it's not quite as exhausting as staying there, and here there's the added benefit of air-conditioning, but being so far from the bustle of real Stone Town makes for a far less authentic experience. Book one of the three sultan rooms on the second (top) floor for space and views; best is Beyt al Chai. The guesthouse is owned by the same people who own Big Blue and adjacent Sultan Sands, two large resorts on the east coast.

Kelele Square, Zanzibar. ✆ **0774/444-111.** Fax 022/40245. www.stonetowninn.com. 5 units. Peak season $196–$265 double; high season $200–$250 double; low season $120–$175 double. Rates include breakfast. Extra bed $75. MC, V. **Amenities:** Restaurant; room service. *In room:* A/C.

Clove House (Value) This quaint no-frills guesthouse offers the best value in its price category, offering clean rooms with small en suite bathrooms and comfortable beds, and a location just a few blocks away from the seafront and Forodhani Gardens. It's personally managed by Dutch owner Lisette Aernaudts (who offers a thorough, if at times somewhat brusque, level of guest care), who is on hand to arrange tours of town or the island. Located in the center of Stone Town and overlooking a small square, it is convenient to most sights (though a tad noisy, as all centrally located guest houses are). Clove House is by no means luxury, but it is head and shoulders above similarly priced alternatives; the suites (comprising two interconnecting rooms with a double bed, two single beds, and a small balcony) are a bargain for both families and couples (plenty of space to spread out). Breakfast is served on a rooftop pavilion typical of Stone Town that affords lovely views; this is also where Lisette runs her honesty bar, so you can enjoy sundowners at one of the tables.

Hurumzi St., or P.O. Box 1117, Stone Town, Zanzibar. ✆ **077/748-4567.** www.zanzibarhotel.nl. 8 units. $65 double; $85 family suite double. Rates include breakfast. Minimum 2-night stay. MC, V.

Serena Inn ★★★ Hands down the best place to stay in Stone Town: two beautifully restored heritage properties, one of them an 18th-century home, located right on the oceanfront, with views of the sparkling sea from every room and most of the public areas, including the pool (the only private one in Stone Town and the site of wonderful Swahili dinners on Friday nights [$30 guests, $35 nonguests]). Aside from the inherently attractive

Set Sail with the Music of Zanzibar

Like so much of the island's architecture and cuisine, Zanzibari music is a fabulous blend of styles from Africa, India, and the Middle East. *Taarab,* roughly translated as "to be moved by music," is attributed largely to the sybaritic nature of Sultan Barghash. Seeking to be entertained while reclining and dining, Barghash imported an ensemble from Egypt to sing him *tarabu* (traditional praise songs) and later sent his own musician, Mohamed Ibrahim, to Egypt, where he learned, among other things, to play the *kanun,* a type of harp, and *qanun,* a kind of zither. Upon his return, Ibrahim formed the Zanzibar Taarab Orchestra, precursor to the Ikwhani Safaa Musical Club (now known affectionately as Malindi), which remains one of the leading Zanzibari *taarab* "orchestras," with 35 active members playing a variety of instruments from Arabic *(sitar, oud, darbuka),* to Latin (bongo drums), to European (violin, accordion, *qanun, nai,* bass).

If the Malindi Music Club (or Culture, another stalwart group I recommend) is performing during your visit, make sure you catch them. Alternatively, listen for recordings of Siti Binti Sadi (1880–1950), who was not only the first to make recordings of *taarab* music, but also the first to sing in the language of the "common people"; in fact, some scholars attribute much of the regional spread of the Swahili language to the huge popularity of Sadi's records.

For a modern interpretation, look out for live performances by the Zanzibar Stars or East African Melody. These artists, as well as many more, perform at both Zanzibar's major cultural festivals, the annual Festival of the Dhow Countries, and Sauti za Busara. Even if you don't catch a live act, a CD (purchase one from Gallery Bookshop on Gizenga St.) is a highly recommended souvenir. As record company manager Andy Morgan wrote in his review on *taarab* in *Roots* magazine, "There's hardly anything in the whole of Africa as uplifting as the swelling sounds of a full *taarab* orchestra in full sail."

historical architecture, the Serena Inn is a member of Small Luxury Hotels of the World, which gives some idea of the breadth of facilities, as well as their investment in staff training; this is perhaps the only place in Stone Town you won't be making excuses for the service levels. Cuisine is also excellent. Even if you don't overnight here, make every effort to enjoy a sundowner at their seaview bar or a meal at one of the restaurants.

Kelele Square, or P.O. Box 4151, Stone Town, Zanzibar. ✆ **024/223-3587** or 024/223-3567. Fax 024/223-3018. www.serenahotels.com. 51 units. High season $570 double, $850–$900 suite; low season $305 double, $750–$850 suite. Rates include breakfast. AE, MC, V. **Amenities:** Restaurant; babysitting; pool; room service; courtesy shuttle between hotel, city center, and airport; free Wi-Fi. *In room:* A/C, TV, hair dryer, minibar.

Seyyida Hotel & Spa ★★★ Finds At the time of writing, the finishing touches were being put on this brand-new boutique-style hotel, with elegant, spacious rooms furnished with a mix of Arabic and Indian influences and cool white marble used judiciously throughout. It's certainly well located (next to the Zanzibar Palace Museum, overlooking the sultan's graveyard and, beyond, the ocean), and if staff can provide the service levels to match the interiors, Seyyida looks set as an incredibly promising entrant into the top-end lodging choices. The rooftop terrace has gorgeous sea views; if you want to enjoy some from your room, book one of the four "balcony seaview" rooms (better value than the similarly priced garden suites). This is also the only hotel in Stone Town with an in-house spa. The only drawback, given how lovely everything else is, is the lack of pool, and the property still has to develop its character.

Rahaleo House Maisara, Stone Town Zanzibar. ✆ **024/223-2375.** Fax 024/223-2577. www.theseyyida-zanzibar.com. 17 units. $190–$250 double; $288 seaview balcony double; $270–$308 suites and family room. Extra bed $50. Supplements during Festive season and Easter. Rates include breakfast. MC, V. **Amenities:** Restaurant; bar; airport transfer ($35); Internet ($5); room service. *In room:* A/C, TV, hair dryer, minibar.

Swahili House ★★ This is an alternative to 236 Hurumzi or Zanzibar Coffee House. Very near to the market, this was clearly the home of either a wealthy merchant (perhaps another belonging to Tharia Topan) or the sultan's family, given its imposing height and space. It opened December 2008 and experienced some teething problems, particularly with water pressure and other plumbing problems, and was closed again for renovations in September 2009. Hopefully this will iron out the small infrastructure problems, as the rooms are lovely: chic, uncluttered Zanzibari furnishings in cool white spaces, some of them double volume, and stained-glass windows letting in lovely light. However, as is the case with most of the hotels in the old historic quarter, staircases are steep, and it's five stories to the rooftop terrace where the bar, restaurant, and Jacuzzi are located (thankfully, an elevator is being installed). Swahili House is part of the Moivaro group, who also own the recommended Unguja Lodge (p. 364) and Fumba Beach Lodge (p. 363) in the south, and you will no doubt spend a night here if you are booking onward to either of these lodges.

831 Kiponda St., Stone Town, Zanzibar. ✆ **077/751-0209.** www.theswahilihouse.com. 19 units. Peak season $135 double deluxe room; $150–$165 suite; high season $105 double deluxe room, $120–$135 suite; low season $75 double deluxe room, $120–$135 suite. All rates include breakfast. Holiday supplements during Christmas and New Year's ($35 per person, per day). MC, V. **Amenities:** Restaurant; Jacuzzi; Wi-Fi (ground floor; $5 per hr.). *In room:* A/C.

Tembo ★★ Tembo gets two stars just for its location, right on the oceanfront; you can walk from the pool (the surrounding hotel looms over this in a rather unfortunate way) right onto the beach (note that Stone Town offers walking rather than swimming beaches). It's an authentically Zanzibari hotel, owned and run by locals. Built in 1834 as the American consulate before housing one of the wealthiest trading companies in East Africa, the building has oodles of character; the combination of old-style colonial architecture (lovely arches, carved frames, colored windows, and tiled floors) framing sea and town views will have you grabbing your camera every few minutes on arrival. That said, much of the furnishings, particularly in rooms, verge on kitsch; this is not the place to come if you like your spaces pared and modern. Some of the rooms are also tiny and dark; be sure to book a "prime room with seaview" ($120). Another drawback, given the sunset-beach location, is that no alcohol is served or permitted, nor at its sister outfit, **Dhow Palace Hotel.** Walking distance away but deeper into the maze, Dhow Palace is no palace, but an atmospheric 140-year-old merchant house turned into a 28-room guesthouse. It lacks the charm of Tembo's beachfront location but offers clean, comfortable rooms and a small courtyard pool (again, very overlooked by the hotel balconies) at slightly lower rates; the spacious triple rooms for $125 may, for instance, suit family travelers, should Tembo be full.

831 Forodhani St., Stone Town, Zanzibar. ✆ **024/223-2069** or 024/223-3005. Fax 024/223-3777. www.tembohotel.com. 37 units. $110–$120 double; $145–$195 suite. Extra bed $30. Rates include breakfast. MC, V. **Amenities:** Restaurant; pool; free Wi-Fi (free); watersports center. *In room:* A/C, TV, hair dryer, minibar.

Zanzibar Coffee House ★★★ Value Located in the heart of the local community, very near the Darajani Market, Zanzibar Coffee House offers a chance to experience truly authentic Stone Town in an old Arabic house (built in 1885), with tasteful interiors and rates that offer the best value for your money. It's not as luxurious as Serena Inn and has no facilities, but you may prefer the character-filled rooms with their handpicked pieces, as well as the more intimate guesthouse atmosphere. It's efficiently run by a group of women who (aside from one surly waitress) go out of their way to make their guests feel at home, as does the Dutch owner, when in residence. There is something endearingly homely about the place; the uncluttered decor and pale whitewashed palette (offset against the thick, black wooden beams) is elegant and soothing. Aside from this, the coffee shop below serves by far the best coffee in town (grown by the owners); breakfasts are also excellent and served on the breezy rooftop teahouse, which has lovely views. Arabica Suite is the best room; entry-level Caturra has a separate bathroom (not en suite, but goes for an incredible $75). All in all, excellent value, and my top choice if you want to be in authentic, lived-in Stone Town. Book early.

1563/64 Mkunazini, or P.O. Box 4047, Stone Town, Zanzibar. ✆ **024/223-9379** or 077/306-1532. www.riftvalley-zanzibar.com. 8 units. $75–$80 double Espresso, Excelsor, and Caturra; $115 double Twin and Macchiato (slightly larger); suite rates vary. Rates include breakfast. MC, V. **Amenities:** Restaurant/coffee shop; free Wi-Fi. *In room:* A/C.

Zanzibar Palace ★★ This is billed as a boutique hotel, and while the compact size (only nine rooms over three floors) and excellent attention to detail warrant this, the decor is a little overstuffed and old-fashioned. If you prefer a more pared look (not to mention rooftop views), you'd be better off at Zanzibar Coffee House or 236 Hurumzi. However, the infrastructure at Zanzibar Palace is of the best in town, with decent plumbing, efficient air-conditioning, and a good Wi-Fi connection. The owner-couple are extremely hands-on, and guests are looked after; they have been on the island for many years and offer really good advice, from where to book a spa treatment to the top tours, and provide generous touches such as free early-morning coffee and tea, one of the best breakfasts in town, and the largest, fluffiest towels. The restaurant (located just off the lobby) has a fairly good reputation but is very pricey; if you're not in the mood to splurge, you are walking distance from a number of other restaurant options, including Tower Tops (see "Where to Dine"). Streets are safe.

831 Kiponda St., Stone Town, Zanzibar. ✆ **024/223-2230** or 077/307-9222. www.zanzibarpalacehotel.com. 9 units. $145 standard double; $260–$330 suite. Rates include breakfast. Surcharge applies Dec 24–Jan 5. MC, V. **Amenities:** Restaurant; airport transfers ($20); room service; free Wi-Fi (laptop provided). *In room:* A/C, TV, DVD player, hair dryer (on request), free Wi-Fi.

JUST OUTSIDE STONE TOWN

Hakuna Matata Beach Lodge & Spa ★ Like Mbweni, this is a small, intimate resort built around a beach, with the silhouette of Sultan Barghash's Chuini Palace ruins on the opposite headland adding a dash of romance. It is located north of Stone Town, however, and, thanks to congestion, takes quite a few minutes longer to get to the center. It is also not as private (there is another guesthouse sharing the beach), nor is it as lush as Mbweni, and some of the rooms here are on the small side. The owner presence is very comforting, though. Fritz and Rose have built the resort from scratch and are very passionate about ensuring a warm and welcome experience; their hospitality has stretched to embrace a delightful herd of donkeys, who graze amid the chalets. Cuisine standards are high (though not everyone will enjoy spending their evening making small talk at a communal table), and there are thoughtful touches such as providing guests with a mobile phone that enables friends and family from home to get in touch with ease (a rare luxury in Zanzibar); the phone is also loaded with some airtime so that you can, for instance, call Rose or Fritz should you want to be picked up once you've had enough exploring.

Bububu, 12km north of Stone Town. P.O. Box 4747, Zanzibar. ✆ **077/745-4892.** info@zanzibar-resort.com. www.hakuna-matata-beach-lodge.com. 12 units. Peak season $280 standard, $320 superior, $350 suite and family suite (2 rooms); high season $190 standard, $290 superior, $360 suite & family suite; low season $220 standard, $260 superior, $280 suite and family suite. Rates include breakfast and dinner buffet. MC, V. **Amenities:** Restaurant; bar; pool; spa; Wi-Fi. *In room:* A/C, hair dryer.

Mbweni Ruins Hotel ★★ **Value** If you are on the island for only a few nights and want to experience both the vibrant nightlife and street life of Stone Town, as well as relax on a classic picture-perfect stretch of beach without having to pack your bags more than once, Mbweni Ruins Hotel is the perfect choice. An unpretentious, old-fashioned, and (most important in this resort-heavy island) *small* hotel, set in tranquil and lush gardens that overlook the beach, Mbweni feels a million miles from the hustle and bustle of Stone Town's narrow alleyways, yet is a 10-minute drive from the center (the hotel runs a regular complimentary shuttle). Rooms are spacious, with bland but comfortable furnishings (king-size beds); all but one have verandas overlooking the garden or sea and writing desks. The best room is the Baobab Suite, with a four-poster bed and rooftop terrace to toast the setting sun (one of the best things about staying on the west coast, as opposed to the many options on the east and south coasts). There are three family rooms, each sleeping four (kids in bunk beds in a separate room). It is also an understandably popular wedding venue.

7km south of Stone Town. P.O. Box 1117, Stone Town, Zanzibar. ✆ **024/223-5478** or -5479. Fax 024/223-0536. www.mbweni.com. 13 units. Dry season $240 double, more than 4 nights $230; green season $200 double, more than 4 nights $190. Extra adult $60; kids 7–16 half rate; under 6 free. Rates include breakfast. Dinner $35 supplement; Baobab Suite $70 double supplement. MC, V. **Amenities:** Restaurant; bar; airport transfers ($15); Internet ($2 per hr.); pool; free shuttle service to town 5 times daily; spa. *In room:* A/C.

WHERE TO DINE

If you're seeing Stone Town only as part of a day trip, you're missing out on the real treat. As evening falls, people gather to gossip and recline on the *barazas* (the raised seating that lines many of the buildings) while the smell of cooking permeates the air. There are a number of good restaurants, the best of which are reviewed below, but if you're looking for a casual beachfront bar/restaurant, **Livingstone's** (✆ **077/316-4939**) is the most buzzy, with canvas safari chairs and timber tables settled into the sand a stone's throw from the water's edge. They serve average fare with the emphasis more bar than restaurant, and the loud pop music pumping from the massive cinema-size TV screen inside can be a bit disconcerting, but head outside and time your visit for a sundowner (those traveling with laptops may want to note that Livingstone's also offers free Wi-Fi). **Mercury's** (named after Queen lead singer Freddy Mercury, Zanzibar's most famous son) is another good sundowner choice and, as it's located farther east, may suit those staying in hotels on that side. Coffee lovers should make a beeline for **Zanzibar Coffee House** in the heart of historic Stone Town (near the market); not only do they serve the best coffee in town, but their selection of cakes and light meals is also some of the best. If you're in the mood for Italian, the most convivial venue is **Amore Mio,** located on the western coast on Shangani Street just before Africa House (✆ **024/223-3666**), which has great ocean views. Pizzas and pastas will run you around $9 to $15 (cash only), and they're open daily 10am to 10pm. Alternatively, head for Kidude (see below). Whatever you do, make sure you spend at least one evening at **Forodhani Gardens night market,** snacking on what is correctly billed by some as the best street food in Africa. Here you'll find numerous small barbecues on which skewers of fish, lobster tails, and prawns are smoking, along with vegetarian *samosas, cassava,* and Stone Town pizza (more a frittata than a pizza). It's vibrant and atmospheric (though frequented by tourists rather than locals) and offers incredible value for money (around Tsh3,000 for a dozen small prawns on a skewer, Tsh12,000 for a lobster tail), but flavors are pretty bland. If you want a superb introduction to Swahili cooking, don't miss the Swahili buffet hosted around the pool at the **Serena Inn.** Much of the food is cooked on barbecues in front of you, so the seafood is fresh and succulent, and the various coconut milk curries typical of Swahili cooking are utterly delicious. Get there early and you'll also catch a great performance by one of the best *taarab* groups.

Beyt al Chai SEAFOOD Located directly opposite Serena Inn is Stone Town's most elegant restaurant, romantically lit, with a menu that will have your mouth watering. Start with crab *millefeuille,* crab meat layered with crispy eggplant and green mango, and follow with pan-fried red snapper served with warm mango pickle and bread-fruit gnocchi, or feast on a plate of giant prawns marinated in garlic and lime (you can opt to have these cooked with Zanzibari spices, but here I recommend you go grilled or steamed for purity of flavor). If you're not a great fan of seafood, there is a small selection of red-meat and vegetarian dishes.

Kelele Square, Shangani. ✆ **077/444-4111.** Main course Tsh14,000–Tsh24,000.

Kidude Café Restaurant ★★ SWAHILI/ITALIAN/SNACKS If you find yourself in the heart of Stone Town, this restaurant, comprising two interleading narrow, high-ceilinged rooms, offers a wonderfully cool (thanks to air-conditioning) respite from the midday heat. Grab one of the comfortable corner tables and order one of the best seafood dishes I've ever had: the baked fish papillote, a filet of kingfish, as kingklip is locally known, baked in parchment with sliced carrots, peppers, eggplant, and an aromatic combination of spices. It's a casual place, also good for wraps and pasta-style dishes; this is the place to order spaghetti bolognaise or penne arrabiata (though, be warned, the latter is pretty spicy), as the chef worked in the kitchen of the Italian Embassy for many years.

236 Hurumzi St. ✆ **074/742-3266.** MC, V (when machine is working). Daily 10am–11pm. Main courses from $6.

Monsoon ★★★ SWAHILI If you're here on a Wednesday or Saturday evening, this warm, laid-back venue, a stone's throw from the beach, is a great place to sample Swahili cuisine while listening to live *taraab* performances by Matone's group; Friday evenings, Mzee Kheri plays the N'goma drums. Kingfish in coconut sauce with a touch of cardamom; tuna topped with tomato *masala*; king prawns marinated in garlic, olive oil, ginger, and a touch of lime; and grilled lobster in a tamarind sauce are all recommended. All mains are served with Swahili-style chapattis, spicy rice, or sautéed potatoes and a choice of four or five spicy vegetarian dishes such as pumpkin in coconut sauce, steamed spinach, cooked green bananas, and snow peas with peanut sauce.

Beachfront, opposite Forodhani Gardens. ✆ **074/447-4441.** Daily 12–3pm and 7–10pm. Cash only. Main courses $12–$20.

Tower Top Restaurant ★★★ SWAHILI/NORTH AFRICAN/INDIAN If you are in Stone Town for only 1 night, this is where you must be: seated under billowing sheets on the rooftop of 236 Hurumzi at this romantic and quirky restaurant. Once the home of Tharia Topan, the most powerful figure in Zanzibari commerce, the building was second in height only to the sultan's House of Wonders and is still one of the highest points in town, affording marvelous views of the rooftops, adjacent temple, and harbor. You can sprawl on tapestry pillows against a crenellated edge, the whole floor a huge Persian rug, and wait as diligent staff see to your every whim, or keep your shoes on to take a seat at one of the tables on a slightly lower rooftop. The menu is set and changes regularly. There are two starters that may include a North African dip and pita bread, followed by soup or *fatoush* salad, main course, and dessert. Main courses are a choice of red meat, fish (the residing chef is a genius with seafood), chicken, or vegetarian, served with rice or potatoes and the vegetable of the day.

236 Hurumzi St. ✆ **074/742-3266.** Cash only. Daily from sunset onward. Mon–Thurs $35 set menu; Fri–Sun $40.

STONE TOWN/ZANZIBAR EXCURSIONS

Zanzibar's old capital is centrally placed for all the island's excursions, from joining the spice tours that take place in the hinterland just northeast of Stone Town, to stroking the leathery heads of giant tortoises on nearby Prison Island. For ease, all excursions are reviewed in this Stone Town section, but you can book any of these trips from any of the beach resorts, all of which have the exact same excursions listed, with small price variations usually related to distances traveled. If you are not overnighting in Stone Town, you should certainly book a half-day walking tour of the historical quarter. Tours usually last 3 to 4 hours and are undertaken on foot; for one person based in Stone Town, the cost is around $30 to $40. (Prices increase the farther away your resort is and decrease for larger groups.) Note that I have not included the sunset dhow cruise, though these are offered, as it is far better value to utilize a dhow experience in conjunction with an actual destination, such as a Safari Blue day trip or a trip to Prison Island. Other day trips from Stone Town include those to the coast, predominantly to Ras Nungwi via **Mangapwani Slave Cave,** where slaves were held illicitly by the sultan after slavery was abolished by the British in 1873, but I recommend you overnight on the north coast rather than spend a cumulative 2 to 3 hours (east and north, respectively) in a car for 1 day.

Safari Blue ★★★

This is one of the most popular and recommended tours. You can be picked up from any place on the island (but it's senseless to do so if you are based in the far north or northeast, in which case the experience will be tempered by long transfers) and taken to one of two launching pads near the fishing village of Fumba, on the southwestern tip of Unguja (also known as Zanzibar main island). Departing at around 9:30am on a locally made traditional *dhow,* you'll take an intensely relaxing sail, exploring Menai Bay, a marine conservation area since 1998. After a 30-minute cruise looking for dolphins (which are spotted 9 times out of 10), you will lounge around on sandbanks (shade set up for you) and snorkel the surrounding waters (equipment provided and properly fitted; guides available). After refreshing yourself with a snifter of fresh *madafu* (coconut), you drop anchor at Kwale Island, where you feast on a huge Zanzibari buffet (predominantly seafood; vegetarian on request) under the tamarind trees. End with a fruit tasting (10–15 tropical fruits available); tide permitting, you will also swim in the island's mangrove

Dive Right In

You'll find some of the best dive sites in Africa in Zanzibar's waters, with experienced divers citing the incredible array of species as one of the main draws. Visibility, ranging from 15m to 60m (49 ft.–197 ft.), is also usually good, and water temperatures range from 25° to 29°C (77°–84°F). The diving season is from September to March, but that's not to say it's not worth diving at other times. The best diving is at **Mnemba Atoll** off the northeast coast, referred to as "the tropical fish capital" of Zanzibar. Surprisingly, the reefs near Stone Town are also very satisfying to dive, particularly **Murogo Reef** and, to a lesser extent, **Boribu Sandbar. Pange Island** is another good site, located 1.5km (.9 miles) southwest of Stone Town, as is Bawe Island, a 30-minute boat ride from Stone Town, where there is a reasonably good snorkeling reef. Aside from fish, these sites offer a great selection of coral; Stone Town also offers wrecks to explore. If you are based on the southeast coast, Jambiani Reef and Stingray Alley (also near Jambiani) are good sites to dive. Essentially, the south offers slightly deeper dives than the north and is better if you're keen to see bigger marine life. But the north is where you see the greatest variety, and aside from Mnemba Atoll, Levan Bank near Nungwi is a must.

One of the oldest and most reputable dive outfits, **One Ocean Zanzibar Dive Center** (✆ **024/22-8374;** www.zanzibaroneocean.com), is also the biggest dive operator in East Africa, with a reputation for excellent dive instructors, tip-top equipment, and a serious attitude to safety. There is a One Ocean Dive Centre in Stone town; there are also a number of One Ocean Dive Centres operating from many of the lodges reviewed under "Where to Stay." Other good dive centers are **Rising Sun** (www.risingsun-zanzibar.com), servicing Breezes, Baraza, and The Palms; and **Reef Leisure Watersports** (www.reefleisure.com), operating at Fairmont, Kempinski, Pongwe, and Matemwe Bungalows.

lagoon. Head back with sundowner in hand (beers and soft drinks only) to disembark around 5:30pm. The cost for one or two persons from Stone Town is around $100 per person. For more, contact Eleanor Griplas (✆ **077/742-3162;** www.safariblue.net).

Snorkeling with Dolphins

Situated on the southern point of the island (about an hour from Stone Town), the laid-back fishing village of Kizimkazi is the site of a 12th-century Shiraz mosque, thought to be the earliest evidence of Islam in East Africa, but it is more famous for the schools of bottle-nose dolphins that swim within a few minutes' boat ride from its shores. If you are lucky, you may be able to jump in and swim quite close to the dolphins, in which case the experience gets three stars. However, while there is an 85% chance of spotting dolphins, it is not always possible to swim with them. Be aware that some of the locals, almost all of whom earn more from dolphin trips than fishing, can be unscrupulous. It is very distressing for the dolphins to be chased or interfered with, particularly during breeding season, so do not insist that your skipper to get closer, and please dissuade others on the boats from doing similar. It is not unknown for tourists to offer to pay the

Tips Snorkel Safety

You can drift for hours mesmerized by the life below, cooled by the ocean currents, and only realize that evening, when the searing pain sets in, how fiercely that sun beats down. Wear a T-shirt or rash vest to protect your back from the sun, and don't forget to slather the backs of your legs liberally with waterproof sunblock. Be careful also of grazing yourself on coral. While it looks like pretty benign underwater flora, corals are actually animal colonies with calcified outer skeletons that have sharp edges; accidental contact can leave a small amount of animal protein and calcareous material in the wound. What appears initially to be a small and harmless graze can develop into a suppurating infected wound that requires specialist intervention. To avoid this, scrub and flush the cut or graze with fresh water, then rinse with vinegar, isopropyl alcohol, or a mixture (50:50) of hydrogen peroxide and water; rinse daily with this mixture. Having suffered from a prolonged infection, I would also apply a topical antibiotic ointment three to four times daily. If the infection persists or spreads, an oral course of antibiotics may be needed; I suggest you make an appointment with your doctor immediately. The best snorkeling sites are Mnemba Atoll in the northeast and Chumbe Island near Stone Town.

skipper more regardless of the dolphins' moods or needs; should you encounter this, I urge you to make your discomfort very clear. Also, do not make a huge commotion by jumping overboard (try to slip in surreptitiously, and not all at the same time). Note that while your chances of seeing the dolphins is not guaranteed, it is highest the earlier you get there; 7am or even earlier is considered ideal, but this makes for an uncomfortably early start if you're coming from Stone Town. If you're really keen for a dolphin encounter, I recommend you book at nearby Unguja Lodge. This means you can get there early and try more than once, and the guys at the dive center are also extremely sensitive to the dolphins' needs. If you visit Kizimkazi, pop into the mosque and look for the remains of an 18th-century stone wall (just above the high-water mark on the beach) that once formed a defensive perimeter around the whole settlement. According to legend, Kizimkazi is named after the merchant who built the wall; when he was captured by the Portuguese, the original Kizimkazi begged for a final prayer session on the beach, whereupon he promptly hopped over his own wall and escaped.

Jozani Forest ★

In the central-east region of Zanzibar (40 min. from Stone Town), the 1,000-hectare (2,470 acre) Jozani Forest protects one of two last remaining pockets of indigenous flora (coastal bushland, mangroves, saline grassland, groundwater forest) that once covered the island. Unless you harbor secret desires to be a botanist, there is not reason enough to spend a couple of hours here; most people are hoping for a close encounter with the forest's red colobus monkeys (though you are just as likely to see these gregarious creatures from the road). Aside from this, if you have been on safari on the mainland, you are unlikely to be excited by the small game, such as Sykes' monkeys, small buck, and bushpigs, that call the forest home. There are three guided trails—Paddock Forest, Monkey, and Mangrove—each taking around 30 minutes. You may want to ask if a visit to ZALA

Park (5km/3 miles south of Jozani entrance; same hours at Jozani Forest; admission $5) is included in your tour; the park has an interesting selection of reptiles including green tree snakes, mambas, pythons, chameleons, geckos, tortoises, striped lizards, and truly prehistoric-looking monitor lizards. Those with kids might also want a quick stop at the Butterfly Park (daily 9am–5pm), a few minutes' north of the Jozani entrance.

From Stone Town, the Jozani Forest trip costs around $70 for one person, $45 per person for a couple, $20 per person for a group of four, with discounts as group numbers grow. It can be combined with a dolphin tour into a full-day tour. If you travel on your own steam, entry is Tsh10,000. Jozani is open daily 7:30am to 5pm.

Spice Tour ★★★

The propagation of spices is, of course, integral to what became known as the Spice Islands, and while a spice tour doesn't sound like the most exciting way to spend a morning, it is surprisingly enjoyable—and hugely popular. None of the spices are indigenous. Clove trees were introduced only in 1818 but flourished in the tropical climate and fertile soil of both Zanzibar and Pemba, and it took less than 40 years for the archipelago to become the world's largest producer of cloves. Other spices, such as cinnamon, cumin, ginger, pepper, and cardamom, were gradually introduced but not as avidly propagated as cloves. A spice tour will take you to one of the Kizimbani plantations (around 30–40 min. drive from Zanzibar town), often via Maruhubi Palace, one of the best-preserved ruins on the island, built by Seyyid Barghash for his concubines, and the Persian baths at Kidichi, built by Seyyid Said for his first wife, Princess Shehrzard, in 1850. Both are in a state of ruin but provide some insight into the lifestyle of the sultanate. If you'd prefer to skip these, simply push on to the spice plantations, where, accompanied by a local guide, you will learn to identify the plants that provide such intense culinary and olfactory pleasure, as well as their cosmetic use and health benefits. This is also the cheapest place to purchase spices and spice oils. Most tours also include a tasting of the many exotic fruits (such as jack fruit, custard apples, and soursop) often produced alongside the spices. Spice tours cost around $50 to $20 per person, depending on group size (set aside a small amount to tip the guide who takes you through the plantation, too) and can be organized by every operator (see "Essentials," above) on the island or through all beach resorts and Stone Town lodgings (who then subcontract to the tour operators they trust or have arranged a good commission with). Given that the exact same excursions are listed everywhere, with small price variations usually related to distances traveled, you may choose to arrange this once you are ensconced in your chosen lodging.

The Islands: Prison (Changuu) ★★, Bawe ★, Chumbe ★★★ & Grave (Chapwani) ★★

About 20 to 30 minutes by boat or dhow from Stone Town, Prison Island (the middle of the three islands you can see from Stone Town's oceanfront; known locally as Changuu Island) is a worthwhile half-day trip, particularly if you feel like combining your sightseeing with a bit of snorkeling. The island was apparently first used by an Arab slave trader to contain and punish the most troublesome slaves before auctioning them in Stone Town's slave market; after this, the first real recorded usage dates back to 1893, when a Mr. Lloyd Mathews, under the orders of the British administrators, was commissioned to build a prison, the ruins of which can be seen today. Like Robben Island and Alcatraz, the island was thought to be an ideal place to contain serious criminals deported from the mainland, but it was never used as such and instead became a quarantine center for yellow fever patients from Kenya, Tanganyika, and Zanzibar. It is worth a visit to encounter the giant Aldabra tortoises (thought to have been imported from the Seychelles by Barghash during the 19th century) and spend some time snorkeling the coral reef that fringes the island: The best snorkeling lies 35m (115 ft.) northwest of the main beach. This half-day tour costs around $25 per person. Note, however, that the resort on Prison Island (currently closed until further notice) has detracted a little from the experience, with the conversion of the former 1930s Quarantine Area into 12 rooms exerting a less-than-benign influence on the historic and natural atmosphere; if you're looking for a more laid-back island trip, Bawe Island (where the tiny resort has also been closed till further notice) sees virtually no day traffic and has a lovely sandy beach and reasonably productive snorkeling reef. But there's no doubt that the best snorkeling to be had is along the reefs surrounding **Chumbe Island,** home not only to one of the most famous eco-lodges in the world (www.chumbeisland.com), but surrounded by the first marine park in East Africa, with pristine coral reefs home to an incredible diversity of species. A permit is required for day-trippers to snorkel in the park (no diving is allowed), which any of the operators in Stone Town can arrange; boats also depart from Mbweni Ruins Hotel (see "Where to Stay," above). The only drawback of actually staying at Chumbe Island lodge is that, like Chole Mjini, which is my favorite eco-lodge island in East Africa (see chapter 14), there is no soft, sandy beach; if this is important, it's a better bet to transfer back to Mbweni Ruins Hotel, which is a charming little resort, and overnight there. Time allowing, another island excursion you may want to look into is Grave Island. Also known as Chapwani Island, this is a pretty little place, home to an atmospheric cemetery reserved in 1879 by Sultan Barghash for the burial of the English colonists; it also offers a good snorkeling site 35m (115 ft.) northwest of the main beach. ***Note:*** Keen snorkelers may also want to inquire about Nyange, an unbuoyed dive site near Stone Town, said to offer some of the best snorkeling outside of Chumbe Island and Mnemba Island in the north.

2 THE UNGUJA (ZANZIBAR) COAST

About 100km (62 miles) from south to north coast

As beautiful as Zanzibar's coastline is, it is no longer a well-kept secret. The northern and eastern shores, lapping the longest stretch of soft sands, are lined with resorts, many of them sharing the same wall, a jigsaw pattern of narrow rectangles that runs for kilometers at a time when seen from the air. Of course, this is not necessarily how you will experience it. Picked up from the airport and whisked directly to your resort, you may remain blissfully unaware of the proximity of an endless line of neighbors, particularly if you are in an intimate little lodge or (possible albeit rare) take a wander along the beach for half an hour before seeing the next resort.

If a sense of remoteness is important to you, choose one of the two lodges I have included on the south coast. Aside from the rocky western shoreline, the south coast is the least populated part of Zanzibar. Based here, you have the added benefit of being close to Kizimkazi and stand the best chance of swimming with the bottle-nose dolphins that frequent its coastline. Board the boat at 6am and you are unlikely to share the experience with day-trippers who are driven down from Stone Town or from the east coast resorts, who arrive from around 8am onward. The south coast also offers some lovely snorkeling opportunities, predominantly in the Minai Bay conservation area (though it

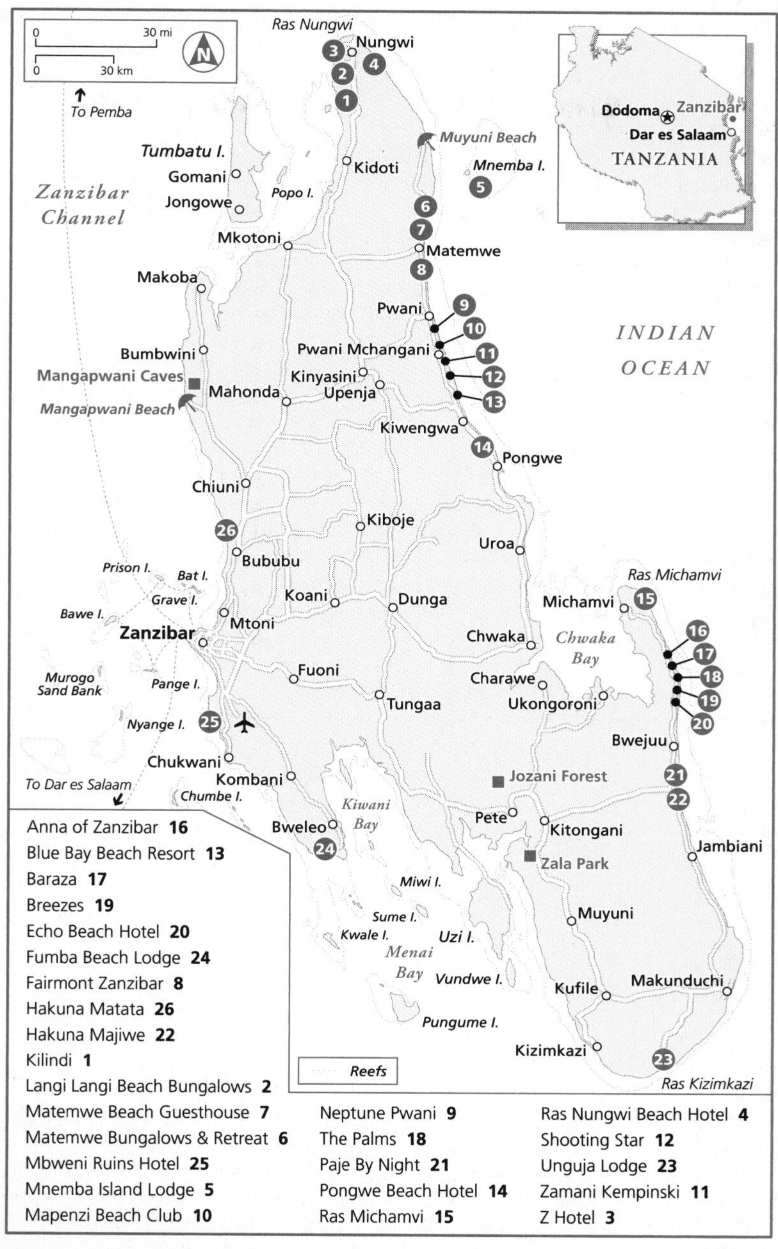
0
30 mi
0
30 km
N
To Pemba
Ras Nungwi
Nungwi
Tumbatu I.
Gomani
Jongowe
Zanzibar Channel
Popo I.
Kidoti
Muyuni Beach
Mnemba I.
Dodoma
Zanzibar
Dar es Salaam
TANZANIA
Mkotoni
Matemwe
Makoba
Pwani
Pwani Mchangani
INDIAN OCEAN
Bumbwini
Mangapwani Caves
Mangapwani Beach
Mahonda
Kinyasini
Upenja
Kiwengwa
Pongwe
Chiuni
Kiboje
Uroa
Bububu
Prison I.
Bat I.
Grave I.
Bawe I.
Koani
Dunga
Ras Michamvi
Michamvi
Zanzibar
Mtoni
Chwaka
Chwaka Bay
Murogo Sand Bank
Pange I.
Fuoni
Charawe
Tungaa
Ukongoroni
Nyange I.
Bwejuu
Chukwani
Kombani
Jozani Forest
To Dar es Salaam
Chumbe I.
Kiwani Bay
Pete
Bweleo
Kitongani
Jambiani
Zala Park
Miwi I.
Sume I.
Muyuni
Kwale I.
Uzi I.
Menai Bay
Vundwe I.
Kufile
Makunduchi
Pungume I.
Kizimkazi
Reefs
Ras Kizimkazi
Anna of Zanzibar 16
Blue Bay Beach Resort 13
Baraza 17
Breezes 19
Echo Beach Hotel 20
Fumba Beach Lodge 24
Fairmont Zanzibar 8
Hakuna Matata 26
Hakuna Majiwe 22
Kilindi 1
Langi Langi Beach Bungalows 2
Matemwe Beach Guesthouse 7
Matemwe Bungalows & Retreat 6
Mbweni Ruins Hotel 25
Mnemba Island Lodge 5
Mapenzi Beach Club 10
Neptune Pwani 9
The Palms 18
Paje By Night 21
Pongwe Beach Hotel 14
Ras Michamvi 15
Ras Nungwi Beach Hotel 4
Shooting Star 12
Unguja Lodge 23
Zamani Kempinski 11
Z Hotel 3

is possible to access this with Safari Blue, regardless of where you are based on the island; see p. 356), and the ocean does not recede for miles at low tide as it does on the east coast. The biggest drawback is the lack of beaches; interspersed among the rocky coastline are small sandy coves, but you don't have the long stretches of the east or north coast. Dive and snorkel sites here are also not the best.

Most people head for popular Ras Nungwi on the northwestern tip. Outside of Stone Town, this is the most densely developed tourist area on the island and, judging by the huge number of resorts built every year, will remain that way well into the next decade. A large sprawling fishing village, more developed than most of the coastal settlements, Ras Nungwi is the dhow-building capital of Zanzibar, with a substantial local population that gives it an edge you won't find in any of the other coastal destinations. While the waters are as azure as on the east coast, this is a place of industry, and the northwestern beach around Z Hotel has small stalls flogging everything from beaded bangles to snorkeling trips, and beach bars vie for customers with music and the lowest seafood and beer prices on the island. As a result, it's by far the most popular destination for budget travelers, with plenty of lodges offering clean but rudimentary accommodation. The whole atmosphere is one of hustle and bustle, and there's a general sense of low-level party. Beaches are less pristine than on the less populated east coast, but the ocean does not recede as far during low tide, and the diving and snorkeling in the area is excellent (don't miss a chance to dive Levan Bank; you are also relatively near Mnemba Atoll off the northeast coast). It's a rare treat to spot a turtle while diving or snorkeling. For a guaranteed encounter, head east from the beach toward the lighthouse, where you'll find the Mnarani Turtle Sanctuary, a fenced-off saline pool in which injured greenback and hawksbill turtles and other marine animals are nursed back to health before being released back into ocean. A little south of Nungwi on the northwestern coast is Kendwa, a smaller fishing settlement experiencing a similar mushrooming of resorts. Near here (look for the signpost along the main road, around 10km/6¼ miles south of the village) are the 16th-century Fukuchani Ruins, also known as Portuguese House; it's said to be well preserved and might be a worthwhile stop for history buffs, but for most of us, the real attraction is back on the beach and in the water.

With the longest unbroken beaches on the island, the east coast is understandably Unguja's most exclusive coastline, and with development a great deal more spread out, the tourist pressure is largely dissipated. When the tide is low, however, the ocean recedes a long way back, and a pool is then essential to cool off. There are two distinct areas here: The southeast stretches from Jambiani and Paje, which used to be where the budget travelers congregated, stretches northward to the more remote Ras Michamvi. From here, you need to drive back via Jozani to get to the road that connects Stone Town with the central-eastern coastal road that starts at Chakwa and culminates in the northeast at Matemwa; then you are ideally situated for the island's best snorkeling and diving on the Mnemba Atoll. This eastern coastline is mostly big-resort territory, lined cheek-by-jowl, but, thankfully, there are still a handful of intimate low-key resorts that I recommend.

WHERE TO STAY

Having tried to describe the benefits and drawbacks of the different parts of the coast, I have divided the lodging options accordingly, but the reality is that where you base yourself geographically is not as important as where you choose to stay: It's the resort rather than the location that will make your beach break. Predictably, I have a preference for smaller, more individualistic places, where service is personal, dining and pool areas are intimate, and you will never feel engulfed by package tours. Note that I dutifully visited all the large resorts; despite finding their vast size and cookie-cutter decor depressing, I have included a few of the best below, with appropriate caveats, should you prefer the anonymity and vast array of facilities that come with these mega-beach lodgings.

Mnemba Island

Mnemba Island Lodge ★★★ (Moments) This small, chic resort, carefully tucked into its picture-perfect island on the edge of Zanzibar's best dive sites, is the most romantic escape in Africa and, despite a hefty price tag, worth every cent (just ask any of the regulars who return every year). A 7-minute boat ride from the northeastern tip of the Zanzibar mainland, the island is tiny (it takes about 10 min. to stroll its circumference), with a coastal forest that sticks out from the powder-soft beaches like a head of unruly hair. Arranged within the forest's cool depths are just 10 beach bungalows, gorgeous raised bedrooms fronted by the most elegant lounges, all open to the elements and reached via a sandy path from your private tanning pavilion. The size is ideal—everything is a short stroll away, either via the beach or through the shady forest—and the sensory pleasures are overwhelming, from the matchless collection of blues to the lush green interior, the gentle lapping of the ocean to the rustling birdsong, the softest sand underfoot to the wonderful in-house masseuse. The dive center is excellent (and, surrounded by a conservation area, you can have the most amazing snorkeling experience right off the beach), food is superb, and staff offer the kind of discreet intelligence that makes you leave feeling sincerely bereft. Make every effort to stay here.

Private Bag X27, Benmore 2010 South Africa ✆ **011/809-4441.** Fax 011/809-4400. www.andBeyond.com. 10 units. $2,200–$3,000 double. Rates include all meals, all drinks, laundry, boat trips, and snorkeling. MC, V. **Amenities:** Bar; dive center. *In room:* Minibar, hair dryer, free Wi-Fi.

South Coast

There are only two good options in the south: Fumba and Unguja (both happen to be sister resorts, though they differ in design and management style). Most of the other lodges on the south coast are looking tired and worn out; some of them are still occupied, pity the poor travelers, but many more are totally deserted and with a forlorn air.

Tip: If you're traveling to Kizimkazi for a dolphin excursion, pop into **Cabs Restaurant** (✆ **077/741-5554;** cabsrestaurant@yahoo.com), which enjoys a great (and prominent) location overlooking Kizimkazi's little harbor and traditional dhow. It's a worthwhile place to slake a thirst (ice available) and choose a snack from the Statar menu or from the Man Coose; lobster *masala* with coconut will run you Tsh30,000, grilled fish Tsh15,000.

Fumba ★ Overlooking a marine reserve, the best thing about this medium-size resort is that it is the only one on this stretch of coast, though its proximity to the Safari Blue launch sites (p. 356) takes away, to some extent, any real sense of exclusivity. That said, I like the intimate, personally run feel and the natural, relaxed atmosphere. It has lots of lovely hammocks and spaces in the organic, unmanicured grounds, including a secluded elevated Jacuzzi for romantic sundowners. However, it will not suit those looking for lots of activities and action (for that, try Breezes, p. 366). The entry-level cottages (preferable to the suites, where the built-in beds are painted a nauseating yellow) are generously sized, basically furnished (each with own bookshelf/library), and open to the environment, which means that mosquitoes can be a problem, so insist on a pristine mosquito net and pack in some coils. It also does not have a proper beach, but access to the sea is otherwise good. It's only 40 minutes from Stone Town.

P.O. Box 3705, Stone Town, Zanzibar. ✆ **077/786-0504** or 077/487-8701. www.fumbabeachlodge.co.tz. 26 units. Peak season $480 double, $550–$580 suite; high season $366 double, $450–$466 suite; low season $260 double, $330–$360 suite. Rates include breakfast and dinner. MC, V. **Amenities:** Restaurant; bar; dive and watersports center; pool; spa.

Unguja ★★★ **Value** The most exclusive and classy option on the south coast, Unguja is wonderfully intimate (only 11 villas) and really the only option worth considering if you have always wanted to swim with dolphins. The spartan villas are organic in style (rounded walls, cement floors) and huge, with a downstairs and upstairs bedroom, a bathroom with good water pressure (rare in Zanzibar), and alfresco areas to enjoy the gorgeous sea views. Most are open to the breeze (and, at night, mosquitoes); if you are used to air-conditioning, book one of the units that have this facility. It has a lovely pool area but a small beach. Unlike the east coast, the sea is very accessible (you can simply step into it via wooden steps at high tide), and snorkeling is possible right in front of the resort, though it is nowhere near as good as at Mnemba. Diving is pretty good, but you have to travel to the best dive sites (ask to go to Dolphin Wall). With great food, excellent hosts, and a romantic atmosphere, this is one of my top choices and is only an hour from the airport.

P.O. Box 675, Stone Town, Zanzibar. ✆ **077/447-7477.** www.ungujaresort.com. 11 units. High season family house and baobab villas $440 double, seaview villa $460; low season all units $350 double. Rates include breakfast and dinner. MC, V. **Amenities:** Restaurant; bar; airport transfers ($60); pool; watersports and dive center; free Wi-Fi (in restaurant area). *In room:* A/C (in some).

Southeast Coast

Approximately 90 minutes' drive from the airport, the southeast comprises a virtually unbroken stretch of wide white sands with three distinct fishing villages situated along it: Jambiani in the south, Paje in the center, and Bwejuu just north of this. Though there are a few good lodging options in Jambiani, this is the largest settlement on this coast, and the beach is very busy, with hawking and other forms of harassment by local villagers common complaints. Many visitors end up taking a taxi to spend the day on the uninhabited beaches farther north, and some end up moving into one of the lodges overlooking this; we suggest you cut this short and just book one from the outset. I have thus reviewed only the lodges running north of Bwejuu, rated one of the top 30 beaches in the world by *Condé Nast Traveler* for its "wide and blindingly white sands," and totally deserted except for the residents of the exclusive accommodations located on it. Of these, the gorgeous Baraza stands head and shoulders above its sister lodges (neighboring The Palms and Breezes) and is the most luxurious lodge on the island, while the tiny Anna of Zanzibar is arguably the most exclusive of the southeast bunch. Note that, at low tide, the ocean recedes for what appears to be miles, and you will then need a pool to cool off. The southeast coast also tends to be buffeted by a nearly constant breeze (hence the many kitesurfing schools that have sprung up along the coast, three alone in Paje); this can either be a welcome relief from the heat or an irritant. The breeze tends to drop during October and November, so don't come during these months if you're keen to try your hand at kitesurfing.

Anna of Zanzibar ★★★ **Finds** If you're looking for a romantic and very pampering break, with hardly any other guests to distract, this beachfront villa, promising "elaborate colonial simplicity," is the best choice on the island. The private holiday residence of two families, Anna's has a wonderfully intimate feel, with a gracious main house where the public areas are located and just four spacious suites leading from the central pool area.

Tips Traveling on a Budget?

Before losing its place to Ras Nungwi as the backpacker destination of choice, the southeast coast used to be the number-one budget traveler destination, and there is still a big cluster of budget options here, of which three are definitely worth looking into. Located in the village of Paje, a 2-minute walk from the beach, the 20-room **Paje by Night** ($70–$95 double, including breakfast, $40 airport transfers, and free Wi-Fi) is the best budget lodge for young travelers looking for some party action along with their beach experience, with disco nights, a pool with large inflatables to sprawl on, sports bar with big-screen TV, 24-hour restaurant, and a convivial crowd; their Friday parties last till 3am, and with no aural escape, you'd best join in. If you're looking for a more laid-back, relaxing, budget experience, there are two good Bwejuu options. The well-managed **Robinson's Place** (✆ **077/741-3479;** www.robinsonsplace.net; $50–$60 double) has no electricity, which makes for romantic evenings lit by paraffin lamps (book Robinson's House for the best sea view); food and service are excellent, making this exceptionally good value. Set back from the beach (less than a minute's stroll), **Mustapha's Place** (✆ **077/437-7442;** www.mustaphasplace.com; $30–$80 double) also serves delicious food, and you won't find more welcoming and accommodating staff on the island.

Each thatched suite, located separately in the well-tended garden, comprises a lounge area as well as an en suite bedroom and dressing area, decorated in elegant colonial-style furnishings, and a sea-facing terrace where early-morning tea or coffee are delivered. It's worth getting up for the sunrise. Staff are excellent, providing warm and very personal service. Cuisine standards are exceptional, given how small the lodge is, with fine dining under the stars and an emphasis on fresh seafood (given notice, however, the staff will prepare any dish you want). Giving five-star service, including a small spa, to a maximum of eight guests is quite a feat.

P.O. Box 3185, Stone Town, Zanzibar. ✆ **077/399-9387.** www.annaofzanzibar.com. 4 units. High season $600–$640 double; low season $540. Christmas supplement. Rates include all meals, afternoon tea, soft drinks, and in-house liquor. MC, V. **Amenities:** Restaurant; bar; *shisha* lounge; airport or seaport transfers (free for minimum 4-night booking, or $68); pool; room service; spa. *In room:* A/C, hair dryer, minibar, free Wi-Fi.

Baraza ★★★ I'm not fond of resorts, but this is a real beauty, and if you like space, opulence, modern conveniences, and great service, this is the number-one choice on the island. It's also the top choice for spa junkies, with the best-looking spa in East Africa and treatments to match. The third project of the Raguz family (the first being Breezes, the second The Palms), the Raguz sisters, Natalie and Paulina, have finessed every detail and gotten the recipe right. No expense has been spared in finishes and furnishings, and the attention to detail is very pleasing. Built along the lines of an Arabian palace (a relief from ubiquitous use of thatch), it has gorgeous symmetry, creamy white walls, and billowing fabrics with varied azure tones of the Zanzibar sea beyond. Bougainvilleas provide splashes of color in every conceivable hue. Villas are huge and plushly furnished, with all the conveniences of a 21st-century luxury suite. It's worth spending extra for a seafront villa rather than the seaview villas that are set back into the garden; seafront villas are literally built right on the beach, the ocean lapping meters from your feet, with private plunge pools, recliners, and shaded double beds. Excellent staff completes the picture. If I must nitpick, the cuisine doesn't quite match the superb standards set everywhere else.

P.O. Box 2284, Stone Town, Zanzibar. ✆ **077/444-0330,** -0331, or -0332. Fax 024/224-0387. www.baraza-zanzibar.com. 30 units. Peak season ocean-front villa 1,025€, oceanview villa 960€, sultan's villa (2 bedrooms) 1,035€, garden-view villa (2 bedrooms) 1,025€; high season ocean-front villa 860€, oceanview villa 800€, sultan's villa 870€, garden-view villa 860€; low season ocean-front villa 685€, ocean-view villa 645€, sultan's villa 695€, garden-view villa 685€. Rates include all meals, afternoon tea, soft drinks, and in-house liquor. MC, V. **Amenities:** Restaurant; bar; fitness center; 2 pools; spa; tennis court; dive center. *In room:* A/C, TV, hair dryer, minibar, Wi-Fi.

Breezes Beach Club & Spa ★ Breezes is popular, likely because it's home to the largest array of facilities on the island, including a highly regarded dive center, a huge array of water sports, an exceptional spa, the best kitesurfing school on the coast, and numerous bars and other public nooks in what feel like vast grounds. The rooms come in three categories, but very few of them have sea views. (Suites are elevated, with some ocean views, but every suite shares a balcony with another and are thus not very private.) Most overlook the scrubby garden and are spread over a huge area, so it can be quite a sweaty hike to get to the beach or public spaces; standard rooms are the farthest away, but plenty of deluxe rooms are, too. If you like small exclusive places, the sheer size of the dining room will feel dehumanizing, and there are many instances where you feel no more than just a number; the security (high walls and tight entrance regulations; guards in uniform wandering around 24/7) is also quite disconcerting. For a beach resort, rules that insist one wear shoes in the restaurant "as a sign of respect" are very silly. However, given the facilities and enduring popularity, this is definitely one of the best options of its type, with a vibrant atmosphere even when others stand empty.

P.O. Box 1361, Zanzibar. ✆ **024/224-0102** or 024/224-0467. www.breezes-zanzibar.com. 70 units. Peak season 350€ superior double, 430€ deluxe double, 480€ suite; high season 256€ superior double, 328€ deluxe double, 382€ suite; low season 154€ superior double, 198€ deluxe double, 244€ suite. All rates include breakfast and dinner buffet. MC, V. **Amenities:** 4 restaurants; 4 bars; airport transfers; babysitting; bikes; fitness center; Internet (dodgy connection; $6 per 30 min.); pool; room service; spa; tennis courts; disco/beach parties; dive center; entertainment center (DVDs on large screen). *In room:* A/C, hair dryer, minibar.

Echo Beach Hotel ★★ Neighboring the large, sprawling Breezes (a 10-min. walk away along the beach), this small resort shares the same awesome beach location but couldn't be more different. Here there are a maximum of 28 guests, all personally looked after by owners Sue and Andrew, both of whom earned a reputation for hospitality and cuisine while running the successful Chambre d'hote in the Loire Valley for 14 years. It's a bit like staying with friends of your parents, only the rooms are bigger and the food is better. The atmosphere is very peaceful, with only 13 rooms arranged in a half-circle around the central kidney-shape swimming pool; for the most privacy, book the top floor of the two double-story units (called first-floor beach-view apartments) or the generous two-bedroom family beach villa. Bathrooms are large and showers have good pressure. It's not as classy as Pongwe or Shooting Star (p. 369), but I love the fact that it's all very personal, with Sue a warm and welcoming mother figure to both guests and staff, and making every effort to ensure a comfortable stay.

Bwejuu, Zanzibar. ✆ **077/359-3260** or 077/359-3286. www.echobeachhotel.com. 13 units. High season $300–$350 double; low season $250–$300. Additional adult $80; additional child $60. MC, V. **Amenities:** Restaurant; bar; Jacuzzi; pool; room service; spa; dive center. *In room:* A/C, hair dryer.

The Palms ★★★ Wedged between Baraza and Breezes, The Palms (not to be confused with Palm Beach Inn) gives you all the luxury of Baraza but, with only six villas, more exclusivity. However, rooms are located too close together (for the most privacy, choose Cinnamon, also the villa closest to the beach) and are not as gorgeously finished and furnished as Baraza's. Note that, with The Palms not having its own facilities, you have to go to Breezes to use shared amenities such as the spa. Food is gourmet and much better than at Baraza, but some complain that it's too much having four-course meals twice a day. Given the price tag, which is hefty, it is all you'd expect from Zanzibar's tiniest boutique beach resort, but for the money, I'd opt for a beachfront Baraza villa or, if you'd prefer something a little more individualistic and funky (but not as comfortable), brand-new Kilindi in the north. Better still, head for Mnemba Island lodge.

Bwejuu, Zanzibar ✆ **077/359-3260** or 077/359-3286. www.palms-zanzibar.com. 6 units. Peak season 1,025€ double; high season 860€ double; low season 685€ double. Extra adult sharing 390€. Rates include all meals, high tea, soft drinks, and in-house spirits, beer, and wines. No credit cards. No children under 16. **Amenities:** Restaurant; bar; pool; Jacuzzi; free Internet; room service; dive center; access to all the facilities at Breezes. *In room:* A/C, TV, DVD, hair dryer, minibar.

Ras Michamvi ★★ (**Value**) If you're looking for a remote hideaway with absolutely no people, this is it. Located right at the northern tip of the southeastern coastal wedge, the atmosphere at this resort is as peaceful as it gets, surrounded by a seemingly endless stretch of deserted beaches (three, including the utterly secluded and private Coconut Beach). Elevated on a coral outcrop (much higher than any of the other east coast lodges), the 15 rooms, clustered in four thatched structures, and public areas are built on the lip of a rather steep incline, making for jaw-dropping views of the turquoise hues of the ocean, but a rather steep and sweaty walk to the pool area (located halfway between the bungalows and the ocean) and beachfront; at least you're burning off meals, which are delicious. Rooms are basic but comfortable, with Zanzibari beds and glorious views from the verandas. There's not much going on, so it won't suit the party animal (head for Breezes), but do note that there's a fabulous beach bar a little south of the resort (follow the music), should you tire of being in the same surroundings.

P.O. Box 635, Zanzibar. ✆ **024/223-1081** or 077/742-8178. www.rasmichamvi.com. 15 units. $180 double. Rates include breakfast and dinner. MC, V. **Amenities:** Restaurant; bar; fitness center; Internet; pool; room service; dive center. *In room:* A/C, hair dryer, minibar.

East Coast

The east coast, a mere 45 minutes from the airport, is classic Zanzibar, where every photograph you take is a visual cliché of perfect white sand and every shade of blue beyond. It is not as quiet as the southeast coast resorts (above), with quite a few beach hawkers in parts, and is also lined with sprawling resorts that all look alike: massive *makuti*-roof reception areas, oversize pools, and double-story bungalows squashed next to each other. When these resorts are full, you feel overwhelmed; when they're half empty, you feel lost. What's more, the huge distances you need to cover between reception and pool, room and beach are far from ideal. On the other hand are resorts that are small enough to not make you feel part of a package tour but that lack the essentials that make for a really relaxing holiday, such as energized and well-trained staff, maintained grounds, and a pool. The latter is really important; as is the case in the southeast, low tide means a 1km to 2km (½–1¼ miles) walk to the reefs. Aside from the time it takes to get there and back (the latter being the more exhausting), sea urchins lurk underfoot, so under no circumstances should this be attempted barefoot. The three top picks, all highly recommended for their intimacy and exclusivity, high service standards, organic rim-flow pools, and barefoot-chic style, are Pongwe Beach, Shooting Star, and Matemwe Beach Bungalows. Travelers watching their budget, however, should look into **Matemwe Beach Guesthouse** (www.matemwebeach.com), a small (just 22 units) and very relaxed option near Matemwe Bungalows; it offers comfortable accommodation right on the beach, is professionally managed (including the dive center), and offers exceptional value ($150–$190 double, $230–$270 suite; rates include breakfast and dinner).

In the large resort category, the bustling Blue Bay/Sultan Sands, organic Fairmont, and upmarket Zamani Kempinksi stand out and are reviewed below, but there are two more large resorts on this coast that may be worth looking into (at least just to see how price competitive they are at the time of booking). The relatively new **Neptune Pwani Beach Resort,** with all the trappings of a custom-built modern resort, and the older, more established (and, therefore, with more character) **Mapenzi Beach Club** are both four-star resorts owned by the Plan Hotel group (www.planhotel.com; both around $260–$500 full board double, depending on season and room) and offer good service and facilities and the same awesome stretch of beach. Rooms at Neptune Pwani closest to the beach or with proper sea views are those on the third floor that end in 51 to 54, 56, 57, 61 to 64, 66, 67, 71 to 73, 76, and 77; on the fourth floor, 51 to 54, 56, and 57.

Blue Bay Beach Resort ★ Located just south of the Kempinski and Fairmont, guests here (and at neighboring Sultan Sands, owned by the same company) have seamless access to both resorts' facilities, putting it on a par with Breezes when it comes to the great choice in dining, swimming, and drinking venues, as well as an excellent spa. Rooms in the superior category are spacious and elegantly furnished, with four-poster Zanzibari beds and dressing rooms, as well as semiprivate balconies. Overall the flow between the public spaces and the beach is far better than at Breezes (where you feel more cut off from the beach), with lovely sea views from most loungers and dining tables, but the resort is far more densely developed than Breezes.

Kinwengwa, northeast coast, P.O. Box 3276, Stone Town, Zanzibar. ✆ **024/224-0240,** -0241, -0242, -0243, or -0244. www.bluebayzanzibar.com. 112 units. Garden rooms $330–$520 double; superior $400–$570 double; Club 24 and suites $450–$700. Rates are seasonal and include breakfast and dinner. MC, V. **Amenities:** 5 restaurants; 6 bars; airport transfers ($55); babysitting; fitness center; Internet ($5 per 30 min.); 5 pools (including children's shallow pool); room service; spa; tennis court; dive center; entertainment center (DVDs on large screen); watersports center. *In room:* A/C, TV, minibar, hair dryer.

The Fairmont ★ Located on the northeast coast, near Matemwe and the Mnemba Atoll dive sites, this is another of the island's bigger resorts (109 rooms), but it gets a thumbs-up for its well-established and mature gardens (lush green with splashes of color that soften the edges), along with prodigious use of stone and adherence to low-level building height. As a result, the resort feels more like a sprawling but well-maintained village than a brand-new housing development (a category far too many fall into). All the rooms have been recently refurbished and are looking good, but the best value are those that are right on the beach (deluxe villas 116–120). There are also a few entry-level rooms (called island cottage) that are a stone's throw from the beach (625, 626, 637, 638, 640, and 641). Staff are fantastic and facilities are just what you'd expect from a large resort; the only quibble is the food, which is mediocre.

P.O. Box 4770, Zanzibar. ✆ **024/224-0391,** -0392, -0393, or -0394. Fax 024/224-0373. www.fairmontzanzibar.com. 109 units. Rates vary hugely depending on how busy the resort is; best to check website. Peak season $300–$400 double; high season $250–$380; low season $225–$350. All rates include breakfast and dinner. MC, V. **Amenities:** 2 restaurants; 2 bars; airport transfers; babysitting; bikes; children's playground w/shallow pool; fitness center; Internet ($5 per hr.); 2 pools; room service; spa; dive center; minigolf. *In room:* A/C, hair dryer, minibar, Wi-Fi.

Matemwe Beach Bungalows & Retreat ★★★ Located virtually opposite the diving mecca of Mnemba, these bungalows are the essence of barefoot chic and the ideal place to unwind if your idea of heaven is a book and a pool, with a snorkeling or island excursion or massage treatment to break up the day. Matemwe does not offer a huge array of facilities, nor do the bungalows represent top-end luxury such as Kempinski, but this is the real deal: just 12 bungalows, each privately located and extremely spacious (more so on both counts than Shooting Star and Pongwe), with organic wall shapes and huge Zanzibari beds, a loft bed alcove, and double hammocks on the sea-facing verandas with views that go on forever. Food in the open-to-the-breeze restaurant is excellent, particularly (of course) seafood; evening entertainment is brought in from Stone Town. If you're celebrating something extra special, book the Retreat, three privately located villas each with its own cocktail bar, air-conditioned bedroom, large bathroom, and plunge pool with shaded beds on a roof terrace. Beaches look gorgeous, but Matemwe is not ideal for swimming, with lots of urchins and coral rock underfoot; opt for snorkel trips by boat to Mnemba.

P.O. Box 3275, Zanzibar. ✆ **077/441-4834** or -4835. www.asilialodges.com. 15 units. High season bungalows $620 double, Retreat $1,050 double; low season $530, Retreat $860. Rates include all meals and certain activities; Retreat rate includes local spirits, wine, and beer. MC, V. **Amenities:** Restaurant; bar; airport transfers; babysitting; free Internet; 2 pools; spa treatments; dive center.

Pongwe Beach Hotel ★★★ Value This unpretentious, laid-back, 16-chalet beach retreat is located on a particularly stunning piece of coast, and while it has none of the luxury of Baraza or the huge list of facilities of the nearby Zamani Kempinski, this is a heavenly place to fulfill a barefoot castaway fantasy. If you can, book one of the 13 beach bungalows, each with a sea-facing veranda (but all sharing walls in clusters) and simply decorated with a traditional Zanzibari bed, flower-strewn and swathed in mosquito netting. It is around the infinity pool, gazing at the many shades of blue, or on the palm-shaded beach, either in the soft sand or strung up in a hammock, that you will laze away your days, wishing you never had to leave. There is no air-conditioning in the rooms, and showers are brackish, but this is easily the most romantic beach hotel on the east coast, though Shooting Star gives it a very good run for its money. Food is also very good—hardly surprising, considering that the in-house chefs receive ongoing training from consultant chefs from Europe. There is one two-bedroom beach chalet, ideal for families; alternatively, two single beds can be put into four of the larger rooms.

P.O. Box 297, Pongwe Beach, Zanzibar. ✆ **0784/336-181** or 077/316-9096. www.pongwe.com. 16 units. Peak season $240 double; high season $210–$220; low season $180. All rates include breakfast and dinner. V. **Amenities:** Restaurant; bar; airport transfers ($50); bikes; pool; Wi-Fi ($5 per 30 min.); dive center; fishing.

Shooting Star ★★★ Value This personally managed beach resort is a classy contender for top choice on the east coast, with a wonderful relaxed atmosphere, excellent rates, and rustic pared island style that resonates with island-hoppers from across the globe. Only 16 rooms, all whitewashed curves with splashes of color, share a number of lovely outdoor spaces: a great infinity pool, two stylish lounge/bars, and *the* most delightful spa (a single whitewashed room within earshot of the ocean). Cuisine is also superb. Rooms are cool and classy, with more facilities than you'll find at Matemwe Bungalows or Pongwe; the ocean and soft sandy beach are also more inviting than at Matemwe (though Pongwe's beach "bay" is the most sublime). Garden rooms are smaller and, therefore, slightly cheaper; given how lovely the public areas are, these represent excellent value, as do the slightly larger seaview cottages, which have great views from their verandas. Four of these are ideal for families, set out on two levels with the ground floor featuring a large air-conditioned double bedroom, shower room, and separate closet, and a twin children's room in the roof space with separate wash basin area. Suites feature two bedrooms, a private plunge pool, and a rooftop with bed and tub. Snorkeling and diving are done at nearby Blue Bay Resort.

P.O. Box 3076, Zanzibar. ✆ **077/74-4166.** www.shootingstarlodge.com. 16 units. High season $215 garden double, $300 seaview double, $575 suite; low season $185 garden, $250 seaview, $520 suite. Rates include breakfast and dinner; B&B and full-board rates also available. MC, V. **Amenities:** Restaurant; bar; airport transfers ($60); bikes; fitness center; Internet ($5 per 30 min.); pool; spa; dive center. *In room:* A/C, hair dryer.

Zamani Kempinski ★ If you want edge-to-edge facilities (including a 60m/197-ft. infinity pool and superb Anantara Spa) and a modern room with TV and Wi-Fi, the all-star Zamani Kempinski will certainly suit. One of the newer resorts on the island, it's all square edges, and no expense was spared in the making. Cool rooms are seriously elegant, and other than size (smallest is 42 sq. m/452 sq. ft.) wouldn't look out of place in one of the great city hotels, making the ocean views from every room a wonderful asset. En suite bathrooms are similarly modern and feature both indoor and outdoor (in private courtyard) showers, as well as a tub. Outside of your cocoon, the Kempinski is big, sprawling over 12 hectares (30 acres), so you'll need a golf cart to get around, which can be a hassle. The jetty bar stretching deep into the ocean (clearly seen from the air as you're flying into Stone Town) is a gorgeous place to settle in for cocktails. Be warned, though, that aside from the quite hefty price, whatever's not included in your package is likely to strike you as steep, and many people report feeling ripped off when faced with the final bill.

P.O. Box 3140, Kinwengwa, Zanzibar. ✆ **077/444-4477.** Fax 024/224-0066. www.kempinski-zanzibar.com. 117 units. Rates vary hugely depending on availability; check the website. $576 garden room double; $700 terrace room double; $985 suite; $2,400–$9,900 for 1-, 2-, and 3-bedroom villas. Rates include breakfast and dinner. MC, V. **Amenities:** 2 restaurants; 3 bars; airport transfers (68€); babysitting; fitness center; free Internet; 2 pools; room service; spa; dive center. *In room:* TV, A/C, hair dryer, minibar, free Wi-Fi.

North

The best choice on this part of the island is the classy **Ras Nungwi** (which is in the fortunate position of facing both the rising and setting sun), though the new **Kilindi,** located a little southwest at Kendwa, may still (once a few teething problems have been sorted) be crowned as best resort on the island. However, if you want to be in the heart of Nungwi's tourist beach, with plenty of independent restaurants (which means you aren't forced into the usual half- or full-board route), as well as a choice of dive centers, **Z Hotel** is the top choice. Aside from these three top-end options (reviewed below), there are a large number of budget accommodations options, most of which are pretty awful unless you're a beachcomber wearing a backpack. However, one midprice option well worth looking into, also located in Nungwi's tourist section (close to the main beach), is **Langi Langi Beach Bungalows** (www.langilangizanzibar.com). Make sure you book one of the nine seaview rooms ($140–$220 double B&B, depending on season and size); they're the latest addition to the hotel, and the views alone are worth the extra money. There's also a good restaurant and a pool.

The Italian Invasion

There are a number of resorts catering almost exclusively to Italian package groups, particularly the Ora group, which owns four hotels in the east (Hakune Majiwe, White Rose, Coral Reef, and the newest, Palumbo Reef) and another soulless edifice in the north (My Blue), in which all signage is in Italian and the Maasai guarding the entrance is as likely to greet you in Italian as Swahili. Also catering to package tours from the continent is the Plan Hotel group, which owns or manages three resorts, all neighboring each other on the east coast (Mapenzi Beach Club, Neptune Pwani, and Dream of Zanzibar), as well as the so-called five-star La Gemma Dell Est, a 138-room resort in the north where haughty reception staff prefer to speak Italian and pumping Eurotrash music drowns out the lapping of the ocean at the beachfront. The collective buying power of these resorts has meant that they are able to, in high season, charter planes to fly direct from Italy to Zanzibar. If you don't mind being in a resort that feels as if you are in Italy, the best of these are Hakune Majiwe (www.hakunamajiwe.net; half-board standard room $185–$275 double, depending on season), which, at 21 rooms, is relatively small; and Mapenzi Beach Club, which, being of an earlier era but recently refurbished, has a little more character than its swisher neighbors, Neptune Pwani and Dream of Zanzibar.

Kilindi ★★★ Zanzibar's new boutique lodge is luxurious enough to be a direct competitor to Baraza and has everyone talking, with (at research time) eight huge and privately placed pavilions, each with gorgeous elevated bedroom, separate "tower" bathroom, shaded lounge, and two plunge pools. The pool/bar/restaurant is the most chic in Zanzibar, with great music, the island's hippest food and beverages manager (who makes the meanest fresh watermelon cocktails), and sublime meals prepared by one of Jamie Oliver's chefs. It's a beautiful resort: younger, funkier, and more personal than the larger, more dignified, more obviously luxurious Baraza. If you want air-conditioning, TV, tub, quality toiletries, and other comforts, then Baraza is a better option, but the atmosphere here is decidedly more decadent. The only drawback is the distance between the rooms and the public area and beach paths—no doubt the price you pay for total privacy (rooms are located as far apart as possible), but it's a sweat in the midday heat. There is also no minibar in the room, and with no telephone, either, it's hard to utilize the personal butler service fully.

P.O. Box 3998, Zanzibar. ✆ **024/223-2473** or -1954. www.kilindi.com. 15 units. Peak season $1,500 double; high season $1,300 double; low season $900 double. Rates include all meals, snacks, specialty dinners, and local spirits (fresh fruit cocktals), wine, and beer. MC, V. **Amenities:** Restaurant; bar; pool; free Wi-Fi (in reception area and business center); cinema.

Ras Nungwi ★★★ This beautiful and well-established resort ticks all the right boxes: small, personal, private, and relaxed, with gorgeous ocean views and plenty of comfortable public areas to enjoy them from. Attention to detail is excellent (the wine list is, for instance, the best on the whole island, without being exorbitant) and service is also spot on: Attentive staff beam with the confidence that comes with delivering a happy guest experience for more than a decade. The four superior deluxe rooms are closest to the beach, but all of the 12 superior chalets have small verandas with chairs to enjoy the sea views; the garden-view rooms are larger and more private, and will suit those traveling with children. All rooms feature extra-width and -length Zanzibari beds, swathed in mosquito nets, but you are likely to spend most of your time in the public areas. Aside from the comfortably outfitted pool and beach areas, the bar/lounge is a very classy space and the ideal run-up to dinner, which is excellent. The dive center is also highly recommended. A pretty faultless experience, but if you're up for a more festive atmosphere, Z Hotel or Kilindi will suit you better.

P.O. Box 1784, Zanzibar, Tanzania. ✆ **024/223-3767,** 22/33-615 or 22/32-512. Fax 024/223-3098. www.rasnungwi.com 32 units. High season garden-view double $390, seaview chalet $480, seaview deluxe chalet $580, ocean suite $990; low season garden-view double $340, seaview chalet $420, seaview deluxe chalet $500, ocean suite $850. Rates include breakfast and dinner. MC, V. Hotel is closed Apr 20–May 19. **Amenities:** Restaurant; 2 bars; airport transfers ($40); pool; spa; dive, fish, and watersports center. *In room:* A/C, hair dryer, minibar.

Z Hotel ★★ This modern hotel, built on stilts right over the beach (somewhat contentiously), is a good alternative if Ras Nungwi or Kilindi falls outside your budget, or you simply want to be in the midst of a little action and a familiarly comfortable room featuring LCD TVs, iPod docking stations, and other modern amenities. Decor is an interesting mix of local design (modern Zanzibari four-poster beds) and international influences (a few pieces by Philippe Starck), with cool travertine floors throughout. The best-value rooms have sea views (only a little more than those with garden views), each with its own balcony. Given the hotel's central location, you are in the middle of everything, with a private pool deck and private beach area staffed with waiters who will bring you any cocktail under the sun. And the sunsets are stunning.

P.O. Box 4807, Zanzibar. ✆ **073/294-0303** or 077/426-6266. Fax 073/294-0171. www.thezhotel.com. 35 units. Peak season $300 garden-view double, $330 seaview double, $390–$480 suite; high season $260 garden-view, $290 seaview, $350–$440 suite; midseason $230 garden-view, $260 seaview, $320–$420 suite; low season $200 garden-view, $230 seaview, $290–$380 suite. Rates include breakfast. Children under 12 by arrangement. Closed May–June 15. MC, V. **Amenities:** Restaurant; bar; pool; spa; dive and watersports center. *In room:* A/C, TV, hair dryer, iPod docking station, minibar, free Wi-Fi.

3 PEMBA ★★★

50km (31 miles) NE of Unguja

Known in Arabic as Al Khundra, the "Green Island," Pemba is exactly that: a lush green gem covered in palms, paddies, indigenous forest, and large clove plantations floating in an azure sea. While it is similar in size to nearby Unguja and blessed with a similarly fertile soil and benign climate, it does not enjoy the same long stretches of sandy coastline. More important, it is ruled with impunity by the Unguja-based government, who see no benefit in encouraging competition for their tourists and are happy to maintain the status quo that sees Pemba producing more than 70% of the archipelago's cloves. Tourism is thus still a fledgling industry here, and despite its beauty, there are just four resorts chasing the tourist dollar.

As a result, the atmosphere is distinctively different. Aside from the lushness of the landscape—a stark contrast to Unguja's deforested and more drought-prone coastline—the island remains largely unsullied by outside influences, is far less populated (the largest town numbers 27,000), and has customs unique to what is largely an insular society. One of the most interesting of these is Pemba's bullfights. Thought to date back to the Portuguese occupation during the 16th and 17th centuries, these are held during important celebrations rather than set dates, though you can probably arrange to see one on New Year's Day. That said, it is not much of a spectacle; the "matador" evades a roped and hornless bull, and the bull is not harmed in any way.

More reserved than the tourist-savvy Zanzibarians, the local populace are focused on agrarian matters rather than the handful of unfamiliar faces that fly past in minibuses on their way to or from their resort, and despite the many living in penury, you are unlikely to be hassled by hawkers or any of the beach boys Western visitors to Unguja often complain of. Aside from offering a far more culturally authentic, less exploited experience, most visitors choose Pemba (either in addition to or as an alternative to one of the lodges near Mnemba) for the superlative diving, for if you're looking for beautiful coral reefs, virtually untouched and free of human presence, Pemba will not disappoint.

If you're looking to dive and snorkel, the best location is Misali Island, lying within the Pemba Channel Marine Conservation Area. Said to be a popular pirates' hide-out during the 17th century, it was apparently referred to as Captain Kidd's Island and said to perhaps still contain his buried treasure. The real jewels, however, are spotted among the sculptural coral reefs, whose variety is on par with that on Mafia. And if you're lucky, you might see a dazzling green and rather rare Fischer's Turaco bird in the trees.

Easiest access to Misali is from Fundu Lagoon, a wonderful resort reviewed below. Other good diving sites are at Uvinje Gap, as well as Panza Island, near the southern tip, which has a superb diving site called Emerald Reef; time allowing, check out the nearby Southern Wreck. Off the northwest coast, Manta Point is named after the giant manta rays that frequent the area. There is also a very good lodge, **Manta Reef Lodge** (www.mantareeflodge.com), which offers good value and is even better than the more popular Fundu if what you really want is solitude.

WHERE TO STAY

Fundu Lagoon ★★★ Whereas some of the lodges on Zanzibar provide a sense of that island castaway fantasy, Fundu Lagoon dishes up the reality. Just getting to this aptly described "beach safari camp" is an adventure. Located on the isolated west coast of Pemba Island, it's a 40-minute taxi journey from airport to harbor and another 20 minutes by speedboat, following an untouched and densely green coastline before Fundu's thatched bungalows peek out of the foliage and its sandy beaches come into view. Once there, you will do nothing but relax, and there are plenty of places to do so, including a wonderfully elevated pool and numerous shaded nooks, along with the friendliest staff to see to your every need. Tented rooms, located along separate pathways in the dense foliage, are indeed beach safari: canvas walls on hardwood, stilted decks, and a palm-thatch roof, each with private balconies overlooking the sea. Obviously, beachfront tents are tops, but given the privacy and views of the hillside tents, these, too, are excellent. Superior suites are more space than you need. It's both a romantic hideaway and a serious divers' destination, but mostly it's a place that makes you feel truly cut off from reality, and that's a rare gift.

P.O. Box 3945, Zanzibar. ✆ **076/359-2820** or 077/443-8668. www.fundulagoon.com. 16 units. High season $740 hillside double, $810 beach-front double, $970–$1,220 suite; low season $610 hillside; $660 beach-front, $850–$1,060 suite. Rates include all meals, in-house drinks, laundry, and selected activities. Closed Apr 16–June 14. MC, V. **Amenities:** Restaurant; 2 bars; airport transfers ($40); free Internet; pool; dive center. *In room:* Minibar.

14

Mafia Island

By Pippa de Bruyn

The very name conjures images of smuggler's coves and illicit peddling of ill-gotten gains. Ironic, really, for while Mafia Island and its surrounding archipelago has nothing to do with a society of secretive Sicilian criminals, it does indeed contain a hidden treasure-trove, its flashing gems hidden in the coral reefs that run the length of the island, from Ras Mkumbi at the northern tip to the islets strewn in the south.

Lapping the largely uninhabited archipelago that lies 200km (124 miles) south of Zanzibar, Mafia Marine Park's waters hold some of the richest reefs in the world, with an extraordinary variety of hard and soft corals and more than 400 species of fish flitting along its shallow reefs and their plummeting walls. Better still, with a grand total of six accommodations options in the entire archipelago, diving these clear waters is a far more exclusive experience than in Zanzibar or even Pemba. Whether it's swimming alongside a whale shark, exulting at the exquisite hues of a butterfly fish, or trailing a rare green turtle, you will savor what is tantamount to a religious experience in relative solitude.

When you've finished exploring this hidden world, there is little more satisfying then lying back on your dhow, listening to the snap of the wind grabbing the unfurled sailcloth and the rhythmical slap of water as the bow carves its way back to shore. As the sinking sun turns the horizon into a vast burning ember, one wonders what one ever found fault with in the world.

But the archipelago is more than just a magical dive site—for centuries, Mafia played a key role in the East African trading routes that linked Zanzibar with Kilwa, the gold- and slave-trading city-state on the mainland's southern coast. The earliest-known settlement on Mafia is thought to have been built in the 11th century at Ras Kisimani, where coins predating the 1300s and minted in Kilwa, China, Mongolia, India, and Arabia have been uncovered, followed by Kua, a settlement established on nearby Juani Island in the 13th century. Little is left of the medieval settlement of Ras Kisimani, destroyed by a cyclone, but Kua's ruins still stand on Juani Island—a wonderfully atmospheric place, the crumbling walls of its palace now in the firm grip of fig tree roots, its only minions wild pig and antelope.

Naturally, these ruins cannot compete with the vibrancy of Zanzibar's Stone Town, but if you're looking for privacy and seclusion, Mafia offers a true respite: a tropical island paradise that lies a mere half-hour flight from Dar es Salaam, but trailing 50 years behind the 21st century, with nothing to distract you from your reverie but the rustle of palm trees or the far-off murmur of fisherman heading out to sea on their dhows. Untouched, remote, and serene, it's the ultimate romantic hideaway and the perfect end to a land-based safari.

ESSENTIALS

VISITOR INFORMATION There is no tourism office on Mafia. Kilondoni has a bank and post office, but you will do any currency exchange or posting through your lodge.

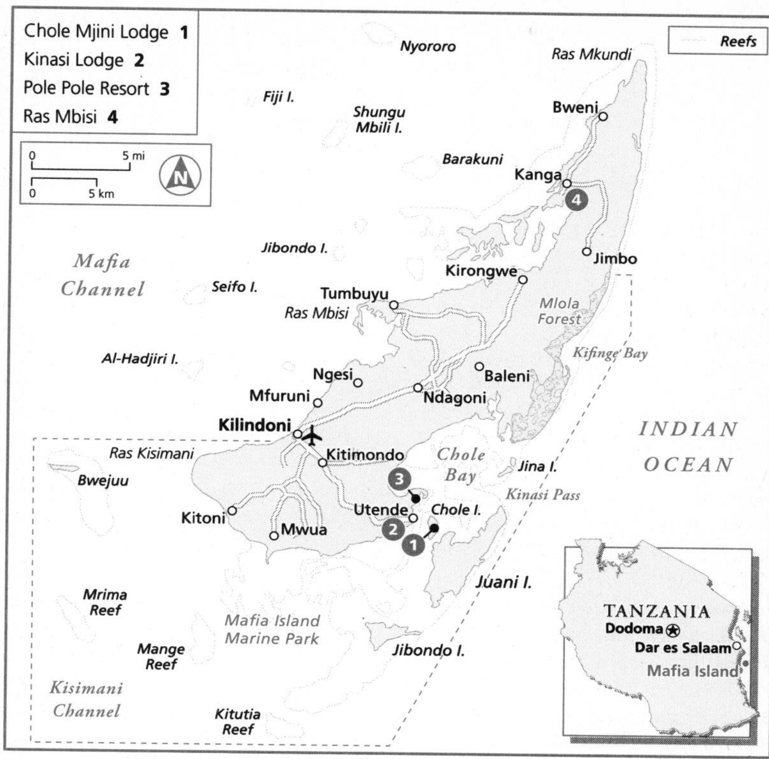

Pole Pole, Kinasi, and Chole Mjini are all within Mafia Marine Park, which costs $10 per person, per day; you will need to prepay this amount in cash on entering the park, so have the figure (in dollars) ready, as the permit will be checked upon departure. For more information on Mafia, visit www.mafiaisland.com or www.zanzibar.net.

GETTING THERE **By Air** The airstrip is located in Kilondoni, "capital" of Mafia, which is no more than a largish village; Utende Beach lies about 20 minutes' drive from here. **Coastal Aviation** (www.coastal.cc) offers a daily scheduled flight to Mafia from Dar es Salaam, arriving at 3pm and departing Mafia at 3:30pm; at press time, the return trip costs $220 per person. (Remember that you may carry only 15kg/33 lb. per person in luggage on these planes, preferably in soft bags.) You can book your flight to Mafia from Arusha, Ruaha, Selous, and Zanzibar, but all flights go via Dar. Kinasi Lodge has its own aircraft, which you can charter if you are staying there, for not significantly more than Coastal Aviation. ***Note:*** The international departure tax ($30) and Safety Fee ($8) are included in ticket prices from Dar es Salaam but not necessarily from Zanzibar, so carry additional cash to cover this eventuality.

Moments **What Century Are We In?**

The sense of stepping outside time starts as you descend to meet the palm-lined sandy clearing that passes for a runway. The pilot taxis up to a whitewashed shed, juddering to a halt near a neatly placed row of white plastic chairs behind a hand-painted sign that reads DEPARTURE LOUNGE. Bumping along dirt tracks in a battered Series 1 Land Rover, past villages and fecund fields and waving children, it is as if you've traveled back 50 years.

By Boat There is no scheduled commercial boat service to Mafia Island.

GETTING AROUND Mafia island is 48km (30 miles) long and 17km (11 miles) at its widest point, with two main dirt tracks running from Kilondoni, the main village (where the airstrip is located): One reaches Bweni in the north, and the other leads to Utende Beach in the southeast, where three of Mafia's lodges lie within 1km (½ mile) of each other (and Chole Island is clearly visible on the other side of the bay). With hardly any vehicles to speak of on the island, your lodge will arrange for your transfer or Mafia Island excursions, in either in a battered Land Rover or private lodge vehicle (Pole Pole includes this transfer in the price, Chole Mjini charges around $30 per car trip, and Kinasi charges 15€ per person). To reach the smaller islands that lie south and west (Chole, Jibondo, Juani, Bwejuu), you will need to charter a dhow; again, your lodge will arrange this.

WHEN TO GO Like the mainland, the island has two rainy seasons: short rains in November and December, and long rains from March to May, when the island's tourism more or less closes down. The temperature on the island is stable, rarely dropping below 20°C (68°F) or rising above 33°C (91°F). June to September is the coolest period; during this time, you can dive only within Chole Bay. The best time of the year for diving is from October to February, when visibility is best—up to 25m (8 ft.)—and you can dive the walls outside the reef that protects Chole Bay. Peak accommodation rates are usually charged in August and the Christmas/New Year period. Most visitors stay 4 to 5 nights.

EXPLORING THE AREA

DIVING & SNORKELING ★★★ With more than 400 species of fish, 40 genera of coral, and five species of marine turtle, scuba diving and snorkeling are the primary reasons most people come to Tanzania's first marine park. The most reliable dive sites are within Chole Bay—a large protected bay with regular water flow but minimal currents, and three types of dive sites (sloping reefs, coral walls, and coral gardens, covering depths of 5m–27m/16 ft.–89 ft.), suitable for both the total novice and the very experienced. If you're here for only a few days, make sure you dive Milimani Reef and Maweni (the latter ideal for beginners and a world-class snorkeling site). Both are located at the mouth of the bay along Mafia's Kinasi Pass, which, in turn, offers three superb dives (for more experienced divers)—South Wall, Utumbi, and Pinnacle. The coral gardens, said to contain the best hard corals in East Africa, offer excellent snorkeling (though, personally, I prefer Maweni). Try to include Milimani and Maweni during your stay, but bear in mind that your dive instructor/leader will decide what's best depending on tides, visibility, and experience levels.

Experienced divers tackle the drops north of Chole Bay, referred to as "outside" dives, but these are available only during certain months of the year (Oct–Feb) due to wind and strong currents.

All the lodges offer dive excursions and courses: Kinasi Lodge has its own dive center, well equipped and superbly organized, but its "like it or leave it" dive master, while very experienced, is not known for his warmth. Pole Pole has access to the dive center at Mafia Island Lodges, run by laid-back and helpful Moez, another experienced diver, but he's not committed to joining every excursion. If you are here to dive, Chole Mjini is definitely where I would recommend you stay—either Jean or Anne de Villiers, the hands-on lodge proprietors, will fit the equipment for comfort prior to every snorkel or dive expedition and personally accompany guests on every dive or snorkel outing, along with their dive crew; they take a maximum of six divers (and then only if they're reasonably experienced) on the boat. Jean, a biologist by profession, is a PADI Master SCUBA Diver Trainer, and after more than 1,000 dives here, he knows Mafia's waters better than anyone. He's excellent at teaching total novices as well as the very experienced (he teaches various specialist diving courses such as navigation and coral reef ecology to U.S. college students twice a year). A single dive with full equipment should cost around $55; a night dive is about $70. There are various dive packages, with prices per dive decreasing the more dives you do (four dives with full equipment will run you $300).

Never dived before? Even if you are here for only a few days and have never dived, you can opt to do so within a 48-hour period if you complete a Discover SCUBA course ($150), which allows total novices to do a deep-sea dive after a few hours' instruction and a verbal test characterized chiefly by its brevity. The Discover SCUBA course is also offered at the Kinasi and Mafia Island Lodges dive centers, but Jean is the only one who refuses to take down more than two novices per dive, which not only is safer, but significantly increases your chances of getting below the surface without panicking.

SWIMMING WITH WHALE SHARKS ★★★ Whale sharks tend to arrive in Mafia waters around November, usually stay until February, and are found in the shallow waters on the northwestern side of the island, facing Kilondoni. If swimming with these gentle giants is your dream, Ras Mbisi, the only lodge on this side of the island, is the place to stay. There is no guarantee that you will see them, but the local fishermen, who follow the movements of whale sharks, are excellent trackers and their skills are utilized to help protect these gentle giants, which feed on plankton a few hundred meters from the shore. This excursion costs $60 to $100 from Mafia Marine park lodges.

SANDBANK PICNIC ★★ Marimbani sand bank is a dazzling strip of white sand, approximately 600 to 700m (1,968–2,296 ft.) long, that appears only during low tide. Your lodge will drop you here with some refreshments and leave you alone to explore the warm crystal-clear waters that surround the bank. The one side of the bank drops off sharply—ideal for swimming—whereas the other side remains slightly submerged, with pockets filled with marine life such as tiger cowries, sea urchins (watch out!), crabs, and starfish; these attract plovers and other seabirds that feed on this trapped bounty. From the Kitutia sand bank (on the Ras Mbisi side of Mafia island, facing Kilondoni), you can even snorkel the surrounding reefs; these have suffered, as they are not as protected as Chole Bay, but in combination with time spent lolling on Kitutia, they offer a good excursion.

CHOLE & JUANI ISLAND EXCURSIONS ★★ Tiny Chole—a short dhow trip across Chole Bay—was once the main settlement in the archipelago, home to a number of wealthy Omani traders who used Mafia Island as their farmland, where they planted the coconut palms that dominate the skyline today. Today Chole is home to a vibrant village and one of the best eco-lodges in Africa, set amid the crumbling ruins of old Arab mansions and massive baobabs, as well as structures built by the Germans from 1892 (the customs house that can be seen on the beach from Chole Bay is currently being transformed into a sunset bar by Jean from Chole Mjini—it's a great spot and, once completed, likely to be featured in any number of glossy magazines' Top 100 Places to Order a Drink).

The atmosphere in the village is very friendly (do bear in mind that it's a Muslim village, so women are asked to cover their shoulders and knees with a wrapped *kikoi,* or light shawl), and visitors are made to feel very welcome. Stop at the boatyard to see how dhows are built much as they have been for centuries. In fact, Mafia boat builders are renowned for their skill; amazingly, they build entirely by eye, using traditional tools and bending timbers into shape. Nearby Jipondo Island is another traditional shipbuilding center and well worth a visit if you're interested in this ancient craft. While on Chole, visit Popo Park, the world's first park for the conservation of the fruit bat, also known as the flying fox; every evening, you will see the bats wing their way from Chole to mainland Mafia, where they feed on crops before returning to Chole Island at dawn. At low tide, you can walk across from Chole to Juani Island, or catch a dhow to explore the 13th-century ruins of Kua, once the Shirazi capital of Mafia and thought to have been founded at the same time as Kilwa, but now a wild and atmospheric ruined village, home to rooting wild pigs and small antelope. The southern point of Juani features a long channel, linking the big inland bay with the open sea; this is where you will find the island's "blue lagoon," effectively a (tidal) swimming pool.

FISHING ★★★ It's been more than 60 years since Conan Doyle set the all Africa record with a 34.2kg (75.4 lb.) dorado; if you're keen to try your hand at breaking this, the deep-sea crescent off Mafia and the Songo Songo archipelago is said to be the best game-fishing grounds in East Africa and one of the most exciting in the world. Kinasi Lodge has a dedicated fishing boat fully equipped with deep-sea and inshore fishing tackle, electronics, and safety equipment for up to four fishermen. Fishing grounds include Mafia Island, Songo Songo islands, Nyuni and Njovi islands, and the channels from the Rufiji Delta south to Lindi. A 7-day fishing license will run you $20.

Moments Swimming with the Biggest Fish in the Sea

It's nothing short of humbling swimming alongside a whale shark, some of which grow to be 150 years old, weigh in at 15 tons, and reach a length of 14m (46 ft.). While it is classified as a shark and has a huge mouth filled with around 3,000 teeth, these gentle giants are totally harmless and feed on enormous amounts of plankton sieved through their gills as they swim. Covering vast distances at a steady 5kmph (3 mph), the whale sharks appear indifferent to the presence of humans paddling alongside.

WHERE TO STAY & DINE

There are only six options; the four best are reviewed below. If you are on a budget, you may want to look at the 1970s government-built **Mafia Island Lodge** (www.mafialodge.com), but I suspect you'll find much better value for your money on Zanzibar. Located on Utende Beach (a 10-min. walk from Pole Pole and Kinasi), it was the first to open on Mafia, and although the airy double-volume public lounge/bar has stood the test of time and remains a great space, the same is not true of the rooms. It's also set too far back from the beach, regardless of the tide—by the time you've reached the lodge, you are perspiring and ready to turn around and head back to the water (admittedly, there is a beach bar to quench your thirst while there). Despite the fact that it is quite a bit cheaper than the other options (126€–150€ double standard room, full board) I don't think these rates fully reflect its inferior position.

On Mafia Island

Kinasi Lodge ★★ (Kids At first glance, this sprawling property—in some ways, the most comfortable lodge on Mafia—looks like a large old-fashioned resort, but there are only 15 cottages spread out under the coconut palms, sharing an impressive range of amenities, including a well-equipped dive center, a dedicated deep-sea fishing boat, kayaks, a snooker table, an extensive wine cellar, massage rooms (an excellent facility run by two Thai ladies), and a swimming pool—the latter essential during the hours when the tide recedes and the sea is a long, hot trudge away. The rooms are great: spacious palm-thatched roof bungalows, well situated, with shaded verandas. My favorite unit is the charming double-story owner's suite; at $255 to $340 (depending on season), it offers good value relative to the other rooms. Entry-level garden-view rooms are tranquil, but if you want a great sea view, book no 6. Public spaces are very comfortable, and there's always someone on hand to help. The main drawback is the resident dive instructor, who seems to dislike most of his clients; this is thus not the best place to come if you want to learn how to dive or are inexperienced and need to feel looked after. Given that the lodge has the most facilities and family rooms (two bedrooms sharing a bathroom), this is a great destination for parents, but a bit commercial if you're looking for a romantic hideaway.

Utende Beach, Mafia Island Marine Park. ✆ **074/74-18256** or 074/12-42977. www.kinasilodge.com. 15 units. Peak season standard room $340–$380 double (depending on view), $360 owner's suite, $360 family room (for 4); standard season $300–$320 double, $320 owner's suite, $320 family room (for 4); incentive season $270–$290 double, $290 owner's suite, $290 family room (for 4). Rates include all meals. Closed after Easter to June 1. MC, V. Christmas/New Year's surcharges apply. **Amenities:** Bar; bikes; dive center; Internet; pool; room service.

Pole Pole Resort ★★ Voted one of the world's top 25 eco-resorts by *The Times,* Italian-owned Pole Pole is the smallest lodge on Mafia, and though it is a classier, more romantic experience than neighboring Kinasi and has more creature comforts than Chole (flushing toilets, a steady supply of ice), it's never at the expense of that island essential: a laid-back, anything-goes atmosphere. It also has—when the tide is high—the most photogenic position on Utende Beach, a palm-lined crescent of sand with shaded traditional loungers and—best of all—wonderful staff on hand to ensure that you soak up the sun armed with whatever you desire (although even they cannot call the tide back in, which is when you'll want a pool if you're not out diving). The beach is also where the billowing massage tents are located—an idyllic place to be pampered, particularly with the lapping from Chole Bay a few meters away. The timber-stilted bungalows are a little close to each other but are reasonably comfortable, though they don't take advantage of the sea views as the rooms do at Kinasi, Ras Mibisi, and Chole Mjini. The lounge enjoys a great view but is not comfortably furnished; thankfully, the open-air bar/dining room is, as this is where you most feel that you've arrived in paradise, with gorgeous views vying with wonderful four-course meals—a sophisticated blend of Italian and Swahili influences, served by attentive staff well trained by the charming Maura.

Utende Beach, Mafia Island Marine Park. ✆ **0787/30-3043.** www.polepole.com. 9 units. Peak season (Aug and Dec 20–Jan 10) 420€ double; high season 360€ double. Rates include all meals; early-morning tea; laundry (2 items per person, per day); tea, coffee, and bottled water; daily excursions in Chole Bay; and transfers to/from the airport. Closed Apr and May. MC, V. Christmas/New Year's surcharges apply. **Amenities:** Bar; airport transfers; room service; dive center.

Ras Mbisi ★★★ The latest lodge to be built on Mafia (in 2007), and the only one currently on the remote and pristine beaches of the island's western shores, Ras Mbisi offers chic-shack accommodation meters from the Indian Ocean, great food (sourced and grown locally), a swimming pool, thoughtful public spaces, and, like Chole Mjini, very hands-on family owner-hosts, headed by Michelle. As Mafia Marine Park is a good hour's drive from the lodge, it's perhaps not ideal if you're here just for the diving (for that, book with Chole Mjini), but the lodge does face the waters favored by whale sharks and humpback whales. There is also snorkeling off the Kitutia sand bank, along with sunset dhow trips and plenty of opportunities to explore unvisited attractions such as the Mlola Forest and the nearby islands of Shungu Mbili and Barakuni. Staff, as at Pole Pole, is excellent. The lodge is intimate, with only nine "open tent" en suite *bandas,* built from sustainable coco wood by local artisans—these are not as privately located as at Chole, but unlike at Pole Pole, they are right on the beach. The fabulous open-air design makes the most of the sea views and breezes.

P.O. Box 16, Mafia Island, Tanzania. ✆ **0754/66-3739** or 0734/28-4397. www.mafiaislandtz.com. 9 units. High season $390 double; low season $330 double; $50 supplement on Dec 31. No credit cards. Rates include all meals, early-morning tea and coffee on your veranda, midmorning coffee and afternoon high tea, transfers, and drinking water. Closed Apr and May. **Amenities:** Bar; dive center; Internet; pool; room service.

On Chole Island

Chole Mjini Lodge ★★★ Kids One of my favorite places on Earth—with no electricity, no road, no water mains (but excellent company)—this is the ideal destination for anyone harboring a castaway fantasy. Reached by boat, you approach the dense mangrove-edged shoreline and start to spot the lodge's treehouses—most of which are built around and into the island's massive baobabs. Aside from the lodge, which can accommodate a maximum of 14 people, only the small village and a large population of fruit bats share the .5 sq. km (¼ sq. mile) island; the focus is very much on diving and snorkeling, with Jean and Anne providing the most hands-on marine experiences in the archipelago. Furniture is sparse but comfortable, and (aside from one ground unit) toilets are of the composting variety. However, if you think that real luxury is living in a large stilted treehouse open to the sea breeze, private enough to enjoy the view naked and near enough to the water's edge to be lulled by the sound of the tide trickling back through the mangrove roots, this is the place for you. The atmosphere also sets this lodge apart. Jean and Anne host the evening dinner every night and are both excellent company—the charismatic Jean is the antithesis of the hospitality-trained sycophants that dominate top-end tourism. As a result (and because they eschew traditional marketing), their guests are of a particular ilk, and the atmosphere is that of a private gathering of hand-picked guests. The only drawback is that there are no beaches for swimming.

Chole Island, Tanzania. ✆ **0748/52-0799.** www.intotanzania.com. To e-mail the lodge directly, send a brief message only to 2chole@bushmail.net, because messages are sent over a very low-speed radio link. 7 units. Peak season $600 double; high season $480 double; low season $400 double. Significant reductions for 6-night and longer stays. Closed Mar 16–June. Rates include all meals, drinking water, laundry, and daily dhow-sailing excursion. No credit cards. **Amenities:** Bar; dive center.

15 The Northern Circuit

by Pippa de Bruyn

Stretching from the snow-capped heights of Kilimanjaro, undulating through Africa's central Great Rift Valley to the shores of Lake Victoria, Tanzania's well-trod Northern Circuit is the country's most popular safari destination, and justifiably so. Blessed with an incredible array of the continent's highlights—world's highest free-standing mountain, largest intact volcanic caldera, oldest hominid footprint, and largest migration of game on Earth—the Northern Circuit is (and should be) a given on any East African itinerary.

Kilimanjaro aside, the Serengeti and Ngorongoro Crater are the circuit's most famous destinations, but with careful planning, you can fit in a great deal more, untrammeled by the large number of visitors this region inevitably attracts, despite the relatively high costs of traveling here.

Within easy striking distance of Arusha, unofficial safari capital of the Northern Circuit, Tarangire National Park is not only one of Tanzania's most beautiful reserves, with baobab-studded yellow plains giving way to lush green swamps, but during the dry season, when large herds of game migrate to the perennial waters of the Tarangire River, your game experiences will rival those of the Serengeti.

The next stop (or penultimate, depending on which direction you're traveling) is Lake Manyara, a shallow soda lake at the base of Gregory Rift, the cliffs of which mark the steep ascent to the volcanic highlands of Ngorongoro. With the country's densest concentration of elephants, all well habituated to the presence of vehicles and humans, close-up encounters with Lake Manyara's resident pachyderms are guaranteed, as are stunning vistas the farther south you travel, culminating in the viewpoints above the Maji Moti hot springs, where pink clouds of flamingos hover above a white soda shoreline and bands of gray and blue meet a cerulean sky. If this inspires a yen for more awe-inspiring landscapes, set aside 2 days and head north to Lake Natron, breeding site for East Africa's flamingos, its caustic waters shadowed by the brooding presence of Ol Doinyo L'Engai. The last in the line of the Rift Valley's active volcanoes, this is the Maasai's sacred "Mountain of God," as compelling as Kilimanjaro in its bleak majesty.

More jaw-dropping landscapes await as you ascend the 800m (2,624-ft.) Gregory Rift to enter the Ngorongoro Conservation Area, an area of some 8,300 sq. km (3,237 sq. miles) stretching from the cool Karatu Highlands to the Serengeti plains in the west. The highlight of the Ngorongoro Conservation Area is the crater after which it is named, but this is also the traditional heartland of the Maasai, and traversing the region you will encounter that quintessential African sight: lone warrior-herders swathed in red, spear and stick held aloft as they stride before their cattle across the vast and empty plains. Also falling within the Conservation Area is

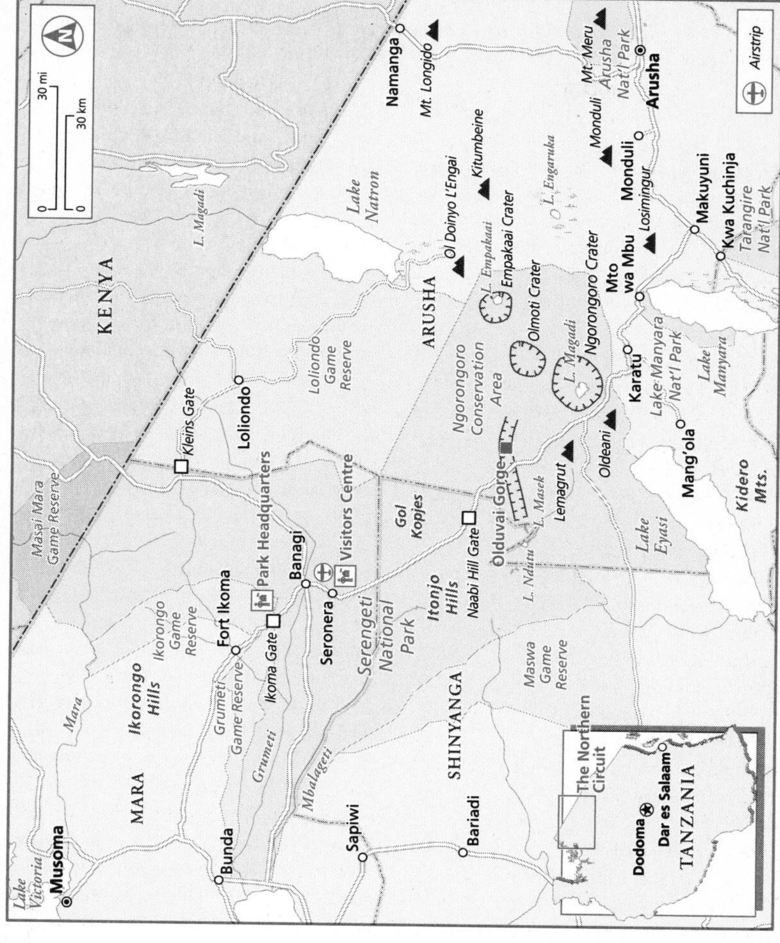

Olduvai Gorge, where Mary Leakey unearthed footsteps made by the earliest proto-humans around 3.6 million years ago, and archaeologists continue to uncover clues to the origins of ancient man.

Finally, it is the Serengeti that will leave you truly dumbstruck: Home to what is regularly vaunted as the greatest wildlife spectacle on planet Earth, this World Heritage Site—umbrella-topped acacias and vast herds in a sea of yellow grass—is the Africa of your dreams, its timeless beauty reassuring in an otherwise rapidly changing world.

1 ARUSHA

80km (50 miles) from Moshi, 647km (401 miles) from Dar es Salaam, 255km (158 miles) from Nairobi, 190km (118 miles) from Ngorongoro, 130km (81 miles) from Lake Manyara, 335km (208 miles) from Serengeti

The first guidebook to Arusha, published in 1929, states somewhat condescendingly that the new visitor "will come into contact with some of the most interesting and picturesque tribes that inhabit Africa, each with their own quaint customs and histories," while The New Arusha Hotel advertised "modern sanitation" and "a teak dancing floor." The dance floor has fallen victim to time, but the Arusha Hotel still stands sentinel opposite the sandstone Clock Tower, built to mark the halfway point between the Cape and Cairo, and the bustling commercial activity you encounter—mainly by the self-same "picturesque tribes"—is a reminder of these heady frontier days, when the journey to Moshi by ox-wagon took a week and farm produce was auctioned in the Arusha Hotel's lounge.

Home to various governmental and nongovernmental organizations (including the headquarters of Tanzania National Parks, East African Community, and the African Wildlife Foundation), as well as the ever-burgeoning number of tourist operators catering to the needs of foreigners here to climb Kili or explore the Northern Circuit's National Parks, Arusha is known as the safari capital of Tanzania. Arusha's International Convention Centre is also where Rwanda's International Criminal Tribunal has been held, but while the 15-year presence of a relatively large and sophisticated foreign contingency has no doubt impacted what some (usually local tourism brochures) smugly refer to as "The Geneva of Africa," Arusha remains a busy but nondescript African town that would see little tourist traffic, were it not for its proximity to the national parks that make up the Northern Circuit.

Given the distances and complexities involved in reaching the Northern Circuit from the Northern Hemisphere, a day for recovery here is virtually essential; thankfully, there are a number of pleasant lodging options in and around town. Many options in the tranquil rural surrounds have views of Mount Meru (also known as *Oldonyo Orok,* "Black Mountain," as the Maasai call Arusha's towering backdrop), or, to the east, Kilimanjaro (known as "White Mountain").

Protected by Arusha National Park, Mount Meru is, at 4,556m (14,944 ft.), Africa's fifth-highest mountain; like Kilimanjaro, it is often swaddled in cloud cover, deigning to show its regal peaks—dusted with snow from June to August—for only a few hours every day. If you are planning to spend a few days in Arusha, make sure you set aside some time to explore Arusha National Park, a small (137-sq.-km/53-sq.-mile) but pretty reserve with dirt tracks leading through the montane forests, its dense canopy inhabited by black-and-white colobus monkeys that crash through the undergrowth, and occasionally opening up to reveal unexpected glades where giraffe, zebra, and buffalo graze. Arusha National Park even has its own crater, Ngordoto, with sweeping views across the caldera from its lip, as well as shallow alkaline lakes that attract a variety of waterfowl and can be circuited by car. Better still, explore the park on foot; like Kili, it will take 4 days to reach Mount Meru's summit, and many seasoned Kili climbers rate it as a more satisfying experience. With stunning scenery, many more wildlife encounters, far fewer people, and awesome views of Kilimanjaro from the mountain's eastern flanks, who can blame them?

ESSENTIALS

GETTING THERE By Plane The closest airport is Kilimanjaro International Airport (referred to as KIA locally, but abbreviated JRO when doing Internet research), 60km (35 miles) east of Arusha center.

Unless you are traveling the Southern Circuit (in which case, your international arrival point would be Dar es Salaam), a more efficient way to get to Arusha may be via Nairobi airport (NBO) in Kenya, with a connecting flight to KIA.

Kenya Airways, in partnership with **Precision Air** (www.precisionairtz.com), operates four to five flights daily from Nairobi to KIA; it is designed as a connector flight, so you should be able to remain in transit and avoid paying for a Kenya visa (for your own peace of mind, double-check this with the airline or your agent before departure; I have heard reports of some visitors being charged by unscrupulous customs officials and paying up simply because they weren't 100% sure). Another option is to utilize **AirKenya**'s daily flight (www.airkenya.com), but this leaves from Nairobi's Wilson general aviation airport. In this case, you will have to go through immigration and purchase a one-way transit visa for $20, as well as a $20 taxi ride to Wilson. Most domestic flights (usually light aircraft arriving from airstrips on the Northern Circuit, as well as Zanzibar, Dar es Salaam, and the Southern Circuit) arrive at Arusha Airport, 10km (6¼ miles) west of Arusha center (20 min.). Recommended domestic airlines are **Precision Air** (✆ **027/250-2541**), **Regional Air Services** (✆ **027/250-2541**), and **Northern Air** (✆ **027/250 8059**).

For information on vaccination (and certificate) requirements and visas, see "Entry Requirements" in chapter 3. Note that the yellow fever vaccination ($50) and visas ($50 most nationalities; $100 U.S. and Irish citizens) are available at KIA.

By Bus Arusha is well connected by bus with every major city, including Nairobi and Dar es Salaam. The latter is a grueling 10-hour trip, with a single 20-minute stop more or less halfway. I'd recommend you fly from Dar, but if you're not squeamish and wish to experience a bit of local life (not to mention save around $170 per person), the best bus operators are **Scandinavia** (www.scandinaviagroup.com for regional office numbers and schedules; Arusha office ✆ **027/250-0153**) and **Royal Coach** (✆ **022/212-4073** or 0754/88-5778); the latter runs a dedicated Dar-Arusha route. For more information, see chapter 16.

It's a far easier transfer by road from Nairobi to Arusha—taking the additional visa costs into account (flying allows you to avoid paying for both Kenya and Tanzania visas, but it will cost you more), you will still save about $100. Several reputable companies operate shuttle bus services daily; the journey takes 4 to 5 hours and costs around $20. Contact **Impala Shuttles** (✆ **0800/221-9000;** www.impalashuttle.com), **Riverside** (www.riverside-shuttle.com), or **Davanu.** In Arusha, contact MD Emmanuel (✆ **0715/40-0318;** emkessy@yahoo.com); in Nairobi (here Davanu operates as **Destination Shuttle**), contact Samuel (✆ **0722/72-9100**) or Nathan at Nairobi International Airport (✆ **0722/31-0234**). Note that you will have to purchase a Kenyan visa (see chapter 5), as well as a Tanzanian visa at Namanga, the border crossing ($50–$100, depending on nationality). It's best to book your shuttle well in advance.

VISITOR INFORMATION The local **Tanzania Tourist Board** office is at 47 E. Boma Rd. (✆ **027/250-3842** or 027/250-3843; ttb-info@habari.co.tz; Mon–Fri 8:30am–4pm, Sat 8:30am–1pm). You can obtain free maps here, as well as the latest information on the various cultural programs on offer. If you haven't already booked a ground operator (someone to do road and local flight transfers), you can also check the credentials of your prospective safari or trekking company here—complaints are registered and repeat offenders blacklisted. Also on the Boma Road is the Ngorongoro Conservation Authority office; **Tanzania National Parks** (TANAPA) headquarters are on Dodoma Road diagonally opposite the Cultural Heritage Centre (© **027/250-1930** or 027/250-1934; www.tanzaniaparks.com).

WHEN TO GO Being equatorial, the region has no summer and winter season, per se, and seasons are defined instead by rainfall. March and April are wet and constitute the only real low season. The second "short rains" fall during November and December, but prices are seldom reduced during this time. For more on the Migration, see p. 172.

GETTING AROUND It is worth prearranging your airport transfer with your lodgings. Arusha center has plenty of taxis; some of them cruise the streets, mostly concentrated outside The Arusha Hotel, at the top of Boma and India roads, along Sokoine Road, along the eastern stretch of Makongoro Road, and along Joel Maeda Street. Fares are not expensive (Tsh1,000–Tsh2,500) and can, if you prefer, be paid in dollars (at an exchange rate of Tsh1,000 to $1).

Fast Facts Arusha

Currency Exchange There are dozens of *bureaux de change* in Arusha—take a walk along Joel Maeda Street to compare rates. Exchange rates are bettered by banks, but commission charges are high, and most do not offer exchange services to foreigners. Standard Chartered Bank on Goliondoi Road does, as does the NBC, at the corner of Soikone Road and School Street—the latter is said to offer the best traveler's check rates. I have found that the rates offered by the Imperial Hotel (in the center of town) are difficult to beat; it is also open daily, whereas banks and foreign exchange bureaus usually operate Monday through Friday 8:30am to 4pm, and Saturday 8am to 1pm. The most popular ATM for visitors is at Barclays, on Serengeti Road.

Emergency Police © **112.** Crimestopper © **111.** For medical emergencies, contact **Flying Doctors** (in Nairobi; © **020/31-5454** or 0733/62-8422). **Directory enquiries © 991.**

Hospital Tanzania is not a country you want to seek serious medical or dental advice in; make sure you're in good health before departure. If you urgently need help in Arusha, contact **Trinity Medical Diagnostic Clinic,** Engira Road (© **027/254-4392**). Alternatively, arrange for an emergency transfer to Nairobi, where services are better (see chapter 5).

Internet Access Most lodgings offer Internet access, but if you want to save money, head for **The Pattiserie,** on Sokoine Road.

Pharmacy **Moona's Pharmacy Ltd.,** Sokoine Road (© **0744/33-4567** or after hours 074/430-9052; moonas_pharmacy@cybernet.co.tz).

Police Dial © **112** or the Arusha police station (© **027/250-3541**).

Post Office The main post office is on Boma Road, near the central Clock Tower; there is an Internet cafe on the first floor. To mail cards or letters, ask staff at your lodging reception. Do not send items of value through the post. For courier services, head to **DHL,** Sokoine Road, next to NBC Bank (© **027/250-6749**).

EXPLORING THE AREA

Most visitors to Arusha are effectively in transit and, as such, do not have the time or inclination to go sightseeing. For those who do, the best attraction by far is a day or morning spent exploring **Arusha National Park**—though it's worth noting here that the park, pretty as it is, pales once you have been to Tarangire National Park, which lies about 2 hours from Arusha. Another pleasant excursion is to the Lake Duluti Forest Reserve (overlooked by Serena Mountain Village; see "Where to Stay"); a pleasant hour-plus amble along its shores or canoe trip should reveal local fishermen at work or, with luck, the majestic fish eagle, responsible for Africa's most haunting cry. Farther afield are a number of **cultural tourism programs** initiated by the Netherlands Development Organization. To learn more about the Wa-Arusha agricultural and cultural traditions, you can visit the villages of Ng'iresi, Ilkiding'a, and Mulala. At Longido and Monduli, you can learn more about the Maasai culture, including a visit to a rural Maasai *boma.* All profits are plowed back directly into the communities. If you have any anthropological or sociological interests, you will likely find these informative and a great opportunity for local communities to share in the tourism bonanza. Some visitors, however, will find the experience slightly artificial. For up-to-date information on all the programs that have itineraries of various durations and costs, visit the Tanzania Tourist Board on Boma Road.

Arusha itself has two museums—the **National History Museum** (Boma Rd.; daily 9am–5pm; $3), of interest primarily for its location in the German Boma (the original military fort, built in 1901, making it the oldest colonial building in Arusha), and the **Arusha Declaration Museum** (off Makongoro Rd.; daily 8:30am–5:30pm; $5). The latter provides some insights into Tanzania's history, with ethnological exhibits that predate the colonial era, as well as interesting artifacts from the 20th century, but a stop here is perhaps warranted only if you are interested in purchasing local art. The building houses the Arusha Cultural Art Association, with artists-in-residence offering their works for sale.

SHOPPING Tanzania offers a wealth of traditional arts and crafts, and Arusha is one of the best places in the country to shop for these. Unless you're traveling the circuit by road, in which case you will find many excellent roadside stalls, consider setting aside a full day in Arusha at the end of your safari just to browse for souvenirs.

Start by trawling the area between the Clock Tower and India Road, where various curio shops offer a huge variety of goods for sale. They are likely to charge slightly more than the roadside stalls that crop up every few miles if you're traversing the Northern Circuit by road, but if yours is a fly-in safari, you won't find better bargains elsewhere. Note that it's best to visit a number of shops to get a sense of relative worth before haggling.

For atmosphere, you can't beat Arusha's **Central Market** (between Somali and Sokoine rds.). Most stalls cater to locals, but you will unearth a few gems, including an Indian-owned shop that sells Maasai blankets to the Maasai at half the price you will pay anywhere else. (Heading north toward the market from Sokoine Rd., it's next to the only bicycle shop.) Do be aware that the area is notorious for pickpockets and rip-off artists; try to visit with a local guide/driver, and watch your belongings.

Another worthwhile stop is **Trade Routes** (Shoprite Shopping Centre, Dodoma Rd.) for high-quality Kenyan goods—look out for bags by Annabels and other Happy Valley–style products. If you're interested in wood carvings, be sure to visit the **Antique Makonde Carvers Workshop** on the Nairobi-Moshi Road (just before the exit to the airport), where you can buy directly from the Makonde craftsmen. The Makonde are famed for their wood carving, a talent and skill that is passed from father to son, and it

Romancing Tanzania's Stone: A Good Investment?

While the U.S. and USSR raced to see who could land the first man on the moon, Mick Jagger whined *Under My Thumb,* and Carnaby Street was awash in the floral fashions of the '60s, Manual d'Souza, a tailor in the sleepy backwater that was Arusha, traded in his scissors for a prospector's hat and headed off to seek his fortune in gold. Some say that, in a bizarre and lucky twist of fate, the hapless tailor's path crossed that of a Maasai cattle herder named Ali Juyawatu, who had picked up a handful of particularly beautiful blue crystals after a fire had swept through the Mererani Hills; others say that D'Souza himself stumbled across them while searching for his gold. Regardless, D'Souza sold the blue stones to John Saul of Swala Gem Traders, who, in turn, sold them to Henry Platt, president of Tiffany & Co. A year later, in 1968, Platt launched tanzanite, a rare new gemstone "from the Kilimanjaro foothills." To this day, the only source of tanzanite in the world is the several-square-mile area in the Mererani (also known as Merelani) Hills, 70km (43 miles) southeast of Arusha, and the pretty blue stone is thus a thousand times more rare than a diamond (and the market, incidentally, just as controlled).

Aside from big company interests, there are some 430 claims mined by nonmechanized miners in Mererani, with daisy-chain workers hand-excavating the mining shafts, an unregulated system shrouded in an atmosphere of treachery and *Deadwood*-style skullduggery until relatively recently, when government officials realized that there was far more tanzanite in circulation internationally than their records could account for, and new systems were set in place. Tanzanite was also at the center of a post-9/11 controversy, when suspicions arose that certain sales were a money-laundering front for Al Qaeda. These have since been repudiated by the U.S. State Department, and tanzanite is once again seen as a "clean" gem, with a concurrent rise in price.

However, there remains a growing concern that supply could be depleted in a few decades, and the gem could represent a potentially lucrative investment. Purchasing it in Tanzania means cutting out the middle man (or men), but be sure to do so from a reputable dealer. And what could be better than purchasing it from **Swala Gem Traders** (www.swalagemtraders.com), the same company, still owned by the Saul family, who first put tanzanite on the market? Today it is an international wholesale trader and export organization, with an outlet in The Arusha Hotel.

is predominantly their work displayed in curio shops and roadside stalls. Themes vary greatly, but all carvers start off by reproducing images of men and women going about their traditional activities, the most famous being the *Ujamaa,* or "Tree of Life." The Makonde hail from southern Tanzania, but many have moved to the "tourist mecca" of Arusha to ply their trade.

Having visited these, set aside a few hours (or, if you have time to make only one stop, head straight there) to explore **Cultural Heritage Company** (Mon–Sat 9:30am–5:30pm, Sun 9am–3pm; ✆ **027/250-7496;** upa@habari.co.tz), the largest and best collection of East African arts and crafts in Arusha (if not the country), located on the Dodoma Road that leads westward from Arusha on the Northern Circuit. Currently in a massive thatched structure, the outlet is due to move into the custom-built monstrosity next door—surely a contender for the most kitsch and extravagant retail outlet on the continent, and proof of just how much money its owner, Mr. Saifuddin Khanbhai, is making. Prices of most items are usually inflated (relative to what you'll pay at many of the roadside stalls, at any rate), but the quality and variety is unbeatable: Makonde and ebony carvings, tanzanite, Tinga Tinga paintings, antique furniture, stone sculptures, fabrics, books, leatherwork, and beading (aside from the Maasai beading, which you're better off buying direct from the Maasai women who will accost you everywhere on the road). Look out for Shanga Shangaa jewelry, a new craft development wherein the beads are made from fabric and recycled glass. Even if you don't buy anything, Cultural Heritage is a useful place to orient yourself in terms of the remarkable breadth of East Africa's crafts and arts, as well as the superb quality available. Items at Cultural Heritage tend to be sourced from the best artists and artisans available, so you are paying for Saif's excellent eye and local knowledge, which (despite his outlandish new building) is clearly considerable. There is also a DHL office right there, making the purchase decision of even very large items that much easier to make.

WHERE TO STAY & DINE

Arusha has a plethora of accommodations options, far too many to cover in detail—rest assured that those listed below truly are the best available in each price category.

Capitalizing on tourist flow into the Northern Circuit, most Arusha lodges differentiate between a high and a low season; some even have a "green" season, which is a euphemism for the wet season (Apr and May) when tourist traffic is but a trickle. Generally, high season is from June to October and mid-December to February, low season is April to July and possibly November to mid-December, but do check with your hotel when booking.

With the exception of The Arusha Hotel and Onsea, which are both in Arusha itself, the top recommended options all lie east of town, between Arusha and Kilimanjaro International Airport. All lodgings listed below offer airport transfers for a fee; I'd utilize these.

Given the tourist numbers, there is a surprising dearth of good restaurants in Arusha, but if you feel like Italian, **Albero's** (Haile Selassie Rd.; ✆ **027/254-8987** or 0762/24-8779) is pretty authentic. The chef-owner, Raffaele Nacarlo, is Italian, and the alfresco

Not-So-Pearly Whites

While potable, the waters that tumble from Mount Meru are extremely high in fluoride. With most of the villages surrounding the mountain reliant on its streams and springs, years of exposure has resulted in the majority of the Arusha population suffering from porous bones, prone to breaking, and brown, stained teeth. A few local NGOs are working hard on finding easily administered solutions to neutralize the high fluoride content for villagers; until such time, a new generation of smiles is in the process of being blighted.

Finds Snacks on Safari

If you're planning a serious road trip, or just browsing for crafts in Arusha and feel like a light meal, the best place to stock up is at **The Patisserie,** on Sokoine Road, near the Clock Tower (© **0754/28-8771** or 0754/250-2757). It's not going to win any prizes for cozy cafe–style atmosphere, but this no-nonsense Indian-owned bakery has the most delicious snacks in town—stock up on *samosas* (various fillings), crispy pies (love the chicken), banana chips (addictive), and "spicy mix" (a traditional Indian snack), or order custom-made sandwiches, made with freshly baked bread or rolls, to pick up before you leave the following day. There's also an inexpensive Internet cafe attached (pity about the terrible coffee). For those with more adventurous tastes, the best road-trip snack is *biltong,* delicious, nutritious strips of dried beef or game. *Biltong* dates back to the great 19th-century road trip of the Afrikaans Voortrekkers, who, desperate to escape the dominance of their new English masters in the Cape, set off north in their ox-wagons to colonize southern Africa. You can purchase *biltong* (ask for it to be carved) from **Meat King** on Goliondo Road (© **078/449-0211**).

dining arrangements are very pleasant; pasta portions are huge and pizzas, made in a traditional wood-burning oven, are the best in Arusha. Owned by a Kenyan-Australian couple, **Stiggy's Thai Restaurant** (Old Moshi Rd.; © **0754/37-5535**) is somewhat of an institution in Arusha, serving Pacific Asian cuisine in a relaxed bar-style atmosphere; Stiggy and Thelma also have a Mexican outlet in the Nduoro Complex. If you're looking for a light meal while curio shopping in Arusha center, try **The Patisserie** (see above), or **Jambo Coffee House** or nearby **Café Bamboo** (© **027/250-6451**), both on Boma Road. Both are open Monday through Saturday from around 8am to 9pm; Café Bamboo is also open Sunday mornings. **Via Via** (© **0754/38-4992**), located on the grounds behind the German Boma, offers a pleasant enough setting if you're in the area (closed Mon). If you like browsing for supper options, Sokoine Road offers a choice of Indian restaurants, as well as a Greek (Greek Hut) and Chinese (Shangai) option.

If you're looking for more of a fine-dining experience, book at **Redds,** the a la carte restaurant at the Arusha Coffee Lodge, or, better still, the intimate candle-lit terrace at **Onsea House,** where celebrated chef Axel serves up gourmet four-course meals with recommended wines for $50 per person; see below for more on both.

Arusha Town

The Arusha Hotel ★★ Located opposite Arusha's historic Clock Tower, this is in the historic heart of Arusha and is the only real five-star hotel in town. Sadly, countless renovations have stripped it of any historical ambience (the hotel received its first guests in 1894), but it offers the weary traveler the security of stepping into a well-bred European- or American-style chain—perfect for those who prefer the bland but soothing anonymity of a well-run hotel. The location is tops: Step outside, and you're in the heart of Arusha; nearby is The Patisserie where you can shop for road-trip snacks, trawl the curio shops for souvenirs and the *bureaux de change* offering the best rate, or just take a stroll to get a sense of life in a bustling African town. Alternatively, you can choose to cocoon yourself in your sound-proof and well-proportioned room, with Wi-Fi and TVs that actually work and a great Indian room service menu. The only drawback is the pool area, which during my stay appeared open to anyone willing to pay an entry fee, turning it into a noisy public mélange on weekends or public/school holidays. Make very sure that you are booked in the original hotel building and not one of the wings near the pool.

P.O. Box 88, Arusha. ✆ **027/250-7777** or 027/250-8870 through -8873. Fax 027/250-8889. www.thearushahotel.com. 86 units. $480 standard double; $600 executive wing double; $960 suite. Rates include breakfast. AE, DC, MC, V. **Amenities:** Restaurant; bar; coffee bar; gym; pool; room service; mini casino. *In room:* A/C, TV, hair dryer, minibar, Wi-Fi.

Ilboru Safari Lodge ★ **Value** On the outskirts of town, yet within walking distance (2.5km/1½ miles) of the center, Ilboru offers the best value in its price category, with friendly staff, lovely lush gardens filled with indigenous birds, and a large, sparkling pool. Accommodations are in circular thatched huts throughout the 2-hectare (5-acre) garden; decor is pretty spartan (twin beds and showers only) but comfortable, with Maasai blankets adding a touch of color. It's worth noting that each rondawel comprises two rooms with a door in the center—great if you're a family, not so if you have inconsiderate and loud neighbors. Food has certainly improved since the new manager took over, but I'd still go for the B&B option and have the choice of either ordering from the snack menu, opting for the restaurant, or taking a taxi (or stroll) to town.

Ilboru Safari Lodge, P.O. Box 8012, Arusha. ✆ **0754/27-0357** or 0784/27-0357. www.ilborusafarilodge.com. 30 units. High season $106 double B&B, $136 half board; midseason $89 double B&B, $119 half board; low season $70 double B&B, $119 half board. MC, V. **Amenities:** Restaurant; bar; babysitting; free Internet (in snack bar); pool; room service. *In room:* TV.

L'Oasis L'Oasis lies at the end of a very bumpy and uncomfortably long dirt track (typical of many Arusha lodgings). However, this particular track provides up-close scenes of rural village life, a fleeting encounter with real Africa that makes the journey more worthwhile. L'Oasis itself is pretty basic, with its own quasi-village feel. Accommodations are in traditionally constructed thatched huts sprawled around a large public space (the best huts are on stilts; avoid those in the main building). Other than the stilted huts, units are quite gloomy, and there are no bedside lamps; best to find a relaxing spot in the garden, in which flamingos, crowned crane, spoonbills, and herons strut about. Once here, it's worth arranging a guided walk to the nearby village of Sekei; this is also the place to be if you're a keen cycler, as the lodge specializes in cycling trips around Mount Meru and Kilimanjaro, as well as farther afield. There is a swimming pool, and being a backpackers' lodge means there are usually other people lounging about. If you are here without a vehicle or driver, you may feel very cut off, which can be nice at a place such as Karama (p. 294), but not as much here.

P.O. Box 1908, Arusha. ✆ **027/250-7089** or 0755/74-9934. www.loasislodge.com. 22 units. $71 double B&B; $103 double half board. AE, DC, MC, V. **Amenities:** Restaurant; bar; Internet; pool.

Onsea House ★★★ **Finds** With only four rooms and a maximum of 12 guests sharing the gorgeous garden and pool, this is the most exclusive option in town (typified by the fact that this is also the only place in town where you can celebrate your arrival with a bottle of Moet). Add intelligent and personalized service, and you're looking at my top pick in Arusha. A family-run enterprise, Onsea was opened in 2006 by Dirk Janssens 2 years after arriving from Belgium with his wife, Inneke. Gregarious and charming, Dirk is a great host, ably assisted by his cousin Axel; both are a mine of information about anything from recommended climbing operators to shopping tips (they also have wonderful objects for sale in the house). If you're watching your budget (or waistline), you could opt for the B&B rate with light meal, but you'd be missing out on a culinary extravaganza—Axel is a Michelin-experienced chef and perfectionist who spends the better part of every day working on the evening's four-course dinner menu—if anything, the only complaint (and only from some) is that the meals are a little overwhelming. If you like it light, indicate when booking. As far as room choices go, my slight preference is for one of the two rooms in the custom-built thatched villa above the pool, but the rooms in the original guesthouse are near the bar, dining room, and open-air Jacuzzi (with lovely views); wherever you end up, you are sure to be delighted. The property is a 7-minute drive from Arusha center and 30km (19 miles) from KIA.

Baraa Rd., P.O. Box 1259, Arusha. ✆ **0784/83-3207.** www.onseahouse.com. 4 units (sometimes 5). Low season $200 double B&B, $300 half board; high season $245 double B&B, $355 half board. Rates include early-morning tea and coffee on your veranda; half board includes recommended wines with dinner. MC, V. **Amenities:** Bar; Jacuzzi; pool; room service; free Wi-Fi (in lobby). *In room:* Hair dryer, minibar.

Outpost Lodge (Value) This is the best budget joint in town, pitched more or less at the same market as L'Oasis, but cheaper and more centrally situated. Marketing itself as a "B&B with a difference," Outpost is a popular backpacker-style destination, with plenty of people around the pool swapping safari stories, and shady gardens in which to write letters and while away the time. The en suite accommodations are basic but spotlessly clean and relatively comfortable (holes in mosquito nets and erratic hot water aside); units in the garden are usually superior to those in main building, but ask to look around before bedding down. Staff are extremely helpful and friendly, and the location, in a peaceful neighborhood around 1.5km (1 mile) from the Clock Tower near banks, shops, and restaurants, is great, so even if the atmosphere (or food) isn't to your liking, you needn't feel marooned.

37A Serengeti St.; P.O. Box 11520, Arusha. ✆ **027/254-8405** or 0748/43-0358. www.outposttanzania.com. 23 units. $66 double B&B; $100 double half board. No credit cards. **Amenities:** Restaurant; bar; mini gym; pool; Wi-Fi. *In room:* TV (in some).

East of Arusha

Hatari Lodge ★★★ It's a bit of a schlep to get here, but what a drive—straight through the montane forests and glades of Arusha National Park, with a few game sightings along the way, you can begin your first game lodge experience 1 hour after touching down. I love almost everything about this lodge. The retro-chic style (featured in numerous magazines) is a funky homage to Hardy Kruger (star of the movie *Hatari,* shot at the neighboring run-down Momela Lodge), whose home this once was. Service is great, food is superb, and the views (including Kilimanjaro's snow-capped dome) a balm. There are no fences between Arusha National Park and Hatari, so you can sit beside a roaring outdoor fire and watch giraffe and buffalo grazing in the near distance. Despite its view onto untouched nature, this is not a real wilderness area, and local communities are, at times, within sight (try to book the honeymoon suite for pure wildlife views). The young and energetic owners, Marlies and Joerg, are involved in various upliftment programs, and just being here helps plow money into the surrounding communities.

Momella Rd., PO Box 3171, Arusha. ✆ **027/255-3456** or 0752/55-3456. Fax 027/255-3458. www.hatarilodge.com. 9 units. High season $560 double; low/midseason $400 double. Rates include 3 meals daily, tea and coffee, mineral water in the rooms and during meals, and concession and community fees. MC, V. **Amenities:** Restaurant; bar. *In room:* Fireplace, hair dryer, minibar.

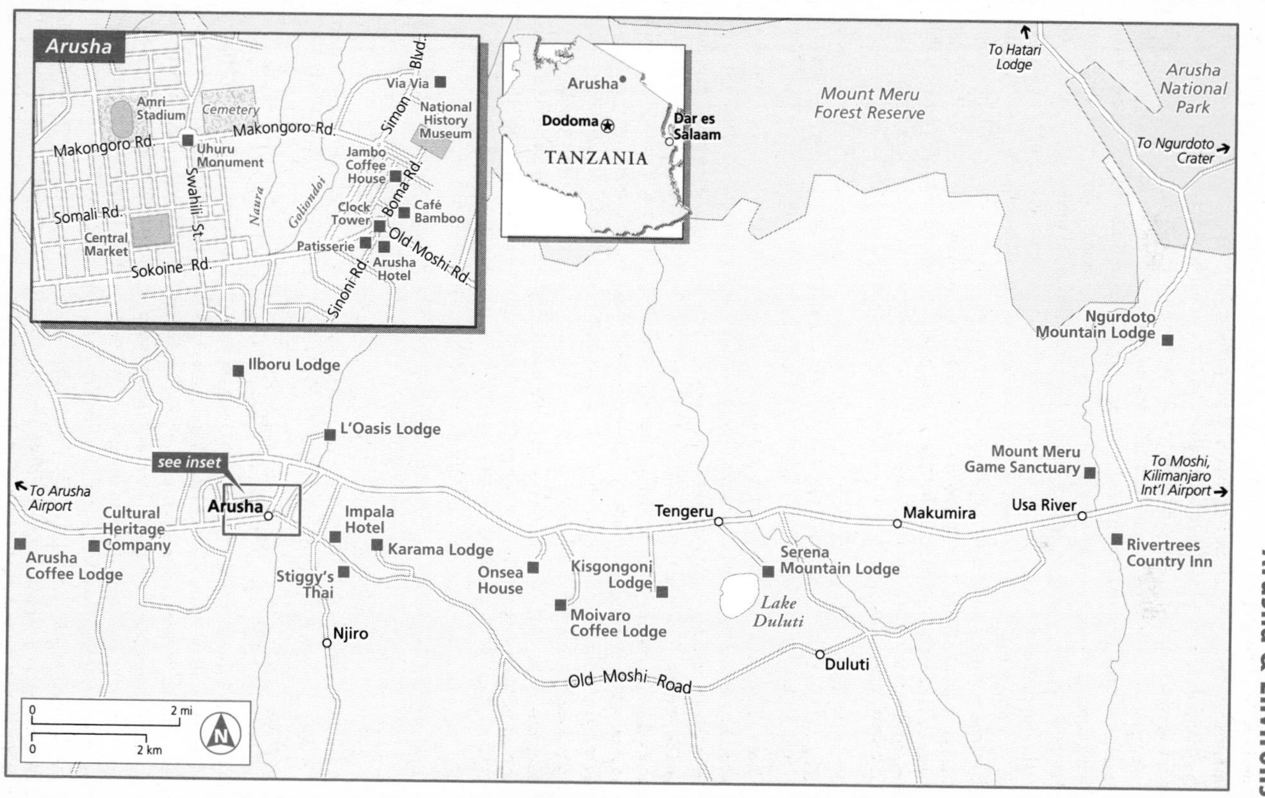

THE NORTHERN CIRCUIT 15 ARUSHA

Karama Lodge (& Spa) ★★ Value In an area where many lodgings can boast of sublime views, Karama Lodge scores very high. It's another long drive up a bumpy track, this time up steep Suye Hill, but the lush rural valley at your feet is reward enough. Accommodation is in basic A-frame timber and thatch cabins on stilts, reached via meandering cobbled and timber walkways. Each cabin has a small furnished veranda with great valley views. It's all very homemade and rough-hewn, but the owners have a really good eye—proof that you don't need a huge budget to create a stylish eco-lodge. Head straight for the large double-volume thatched lounge/bar, open to the breezes that come off the valley floor. With twinkling lights below at night, this is a romantic, comfortably furnished space, a great place to curl up with a book or a beer. You can eat up here or downstairs in the restaurant, where floor-to-ceiling picture windows show off the lush green surrounds. Food (of the organic, locally sourced variety) is excellent, some of the best in Arusha (try the oven-baked organic farm trout in butter), and staff are very friendly. The only drawback is the lack of reading lights (insist on these being installed next to your bed when booking) and pool; if you're keen on a big social scene, you also won't like the sense of being totally cut off. The long-awaited spa should (hopefully) be open by the time you read this.

P.O. Box 1573, Arusha. ✆ **027/250-0359** or 0754/47-5188. Fax 027/250-5578. www.karama-lodge.com. 22 units. High season $135 double B&B, $175 half board; low season $108 double B&B, $148 half board. MC, V. **Amenities:** Restaurant; bar.

Kigongoni Lodge ★★ Almost every lodge in Tanzania will tell you about the community projects they support (usually an integral part of getting land tenure), but Kigongoni virtually grew out of its community project. Built by Dutch couple Claudia Verbraak and Sander Hammer to support the neighboring Sibusiso Foundation, which cares for mentally and physically challenged children and their families, a stay at Kigongoni has a real feel-good aspect to it. The beautifully constructed and spacious cottages (cool, roughly plastered whitewashed walls and half-timber beams, each with private veranda) are spread along the 28-hectare (69-acre) hilltop site that drops quite steeply below the public areas. It's best to specify if you want a unit near the pool and dining area, as these are located at the top of the hill. On a clear day, you can see Mount Meru and Kili; once the views must have been splendid, but the valley below is now carpeted in ugly plastic tunneling. As charming manager Sander pragmatically put it, "Kigongoni is a transition lodge. People come here to recover from their flight or prepare for their return." And given the lovely standard of accommodations and peaceful atmosphere, this is a very pleasant place to do so.

P.O. Box 11952, Arusha. ✆ **027/255-3087.** Fax 027/255-3073. www.kigongoni.net. 18 units. High season $244 double B&B, $288 half board; low season $214 double B&B, $258 half board; green season $160 B&B, $204 half board. MC, V. **Amenities:** Restaurant; bar; pool. *In room:* Fireplace.

Mount Meru Game Lodge & Sanctuary ★★ If your ideal is to arrive and immediately immerse yourself in an old-fashioned safari-like experience, Mount Meru is a great option (though, for my money, Hatari is better). Mount Meru does have game grazing a few meters beyond its lawns, but it's definitely more sanctuary than game lodge. That said, its separate cottages in the garden, with comfortable four-poster wrought-iron beds, offer a great place to recover from jet lag. The more attractive units are in the front (no. 3, nearest the game area, is the best, with lovely outdoor fireplace beneath massive buffalo horns, followed by the cottage shared by nos. 5 and 4); the only drawback of being so close to the game is the possibility of being awakened by an ostrich pecking at your bedroom window. Rooms at the back of the lodge are more tucked away from public view, and you'll be lulled to sleep by the Usa River. You can watch zebra and various antelope graze from the open-sided lounge area while using the hotel's free Wi-Fi (typical of the generosity that permeates the lodge). It's a tranquil retreat, well managed by Evelyn and spoken of with respect even by its competitors. And like Rivertrees (their entrances are located opposite each other), it's an easy 20-minute drive from KIA.

P.O. Box 2747, Arusha. © **027/255-3643.** Fax 027/255-3885. www.intimate-places.com. 17 units. Peak season (Christmas and New Year's period) $275 double B&B, $315 double half board; high season $237 double B&B, $277 double half board; low season $174 double B&B, $214 double half board. MC, V. **Amenities:** Restaurant; bar; hair and beauty treatments; pool; free Wi-Fi; satellite phone for cheaper calls.

Ngare Sero Mountain Lodge ★★ Built between 1905 and 1912 by August Leue, first administrator of the area, Ngare Sero offers rare proof of Tanzania's turn-of-the-century German colonial history. Like so many of Arusha's lodgings, it's located a long way off the main road, down a bumpy track past other (inferior) lodgings, but again the rough ride there is rewarded by the destination: an almost baronial barnlike structure (pretty much unchanged in 100 years), surrounded by parklike grounds that lead to a sparkling trout-filled lake (Ngare Sero means "Dappled Water" in Maa) and riverine forest. Accommodations are split between two suites in the original farmhouse and the better-value garden custom-built suites; given that everyone has access to the deep veranda overlooking the lake and lounge, with its huge stone fireplace, there seems little reason to shell out for the upstairs suites, which are grand but a little stark. The pool is the prettiest in Arusha, and the broad stone staircase leading down to the lake a grand folly from a bygone era. There is a resident yoga instructor, and you can pre-arrange for guided yoga and meditation sessions in Mount Meru's crater. Part living museum, part organic trout farm, part yoga retreat, Ngare Sero will not suit anyone looking for social life or hotel-standard service, but as a low-key place to rejuvenate, it is hard to beat.

P.O. Box 425, Arusha. © **027/255-3638** or 0787/56-0055. www.ngare-sero-lodge.com. 12 units. $150 double; $200 suite. Rates include all meals. MC, V. **Amenities:** Restaurant; airport transfers; babysitting; pool; room service; Wi-Fi.

Ngurdoto Lodge ★★ Finds Not to be confused with the cavernous, soul-less Ngurdoto Mountain Lodge, little Ngurdoto Lodge is a relative newcomer to the Arusha scene but is a special rural retreat consistently wowing visitors. Situated on the high foothills of Mount Meru (29km/18 miles east of Arusha), it's owned by the U.S.-born Novaks, who have spent the past 40 years traveling and living in Africa and the Middle East. The six individually situated "Meru-style guesthouses"—all with views of Arusha National Park forest, backdropped by Mount Meru—are spacious and furnished with queen or

Recommended Safari Operators

For a list of a few choice operators I have no trouble recommending, based on personal experience (such as Simba Safaris, who bent over backward to accommodate this researcher's grueling itinerary) and anecdotal evidence from trusted sources, see chapter 3.

Moments When Kilimanjaro Comes Out to Play

"Look, from here you will have a one of the best photographs of Kilimanjaro." Our driver, who has just pulled up on the verge, points to the dense cloud cover towering above the horizon. "Shall we wait a bit? See if the mountain comes out?" he asks. "No," I answer curtly, thinking of my (very long) list of things to do. But a few hours later, driving through Arusha National Park, he points to the horizon again, and my heart does a jolt. Rising above the cloud cover, finally, is the snow-capped dome of Kilimanjaro. I did not expect to be so affected by my first sighting of the world's tallest free-standing mountain, but the contrast between driving through a tropical forest, monkeys crashing through the undergrowth, and seeing those white powdered peaks floating above the clouds is nothing if not surreal, and one of those moments you treasure for life. For more on Kilimanjaro, see chapter 16.

twin beds, with the exception of one, which is a double bedroom unit (three twin beds in each bedroom) linked by a central lounge and fireplace; it's ideal for families or friends traveling together. Surrounded by 4 hectares (9¾ acres) of tranquil bird-filled gardens, there are pretty much views everywhere you look from the main lodge, including the snow-capped dome of Kilimanjaro some 50km (31 miles) away—best enjoyed from a comfortable seat on the wraparound veranda. Another lovely swimming pool, great home-cooked food (special diets are well catered for), and hands-on management by Dick and Dolores complete the picture.

P.O. Box 515, Usa River. © **027/255-3701** or 074/447-6677. www.ngurdoto.com. 6 units. $320 double full board; $192 double half board. MC, V. **Amenities:** Limited Internet access; pool; room service. *In room:* Hair dryer.

Rivertrees Country Inn ★★★ Value A rural-style idyll set on 4 hectares (9¾ acres) of natural gardens on the banks of the Usa River, Rivertrees is a very stylish option (less safari-themed than Mount Meru, more individual than Serena Mountain Village), thanks to the impeccable taste of hands-on owner Martina Gerkin-Trappe. Small and quirky, it's more a rambling house than a hotel, with a lovely, laid-back atmosphere. The original farmhouse in which the public spaces are housed is beautifully furnished with eclectic antiques, photographs, and artworks. Rooms are in whitewashed cottages dotted around the garden and feature cool uncluttered decor. No room is the same, but all share a few touches of decadence—big galvanized buckets brimful with fresh roses, and rose petals scattered on the romantically mosquito-sheathed four-poster beds. Besides the farmhouse, there is a great open-air kitchen and dining area, as well as a large open-sided thatched bar–cum–dining room, furnished with mismatched chairs, huge *kelims,* and a roaring fireplace with sofas for lounging about with pre- or post-meal drinks. There's not a huge staff-to-guest ratio, so don't arrive expecting hotel service standards, but the wonderful Zablon will bend over backward to make your stay comfortable. Excellent value.

P.O. Box 235, Arusha. © **027/255-3894** or 0713/33-9873. Fax 027/255-3893. www.rivertrees.com. 12 units. $195 double. Rates include breakfast. MC, V. **Amenities:** Bar; Internet. *In room:* A/C, hair dryer.

Serena Mountain Village ★★★ *Gracious* is the first word that comes to mind when wandering through the grand colonial-era farmhouse that is the centerpiece of Serena's award-winning "village," and it is apt. Unlike say, Rivertrees, this is very much a resort, but it's an extremely well-bred one. From the well-maintained upholstery of the reproduction antiques and turned-wood tables supporting vases filled with fresh roses to the plush red carpets and polished timber balustrades, this is one of Arusha's classiest options. The 20-hectare (49-acre) grounds are similarly manicured. Rooms are in circular ivy-clad cottages with diamond-pane windows; try to book room nos. 19 to 28, as they have lake views. Furnishings follow the same country manor house style—good quality, if somewhat forgettable, and showers are generous. Situated deep within a coffee plantation (45 min. from KIA; 20 min. from Arusha), the stone-clad manor house has views toward Mount Meru and Kilimanjaro and overlooks Lake Duluti—a very photogenic sight, and one that will have you wondering whether you should not perhaps have booked another night here and spent some time exploring the lake and forest reserve behind it. Definitely my favorite in the Serena chain.

P.O. Box 2551, Arusha. ✆ **027/255-3313,** -3314, or -3315. Fax 027/255-3316. www.serenahotels.com. 42 units. High season $320 double B&B; low season $260 double B&B. Holiday surcharge at Easter ($35 per person, per night) and Christmas ($40 per person, per night). MC, V. **Amenities:** Restaurant; babysitting; pool; room service; currency exchange. *In room:* Minibar.

West of Arusha

Arusha Coffee Lodge ★★ Arusha Coffee Lodge (not to be confused with Moivaro Coffee Lodge, on the eastern side) is a popular choice with upmarket travel agents, not least because it is located 5 minutes from Arusha Airport (the small strip utilized by local charters and light aircraft). It also houses what is generally considered the best restaurant in Arusha (Redds), and the split-level accommodation units—attractive, dark timber plantation-style cottages off a winding garden path—are spacious and comfortably outfitted. Despite the fact that it is billed as being "cradled in the endless acres of Tanzania's biggest coffee plantation," the lodge has been built right on the edge of the farm, next to busy Dodoma Road, where trucks thunder past at all hours—a real comedown if you've just returned from safari. The units also all face each other rather than onto the plantation, so verandas offer no privacy, and curtains need to be kept closed for much of your stay. Service is also not what you'd expect, given the heavy price tag. I'd opt first for any of the other Frommer's two-star rated options.

99 Serengeti Rd., Sopa Plaza; P.O. Box 12814, Arusha. ✆ **027/254-0630** or -0639. Fax 027/254-8245. www.elewana.com. 18 units. Peak season $500 double B&B; high season $426 double B&B; low season $355 double B&B. MC, V. **Amenities:** Bar; babysitting; pool; room service; Wi-Fi. *In room:* Fireplace, hair dryer, minibar.

2 TARANGIRE NATIONAL PARK

118km (73 miles) SW of Arusha, 90km (56 miles) E of Lake Manyara, 150km (93 miles) SE of Ngorongoro Crater

While the focus for most travelers on a Northern Circuit safari is the Serengeti, many come away claiming that Tarangire was, in fact, the highlight of their trip.

Named after the life-giving river that flows its length, the 2,642-sq.-km (1,030-sq.-mile) Tarangire National Park is Tanzania's fifth-largest park—though if you include the unfenced game-controlled areas that border it, the larger ecosystem is closer to 35,000

Fun Facts The Tsetse Fly: Guardian of the Wilderness

Aside from mosquitoes (and these only in certain locations or times of the year), the biggest pest you will encounter on safari is the tsetse fly (pronounced *tset*-see), which delivers a very painful bite. They are almost everywhere on the Northern Circuit, particularly in woodland areas; stop to have a picnic in the shade, and within minutes you will have to flee to open savannah. Thankfully, the tsetse is easy to identify. Similar in shape but slightly larger than your common housefly, the wings fold one on top of the other over the abdomen when resting, and you'll notice the long proboscis that sticks out from a distinct bulb at the bottom of the head. Unlike mosquitoes (and rather like horseflies), they have relatively large "scalpels" to make their incision, so you feel the bite before it actually happens and can flick or kill the offending insect before it can render any further damage. Travel with insect repellent and (I kid you not) a fly swatter. Do not wear dark clothes (they're attracted to dark colors), try to keep the vehicle moving through woodland areas, and have fun swatting them. While they are an irritant, it's worth bearing in mind that it is thanks to the tsetse fly that huge tracts of wilderness have been left in their pristine state. Its ability to decimate domestic animals as well as cause sleeping sickness in humans ensured that areas such as the Serengeti and Tarangire were spared the type of European encroachment that happened around other riverine areas (aside from the Maasai, who seem immune to them).

sq. km (13,650 sq. miles)—enough to host some migratory movement of herds. Sometimes referred to as a "mini Serengeti," Tarangire also shares some topographical similarities with its big brother, the most arresting being the short-grass plains you find mostly in the north, their expanses broken only by the shapely "umbrella" acacia tree—a picture-perfect backdrop for game viewing. A striking contrast to these golden plains, and not found in the Serengeti, are Tarangire's lush green swamps—Gursi, Larmakua, Nguselorobi, and Silale—where elephants stand thigh-high in juicy grasses that act as a magnet for herds of buffalo, wildebeest, and zebra, with predators usually in close attendance. The farther south you travel, the landscape becomes more densely vegetated and game sightings drop accordingly, though there are areas of open savannah, and the tracks are mercifully free of day-trippers.

It's a beautiful park, typified by century-old baobabs that stand sentinel above the open grass plains and riverbeds, and varied habitats that play home to 94 mammal species, huge numbers of which concentrate around the permanently flowing waters of the Tarangire, particularly during the dry season. In fact, given its dense concentrations of animals—second only to Ngorongoro—there is every chance that you will enjoy a higher incidence of sightings than in the Serengeti; elephants are particularly common, with herds numbering in the hundreds. Tarangire is also an ornithologists' haven, boasting a greater variety of birds than even Lake Manyara, with upward of 500 species to look out for—many of them, like the kohl-eyed lilac-breasted roller, orange-bellied parrot, and malachite kingfisher, flashing like gems in the undergrowth. Tarangire is a worthwhile

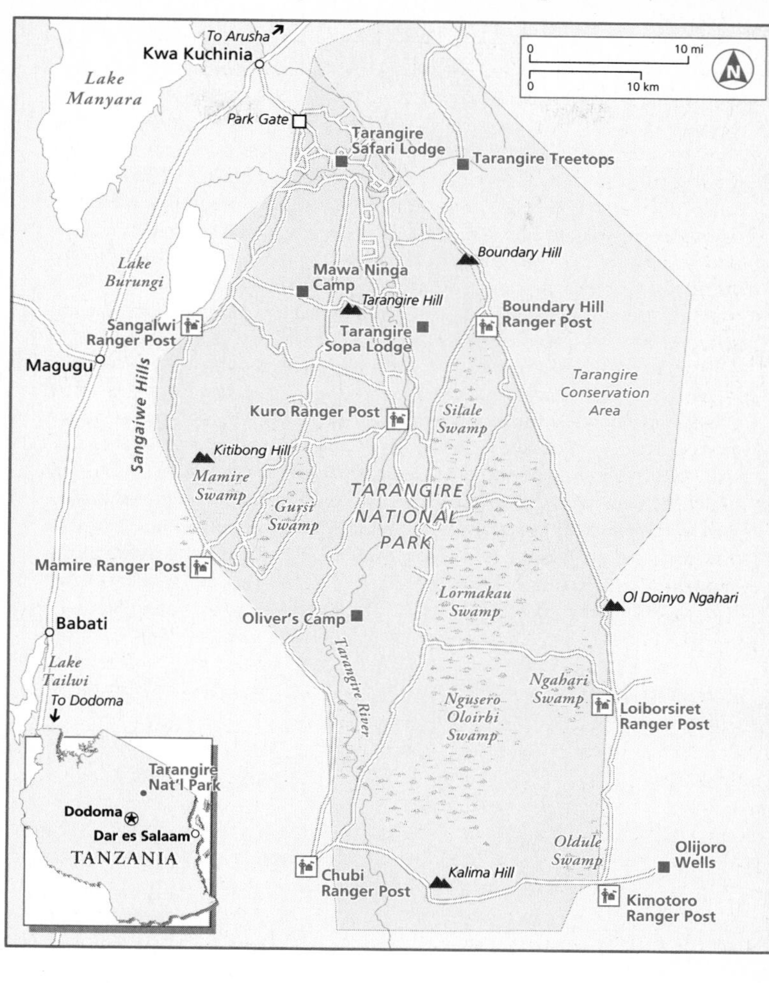

addition to any Northern Circuit itinerary, but during the driest months (usually Sept and Oct)—when the Serengeti herds have usually migrated north into Kenya's Masai Mara and animals from throughout the Tarangire ecosystem slake their thirst in the waters of the Tarangire river—you should make a few days here a priority.

ESSENTIALS

The nearest airport is Arusha, which is less than 2 hours' drive from the entrance (3 hr. from KIA), so unless you're in a rush, you're unlikely to utilize Kuro Airstrip in Tarangire. To get there, exit Arusha west and travel for an hour (100km/62 miles) on the tarred Great North Road that runs from Arusha to Dodoma (capital of Tanzania), looking for

Tree of Life

The most iconic tree you will see in Tarangire is the **baobab,** its thick, silvery trunk, capable of reaching more than 15m (49 ft.) in diameter, sprouting smooth branches that look not unlike roots, hence its "upside-down tree" moniker. According to one legend, God planted the baobab tree upside down—some say by accident, others to stop the tree from complaining.

The baobab has inspired myths and legends throughout Africa, a function not only of its strange appearance, but of the age that radiates from its massive trunk. Like all ancient life forms, it is hard to comprehend that many germinated before Christ was born, according to radiocarbon dating (though I have also heard that some reports are apocryphal, given that the baobabs have no growth rings and leave behind no fossils).

The Tree of Life, as the baobab is also aptly known, is very useful. Behaving much like a giant succulent, it can store up to 300 liters (79 gallons) of water, enabling it to live through long periods without rain. Chewing the wood is a source of moisture for humans and animals alike. This is also why the circumference of a single tree—which can take up to 10 humans to embrace—can vary significantly between wet and dry seasons. The trunk of mature trees is often hollow, providing living space for numerous animals and humans alike. The fire-resistant bark is used for weaving and rope, and the young leaves for condiments and medicines. It flowers only during the rainy season, and flowers last 1 day, pollinated at night by fruit bats. The fruit has a furry coating around a tough, gourdlike shell that shields a soft pulp inside called "monkey bread." The oil-rich seeds are high in citric acid and are fermented as a spice or roasted as coffee replacement.

the turn-off to the main park entrance at Kwakuchinja village. It's about a 20-minute drive on dirt from this point, and you might allow time to stop for curios.

The main entrance gate has spotlessly clean ablutions; you can also purchase booklets, films, maps, and postcards here. Cost of the 24-hour entry permit for each person to Tarangire National Park is $35. Park hours are 6:30am to 6:30pm; entry and exit outside these times is not possible, and vehicles are not allowed to drive inside the park after dark, so plan your schedule accordingly. Though the gates are manned 24 hours (useful to know should you be running late), hours are strictly enforced by park wardens.

You could choose to use Tarangire as a base to visit Lake Manyara National Park (90km/56 miles; about 1½ hours away) and even Ngorongoro Crater (150km/93 miles; about 2½ hours away); Serengeti National Park is a bone-jarring 295km (183 miles) away, a drive that will take at least 6 hours.

Like the Serengeti, Tarangire has no real winter or summer seasons, but has a bimodal rainfall pattern, comprising brief rains during November or December and a heavier rainfall period from mid-March to May. During the dry season (June–Nov or Dec), game is concentrated along the river, including large elephant herds, prompting many to site this as one of the finest game-viewing parks in Africa. January to March, after the short rains have greened the park, are particularly beautiful months, game numbers are dis-

Another tree with an interesting-shape fruit is the **Sausage Tree,** which occurs along the Tarangire River and its tributaries, and appears to have sausages dangling from thin stalks. The trees are beautiful when in flower from July to October, when dark-red trumpet flowers hang in long, drooping sprays from its branches, opening to release their scent at night. The sausage-shape fruit these produce—gray-green to pale brown in color, and weighing up to 6.8kg (15 lbs.)—grows up to 60cm (24 in.) in length and 10cm (4 in.) in diameter. Fruit falls from the trees in March and April of the following year and lies undamaged on the ground for many months. Ripe fruit is eaten by baboons, monkeys, porcupines, and bushpigs; humans find them inedible but use them to ferment beer. The skin is also ground and used externally for medicine, while the fruit is burned and the ashes pounded by a mortar with oil and water to make a paste that is then applied to the skin.

Another personal favorite is the rather unfairly named **Fever Tree.** Along with the flat-topped acacia, this is one Africa's most attractive thorn trees, immediately recognizable for its almost luminous lime-green to greenish-yellow bark and the bright-yellow sweetly scented flowers it produces from August or September to November. The Fever Tree grows in shallow swampy pans, where underground or surface water is present, and along the margins of lakes and on river banks. It is this accident of location that earned it the unfair *fever* sobriquet—early settlers mistakenly associated the onset of malaria with the tree rather than the swampy surrounds that bred the malaria-carrying mosquitoes.

persed but reasonable, and, given low visitor numbers, this period can make for a very exclusive safari experience (be warned: insects can be unbearable). During the April and May rainfall period, animals are more widely dispersed and Tarangire is not really worth including in a Northern Circuit itinerary—as the timing of rainfall can be erratic, it is best to check with a local ground operator if your dates are anywhere near this period.

If you spend 3 nights in Tarangire, you won't regret it, but unless you are here on a fly-camp walking safari with Oliver's (p. 402), 2 will suffice. This allows you sufficient time to explore the northern section of the park, which is both more scenic and more game rich.

WHERE TO STAY & DINE

A number of places advertise with a Tarangire address but are actually located well outside the park, where dust clouds are far more likely to be Maasai cattle being herded to the riverbed than thirsting buffalo or wildebeest. Most are around a 20-minute drive from the main entrance gate, usually along a rutted track, which makes for a later start to your game drive than ideal. Also, having to enter through the main gate every time you want to enter the park puts you in the thick of the safari traffic, which can be busy, given that Tarangire can be done as a day trip from Arusha. It's true that accommodations options outside the park can offer night drives, which are not allowed in Tarangire, but these are seldom that productive. With the exception of Tarangire Treetops, which is included because the accommodation is so attractive, I strongly urge you to stay inside the park.

Mawe Ninga Camp ★★ Value Mawe Ninga enjoys a superb elevated position on Tarangire Hill, with views of the small soda lake (Burungi) and, on a clear day, Lake Manyara. It's a great deal more off the beaten track than Tarangire Safari Lodge (in a similar price range), yet within easy reach of the park's prime game-viewing areas. It's a wonderfully intimate camp—something only the most exclusive camps (some of whom charge double a day) offer, with just 12 tents on stilted timber platforms built among the black granite rocks (after which the camp is named). Palm-thatch roofing aids insulation, but (like sister camp Olduvai in Ngorongoro), there is no overture to luxury. Interiors, divided into bedroom and bathroom/dressing area, are basic, with twin beds, chemical toilets, and bucket showers, but the location is everything. Some of the tents are virtually cantilevered off the hill to make the most of the views, and in the evening, a campfire is lit right on the lip for spectacular sunsets. There are no resident guides or vehicles, and you can't expect engaged service levels or memorable meals, but if you're looking for an unpretentious option that is both comfortable and authentically connected with the bush experience, Mawe Ninga Camp is the best value in Tarangire.

Bookings only through Tanzania specialists. ✆ **888/487-5418** in the U.S. and Canada, or 01306/880770 or 0208/232-9777 in the U.K. www.africatravelresource.com or www.expertafrica.com. 12 units. $720–$930 double, depending on season. Rates include driver/guide, private vehicle, all meals, and park fees. **Amenities:** Restaurant; bar.

Oliver's Camp ★★★ "Camping" simply doesn't getter better than this. Oliver's combines luxurious touches (a decanter of port on the writing desk in your tent) with the thoughtful (deck chairs that actually recline in front of your privately situated tent). The whole camp is beautifully furnished, service is excellent, and tents are carefully placed in such a way that you are unaware of your neighbor and enjoy unimpeded views (especially from the outdoor fire pit). Oliver's is located in a Tarangire wilderness area, so the luxuries of top-quality linens and toiletries are offset with the authentic safari experiences of bucket showers and composting toilets (the latter a concession to TANAPA allowing Oliver's to set up in a wilderness area). Oliver's has a license to offer walking safaris inside the park, and visitors can either complete a few hours' circuit or head off across the plains to overnight at a specially set up fly-camp where the tents are made of heavy-duty mosquito netting so you can admire the stars in comfort. Though ablutions are basic, you enjoy relative luxuries such as ice-cold drinks and hot showers, comfortable beds, and gourmet cuisine. Located in the eastern section of the park, far from any other lodging, at the end of a dirt track that has scenery and game that will have you stopping

Tips Prime Picnicking

If you're looking for a beautiful spot to picnic, pick the site at Silale Swamp. It's relatively quiet, the tables and chairs have great views, and the public facilities are spotless.

to take pictures every few minutes, Oliver's is not cheap, but the combination of real authenticity and sheer luxury is worth every cent.

Farm No. 175, Olasiti. ✆ **027/250-4118** or -4119. Fax 027/250-2799. www.asilialodges.com. 9 units. High season $1,170 double game package, $940 double full board; low season $970 double game package, $800 double full board. MC, V.

Swala Camp ★★ If privacy is paramount, Swala's location, deep in the southwest of Tarangire (67km/42 miles from the entrance) at the edge of the Gurusi wetlands, will certainly satisfy. Furnishings in this small tented camp are more understated than those at Oliver's (p. 402), but there are other luxuries (flushing toilets, a personal butler, silver service dinners). Managers Maryna and Steve, who've spent many years in Botswana's Delta, are warm and accommodating but discreet—dinners are private unless they notice a rapport between particular guests, in which case a communal table may be set. The only drawback here (aside from a rather large bill) is that much of the drive here and back—through predominantly acacia woodland—is boring. That said, once there, the sense of isolation is wonderful, as is the waterhole—a permanent source of water that attracts a huge variety of animals. Knowing that you will want to spend the day exploring the game-rich northern sections, guests are provided with the most luxurious picnic in Tarangire and head off for the day before returning to camp for sundowners, watching as elephants and other regulars arrive for their evening drink at the watering hole.

✆ **027/250-9816** or 027/250-9817. Fax 027/250-8273 or 027/250-4112. www.sanctuarylodges.com. 9 units. Peak season $1,300 double full board; high season $1,220 double full board; low season $880 double full board. Holiday supplement during Christmas ($40 per person) and Easter ($25 per person). Closed April–May. **Amenities:** Bar; room service.

Tarangire Safari Camp ★★ Value Kids With public spaces and accommodation units built all along the ridge of a hillock in the northern section of the park, providing sweeping views over the central Tarangire River valley (literally crawling with animals during the dry season), this is one of the finest locations in Tarangire. However, its size makes it rather impersonal, attracting a lot of package deals, and its location (very near the main entrance) doesn't feel remote enough. Tents are comfortably outfitted (though only four have a double bed) with en suite, solar-heated showers and flush toilets, but are too close together; given how little soundproofing canvas provides, you will share more than you wish of your neighbor's day come evening. That said, if you're a nervous initiate to tented camps, you might enjoy the greater security that comes with this proximity; alternatively, book one of the five solidly built stone bungalows (each sleeps three adults and has a separate thatched veranda) to enjoy the view. The pool area isn't large, but the slide is constantly occupied with happily screeching kids (youngsters also have earlier mealtimes); the huge thatched open-air dining and lounge area—open to the view—is equally busy. Luncheons are buffets; dinner is a three-course meal. Safari Camp offers excellent value but no exclusivity, and despite being a tented camp, this is not where you'll have your true safari experience; if you're more intrepid, Mawe Ninga (below) may be a better option.

P.O. Box 2703, Arusha. ✆ **027/253-1447.** Bookings 0784/20-2777 or ✆/fax 027/254-4752. www.tarangiresafarilodge.com. 40 units. High season $260 double half board; $290 double full board; low season $180 double full board; kids sharing $55–$63. V. **Amenities:** Restaurant; bar; pool.

Tarangire Sopa Lodge Overrated Aimed, like all Sopa lodges, squarely at the package tourist market, the Sopa Lodge is just a resort in the bush. As such, it doesn't inspire much excitement, with heavy-handed adobe and thatch structures that cut you off from any sense of being in a wilderness area. Architecture and decor is dated, though perfectly comfortable (two queen-size beds per room) and quite spacious. The flirtatious red-headed agama lizards that seem to love the lodge are a delight, and the pool is large and refreshing. Perhaps this property appeals to the type who feels safe in the bush only when in an apartment block rather than a freestanding tent or bungalow, but this falls squarely into the concrete monstrosity category. Given that one could, for more or less the same money, be at Safari Lodge or Mawe Ninga, it beats me why anyone would book here.

99 Serengeti Rd., Sopa Plaza, P.O. Box 1823, Arusha. ✆ **027/250-0630** or -0639. Fax 027/250-8245. www.sopalodges.com. 75 units. Peak season $550 double full board, $530 half board; high season $450 double full board, $430 half board; low season $200 double full board, $180 half board. Holiday supplement during Christmas ($45 per day) and Easter ($40 per day). MC, V. **Amenities:** Restaurant; bar; babysitting; pool; resident nurse. *In room:* Hair dryer, minibar (stocked on request).

Tarangire Treetops ★★ Despite a hefty price tag that makes it by far the most expensive option in the area, and the fact that it is not in within the park, Tarangire Treetops is an incredibly popular lodging option. The lobby, built around a 700-year-old baobab, is inhabited by a colony of bats; it sounds scary but is actually quite magical. Accommodations are in huge stilted treehouses, each the size of a small house, individually situated, and reached via sandy pathways. Some of them are accessed by steep spiral staircases, often through a trapdoor that opens onto the front porch (not ideal if you are unsteady on your feet—thankfully, there are plenty of porters to deal with getting the luggage up). The rooms are extremely comfortable, with king-size beds and open-plan his-and-hers drench showers (with decent water pressure). Much of the room zips open (walls are canvas) to reveal a big timber balcony where you can enjoy a complimentary nightcap after dinner, gazing at a zillion stars. Food is a bit hit or miss, but the staff are incredible, and the warm South African management couple are really passionate about the lodge, park, and country. Treetops is situated in a 23,000-hectare (56,810-acre) Maasai-owned conservation area that borders the national park, and you may be lucky enough to witness a Maasai group singing and dancing before dinner. Huge open-air public spaces overlook a bustling waterhole. The only negative is that it takes around 20 minutes to reach the Boundary Hill entrance to the park.

99 Serengeti Rd., Sopa Plaza; P.O. Box 12814, Arusha. ✆ **027/254-0630** or -0639. Fax 027/254-8245. www.elewana.com. 20 units. Peak season $1,690 game package double, $1,490 full board; high season $1,560 game package, $1,360 full board; low season $1,460 game package, $1,260 full board. MC, V. **Amenities:** Restaurant; bar; pool; room service; free Wi-Fi. *In room:* Hair dryer, electricity converter.

3 LAKE MANYARA NATIONAL PARK ★★

160km (99 miles) from Arusha, 69km (43 miles) from Tarangire, 60km (37 miles) from Ngorongoro, 145km (90 miles) from Serengeti (entrance gate)

Curling along the western shores of a shallow soda lake, the emergence of the Gregory Escarpment—a sheer 500m (1,640-ft.) drop, making this the most impressive wall in the Rift Valley—signals your approach to Lake Manyara, heart of Tanzania's second-oldest national park. A shallow 390-sq.-km (152-sq.-mile) expanse, of which 230 sq. km (90 sq. miles) fall within the national park boundaries, Lake Manyara lies in a closed basin with no outlet. Fed by waters that percolate through the volcanic ash and lava of the Ngorongoro Highlands before seeping and spilling from the ever-eroding walls of the Rift Valley, the lake is highly alkaline, its chemical salts further distilled by the high rate

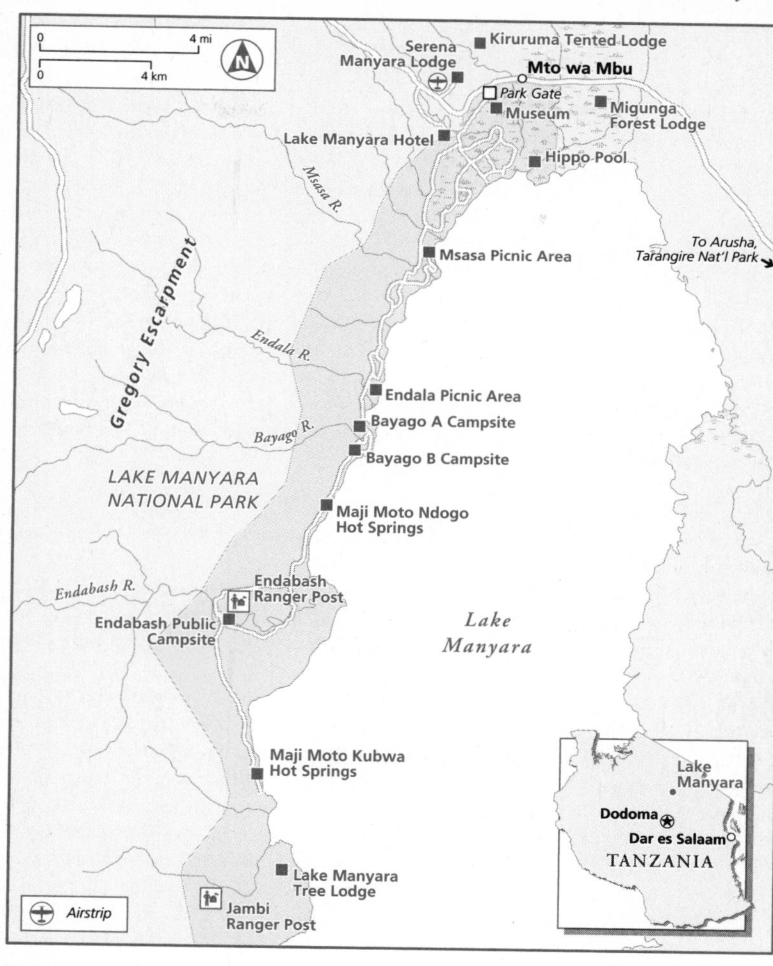

of evaporation—hence the tell-tale crusty white soda deposits that line the lake's shores during the dry season. The ideal breeding ground for blue-green algae and other microorganisms, the lake is thus a nutrient-rich home to large numbers of fish (including an endemic species of tilapia), which, in turn, attract an astonishing variety of waterbirds. Of these, the most spectacular visitors are the migrant flamingos, who hover like pink clouds in and above the blue-gray bands of Manyara's lakeshore.

Despite the fact that the lake covers two-thirds of the park, the slim wedge of land between the shore and the baobab-studded escarpment wall offers a remarkably varied ecosystem: Visitors enter the lush groundwater forest in the north, crossing rivers and pools to traverse stretches of acacia woodland and bushland, and finally emerge to sweeping views of floodplain grasslands, its thin strips of yellow and green blending into a soaring skyline.

Along the way, you are sure to encounter elephants, whose numbers have recovered dramatically since the ban on ivory trade stopped what East African conservationists somewhat dramatically refer to as the "poaching Holocaust" of the '70s and '80s, as well as olive baboons. The park has the highest density of baboons anywhere in Africa, with troops numbering up to 200 family members. Another large mammal species you are assured of seeing are hippos, lazing in and around the aptly named Hippo Pool. Stream-fed with freshwater, this area is not as alkaline as the deeper waters of Lake Manyara, and hence favored by these lumbering amphibians. In the dry season, the park's most prolific herbivores—wildebeest, zebra, and buffalo—are spotted grazing on tender new grass shoots on the floodplains, keeping a wary eye out for approaching predators, while lone giraffe nibble on acacias that line the shore. Lake Manyara is also known for its prolific butterflies that float like confetti in the groundwater forest or acacia woodland, and, of course, its famous tree-climbing lions—a taught behavior, virtually unique to the lions of Lake Manyara, and one of the primary reasons why, despite not being a true wilderness park like Tarangire or Serengeti, this is considered an important stop on the Northern Circuit itinerary.

ESSENTIALS

There is only one entrance to the park, located at the northern end, near the main road and on the outskirts of the nearest village, Mto wa Mbu. (Note that Mto wa Mbu is lined with wall-to-wall curio stalls, the density of which may tempt you to stop—don't; there is unpleasant pressure to purchase, and you'd be well advised to hold on tight to your belongings, as there is a slightly menacing atmosphere. This is not the case at most other roadside stalls).

Direct from Arusha, the road trip takes around 2 hours; Tarangire's main entrance lies just more than an hour away. Entry is $35 per person, per day ($10 for ages 5–16; under 5 free). Given the small traversing area and heavy tourist traffic it experiences, I'd strongly advise you to overnight within easy striking distance so that you can aim to be there when the park gate opens at 6:30am. As is always the case on safari, the early bird is well rewarded, not only with potentially great game sightings, but also with the peace and privilege of having the park to yourself—a notion that will be dispelled from 8am onward, as the post-breakfast hordes descend from the escarpment lodgings. Better still, spend the night in the park; this way, you have the park to yourself in the morning as well as late afternoon, by which time traffic is dispersed from the southern end of the park. Note that the park is one of the first in Tanzania to offer night game drives and walking safaris. **Green Foot Print Adventure** (www.greenfootprint.co.tz) has a license to offer both these activities; inquire at the park entrance or book through Serena Lake Manyara Lodge (p. 408). The park fees for night game drives are in the range of $50 per person, with a further $50 per person for the park vehicle (this reduces depending on number of guests); walking safaris cost $20 per person, plus the group or individual fee for the guide, at $20.

Generally, the northern section of the park sees the most tourist traffic and, from a landscape viewpoint, is the least rewarding. Make sure you get as far south as the Maji Moto hot springs, where waters, having circulated deep in fissures below the earth finally resurface at 60°C (140°F; hot enough to boil an egg) and provide ideal breeding

Fun Facts — Two Commonly Asked Questions

Why is it called Manyara?

Manyara is the Maasai name for a rather unassuming thin succulent cactus *(euphorbia tincalli)* that the Maasai plant as a living stockade to keep their cattle from straying. You will see one, clearly marked, growing at the park entrance.

Why do Manyara's lions climb trees?

Unlike leopards, lions do not typically climb trees, preferring to rest under them during the day. The reason for the unusual behavior in Lake Manyara National Park is thought to have arisen during a major tsetse fly epidemic: Blood-sucking tsetse flies appear not to bother the lions once they have ascended 5m (16 ft.) or higher. Manyara's lionesses now teach their cubs from a young age, seeking out trees that offer maximum shade, good views, and a relatively easy climb, and the image of a lioness in a tree has become synonymous with Lake Manyara.

temperatures for the algae the flamingos feed on. Flamingos aside, the views of the flood-plains are well worth the journey (if you like huge barren landscapes), but if you don't have the time to travel this far south (and, preferably, overnight at &Beyond's Tree Lodge), you can exclude Lake Manyara from your itinerary without serious regret. Certainly, there is no point in seeing the park as part of a package tour, where you will be wheeled around to all the predicable points, probably at the same time everyone else is.

WHERE TO STAY & DINE

There are only two ways to spend the night within the park: camping or in one of the most luxurious lodges on the Circuit. Adventurous campers can choose to overnight with **Manyara Bivouac,** a mobile camp erected on request, in which you sleep in simple dome tents on stretcher beds and share very basic ablution facilities (www.africatravelresource.com). Those seeking more luxury should inquire about a mobile camping trip with **Nomad** (www.nomad-tanzania.com), with walk-in tents, comfy mattresses, and en suite bathrooms (short-drop toilet and bucket shower). Both options require group bookings of at least four to eight and are a far cry from overnighting in one of **Manyara Tree Lodge**'s ultrachic forest cabins, where you can dial up your private butler and demand more ice. At around $455 (including all meals, private vehicle and guide, and park fees), the Bivouac camping experience costs the least and is the most authentic, but you can easily guess which of the three options I'd recommend.

Given that camping and the Tree Lodge represent two extremes in the market, most visitors opt for one of the four lodges built along the lip of the escarpment, the best of which are reviewed below. Given the views—Lake Manyara shimmering 500m (1,640 ft.) below, dissolving into the Rift floor valley, which stretches all the way to Mount Losimingori—not to mention cooler temperatures and fewer insects, these escarpment lodgings are no bad consolation prize.

There are also a handful of options available on the lake's northeastern shore (which falls outside the park), of which only Mbunga is worth considering. The cheapest accommodations options are in Mto wa Mbu but are recommended only if you're on a serious cost-saving mission (Mto wa Mbu means "Mosquito Waters"—spend the night here and you'll see why).

It's also worth nothing that Karatu, gateway to Ngorongoro, lies about 40 minutes from here, so, having traversed the park, there is no reason not to proceed directly to one of guesthouses here, or even direct to the crater rim; best options are discussed under Ngorongoro, below.

Near the Shores

Lake Manyara Tree Lodge ★★★ If you're prepared to splash out, look no further than Tree Lodge, the best in the area by a large margin and worth the outlay. Not only is it the only permanent option inside the park, but it enjoys a location deep in the southern section where the most picturesque landscapes are, so the drive here is part of the pleasure. The stilted timber rooms—great examples of the best in safari chic—comprise an open-plan lounge and bedroom, with large en suite bathroom; doors from all three open onto a private veranda. These units are equipped with everything, including a telephone to summon your private butler, which is more or less what you'll come to expect from &Beyond, the luxury safari company that offers (along with Singita) the best permanent lodgings on the Northern Circuit. Situated within an evergreen forest of mahogany, wild mango, and fig trees, Tree Lodge is quite a contrast to anything you'll experience in Tarangire, Serengeti, or Ngorongoro, where a huge vista of endless plains is the view of choice. Rooms are privately situated, and each is so luxurious and romantic that you'll be more than happy to forgo any activities and cocoon—but as the guides are some of the best in Tanzania, be sure to book at least one game activity while here. Dinner is a real highlight: served in the *boma,* open to the sky, with three huge open-air fireplaces, constantly fed by tree trunks. The atmosphere is almost a movie set, and the food is superb.

Private Bag X 27, Benmore, Johannesburg, 2010, South Africa. ✆ **011/809-4300** or U.S. toll-free 888/882-3742. Fax 011/809-4400. www.andbeyond.com. 10 units. High season $1,990 double; midseason $1,640 double; low season $1,310 double. Rates include all meals and drinks, laundry, scheduled safari activities, emergency medical evacuation insurance, and transfers from Manyara airstrip to Lake Manyara Tree Lodge. **Amenities:** Bar; babysitting; pool; limited currency exchange. *In room:* Mobile gym, hair dryer.

Migunga Tented Camp ★ Located in a lush, shady glade, near the northeastern shores of the lake, Migunga is a peaceful tented camp and campsite that offers easy access to the park (entrance is 10 min. away) at a very good price. The large thatched public area—housing a bar and dining area, its front entirely open and facing a tall stand of fever trees—is where guests spend their evenings swapping safari notes. The original tents, ranged to the left and right of this building, are best avoided. Since the Moivaro group took over the camp, 11 new tents have been added, and these (nos. 6–16) are vastly preferable. They are farther away from the dining/bar area, but it's a pleasant walk (accompanied by an *askari* at night), and they are bigger and more private, allow in more natural light, and have much nicer bathrooms (flushing toilet, generous shower area, basin sunk into wood, large mirror). There are no reading lamps, though—only a bare overhead bulb. Migunga doesn't feel as well loved as Kirurumu (below), but it is clean, functional, and a good option for cyclers, with mountain bike tours of the northeastern shore, where you may come across zebra, giraffe, and wildebeest. Note that from February to May, mosquitoes are usually rife.

P.O. Box 11297, Arusha. ✆ **027/250-6315** or 027/250-6386. Fax 027/250-6378. www.moivaro.com. 19 units. High season $257 double half board, $287 double full board; low season $150 double half board, $180 double full board. **Amenities:** Bar; room service.

On the Escarpment

Kirurumu Tented Lodge ★ Relative to its escarpment neighbors, Kirurumu is an intimate camp, with just 22 units (mostly tents) spread over the property and views to the east of Lake Manyara. It also has no gardens, opting instead for walkways through natural bush, which has its drawbacks. Most tents probably enjoyed great views when they were first erected, but with trees allowed to grow willy-nilly, the only place to ensure that you have an unobscured view of the Rift Valley is from one of the two honeymoon suites, custom built right on the edge. Alternatively, ask for units 1 to 8 or 16 to 20; located nearest the escarpment rim, these are likely to have better views.

Tents, built on timber platforms, are very spacious, with plenty of bedding permutations to suit families or friends prepared to sleep in the same room, en suite bathrooms (shower, flush toilet, double basin), and comfortable outdoor furniture on the veranda (fabrics are a little tired, though). Interiors are well thought out (two luggage racks, ample hanging space, umbrellas) and feature sturdy timber furniture with Maasai blankets (both practical and colorful). Meals are simple but adequate and a welcome relief from a buffet. The thatched public spaces, open to the elements, are small but lovely, with leather chairs, a well-stocked bar, a small library, and fantastic views. Though not quite as well positioned as the Serena and Lake Manyara Hotel, this is certainly the best value on the escarpment.

P.O. Box 2047, India St., Arusha. ✆ **027/250-7011** or 027/2507541. Fax 027/254-8226 www.kirurumu.net. 22 units. High season $264 double B&B, $332 double half board, $396 double full board; shoulder season $240 B&B, $300 half board, $350 double full board; low season $190 half board, $210 full board. **Amenities:** Bar.

Lake Manyara Hotel ★★ Built by the Tanzanian government in the early '70s, this was the first hotel built to service tourist traffic to Lake Manyara, and boy did they choose a great location—on the escarpment directly above Lake Manyara, its migrant flamingoes like pink clouds on the water, it cannot be beat. Location aside, the hotel has not enjoyed good press over the years, but a massive investment in 2008 could change all that. All four government-constructed safari lodges (one in Ngorongoro; the other two in Serengeti) were nationalized a few years back, and the current owner, Mr. Kotak, has embarked on a huge renovation and refurbishment program. The architecture is classic early '70s modernism, with plenty of glass, stone, and timber, and the sensitive renovations build on these existing architectural strengths. The interlinking lobby/bar/restaurant areas are huge and airy, with plenty of leather and heavy Indo-African antiques, but the best improvement has to be the new raised bar built right on the escarpment edge, making the most of the expansive views, as well as the immaculate gardens that surround the pool. Room size is classic of the era (small, with tiny shower-in-tub bathroom), but rooms enjoy a sense of space thanks to the floor-to-ceiling wall of glass that slides open to a small veranda. Make sure you get an elevated lake view (rooms 58–66 are good, as are 45–48 and 17–32). The self-service buffet-style food is not memorable, and service is slow and indifferent; the new Italian manageress, Margherita Olivieri, may put an end to this, however.

2nd Floor, Summit Centre, Sokoine Rd., P.O. Box 2633, Arusha. ✆ **027/254-4595,** -4807, -4798, or -4795. Fax 027/2548633. www.hotelsandlodges-tanzania.com. 100 units. High season $440 double B&B; low season $240 double B&B. **Amenities:** Restaurant; bar; babysitting; pool; currency exchange; nurse.

Lake Manyara Serena Safari Lodge ★★ The spectacular pool area—so near it appears virtually cantilevered over the escarpment rim—is the best reason to book here, with views from the bar and sun loungers to rival those of Lake Manyara Hotel. The Serena also has a far greater range of activities on offer, from scenic flights over the lake in a micro-light (you can even fly to Ngorongoro, or over Ol Doinyo L'Engai) to night game drives in the park in an open vehicle. Rooms are spacious and beds are comfortable, but the dated decor doesn't invite lingering, and (unlike at Lake Manyara Hotel) there's no chance of enjoying the view from your bed; even from the small balconies, views are generally obscured by trees and undergrowth. Part of the Serena chain, this is very much a resort aimed at higher-end package tours and, as such, is a well-maintained machine. Some may find the architecture, apparently inspired by "the gentle concentric patterns of traditional Maasai *bomas,*" somewhat dated, others charming—certainly, no one can call it characterless. Cuisine is good, service a little complacent. However, with Hotel Lake Manyara's refurbishment finally complete, Serena now faces competition.

P.O. Box 2551, Arusha. ✆ **027/253-9161,** -9162, or -9163. Fax 027/253-9164. www.serenahotels.com. 67 units. Peak season $635 double full board; midseason $480 double full board; low season $340 double full board. **Amenities:** Bar; Internet; pool. *In room:* Hair dryer.

4 NGORONGORO CONSERVATION AREA ★★★

60km (37 miles) NW of Lake Manyara, 170km (105 miles) W of Arusha, 145km (90) SE of the Serengeti

Designated as a "multiple land use area," the Ngorongoro Conservation Area stretches from the precipitous barrier that is the Great Rift Valley wall, encompassing a high-altitude plateau of dramatic volcanic highlands and craters before gently descending to the contiguous plains of the Serengeti in the west. It is a vast and untouched region, much of it appearing harsh and barren, yet what makes the Ngorongoro Conservation Area so unique is that it is a refuge for both animal and man.

With no physical borders, the Ngorongoro Conservation Area is very much part of the greater Serengeti ecosystem and hosts the annual Migration as it passes through from Loliondo in the north to the breeding grounds surrounding Lake Ndutu in December, before returning north and west some 12 weeks later. In fact, the entire Ngorongoro Conservation Area initially fell within the Serengeti National Park, but the inevitable conflict that arose between the newly formed park authorities and long-resident Maasai inhabitants resulted in a new agreement being signed by the Maasai elders in 1958. The following year, the Maasai herded the last of their animals across the Serengeti and resettled in the newly designated Ngorongoro Conservation Area, which included their most sacred of mountains, Ol Doinyo L'Engai (literally, "Mountain of God"; p. 420), the last remaining active volcano in the Rift Valley. Government officials then tried to stop the Migration from moving into Ngorongoro, putting up mile upon mile of barbed-wire fencing, which the wildebeest, in their millions, simply trampled. "It's marvelous the way those animals have smashed it flat," was the sardonic response of Myles Turner, then deputy chief game warden of Serengeti, adding, "I use the fence posts for firewood now."

Seen at the time as a radical compromise, Ngorongoro was, and still is, the only conservation area in Africa to provide full protection status for resident wildlife as well as the interests of its indigenous pastoralists, who live as traditionally as ever, free to roam anywhere in the NCA (crater excepted), herding their cattle, donkeys, goats, and sheep. Thanks to the Maasai's innate conservation ethic, it has been a remarkably successful

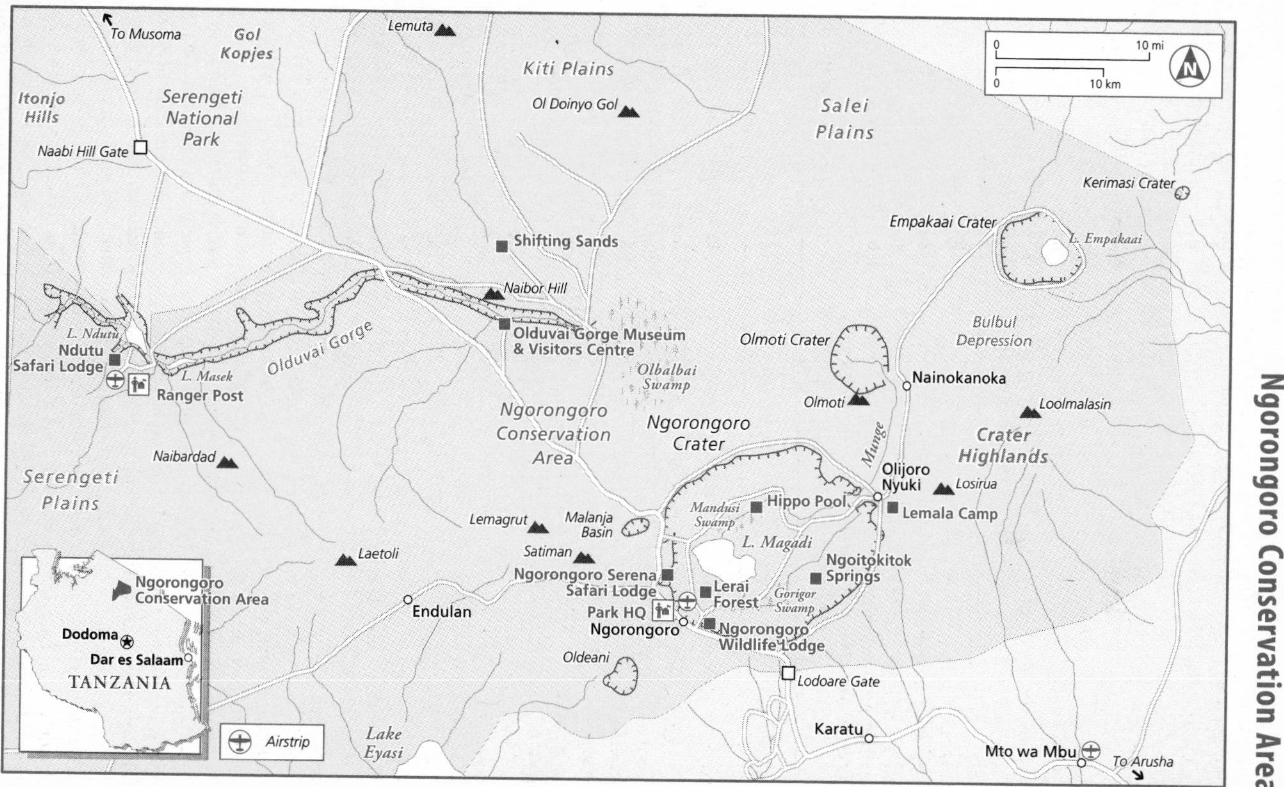

To Musoma
Gol Kopjes
Lemuta
Kiti Plains
Ol Doinyo Gol
Salei Plains
0 10 mi
0 10 km
Itonjo Hills
Serengeti National Park
Naabi Hill Gate
Kerimasi Crater
Empakaai Crater
L. Empakaai
Shifting Sands
Naibor Hill
L. Ndutu
Ndutu Safari Lodge
Olduvai Gorge
Olduvai Gorge Museum & Visitors Centre
Olmoti Crater
Bulbul Depression
L. Masek
Ranger Post
Olbalbai Swamp
Nainokanoka
Olmoti
Loolmalasin
Ngorongoro Conservation Area
Ngorongoro Crater
Munge
Crater Highlands
Naibardad
Olijoro Nyuki
Losirua
Serengeti Plains
Mandusi Swamp
Hippo Pool
Lemala Camp
Lemagrut
Malanja Basin
L. Magadi
Laetoli
Satiman
Ngoitokitok Springs
Ngorongoro Conservation Area
Ngorongoro Serena Safari Lodge
Lerai Forest
Gorigor Swamp
Endulan
Park HQ
Dodoma
Ngorongoro
Ngorongoro Wildlife Lodge
Dar es Salaam
Oldeani
TANZANIA
Lodoare Gate
Airstrip
Lake Eyasi
Karatu
Mto wa Mbu
To Arusha

When Louis Met Mary: The Start of a Paleontological Dynasty

In 1929, an enthusiastic Cambridge graduate named Louis Seymour Bazett Leakey traveled to Berlin to bet fellow archaeologist Hans Reck, who had a few years back extricated some particularly interesting fossils from a gorge in Tanzania, that the same gorge would reveal more of its secrets to Leakey within 24 hours. Reck accepted the bet, and he and Louis duly set off to what the Maasai called Olduvai Gorge, after the sisal-type plant that grew here. Reck lost the bet, which cost him all of £10. Louis, born of missionary parents in Africa at the turn of the century and initiated at age 13 into the Kikuyu tribe he grew up with, wanted more. He was determined to prove that *homo sapiens* originated in Africa—a concept we now take for granted, but one met with total skepticism at the time.

A Christian and Darwinian, Louis was, by all accounts, a complex, charismatic figure. When he met the young Mary Nicol in 1933, he was looking for an illustrator, his wife having taken ill with morning sickness. Mary, the daughter of an English landscape artist who had spent a lot of time at Les Eyzies and the Dordogne, was fascinated with prehistory as a child, and after the death of her father when she was just 13, became what her mother described as "a difficult child." She was expelled from two consecutive convent schools for minor misdemeanors (refusing to recite poetry, creating explosions in the chemistry lab) and proved impossible to tutor privately. Mary wanted nothing more than to draw and study archaeology, but as her academic history ruled out a university education (ironically, she would be awarded many doctorates from these very universities), she turned to scientific illustration, which is why she was recommended to Louis when he was looking for a replacement illustrator for his book, *Adam's Ancestors.* The attraction between the two free-spirited individuals was immediate. Louis left his wife, and after she granted him a divorce in 1936, he and Mary were married in a civil ceremony witnessed by the son of a Kikuyu chief. They spent all the time they could at Olduvai: 2 decades on and off, patiently scouring the 48km (30-mile) gorge for the tools and fossils of ancient hominids, and raising a family of three sons.

cohabitation experiment, attested to by the NCA's status as a UNESCO World Heritage Site (1979), followed by its recognition as an International Biosphere Reserve in 1981.

Although the Conservation Area covers a vast 8,288 sq. km (3,232 sq. miles), virtually all tourist traffic is centered on and around the crater after which it is named: The Ngorongoro Crater is not only the world's largest unbroken volcanic caldera, but it is also home to one of the densest wildlife populations on Earth, some 250,000 wild animals. Created 2 million to 3 million years ago, the crater walls drop a sheer 610m (2,001 ft.), a circular embrace enclosing a 260-sq.-km (101-sq.-mile) valley, in which even a 6-ton elephant appears no larger than an ant. Standing on the lip and gazing into this vast natural arena, the opposite walls of which rise almost 20km (12 miles) away, one is struck not only by the sheer size and symmetry, but also by the visible ecosystems that sustain

It was the chain-smoking Mary who finally made the discovery that would catapult the Leakey name into the annals of paleontology. A fragment of bone caught her eye and, hours of careful brushing later, she discovered a set of hominid-looking teeth. With great care, Mary and Louis uncovered *Australopithecus boisei,* "Nutcracker Man," who would finally prove, without doubt, the existence of hominids some 2 million years ago in East Africa. Mary had proven Louis right.

Louis needed more than just painstaking excavation to sustain him, and a year after Mary's major discovery, they agreed that she would become director of excavations at Olduvai while he would head off to raise awareness and funds. Convinced that field research in primates was key to unraveling the mysteries of human evolution, Louis particularly fostered female researchers, including Jane Goodall, Dian Fossey, and Birute Galdikas; at least two of them became known as "Leakey's Angels" and became romantically linked to him.

When, dogged by ill health, Louis died of a heart attack in London in 1972, Mary kept working in Olduvai, and in 1976 she discovered the Laetoli hominid footprint trail, left in volcanic ash some 3.6 million years ago. Mary finally retired in 1983 at age 70, passing the baton to second son Richard, who had led his first fossil-hunting expedition in 1964 and married archaeologist Margaret Cropper in 1966. When this relationship failed, he married primate researcher Meave Epps, whose own paleoanthropological discoveries included *Australopithecus Anamensis* (1995) and *Kenyanthropus platyops* (2001). When their daughter, Louise, completed her Ph.D. in paleontology in 2001, she took her place in what has, to all intents, become the family "business"—uncovering the story of man's genesis.

Today **Olduvai Gorge** (entry Tsh3,000) is still under excavation, with three international groups working here between June and August, but anyone can visit the gorge, either as a day trip from the Ngorongoro Crater (about 90 min. away) or en route to Serengeti. It's a worthwhile stop, with a good talk and a basic museum attached, but little to evoke the passions that flowed within and between the Leakey family who made the sight so famous.

its incredibly varied wildlife. From the dark montane forests that clad the southern crater walls to the open yellow grassland and acacia thickets in the basin, intersected by veins of freshwater streams, and the tell-tale white crust of its very own salt lake, Ngorongoro's great caldera falls into the archetypal realm of an isolated Lost World, only without the dinosaurs. That said, descend to the valley floor, and you will probably have one of the most productive game drives in Africa. The fertile pasture and permanent water supply support a population of approximately 25,000 grazers, mostly zebra and wildebeest, but also buffalo, gazelle, eland, kongoni, and warthogs. Swamps and forest are home to hippos, elephants, waterbucks, reedbucks and bushbucks, baboons, and vervet monkeys. Thanks to the abundance of grazers, lion, leopard, cheetah, and hyena lead a rather idyllic life (though, sadly, stagnation has led to genetic inbreeding of the lion population), and they are so habituated to vehicles that you are likely to capture them on film without the use of a zoom. This is also the only area in the Northern Circuit park (aside from the Grumeti) where you are virtually guaranteed a sighting of that most prehistoric of living creatures—the black rhinoceros. In fact, with the exception of impala, topi, oribi, giraffe, and crocodile, almost every species found in East Africa is present here. The cooler temperatures on the rim are also very agreeable, so much so they prompted great African explorer Frederick Courtney Selous to recommend a sojourn here as "an essential respite from the heat and repetitive bouts of malaria."

The main drawback—and it is a very real one—is the equally large population of tourists the crater attracts—400,000 at last count, earning the country a whopping $30 million. Park authorities have reduced volumes on the crater floor somewhat with their ever-escalating fees, making this the most expensive game drive you'll take in East Africa, but if your idea of experiencing the wilds precludes doing so in full view of other vehicles, I would recommend you traverse the rim road, with regular stops to take in the stupendous views, particularly in the late afternoon (or at least well after the morning fog has cleared). Having spent the night at one of the lodges recommended below, head on to the Serengeti, either by charter flight or, if you are driving, with a scheduled stop at Olduvai Gorge (see "When Louis Met Mary" box above), considered one of the most important archaeological and paleontological sites in the world.

ESSENTIALS

The road from Arusha to the Lodoare Entrance Gate is now paved and takes just more than 2 hours; the crater can be reached in a sedan, but beyond the crater (to Serengeti) you will need a 4×4 vehicle. Traveling to Ngorongoro by vehicle is recommended, as it will give you ample opportunity to shop for crafts along the way and allows you to set your own pace, taking whatever detours you deem worthy (note that Karatu, the nearest town to Ngorongoro Conservation Area, has a 24-hour ATM on the main road; it may not be operational, so don't rely on this, but it will be the last source of cash till Lake Victoria). By contrast, the road from the crater to the Serengeti is quite possibly the worst in Africa—no one drives on the demarcated road, and even the tracks that have been made on either side of this are corrugated hell.

Aside from the atrocious state of the roads between the crater to the Serengeti, the conservation area is professionally run, with an excellent website, www.ngorongorocrater.org (or the slightly less user-friendly www.ngorongoro-crater-africa.org; in the unlikely event this does not answer all your queries, call ✆ **027/253-7046** or 027/253-7019, or write to ncaa_faru@cybernet.co.tz).

We're People, Not Wildlife

While traveling the Northern Circuit it is impossible not to fill your camera with images of the most awesome landscapes and wildlife encounters, but resist the urge to take photographs of people on the roadside (the Maasai, in particular) without first asking permission. Permission may not be granted, or will be for a fee, sometimes as high as $10 per person, in which case you may refuse with good grace. However, to take a photograph without permission is considered the height of rudeness and is asking for trouble.

Overrated Hadzabe: Stuck Between a Rock and the Stone Age?

Lake Eyasi, located on the edge of the Ngorongoro Conservation Area, is neither as attractive or game-rich as Lake Manyara, nor as significant as Lake Natron. However, it still attracts a fair number of visitors, thanks to the inhabitants living near its shores. The 200-odd Hadzabe families are among the last remaining hunter-gatherers on the continent and have lived in this area relatively undisturbed for more than 10,000 years—though the last 50 years have not been kind. They resisted the forcible settlement policies that Julius Nyere implemented in the 1970s, but their traditional way of life remained under serious threat—not only from conservationists who disapproved of their hunting and government officials desperate to enroll the new generation in school, but more recently from the burgeoning tourism industry that has sprung up around them. What was initially irregular contact, usually with individual travelers with an anthropological interest in understanding their customs, the "Meet the Hadzabe" experience has been turned into a package tour event, with Westerners gawking at the hunting and survival methods of "Africa's last remaining primitive Stone Age tribe." The effect of this fishbowl treatment, as well as the money that has entered the Hadzabe's previously cashless social system, has had a disastrous impact on the lifestyle people are so keen to witness, and most reputable tour operators no longer participate in what some have described as cultural rape, others as simply a waste of the client's money. That said, **Kisima Ngeda** (www.kisimangeda.com), the tented camp on Lake Eyasi's shores, is a remote and peaceful camp, and a great way to spend a day or two unwinding pre- or post-safari.

Daily entry permit to NCA costs $50 per person ($10 for children 5–16, 4 and under free) plus an additional daily vehicle permit fee ($40–$300, depending on weight). To visit the crater, you will need to fork out an additional $200 per vehicle.

Note that NCA wardens will not allow vehicles into the crater before 6:30am, and all vehicles need to be out by 6pm (latest descent is at 4pm). As is the case at Lake Manyara, an early start is well rewarded. Most visitors depart after breakfast and take a packed lunch; to miss the crowds, ask your lodge to pack a breakfast, leave early enough to start your descent through the mists at 6:30am, and return for a late lunch.

Aside from the wildlife in the crater, you may wish to visit a Maasai cultural *boma;* the entrance fee is hefty (around $100 per person), and some report that the Maasai can be rather pushy about buying souvenirs. As fascinating as the Maasai culture is, I have always found the "meet the tribe" routine a little fake and awkward, but if you wish to experience it firsthand, there are four good options. The first two are conveniently situated on the road to Serengeti (but, as a result, are the most tourist savvy): Kiloki Senyati Cultural Boma is 7km (4¼ miles) southwest of the Olduvai Gorge Information Center, while Loonguku Cultural Boma is 10km (6¼ miles) before the turn-off to Olduvai

Gorge. Irkeepusi Cultural Boma is 2km (1¼ miles) northeast of the Lemala mini gate, on the main road to Empakaai, and Seneto Cultural Boma is just west of the Seneto Gate, within the Malanja Depression. There are two more craters you may wish to visit, both of them rarely included in itineraries and, therefore, wonderfully solitary experiences. Olmoti Crater is about an hour's drive from Ngorongoro Crater and must then be approached on foot, but the more spectacular is Empakaai Crater, a 2-hour drive on rough roads (4×4 only). This crater floor lies 300m (984 ft.) below the forested rim and is almost 6km (3¾ miles) across, half of it (depending on rain) a soda lake; even more stunning than the crater itself are the views of Ol Doinyo L'Engai (p. 420).

WHERE TO STAY & DINE

If money is no object, there is only one choice: Ngorongoro Crater Lodge. A destination in its own right, its location, right on the crater rim, is unsurpassed. If you want to enjoy the same sublime views but not blow the budget, there are four more options along the rim, three of them reviewed below, of which Lemala Camp, while not the least expensive, offers the best value for your money.

Ngorongoro Sopa is a huge cavernous lodge that enjoys the same fabulous views as the Crater, Serena, and Wildlife lodges, but interiors and exteriors are ugly, and despite recent refurbishments to rooms, decor is still dated and drab. Before the Lemara Camp (reviewed later in this chapter), **Sopa** (www.sopalodges.com) was the only lodge close to the eastern route to the crater, which meant that you could be the first down, but Lemara now offers this and so much more. Given that the rack rates are usually only around $50 per person, per night lower than at the superior Serena, Sopa is not reviewed here. However, if all the recommended options below are full, or if you are cherry-picking for bargains (which Sopa at certain times of the year offers), take a look at their website. Note also that Rhino Lodge, an ugly new lodge located in indifferent surrounds near the crater rim, is *not* worth booking—prices (around $180 double) are great, given that you are in the NCA, but the stark low-budget accommodations are depressing and there are no views. A far better option is to base yourself in one of the lovely farmhouse-style guesthouses that lie in the highlands above Karatu, the nearest town to the NCA, all about 30 minutes from the crater rim (more than an hour to the floor). The top three are reviewed below, but if you're watching your budget, also take a look at **Bougainvillea Lodge** (www.bougainvillealodge.net), on the main road leading into Karatu. It comprises 24 en suite cottages built around a central pool, each with fireplace and veranda. Units are comfortable and a good value ($146 double half board; $173 full board); I'd take at least one meal at Gibb's (see below), however. Lastly, if you're a little more adventurous, **Olduvai Camp** (book through www.africatravelresource.com), located beyond the crater (walking distance from the famous archaeological dig, which you can visit with one of the resident Maasai), is a highly rated back-to-basics experience, with a relaxed and welcoming Maasai staff (one of the best reasons to come) and awe-inspiring views of the

Tips Blowing Hot & Cold

Between 1,580 and 3,600m (5,184–11,811 ft.) above sea level, temperatures on the Ngorongoro plateau can get decidedly chilly, particularly at night and in the mornings. It's best to dress in layers, as temperatures can rise to T-shirt level by noon.

surrounding plains and volcanic highlands. Accommodations are classic East African safari-style tents—big enough to walk in, with relatively basic furnishings. The new flush toilets are welcome, albeit erratic, and bucket showers during dry season are sometimes, well, dry. However, mealtimes are generally wonderful affairs shared around a communal table. This is a great camp to meet similar-minded folk from all over the world. If large lodges and four walls leave you cold (and Lemara is too pricey), this is the perfect stop-over on your way to or from the crater. Rates range between $900 and $1,200 for a double, including all meals, park fees, private vehicle, and driver.

Around Karatu

Gibb's Farm ★★★ The utterly charming Gibb's, usually booked as an overnight stop for visitors traveling between the Serengeti and Manyara/Tarangire, will have you wishing you were staying for a week. Most visitors to the Conservation Area want a crater view, but, with the exception of Crater Lodge, Gibb's is a superior accommodation experience in every way. If you're the kind of person who is thrilled by the sight of six grinning kitchen staff sharing the burden of three huge woven baskets, each brimming with organic vegetables just plucked from the fertile Karatu soil, this "respite from the rigors of safari" is a must. Food is home-style and consistently the best you'll eat on the entire Northern Circuit, and everyone dines from the same menu/buffet. Accommodations, centered on the 80-year-old farmhouse, are the kind you'll be reticent to leave: huge cottages in the midst of lush gardens, with tasteful furnishings (Martha Stewart would love it), every comfort (bedroom with two queen beds, bay-window dining area, wrap-around fireplace—some even have a secondary fireplace next to the tub), and garden bathrooms. Standard rooms are not in the same class but offer superb value (though they plan to renovate these into farm cottages). My only complaint is that the new African Living Spa reeks of marketing gimmick rather than medicinal healing. Then again, if it feels good, who cares?

P.O. Box 280, Karatu. ✆ **027/253-4040** or 027/253-4397. Fax 027/253-4418. www.gibbsfarm.net. 22 units. Farm cottages $744 double full board, $702 double half board; standard rooms $356 full board, $314 half board. MC, V. **Amenities:** Bar; spa treatments. *In room* (cottages only): Fireplace, hair dryer, Wi-Fi.

Ngorongoro Farm House ★★ The best Northern Circuit property in the Tanganyika Wilderness Camps portfolio, Ngorongoro Farm House is a well-established watering hole on the Northern Circuit tour (though I'd much rather stay in a standard room in Plantation Lodge or a standard room at Gibb's, both of which offer even better value). Given that this property is twice the size, it has more of a resortlike atmosphere than the "boutique farm" experience that Gibb's and Plantation Lodge offer, but it's still an oasis of calm, and certainly next in line. The main lodge with huge dining room and inviting pool area is surrounded by soft green lawns shaded by huge jacarandas (when in bloom, they transform the lawns into a purple carpet). Meandering walkways lead from here to the garden rooms—some are distant from the main dining and pool area, so do specify if you don't want to walk too far. Rooms are wonderfully spacious, most with mosquito-swathed four-poster king-size beds (newer rooms have twins only), a sitting area, desk, and a semiprivate veranda with garden and farm views. There are a number of interconnecting rooms for families. Showers are generous and decent water pressure a treat. At night, fires are lit in the outdoor pit, and there is usually live entertainment from the nearby village. All in all, this is a very satisfactory choice (unlike sister lodge Tloma, also in Karatu highlands, which is an inferior choice for the same rate).

P.O. Box 8276, Arusha. ✆ **027/254-4556** or 078/420-7727. www.tanganyikawildernesscamps.com. 50 units. Peak season $500 double full board; high season $440 double full board; low season $220 double full board. MC, V. **Amenities:** Bar; Arusha transfers; Internet; pool.

The Plantation Lodge ★★★ Value Karatu's other class act is, like Gibb's, located on a farm surrounded by working coffee plantations, with cottages in lush gardens surrounding the original farm house. This, however, is a more pared version, with interiors featuring predominantly cool whites and natural wood finishes. Service and facilities are not as slick as at Gibb's, but many find it less commercial and enjoy the more laid-back atmosphere and intimate "boutique farm" atmosphere. It's the kind of place you're served tea and homemade biscuits under a leafy canopy and drift off, surrounded by expansive lawns and flowerbeds filled with birdsong. Cottages are spacious, with plenty of windows and French doors letting in natural light and lovely garden views; the standard rooms offer exceptional value, whereas suites are gorgeous. Food is healthy, home-style fare; for a romantic occasion, request to be served in one of the many intimate locations in the garden. This place would be my personal pick for those who can't afford Crater Lodge.

P.O. Box 34, Karatu. ✆ **078/494-7125** or 027/253-4405. www.plantation-lodge.com. 16 units. $315 double half board; $390 double full board; $520–$800 suite. No credit cards. Suite rates include all meals, drinks (with the exception of imports), and laundry. **Amenities:** Bar; Internet; pool. *In room:* Fireplaces (in some), fridge (in suites), hair dryer.

Ngorongoro Crater Rim

Lemala Ngorongoro Camp ★★★ This classy newcomer, operated by Grumeti Expeditions, is a fantastic addition to the Ngorongoro (and Serengeti) options. Located in a private campsite in a lush acacia forest on the eastern edge of the crater, the views to the crater floor are not as unobstructed as at its lodge counterparts, but this is a really exclusive experience: You are one of a maximum 20 privileged guests, and the camp's descent road into the crater is 5 minutes away, which means you can get into the crater by 7am (a huge advantage during high season). Thus, you'll encounter far fewer vehicles than on the traffic-logged road shared by three big lodges on the western side. The styling and design of the tents are fabulous, with all the luxuries you will come to expect from the best tented camps—comfortable upholstered sofas in the mess tent, cut-crystal stemware, comfortable king-size (or twin) beds, rugs, dressing areas, flush toilets, shower and basin with running water, solar-generated electricity, and excellent service standards. A word of warning: It gets pretty cold at night, and although every tent has a heater and beds are covered in polar blankets, down duvets, and stuffed with hot water bottles, you will still need to pack plenty of warm clothes (insulated camp jackets are on hand if you don't want to pack bulk). It's the most authentic safari experience you can have on the crater, replete with regular camp visits from big tuskers and roaring camp fires.

Grumeti Expeditions Tz Ltd.; P.O. Box 14529, Arusha. ✆ **027/254-8952.** Fax 027/254-8939. www.lemalacamp.com. 9 units. High season $1,390 double game package, $1,100 double full board; low season $1,190 game package, $960 full board. Full board rates include all meals and beverages, camping fee, and laundry. Closed Nov 16–20 and Apr 16–May 31. **Amenities:** Bar.

Ngorongoro Crater Lodge ★★★ Arguably the most over-the-top lodge in Africa, this wonderful mix of hobbitlike craftsmanship and baronial-style splendor (famously described as "Versailles meets Maasai") is a wonderful counterbalance to the stunning crater views that vie for your attention. The lodge comprises three totally separate camps, with 12 suites in both North and South camps, served by identical but separate public areas. (The intimate six-suite Tree Camp is aimed at a group or family and is totally self-functioning). So while the full guest complement is 60, the feeling remains one of an intimate gathering on the edge of heaven. Each stone-and-thatch suite is wonderfully ornate (dripping chandeliers, teak paneling, raw silk curtains, Persian carpets, gilt mirrors) and combines three circular rooms—bedroom, bathroom, and toilet—with tall glass windows and doors opening to views of the crater and the grazers who frequent the camp. Guests enjoy the services of a private butler who will light the fire before you return to your room at night, or surprise you with a bubble bath after a game drive or a superb meal in a room romantically lit with three fireplaces. Guides, too, are impeccable, but this is one lodge where you will want to forgo game drives (and feel free to do so).

Private Bag X 27, Benmore, Johannesburg, 2010, South Africa. ✆ **011/809-4300,** or U.S. toll-free 888/882-3742. Fax 011/809-4400. www.andbeyond.com. 30 units. High season $2,690 double; peak season $3,000; low season $1,370. All rates are game package and include all meals and drinks, laundry, scheduled safari activities, emergency medical evacuation insurance, and transfers from Ngorongoro airstrip. **Amenities:** Bar; babysitting; pool; limited currency exchange. *In room:* Fireplace, hair dryer, iPod docking station.

Ngorongoro Serena Lodge ★★ This stone-clad lodge, with equally superb crater views, is typical of the Serena chain: perfectly comfortable, but very much a resort experience, with facilities aimed at the package tour market. Exteriors are covered in indigenous foliage, with the river-stone facades sitting right into the crater edge, an attractive camouflage that makes what is the second-biggest lodge on the rim look deceptively small. Serena is also the closest lodge to the western descent road, which means you can be one of the first to get to the floor on this side of the crater (assuming you get up in time). Interiors are less successful, with faux bushman painting, stained-glass lamp sconces, and the same heavy, clumsy furniture as found in sister lodges Seronera and Lake Manyara—but the views are what this is all about (the telescope on the terrace is a boon, and the views from the dining room are truly fabulous). Besides, some find the whole Flintstones styling rather quaint. Rooms are bland but comfortable, with small balconies, all with crater views. If a crater view is what you want, this is the best option in its price category, but I'd look at making an even bigger savings by booking at Ngorongoro Wildlife Lodge, assuming their renovations are complete, or give up the view and opt for Plantation Lodge.

P.O. Box 2551, Arusha. ✆ **027/255-3313,** -3314, or -3315. Fax 027/255-3316. www.serenahotels.com. 75 units. Peak season $635 double full board; midseason $560 full board; low season $360 full board. Holiday supplement at Easter ($30 per person, per night) and Christmas ($40 per person, per night). MC, V. **Amenities:** Restaurant; babysitting; room service; Wi-Fi; currency exchange.

Ngorongoro Wildlife Lodge ★ Value Wildlife Lodge has a similar location to its far pricier neighbor, Crater Lodge, but that's where the similarity ends (and abruptly). Another of the original government hotels dating back to the late '60s, now nationalized and owned by Mr. Kotak, the Wildlife Lodge was undergoing extensive renovations in 2009. The architecture is very much '60s resort, with a massive A-line sheet of roof on approach and interiors featuring huge stone fireplaces with brass detailing. If you like this kind of thing, the Wildlife Lodge represents the best value for your money on the circuit. Design-wise, the public spaces have stood the test of time far better than the younger Serena and Sopa, but the real reason you are here is the view, and it is stupendous. Rooms are very small but have floor-to-ceiling windows looking out on the crater (try to book a room located away from the public spaces, which can be noisy); bathrooms are similarly tiny (shower over tub), and water pressure fluctuates. Food is mediocre, packed lunches awful. But the main drawback (at least, at research time) is the massive construction—no one wants to go on holiday with builders and scaffolding, and the whole service aspect was in disarray, so do check that renovations (including room refurbishments) are complete before booking here.

2nd Floor, Summit Centre, Sokoine Rd., P.O. Box 2633, Arusha. ✆ **027/254-4595,** -4807, -4798, or -4795. Fax 027/254-8633. www.hotelsandlodges-tanzania.com. 72 units. Peak season $460 double full board, $450 double half board; high season $400 full board, $390 half board; low season $240 full board, $230 half board. $40 surcharge Dec 24–26 and 31. **Amenities:** Restaurant; bar; currency exchange.

A SIDE TRIP TO THE MOUNTAIN OF GOD ★★★

The 2½-hour drive from Mto wa Mbu to Lake Natron, East African flamingo breeding site in the valley of Ol Doinyo L'Engai (the Maasai "Mountain of God"), is not for everyone. But if you like getting right off the beaten track and revere stark and desolate landscapes (and can take hostile heat, bumpy roads and relentless dust), this is arguably the most rewarding experience you will have in East Africa.

Technically, you can travel the 120km (74 miles) from Mto wa Mbu to Engaresero (also known as Ngare Sero, the nearest village to Lake Natron) overnight, then set off across more bone-jarring tracks to Klein's Gate in the northern Serengeti, but the latter half of this drive—which can take 5 to 7 hours, depending on road conditions—is demanding on backs, vehicles, and tempers; most operators will try to persuade you to back-track from Lake Natron, heading back (on the same road) to Mto wa Mbu. If you are an intrepid traveler and inveterate camper, it's worth finding a reputable operator who will traverse the Ngorongoro Conservation Area from Mto wa Mbu to Klein's Gate, as I have met a number of people who have done the journey—some more than once—and all rate it as "awesome" (one of the best people to arrange this through is Horst, proprietor of Meru View; africanview@habari.co.tz or www.matembezi.co.tz). However, returning the way you came the following day (or later, if you want to climb Ol Doinyo L'Engai) is no hardship, given the jaw-dropping landscapes, now seen from the reverse angle and probably in a different light.

Aside from the sheer scale and brutality of the landscape, there is the luxury of savoring it all on your own; there are no road-side stalls or signs of tourist activity en route, and you are unlikely to pass more than a handful of other vehicles during the entire round-trip. What you will encounter are some of your most treasured memories of the Maasai. Traversing seemingly barren valleys, Maasai men stride like kings before their cattle, their tall, lean frames draped in artful shades of red, a startling contrast against the parched backdrop; similarly, the women are usually wrapped in blue, their white-beaded manacles gleaming against their elongated necks and slim wrists.

With the exception of Engaresero village, the Maasai here live pretty much untrammeled by the cultural tourism that has turned villagers living within easy reach of the Ngorongoro Crater into attractions. Trigger-happy photographers are urged to practice the utmost restraint. (Note that some Maasai living here prefer not to have their photographs taken; others, like elsewhere, will expect to be paid. Always ask first, and respect the response.)

Most visitors travel this way ostensibly to get a close-up look at Lake Natron, breeding ground for the Rift Valley's 2.5 million endangered lesser flamingo. Along the way, you will also pass by the 500-year-old Engaruka Ruins. Once a thriving terraced city with a sophisticated irrigation system, it is today of limited interest to visitors without a strong archaeological bent. Of far more importance is the approaching bulk towering 2,878m (9,440 ft.) above the blackened plains—Ol Doinyo L'Engai, the last remaining active volcano in the Great Rift Valley.

Active for more than a century (the first recorded observation dates back to 1883; the last smoke seen spewing from the mountain was in June 2008), the rumblings emitted by the mountain are believed by the Maasai to be the voice of their female deity (eruptions seen as her fury). Aside from its spiritual significance, the beautiful symmetry of the mountain is one of the most arresting sights in East Africa. Entirely barren, its single-cone peak dusted in white ash, the triangulated shape rises from flat plains that are blackened and strewn with volcanic rock. Hot and hostile, it is as humbling as any of Earth's great natural wonders, a truly surreal and post-apocalyptic vision that will have you stopping your vehicle every few minutes to try, yet again, to capture it all on film.

By contrast, Lake Natron, its shallow, caustic waters surrounded by sludge-gray volcanic ash and pink and white crusty salts, is, unless seen from the air, not a photogenic destination, but a fascinating natural phenomenon nevertheless.

Like all Rift Valley lakes, Natron has no outlet, and during the driest months, when evaporation is at its highest, the pH concentration can shoot as high as 11, turning its waters as alkaline as ammonia. Even mud temperatures can reach 60°C (140°F), an inhospitable environment for most living organisms, but an ideal nursery for salt-loving microorganisms, including cyanobacteria, whose red pigment produces the deep-red colors seen in the central parts of the lake, changing to orange in shallower water. The saline waters are also much loved by the blue-green algae with red pigments that forms the primary diet of the lesser flamingo and gives its feathers its glamorous pink hues.

Flamingo breeding season is usually around June, when they congregate in the center of the shallow waters, the caustic and hot muddy surrounds safeguarding them from predators, before moving to the southern shorelines and finally migrating to other soda lakes in the Rift Valley. You can arrange excursions to the breeding grounds (a drive of 25km/16 miles from the village) or, depending on time of year, to the southern shoreline, from Lake Natron Camp (see below). If the flamingoes are resident on the southern shoreline, a wonderful excursion is to walk, accompanied by a guide, to the lake in the late afternoon, when the softer light and lower temperatures transform what is otherwise a physically inhospitable environment. The walk takes approximately 90 minutes; set aside some more time to photograph the waterfowl (aside from flamingoes, you will see plenty of egrets, herons, and pelicans), then settle down at the table that has been set up for you by camp staff and enjoy a chilled bottle of wine before being transferred by vehicle (or you may opt to walk) back to camp.

Lake Natron Camp will also make all the arrangements, should you wish to climb Ol Doinyo L'Engai. Ascending more than 2,000m (6,560 ft.) in 5 hours, this is a tough, steep climb, rated by some as the best 1-day trek in Africa and more exhilarating than conquering Kilimanjaro. Due to the heat the lunar-like landscape radiates, climbers set off at midnight, reaching the summit at dawn, making the 2-hour descent before the sun climbs too high.

Erupting with Anger

"There must have been more than enough reason for God to have unleashed Her anger on us, and all we could do was pray for mercy."

–Tepilit Ole Saitoti on the 1966 eruption that devastated the Maasai's livestock, from *Worlds of a Maasai Warrior*

Flamingos Facing Ground Zero?

Despite the fact that the lesser flamingo is on the IUCN Red List and that Lake Natron is the only site in East Africa where it can breed successfully (one of only five sites in the world), a development proposal by Tata Chemicals Ltd., India's leading manufacturer of inorganic chemicals, and the National Development Corporation of Tanzania, is currently under serious consideration. Making the usual deal-sweetener promises (local investment and job opportunities), Tata wants to build a soda ash plant on Lake Natron's shores for the production and export of sodium carbonate, or washing soda, used predominantly in the manufacturing of glass and in swimming pools to reduce the effects of chlorine and raise pH. In addition to the actual plant, which will pump water from the lake, this would involve building housing for more than 1,000 workers and a coal-fired power station to provide energy for the plant complex. In addition, there is a possibility the developers may introduce a hybrid brine shrimp to increase the efficiency of extraction. Naturally, experts rate the chance of the lesser flamingoes continuing to breed in the face of such mayhem as "next to zero." As a result of this commercial pressure, the Ngorongoro Conservation Area Authority (NCCA) has stepped in and proposed that Ol Doinyo L'Engai and the lake be incorporated into NCAA, which will then place "periodical tourism activities under official control." While this will certainly protect Lake Natron, and their efforts to do so are lauded, it is unclear how it will affect the villages living in the shadow of their Mountain of God, not one of which wishes to be moved despite the NCAA having declared their home "hostile and unsafe for humans." What is clear is that it will become a great deal more expensive to travel here, should the NCAA succeed.

Natron Tented Camp ★ With the nearby windswept Ngare Sero Camp virtually unusable (no shade, and tents that look like relics from a lost war), Lake Natron Camp is not only the best option, but effectively your only option. Accommodation is rudimentary, but by the time you arrive, hot and thirsty, every crevice covered in dust, to find a shaded oasis, replete with barman and ice, and sprinklers watering a patch of grass surrounding a small rock pool, you will experience the pleasure normally evoked by five-star pampering. If you can, prebook tent C—vastly superior to anything else on offer, with a thatched roof to aid insulation, a view from the small veranda, a comfortable king-size bed, and the best bathroom in the camp. The mobile tents are hot but adequate; the flytents are like sleeping in a plastic bag. The shaded bar, within view of the pool, is the most pleasant place to pass the hottest part of the day. It's located on land belonging to Enkaresero village, with a percentage of profits going directly to the village. All excursions are led by local Maasai (though don't expect traditional garb); aside from climbing expeditions, there are guided walks to Ngare Sero waterfall (pack a bathing suit), Maasai *boma,* and various Lake Natron options.

P.O. Box 11297, Arusha. ✆ **027/250-6315** or 027/250-6386. Fax 027/250-6378. www.moivaro.com. 24 units. High season $300 double half board, $330 double full board; low season $180 half board, $210 full board. **Amenities:** Bar.

5 SERENGETI ★★★

335km (208 miles) from Arusha, 245km (152 miles) from Tarangire, 175km (109 miles) from Lake Manyara, 90km (56 miles) from Ngorongoro

Take it from an African: The Serengeti is the greatest game park on the continent. It's not just the wildlife, though the sight of more than two million animals moving across the plains is regularly cited as the greatest wildlife spectacle on Earth. Nor is it the size, although, at 14,763 sq. km (5,758 sq. miles), the park is almost the size of Hawaii, and the greater ecosystem—an area encompassing the Ngorongoro Conservation Area; Maswa Game Reserve; Loliondo, Grumeti, and Ikorongo Controlled Areas; and Maasai Mara National Reserve in Kenya—is double that.

It was the Maasai who called it Siringitu (The Place Where the Land Moves on Forever), and it is precisely this sense of vastness that will blow you away. The sheer expanse of the short-grass plains, like a yellow sea, is broken only by occasional rocky outcrops and elegant acacia trees, like giant bonsais sculpted by some invisible hand. And above it all is "the high noble arc of the cloudless African sky," as the American hunter-turned-conservationist Stewart Edward White so lyrically put it in 1913. The first man to encounter the great Migration moving through the Serengeti, White was clearly bowled over: "Never have I seen anything like that game. It covered every hill, standing in the openings, strolling in and out among groves, singly, or in little groups. It did not matter in which direction I looked, there it was, as abundant one place as another. Nor did it matter how far I went, over how many hills I walked, how many wide prospects I examined, it was always the same. I moved among those hordes of unsophisticated beasts as a lord of Eden would have moved."

The Migration is central to the Serengeti's appeal. It's a virtually continual movement of some 1.3 million wildebeest, 200,000 zebra, 300,000 Thomson's gazelle, and thousands of eland, kongoni, and topi, all following a millennia-old instinct to seek new pasture as the life-sustaining rains that come twice a year sweep across the greater Serengeti. Contrary to the popularly held promise that the Migration is an "event" that takes place at a certain time of year, it is a slow, vaguely counterclockwise cycle, starting (or ending) near the Ndutu and Masek soda lakes that lie in the volcanic plains west of the

Fun Facts Are Those Hippos Sweating Blood?

Hippos spend hours submerged up to their nostrils in tropical rivers because their thin skin is highly susceptible to sunburn. They do, however, like to spend time basking on sandbanks (or may not be able to fully submerge their 1-ton-plus bodies). Either way, when skin is exposed like this, the hippo's subdermal glands release a reddish secretion that keeps the skin moist and protects the hippo from U.V. damage. Due to the color of this secretion, it was once thought that hippos sweated blood. It has been suggested that these secretions also have extremely effective antibiotic properties, given that the wounds inflicted during fights seldom become infected, despite the less than savory conditions of the tropical waters in which they spend their days. For more interesting facts on the hippo and other wildlife, turn to chapter 19.

Fun Facts The Mystery of the Disappearing Wildebeest

There are a number of theories about why the zebra has evolved its stripes, but perhaps the most interesting is that posited by Dr. Tony Sinclair, long-time mammal researcher in the Serengeti. Using night-vision goggles to study the nocturnal habits of buffalo and wildebeest, which rendered the animals as black blobs against a green skyline, Dr. Sinclair was surprised when the wildebeest he was observing would suddenly just disappear, then reappear a little farther away, a few seconds later. After a few nights puzzling over this mysterious ability of the wildebeest to just "disappear," Dr Sinclair commandeered a powerful spotlight, which he switched on the moment the wildebeest did its disappearing act. Standing alongside the wildebeest was a zebra, which appeared invisible when seen through the goggles, its stripes a perfect camouflage for night, when predators, whose eyes may very well interpret light in the same way, are most likely to hunt.

Ngorongoro Crater. Following the short rains that usually drench the southern plains during November and December, turning yellowed plains into green pastures brimming with nutrient-rich grass, breezes filled with moisture call the wildebeest south. Already heavy with calf, the wildebeest arrive in their thousands during December, ready for the annual population explosion that occurs in January, when up to 8,000 calves are born daily. Predators are in close attendance, patiently awaiting any opportunity to sink their teeth into this abundance of vulnerable flesh—a great time to experience the thrill (or, for the squeamish, horror) of the primal brutality of nature, in which the weak and vulnerable are essential to the survival of the hunter.

As the Ndutu plains start to dry and the soda lakes turn salty, the animals start their 1,000km (620-mile) annual pilgrimage, and million-strong herds begin to move northwest in anticipation of the heavy rains that will soon transform the central Serengeti. April to mid-May, thundershowers sweep the park, sustaining the herds as they move through the central Seronera plains and up through the Western Corridor, plunging into the crocodile-infested waters of the Grumeti around June, while others veer northeast, walking via Lobo through to the Mara River. Regardless of where they find themselves, the nodding wildebeest columns—some as long as 40km (25 miles)—are all headed north, reaching the waters of the Mara by September or October, traditionally the driest months for the Serengeti National Park. Here they remain until they sense the coming rains and head south to the breeding grounds of the southern plains, timing their arrival with its transformation into lush pasture.

Aside from the migrating herds, the park sustains stable populations of many other species, and you will certainly encounter giraffe, warthog, olive baboon, vervet monkey, and buffalo, as well as elephant (though the latter are not as commonly encountered as at Tarangire or Lake Manyara). More important, for most, at least, is the large population of predators. An estimated 2,000 lions alone prowl within the park, many of them territorial and well habituated to human presence; aside from encountering them during the day, you will almost certainly hear them roar at night—a powerful and thrilling sound that can reverberate across the plains 5km (3 miles) or more. Hyenas and jackals are also plentiful. Cheetahs, mostly encountered on the plains, are more elusive; leopard, while more plentiful in number, are even more so. Moru Kopjes is where you will encounter

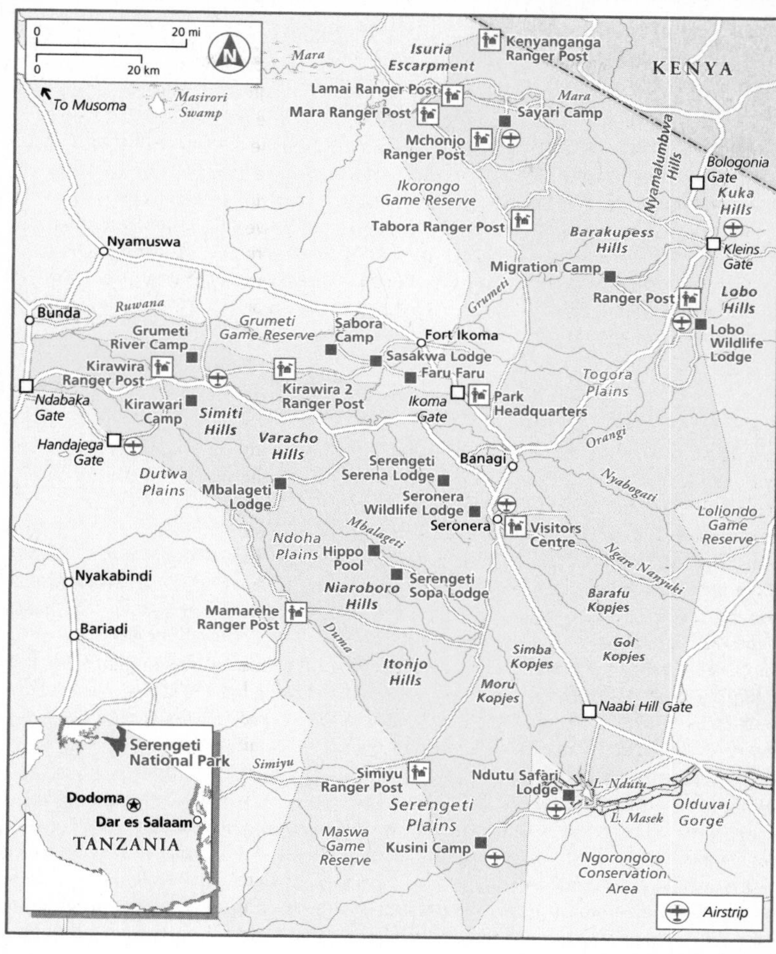

the park's small rhino population; hopefully, with plans afoot to boost their numbers, these great prehistoric mammals will become more prevalent. Serengeti is also an ornithologist's paradise, with the chance of sighting more than 500 species, from the world's largest bird—the ostrich, with its pink legs during mating season—to some of the strangest (look out for the secretary bird, its officious strut and old-fashioned elegance marking it as a character from a Dickens novel).

Given this abundance, it is hardly surprising that Tanzania's oldest game park is also the most popular (though visitor numbers are still nowhere near those in Masai Mara). Despite its popularity, it is still possible to enjoy a more exclusive safari in Africa's finest game park, but choosing where and when you go has never been more important.

ESSENTIALS

GETTING THERE By Car Most visitors traveling by road enter the Serengeti through Naabi Hill Gate, which lies in the southeastern part of the park. Were you to drive straight through from Arusha (not recommended), the 325km (202-mile) drive would take 7 to 8 hours; the flight takes just more than an hour. Naabi Gate is about 2 hours from Ngorongoro, 4 hours from Lake Manyara, and 6½ hours from Tarangire.

By Plane There are airstrips throughout the park, allowing visitors to fly within easy reach of whichever camp or lodge they have booked. Kusini and Ndutu airstrips are located in the south; Seronera airstrip is in the center; Lobo, Kleins, and Kogatende serve the north; and Grumeti and Sasakwa airstrips serve the Western Corridor. You can fly in from Arusha, Kilimanjaro, Tarangire, Lake Manyara, or Ngorongoro, or fly within the park for relatively little money (a round-trip from Arusha to Kogatende, near the Mara River, will run you around $250).

Regional Air Services (www.regionaltanzania.com) has the biggest fleet of twin-engine, turbo-prop aircrafts servicing all the Serengeti airstrips. You can book charter flights or check out (and book online) the daily scheduled flights between Serengeti and Manyara, Zanzibar, and Dar es Salaam. **Northern Air** (northernair@habari.co.tz) is another very professional charter company based in Arusha, operating three Grand Caravans (13 seats) and one Cessna 206 (five seats), all in mint condition. **Precision Air** (www.precisionairtz.com), Tanzania's fastest-growing airline, operates scheduled flights to Grumeti and Seronera (from Kilimanjaro, Arusha, and Lake Manyara).

VISITOR INFORMATION Park fees, payable in advance at the gates, are $50 per person, per day. The park headquarters is located at Seronera. It's worth stopping here to take a look around the visitor center and take the elevated walkway that leads you past informative displays. These are filled with interesting tidbits about various animals and the park itself, such as the role played by the Frankfurt Zoological Society (FZS), which has supported TANAPA's efforts ever since Professor Bernhard Grzimek, then the society's president, first came to the Serengeti in the 1950s and campaigned for its protection. There is also a coffee shop and picnic site. For more information, visit www.serengeti.org.

GETTING AROUND If you are on a game package, your price will include a transfer from the closest airstrip, as well as scheduled game activities (either a full-day game drive or morning and late-afternoon drives), so you need not concern yourself with the practicalities of how to get around (though it's worth knowing that you may not drive around after 7pm or before 6am). If you are being transferred by a ground operator (driven by an Arusha-based guide), you can choose to travel by road between camps or fly while your driver catches up via road. Personally, I like traveling by road within the Serengeti—it's effectively a game drive taken at a bit of a lick, so you can flip open the lid and feel the wind in your hair while looking out for animals. And once you've negotiated the hell that is the Ngorongoro-Naabi gate road, the Serengeti roads, though not perfect, are relatively smooth. Not everyone agrees with me on this, however, and if you're at all unsure about spending time on bumpy roads, opt to fly.

EXPLORING THE PARK/UNDERSTANDING THE PARK LAYOUT The park can be geographically divided into four areas: the Southern plains, the central Seronera valley, the Western Corridor, and the northern parts, extending from Lobo northward to the Masai Mara.

Visitors traveling by vehicle usually enter the Serengeti through the Naabi Hill Gate, gateway to the undeveloped **southern plains** (they contain only one permanent lodge,

Fun Facts Black Is Back

The poaching onslaught of the '70s and '80s decimated black rhino numbers in Tanzania, and within these 2 decades, this stately mammal species, which had grazed the plains for 4 million years (2 million years before the earliest species of lion or elephant made an appearance), looked close to being declared nationally extinct. Serengeti authorities had given up hope until two female rhinos made their appearance in the Moru area (Central Serengeti) in the '90s. Much to the delight of the park wardens (and, no doubt, the rhino ladies), a Ngorongoro bull—chased away by the dominant male in the crater and following traditional routes—made his way west to Moru, where he chanced upon his small but ready-made harem. Since Rajabu's appearance (as the wardens have named him), four calves have been born, bringing the estimated rhino population throughout the greater ecosystem of the Serengeti (most of them residing in Kenya's Masai Mara) to around 100. However, many of these herds, including Rajabu's, are too small for a founder population. In an effort to conserve these, South Africa, which, along with Namibia has made the greatest strides in protecting the rhino, offered to donate 45 black rhinos, 18 of them females, to TANAPA. The project will be supplemented by the rhino repatriation program currently in place at Grumeti Private Game Reserve in the Western Corridor, where captive-bred East African black rhinos have been returned to their homeland and are currently adapting to their new environment before being released.

Ndutu, but also a number of mobile camps, as well as the remote Kusini Camp). The wide-open southern plains, interspersed with rocky kopjes and acacia woodland, blend seamlessly into the short-grass plains of the **central Seronera valley** (which is why many choose to lump these regions together), but unlike the southern plains, the Seronera valley has a network of rivers to sustain its incredibly varied and stable wildlife population, with great game sightings virtually guaranteed all year. It's also very accessible (the drive from Naabi Gate to Seronera takes around 1½ hours), making this region the most popular with tourists, with far too much vehicle action for safari buffs. Naturally, this is also where all the big commercial lodges are located. Note that there is a fuel station at Seronera, and you can also opt to do a hot air balloon trip here.

Stretching beyond Lobo (the other refueling point in the park, reached from Naabi Gate in around 4 hr.) are the more vegetated **northern parts** of the Serengeti. Around the Lobo Hills are open clearings where you will see lions, but large swathes are dominated by woodland, which are good areas for giraffes, impalas, elephants, and dik-diks. Previously inaccessible, the area known as Wogakuria, close to the Masai Mara border, has been opened up with flying safari options to superb tented camps such as Sayari and Lemala. This is a beautiful environment, particularly after the rains, when the green parkland is carpeted in flowers, and its relative inaccessibility makes it the least busy part of the park, with only a handful of operators setting up exclusive mobile camps, their impact negligible. This is then—along with the southern plains from December through

March—a most attractive destination, and it's worth timing your visit for June and July to September and October, when camps are operational in this area. The **Western Corridor** is also less busy than the central plains but sustains relatively stable populations with its varied landscapes (it's also possible to see from a hot air balloon). The area, however, really comes into its own during June and July, when the Grumeti River crossing occurs. The exception to this is at the Grumeti Private Game Reserve (north of the river), where game sightings and photography opportunities are enhanced by the fact that vehicles can go off-road to approach animals (with care), and walking and riding safaris as well as night game drives are offered, making it the most exclusive experience in the greater Serengeti.

Balloon safaris are a great way to see the Serengeti (essential if you're doing all transfers by road, less so if you're flying in or out by plane), a truly romantic experience as you float above the vast plains tinted pink by the rising sun, heading whichever direction the winds take you. It's a real treat (aside from the 5am wake-up call), lasting about an hour before descending to your champagne breakfast in the bush; you should be back in camp at 9:30am. There are only three balloons operating at any given time; to include a balloon safari ($499 per person) you need to overnight at one of the lodges or camps in central Serengeti (Serena Lodge, Seronera Wildlife Lodge, Sopa Lodge, Mbuzi Mawe Camp, or any central Serengeti camp site) or one of the Western Corridor camps (Grumeti River Camp, Kirawira Camp, Mbalageti Camp). Book ahead at www.balloonsafaris.com.

WHEN TO GO Given that the Migration is not an event so much as a continuous (and unpredictable) cycle, *where* is as important as *when* (which is why I've included month indications on when best to visit next to locations under "Where to Stay & Dine").

Obviously, you'll want to time your stay and location with the animal movement, but lodges and camps cash in on this, and peak season does not come cheap. If you're strapped, you're best off booking one of the large lodges in the central plains, where stable animal populations mean plenty of productive game drives. Even if you have shelled out for a position close to the Migration, bear in mind that some years the Migration can be dispersed in pockets with huge empty areas between, but if you are prepared to drive long distances (and it is worth it), you will always find them. Allow at least 3 days to be assured of seeing them.

Calving season usually occurs **January to March** in the southern plains. This is an incredible time to be in the Serengeti, with thousands of calves being born every day, and—thanks to the short-grass plains—the clearly viewed predator action riveting. This is also the most predictable timing of the Migration, as calving must occur during this time. But with virtually no water source other than rain, the plains start to dry and the lakes become too saline to drink, forcing the herds to move north to the grasslands of the central area, soon to be replenished by rain.

April to May is when the main rainfall occurs and is low season for the camps and lodges in the Serengeti, many of which close down for refurbishment at this time. Animals are widely dispersed throughout plains, but the wildebeest rut—done on the hoof and usually occurring in May—is something to behold (and hear), as is the transformation of yellow savannah into lush green parkland.

Toward the end of May, when the rains abate, the Migration moves north or into the Western Corridor. If it's a dry year, the Migration could be at the Mara and Grumeti rivers in **June,** but this usually happens in **July.** If you're lucky, you'll be there when it happens, as the sight of thousands of animals plunging into waters infested with some of the biggest crocodiles in Africa is for many the eponymous moment of the "greatest wildlife spectacle." However, if the April and May rains have been good, the migration can spread out very slowly from the Seronera, reaching the river only by **August.** Between **August/September** and **October,** the herds are at the Mara River, equally infested with monster crocodiles, and over these months they cross backward and forward, in and out of Kenya, drawn by localized rain showers. In **November,** when the rain clouds usually gather to green the south, they again cross the Mara, passing through the eastern Serengeti and Loliondo, to return to the short-grass plains of the southern Serengeti in **December.**

WHERE TO STAY & DINE

As is the case in Tarangire, it is preferable to be based within the Serengeti National Park rather than in one of the game-controlled areas that adjoin it, where livestock is as predominant—if not more so—than game, and pressure on water resources and poaching keeps predator numbers low. The exceptions to this are &Beyond's Klein's Camp in the north and the Singita's camps in the west; these operate on what are effectively private game reserves bordering the Serengeti, with no human habitation allowed. They offer exclusive traversing rights for their clients, making these the most desirable destinations in Tanzania. At research time, the park had four large lodges catering to the package deal tourist, all reviewed below; the fifth, the 74-room **Bilila Lodge Kempinski** (**© 0778/88-8888;** fax 0778/77-8866; www.kempinski-bililalodge.com), opened in June 2009 and features an infinity pool, wine cellar, art gallery, bar, *boma,* restaurant, lobby lounge, and spa. Rooms are en suite, and rates are full board and range upward from $572.

While it is true that these lodges all enjoy superb locations—mostly sprawled in the game-rich central plains, which are least affected by the vagaries of rainfall—it would be a pity if this was your sole experience of Africa's most exhilarating game park. Unless you have a particular penchant for impersonal resorts that could, view aside, be anywhere, and don't mind seeing plenty of other vehicles on game drives, these options should be at the bottom of your list. Preferable by far is a smaller, more exclusive lodge located in a more remote area, such as Migration Camp in the north, Grumeti River Camp and Mbalageti in the west, or Kusini in the south, but be aware that, outside of the central Seronera, your choice in camp must ultimately be led by the Migration timing. There is no point in being in the Western Corridor if the animals are on the southern plains, or booking in the south when the animals are crossing the Mara in the north. That said, the unpredictability of the rains makes it impossible to guarantee that you'll be in the midst of the Migration, but with a good ground operator (and using common sense and rainfall guidelines), you should be within striking distance. Alternatively—and here is my number-one recommendation—book with one of the reputable companies that sets up

Fun Facts **Is That Lion in Our Camp?**

If you hear a lion roaring at night (and, no doubt, you will), there is no need for concern, even if it sounds as if it is relatively nearby. A lion's roar can reach 115 decibels and is carried across the plains 5km (3 miles) or more; if you're close enough, you will feel your entire body vibrate. It is thought that both females and males roar to advertise their territory ownership to rivals of the same sex and possibly to recruit aid from distant companions.

Fun Facts Do Your Bit for Conservation: Shoot a Cheetah

Tanzania is thought to hold 10% of the world's cheetahs—along with wild dogs, Africa's most threatened carnivore. The Serengeti Cheetah Project is a 27-year-old study of individual cheetahs (all recognizable due to their unique spot patterns) run by the Tanzania Carnivore Conservation Project at the Tanzania Wildlife Institute. But they need all the help they can get, and tourists can be as helpful as park authorities. With their Cheetah Watch Campaign, anyone on safari in Tanzania can help ensure their survival by adding to the knowledge base. It's simple: If you spot a cheetah, no matter where, take a picture of it. (Whatever you do, don't disturb it/them in the process; not only are cheetahs shy, but they hunt during the day, and a vehicle can scare off its prey.) Make a note of where you are (your driver will be able to assist if you're not sure), as well as the date. When you get back home, e-mail your cheetah image(s) along with the "where and when" information, and the safari company/guide you were with, to carnivores@habari.co.tz; if you are okay with your photograph and information being posted on their website, say so. If the cheetah is identified, they will write and tell you a little about that cheetah's history.

small semi-permanent camps in locations that follow the seasonal migration of Serengeti's superherds. Or for unabridged luxury, book a few nights at Singita's Sabora Camp, the best tented camp in Africa. It's camping, but not as you have ever known it (see "The Argument for Tented Camps," below, as well as the reviews of recommended tented camps later in this chapter).

There is simply no better way to experience the Serengeti than to book a few nights in one of the small tented camps that move, following the general pattern of the Migration. Most of these camps are set up in the northern Serengeti from June and July to October and November, and move south to the short-grass plains around Ndutu from December to March, after which they close down for tent maintenance and upgrades during April and May. **Nomad** moves more frequently to ensure proximity, but—as is the case with all semi-permanent camps—never while guests are there. Aside from the exclusivity of the semi-permanent camps (there are only 4–10 tents per camp), you will enjoy the decadence of a beautifully furnished mess tent, replete with carpets, plush sofas, and small libraries with books, board games, and table lamps. Dining is a surreal experience, seated under the stars at a table with a crackling fire nearby, served with crystal and fine china in the midst of (or near) mass animal movement.

Lemala and **Nomad** offered the best value at press time, but it is worth checking with the following top operators for their fly-in deals and comparing these for the dates you have in mind (or asking your operator to do so). **Serengeti Under Canvas** has always been the priciest option, but bear in mind that booking more than one **&Beyond** camp (and they are all excellent) can offer significant savings. (Note that if you want a truly mobile tent experience, wherein the same camp moves to a new location every 2 days, Nomad is one of the best companies offering these traditional mobile tented camps.)

Asilia Olakira/Suyan/Sayari Camps ★★★ Not quite as luxe with their detailing as Lemala or Under Canvas, Asilia is still about as comfortable as the tented safari can get, and its semi-permanent camps offer a very exclusive experience, with a mere six tents (plus two common-area tents) and camping locations that make for different experiences. Olakira (a great camp) moves from the southern plains (Dec–Mar) to northcentral Serengeti (June–Nov), which has a high density of game year round. This is by far the best place to experience this otherwise heavily touristed area, but note that when the Migration moves north, Olakira's central location won't give you access to it; try to book this part of the camp early or stay elsewhere. The Suyan camps (my least favorite in the Asilia roster) move within the Loliondo Game Controlled Area, between Olosokwan in the north and Piyaya in the south. Only concession holders can drive in Loliondo, so only a game package is offered here. Loliondo allows for night drives and game walks, but poor resident game makes for a compromised experience outside of Migration time (though Suyan Olosokwan is very close to the national park entrance). The jewel in the Asilia crown is their permanent Sayari camp in the remote Wogakuria region near the Mara River (see full review below). From December to March, you may choose to visit its southern counterpart, in the Moru Kopjes on the western edge of the southern plains. Currently known as Sayari South (due for a name change to Sayari), it is another highly recommended camp.

✆ **027/250-4118** or 027/250-4119. Fax 027/250-2799. www.asilialodges.com. Olakira and Suyan Camps high season $1,290 double game package, $1,160 double full board (full board available for Olakira only); low season $980 double game package, $860 double full board. Asilia camps close for maintenance Apr–May.

Lemala Camps ★★★ **Value** This is my top pick, combining fantastic tented accommodations—a lovely eye for detail, both design-wise and for comfort—with luxury touches in the lounge (mini chandeliers!) and dining tents, and the best value for money. Tents are very comfortable, with proper king-size beds (or twins) covered in pretty *kikois* and cushions, and bedside lamps with 24-hour solar power. The en suite bathroom has a flush toilet and running water for basins. Each camp has 10 tents, including a family tent that can accommodate up to five. Views from the Ndutu camp are across the spillway that extends from Lake Ndutu, attracting huge amounts of game; the Mara camp is minutes from the river, and you may witness a river crossing in solitude (something the Masai Mara certainly cannot claim). You can opt to drive in with your own guide/driver, which may represent a savings, or go for convenience and utilize their game package.

✆ **027/254-8966** or 027/254-8952. Fax 027/254-8937. www.lemalacamp.com. Lemala Ndutu high season $1,090 double game package, $950 double full board; low season $930 double game package, $790 double full board. Lemala North Serengeti high season $1,190 double game package, $1,050 double full board; low season $930 double game package, $790 double full board. Camps close mid-Apr to May and Nov.

Serengeti Safari Camps ★★★ Although accommodation tents are a little more basic than with Lemala, &Beyond, or Asilia (some camps have short-drop toilets rather than flush), Nomad is the only operator to guarantee each group (even if comprising only two) its own private guide and exclusive use of a 4×4 vehicle. This is a huge bonus to your game drive experience (but is not necessary if you're arranging a self-drive from Arusha, in which case Asilia or Lemara is a better option). Camp positions, said to change every 2 to 3 weeks (but never during guests' stay), are, for the most part, fabulous. December through April, camp is on the southern Serengeti plains or NCAA, depending on the animals; from May to early July, the camp moves to the Moru area or Western Corridor, depending on where the animals are. Mid-July to November, the camp moves close to the Mara or Bologonja rivers to view the back-and-forth crossing of the rivers.

During Migration, camp may move into the Loliondo (Olosokwan in the north to Piyaya in the south), an area that I am not so keen on. Nomad also likes to compliment a stay at their semi-permanent camps with a night or two at the permanent camp, **Nduara Loliondo,** which is in the Olosokwan area. Though Nduaro is a gorgeously designed and furnished camp (featured in *Tatler* and the like), the surrounds are rather bleak and game poor, so I would avoid this and opt instead for a combination with any of the other camps elsewhere in Tanzania (Nomad has an excellent array). ***Note:*** If you're traveling as a family or small group, Nomad also offers exclusive mobile safaris with their own car, guide, and camp, which can move every 2 days; it's pricey (around $2,300 per night for an all-inclusive game package for two, $2,745 for three or a family of four with children under 12), but what an experience.

Ⓒ **027/255-3819.** www.nomad-tanzania.com. Peak season $1,480 double game package; high season $1,200–$1,320 double game package; low season $900 double game package. Discounted combination rates for minimum 5 nights of around $100 per night.

Serengeti Under Canvas ★★★ This has all the hallmarks of &Beyond, with elegantly styled camps, excellent food, and—with a private butler to see to your every whim—superb service. With only four tents per camp in the Wogakuria and Ndutu regions, this is a truly exclusive experience, and the staff go all out to treat you as if you are king and queen of all you survey. Note that if you're in the Ndutu area in March (calving season), the low-season rate represents good value. Although every effort is made to secure vehicle exclusivity, you may have to share your 4×4 with other guests, which is a little churlish, given the rate, but the knowledge and passion of the &Beyond guides is always inspiring. Note that no drive-ins are allowed, meaning that the game package is compulsory. Should you arrive with a driver/guide from elsewhere, he will not be allowed to take you on game drives.

Ⓒ **888/882-3742** toll-free in U.S., or 011/809-4300 in South Africa. www.andbeyond.com. High season $1,800 double game package; midseason $1,500 double game package; low season $1,250 game package.

THE SOUTHERN PLAINS (IDEAL TIME: DECEMBER TO MARCH)

Despite the fact that most vehicles enter through the south, this is—due to the lack of game action for much of the year—a seriously underdeveloped part of the park, much of it unvisited. But come the short rains in November and December, the herds are summoned back to their breeding ground. The plains teem with wildebeest, zebra, and antelope, followed by predators and tourists, the latter of whom can opt to stay in one of the exclusive semi-permanent camps, described above, or one of only two permanent options. Note that Serengeti Sopa (described under "The Central Lodges") is the most southern of the big lodges and could ostensibly fall under this region.

Ndutu Safari Lodge ★★ Value Despite the fact that it is far from luxurious, the atmosphere and staff are just so welcoming and the price so fair, I couldn't resist giving this unpretentious and excellent-value lodge a two-star rating. Strictly speaking, the lodge falls outside the Serengeti National Park boundaries and within the Ngorongoro Conservation Area (NCA), but it is superbly located for witnessing the Migration during the breeding season, with views of the animals from your veranda and the communal areas, and within easy striking distance of a variety of habitats (which is, along with the fact that you can drive off-road in the NCA, why so many professional photographers and filmmakers choose to make this their base). With so few rooms, it has a relatively exclusive feel, with rudimentary brick-and-thatch rooms extending from the convivial open-sided bar/lounge/dining room. Interiors are pretty rudimentary. Only four rooms have king-size beds (try to book no. 35); the rest are twins. Rooms are not, however, the focus here; the bar and outdoor fireplace is where everyone gathers, where the relaxed and friendly staff is as much a pleasure as the views of Lake Ndutu. Spotting the resident family of genets—a rare and privileged sight, given how shy these nocturnal animals are—is yet another bonus. The only downside is that, should you wish to enter the Serengeti National Park, you will have to pay $50 per day, despite already having paid $50 per day to be in the NCA.

P.O. Box 6084, Arusha. ✆ **027/250-6702** or 027/250-2829. Fax 027/250-8310. www.ndutu.com. 34 units. High season $385 double full board, $347 double half board, $295 double B&B; low season $302 full board, $264 half board, $212 B&B. MC, V. **Amenities:** Bar; Internet.

Kusini Tented Camp ★★ Owned and operated by Abercrombie & Kent (Sanctuary Lodges), this is, like sister outfit Swala in Tarangire, located in the most remote, least-visited part of the park; once here, the sense of total isolation is a privilege afforded very few who visit the Serengeti. Like &Beyond, each Sanctuary Lodge tent comes with a private butler, and the result is a discreet but constant sense of pampering. The tents, located at the base of massive boulder outcrops (on which sundowners are enjoyed), are privately situated and as luxurious as you'd expect from A&K. Gourmet meals, served candlelit in the dining tent or under the stars, are quite incredible, given how far the nearest supermarket is. There are two vehicles permanently available for game drives if you fly in, and a nearby Maasai village (just outside the park) is worth a visit, given that they don't see much tourist traffic. This is an incredible option during the breeding months, but even when the herds move north, it remains a wonderful camp to unwind in (particularly if your need is exclusivity and peace), and a fair number of wildlife sightings (like buffalo) is guaranteed year-round.

Sanctuary Lodges. ✆ **027/250-9816** or 027/250-9817. Fax 027/250-8273 or 027/250-4112. www.sanctuarylodges.com. 9 units. Peak season $1,430 double game package, $1,190 double full board; high season $990 game package, $770 full board. Holiday supplement during Christmas ($40 per person) and Easter ($25 per person). Closed Apr–May. **Amenities:** Bar; room service.

THE CENTRAL LODGES (IDEAL TIME: YEAR-ROUND)

With permanent water, the central plains support a stable population of wildlife, making this the most reliable year-round destination, though you should still not miss seeing the large numbers that only the Migration can provide. It's worth knowing that the Migration usually moves through this region on its way north from March to May, and possibly on the way south in September and October. However, given a truly central location, you could also (unless herds are in the far north) reach the Migration by vehicle, wherever it is, if you are prepared to spend a day traversing bumpy roads.

The first area to be developed in Serengeti, the central plains is busy, with three large lodges, all aimed at the mass market. Despite the hefty entry fee increases seen in the past few years, which raised hopes that TANAPA was moving in the direction of Botswana's high-end, low-impact tourism model, plans for another large lodge were approved in 2006, and the 74-room **Kempinski Bilila Lodge** duly opened in mid-2009 (possibly worth combining with a few nights in a tented camp such as Sayari). For semi-permanent camp options, see the box on p. 429.

Mbuzi Mawe Tented Camp ★ (Value) Managed by the Serena group, this tented camp is a far more intimate experience than its sister lodge and is the most inexpensive tented camp in the Serengeti—a good choice if you're on a budget and want a more authentic safari experience than the resortlike lodges. Don't expect the same level of luxury as other tented camps offer, however. Although the tents, built on concrete platforms, are generously proportioned (with two double beds, a desk and sitting area, en suite bathroom with two basins and large shower, and a large veranda), they are placed far too close together (you'll hear your neighbors waking up for the 4am balloon safari call) and show some signs of wear; at night, they creak and groan (it's often windy), which can be a little disconcerting. Though within easy reach of the central plains (an hour from the Seronera Visitor Centre), Mbuze Mawe falls just north of the short-grass plains and is surrounded by boulders inhabited by klipspringers, the small antelope after which the camp is named, as well as rock hyrax and baboons. Staff are eager to please, but service is patchy, and irritants like running out of ice are a liability; a pool would also be a great addition.

P.O. Box 2551, Arusha. ✆ **027/255-3313,** -3314, or -3315. Fax 027/255-3316. www.serenahotels.com. 75 units. Peak season $635 double full board; midseason $560 full board; low season $340 full board. Holiday supplement over Easter ($35 per person, per night) and Christmas ($40 per person, per night). AE, DC, MC, V. **Amenities:** Bar; room service; Wi-Fi; currency exchange.

Seronera Serena (also known as Serengeti Serena) ★★ This large "Afro-hobbit" themed resort is the most popular of the park's large lodges, and if you want a hotel rather than a safari experience, this is the best base for those who want to be in the central plains (though be sure to consider similarly priced Mbalageti in the west, for a more exclusive experience). Rooms come three apiece in circular thatched huts, all facing west. If you can possibly book an upstairs unit, do so; these have small verandas from which to take in the views and sunsets, while the two below have no views to speak of, though they are slightly larger and offer the possibility of being interconnected for families. Decor is a little dated. The pool area is fantastic, with amazing views of the plains below. The pool area is also where the massage tent is set up—second only to Mbalageti for best-located massage in Serengeti. There's a slightly smug service attitude (package tours mean the lodge enjoys very high occupancy), and one suspects that there is little incentive to improve. It's too big for my liking (if you want a more intimate camp, take a look at Mbuze Mawe), and personally I don't like the style, but the location (20 min. from Seronera), pool views, and price make this worth considering. If you haven't seen what else is out there, you will more than likely be very happy here.

P.O. Box 2551, Arusha. ✆ **027/255-3313,** -3314, or -3315. Fax 027/255-3316. www.serenahotels.com. 67 units. Peak season $635 double full board; midseason $560 full board; low season $340 full board. Holiday supplement over Easter ($35 per person, per night) and Christmas ($40 per person, per night). AE, MC, V. **Amenities:** Restaurant; babysitting; room service; Wi-Fi; currency exchange. *In room:* Hair dryer.

Seronera Wildlife Lodge ★ (Value) Assuming that you don't expect luxury, and that the renovations are completed, this is by far the best-value lodge in the Serengeti, with an unbeatable location and the '70s architecture a great deal more pleasing than the heavy-handed concrete Sopa or theme-park Serena. Artfully built into a kopje, the huge boulders that jut into the building give it an almost film-set atmosphere (pity about the obviously faux rock-art paintings, which detract from their natural grandeur). Although public spaces afford great sunset viewing, rooms are on the small size, with paper-thin walls and tiny bathrooms with erratic water pressure; that said, this is a clean, comfortable place to rest your head. Room nos. 20 to 34 and 35 to 43 enjoy the best views. The

Wildlife Lodges are not known for the quality of their meals, but Seronera is the best in the chain. It's right in the heart of the park's prime game viewing, and you will see plenty of animals (and many other tourists), but if you want to stay in a lodge rather than a tented camp, this is—given the Serengeti prices—a relative bargain.

2nd Floor, Summit Centre, Sokoine Rd., P.O. Box 2633, Arusha. ✆ **027/254-4595,** -4807, -4798, or -4795. Fax 027/254-8633. www.hotelsandlodges-tanzania.com. 75 units. Peak season $460 double full board, $450 double half board; high season $400 full board, $390 half board; low season $240 full board, $230 half board. $40 surcharge Dec 24–26 and 31. **Amenities:** Restaurant; bar; small gym; pool; currency exchange. *In room:* Hair dryer.

Serengeti Sopa ★ The concrete hulk that is Sopa makes no overtures to the gorgeousness of its surrounds, but once inside, the views of the plains are absolutely fabulous. Located on the very southern edge of the central plains, with plenty of wildlife but not as many people traversing them (at least, not as many as in the central Seronera), it's a slightly quieter destination. However, Sopa here is, like elsewhere, very much a resort, with a soulless atmosphere, and despite the fact that interiors were recently refurbished, everything looks outdated already. The spotlessly clean rooms are spacious, with two double beds. Buffet-style dining is adequate for appetite but boring. March, when Migration should be within easy striking distance, offers good value, but if you are watching your budget (and happy to have a hotel rather than camp experience), I'd opt for one of the Wildlife Lodges.

99 Serengeti Rd., Sopa Plaza, P.O. Box 1823, Arusha. ✆ **027/250-0630** or -0639. Fax 027/250-8245. www.sopalodges.com. 75 units. Peak season $550 double full board, $530 half board; high season $450 full board, $430 half board; low season $200 full board, $180 half board. Holiday supplement during Christmas ($45 per day) and Easter ($40 per day). MC, V. **Amenities:** Restaurant; bar; babysitting; pool; resident nurse. *In room:* Hair dryer, minibar (stocked on request).

THE NORTH (IDEAL TIME: JULY TO OCTOBER/NOVEMBER)

The far north, particularly the remote northeastern area on the Mara River known as the Lemai Wedge, is beautiful and virtually untouched by tourists, despite the growth in semi-permanent camps. (Other than Asilia's now permanent Sayari Camp, Serengeti Under Canvas operates here in season, as does Nomad; the Thomson's camp here is in a bad state and best avoided). Note that many northern camps that advertise themselves as Serengeti camps are actually in the Loliondo Game Controlled Area, which borders the Serengeti National Park on the east. Strictly speaking, this claim is not incorrect—Loliondo is part of the greater Serengeti ecosystem and, depending on the arrival of the short rains, usually sees the Migration moving through here (and Lobo) around November as it moves south. However, Loliondo (like Ngorongoro Conservation Area) is home to the Maasai and their livestock, and game viewing is definitely not on par with that in the national park. This means that you have to travel 30 minutes or more before entering the park—and travel many more hours if you want to get to the Mara. So unless you are making a last-minute booking and know that the Migration is currently moving through Loliondo, my advice is to stick to the camps within the park. The exception to this is Klein's, which is on a private concession that offers superb game-viewing opportunities, and Grumeti in the west, discussed later in this chapter.

Klein's Camp ★★★ Perched at the top of the Kuka hills, with one of the greatest views in Africa, Klein's Camp deserves its top-star rating because of the incredible game-viewing opportunities afforded here. The camp is set in an exclusive private concession neighboring the northeastern part of the park. Rangers are allowed to drive off-road, allowing you to get really close to animals, and night drives and guided walks are allowed (and included in the price). Add to that top guides (typical of &Beyond's stringent selection and training) and exclusive sightings (only ever shared with the handful of others privileged enough to stay at Klein's). An inherited lodge (as opposed to one built by &Beyond), rooms are not quite up to &Beyond standards. The round stone cottages are a little too close together for aural privacy and make far too little of the views; there's no tub, outdoor shower, or writing desk; reading lamps are poor; and rooms have a generally underfurnished air. But step into the cozy lounge/bar and all is forgiven, with deep wingback chairs in which to settle and enjoy the stupendous views and, at night, a roaring central fireplace creating a very romantic ambience. Service is not up to &Beyond standards (the lounge/bar is often unmanned, the private butler hard to summon), but the cuisine sure is.

Private Bag X 27, Benmore, Johannesburg, 2010, South Africa. ✆ **011/809-4300,** or U.S. toll-free 888/882-3742. Fax 011/809-4400. www.andbeyond.com. 10 units. High season $1,990 double; low season $1,310 double. **Amenities:** Bar; babysitting; pool; limited currency exchange. *In room:* Hair dryer.

Lobo Wildlife Lodge ★ Value If you want to be close to the game, yet not in the midst of heavy tourist traffic, the Lobo Hills are a great destination, and their Wildlife Lodge is not only the most affordable option in the north, but architecturally more interesting than Sopa or Serena. Like sister outfit Seronera Wildlife Lodge, the lodge is built right into a kopje (rocky outcrop), which affords some striking architectural twists, plenty of resident wildlife, and great views. The property has an inviting lounge/bar area, with a copper fireplace surrounded by leather wingbacks, tapestry cushions, *kelims,* and a grand piano played at sunset. Pity the refurbishment hasn't stretched as far as the rooms, which remain small with basic furnishings and fittings (but clean, and great views) and thin walls; the usual caveats regarding Wildlife Lodge bathrooms apply. The dining room features a double height wall of glass—great for views, bad for ventilation. Like all the Wildlife Lodges, it has been undergoing extensive renovations, so do check that these are complete; at research time, these were still in full swing, and service and cuisine were definitely not up to par.

2nd Floor, Summit Centre, Sokoine Rd., P.O. Box 2633, Arusha. ✆ **027/254-4595,** -4807, -4798, or -4795. Fax 027/254-8633. www.hotelsandlodges-tanzania.com. 72 units. Peak season $460 double full board, $410 double half board; high season $400 double full board, $375 double half board; low season $240 double full board, $230 double half board. $40 surcharge Dec 24–26 and 31. **Amenities:** Restaurant; bar; currency exchange.

Fun Facts It's Not the Length, It's the Color

In 2004, researchers from the University of Minnesota placed four life-size male toy lions in the Serengeti—one with a long, dark mane; another with a short, dark mane; the third a long, pale mane; and the last a short, pale mane. Lionesses were initially fooled by the life-size toys—long enough for the researchers to observe them flirting. They were most attracted to the lions with dark manes, regardless of length. When researchers then took samples of blood from real lions, they found that lions with dark manes had more testosterone and were better able to withstand being wounded. Therefore, a litter produced by a black-maned male stands a better chance of surviving.

Sayari Camp ★★★ Located on the south bank of the Mara River, in the remote northwest known as the Lemai Wedge, Sayari Camp enjoys an incredible location, with rolling parkland interspersed with riverine woodlands—pure paradise. The landscapes are less typical of the Serengeti, but many regulars claim the Wedge as the most beautiful part of the park, with the permanent waters of the Mara attracting huge numbers of animals but only (long may it last) a relative trickle of tourists—no doubt why it was chosen as one of the "Special Places" in Africa by *Africa Geographic*. After a full refurbishment in 2009, furnishings in the public spaces are cool and modern—more urban bar than Hemingway safari. Accommodation tents, placed at least 20m (66 ft.) apart, are supremely comfortable (this is the only tented camp that has a sofa-bed and soft chairs on the veranda—the ideal place to enjoy the view and breeze), with full en suite luxuries from double basins and separate toilet to bathtubs (hard to believe you're in a tent, really). Service is excellent, and the pool, which was set to be completed at press time, is the ultimate luxury in what is—along with Singita's Sabora Plains—the best tented camp in the Serengeti.

Farm No. 175, Olasiti. ✆ **027/250-4118** or -4119. Fax 027/250-2799. www.asilialodges.com. 15 units. High season $1,240–$1,290 double game package, $1,160–$1,120 double full board; low season $980 game package, $860 full board. MC, V. **Amenities:** Laundry; pool.

Serengeti Migration Camp ★★★ Ideal for those who would like to try a tented camp but want more standard hotel-type facilities, Migration is a class act, with great accommodations, excellent location, and fantastic service levels. It is hardly surprising that it was named Best Resort in East Africa by readers of *Condé Nast Traveler* in 2008. The huge elevated open-air public lounge (with lots of overstuffed leather and wicker chairs with *kuba* cloth cushions) overlooks the pool terrace and surrounds, and the dining area enjoys similarly elevated views—all lovely spaces, but usually rather empty, given how comfortable the massive canvas and timber suites are, with double doors opening onto your private deck and the call of the hippo to remind you just how close you are to the Grumeti River. Rooms are much bigger and better designed than Klein's, but it can get oppressively hot and can't compare with Klein's in terms of game-viewing opportunities, unless the Migration is moving through. Service is far more attentive than Klein's, though, and it's cheaper (though, to be honest, I'd rather be at Sayari or Lemara, which win on location and rate, and are real camps).

99 Serengeti Rd., Sopa Plaza; P.O. Box 12814, Arusha. ✆ **027/254-0630** or -0639. Fax 027/254-8245. www.elewana.com. 20 units. Peak season $1,690 double game package, $1,490 full board; high season $1,560 game package, $1,360 full board; low season $1,460 game package, $1,260 full board. MC, V. **Amenities:** Restaurant; bar; pool; room service; free Wi-Fi. *In room:* Hair dryer.

THE WESTERN CORRIDOR (IDEAL TIME: JUNE TO AUGUST; GRUMETI, YEAR-ROUND)

Time your stay with the Migration moving through the Corridor, particularly crossing the Grumeti, and you will have the safari of a lifetime, with the photographs to prove it. Aside from the options below, it's worth mentioning **Ikoma Bush Camp** (www.moivaro.com), located just outside the national park (a few minutes' drive from Ikoma Gate). It's a camp comprising 31 basic en suite East African tents, each with a private veranda and savannah views. It's not luxury and it's not in the park, but at $286 double full board in the peak months of July and August ($251 in high; $176 in low), it offers exceptional value.

If you're fortunate enough to have a rather cavalier attitude to budget constraints, make a beeline for the 138,000-hectare (340,860-acre) Grumeti Private Reserve, the

Side Trip to Lake Victoria: In or Out?

With Mwanza, the biggest port on Lake Victoria, under 2 hours' drive from the Western Corridor, the question arises, should one set aside the better part of a day (or more) to say you have cast eyes on Africa's largest lake? The answer is, no. Unless you are in the enviable position of spending months traveling the East African circuit, or are a keen angler, Lake Victoria should enjoy minimal priority. This is largely due to the quality of the water. Unlike the waters of Lake Tanganyika, so clean and clear that you can snorkel and scuba-dive, you cannot swim the murky waters of Lake Victoria without risking bilharzia. It's also awkward to get to and around the lake. You could fly to Arusha or Dar es Salaam from Mwanza, but with little point: The flight will cost more than your flight from the nearest airstrip in the Serengeti. Road conditions west of Mwanza are also poor, so circumventing the lake is an ordeal, besides which there is no strong drawcard along its shoreline. The three main lake ports—Mwanza, Musoma, and Bukoba—are classic African towns, for the most part a scruffy sprawl, their colonial-era buildings in decay, with no distinguishing cultural or historical characteristics and little by way of scenic beauty or shopping. As a result, there is no developed tourism infrastructure, and the ferries that ply the lake, passing the admittedly alluring islands that dot its shores, are pretty hardcore by middle-class Westerner standards. That said, Mwanza is Tanzania's second-largest city, and an important travel hub that you will certainly pass through if your travel plans include an overland trip to Uganda (or if you just want to get off the well-worn Northern Circuit route); it is also 20km (12 miles) west of the **Bujora Sukuma Museum.** Initiated by Father David Clement in the '50s, it is aimed at Sukuma visitors interested in understanding their royal lineage and traditional customs rather than Western tourists. As such, it offers authentic insights into Tanzania's most populous tribe and is a highly recommended stop if you are in the area (signposted from Kissesa on the Mwanza-Musoma Rd.), particularly on Saturdays, when you might catch the Sukuma Snake Dance performance.

If you find yourself in Mwanza for the night, the best place to stay is at the lakeshore **Hotel Tilapia** (www.tilapiahotel.com). Another property in the Sandhu family portfolio (though these accommodations cannot compete with their Mbalageti Lodge in Serengeti), Tilapia enjoys a better location than any of the other city hotels (1km/1 mile from the center, but on a tranquil position on the lake), and it offers clean and comfortable rooms from $95 double. Alternatively, there's the newer **Isamilo Lodge** (www.isamilo-lodge.com), on a hilltop 3km (1¾ miles) from the city center, with lovely lake views and rooms ranging

concession that borders the Serengeti in the northwest, which has exceptional resident game throughout the year. An ardent conservationist, billionaire hedge-fund trader Paul Tudor Jones has invested enormously in his concession, paying the Tanzania government for every head of animal estimated to be on it, setting up an anti-poaching team, and reintroducing black rhino. He built his own "villa-lodge" Sasakwa and then teamed up between $80 and $120 double. Or if you don't mind being 12km (8 miles) out of town, **Tunza Lodge** (http://tunzalodge.com; $120 double) is popular with the fishing set, with just 12 bungalows surrounded by lush gardens and green lawns that line a pristine sandy beach. If you're here for the fishing (or birding), the place to be is **Wag Hill** ★★ (www.waghill.com). A real find, with just three large bungalows sharing 17 hectares (42 acres) of protected indigenous forested hillside, a comfy open-air dining area overlooking the lake, and great pool, this tiny eco-lodge is the most tranquil place to be near Mwanza, with only birds and monkeys disturbing the peace. Staff will pick you up from the Mwanza Yacht Club by boat. Boat transfer, fishing lessons, all excursions, beverages, meals, and laundry are included in the price of $550 double.

If you have no desire to see Mwanza but simply cannot resist seeing (or fishing) Lake Victoria's waters or are traveling to or from Kenya along its shoreline, you could consider booking one of the eight bungalows (avoid the tents) that line the sandy cove that faces Speke Gulf (named after explorer John Hanning Speke, who, in 1858, discovered Lake Victoria to be the source of the Nile). **Speke Bay Lodge** (www.moivaro.com) is 15km (9[1/4] miles) directly west of the Serengeti National Park's gate (125km/78 miles northeast of Mwanza), so you could even use this as a base to visit the park, perhaps passing through to Ikoma, another budget Moivaro property that lies within spitting distance of a park gate and costs significantly less than those within the park.

Other than the simple fact that it is the second-largest freshwater lake in the world (after Lake Superior in the U.S.), Lake Victoria's chief attraction (at least, in the area that falls within Tanzania) is **Rubondo Island National Park,** a tropical forested island paradise with sandy beaches, somewhat inconveniently located in the far southwestern corner of the lake. Rubondo Island is primarily a great birding destination; you can ostensibly go chimpanzee tracking here, but the Rubondo's primates are notoriously shy, and you will almost certainly have better luck at Mahale and Gombe, near Lake Tanganyika. More problematic is the fact that what was touted as Rubondo's first luxury lodge, opened by Flycatcher Safaris a few years back, has sadly changed hands and, due to a lack of interest, closed down. You can still camp or stay in one of the grubby National Park *bandas* on the island, but given how long it takes to reach Rubondo (by vehicle and then by boat), this hardly seems worth the time and effort. Should the lodge reopen, with flights to service it, I will certainly endeavor to visit and review it in the future.

with Singita (the group that set the bar with their South Africa camps, regular recipients of "Best Destination in the World" as voted by *Travel + Leisure* and *Condé Nast Traveler* readers). Located in the most stunning East African landscape, the Grumeti camps take the Singita experience to a whole other level. Not only are they exclusive (only a handful exploring an area that is not a great deal smaller than the entire Masai Mara), but guides are unparalleled, and as they are allowed to drive off-road, they can track and ensure that you enjoy up-close encounters all year.

Grumeti Serengeti Tented Camp ★★★ Located right on the banks of a major Grumeti tributary, with honking hippos in clear view, this &Beyond camp enjoys a magical lush riverine setting, very different from Kirawira and Mbalageti's huge savannah views, but very productive for game viewing. Its location and atmosphere are the main draws, with the river attracting a variety of animals coming to slake their thirst and the hippos a constant source of entertainment (though they are noisy, which some killjoys find an irritant); at research time, the choice units (those with clear river views) were 7, 9, and 10. Comprising only 10 "tents" (canvas walls are the only clue), the camp is far more laid back and intimate than the similarly sized Klein's, and service is warm and personal. Cuisine is as good as you'd expect from &Beyond. Given &Beyond's exacting standards, the whimsical decor is looking a little dated and bright colors a little faded; according to the camp manager, the entire camp was due for a massive overhaul at press time, with brand-new luxury units planned.

Private Bag X 27, Benmore, Johannesburg, 2010, South Africa. ✆ **011/809-4300,** or U.S. toll-free 888/882-3742. Fax 011/809-4400. www.andbeyond.com. 10 units. High season $1,990 double; midseason $1,640 double; low season $1,310 double. **Amenities:** Bar; babysitting; pool; limited currency exchange. *In room:* Hair dryer.

Kirawira Luxury Tented Camp ★★ Perched high on a hill, Kirawira (like Mbalageti, Sasakwa, Klein's, and Sopa) enjoys a classic view of the "endless plains" that typify the Serengeti, a great place to watch the Migration or just drink in the vastness of it all. Styling is Edwardian/Victorian (though not on par with the similarly themed and far more luxurious Singita Sabora), with tents ranged below a pretty public lounge/bar. The spacious tents are constructed on stilted timber platforms (ask for one with an unobstructed view; nos. 7, 8, and 9 offer particularly good panoramas), but while there is no doubt that this is a luxury option (it's even a member of Luxury Hotels of the World), it feels—from both a design and service point of view—a little too much like it's been built and run by people who understand only the mass market but are charging prices usually associated with the more discriminating end. I have heard that Kirawira offers good deals out of season, far better than the rack rate quoted below; if you can get it at a reduced rate, it's certainly worth considering—personally, though I'd rather be at Sayari Camp or one of the semi-permanent camps, or Mbalageti, if the Migration is here. Even better, choose Sabora or Faru Faru—they will cost around $100 more per person, per night, but the improvement on every level is stratospheric.

P.O. Box 2551, Arusha. ✆ **027/255-3313** or 027/255-3314. Fax 027/255-3316. www.serenahotels.com. 25 units. High season $800 double full board; low season $330 double full board. Holiday supplement over Easter ($35 per person, per night) and Christmas ($40 per person, per night). Rates include airstrip transfers; tea, coffee, soft drinks, and select wines, beers and spirits; 2 game daily game drives; and laundry. AE, MC, V. **Amenities:** Restaurant; bar; babysitting; Internet; room service. *In room:* Hair dryer.

Mbalageti Lodge ★★ Value Circling the top of Mwamyeni hill like a necklace, with jaw-dropping views of the Dutwa plains below, Mbalageti offers excellent value. Price-wise, it's on par with Serena, but it's half the size. Each tented unit is privately located on its own platform, with stunning sunset or sunrise views of the plains from the veranda and bed. Game viewing outside of the Migration is not as guaranteed as on the central plains, however (80km/50 miles away), and the downside of the privacy everyone enjoys with this spread-out layout is the distances most have to walk to get to the public areas (no bad thing if you've been sitting in a vehicle all day). Public areas make the most of the stunning views, with a pool right on the lip of the deck and surrounded by loungers and the bar; the dining area has a massive deck so you can watch the grazers while doing same. There is a privately located outdoor massage/wellness area with sunken plunge pool—ideal for romantic couples. Mbalageti cannot offer the personal touch of a small camp, but it is very efficiently managed by Shamez, and taking account of location and views, comfort of tented units and bathrooms (Victorian bathtubs strategically placed next to picture windows are a nice touch), public areas, and rates, this is the best lodge in the Serengeti. Note that while standard lodge rooms represent a savings, you will have no view or privacy, which negates the whole Mbalageti Lodge experience.

P.O. Box 775, Mwanza. Reservations: ✆ **027/254-8632** or 0748/98-2211. Lodge ✆ **028/262-2387** or 028/262-2388. www.mbalageti.com. 27 tented chalet units (plus 14 standard lodge rooms). Peak season $550 tented chalet double, $385 lodge room double; high season $450 tented chalet, $360 lodge room; low season $370 tented chalet, lodge rooms not available. All rates include full board. **Amenities:** Restaurant; bar; Internet; pool.

Singita Sabora Plains, Faru Faru & Sasakwa ★★★ Singita is certainly not the cheapest option, but as it leaves every other camp and lodge in the Serengeti standing in the dust, it actually represents good value. If you can afford it, you are guaranteed an incredible experience, on par with the world's top destinations, in the most beautiful, remote part of Africa. Whether you are judging it by game-viewing (it's a private concession, so you can get really close to animals, and you will not find better-trained or -informed guides), accommodations (you won't want to leave your suite for *anything*), or service (it's not just attentive, flexible, and discreet, but that rarest type—intelligent), there is simply no comparison.

Sasakwa is the flagship lodge, set atop a high plateau with sweeping views of the plains below (with plenty of animal action). It's a huge, rambling, ultra-luxurious ranch-style lodge, with each unit actually a private cottage with its own swimming pool. (There's also a massive central one on the lip.) It has relatively few rooms, yet there's a superb equestrian center (this is the only place to do horseback safaris in Serengeti), tennis courts, a spa, fine dining (the restaurant's chef is Michelin starred), several libraries, a pool table and computer room, and in-room telephones with free international calls. It's impressive, but not as unusual as Sabora Plains Tented Camp and Faru Faru Lodge (both developed by the Singita team). With every article of furniture made with brass hinges to fold up (in keeping with its Victorian safari theme) and each tent comprising a huge bedroom; separate bathroom; and separate lounge/library filled with books, games, fresh roses, and treats, Sabora is quite simply the most decadent, opulent, and beautiful tented camp on the planet. Faru Faru is more hip, with gorgeous glass-box suites, with styling similar to Sweni and Lebombo in the Kruger. Both Faru Faru and Sabora are a great deal more intimate than Sasakwa (and all guests have access to all Sasakwa facilities), but grand and gracious Sasakwa will satisfy urban appetites more. It's very hard to choose a favorite, as they are all so completely different you could happily hop among them—certainly try not to book any other safari destination after a stay at any of the Singita camps; it's likely to be a real let-down.

P.O. Box 23367, Claremont 7735. ✆ **021/683-3424** or direct 013/735-5500. Fax 021/683-3502. www.singita.co.za. Sabora 6 units; Faru Faru 9 units; Sasakwa 9 units. Sabora and Faru Faru $2,090 double game package (all-inclusive except French champagne); Sasakwa $ 3,300 double game package. AE, MC, V. **Amenities:** Bar; Internet; spa therapies; pool; room service. *In room:* TV (at Sasakwa), hair dryer, Wi-Fi.

16

Kilimanjaro

by Pippa de Bruyn

On October 22, 1959, 2 years before he would become chief minister of a newly independent Tanganyika (soon to become Tanzania), Julius Nyerere addressed the Legislative Assembly, saying, "We, the people of Tanganyika, would like to light a candle and put it on the top of Kilimanjaro, which would shine beyond our borders, giving hope where there was despair, love where there was hate, and dignity where before there was only humiliation."

The speech was to inspire Africans throughout the continent. As Joaquim Chissano—inaugurated as president of independent Mozambique in 1986—would say in an emotional speech to Tanzanians years later, "Kilimanjaro carried the torch that liberated Africa."

Today Kilimanjaro's snowcapped dome—when she deigns to appear from behind the clouds that swaddle her for much of the day—continues to be one of the most inspiring sights in Africa. It is the combination, perhaps, of the viewer being physically immersed in equatorial heat while high above the cloud cover—towering 5,895m (19,336 ft.) above the plains—and the other-worldly glow of snow and ice. The tallest freestanding mountain in the world, Kilimanjaro is just 3 degrees south of the sweltering equator. It's hardly surprising that early-19th-century explorer-missionaries relayed tales of "a mountain topped with silver." Even the most celebrated among them, David Livingstone, attributed the mountain's white crown to "a mass of white rock, somewhat like quartz."

Fascinated by local accounts of this mysterious mountain, Johann Rebmann, a Swiss-German missionary whose taste for adventure apparently outweighed his religious zeal (he notched a mere seven converts during his 12-year sojourn in Africa), set off to find it with his guide, Bwana Kheri, on April 27, 1848. Two weeks later, Rebmann became the first white man to look upon Kilimanjaro, writing in his diary, "I observed something remarkably white on the top . . . and first supposed it was a very white cloud." On closer inspection, Rebmann correctly identified it as snow, an observation that was dismissed out of hand by armchair geographers in Europe as the "visions of his imagination." It was to take another 12 years before Rebmann's report was finally verified by two more avid explorers, Briton Richard Thornton and the German Baron Carl Claus von der Decken. The two men climbed to 2,500m (8,200 ft.) before they were forced to turn back, the bottle of champagne they carried consumed in solace rather than celebration. Only the Baron attempted the climb again, this time reaching 4,200m (13,776 ft.) before a heavy snowfall forced yet another disappointing retreat.

The mysterious allure of Kilimanjaro's snowcapped peaks drew many more suitors keen to conquer her summit, but weather, porters, and local chieftains defeated their ambitions until 1889, when Dr. Hans Meyer and Ludwig Putscheller finally scrambled to the top, proudly planting the German flag on what the

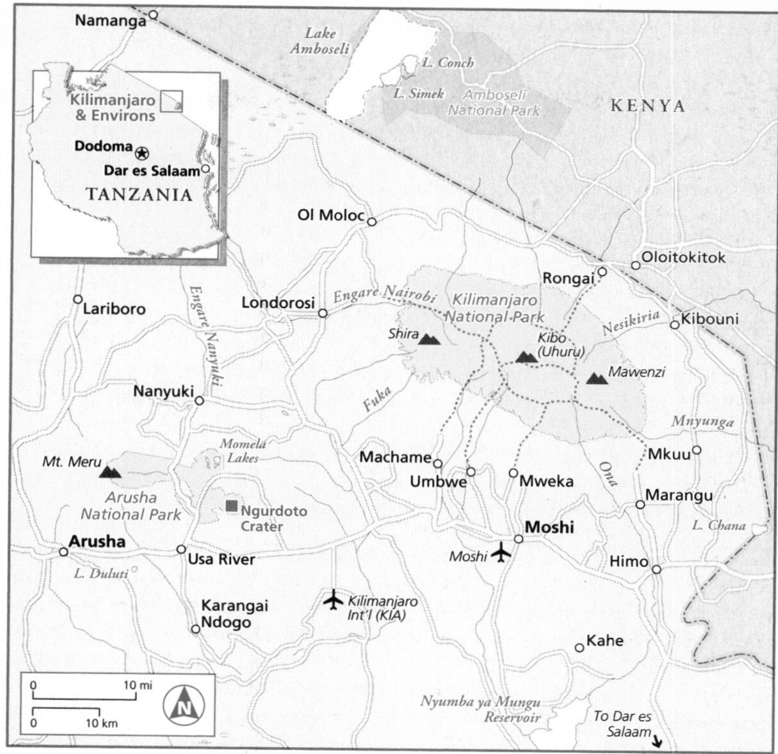

local Chagga tribes called Kipoo (Kibo) and naming it Kaiser Wilhelm Spitze. The climb took them 6 weeks. Thanks in part to the shrinking snowline, the ascent is much easier today, but one cannot help but wonder what the two intrepid climbers would make of the fact that the summit can be reached in 4 days today; that some 25,000 climbers now head up these slopes every year (though only around 60% make it to the top); and that record-holding victors include 87-year-old Valtee Daniel, 9-year-old Joshua Schumacher, and quadriplegic Bern Goosen, the first wheelchair user to make it to the summit.

Despite its exotic "highest mountain in Africa" moniker, Kilimanjaro is unique in the pantheon of great mountains, in that it can be scaled by virtually anyone with the drive to do so. No mountaineering skills or special preparations are needed, though you do need to be in relatively good health and able to complete a hard hike. Being super-fit can be a drawback, as pace is everything—the slower, the better. That said, the relative ease with which she can be conquered should not engender a careless, gung-ho approach. Aside from enduring the debilitating effects of altitude, a serious onset of pulmonary and cerebral edema can be lethal. If you plan to climb

"Kilimanjaro Is in Tanzania, Because Mombasa Is in Kenya"

Many visitors to East Africa are surprised to discover that access to Kilimanjaro is from Tanzania rather than Kenya. This is not so much due to a poor grip on geography as to a rather active and canny Kenyan tourism board. Kenya's tourism authority (which predates its socialist neighbor by many years) has often marketed itself with great images of wildlife taken in Amboseli, the Kenyan reserve bordering Northern Tanzania, with the alluring backdrop of a snowcapped Kilimanjaro shimmering in the distance, thereby entrenching the East African landmark with the Kenyan brand.

Romantic history would have us believe that Kilimanjaro was given to Tanzania (previously German East Africa) by Queen Victoria (who "owned" Kenya) because she wanted to give her German grandson a special gift on his birthday. In reality, the British and the Germans both wanted seaports, and when the British claimed Mombasa, the Germans agreed, as long as they could have Dar es Salaam and Lake Victoria, in a compromise negotiated by Sir Percy Anderson in 1886. The northern border was thus a line drawn straight from the Indian Ocean, with a slight wiggle around the mountain, to Lake Victoria in the west. "Now it becomes evident why Kilimanjaro is in Tanzania: because Mombasa is in Kenya," quipped Dr. Heinz Schneppen, German ambassador to Tanzania, looking at the records of these negotiations more than a century later.

its summit, come prepared, and book your trip with a reputable company, as recommended below. Alternatively, you could spend a pleasant few days rambling the foothills and lush forest that ring the lower slopes, stopping well before the 3,000m (9,840 ft.) moorlands zone, where the effects of altitude begin to set in. For the more sedentary, it's uplifting enough just to raise a toast to Kili as she shows herself in the late afternoon, her still-snowcapped dome tinged pink by the setting sun. As the popular T-shirt for Kilimanjaro Beer, one of Tanzania's most refreshing home-brewed beverages reads, "If you can't climb it, drink it!"

1 MOSHI & MARANGU

Most of Kilimanjaro's dedicated climbing operators are based in the small town of Moshi, a 45-minute drive south of the entrance to the Kilimanjaro National Park. Located in the heart of Tanzania's predominantly coffee-growing region, and surrounded by wheat, maize, sugar, banana, and coffee plantations, Moshi is the scene of vigorous bidding as international buyers vie for the region's seasonal wholesale coffee. Despite being the gateway to Tanzania's most visited national park, it feels less dependent on tourism dollars than nearby Arusha, with fewer tourism operators and foreign exchange bureaus, and only the occasional tout hawking tat to irritated tourists. Moshi's peaceful atmosphere can also be attributed to its relatively tiny population—a mere 150,000 strong, with a harmonious mix of Muslims, Hindus, and Christians providing a low-key but bustling street scene.

Given its proximity to Kili, Moshi is surprisingly hot and humid, with the run-down charm and laid-back atmosphere typical of subtropical climates. Surrounding Moshi's small shopping and business center (don't miss a wander through the vibrant African market, located on the double roads near Chagga St.) are leafy suburbs, their pavements periodically covered in carpets of purple jacaranda blossoms.

While Moshi is a one-horse town in comparison to Arusha, it remains a great deal more urban than Marangu, the sprawling village located at the foot of Kilimanjaro (40–50 min. from Moshi), above and below the main entrance to the national park. Fed by numerous streams that gush down from the mountain, Marangu (meaning Land of Water in the local Chagga dialect) is perennially lush and cool, with mornings shrouded in mist and doused with overnight rainfalls. It's a great deal more romantic than Moshi—ideal if you prefer a more rural atmosphere, with most of the accommodations options conveniently within a 5km (3-mile) radius of the park entrance. This makes it an ideal base for those who wish to explore the foothills and forests of Mount Kilimanjaro. If you don't wish to fork out for park fees, it's worth noting that there are also a number of walks to waterfalls that fall outside the park, which can be reached on foot from Marangu lodgings.

But be warned: You are likely to be rather disappointed by the food on offer at Marangu lodgings; despite the fertility of the soil that produces much of the food on your table, the old-school colonial training that prevails in most kitchens means that much of it reaches your plate nutrient-depleted and stripped of flavor. Climbers, so focused on conquering (or celebrating) their ascent, appear indifferent to the bland cuisine and predominantly spartan sleeping quarters that most Moshi and Marangu hotels offer; if you're not one of these, it's worth looking into basing yourself at one of the rated options in and around nearby Arusha, where the well-heeled are fed and watered before flying or driving onward to their Northern Circuit destinations. See chapter 15 for recommendations.

ESSENTIALS

GETTING THERE **By Air** The closest airport to Moshi is Kilimanjaro International Airport (referred to as KIA locally, but JRO is the official abbreviation), 45km (28 miles) from Moshi (more or less halfway between Moshi and Arusha) and 90km (56 miles) from Marangu. Facilities include a post office, bank, and *bureau de change*. International carriers KLM, Air Tanzania, Air Kenya, and Ethiopian Airways land here daily; others land at Dar es Salaam International Airport, from where visitors need to charter a flight to KIA or Arusha Airport (the latter servicing light aircraft only and located on the western outskirts of Arusha). Unless traveling to the south, it makes more sense for visitors to Kili and the Northern Circuit to fly to Nairobi airport (NBO) and then catch a connecting flight to KIA. Kenya Airways, in partnership with a Tanzanian airline called **Precision Air,** operates four or five flights daily on this route; it is designed as a connector flight, so if you are arriving on an international flight, you should check to see if you can remain, in transit to avoid paying for a Kenyan visa. You can book directly with Precision (pwreservations@precisionairtz.com). Another option is to connect with **AirKenya** (note that this is different from Kenya Airways), which offers a daily flight that leaves from Nairobi's Wilson General Aviation Airport (at press time, around 12:30pm). The drawback is that this means going through immigration and getting at least a one-way transit visa for $20 (full visa for most nationalities is $50), as well as a $20 taxi ride to Wilson. To book, e-mail resvns@airkenya.com. Expect to pay around $220 one-way for these connector flights.

Vaccination Alert

Travelers arriving at KIA direct from Europe (such as the daily KLM flight from Amsterdam) do *not* need a yellow fever vaccination certificate. Any traveler who transits through an endemic country (such as arrivals on Ethiopian Air via Addis, or arrivals via international flight to Nairobi such as British Airways, Swiss Air, Kenya Airways, and so on) who then connect onward to KIA by charter or other connecting flight will, however, need a yellow fever vaccination certificate. It is preferable (and far cheaper) to have the vaccination done at your local travel clinic or private doctor back home, but the vaccination is available at Kilimanjaro Airport at a cost of $50 per vaccination (as are visas, which are $50 for most nationalities, $100 for U.S. and Irish citizens).

It is worth prearranging your **airport transfer** with your lodgings, particularly if you are heading for Marangu. A taxi from KIA to Moshi should cost around $60; transfer from KIA to Machame should cost $70. Moshi to Marangu costs around $40, around $80 to $120 (depending on hotel) for transfer to or from KIA to Marangu, and $130 from Arusha Airport to Marangu.

By Road Moshi is an important transport hub, well connected by bus with both Arusha (which, in turn, is well connected with Nairobi) and Dar es Salaam. Marangu is a bit trickier, and you'd be well advised to prearrange this transfer before arrival, either with **Davanu Shuttle** (see below, under "From Nairobi," for full contact info) or direct with your lodgings.

From Dar es Salaam: The bus ride from Dar es Salaam is a rather grueling 8 hours, with one 20-minute stop more or less halfway. Toilets at this designated stop are squat-style pit latrines and are extremely daunting for anyone with sensitive olfactory senses. If you're at all squeamish, fly. That said, the savings are rather substantial—it costs a mere $30 for a one-way bus ticket from Dar to Moshi (versus around $200 for the flight), and it's a more adventurous way to get to know the country. Make sure you book well in advance (this holds even more true when departing the Moshi bus station, known for its ruthless touts), and try to book the front row seats (1–4) for the best views. The only bus operators I'd recommend (don't expect much in terms of condition of the bus, but the drivers are known for their safety-first approach) are **Scandinavia** (✆ **0722/286-1947**; www.scandinaviagroup.com) and **Royal Coach** (✆ **022/212-4073** in Dar, 0754/88-5778 in Arusha, or 0754/29-8274) in Moshi; Royal Coach even has a toilet on board. If you are bound for Marangu, you could wait for one of the unscheduled buses (see "Getting Around," later in this chapter).

From Nairobi: Several companies operate shuttle bus services daily from Nairobi to Arusha, with some going on to Moshi. Buses depart Nairobi at 8am and 2pm from the main depot (Parkside Hotel). Shuttles pick up at a number of Nairobi hotels and the International Airport and arrive at Arusha 4 to 5 hours later; the full journey to Moshi is 7 hours (or longer, depending on how long the stop is at Arusha). You will cross the border at Namanga, where you can buy a Tanzanian visa for $50 to $100, depending on your nationality (see above).

Impala shuttles (✆ **800/221-9000;** www.impalashuttle.com) transfer from Nairobi to Arusha for around $20; Arusha to Moshi is around $4. The Marangu Hotel has a long-standing relationship with **Davanu Shuttle,** which charges $80 from Nairobi to Marangu (a great price, but, with many stops and a few bus changes, it can take as long as 9 hr.). In Arusha, contact MD Emmanuel (© **0715/40-0318;** emkessy@yahoo.com); in Nairobi (here Davanu operates as **Destination Shuttle**), contact Samuel (© **0722/72-9100**) or Nathan at Nairobi International Airport (© **0722/31-0234**). **Riverside** (www.riverside-shuttle.com) is another reputable shuttle company. Book at least 1 day in advance.

VISITOR INFORMATION There is no visitor information office in Moshi or Marangu. **Kilimanjaro National Park Headquarters** (www.tanzaniaparks.com) is located at the park entrance gate in Marangu. Office hours are from 7am to 7pm (though you can obviously leave after hours for altitude reasons). At present, you need to prebook for only the Marangu route; on camping routes, you can simply turn up, with no limit on climbing numbers.

FAST FACTS There are several **Internet** cafes, charging around Tsh1,500 per hour. **Twiga,** the first Internet cafe in Moshi, located on Old Moshi Road, is still a good choice. (They also rent out novels, movies, and trekking/camping equipment.) Alternatively, head for the Tanzanian Coffee Lounge on Chagga Street, where you can enjoy a cup of Tanzanian coffee (Tsh900) or cappuccino (Tsh1,200) while checking or sending e-mails (Tsh500 per 15 min.). But be warned: Moshi suffers from regular power outages.

NBC is located directly opposite the Clock Tower; several more **banks** (and ATMs) are located along Boma Road leading from the Clock Tower. They all accept international debit cards accredited with the Plus logo and Visa credit cards.

WHEN TO GO The park is open year-round. January, February, and September are considered the best months to climb, followed by July and August. It is most difficult to ascend in the rainy months (Apr and May), when visibility is not great; on the upside the flowers are out and there is far less traffic during these months, so you may even get to savor your ascent in relative solitude. Bear in mind, however, that April and May are not ideal if you want to add on a Serengeti safari.

GETTING AROUND Moshi is small enough that pretty much anywhere can be reached on foot. The same holds true for Marangu. Buses run between Moshi and Arusha, as well as between Moshi and Marangu. There is no scheduled departure time for

Tips Money Matters

Credit cards are not very welcome in Northern Tanzania, with many places refusing to process a payment under $50 (or even $80); there will also be a 5% to 7.5% surcharge on the bill. Visa is more accepted than any other card, MasterCard less so, and American Express seldom. Absolutely everyone accepts U.S. dollars as payment (parks will accept only U.S. dollars, though not in cash), so it's worth bringing a certain amount in cash and/or traveler's checks. If you bring euros or sterling, you will have to convert it to shillings and then to dollars—far from ideal, so change into dollars before leaving your country of origin, and try to pay for major expenses via credit card or EFT *before* arrival. Note that most street vendors and even some hotels take a very relaxed attitude to actual conversation rates and will simply knock off three zeros (for example, Tsh1,000 = $1).

these; the bus leaves when it is full. A transfer between Marangu and Arusha costs around $120, between Moshi and Marangu $40. If you're here to climb, note that most standard packages include transfers to and from the starting point of your ascent.

WHERE TO STAY & DINE

If you are here to climb Kilimanjaro, the following lodgings offer both comfortable accommodations and all-inclusive climbing packages. If you don't wish to reach the summit but would prefer to explore the lower reaches, or you just want to say you spent a night at the foot of the mountain, the Marangu Hotel is the best option.

I have noted elsewhere that climbers should also look at options in Arusha. Aside from those reviewed (see "Where to Stay & Dine" under "Arusha," in chapter 15), the **Meru View Lodge** (✆ **0784/19-232;** www.meru-view-lodge.de; from $130 B&B double), adjacent to the Arusha National Park, is worth highlighting. This is a highly recommended climbing base, very efficiently owner-managed by Horst and Deborah Bachmann. Horst is a regular climber of both Kilimanjaro and Mount Meru, as well as a seasoned self-drive fly-camper throughout the Northern Circuit. His advice on everything from routes to road conditions is invaluable. He utilizes Zara Tours, so you get exactly the same climbing deal as you would at Springlands, though you pay more for the privilege of starting and ending in the more peaceful atmosphere of this small (15-unit) lodge, with accommodation in separate huts dotted in the garden around the pool.

Marangu

The sprawling village of Marangu has limited accommodation options. Aside from the two listed below, you may want to take a look at the 42-room **Kilimanjaro Mountain Resort** (✆ **027/275-8950;** $154 double full board). Opened in 2003, it is younger than the Kibo or Marangu by many decades and is in some ways the most comfortable lodging in Marangu, with modern amenities such as flatscreen TVs, minibars, and hair dryers in every room; an Internet cafe; and a small fitness center. Its lush mountainside location is best enjoyed from an elevated position; ask for rooms on the second or third floors. The two family loft rooms, sleeping four, are quaint. However, the property is set at the end of a bone-jarring track, 15 minutes' drive from Marangu gate; rooms (aside from those in the loft) are utterly characterless; and service, staff, and food are also lackluster. The rest of Marangu's lodgings are not worth a look.

Kibo Hotel ★ Built by a German family in the late 1800s, this dowager is a throwback from another era, retaining all her original signage, a huge 360-degree open fireplace in the bar/lounge (nights can be chilly, at 1,550m/5,084 ft.), tall arched windows, and plenty of dark wood paneling. Climbs are arranged through two reputable Arusha-based operators, and the dining room walls are covered with signed memorabilia from the many hotel guests who've made it (as well as a large sign at the entrance welcoming their most famous guests, Jimmy Carter and his wife, Roselyn, who completed their climb in 1988). The best rooms range along the front of the building on the second floor (6–11); these are spacious, with a door opening onto a furnished balcony with lovely views—even the toilet has a great view. It must be said that furnishings and fittings do look a little tired, and the hotel is in need of TLC. Kibo won't suit the traveler looking for modern amenities and decor (for that, you're far better off at the Kilimanjaro Mountain Resort up the road, or the Protea in Machame, reviewed later in this chapter). But if you're a sucker for character and nostalgia, you will thoroughly enjoy staying in the kind of gracious spaces and old-fashioned decor that predates the bland cookie-cutter hotel rooms built in their billions these days.

P.O. Box 102, Marangu. ✆ **027/275-1308.** 44 units. $72 double B&B; $93 double dinner and B&B; $120 double full board. Third person supplement $32–$40. MC, V. **Amenities:** Bar; airport and Kili transfers; limited phone and Internet services; pool.

Marangu Hotel ★★ (Kids) This is the most popular hotel in Marangu, with an unblemished reputation for getting climbers safely up and down the mountain that stretches back 80 years (see recommended operators). The sprawling "hotel"—a converted 19th-century farmhouse, surrounded by a rambling English-style garden, in which clusters of ivy-clad bungalows were built as time and money became available—is ideal for sedentary types, keen to ramble rather than trek. Despite (or probably due to) its slow metamorphosis, the grounds remain steeped in colonial farmhouse atmosphere, and seated on the shaded lawns as Kili shows herself at dusk, you feel less like a tourist and more like a guest of some unknown relative in the "colonies." Accommodation is Spartan, but the important bits are there: comfortable mattresses (mostly twin; specify when booking if you want a double), bedside lighting, and a spotlessly clean bathroom (shower only; water takes some time to heat on the donkey boiler system). It's all rather utilitarian, but I love the authentic, nonhotel atmosphere. Favorite rooms (front patios with good garden views) include nos. 25, 27, 37, and 38. The biggest drawback is the food, which is considerably below par; consider ordering from the snack menu (burgers looked great), but note that the last order is at 6pm, and you're probably paying full-board rate anyway.

P.O. Box 40, Moshi. ✆ **027/275-6594** or 027/275-6361. www.maranguhotel.com. 26 units. High season $120 double; low season $90 double. Children under 5 free; 6–12 sharing 50% discount. Rates include dinner and B&B. Note that low-season rates are applicable when accommodation is taken in conjunction with a fully equipped climb. AE, MC, V. **Amenities:** Bar; limited phone and Internet services; pool; airport and Kili transfers.

Moshi

If the following options don't suit or are full, another worth looking into is **Sal Salinero** (http://salsalinerohotel.com; $115 double dinner and B&B), also located in Moshi's leafy suburbs in what must once have been the private home of a somewhat eccentric art lover. The gardens are dotted with interesting sculptures, and the double-volume dining area is very dramatic, with more imposing artworks. The seven rooms are generously sized but not in ship-shape condition; staff are well meaning but clearly not that well versed in Western hospitality standards. That said, it has a great pool and is certainly one of Moshi's more interesting options. Climbs are arranged through a sister company.

If you are not on a full board package or simply want a break from your lodgings, the best restaurant in town is the veranda at the **Impala Hotel** (noon–11:30pm; average main course $6.50). Order the Hara Bhara Chicken, tender cubes of chicken cooked in coriander and creamy yogurt with subtle spices, or the Handi Lazeez, chicken marinated in yogurt and cooked in a sublime gravy of cardamom and cashew nuts. Vegetarians are naturally well catered for, and the *dhingri kaj mutter,* mushrooms and peas simmered in subtly spiced cashew gravy, is out of this world. Chef Kamal Singh, trained in Mumbai, came to Tanzania for a year-long contract; that, thankfully, was 5 years ago. If you feel like pizza, **IndoItaliano** (New St., opposite the Buffalo Hotel; ✆ **027/275-2195;** daily noon–11:30pm) is a good bet (the Indian isn't bad, either). The average main course is around $3 to $4; try for a table on the balcony.

Impala Hotel The best reason to stay at this small Indian-owned hotel, located 2km (1¼ miles) from the town center, is the food. The Mumbai-trained Indian chef produces meals in his outdoor kitchen to equal the best in India and the most refreshing masala tea this side of Kolkata. The architecture is that of an embassy home, built for the ambassador of a minor country—solid and well crafted, if a little unimaginative. The L-shape house and separate wing are arranged around the central lawn area with pool, which includes a deep veranda where meals are served. Rooms are comfortable albeit a little gloomy, with plenty of dark wood detailing around the windows, parquet floors, and heavy, dark furniture. Staff is welcoming and service is attentive (but a tad slow). Although the hotel does not arrange climbing tours, the travel desk will put you in touch with their sister company, **Classic Tours and Safaris** (www.theclassictours.com), whose representatives will come to the hotel and brief you on their services. Part of a larger hotel group (the smart younger sister of the big slightly has-been Imperial in Arusha), the travel desk is more savvy than most and offers good-value shuttles to and from Arusha and Nairobi.

Old Moshi Rd. P.O. Box 7302, Moshi. ✆ **027/254-3082** to -3087. Fax 027/254-3088 or -3089. www.impalahotel.com. 11 units. $110 double dinner and B&B. MC, V. **Amenities:** Restaurant; bar; pool; room service. *In room:* TV, A/C, minibar (in some).

Keys Like Springlands, this is a relatively efficient, no-nonsense base for climbers who are serious about reaching Uhuru and don't want to spend buckets of money doing so. Located in the center of Moshi, there are no views or gardens to speak of, and rooms—despite having small TVs, air-conditioning, minifridges, mosquito nets, and desks—are by no means luxurious, with fittings in the en suite bathroom cubicles (small, shower-only) showing their age. The best rooms, as always, are corners—rooms 101 and 110 are quieter, 102 and 108 are on the street side. Whatever you do, make sure you're not booked into one of the newer ground-floor rondawels; these stark units, clustered together in a sea of paving, are depressing. But everything is scrupulously clean, and the downstairs dining/bar area has some charm, particularly in the evenings. Thanks to its reputation, Keys is a popular choice (though currently outpriced by Springlands), which means that the public area really comes into its own at night, when aspirant climbers and exultant finishers congregate to swap tales around the bar and pool table. For dinner, opt for one of the Indian choices on the menu; prices at average Tsh6,000 are good, as is the wine list (order the reliable Nederberg options from South Africa).

P.O. Box 933 (Mbokomu Rd.) Moshi. ✆ **027/275-2250,** -1875, or -1909. www.keys-hotel-tours.com. 30 units. $85 double B&B; $100 dinner and B&B. MC, V. **Amenities:** Bar; pool. *In room:* A/C (on request), TV, minibar (stocked on request).

Kilemakyaro Mountain Lodge Located 9km (5½ miles) north of Moshi center, on the top of a hill, with arguably the best views of Kili, Kilemakyaro likes to think of itself as rather grand (and prices itself accordingly), but is disappointingly bland, with plenty of kitsch touches such as the liberal use of leopard print and faux elephant in the garden. The reception and dining areas are housed in the original 1880s home of the Kifumu Tea Estate owner, but renovations have taken their toll. Today there's little sign of what is said to have once been a gracious homestead. Accommodation is in custom-built rondawels (round chalets; two units per chalet; shower only) reached via pathways that wind throughout the garden; they are very comfortable and are more attractively furnished than the main house. The best part is the pool, which enjoys great views of Kili. Kilemakyaro is the most expensive option in Moshi and is geared toward European package tours (they won't take on single climbers), but being Swiss-owned and -managed, it is a pretty professional outfit, dedicated to getting its guests up the mountain as efficiently and painlessly as possible. It also offers 3-day Mount Meru packages.

P.O. Box 6611, Moshi. ✆ **027/275-4929** or -49. www.kilimanjarosafari.com. 39 units. $120 double dinner and B&B. MC, V. **Amenities:** Bar; pool. *In room:* TV, minibar (stocked on request).

Springlands Hotel ★ Value Located on the outskirts of Moshi, Springlands is not only great value, but—visually hidden from passing trade—a real surprise. Enter through the fortresslike gates (bolted and guarded, with no signage), and you are immediately struck by the low-level bustle of many-language foreigners gathering and dispersing into the lush central courtyard divided into outdoor rooms by gravel pathways lined with low clipped hedges or wrought-iron edging. Owner Zainab is an entrepreneurial powerhouse, and her warrenlike hotel (she seems to add a new wing every 4 years or so) is continuously abuzz with the low-key adrenaline of aspirant climbers gathering around tables or poolside to discuss the next day's ascent. The en suite rooms are basic and functional (two or three single beds, lamp, two plastic chairs, central fan, mosquito netting), a simple "sleep 'n' shower" zone. Although room nos. 7 to 12 have a balcony that runs the length, with great views of Kili at dusk, most guests unwind before or after their ascent by the pool, at the garden bar, or among any of the many tables in the courtyard. Plenty of facilities and services (there's even Wi-Fi in the corridors) are on offer; food is not, however, what you're here for. **ZARA Tours** (✆ **866/550-4447** or 027/27-50233; www.zaratours.com), Zainab's tourism outfit, aimed at budget travelers, is also based on the premises.

P.O. Box 1990, Moshi. ✆ **027/275-0233** or 075/445-1000. www.springlandshotel.com. 79 units. $72 double B&B. **Amenities:** Bar; bikes; small gym; Internet and phone services; massage and beauty treatments; pool; sauna; shuttle to Moshi center.

Machame

Protea Hotel Aishi Machame ★★ Value Kids This family-built hotel, located on the western slopes of Kili, 7km (4¼ miles) from the Machame Gate (20 min. west of Moshi; 25 min. from KIA), was taken over by the South African hotel chain Protea and fully refurbished to their bland but exacting standards. With gorgeous, immaculately groomed gardens, lovely views, walkways over ponds, attractive shingle roofing, and comfortable and well-equipped en suite rooms (shower only), this is by far the most upmarket option for climbers and is better value than Kilemakyaro (above). As such, this will suit the older traveler or anyone who appreciates simple creature comforts, such as direct-dial telephones and working TVs in every room, minibars and room service, a huge (and private) solar-heated pool, and well-trained staff. Best rooms are the corner rooms: 8, 9, and 11 on the first floor, and 16, 17, 20, and 21 on the second. The hotel-only rate is a bit higher than the more characterful but relatively stark rooms at the Marangu Hotel, but when you compare climbing packages, the Protea hotel offers excellent value—for the 5-day Marangu Route, the Protea currently shaves almost $400 off the bill compared to the otherwise highly recommended Marangu Hotel (above). Food, while nothing to write home about, is also of a higher standard here.

P.O. Box 534, Moshi. ✆ **027/275-6941** or -6948. www.proteahotels.com/aishi. 30 units. $145 double B&B; children 5–11 50%. MC, V. **Amenities:** Bar; airport transfers ($25 per person; minimum 2); babysitting; bikes; mini gym; Internet; pool. *In room:* TV, hair dryer, minibar (stocked on request).

Tips to Help You Get to the Top

Choose a reputable operator Don't fall for the cheapest option—at best, you may have a horrific and stressful experience; at worst, you're gambling with your life. Climbing the mountain is expensive, but this is because the mandatory fixed costs (daily park fees, hut fee, guide entrance fee, rescue fee) are already very high. Like most things, you get what you pay for. Squeezing any profit from your tour is bound to end in tears. Check that your package includes transport to and from the gate, equipment, food, all park fees, a guide, and two porters per person; hotel packages will usually include 2 nights (first and last) at the lodging.

Pack the right gear Although you don't need mountaineering equipment, the following gear is essential: sturdy, well-worn walking boots; layers of warm clothing (thermal underwear, three pairs of warm trousers, two sweaters, six pairs of warm socks, a wind-proof jacket, gloves, scarf, balaclava); adequate sun protection (ski sunglasses/goggles, sun hat, sunscreen); headlamp (with spare battery); daypack; and 2-liter water bottle. Even if it's included in the package, consider bringing your own well-insulated sleeping bag and, if you're camping, an insulation mat. Adjustable climbing poles are useful.

Sweet treats Pack a good supply of high-energy treats—chocolate, cookies/biscuits, boiled sweets, energy bars, and so on. This is not so much a reward for completing each day's hike—though, heaven knows, you deserve one—but an appreciated boost for your body. Snacks will also come in handy as you may struggle to eat what's prepared for you on the mountain—some visitors find the food thoroughly unappetizing, a situation exacerbated by a real loss in appetite due to the altitude.

Get the pace right Climbing Kili is an endurance test, and as any endurance athlete knows, pace is everything. A super-fit person in his or her 20s stands a higher chance of altitude-related illness than an averagely fit person twice his or her age. This is simply because younger, fitter contenders tend to

2 ASCENDING KILIMANJARO

Climbing Kilimanjaro is not just about conquering Africa's highest mountain—it's a trek through five distinct eco-zones (enjoy it, but be aware of the potential for exhaustion).

You are likely to drive through the predominantly populated and farmed **lower slopes** (900–1,800m/2,952–5,904 ft.), the zone below the entrance gate closest to your chosen route. Most routes start their ascent beyond this, in the lush and fertile montane **forest zone** (1,800–2,800m/5,904–9,184 ft.). The forest that rings the mountain is the recipient of the mountain's highest rainfall (1,000–2,000mm/40–80 in. a year) and, in turn, provides 90% of the water that streams down Kilimanjaro's slopes, with a girdle of cloud cover ensuring year-round damp conditions. This is also the most likely place to see the mountain's fauna—look out for duiker, bushbuck, black-and-white colobus monkeys, blue approach the climb with more gusto, relishing their ability to "power walk"—until they get above 3,000m (9,840 ft.), when the debilitating effects of altitude sickness set in. The trick is to walk at a slow, steady pace and rest frequently to acclimatize.

If at first you don't succeed If you feel a strong bout of altitude sickness setting in (fatigue, nausea, swelling, headaches) or, worse still, pulmonary or cerebral edema, caused by ascending too rapidly (symptoms include labored breathing even at rest, poor coordination, disorientation, hallucination, coughing up frothy spit or blood), descend immediately—even a 100m (328-foot) drop can make a huge difference. If you feel better after a brief rest, start up again slowly; if not, descend and seek immediate medical attention.

Hydration You should drink 2 to 3 liters of water every day; make sure your porters are carrying adequate supplies, and take your own water bottle, which you should replenish regularly. If you're sweating, remove a layer to retain water.

Pills and thrills A decent operator will ensure that your guide is equipped with a well-stocked medical kit, but it's worth packing your own supply of good quality plasters, nausea and diarrhea medication, rehydration sachets, and headache tablets. Glucose powders will give your body a much-needed energy lift.

Give yourself an extra day It's not just the altitude that exhausts; during the final 24-hour approach and descent from the summit, you are—regardless of route—walking for a cumulative 14 hours, quite possibly with no sleep (sleeplessness being a common symptom at these altitudes). Speak to regular climbers of Kilimanjaro, and they all emphasize the importance of taking an extra day to acclimatize, and that the benefits outweigh the increase in cost (a hefty $165–$230, depending on your operator). Some say it will increase your chances of getting to the top; even if this is supposition, the reality is that a longer-duration climb will, without a doubt, be that much more enjoyable. Like life, this is ideally what conquering Kilimanjaro should be.

monkeys, and troops of baboons. Above the 2,700m (8,856-ft.) contour line, the mountain is protected from human habitation or interference by Kilimanjaro National Park.

At around 2,800m (9,184 ft.), you enter the **heath and moorland zone,** rising to 4,000m (13,120 ft.). During the latter part of this ascent, you will start to feel the effects of altitude and will need to protect yourself from both frost and sunshine. But any discomfort is more than made up for by the alpine meadows and stunning vistas that now unfurl above the clouds that encircle the forest zone (though this is not, of course, guaranteed) and the flora (which is). The flora is rich in variety, including red-hot pokers, the pink-flowered iris, pale wild protea, and, beyond, in the moorlands, the endemic lobelia *deckenii,* its specially adapted rosettes closing at night to protect the delicate inner bud from frost. There are also a number of interesting geological features in this zone, such as the Maundi Crater, the glassy, crystal-like rock visible below Horombo Hut and Zebra Rock, its stripes created by water flowing over the dark lava rock.

The grueling 4,000 to 5,000m (13,120–16,400 ft.) **highland desert zone** follows. Nights here are below freezing, but daytime temperatures rise to 40°C (104°F); water is scarce, and only the hardiest flora thrive in this lunarlike landscape. Lichens, which need no soil, add splashes of color to lava rocks in the Saddle area and around Kibo and Mawenzi Huts; hardy tussock grasses feed off their own dead matter, while free-moving moss balls are sustained by a few granules of soil. From here you are now in full view of the Kibo glaciers and Mawenzi "dykes"—prominent pinnacles and carved "walls" leading up to the peak. Having traversed the inhospitable and bleak boulder-strewn Saddle (literally straddling the two peaks), you head into the **summit zone.** Arctic conditions prevail above 5,000m (16,400 ft.): Subzero temperatures at night are followed by blistering solar radiation. Oxygen levels are half what they are at sea level. Very little can survive for long here, though there have been reports of wildlife sightings—mostly famously in 1926, when ex-officer Richard Reusch, a Lutheran missionary who had recently dropped out of the Cossack Army of Imperial Russia, is said to have discovered a frozen leopard near the summit. Reusch apparently tried unsuccessfully to behead it, then cut off an ear as a souvenir, an inglorious end for the intrepid big cat, later to be immortalized in Hemingway's *The Snows of Kilimanjaro.*

The number of people wanting to climb Kilimanjaro has doubled in the past decade, and while the environmental impact is of concern, the mountain earns more in income than all of the other national parks combined, thereby subsidizing parks that are less popular but no less worthy of protection. As a compromise, the park tries to control numbers. Currently, a maximum of around 65 hikers per day are allowed to use the Marangu Route because accommodation must be juggled among the huts, but there is less control on the other routes, with Machame, in particular, very busy; if you'd prefer to climb and camp in solitude, Mount Meru is a much better bet. You can arrange your climb through the park headquarters at the Marangu entrance gate, but most visitors utilize a reputable operator. It is compulsory to hire an authorized guide (he should have a small walletlike document proving that he is registered), and no one intent on actually enjoying at least part of the climb would attempt to do so without porters. Bringing your own equipment and purchasing food in Moshi does, however, significantly reduce the cost.

If you are not in peak health, or you simply don't wish to experience the effects of altitude, 3,000m (9,840 ft.)—roughly the upper limit of the forest—should define the limit of your ascent. Needless to say, picking flowers or destroying any vegetation is forbidden, as is littering. Great care must be taken where fires are lit.

3 CHOOSING YOUR ROUTE

There are six established routes up the mountain: Marangu, Machame, Rongai, Shira, and Umbwe. Of these, the popular **Marangu Route** (also sometimes referred to as the Tourist Route or snidely as the Coca-Cola Route) has the easiest gradient and is the only route with accommodation in huts, which—along with the fact that it can be completed in 5 days—makes it the cheapest option. In recent years, the **Machame Route** (or "Whisky Route") has almost equaled it in popularity, and the convergence of routes has made it almost as busy on the final days. The gradients are steeper, but you have an extra day built in, giving you more time to acclimatize, and it is generally considered more scenic. Given that you have to camp, it also feels more adventurous.

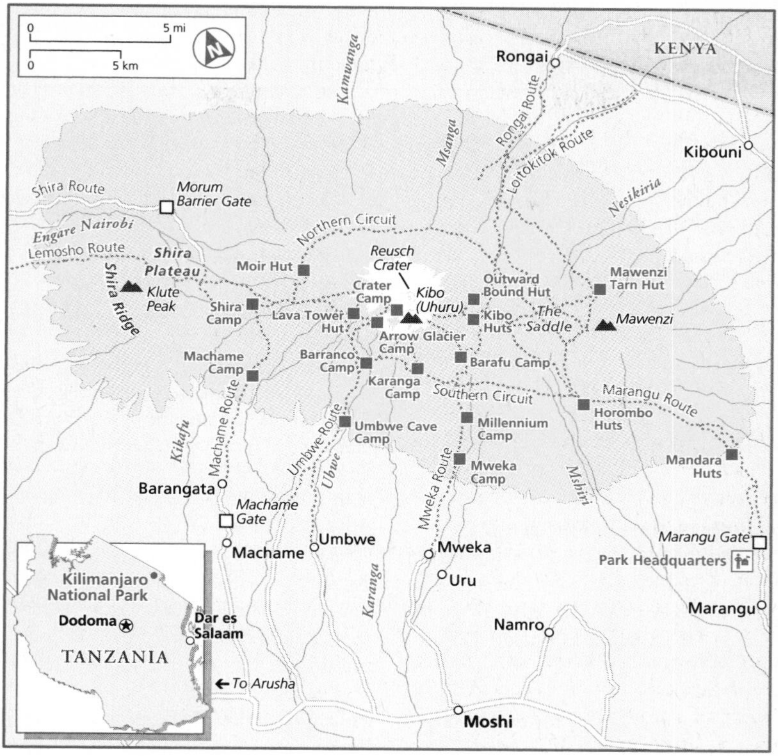

I have heard a number of regular climbers assert that **Rongai** is a great route because it is the only one that kicks off on the north side and is, therefore, the least busy, but with the final ascent of the Western Breach Route recently reopened with strict new rules (following a bad accident in 2006), it usually converges with the busy Marangu Route on day 5 (though some say that 4 days of solitude on the mountain more than make up for this). Similarly, the **Shira Route** is said to cross through beautiful scenery, but the strictures of the final ascent on the Western Breach Route have similarly robbed it of its exclusivity and—unless you are with a reputable company following the new guidelines (see below)—you will converge with the Machame Route the third night. The **Umbwe Route** is the most direct, but also the steepest, and is therefore traditionally considered the most difficult route (and very scenic). It appeals primarily to those keen to flaunt strong machismo levels. However, it currently converges with the Machame Route on the second night and is therefore not described in detail below.

It's worth noting that if you're looking for real exclusivity and a more scenic climb, Mount Meru is considered by locals to be a far more satisfying experience; some rate climbing the active volcano, Ol Doinyo L'Engai, the Maasai's Mountain of God, the most exhilarating. Kilemakyaro Mountain Lodge in Moshi, Meru View Lodge, and Hatari arrange climbs on Mount Meru; for details on Hatari lodgings, as well as Ol Doinyo L'Engai, see chapter 15.

MARANGU ROUTE (60KM/37 MILES IN 5 OR 6 DAYS)

Day ❶: Marangu Gate to Mandara Hut (1,700–2,740m/5,576–8,987 ft.) in 3 hours

After breakfast, you will be taken to Marangu Park Gate to register. Enter the forest for the gentle walk to the 84-bed Mandara Hut via forest or main trail. Once here, you may like to walk to the Maundi Crater at the upper edge of the rainforest (a 30-min. walk from the hut) for the first of many lovely views, or rest. (Huts are basic but comfortable; lighting is solar-powered; and all but Kibo hut, reached on Day 3, have running water and flush toilets.)

Day ❷: To Horombo Hut (2,740–3,700m/8,987–12,136 ft.) in 5 hours

Depart the Mandara encampment at about 8am for the 5-hour walk to the 84-bed Horombo encampment. The first 30 minutes continues through the forest; after this, you skirt the Maundi Crater, crossing a meadow and wooded stream before emerging into the moorlands zone. Look out for the many flora species; if the day is clear, there are also splendid views to enjoy. As you go higher, the vegetation thins, and you may experience shortness of breath—this is common, but keep your guide informed if you are at all worried. If you opt for the 6-day alternative, Horombo hut is where you spend the extra day to acclimatize, walking upward toward the Saddle, then returning to the hut to overnight.

Day ❸: To Kibo Hut (3,700–4,700m/12,136–15,416 ft.) in 5 hours

Terrain is very similar to that seen the previous day. Take the left fork until you reach the lunar landscape of the Saddle, from where you can see Kibo Hut (it's worth knowing that it appears closer than the few hours' walk away it really is). Most find the last 30 minutes to the hut very tiring, and the sight of the next day's path can appear pretty daunting. Try to get as much rest as possible.

Day ❹: To Summit; Descend to Horombo Hut (4,700–5,895–3,700m/15,416–19,336–12,136 ft.) in 8 to 11 hours

Wake at midnight to complete the final trek to reach Gillman's Point on the crater rim. The first part of the ascent is to the Hans Meyer cave, weaving around large rock outcrops. The surface is loose and hard going (don't push too hard); you should witness sunrise from behind Mawenzi. After the cave, the scree slope becomes extremely steep; climbers move up in a zigzag fashion to Gillman's Point—at 5,895m (19,336 ft); this is acknowledged to be the top, and you will receive your certificate at the gate to prove it. After a rest, enjoying the splendid views of the ice cliffs across the crater, you may—if you feel able and/or weather and time permit—attempt to reach Uhuru Peak. Uhuru (meaning "Freedom" in Swahili) is where a symbolic torch and the flag of the newly independent Tanganyika were hoisted on December 9, 1961; climbers reaching this point receive a gold certificate to commemorate the achievement. Before attempting this 2-hour walk around the crater rim, bear in mind that the descent is, in some ways, as difficult as the ascent. After a rest at Kibo Hut, you continue to Horombo Hut, this time by the more direct route.

Day ❺: Descend to Marangu Park Gate in 3 to 5 hours

Collect your certificate and return to your lodgings, hopefully to a prebooked massage.

The route below does not include the final ascent of the Western Breach Route, considered a difficult and potentially dangerous climb. Following a serious rock fall accident on the mountain in January 2006, park authorities closed this section; it has been reopened but is subject to strict conditions laid down by the national park. Quite a few operators are using the route again—make sure they fulfill the training and equipment regulations specified. These include using guides trained in rock-fall protocol and briefing clients and porters before they embark for the crater's summit. Companies have been asked to consider reducing the number of support staff accompanying clients during the hike from Arrow Glacier to the crater rim, to reduce the number of porters subjected to high risks and reduce the number of dislodged rocks in this area. Porters should carry luggage in rucksacks to keep their hands free. Every group must have at least two ice axes to help cut steps in the icy conditions to create stable footholds for climbers. Every group must have life-saving equipment (Gammov bag, oxygen cylinder, first-aid kits) during the crater summit attempt, and there should be a written emergency response plan. If the company you are climbing with offers this route without fulfilling their obligations, insist on following the route below.

Day ❶: Machame Gate to Machame camp (1,830–3,100m/6,002–10,168 ft.) in 5 to 6 hours

The first day is a gentle walk, gradually ascending through the forest to a ridge between two streams and then onward to the campsite, just clear of the forest. Note that the forest walk can be muddy, in which case trekking poles may be useful.

Day ❷: To Shira camp (3,100–3,840m/10,168–12,595 ft.) in 5 to 6 hours

Ascend the steep, rocky ridge from Machame camp, through the moorland zone, heading straight toward the peak. After about 4 hours (at around 3,600m/11,808 ft.), the path veers to the left, flattening out into a gorge and ascending more gradually to Shira camp on the Shira plateau, to the west of Kibo.

Day ❸: To Barranco camp (3,840–3,950m/12,595–12,956 ft.) in 5 to 6 hours

The path continues directly up the ridge toward Kibo. After about 4 hours, the path forks to the right and descends into a gorge (barranco), where you will spend the night at Barranco camp.

Day ❹: To Barafu camp (3,950–4,600m/12,956–15,088 ft.) in 6 to 7 hours

Cross the Barranco Valley, climb the Barranco Wall, then follow the Kibo South Circuit. If the weather is clear, the views of Kibo's southern glaciers are wonderful. Lunch next to the river in the Karanga valley, then continue to the intersection of the South Circuit with the Mweka ascent path. Turn left and climb up a ridge for about 2 hours to Barafu camp. (Climbers keen to enjoy rather than endure can opt to split this ascent into 2 days and camp out at Karanga. This means that Day 4 is only a 3- to 4-hr. walk, and Day 5 to Barafu is a mere 3-hr. walk, with plenty of time to acclimatize.)

Day ❺: To Summit, and descent to Mweka camp (4,600–5,895–3,100m/15,088–19,336–10,168 ft.) in 10 to 13 hours

Leave your hut at 1 or 2am. The day starts with a steep climb over scree and rock toward the Rebmann Glacier, passing a cliff before entering the gap between the Rebmann and Ratzel glaciers, arriving at the crater rim near Stella Point (about 6–7 hr.). One more hour of hiking takes you to Uhuru. Descend via Barafu hut (1–2 hr. from Stella Point) and then continue for another 3 or 4 hours to Mweka camp.

Day ❻: Descend to Mweka gate

Climbers will find the Mweka College of Wildlife Management.

RONGAI ROUTE (65KM/40 MILES IN 5 OR 6 DAYS)

Day ❶: Naremoru gate to first camp (1,800–2,800m/5,904–9,184 ft.) in 3 to 4 hours

Climbers are dropped off at the Naremoru entrance gate, a journey of around 2 hours from Marangu. From there, it is gradual ascent through the forest; the camp is just clear of the forest.

Day ❷: To Kikelewa (Third) Cave (2,800–3,690m/9,184–12,103 ft.) in 5 to 7 hours

The path goes through the alpine-like moorland zone, similar to that found on the Marangu route, with views of Kibo, the Eastern Ice Fields, and Mawenzi (on a clear day), to Second Cave at 3,500m (11,480 ft.). After a lunch stop there, the path forks left toward Mawenzi (this is not the most direct route but is better for acclimatization). The campsite near Kikelewa Cave is reached after about 3 hours. Total distance is about 15km (9¼ miles), making it a rather hard day, but most of the altitude gain is achieved before lunch.

Day ❸: Kikelewa Cave to Mawenzi Tarn (3,690–4,320m/12,103–14,170 ft.) in 3 to 4 hours

From Kikelewa, the path climbs a steep ridge directly toward Mawenzi. At the top of the ridge, you traverse left across the rocky landscape to descend into the Tarn Valley to camp. The distance covered on this day is only about 5km (3 miles) but is difficult because of the steep incline and altitude.

Day ❹: Mawenzi Tarn to Kibo Hut (4,320–4,700m/14,170–15,416 ft.) in 4 to 5 hours

Retrace your path for a short distance, then descend to the Saddle between Mawenzi and Kibo. A 6km (3¾-mile) walk across the gradually ascending high-altitude desert brings you to Kibo Hut, where camp is made.

Day ❺: As per Marangu Route, Day ❹.

Day ❻: As per Marangu Route, Day ❺.

Note: Should you wish to save a day, it is possible to climb direct from Kikelewa Cate to Kibo Hut in about 5 to 6 hours, completing the climb in 5 days.

SHIRA ROUTE (55KM/34 MILES IN 7 DAYS)

As with the Machame Route, the strictures on the final ascent of the Western Breach have meant altering the Shira route as below. If you wish to tackle the Western Breach, make sure it's with a reputable company.

Day ❶: Londorossi gate to Mti Mkubwa (1,800–2,750m/5,904–9,020 ft.) in 3 to 4 hours

Climbers are taken to the entrance gate and then to the trail head at Lemosho Glades. From there you ascend quite steeply through the forest. Camp is made in a clearing in the forest dominated by a large tree known as Mti Mkubwa.

Day ❷: To Shira One campsite (2,750–3,500m/9,020–11,480 ft.) in about 6 hours

Continue climbing the moorland above the forest, then detour northward around the Shira ridge before dropping down onto the beautiful Shira plateau. Camp is made by a stream at Shira One campsite.

Day ❸: Shira One to Shira Hut (3,500–3,800m/11,480–12,464 ft.) in 3 hours

The trail continues across the plateau toward Kibo. After about 2 hours, the edge of the plateau is reached and the path climbs for about 40 minutes to Shira hut. It is 3 hours if the direct route is taken. However, this day affords the opportunity to branch off the trail to climb Shira Cathedral and Shira Needle and look down the Machame Ridge, or visit Cone Place, center of the extinct Shira volcano, and admire the highest parts of the Shira plateau.

Day ❹: As per Machame Route, Day ❸

Day ❺: As per Machame Route, Day ❹

Day ❻: As per Machame Route, Day ❺

Day ❼: As per Machame Route, Day ❻

4 THE COST OF CLIMBING

Climbing Kili is an expensive business, and it gets more so every year. At press time, the park fees alone were $525 for a 5-day climb, $635 for a 6-day climb, and $745 for 7-day climb. In addition, tour operators' costs cover guides, porters, equipment, transport, and catering.

It is usually easier to do a climb with a hotel specializing in climbs, as packages are all-inclusive and experienced staff guaranteed. At press time, you could expect to pay the following for the two most popular routes, which should provide a guideline. These include 2 nights' accommodation pre- and post-climb (1 night each), park fees, mountain accommodations, a guide, two porters per person (to carry max 15kg/33 lb.; if you exceed this, you will need another porter), park transfers, equipment, and food and catering on the mountain. When comparing rates, make sure that they all include the above.

Tips Saving Money on Your Climb

Besides opting for the cheapest route (Marangu), you can save money by getting a group of friends together or bringing your own sleeping bag and food and catering equipment, and catering for yourself—unless you are a serious camper, with the right gear for arctic conditions, this is worth considering on the Marangu Route, where accommodation is in huts. If you opt for this, book with the Marangu Hotel, which charges $820 for what they rather discouragingly refer to as a "hard way" climb; this includes park fees for a 5-day climb ($985 for 6 days), a guide and two porters, and hut bookings. This rate is for a single climber; the per-person rate is reduced with each additional climber. Be sure to budget for an additional porter for your guide.

Tips Tipping

Quoted rates never include tips for the guides and porters. Tipping, of course, is a discretionary matter and presupposes good service, but you are likely to be very grateful for the services rendered, so be prepared and budget accordingly. As a guideline, you can expect to pay $10 per day per guide, $8 per day per assistant guide and cook, and $5 per day for the porters. Everyone understands that single travelers and members of small groups may not be able to give as much as larger groups, whereas, with larger groups, each participant needs to contribute less while still providing a satisfactory tip ($150 per climber is about right for a 1- to 4-person group on camping climbs where crews are larger than on the Marangu Route; the amount on the Marangu Route in a small group would be closer to $100 per person). Porters are the lowest link in the food chain and, therefore, open to abuse. Please ensure that your porters are adequately looked after. To ensure that minimum working conditions are met, visit www.kiliporters.org, the website of the Kilimanjaro Porters Assistance Project, an initiative of the International Mountain Explorers Connection, a nonprofit organization based in the U.S.

THE 5-DAY MARANGU ROUTE For one climber: $1,087 (Machame Protea), $1,172 (Springlands), $1,188 (Kibo Hotel), $1,440 (Marangu Hotel).

For two climbers: $1,021 Machame Protea, $1,122 Springlands, $1,158 Kibo Hotel, $1,295 Marangu Hotel, $1,395 Kilemakyaro Mountain Lodge.

For three climbers: $1,010 Machame Protea, $1,013 Kibo Hotel, $1,122 Springlands, $1,230 Marangu Hotel, $1,335 Kilemakyaro Mountain Lodge.

An extra day could cost between $165 and $230, depending on the hotel and number of climbers.

THE 6-DAY MACHAME ROUTE For one climber: $1,400 Machame Protea, $1,447 Springlands, $1,698 Kibo Hotel, $2,040 Marangu Hotel.

For two climbers: $1,370 Machame Protea, $1,397 Springlands, $1,643 Kibo Hotel, $1,955 Marangu Hotel, $1,850 Kilemakyaro Mountain Lodge.

For three climbers: $1,365 Machame Protea, $1,397 Springlands, $1,493 Kibo Hotel, $1,800 Marangu Hotel, $1,905 (Kilemakyaro Mountain Lodge).

An extra day could cost between $175 and $250, depending on the hotel and number of climbers.

5 RECOMMENDED OPERATORS

The number of mountain operators has multiplied dramatically in recent years—faster than the number of skilled experienced guides coming up through the ranks, so it's advisable to stick to a company with an established track record.

Chagga Tours LTD Chagga Tours was founded by mountain guide Michael Nelson Ntiyu of Tanzania and investor-hiker Christina Helbig of Germany. Michael, a Chagga who grew up on the mountain, has successfully guided hundreds of groups up the mountain (he has also climbed Mt. Everest) and is very attuned to the needs of climbers. Christina Helbig climbed with him twice and was so impressed by his leadership skills that she decided to build a tour company with him. Tours are not just mountain treks but can include stops at the cultural achievements of the Chagga, like the irrigation canals, built hundreds of years ago, which seem to flow uphill, and the terraced cultivation of plants in the Chagga farmlands. www.chagga-tours.com.

Marangu Hotel The family-run Marangu Hotel offered the first commercial climbs from their farmhouse in the 1930s, and their most senior guides have been working with the hotel for more than 40 years. Their climbs are not the cheapest (though they are certainly competitive), but they provide highly professional service with experienced guides and porters who queue up to work here (Marangu Hotel is a partner with the Kilimanjaro Porters Assistance Project). You have to stay at the Marangu Hotel to utilize their climbs; see p. 449. www.maranguhotel.com.

Nature Discovery This highly ethical company has been climbing since 1992 and focuses on top-end personalized expeditions. Kili climbs are only via the Machame and Shira routes and include the Western Breach ascent, with all safety precautions. Their cooks are said to be the best on the mountain, and their equipment is tip-top, from the modern mountaineering tents with ground sheets and cold-weather sleeping mats to large mess tents furnished with aluminum tables and chairs (with backs and armrests) and sanitary portable flush toilets inside enclosed tents. All guides are fluent in English and receive ongoing training. Their camping and lodge safaris are also highly rated. www.naturediscovery.com.

Hoopoe Adventure Tours The eco-friendly Hoopoe Safaris (now merged with Tropical Trails) is known for its semi-luxury safaris under canvas in Tanzania's National Parks. It also offers high-quality Kili climbs, with thick foam mattresses for all the igloo tents, a toilet tent, mess tent complete with tables and chairs, and high-frequency two-way radios for communication with base. Packages include overnight stays at The Arusha Hotel, the best hotel in Arusha center. www.hoopoe.com.

Jo Anderson Safaris Jo Anderson is a keen botanist who, after 50 climbs, is well versed on Kili flora and has three guides trained to do what he does so well: making the journey as special as the arrival at the summit. Safety is a top priority, and his team carries oxygen, a high-altitude pressure chamber, and a full wilderness medical kit on every climb. All support staff have first-aid qualifications and practical experience in wilderness first-aid. Flowers bloom at different times, but March through May is great for some (low season on the mountain), as is September and October. For more information on the best times to climb with Kili flora in bloom, contact him at jo@jo-anderson.com.

Zara Tours Owned by the dynamic Zainab, Zara Tours has been cornering the budget market for 2 decades and is, in this sense, by far the most successful outfit in Moshi, proudly claiming to put more people on the summit than anyone else. And Zara does offer a very competitive package, including airport transfers and 2 nights at their hotel (Springlands, p. 451), with add-on tours elsewhere in Tanzania, though again, these are very much focused on the budget mass end of the market. You do not need to stay at Springlands to utilize Zara Tours, but it makes sense to, given that the accommodation is also geared toward saving money. www.zaratours.com.

6 OTHER EXCURSIONS

KILIMANJARO FOOTHILLS

A number of Cultural Tourism Programmes in which visitors are taken by a local guide to meet villagers and understand their traditional way of life were set up with the assistance of Dutch agency SNV a few years back. Most are around Arusha, but there are also a few in Marangu and Moshi that enable visitors to explore the lower foothills of the mountain while gaining some insight into the traditional lifestyle and culture of the Chagga (the local residents of the mountain) while simultaneously benefiting the local community, thanks to the presence of a local guide. To find out more, type in the unbelievably long www.tourismwebservices.com/dev/TCTP/index.php?option=com_frontpage&Itemid=1, or visit the Tanzania Cultural Tourism Programmes offices in the Museum Buildings on Boma Road in Arusha (see chapter 15 for Arusha tourism office details).

There are number of guided walks worth considering, the best of which is a trip to the **Kuringe Waterfall,** located beyond the village of Materuni, 15km (9¼ miles) from Moshi—though this requires a half-day commitment to reach it, it is well worth the time. You could also extend this into a full-day excursion, walking through the cultivated fields of subsistence farmers to visit a Chagga homestead on the lower slopes of Kilimanjaro, where you stop for lunch, then spend the afternoon exploring the Rau Forest (**www.akarotours.com**). If you don't have a full day at your disposal, there are a few waterfalls within walking distance of most Marangu lodgings—if pressed for time, give the pretty 15m-high (49-ft.) Kinukamori Waterfall a miss and head instead for the more impressive **Kilasia Waterfall,** with its 30m (98-ft.) drop into an attractive pool surrounded by lush vegetation, said to be safe for swimming ($4; kilasiawaterfalls@yahoo.com). Protea Machame offers picnic trips to Kukuletwa Hot Springs, a natural spring whose warm water invites a dip. Dedicated safari lovers may want to schedule a visit to Mweka College of Wildlife Management (or pop in after descending the Machame or Shira routes, Mweka being their finishing point)—most of the best local safari guides are graduates of this respected tertiary establishment, and a small wildlife museum is attached to the college.

FARTHER AFIELD

An hour to 90 minutes' drive away, on the Kenyan border, **Lake Chala** is a small crater lake, beautiful but with an eerily desolate air. A number of operators offer picnic excursions here, and the views of the lake—an intense and unsettling turquoise color, rimmed by verdant green cliffs—are spectacular. Don't be tempted to take a dip—in 2002, a hapless British tourist, unaware that crocodiles lurk in its attractive depths, couldn't resist and never lived to tell the tale. A lodge has been under construction here for years, and the abandoned structures only add to the eerie atmosphere. Most lodgings offer day trips to Chala; rates vary on distance covered. Keen birders should also consider a trip to **Lake Jipe,** a 16km-long (10-mile) shallow alkaline lake that shares a border with Kenya. You can book these excursions through your lodging.

17

The Southern Circuit

by Philip Briggs

Were they relocated to practically any other African country, the diverse cluster of national parks and game reserves set in the scrubby southeast Tanzanian lowlands and lush Lake Tanganyika hinterland would form the cornerstone of a national tourist industry. As it is, however, the fine reserves of the southern and western safari circuits inhabit the same country as the Serengeti, Ngorongoro Crater, Lake Manyara, Mount Kilimanjaro, Zanzibar, and other big names of the Northern Circuit, and they are overshadowed by them completely. The Southern Circuit attracts a tiny fraction—recent statistics suggest as few as 1%—of tourists who visit Tanzania.

So much the better for those adventurous souls who forsake the well-trodden attractions of the northern safari circuit and instead head south. For here they will find the most untrammeled safari circuit of comparable quality anywhere in Africa—a complex of parks and reserves whose combined area of more than 77,000 sq. km (30,030 sq. miles) is serviced by a mere two dozen exclusive bush camps boasting the collective bed capacity of the average urban Hilton or Sheraton.

The centerpiece of the south, the immense Selous, is the largest game reserve in Africa, and it offers a more varied menu of activities than any northern reserve, with motorboat trips on the mighty Rufiji River, expertly guided walks, and wild fly-camping expeditions supplementing the more standard fare of twice-daily game drives. In pure game-viewing terms, Selous takes second place to Ruaha National Park, a rugged baobab-studded thirstland notable for its high predator densities and unusually varied selection of antelope and other ungulates.

The area has two other fine safari destinations in the form of Mikumi and Katavi National Parks, whereas the Mahale Mountains and Gombe Stream, set on the scenic shores of Lake Tanganyika, offer the world's best wild chimpanzee viewing. More esoteric attractions include the forested slopes of the Udzungwa Mountains, home to a dazzling array of endemic birds and mammals, and the brooding island-bound ruins of Kilwa Kisiwani, relics of the most important medieval gold trading center anywhere along the Swahili Coast.

1 SELOUS GAME RESERVE

The largest game reserve in Africa, Selous extends over 45,530 sq. km (17,757 sq. miles) of southeastern Tanzania, at the core of the thrice-larger Selous-Niassa ecosystem, which also incorporates Mikumi and Udzungwa National Parks, the swampy Kilombero Game Protected Area, the 37,660-sq.-km (14,687-sq.-mile) Niassa Game Reserve in northern Mozambique, and various other protected game corridors. This vast tract of untrammeled bush supports some of the world's most prodigious wildlife, with an estimated 120,000 to 150,000 buffalo, 70,000 elephant, 50,000 puku antelope (centered mainly on Kilombero), 40,000 hippo, 8,000 sable antelope, and 4,000 lion forming what are probably the largest extant populations of these species. In addition, the 1,300 African wild dogs that roam the Selous represent at least one-quarter of the noncaptive population of this endangered canid.

To some extent, the oft-quoted statistics about Selous—a game reserve four times larger than the Serengeti and twice as large as Switzerland—flatter to deceive. What the marketing folk generally neglect to mention is that 95% of this vast reserve is actually carved into hunting concessions and leased exclusively to private operators. This means that ordinary photographic safaris have access only to the relatively small portion of the Selous north of the Rufiji River, and all the camps and lodges catering to the general public lie within a few hours' drive of each other, making for a somewhat less exclusive experience than if they were more widely scattered.

All the same, coming from the likes of the central Serengeti or Masai Mara, the Selous does come across as refreshingly untrammeled. More significant for tourists, it offers perhaps the most varied range of activities of any safari destination in the region—not just game drives, but boat excursions on the wide and sluggish Rufiji, Tanzania's largest river, as well as guided bush walks and fly-camping on the lakes, activities that are forbidden in most of the region's savannah national parks. Furthermore, whereas the Northern Circuit of Tanzania is dominated by large impersonal lodges that feel removed from their wilderness surroundings, accommodation in the Selous is uniformly down-to-earth, consisting of around half a dozen exclusive eco-friendly small camps.

Game drives in the Selous focus on a labyrinthine complex of five lakes and interconnecting channels fed by the Rufiji. Elephant, buffalo, giraffe, impala, common waterbuck, bushbuck, wildebeest, eland, greater kudu, and zebra are all common here, but the area is less reliable for big cats than many other reserves. Leopards are present but shy, while cheetahs haven't been recorded in the pubic part of the reserve in decades. Lions, by contrast, are very common, typically darker than average and with scragglier manes, and chances of seeing a kill are good during the dry season, when prides wait in the shady lake verges and pounce opportunistically on any thirsty animal that strays close by. Another plus is the high probability of spotting a pack of African wild dog, especially during the denning season from June to August.

For many, the highlights of a Selous safari are boat trips along the Rufiji, its muddy waters populated by high densities of crocodiles and hippos. Elephant, buffalo, and giraffe regularly come to drink at the riverbank, which is lined with tall borassus palms, and the birdlife is fantastic, ranging from shorebirds such as yellow-billed stork and African skimmer, to the fish eagles and palmnut vultures that perch high in the riverine trees, to the colorful bee-eaters and kingfishers that nest seasonally along the mud banks. Guided game walks are even more thrilling, offering a good chance of encountering the likes of elephant and lion on foot, but the ultimate Selous experience—offered by all camps, ideally by advance arrangement—is fly-camping on the lakeshore, separated from the surrounding bush by little more than a mosquito net.

The northern Selous was first proclaimed as a reserve in 1905, a gift from Kaiser Wilhelm of Germany to his wife, leading to its Swahili nickname of *Shamba la Bibi* (Field of the Wife). It was later named after Frederick Courtney Selous (pronounced "sel-*oo*"), a British-born professional hunter who died in battle in the 1917 Battle of the Bundu that took place there between German and British troops during World War I. Five years after Selous's death, the reserve was extended south of the Rufiji, and it attained

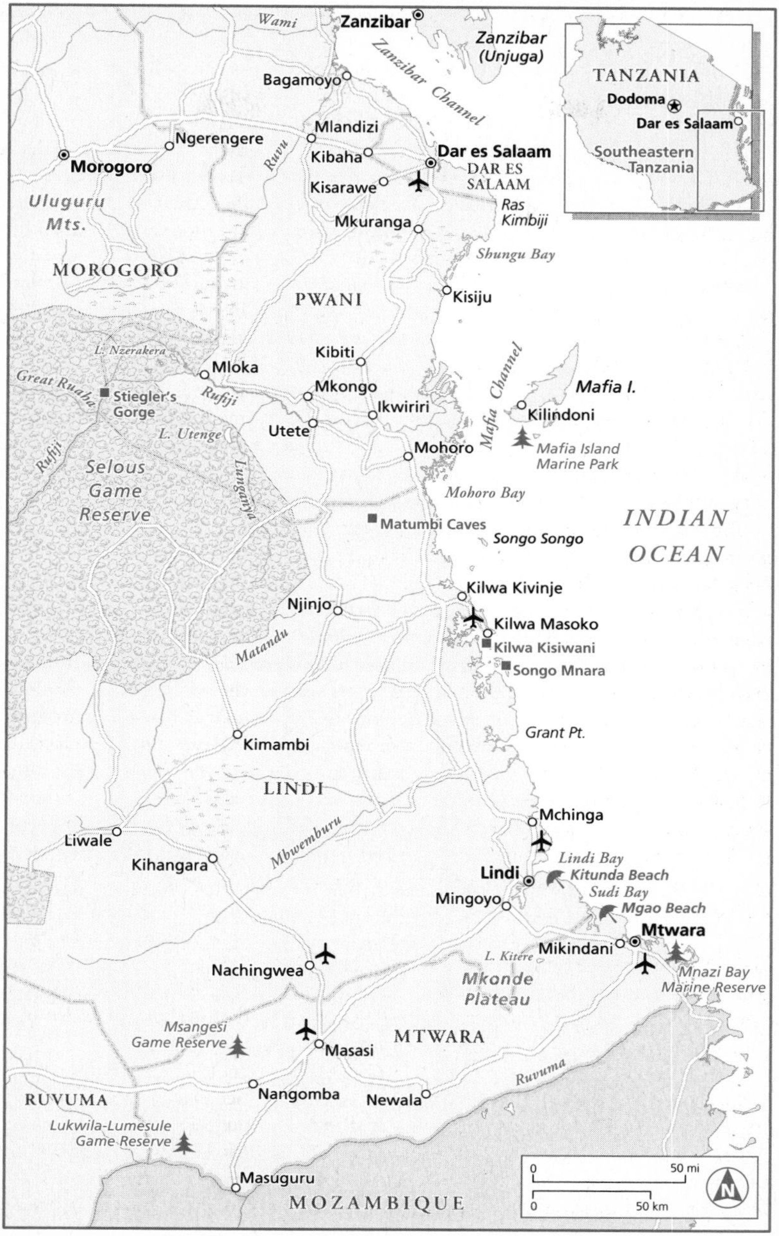

Wami
Zanzibar
Zanzibar (Unjuga)
Zanzibar Channel
Bagamoyo
Mlandizi
Ngerengere
Morogoro
Ruvu
Kibaha
Dar es Salaam
DAR ES SALAAM
Kisarawe
Uluguru Mts.
Ras Kimbiji
Mkuranga
Shungu Bay
MOROGORO
PWANI
Kisiju
L. Nzerakera
Kibiti
Mloka
Great Ruaha
Stiegler's Gorge
Rufiji
Mkongo
Mafia Channel
Mafia I.
Ikwiriri
Kilindoni
Utete
L. Utenge
Mohoro
Mafia Island Marine Park
Rufiji
Selous Game Reserve
Lunganya
Mohoro Bay
Matumbi Caves
INDIAN OCEAN
Songo Songo
Kilwa Kivinje
Njinjo
Kilwa Masoko
Kilwa Kisiwani
Matandu
Songo Mnara
Grant Pt.
Kimambi
LINDI
Mchinga
Liwale
Lindi Bay
Kihangara
Mbwemburu
Lindi
Kitunda Beach
Sudi Bay
Mingoyo
Mgao Beach
Mtwara
Mikindani
L. Kitere
Nachingwea
Mkonde Plateau
Mnazi Bay Marine Reserve
Msangesi Game Reserve
Masasi
MTWARA
Ruvuma
Nangomba
Newala
RUVUMA
Lukwila-Lumesule Game Reserve
Masuguru
MOZAMBIQUE
0 50 mi
0 50 km
N

TANZANIA
Dodoma
Dar es Salaam
Southeastern Tanzania

its present size and shape in the 1940s, when the colonial government evacuated the area to curb a sleeping sickness epidemic. Selous Game Reserve became a UNESCO World Heritage Site in 1982.

ESSENTIALS

VISITOR INFORMATION An entrance fee of $50 per person per 24 hours is levied. Internal roads often become impassable toward the end of the rainy season, and most camps close during April and May.

GETTING THERE & AROUND **By Air** Game drives and other activities are included in the standard rate offered by all Selous's camps, which means that the simplest and most popular option is to fly down from Dar es Salaam or elsewhere. The main flight operators are **Coastal Aviation** (www.coastal.cc) and **Safari Air Link** (www.safariaviation.info), both of which offer flights as charters or as part of all-inclusive packages.

By Car It is also possible to visit Selous on a road safari from Dar es Salaam, but it is a long, bumpy trip that consumes at least half a day in either direction, and there are few advantages to driving unless you also want to visit Kilwa and the south coast.

If you do drive, the most direct route is the 240km (149 miles) easterly road via Kibiti and Mloka to Mtemere Gate, which typically takes about 6 hours. However, if you are combining a Selous safari with other southern reserves such as Mikumi or Ruaha National Parks, then the best road for making these connections runs for 140km (87 miles) between the Morogoro town to Matembwe Gate via Mkuyuni and Kisaki. Recommended operators for road safaris are **Kearsley's** (www.kearsleys.com), **Hippo Tours** (www.hippotours.com), and **Authentic Tanzania** (www.authentictanzania.com).

WHERE TO STAY & DINE

The Selous is serviced by a growing number of camps, all of which are small and personalized, with a real bush atmosphere. In addition to the established places listed below, two new camps are currently scheduled to open in the far west of the reserve and should be worth a look. These are the 12-room **Mivumo River Lodge** (www.malalaluxurylodges.com), overlooking the Rufiji panhandle at the entrance to Stiegler's Gorge, and the luxurious 12-room **Amara Selous** (www.amara-tanzania.com), on the banks of the Great Ruaha before its confluence with the Rufiji.

Beho Beho Camp ★★★ This is one of the oldest lodges in the Selous, and following extensive renovations, it is also perhaps the most overtly luxurious. Set in the footslopes of the Beho Beho Hills, it is one of the few lodges without a riverine location, a negative in terms of intimate wilderness atmosphere, but compensated for by the breezy hillside climate, stunning views over the plains to Lake Tagalala, and the plentiful wildlife that congregates at a nearby waterhole. Another plus associated with the camp's location is its remoteness from other camps. This means that few tourist vehicles cover the same ground on game drives, which generally focus on Lakes Tagalala and Manze. Nervous first-time safarigoers generally find the stone cottages here more reassuring than the tented accommodation at most other camps in the Selous. The spacious cottages are attractively decorated in faux-colonial style, and the common areas also exude Edwardian elegance. Game walks and boat trips on crocodile-infested Lake Tagalala are offered, and the lodge lies close the grave of the reserve's namesake, Frederick Courtney Selous.

P.O. Box 2261, Dar es Salaam. ✆ **022/260-0352.** www.behobeho.com. 8 rooms. $1,400 double full board. Rate includes all activities. MC, V. **Amenities:** Restaurant; bar; pool. *In room:* A/C.

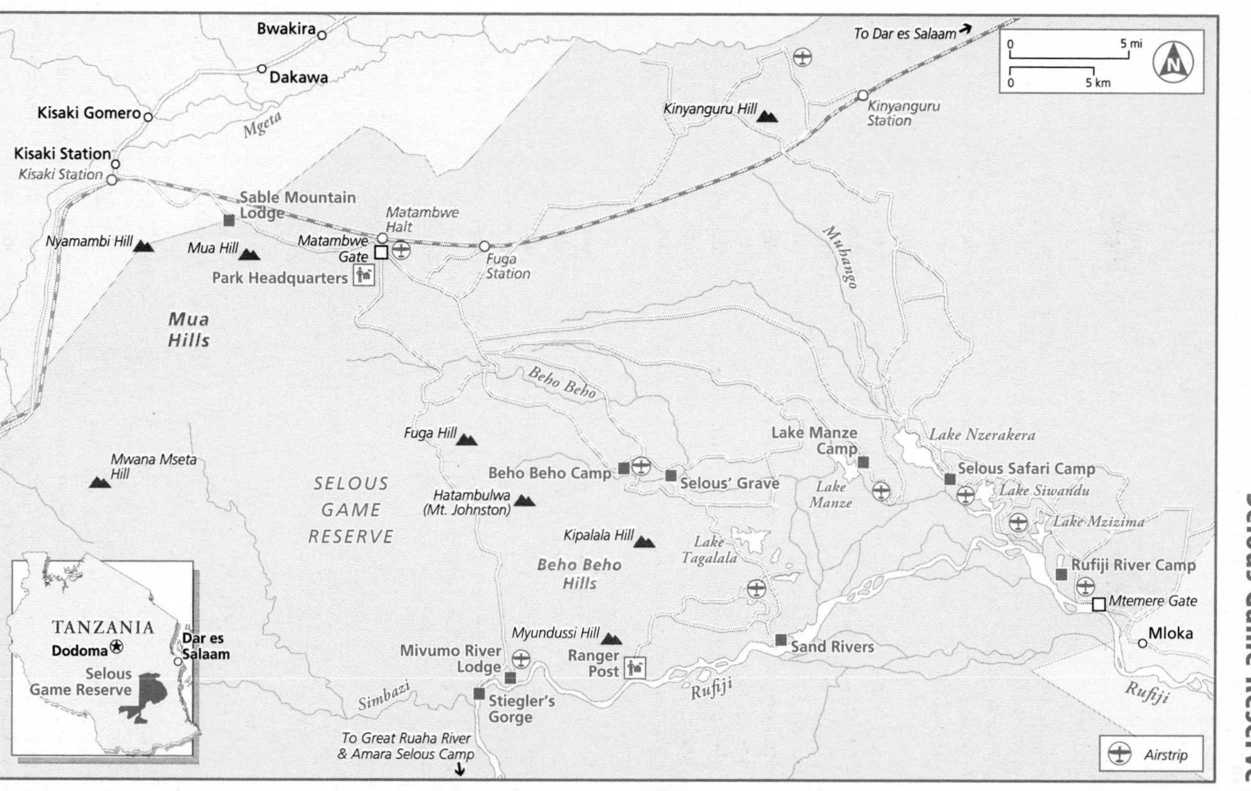
Bwakira
Dakawa
Kisaki Gomero
Kisaki Station
Kisaki Station
Mgeta
Sable Mountain Lodge
Matambwe Halt
Matambwe Gate
Nyamambi Hill
Mua Hill
Fuga Station
Park Headquarters
Mua Hills
To Dar es Salaam
0 5 mi
0 5 km
Kinyanguru Hill
Kinyanguru Station
Muhango
Beho Beho
Fuga Hill
Mwana Mseta Hill
SELOUS GAME RESERVE
Beho Beho Camp
Selous' Grave
Hatambulwa (Mt. Johnston)
Kipalala Hill
Beho Beho Hills
Lake Manze Camp
Lake Manze
Lake Nzerakera
Selous Safari Camp
Lake Siwandu
Lake Mzizima
Lake Tagalala
Rufiji River Camp
Mtemere Gate
Mloka
TANZANIA
Dodoma
Dar es Salaam
Selous Game Reserve
Myundussi Hill
Mivumo River Lodge
Ranger Post
Sand Rivers
Simbazi
Stiegler's Gorge
Rufiji
Rufiji
To Great Ruaha River & Amara Selous Camp
Airstrip

Lake Manze Camp ★ One of the newer options in Selous, this delightfully rustic small camp opened in 2007 on the palm-fringed shores of Lake Manze, a beautiful location that supports a rich and varied fauna, including innumerable hippos and elephants, and is regularly visited by African wild dog. It has an exposed bush atmosphere aimed at those who want to truly immerse themselves in the wilderness experience—as such, it might seem a little daunting to nervous first-time safarigoers. The no-frills standing tents all have double or twin beds with walk-in netting, a private stone balcony, and an en suite solar-powered hot shower, but otherwise no electricity. The large thatched lounge, with a library, charging points for cameras, and views to the hippo- and croc-infested lake, has an open feel in keeping with the accommodation.

P.O. Box 40569, Dar es Salaam. ✆ **022/245-2005.** www.adventurecampstz.com. 12 units. Low season $610 double; high season $670 double. Rates include all meals and activities. MC, V. **Amenities:** Restaurant; bar; intermittent satellite Internet access by request.

Rufiji River Camp ★ The oldest permanent accommodation in the Selous is the ever-popular Rufiji River Camp, which was operated by its Italian founders until late 2008, when it was bought out by the Fox family, who also operate long-standing lodges in Ruaha, Katavi, and Mikumi. The focus here is on a comfortable but relatively affordable wildlife experience rather than the overt luxury offered by pricier lodges, and that is unlikely to change under the new management, though a program of upgrades is currently underway and will include relocating 6 of the 20 tents to a discreet second camp about a mile farther upriver. Situated at the eastern extremity of the reserve, the camp overlooks a hypnotic stretch of the Rufiji River, and all tents offer a view of the riverside action, which is dominated by hippos, crocs, and elephants. The en suite standing tents are protected by thatch roofs and have twin or double beds with walk-in netting, solar-heated water and electricity, and a private veranda. There's a swimming pool, too.

P.O. Box 10270, Dar es Salaam. ✆ **0784/23-7422.** www.rufijirivercamp.com. 20 units (soon to be split across two camps). Low season $550 double; high season $640. Rates include all meals and activities. MC, V. **Amenities:** Restaurant; bar; satellite Internet (in main structure); pool.

Sable Mountain Lodge ★ This small and affordable camp has a hillside location about 1 mile outside Matembwe Gate on the reserve's western boundary. There are eight stone cottages and five tented rooms, all with en suite hot shower and toilet, and 24-hour electricity fed by solar power. It lies in an area characterized by dense miombo woodland inhabited by black-and-white colobus monkey, checkered elephant-shrew, and many forest birds. It is also the one public part of Selous where the handsome sable antelope is sometimes seen, most often in November and December. The camp has two dining areas, a large swimming pool fed by spring water, and a treehouse overlooking a waterhole that's regularly visited by buffalo and elephant. Game drives concentrate on the plains north of the main cluster of lodges, which can be very worthwhile seasonally, with very few other vehicles around. Fly-camping is also available, as are boat trips on the Mbega River during the wet season.

P.O. Box 40525, Dar es Salaam. ✆ **022/211-0507.** www.selouslodge.com. 13 units. $290 stone cottage double; $350 luxury tent double; $390 luxury tent honeymoon suite. All rates full board; add $300 double for activities to be included. V. **Amenities:** Restaurant; bar; limited Internet; pool.

Sand Rivers ★★★ Perched dramatically above a wide, sandy bend in the Rufiji, this exclusive camp has an isolated location southwest of the other camps and wonderful in-house game viewing, with hippos grunting in the foreground, massive crocodiles lining the sandbanks, and elephants regularly coming down to drink. Accommodation is in spacious open-fronted cottages with stone walls, a thatched roof, and a stilted wooden floor that extends to a wide deck above the riverbank. Rooms all have king-size beds with walk-in netting, pastel-shaded cloth seating, and wooden furnishings. In addition to the five luxurious standard units, there are two suites with private plunge pools, as well as Rhino House, which offers private dining, too. Walking safaris are the main activity at Sand Rivers, which is known for its high standard of guiding, but game drives are also offered in a part of the reserve that sees little other tourist traffic and supports a large number of rhinos. It is the only lodge offering boat trips through Stiegler's Gorge, home to leopard and black-and-white colobus monkey. A recently opened sister lodge called Kiba Point, catering to families or groups of friends, consists of four cottages sleeping a total of eight and is bookable on an exclusive basis only.

P.O. Box 681, Usa River. © **022/286-5156.** www.nomad-tanzania.com. 8 units. $900–$1,900 double; $1,440–$2,030 suite; $3,500–$4,200 Rhino House; $6,000–$8,635 Kiba Point. Rates depend on season but are full board, inclusive of activities. MC, V. **Amenities:** Restaurant; bar; pool. *In room:* A/C.

Selous Safari Camp ★★★ Situated in a lush palm forest alongside Lake Nzerakera, this classic luxury bush camp maintains a highly personalized atmosphere by splitting accommodations into separate North and South Camps, consisting of only six and seven tents, respectively. Each camp is a self-contained entity, dominated by a fabulous stilted treehouse-like dining area; bar and lounge offering far-reaching views over the lake; and its own swimming pool, kitchen, host, and game-viewing activities. The stilted tents are widely spaced and have front and back verandas offering shady outdoor seating at all times of day, king-size beds with walk-in netting, ceiling fan, en suite hot bath, and outdoor shower. The camp is well positioned for game viewing, with plenty of wildlife wandering through, and the usual Selous cocktail of guided drives, walks, and boat trips on offer.

P.O. Box 1192, Dar es Salaam. © **022/212-8485.** www.selous.com. 13 units in 2 camps. Low season $1,040 double; high season $1,440 double. Rates include all meals and activities. AE, MC, V. **Amenities:** Restaurant; bar; limited Internet access; pool.

2 KILWA & THE SOUTH COAST

Stretching for almost 650km (403 miles) between Dar es Salaam and the Rovuma River on the Mozambican border, the south coast of Tanzania has all the attributes one would expect of a tropical Indian Ocean idyll. There are endless white beaches lined with tall swaying palms, offshore reefs writhing with brightly colored fish, remote islands whose fisherfolk inhabitants cross to and from the mainland in dhows with billowing white sails, and any number of time-warped Swahili ports evoking the area's long history of maritime trade. Indeed, it could be argued that the most significant difference between the remote south coast of Tanzania and the better-known beach resorts of Zanzibar and Mombasa is simply a lack of publicity and the longstanding absence of anything resembling a conventional tourist infrastructure.

The south coast has long been a rewarding destination for travelers tolerant of challenging on-the-ground conditions. But this situation is slowly changing. The recent upgrade of the main road connecting Dar es Salaam to the Mozambican border (all but 48km/30 miles of which is now paved) has greatly improved access to the region, and there are also scheduled flights to Mtwara, the country's largest and most southerly port. Furthermore, the last few years have seen the opening of several new upper-midrange lodges aimed squarely at tourists, especially in the small towns of Kilwa Masoko and Mikindani.

For the architecturally and historically minded, the most worthwhile target along the south coast is Kilwa Kisiwani, which can easily be incorporated into a road safari to Selous. This small offshore island houses the most important ruins anywhere along the Swahili Coast of East Africa, the relic of a medieval gold-trading emporium described as "one of the most beautiful and well-constructed towns in the world" by the 14th-century globetrotter Ibn Buttata. The island lies directly opposite the well-facilitated mainland port of Kilwa Masoko, a crossing that takes about 10 minutes by motorboat, or anywhere from 15 to 60 minutes by dhow, depending on wind conditions.

From the mid–13th to early 16th century, Kilwa Kisiwani (literally "Kilwa on the Island") stood at the hub of a gold-trading network that linked the gold fields of the present-day Zimbabwean interior to Arabia and Asia. The decline of Kilwa was triggered by the Portuguese sacking of 1505 and sealed by the culinary attentions of the cannibalistic Zimba in 1587. Yet the haunted ruins that remain more than 4 centuries later form a peerless and compelling example of medieval Swahili architecture, one inscribed as Tanzania's second UNESCO World Heritage Site in 1981, yet still almost totally neglected by the tourist industry.

An imposing partially collapsed fort, known locally as the Gereza, dominates the shoreward side of Kilwa Kisiwani. This is a relatively modern building, built around 1800 during a brief Omani occupation of the island. A short footpath uphill leads from here to the main ruins, which include several mosques and palaces, as well as the ornately carved tombs of a succession of powerful sultans. The centerpiece of the old city, today as it was 7 centuries ago, is the Great Mosque, whose exquisite multidomed roof, supported by bays of precisely hewn arches, stands as the apex of medieval Swahili architectural aspirations. Ten minutes away, the cliff-top Husuni Kubwa (literally "Big House") was once the palace of the Sultan of Kilwa, and its sprawling floor plan includes a swimming pool and sunken audience court.

Back on the mainland, Kilwa Masoko (Kilwa of the Market), serviced by a quartet of fairly new tourist resorts, is the obvious base for exploring. From here, it is also possible to arrange diving and snorkeling excursions into the reefs of the Songo Songo Archipelago, where Songo Mnara Island has some well-preserved ruins contemporaneous with those on Kilwa Kisiwani. Also worth a visit, about 16km (10 miles) away by road, Kilwa Kivinje (Kilwa of the Casuarina Trees) is an atmospherically time-warped fishing village dotted with crumbling Omani and German mansions built during its 19th-century heyday as the terminus of the slave caravan route to Lake Niassa.

What limited tourist development exists south of Kilwa is centered on Mikindani, a sleepy Swahili port whose narrow alleys lined with two-story 19th-century homesteads evoke a far greater sense of place than the larger town of Mtwara, only 10km (6¼ miles) to its south. Literally "Place of Palm Trees," Mikindani was the starting point of the final ill-fated expedition into the African interior led by Dr. David Livingstone, who described it as "the finest port on the coast" but was rather less enamored of its "wretched" inhabitants. It is a beautifully sited port, home to a British nonprofit organization called Trade Aid, which funds community projects through sustainable ecotourism centered on the restored German Boma, and a diving center called eco2 that offers diving and snorkeling expeditions in the remote but ecologically pristine Mnazi Bay–Ruvuma Estuary Marine Park on the Mozambican border.

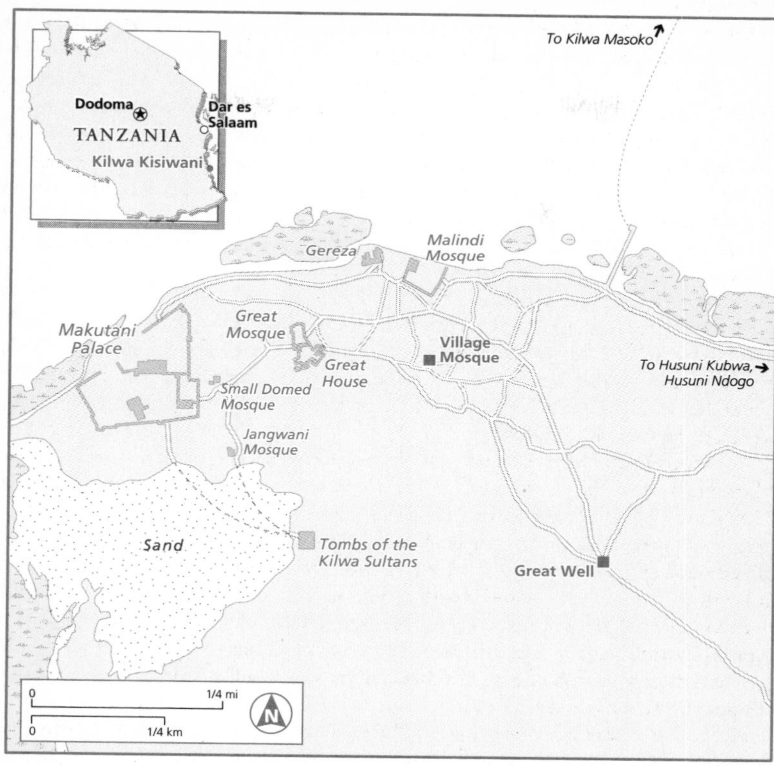

ESSENTIALS

VISITOR INFORMATION The Old Boma operates a very useful website, **www.mikindani.com**, with up-to-date information about getting there from Dar es Salaam, and other practicalities.

GETTING THERE & AROUND Both Kilwa and Mikindani are most easily reached by air from Dar es Salaam, though, oddly, there are no scheduled connecting flights between the two. **Coastal Aviation** ($130 one-way; www.coastal.cc) operates a daily return flight between Dar es Salaam and Kilwa Masoko, stopping at Mafia or continuing to Zanzibar by request. **Precision Air** (✆ **022/286-0701;** www.precisionairtz.com; about $140 one-way) flies a few times a week between Dar es Salaam and Mtwara, as does the less reliable **Air Tanzania (022/211-8411;** www.airtanzania.com), placing you less than 10 miles from Mikindani. Taxis usually meet incoming flights at Mtwara but not at Kilwa Masoko, though the safest bet in both cases is to prearrange a transfer with your hotel. If you fly down, there is no need to involve a safari operator unless you actively want to—by prior arrangement, your lodge will be able to arrange all transport and activities on the ground.

Any safari operator can tag a visit to Kilwa onto a road safari to Selous Game Reserve or set up a standalone road trip there. Kilwa lies about 290km (180 miles) south of Dar es Salaam along a road that is newly surfaced for all but 48km (30 miles). The drive should take 4 to 5 hours in a private vehicle. You don't need a 4×4 unless you are coming from Selous, which is a perfectly feasible drive of at least 4 hours, depending on which camp you leave from. Self-drivers should note that Kilwa Masoko is not on the main coastal road, but is reached along a good 11km (6¾-mile) side road branching left at Nangurukuru. Mikindani is another 260km (161 miles)—at least 3 hours—south of Kilwa along a mostly good road passing through the more substantial port of Lindi.

WHERE TO STAY & DINE

You won't find five-star resorts in this remote part of Tanzania, but the situation is greatly improved from a few years back, when accommodations options were limited to a few basic local guesthouses. Standalone restaurants remain somewhat thin on the ground, but all the lodges mentioned below serve adequate to good meals, with seafood being something of a specialty.

In addition to the options reviewed below, there are two good midrange hotels in Kilwa Masoko. The 12-room **Kilwa Seaview Resort** (© **022/265-0250;** www.kilwa.net; $90 double B&B) is an attractive beachfront lodge with accommodation in spacious en suite bungalows with tall *makuti* roofs, a good restaurant, and camping space ($5 per person). Farther out of town, **Kilwa Dreams** (© **0784/58-5330;** www.kilwadreams.com; $60 double B&B) is a small owner-managed lodge with an isolated location offering accommodation in seven blue seafront cottages on Pwani Beach. In Mikindani, **Ten Degrees South** (© **0746/85-5833;** www.tendegreessouth.com; $60 double B&B) is a pleasant waterfront lodge whose English owner-manager also runs the eco2 diving center and plans to build a new self-catering lodge on a hilltop plot overlooking the bay.

Kilwa Ruins Lodge ★ Catering first and foremost to anglers but also well placed to explore the area's historical attractions, this is the smartest lodge in Kilwa, standing immediately outside Kilwa Masoko on a lovely swimming beach with views across to Kilwa Kisiwani. Charter boats are available for fishing and other expeditions, as is a variety of watersports equipment. It is comfortable rather than luxurious, with an attractive swimming pool and dining area on the beachfront. Three types of en suite air-conditioned accommodation are available. The mahogany-clad fishing bungalows are rather cramped but have sea-facing verandas. More spacious are the two-bedroom beach bungalows and deluxe six-person beach chalets.

P.O. Box 44, Kilwa Masoko. © **0785/97-2960.** www.kilwaruinslodge.com. 14 rooms. One-bedroom fishing bungalows; $160 full-board double; 2-bedroom beach bungalows $240 full-board double; beach chalets $280 double. All rates include a free transfer from Kilwa airport and complimentary laundry. No credit cards at press time. **Amenities:** Restaurant; bar; airport transfers; pool. *In room:* A/C.

Kimbilio ★ The newest lodge in Kilwa, this place opened in 2008 practically next door to the Kilwa Ruins Resort, and it has a similarly attractive beachfront setting on the outskirts of Kilwa Masoko. It offers simple but very comfortable accommodation in *makuti* beachfront huts with netting, positioned to take advantage of the natural ventilation. The Italian manager is a qualified chef; the seafood and pasta dishes are superb. The only diving operation in Kilwa operates out of this lodge (though it is open to guests at other hotels), and fishing trips and Kilwa Kisiwani excursions to the ruins are offered.

P.O. Box 86, Kilwa Masoko. © **0787/03-4621.** www.kimbiliolodges.com. 6 rooms. $120 double B&B; $180 full board double. No credit cards at press time. **Amenities:** Restaurant; bar; Wi-Fi (when satellite connection is working). *In room:* A/C (1 room).

The Old Boma ★★ The most atmospheric lodge on the south coast, the Old Boma is housed in the former German Boma (administrative building) in Mikindani, built in 1895 on Bismarck Hill, a few hundred meters from the harbor and main road. This handsome colonial building remained in service into the late colonial era, first as the regional administrative headquarters, then as a police station, but it was allowed to fall into disrepair in the 1980s. In 1998, the building was leased by Trade Aid and restored to its full whitewashed colonial splendor, complete with genuine Swahili-style furnishings and a lovely garden graced by a swimming pool. The en suite rooms vary greatly in size, but all have netting, a fan, and a hot bath. There is also an excellent restaurant, with the option of eating indoors or on the attractive terrace.

P.O. Box 44, Kilwa Masoko. ✆ **0784/36-0110.** www.mikindani.com. 8 rooms. £70–£110 double B&B, depending on room size. MC, V. **Amenities:** Restaurant; bar; Internet access; pool.

3 MIKUMI & UDZUNGWA NATIONAL PARKS

These relatively underpublicized national parks both extend westward from the Selous Game Reserve, but they are otherwise very different in character. The more conventional safari destination, gazetted in 1964, Mikumi is the country's fourth-largest national park, protecting some 3,260 sq. km (1,271 sq. miles) of open grassland and wooded slopes flanking the main highway through southern Tanzania, immediately east of the small junction town after which it is named. By contrast, the 1,915-sq.-km (747-sq.-mile) Udzungwa Mountains National Park, created in 1992, protects the forested northeastern block of Tanzania's most extensive mountain range, an area known for its immense biodiversity and wealth of endemic plant and animal species.

Wildlife moves freely across the common border between Mikumi and Selous, but the two reserves are mutually inaccessible by road. However, Mikumi is easily accessed from the Tanzam Highway, and though it is seldom marketed as a standalone safari destination, it is a place to break up the long drive between Dar es Salaam and Ruaha National Park. The main game-viewing circuit loops northwest of the main road, through the Mkata Floodplain, a landscape of swaying grass and isolated trees reminiscent of the Serengeti. The floodplain supports large numbers of elephant, giraffe, buffalo, zebra, wildebeest, eland, impala, waterbuck, reedbuck, warthog, and yellow baboon, as well as healthy populations of lion and spotted hyena. Occasional transient packs of African wild dog are seen, too, whereas patches of miombo woodland harbor the impressive greater kudu and sable antelope. Among the more visible of 400-plus recorded bird species are the handsome bateleur eagle, outsized ground hornbill, and colorful lilac-breasted roller.

Spanning altitudes of 245 to 2,780m (804–9,118 ft.), Udzungwa is the largest of the Eastern Arc Mountains, a series of a dozen crystalline ranges that rise from the coastal belt of Tanzania to support East Africa's most ancient and biologically diverse forests. Although three-quarters of Udzungwa's forest cover has been chopped down over the course of the past two millennia, around 2,720 sq. km (800 sq. miles) is still intact, most of it protected within the national park or adjoining forest reserves. The forest of Udzungwa is home to several endemics (species that occur nowhere else), including two monkeys, Uhehe red colobus and Sanje crested mangabey, and several birds, of which the Udzungwa forest partridge, discovered as recently as 1991, is the most remarkable. And this list of endemics is still growing: Recent discoveries include the Matunda dwarf galago, first described in 1996, and the world's largest species of elephant shrew, first photographed in 2005; the kipunji monkey was simultaneously discovered in a forest reserve in the western Udzungwa and on the more southerly Mount Rungwe area in 2004.

For all its ecological significance, Udzungwa remains a somewhat unsung gem. There are no roads within the national park, but a network of walking trails traverses the forested eastern slopes, mostly starting at the Mang'ula entrance gate. These include the self-guided Prince Bernhard Waterfall Trail, which leads to a small but pretty waterfall less than 1 mile from the entrance gate, and offers a good chance of sighting the endemic red colobus monkey and a variety of birds, including green-headed oriole. The guided Sanje Waterfall Trail is a 4-hour round-trip hike leading to a cascade that drops about 305m (1,000 ft.) over three stages into a pool where swimming is permitted. The longest hike is the Mwanihana Trail, which ascends to the second-highest point in the range and involves camping for 2 nights in areas that offer a good chance of spotting the endemic mangabey, the rare Abbott's duiker, and larger mammals such as elephant.

ESSENTIALS

VISITOR INFORMATION An entrance fee of $20 per person per 24 hours is payable at both parks. At Udzungwa, the daily guide fee is $10 per party, and an armed ranger is required for longer hikes, costing $20 per party. For more information, visit www.udzungwa.org.

GETTING THERE & AROUND Mikumi National Park lies about 290km (180 miles) southwest of Dar es Salaam, a 3- to 4-hour drive on a fairly surfaced road that goes right past the main entrance gate. A 4×4 may be required inside the park, and internal roads may sometimes become impassable during the rainy season. Any operator in Dar es Salaam can organize a road safari to Mikumi, whether in isolation or as part of a package that also includes Ruaha. Alternatively, **Safari Air Link** (✆ **022/550-4384;** www.safariaviation.info) runs a daily shared charter flight between Dar es Salaam, Selous, and Mikumi during the high season ($160 per person).

There are no flights to Udzungwa, and accommodations close to this park are rather basic, so most tourists visit as a day trip from one of the more upmarket camps in Mikumi National Park, following the B127 south from Mikumi town to the park entrance gate at Mang'ula. The road is paved as far as Kidatu, about 35km (22 miles) south of Mikumi, but the last 24km (15 miles) to Mang'ula is quite rough—expect the drive to take around 1 hour in either direction.

WHERE TO STAY & DINE

There are two good tented camps in Mikumi National Park, both run by the Fox family and well priced by Tanzanian standards. Most people visit Udzungwa as a day trip out of Mikumi, but those who want to explore the park more thoroughly could base themselves at the **Udzungwa Mountain View Hotel** (✆ **023/262-0218;** www.genesismotel.com; $30 en suite double B&B; $5 per person camping), a decent, locally run place only 10 minutes' from walk from Mang'ula and park headquarters.

Note: Because this is the bush, in most cases, there is either no electricity in the room or a limited solar or generator supply.

Stanley's Kopje ★★ Formerly Foxes Safari Camp, this accommodation option reopened in August 2009 after being gutted by fire in 2008, and remains the top choice in Mikumi. Accommodations, set around the slopes of a rocky kopje (small hill), are in smart en suite tents set on stilted wooden platforms, sheltered by thatch canopies, and containing two king-size beds and hot showers. The swimming pool and thatched restaurant/bar stand on the top of the hill and offer panoramic views across the animal-rich Mkata Plains to the Mwanambogo dam. Unlike the other camps in Mikumi, Stanley's Kopje lies far enough from the Tanzam Highway that traffic noise doesn't disturb the tranquil bush atmosphere.

P.O. Box 10270, Tazara, Dar es Salaam. © **022/286-2357.** www.tanzaniasafaris.info. 12 units. $310–$350 double full board; $490–$510 double including all activities. MC, V. **Amenities:** Restaurant; bar; satellite Internet (in the main structure); pool.

Vuma Hills Tented Camp ★ Owned by the Foxes, the same family that runs Stanley's Kopje, this attractive camp stands on the miombo-lined Vuma Hills, a short distance southeast of the Tanzam Highway. It is a family-oriented setup, and the large standing tents, perched on stilted wooden platforms, all have one double and one single bed, en suite bathroom with hot shower, and a shaded veranda offering a fabulous view over the wooded plains below. The excellent food is made using fresh produce sourced from the nearby highlands, and there is a small swimming pool. Traffic from the main road is often audible, and the game viewing in this part of the park is rather slow compared to that of the Mkata Floodplain.

P.O. Box 10270, Tazara, Dar es Salaam. © **022/286-2357.** www.tanzaniasafaris.info. 16 units. $310–$350 double full board; $490–$510 double including all activities. MC, V. **Amenities:** Restaurant; bar; satellite Internet (in the main structure); pool.

4 RUAHA NATIONAL PARK

Ruaha is the country's largest national park, following the recent incorporation of several adjoining game reserves to double its original area to 20,540 sq. km (8,011 sq. miles). It has the wildest and most rugged feel of any Tanzanian safari destination, all semi-arid rocky slopes and baobab-studded plains, a harshly beautiful landscape alleviated by the near-perennial Great Ruaha River, which follows the park's southeast boundary for 160km (99 miles), and several small seasonal tributaries. Ruaha also offers some of the finest game viewing in the region, with large concentrations of wildlife—elephants, in particular—complemented by low tourist volumes by comparison even to Selous.

Ruaha vies with the Serengeti when it comes to large predators. Lion prides containing more than 15 individuals are a feature of the park, and leopards and cheetah are regularly seen and are generally habituated to vehicles. The park also forms the core territory for an estimated 100 African wild dogs, and though the movements of these wide-ranging animals are unpredictable, at least one pack regularly moves into the Mwagusi area; sightings are especially good in denning season in June and July. Other common carnivores include black-backed jackal and spotted hyena, and the park lies at the southern extreme of the range of the uncommon striped hyena. An estimated 12,000 elephants inhabit the greater Ruaha ecosystem, and the heftiest pair of tusks recorded in the 20th century, with a combined weight 201kg (443 lbs.), came from an individual shot in Ruaha in the 1970s.

In ecological terms, the vegetation is transitional between the southern miombo woodland and eastern savannah biomes, leading to a great floral variety reflected in the varied wildlife. It lies at the southernmost range of typical East African ungulates such as lesser kudu and Grant's gazelle, but it also hosts several species that are rare farther north, including greater kudu, roan, and sable antelope. A similar dichotomy is noted among the 450 recorded bird species, with north-central Tanzania endemics such as black-collared lovebird, ashy starling, and Tanzania red-billed hornbill occurring alongside typical southern African species such as the perpetually trilling (and very colorful) crested barbet.

Visitors driving to Ruaha might want to explore two sites of interest close to Iringa. The first is the **Isimila Stone Age Site** (entrance around $3), where a seasonal watercourse cuts through sedimentary layers deposited on the bed of a shallow lake over several thousand years before it dried out around 60,000 years ago. The site has yielded one of the world's richest assemblages of Acheulean hand axes and other stone tools, along with the fossilized bones of several extinct large mammals, including a gigantic pig, a giraffe-like ungulate with large antlers, and a hippo with telescoped projecting eyes. The site museum houses a varied selection of these finds, while nearby a scenic gully hosts several magnificently eroded sandstone pillars up to 10m (33 ft.) high.

The more recent past is evoked at the small village of **Kalenga,** set on the banks of the Ruaha along the road between Iringa and Ruaha. This was once the fortified capital of King Mkwawa, the Hehe leader who acquired legendary status in the late 19th century for his concerted resistance to German rule. Kalenga was razed by German cannon fire in 1894, but Mkwawa stayed on the loose for another 4 years, inflicting occasional guerrilla attacks on the Germans until June 1898, when his camp was surrounded by a German garrison and he shot himself in the head rather than being taken captive. Today a small site museum in the village houses several of Mkwawa's personal effects, including some of his clubs, spears, and guns, and the village is scattered with relics of Mkwawa's rule, including the remains of fortified walls and the foundations of his house. About ½km (.3 miles) from the museum is the tomb of the German Commander Erich Maas, who died in the battle of Kalenga.

ESSENTIALS

VISITOR INFORMATION In addition to the official website www.tanzaniaparks.com, the Selous Safari Company, which operates Jongomero Tented Camp, maintains a highly informative website (www.ruaha.com). An entrance fee of $20 per person, per 24 hours is levied.

GETTING THERE & AROUND As with Selous, all camps in Ruaha offer all-inclusive game packages, and the easiest way to get to them is by air. The main flight operators are **Coastal Aviation** (www.coastal.cc) and **Safari Air Link** (www.safariaviation.info), and both can fly you between Dar es Salaam or Ruaha in isolation or as part of a broader package safari package including Selous, Katavi, and/or Mahale. A minimum stay of 3 nights is recommended.

Standalone 4×4 safari packages to Ruaha are less attractive than to Selous, mainly because of the distances involved. It's a 580km (360-mile) drive from Dar es Salaam via Iringa, the last 100km (62 miles) is on rough dirt, and it will take 10 to 12 hours in either direction. Driving down makes a great deal more sense if you have about a week to spare and plan to visit Ruaha in combination with Mikumi and Udzungwa. Any safari operator in Dar es Salaam can set up a trip of this sort; I recommend **Kearsley's** (www.kearsleys.com) and **Authentic Tanzania** (www.authentictanzania.com).

WHERE TO STAY & DINE

Jongomero Tented Camp ★★ This is the most luxurious lodge in Ruaha, and it has the only swimming pool, a welcome feature in this hot climate. Accommodations are in palatial standing tents with private balconies carved into the dense woodland that

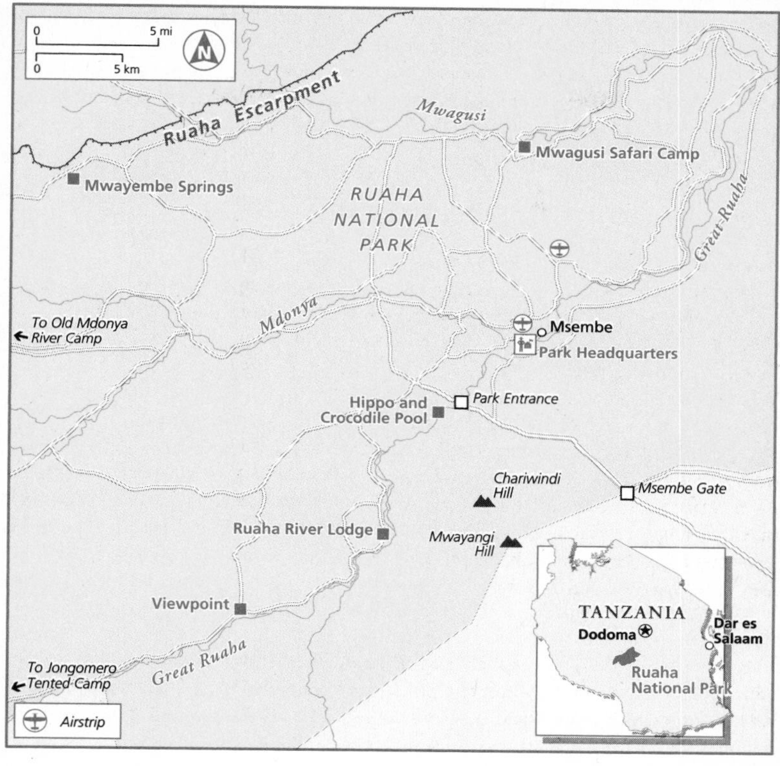

hems in the seasonal river Jongomero near its confluence with the Great Ruaha. The camp has an isolated location in the western part of the park, and the road back toward the entrance gate is good for elephant and buffalo, whereas game drives south of camp are notable for the untrammeled feel of the bush rather than great volumes of wildlife. The food is superb here, and most meals are served on the wooden deck overlooking the river, though it also has regular bush dinners.

P.O. Box 1192, Dar es Salaam ✆ **022/212-8485.** www.selous.com. 8 tents. Low season $940 double; high season $1,140. Rates include all meals and activities. AE, M, V. **Amenities:** Restaurant; bar; limited Internet access; pool.

Mwagusi Safari Camp ★★★ Not quite as luxurious as Jongomero, this owner-managed lodge on the north bank of the seasonal Mwagusi River approaches it in terms of amenities, but is totally unrivalled when it comes to its compelling bush atmosphere, high quality of guiding, and superb wildlife sightings. Accommodations are in spacious walk-in tents, strung along the riparian woodland fringing the river, and enclosed in a wood, thatch, and reed shelter. Each unit has a large bathroom with hot shower and a private balcony for game viewing (the lovely greater kudu antelope favors the riverine bush here). Attentive service and great food are the hallmarks of the bush dinners, served below the stars around a campfire in a bush clearing in the riverbed. The area is good for wild dog, lion, and leopard sightings, but sufficiently isolated from other camps so you feel you have the place to yourself. This place is one for the safari connoisseur.

15 James Rd., Whitchurch, Tavistock, Devon PL19 9NJ. ✆ **1822615721** in the U.K. www.ruaha.org. 10 tents. Rates on request but range btw. those of Jongomero and Ruaha River Lodge. **Amenities:** Restaurant; bar; pool.

Old Mdonya River Camp ★★ This low-key camp has an isolated location in the west of the park on the wooded banks of a sandy watercourse that hasn't really flowed since the Mdonya River changed course a couple of decades ago. Placing first priority on the bush experience and game viewing rather than fancy food and slick accommodation, the camp consists of 10 en suite standing tents with double or twin beds, hot showers, and a private balcony, while tasty country-style meals are eaten communally beneath the stars. The camp offers good access to the superb Mwagusi River game-viewing circuit, wonderful woodland birding, and plenty of wildlife passes through, including the occasional lion or elephant and nocturnal visitors such as porcupine or bushpig.

P.O. Box 40569, Dar es Salaam. ✆ **022/245-2005.** www.adventurecampstz.com. 10 units. Low season $340 full board double; high season $400; extra $240 double for game drives. MC, V. **Amenities:** Restaurant; bar; intermittent satellite Internet (by request).

Ruaha River Lodge ★★ The oldest accommodation in Ruaha, this pioneering camp, founded (and still owned and managed) by the Fox family, has a scenic location overlooking a set of rapids on the Great Ruaha River about 16km (10 miles) from the entrance gate. It retains an unpretentious bush feel, offering accommodation in comfortable en suite stone cottages with private balconies. The property is divided into two camps, both of which have their own restaurant and bar. The riverside camp is best for in-room game viewing, but the hillside units have more expansive views and feel less exposed in terms of tripping over wildlife as you walk between your room and the main dining area. This is one of the best-value lodges anywhere in the country, offering great in situ game viewing (hippos are resident on the river, and elephants maintain a more-or-less permanent presence), and it is also well located for game drives.

P.O. Box 10270, Dar es Salaam. ✆ **022/286-2357.** www.tanzaniasafaris.info. 20 rooms split btw. two camps. Low season $320 full board double; high season $380; extra $200 double to include game drives. MC, V. **Amenities:** Restaurant; bar; satellite Internet (in the main structure); pool.

5 WESTERN SAFARI CIRCUIT (KATAVI, MAHALE & GOMBE NATIONAL PARKS)

The far west of Tanzania features three of the most remote and least-visited national parks anywhere in Africa, namely Gombe Stream and Mahale Mountains, with their habituated chimpanzees, and a more conventional safari destination in the form of Katavi. Geographically, the west is dominated by Lake Tanganyika, which follows the Rift Valley floor for 675km (419 miles)—the world's longest freshwater body—to form the border with the Congo. Hemmed in by tall green hills, this beautiful lake is reputedly the least polluted in the world, with crystal-clear water to substantiate this claim and entice swimmers. At least 3 million years old, Tanganyika is also perhaps the world's most biologically rich aquatic habitat, supporting at least 500 fish species, of which the great majority

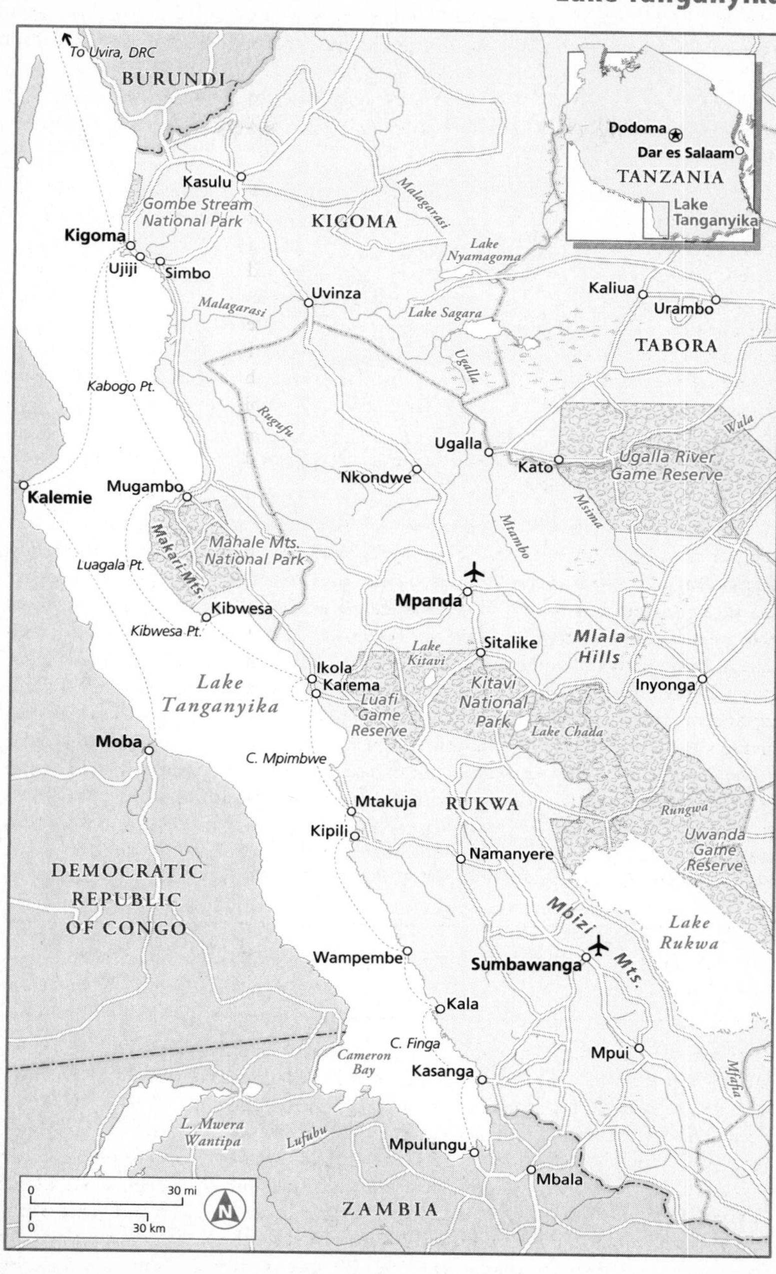

To Uvira, DRC
BURUNDI
Kasulu
Gombe Stream National Park
Kigoma
Ujiji
Simbo
KIGOMA
Malagarasi
Lake Nyamagoma
Uvinza
Malagarasi
Lake Sagara
Kaliua
Urambo
TABORA
Ugalla
Kabogo Pt.
Rugufu
Ugalla
Kato
Wala
Ugalla River Game Reserve
Nkondwe
Kalemie
Mugambo
Msima
Makari Mts.
Mahale Mts. National Park
Mtambo
Luagala Pt.
Mpanda
Kibwesa
Kibwesa Pt.
Lake Kitavi
Sitalike
Mlala Hills
Ikola
Karema
Lake Tanganyika
Luafi Game Reserve
Kitavi National Park
Lake Chada
Inyonga
Moba
C. Mpimbwe
Mtakuja
RUKWA
Kipili
Rungwa
Uwanda Game Reserve
Namanyere
DEMOCRATIC REPUBLIC OF CONGO
Mbizi Mts.
Lake Rukwa
Wampembe
Sumbawanga
Kala
C. Finga
Cameron Bay
Kasanga
Mpui
Mfafua
L. Mwera Wantipa
Lufubu
Mpulungu
Mbala
0
30 mi
0
30 km
N
ZAMBIA
Dodoma
Dar es Salaam
TANZANIA
Lake Tanganyika

occurs nowhere else. At night, this undeveloped lake is scattered with hundreds of lamp-lit fishing boats bobbing like a distant swarm of fireflies.

Kigoma, though not exactly a metropolis, is the largest port on the east shores of Lake Tanganyika. The gateway to Gombe Stream, the town is seldom visited by tourists now that there are direct charter flights to Mahale and Katavi, but it's a very pretty and amiable spot, set on green slopes enclosing a deep natural harbor. Kigoma is also an important public transport hub, serviced by daily flights and a railway from Dar es Salaam. It's also the main terminus for the venerable lake steamer MV *Liemba,* which was railed up from the coast in the dying years of German colonial rule, and still plies passengers and goods up and down the lake once a week.

Kigoma was chosen as regional administration center by the Germans, in favor of the older port of Ujiji, a 19th-century Arab slave trading center situated just 6km (3¾ miles) farther southeast. Unimposing as it is today, Ujiji is the site of arguably the most famous enquiry ever made on African soil: "Doctor Livingstone, I presume?" as posed by Henry Stanley to the mislaid Scottish explorer on November 10, 1871. The site where Stanley met Livingstone is marked by a shady mango tree and brass plaque, as well as the somewhat undercooked Livingstone Museum, whose centerpiece consists of life-size *papier-mâché* statues of the explorers' doffing their caps in greeting. Also worth a look is the traditional harbor, where local fishermen and boat builders ply their trades.

Only 52 sq. km (20 sq. miles) in extent, Gombe National Park—also known as Gombe Stream—is renowned for the groundbreaking chimpanzee behavioral research project initiated there by Jane Goodall in 1960. Despite its association with this renowned primatologist, Gombe is too inaccessible to attract significant numbers of tourists, but—along with the more southerly Mahale—it is undoubtedly the finest chimp-tracking destination in Africa. First habituated by Goodall, the 45-strong Kasekela community (the largest of the park's three chimp communities) is still remarkably approachable and relaxed with human visitors, making for a wildlife encounter as exciting and evocative as any in Africa. Locating the chimps can be quite strenuous, however, and it may involve hiking for an hour or three along steep, rocky slopes covered in thick miombo woodland and pockets of riparian forest. Accessible only by boat and explorable only on foot, Gombe supports good populations of olive baboons, often seen beachcombing on the lakeshore, as well as red-tailed, blue, and red colobus monkeys, and around 200 bird species.

Roughly 30 times larger than Gombe, and at least its equal as a chimpanzee-tracking destination, Mahale Mountains National Park is also wonderfully scenic, rising from the deserted sandy beaches of the 700m (2,296-ft.) lakeshore to the 2,441m (8,006-ft.) summit of Nkungwe in the Mahale Mountains. The park is home to around 1,000 chimpanzees, split among more than a dozen communities, one of which, comprising around 80 individuals, has been habituated and studied by primatologists from the University of Kyoto since 1965, and is also used for tourist visits. This community is no less habituated than its counterpart in Gombe, but it does occupy a larger territory, so it may take longer to locate them, especially during the wet months from November to April, when hiking is tougher. Chimps aside, Mahale supports varied fauna, including eight other primate species, including yellow baboon, red colobus, blue monkey, red-tailed monkey, vervet monkey, an endemic race of Angola colobus, and two types of galago. It is also home to forest creatures more typical of West Africa, such as brush-tailed porcupine and giant forest squirrel, alongside familiar East African species such as elephant, lion, buffalo, roan antelope, and giraffe. At least 230 bird species are present.

Inland of Lake Tanganyika and southeast of Mahale, the 4,530-sq.-km (1,767-sq.-mile) Katavi National Park is the most underpublicized of Tanzania's major savannah reserves, attracting fewer than 20 parties of tourists per calendar year for much of the 1990s. The park's profile is a little higher today, but not much—and it remains ideally suited to safarigoers seeking a genuine wilderness experience. The main vegetation cover is dense miombo woodland, interspersed with a series of wide floodplains that flank the Katuma and Kapapa rivers and form lush marshes during the rain, but retreat almost completely during the dry season from June to November, when they attract immense herds of wildlife. Elephant, buffalo, zebra, giraffe, and various antelope are abundant, and lion and spotted hyena are also likely to be seen on a daily basis, while residual riverine pools attract mind-boggling aggregations of several hundred huddled hippo. Away from the floodplain, game is less plentiful, and the thicker vegetation is favored by the park's legendarily vicious tsetse flies. Katavi is best avoided in the rainy season from November to April, when game-viewing tracks often become impassable and the mosquitoes go mental.

ESSENTIALS

VISITOR INFORMATION Further information about all parks is obtainable at **www.tanzaniaparks.com**; see also the more dedicated sites **www.mahalepark.org** and **www.katavipark.org**. Gombe charges an entrance fee of $100 per 24 hours, the highest for any Tanzanian National Park, though this is applicable only to time spent in the forest, not to time spent in camp. The entrance fee for Mahale is $80 per 24 hours. Both parks charge an additional guide fee of $20 per party for chimpanzee tracking. Entrance to Katavi is set at $20 per 24 hours.

GETTING THERE & AROUND Gombe Stream is normally visited out of Kigoma, which is only 16km (10 miles) from the southern park boundary and accessible from Dar es Salaam by daily flights with **Precision Air** (✆ **022/286-0701;** www.precisionairtz.com; $130 one-way). Less comfortable and far less efficient is the thrice-weekly rail service from Dar es Salaam to Kigoma, which usually takes upward of 40 hours one-way. Once in Kigoma, the **Kigoma Hilltop Hotel (022/213-0553;** www.mbalimbali.com) operates the only upmarket camp at Gombe and arranges motorboat transfers (25 min. in either direction).

Mahale, like Gombe, is inaccessible by road. It can be reached from Kigoma by motorboat with the Kigoma Hilltop Hotel, which also operates a camp there, or on the MV *Liemba* (the latter being a tough and unreliable ride). Katavi is technically accessible by road, but it's a long, rough ride and cannot be recommended to all but the hardiest of adventurers. Most visitors to Mahale or Katavi opt for a fly-in package; the two parks can be visited either singly or together, and are often treated as an add-on to a safari to Ruaha (linked by flights to Katavi). It is best to arrange safaris to this specialized area with a company that knows it well, such as **Nomad Tanzania** (www.nomad-tanzania.com), **Foxes African Safaris** (www.tanzaniasafaris.info), or **Mbali Mbali** (www.mbalimbali.com), all of which operate camps and flights in the region.

WHERE TO STAY & DINE

The far west has been a huge growth area in terms of tourist facilities over recent years, though the emphasis is firmly on small, exclusive, and rather costly tented camps rather than midrange package hotels and lodges. There's plenty of accommodation in Kigoma, but only one hotel that could be described as tourist class. Gombe Stream has only one tented camp, whereas Mahale and Katavi boast two and three, respectively. For independent budget travelers, all three parks offer simple hut accommodations or camping sites for $20 per person; see the national park website www.tanzaniaparks.com for details.

Chada Katavi Camp ★★★ Offering one of the most truly wild upmarket safari experiences in Africa, this small old-style tented camp is the oldest in Katavi, established in the mid-1990s. It has a peerless location in a buffalo thorn glade overlooking the seasonal Chada floodplain. The standing tents have king-size beds with walk-in netting, private balconies, private open-air hot showers, and long-drop toilets. There are no fences and no permanent structures, and the bush here—untainted by footpaths or lawns—is regularly traversed by elephant, buffalo, and other large mammals. It's not for the faint of heart, but if the in-your-face wilderness atmosphere doesn't faze you, it's difficult to beat. In addition to game drives (in an open 4×4) and guided walks onto the game-rich floodplain, the camp sets up fly-camp safaris and game drives into the new park extension toward Lake Rukwa.

P.O. Box 681, Usa River. ✆ **022/286-5156.** www.nomad-tanzania.com. 6 tents. $900–$1,900 full board double, depending on season. Rates include game rides and walks and all drinks. No credit cards. **Amenities:** Restaurant, bar.

Gombe Forest Lodge ★ This luxury tented camp is situated on Mitumba Beach, on the northern park boundary, and is well positioned for chimpanzee tracking and other guided forest walks, as well as for relaxing on the lovely beach. The only tourist lodge serving Gombe, it is operated by Mbali Mbali and consists of six standing tents with double beds protected in walk-in nets, writing desks, and private patios with lake views.

P.O. Box 20965, Dar es Salaam. ✆ **022/213-0553.** www.mbalimbali.com. 6 units. Jan–Feb $700 full board double; May–Dec $890. Closed Mar–Apr. Minimum stay 2 nights. Credit cards not accepted. **Amenities:** Restaurant; private beach.

Greystoke Mahale ★★★ Part of the exclusive Nomad Tanzania chain, this rustic yet luxurious small camp lies on a sandy private beach in the heart of the national park. Accommodations, spaced widely along the forested beachfront, are in spacious wooden huts, with tall *makuti* thatch roofs, king-size bed with walk-in netting, private balcony, en suite bathroom with hot water, and an upstairs "chill-out" deck accessible by ladder. The dining area and bar is a two-story wooden structure. In addition to chimp tracking and other walks, visitors can snorkel in the lake from a large dhow.

P.O. Box 681, Usa River. ✆ **022/286-5156.** www.nomad-tanzania.com. 6 units. $900–$1,900 full board double, depending on season. Rates include activities. No credit cards. **Amenities:** Restaurant; bar; private beach.

Katavi Wildlife Camp Owned by the Fox family, along with a string of other camps in southern Tanzania (daily flights connect them all), this rustic tented camp is smartly situated near the Ikuu ranger post. Each of the raised en suite tents is hidden in the trees overlooking a flood plain, which allows for exceptional game viewing right from your private balcony. Game drives and guided walks in this part of the park are also reliably exciting.

P.O. Box 10270, Dar es Salaam. ✆ **022/286-2357.** www.tanzaniasafaris.info. 6 tents. Low season $440 full-board double; high season $500; extra $250 per double includes all activities. MC, V. **Amenities:** Restaurant; bar; pool; satellite Internet (in the main structure).

Kigoma Hilltop Hotel The only tourist-oriented accommodation in Kigoma, this place doesn't quite match its four-star billing, but it's a competent and well-managed hotel with a lovely cliff-top location about 2.5km (1½ miles) south of the town center.

Accommodations are in well-equipped en suite chalets surrounding a central garden inhabited by a small, friendly herd of zebra. The attached restaurant serves good Indian and Western dishes, and although alcohol isn't sold, guests are permitted to bring their own.

P.O. Box 20965, Dar Es Salaam. ✆ **028/280-4357.** kht@raha.com. 30 units. $90 double B&B; $110–$150 suite B&B. Credit cards not accepted. **Amenities:** Restaurant; boat transfers to Gombe and Mahale; gym; pool; private beach. *In-room*: A/C, satellite TV, fridge.

Kungwe Beach Lodge ★ Formerly Nkungwe Camp, this is an idyllic tented camp, not quite so effortlessly classy as Greystoke, but still very comfortable and less stratospherically priced. It stands on a secluded sandy beach, ideal for swimming, near the Sisimba River mouth about a mile from Greystoke. The furnished standing tents each have a large double bed with nets and en suite flush toilet and shower. The dining and lounge area consists of a large raised wooden construction on the beach.

P.O. Box 20965, Dar es Salaam. ✆ **022/213-0553.** www.mbalimbali.com. 6 units. Jan–Feb $780 full board double; May–Dec $930. Rates include most activities. Minimum stay 3 nights. Credit cards not accepted. Closed Mar–Apr. **Amenities:** Restaurant; private beach.

18

Fast Facts: Kenya & Tanzania

1 FAST FACTS: KENYA

AREA CODES Nairobi, 020; Mombasa, 041; South Coast, 040; Malindi, 042; Nakuru, 051; Nanyuki, 062; Naivasha, 050; Kisumu, 057. If you're calling a cell-phone number from abroad, you don't need to add the area code before the cell-phone code, but you do need to drop the first 0.

BUSINESS HOURS Standard shopping and business hours are Monday to Saturday 8:30am to 5pm, though many shops open Sunday morning, too. Some shops may close on Friday afternoons due to prayers. Bank hours are Monday to Friday 8:30am to 1:30pm and Saturday 8:30 to 11am.

DRINKING LAWS Alcohol is sold in bars, hotels, restaurants, and supermarkets with no restrictions. Away from the large resorts on the coast, small Muslim-owned restaurants may not offer liquor. The Lamu Archipelago is predominantly Islamic and largely nonalcoholic except for a handful of European-run resorts and hotels.

DRIVING RULES See "Getting There and Getting Around," p. 29.

ELECTRICITY Kenya operates on 220-voltage electricity and takes square three-pin plugs (same as in the U.K.). While some safari properties provide adapters, you're advised to bring your own for charging equipment. If you're bringing electrical equipment from the U.S., you'll also need a convertor. Consult www.walkabouttravelgear.com for information on converters and adapters.

EMBASSIES & CONSULATES All embassies are located in the nation's capital, Nairobi.

United States Embassy: United Nations Avenue, off Limuru Road, Gigiri, Nairobi (© **020/363-6000;** http//:Nairobi.usembassy.gov).

British High Commission: Upper Hill Road, Nairobi Hill, Nairobi (© **020/284-4000;** www.ukinkenya.fco.gov.uk).

Canada High Commission: Limuru Road, Gigiri, Nairobi (© **020/336-3000;** www.canadainternational.gc.ca/kenya). **Australia Embassy:** ICIPE House, Riverside Drive, Westlands, Nairobi (© **020/444-5034;** www.kenya.embassy.gov.au).

EMERGENCIES For all emergencies (ambulance, fire, and police), dial **999.**

GASOLINE (PETROL) Taxes are already included in the price. One U.S. gallon equals 3.8 liters or .85 imperial gallons.

HOLIDAYS The Kenyan coast is predominantly Muslim, and many vacations are determined by the Islamic calendar, which shifts from year to year. These include Eid El Adha (Feast of the Sacrifice), Ras El Sana (Islamic New Year), Moulid El Nabi (Prophet's Birthday), and Ramadan (fast during the ninth month of the Islamic calendar), followed by **Eid al Fitr** (Feast of the Breaking of the Fast after

Ramadan). Public holidays are New Year's Day (Jan 1), Good Friday and Easter Monday (sometime in Mar or Apr), Labor Day (May 1), Madaraka Day (June 1), Moi Day (Oct 10), Kenyatta Day (Oct 20), Jamhuri (Independence) Day (Dec 12), Christmas Day (Dec 25), and Boxing Day (Dec 26). For more information on annual events, see "Calendar of Events," in chapter 3.

HOSPITALS See "Fast Facts" in specific destination chapters.

INSURANCE Travel insurance is imperative for Kenya and should include coverage for theft or loss of valuables, full medical coverage in the event of an emergency, and medical repatriation to your home country. For more information on traveler's insurance, trip cancelation insurance, and medical insurance while traveling, please visit www.frommers.com/planning and p. 37.

INTERNET ACCESS For information on staying connected while on safari in Kenya, see p. 52.

LANGUAGE Swahili (or, more correctly, Kiswahili, meaning "Swahili language") is the official national language and is taught in primary schools. However, English is taught in secondary schools, is widely spoken, and is the language of government, most media, and businesses. Some safari guides and hotel staff on the coast speak other European languages, too. Signs are usually in English. As in any country, it's always appreciated if you learn a few local phrases; most people will recognize *Hakuna matata* from *The Lion King,* which means "No problem!" in Kiswahili. For "Useful Swahili Terms & Phrases," see p. 508. For those wanting to go further, the *Swahili Dictionary,* compiled by D. V. Perrot (Hodder and Stoughton), contains a concise grammar and a guide to pronunciation, as does *Teach Yourself Swahili,* by Joan Russell (McGraw-Hill). The *Swahili Phrasebook,* by Martin Benjamin (Lonely Planet), has some useful phrases.

LEGAL AID If you get into trouble with the law, contact your consulate or embassy, which, if necessary, can refer you to a qualified English-speaking attorney. Also bear in mind that if you are dealing with the police, even if reporting a crime (like a theft) against yourself, it is customary to address the police formerly—that is, calling a policeman "sir" and policewoman "madam." Ranting and raving that they should do something about a situation will get you absolutely nowhere.

MAIL The Kenyan postal service is cheap and reasonably efficient. Having said that, *never* send anything of value though the post; always use a courier service. An airmail letter will take about a week to Europe and about 10 days to North America and Australia. The bulkier your mail, the longer it will take to arrive. A postcard or letter costs around 90¢ to Europe and $1.20 to North America or Australia. International surface parcels cost about $14 per kilogram, and parcels by airmail are about $40 per kilogram. Post offices are open Monday to Friday 8am to 5pm and Saturday 9am to12pm.

NEWSPAPERS & MAGAZINES Kenya has a number of English-language newspapers, of which the best is ***Daily Nation*** (www.nation.co.ke). ***The East African*** (www.theeastafrican.co.ke) is a weekly newspaper covering news throughout Kenya, Tanzania, and Uganda. Kenyans themselves are avid newspaper readers, so papers can be bought on any street corner or from wandering vendors in the cities and towns. Rather delightfully, you will see groups of men reading the same newspaper and discussing its contents.

POLICE See "Emergencies," above.

SMOKING Kenya's ban on smoking in public places is harsher than in other countries, as it includes not only smoking in public buildings, but also smoking on the street. Smokers can smoke only in designated places, such as outside areas of some restaurants and bars or on hotel balconies.

TAXES Value-added tax (VAT) of 16% is included in all prices of goods and services.

TELEPHONES See "Staying Connected," on p. 52.

TIME Kenya is 3 hours ahead of Greenwich Mean Time.

TIPPING It is customary to tip guides, drivers, and support staff on your safari. That said, the decision to tip—and how much to give—is a personal matter and not an obligation. Most lodges and camps will indicate (usually with an in-room note) an amount that is considered appropriate. Unlike the U.S. and Europe, where gratuities are akin to wages and are almost mandatory in many places, in Kenya tips are gifts, and the people you meet will generally work incredibly hard for them. Typically, you will be asked to give any gratuities to your host (or the lodge manager) upon departure from each safari property, and these monies will then be distributed among all staff members. At some places, guides should be tipped separately, and you're often encouraged to hand over their tip personally. Guides can make or break a trip, so it's a good idea to bring extra money to reward a stellar guiding experience. Allow $10 and $20 per day (for each person in your party) for a guide, plus an additional $5 to $10 per person for drivers and, on budget camping safaris, cooks. In cities and on the coast, 10% of the bill is standard for restaurants, and you can hand over $1 for porters and similar services. Taking pens and sweets to give out freely to children in Kenya is not advised, as this encourages begging. If you want to contribute to any cause in Africa, it's always best to make a donation to a reputable charity. Your tour operator should be able to help you with this.

TOILETS You'll find few public toilets while on safari—or anywhere in Kenya, for that matter. Generally speaking, you'll want to avoid any type of public restroom unless it is in a hotel, resort, or safari lodge or camp. Upmarket restaurant facilities in larger towns and cities are generally acceptable, but never assume that you're going to encounter a decently managed toilet.

VISAS Visas are most easily obtained on arrival in Kenya (p. 27).

U.S. residents looking for more information on Kenyan visas can go to www.passportsandvisas.com. Alternatively, visit www.kenyaembassy.com, and click on "Consular Info—Visa Information." You can also contact the Embassy of Kenya, 2249 R St. NW, Washington, DC 20008 (✆ **202/387-6101**). You can also contact one of two Consulate General facilities: either in L.A. at Park Mile Plaza, Mezzanine Floor, 4801 Wilshire Boulevard, Los Angeles, CA 90010 (✆ **323/939-2408;** www.kenyaconsulatela.com), or in New York at 866 U.N. Plaza, Ste. 4016, New York, NY 10017 (✆ **212/421-4741**).

Australian and New Zealand citizens can obtain up-to-date visa information from the **Kenyan High Commission,** Level 3, Manpower Building, 33–35 Ainslie Place, Civic Square, Canberra ACT 2601, Australia (✆ **61/02/6247-4788**), or by checking the High Commission's website at www.kenya.asn.au.

British subjects can obtain up-to-date visa information by calling the Visa Section of the U.K.'s **Kenya High Commission,** 45 Portland Place, London W1B 1AS (✆ **020/7636-2371**), or by visiting www.kenyahighcommission.net.

Canadian citizens should contact the Kenya High Commission, 415 Laurier Ave. East, Ottawa, Ontario K1N 6R4 (✆ **613/563-1773**), or visit www.kenyahighcommission.ca/visas.htm.

Irish citizens can obtain up-to-date visa information through the **Embassy of Kenya,** 11 Elgin Rd., Ballsbridge, Dublin 4 (✆ **01/613-6380**), or by checking the "Consular Services" section of the website at www.kenyaembassyireland.net.

VISITOR INFORMATION Your first port of call will probably be the Kenya Tourist Board's website (Kenya-Re Towers, Ragati Rd., Nairobi; ✆ **020/271-1262;** www.magicalkenya.com), although you'll soon discover that many of the tour operators specializing in Africa (or Kenya, specifically) carry similar, or even better, information on their websites. The Kenya Tourist Board will send you some brochures on request, so it's worth contacting them in advance. **U.S. and Canada:** Kenya Tourist Board, c/o Carlson Destination Marketing Services, P.O. Box 59159, Minneapolis, MN 55459-8257 (✆ **866/445-3692**). **U.K.:** Kenya Tourist Board, c/o Hills Balfour, Notcutt House, 36 Southwark Bridge Rd., London SEI 9EU (✆ **0207/202-6362**). If your primary interest is in game-viewing safaris, check out the website of **Kenya Wildlife Services** (www.kws.org). Other general destination websites with extensive information about Kenya include **www.kenyalogy.com** and **www.kenyatravelideas.com.**

WATER Do not drink any tap water unless you have been given the thumbs-up by your host. There are only a few hotels, resorts, and lodges that treat, filter, or purify their tap water. (Tortilis in Amboseli National Park, p. 109, supplies naturally sourced mineral water direct to their bathrooms.) Nearly every safari property and beach resort will supply rooms with either a jug of filtered water or bottled mineral water. Remember that it is more environmentally friendly to use the filtered water if given a choice; some places make the extra effort to treat and filter their water and then bottle it in glass (remember that all plastic requires an elaborate disposal and recycling process). Always carry sufficient liquid with you when heading out for the day, since you never know how long it will be before you find a supply of drinkable water. Some river, stream, and mountain water may be safe to drink; however, remember that rivers may be used for human ablutions and bathing, and that hippos defecate in water. Also see "Dietary Red Flags" on p. 39.

2 FAST FACTS: TANZANIA

AREA CODES Dar es Salaam, 022; Bagamoyo, Mafia Island, and south coast, 023; Zanzibar and Pemba, 024; Moshi, Arusha, and Ngorongoro Crater Conservation Area, 027; Serengeti National Park and Lake Victoria region, 028; central and southwestern Tanzania and Lake Tanganyika, 026. If you're calling a cellphone number from abroad, you don't need to add the area code before the cellphone code, but you do need to drop the first 0.

BUSINESS HOURS See "Business Hours," above.

DRINKING LAWS On mainland Tanzania, alcohol is sold in bars, hotels, restaurants, and supermarkets with no restrictions. The exception is the coast and Zanzibar, where, away from the large resorts, small Muslim-owned restaurants generally do not offer liquor.

DRIVING RULES See "Getting There and Getting Around," p. 29.

ELECTRICITY Outlets in Tanzania supply 230 volts of electric current. New sockets take square three-pin plugs (same as the U.K.), but you may find large round three-pin and small two-pin sockets in older hotels. Bring a multi-adaptor/converter with power surge protection, as Tanzania can experience power surges. Consult www.walkabouttravelgear.com for information on converters and adapters.

EMBASSIES & CONSULATES All embassies are located in Dar es Salaam, the capital.

U.S. Embassy: 686 Old Bagamoyo Rd., Msasani (© **022/266-8001;** http://tanzania.usembassy.gov).

U.K. Embassy: Umoja House, Garden Avenue (© **022/211-0101;** http://ukintanzania.fco.gov.uk).

High Commission of Canada: 38 Mirambo St. (© **022/216-330;** www.canadainternational.gc.ca/tanzania-tanzanie).

Australia Embassy: Australia does not have an embassy or consulate in Tanzania; the Canadian embassy provides consular assistance to Australians.

EMERGENCIES For all emergencies (ambulance, fire, and police), dial **112.**

GASOLINE (PETROL) See "Gasoline," above.

HOLIDAYS Zanzibar and the Tanzanian coast are predominantly Muslim; see "Holidays," earlier, for a list of Islamic holidays. Tanzania shares some public holidays with Kenya. Exceptions are Nyerere Day (Jan 1), Zanzibar Revolution Day (Jan 12; Zanzibar only), Union Day (Apr 26), Industrial Day (July 7), and Farmer's Day (Oct 14).

HOSPITALS In Dar es Salaam: IST Clinic, Ruvu Street, International School of Tanganyika Campus, Masaki (© **022/260-1307** and 022/260-1308, or, in emergency, 0744/783-393; www.istclinic.com); and Nordic Clinic, Valhalla House 30 (© **022/260-1650** and 022/260-0274, or mobile 0741/325-569; www.nordic.or.tz).

In Arusha: Selian Hospital Clinic (© **027/250-3726**).

INSURANCE See "Insurance," above.

INTERNET ACCESS For information on staying connected while on safari in Tanzania, see p. 52.

LANGUAGE See "Language," above.

LEGAL AID If you get robbed, lose your passport, or get into any kind of trouble, contact the police. The Tanzanian police are responsible for investigating and prosecuting local crimes, and to make an insurance claim, you will need to get a police report for theft. For anything more serious, embassy officials can provide some basic assistance, such as recommending an English-speaking attorney.

MAIL A postcard or letter costs $3 to Europe and $3.50 to North America or Australia. International surface parcels cost about $6 per kilogram, and parcels by airmail are about $12 per kilogram; note that this is considerably cheaper than in Kenya. For hours and more information, see "Mail," above.

NEWSPAPERS & MAGAZINES Tanzania has two daily English-language newspapers: ***Daily News*** (www.dailynews.co.tz) and ***Guardian*** (www.ippmedia.com). ***The East African*** (www.theeastafrican.co.ke) is a weekly newspaper covering news throughout Kenya, Tanzania, and Uganda. Kenya's daily, ***The Nation,*** is also available in the cities. Newspapers can be bought on any street corner or from wandering newspaper vendors in the cities and towns.

POLICE Dial **999.**

SMOKING Smoking in public and in the workplace is banned in Tanzania, although hotels provide smoking rooms, and most restaurants and bars permit smoking in designated areas.

TAXES Value-added tax (VAT) of 20% is included in all prices of goods and services. However, if organizing a safari or Kilimanjaro climb locally, make sure the tour operator includes the VAT when making a quote.

TELEPHONES See "Staying Connected" on p. 52.

TIME Tanzania is 3 hours ahead of Greenwich Mean Time.

TIPPING Wages in Tanzania are generally low, so tipping for good service will be much appreciated. In general, you should leave a 10% to 15% tip at restaurants and bars, even if the service charge is already included. If you're staying at an upmarket hotel or lodge, tip a few dollars to the luggage porter and chambermaid. See "Tipping," above, for information about tipping on safari, and consult chapter 16 for advice on tipping guides and porters when climbing Kilimanjaro.

TOILETS Public bathrooms are rarely available and can be quite smelly and dirty; some are long drops that you have to squat over, with no toilet paper on hand. If you need a toilet, try to find a nearby restaurant or hotel.

VISAS Visas are most easily obtained on arrival in Tanzania (p. 27).

VISITOR INFORMATION The Tanzania Tourist Board will send you some brochures on request, so it's worth contacting them in advance, and their website, **www.tanzaniatouristboard.com**, is a good source of general information. Some of the tour operator websites, however, are as good, if not better. There are drop-in tourist offices in Dar es Salaam (p. 306), Arusha (p. 385), and Zanzibar (p. 342) where you'll be able to talk to the staff and pick up a few brochures and fliers. For information about the national parks, including accommodations and tariffs, visit the website for **Tanzania National Parks** (www.tanzaniaparks.com). Other useful resources on the Internet include **www.zanzibartourism.net**, which is the official website of the Commission for Tourism and is published in a number of languages, and **www.absolutetanzania.com**, which has not only tourist information, but also interesting articles about conservation, the government, and the economy.

WATER See "Water," above, and "Dietary Red Flags," on p. 39.

3 AIRLINE, HOTEL & CAR RENTAL WEBSITES

MAJOR AIRLINES

Air India
www.airindia.com

British Airways
www.british-airways.com

Delta Air Lines
www.delta.com

EgyptAir
www.egyptair.com

Emirates Airlines
www.emirates.com

KLM
www.klm.com

Lufthansa
www.lufthansa.com

South African Airways
www.flysaa.com

Swiss Air
www.swiss.com

Virgin Atlantic Airways
www.virgin-atlantic.com

MAJOR HOTEL CHAINS

Hilton Hotels
www.hilton.com

Holiday Inn
www.holidayinn.com

Hyatt
www.hyatt.com

InterContinental Hotels & Resorts
www.ichotelsgroup.com

Marriott
www.marriott.com

Sheraton Hotels & Resorts
www.starwoodhotels.com/sheraton

CAR RENTAL AGENCIES

Avis
www.avis.com

Budget
www.budget.com

Hertz
www.hertz.com

19

Wildlife Guide

By Pippa de Bruyn and Lee Fuller, Private Guide and Singita's East Africa Guide Trainer

Everyone who comes to Africa wants to see the Big 5—elephant, lion, leopard, rhino, and buffalo—a term coined during the great hunting expeditions of the last century, when these animals were considered the most dangerous to kill and, therefore, the most prestigious trophies. Thankfully, the majority of hunters today aim only cameras, but the thrill of watching these magnificent creatures survive in a wild and untouched African landscape remains. But while almost everyone arrives wanting predominantly to tick off the Big 5, East Africa has more large mammals than virtually anywhere else on Earth, and the variety and concentration of its birdlife is unequalled. Included here are some of the more common predators and their prey—some of them occurring in their thousands—as well as a few of the more rare creatures you may be fortunate enough to track down.

To get the most out of your safari, consider purchasing *The Safari Companion: A Guide to Watching African Mammals, Including Hoofed Mammals, Carnivores, and Primates* (University of California Press), by Richard D. Estes, one of the excellent Collins Field Guides to large mammals of Africa, or East Africa–specific guides to birds, butterflies, wildflowers, and reptiles and amphibians.

1 CARNIVORES

Aardwolf, or *Fisi Ankole* in Swahili *(Proteles cristatus septentrionalis)*

Aardwolf

The aardwolf, whose name in Afrikaans means "earth wolf," looks like a small striped hyena, with vertical black stripes, a bushy black-tipped tail, and a long, coarse mane along the length of its back. That, however, is where the similarity ends, as the shy aardwolf is, strictly speaking, an insectivore, living on a diet of harvester termites (workers only) and other insects—up to 200,000 per night. The aardwolf lives in an underground burrow and is usually solitary but may forage in small packs; males are known to baby-sit pups at the den entrance while females forage. Gestation is 90 to 100 days; the litter generally consists of three or four young. The aardwolf has unusually acute hearing due to its large external ears and bony capsule enclosing the inner ear—this can become a liability when it rains, as the patter of raindrops masks the sounds of termites.

Banded Mongoose, or *Nguchiro (Mungos mungo)*
There are more than 30 species of mongoose, of which the most commonly seen (and the most social) is the banded—so called because of the light and dark stripes on its otherwise gray-brown torso and rump. The banded mongoose lives in family groups headed by a dominant male and three or four dominant females; group size can go up to 40, after which they split into two smaller groups. Members of a group recognize each other by a distinctive scent. The banded mongoose is diurnal, but on hot days it is active only during the morning and evening. You will often find them near baboons—they forage together and alert each other to danger. Gestation is 8 or 9 weeks; two to four young are born, all collectively suckled by the milk-producing females of the group. Aside from the banded mongoose, the other highly social mongoose you may encounter is the 32cm (1 ft.) dwarf mongoose, who live in family groups of 10 to 15—aside from its size, it is easily identified by its russet-orange hue. The Egyptian mongoose, at 1.6m (5½ ft.) the largest mongoose in East Africa, and diurnal, is another you are likely to encounter; while these are sometimes seen in small groups of six, they are more often alone.

Banded Mongoose

Bat-Eared Fox, or *Mbweha Masikio (Otocyon magalotis virgatus)*
Immediately identified by its large (13cm/5 in.) ears, the bat-eared fox occurs predominantly in open savannah and woodland, and often near large herds of zebra, wildebeest, and buffalo, where it feeds on the insects attracted by their droppings. The bat-eared fox is the only canid to prefer insects over mammalian prey. Insects, particularly harvester termites and dung beetles, make up to 80% of its food intake, supplemented by rodents, lizards, birds and eggs, and sometimes fruit. It has more teeth than most other mammals (about 50), exceeded only by marsupials, and can crush insects with rapid jaw snapping (five times per second). It is well adapted to dry conditions, as most of its water intake comes from the food it eats. The bat-eared fox is predominantly nocturnal (although it is active on cloudy days or in twilight) and, like the jackal, lives in monogamous pairs, raising (one to five) pups aided by the last litter. With an average 6 years, its lifespan is considerably shorter than that of the jackal.

Bat-Eared Fox

Black-Backed Jackal, or *Mbweha Nyekundu (Canis mesomelas)*
This medium-size canine is, along with the golden jackal, the most common carnivore in Africa, due to its ability to adapt to almost any environment, its ability to hunt and scavenge at any time of the day or night, and a very unfussy approach to its omnivorous diet—fruits, small to medium-size mammals, birds and reptiles, carrion, and human refuse. Black-backed jackals are monogamous, living together in pairs

Black-Backed Jackal

that last for life, but they tend to occur in small family groups, with last season's litter (breeding is annual) staying on as helpers for when the mother has the next litter of puppies. These helpers assist in hunting and scavenging, as well as protecting and bringing food to the pups (which is regurgitated in response to the pups begging, which they do by licking the mouths of the helpers and parents). Dominant siblings will leave first unless resources are scarce, in which case they will push the submissive siblings out of the pack. The dominant breeding pair is very territorial and will defend their territory vigorously, particularly the den—black-backed jackals have been known to attack potential predators as large as hyenas to protect their young and siblings. They can live up to 19 years. After a 60-day gestation, females bear 1 to 6 pups.

Cheetah, or *Duma (Acinonyx jubatus)*

Cheetah

The critically endangered cheetah is the fastest animal on land, reaching a top speed of 90 to 110kmph (56–68 mph). More impressively, they can accelerate from 0 to 110kmph (68 mph) in 3 seconds flat (a Formula 1 car takes 3.2 seconds to do the same). The cheetah is sometimes confused with the leopard, but it is smaller and has a leaner, greyhound-like physique; smaller spots; and a distinctive black "tear" running from the inner aspect of each eye down to the mouth. It also makes a most unlikely sound—like a bird's chirp or a dog's yelp. Unlike most cats, which are nocturnal, cheetahs are primarily diurnal, preferring to hunt at sunrise and sunset, usually on open plains where they can approach stragglers by running them down with a short burst of speed within a 400m (1,312-ft.) range. Being a very timid and non-confrontational cat, the cheetah also has a large percentage of kills stolen by lions and hyenas; even baboons and vultures can drive them away. Interestingly, the cheetah is a picky eater, leaving the skin, bones, and entrails of its prey. While females shun company (with the exception of their cubs), males usually cohabit in groups of two or three. Unlike leopards, they seldom climb trees and are averse to water. Gestation period is similar to that of leopards (95 days), with cubs suffering the same vulnerability; cheetahs are genetically uniform throughout their wide distribution and are, therefore, susceptible to epidemic disease outbreaks.

Golden Jackal, or *Mbweha Wa Mbuga (Canis aureus)*

Golden Jackal

The golden jackal (also known as the Asiatic, Oriental, or common jackal) is similar in appearance to the black-backed jackal (slightly larger, without the black stripe/saddle) and is the most desert-adapted, found farther north than its black-backed cousin (the head of the golden jackal was depicted as Anubis, the Egyptian god of death). It is the only jackal to occur outside of Africa. Golden jackals are even more opportunistic feeders and include plant matter such as fruits and berries in their diet. The courtship and reproductive behavior of golden jackals and black-backed jackals are very similar, and they also tend to have sibling helpers to protect and raise their young. Lifespan is shorter than that of the black-backed jackal.

Leopard, or *Chui (Panthera pardus)*

Leopard

Africa's most adaptable cat, the leopard has withstood human encroachment due to the fact that it can inhabit a large variety of habitats, from coastal plains to high-altitude mountains, semideserts to tropical rainforests. Another important part of their survival success is the huge variety in their diet—there is not much they will not eat, including insects, birds, reptiles, and fish (yes, they can fish, and they catch what is known as catfish). The bulk of their prey, however, is medium-size antelope, with impala particularly favored; warthog is another delicacy. Prey seldom exceeds their own body weight (they have to hoist carcasses into trees to keep their meal safe from hyenas and, to a degree, lions), but they have been recorded killing young buffalo and giraffe, as well as adult wildebeest and waterbuck. Except for a brief time during mating and when the female is rearing her young, the leopard leads a solitary life within a defined territory, marked by urine. When the female is in heat, the male picks this up from her urine and will spend 6 or 7 days with her. Birth takes place in a hidden lair after a gestation period of 3 months, enabling her to return to the hunt, but leaving the sightless cubs vulnerable. Leopards tend to lie under dense cover during the day, making them exceptionally difficult to see (they are more often viewed at night)—if you've spotted a leopard, you've had a very productive game drive.

Lion, or *Simba (Panthera leo)*

Lion

Africa's largest carnivore is a very inefficient killer, which may account for why the lion is also the only truly social cat: Hunting as a pride is far more effective, allowing them to tackle larger prey, such as buffalo, giraffe, and eland. Male lions rarely participate in the hunt, but once the kill is made, they eat first. The dominance males enjoy at mealtimes probably has more to do with sheer size than any deference to their sex: The average male weighs 190kg (420 lb.)—60kg (130 lb.) more than the average female. Male lions, their manes designed to protect the head and neck during fights with other males, become sexually mature at about 2 years old but have to wait another 3 to 5 years before mating; females become pregnant at around 4 and produce small litters every 2 years (after a 3-month gestation) until they are about 15. Copulation occurs frequently—every 15 minutes over a period of several hours—but the conception rate is low. The mortality rate is also very high; underdeveloped cubs are born blind and are very dependent on the lioness, who often has to leave them to hunt. If a new male lion enters the pride, he will usually eat the cubs of the male he ousted, to destroy the bloodline. This induces the lionesses into estrus in as little as 24 hours. Cubs begin to move around at 1 month of age and are able to follow the mother at about 2 months, when their chances of survival increase substantially.

Nile Crocodile, or *Mamba (Crocodylus niloticus)*

The maximum size and weight of the world's largest living reptile has been a matter of much debate (and exaggeration), with early hunters claiming to have bagged critters well over 7m (23 ft.), but the general consensus is that the average Nile croc measures around 5m (16 ft.) and weighs about 1 ton. It looks prehistoric and is: Fossil forms dating back more than 100 million years look remarkably like the basking menace you'll spot near riverbanks today. The crocodile is the only animal in the wild that counts humans as part of its list of food items, so be wary of approaching water, particularly rivers. Generally, river crocodiles are more dangerous than those in lakes; the cleaner, clearer water in lakes means a greater proportion of fish in their diet, whereas the muddier and dirtier water of rivers leads to a greater reliance on mammals. The crocodile can stay underwater for up to 30 minutes if threatened; if they remain inactive, they can hold their breath for up to 2 hours. They have an ectothermic metabolism, so they can survive a long time between meals—though when they do eat, they can eat up to half their body weight at a time. After a 3-month incubation period, 30 to 50 eggs hatch; the temperature at which the eggs are incubated will determine the sex of the hatchlings, with males produced between 31° and 34°C (87–93°F) and females between 26° and 30°C (78°–86°F). Crocodiles live for 60 to 70 years, with reports of some reaching a century. If you spot a croc's hind foot tracks, you can roughly estimate overall body length (1 in. in the track = 1 ft. of body length).

Nile Crocodile

Pangolin, or *Kakakuona (Manis temminckii)*
The nocturnal pangolin, or "scaly anteater," is a fascinating-looking mammal. Aside from its tiny head (though it has good hearing, it has no external ears), it is covered with hard, movable, plate-like armor—the only mammal covered in scales. Made of keratin (like human fingernails), it is said the scales can deflect a bullet from a .303 rifle fired from 100m (328 ft.). Pangolins have short legs, with sharp claws for burrowing—these claws are so long that they have to walk with their forepaws curled over. The pangolin locates termite and ant mounds with its excellent sense of smell. It has no teeth but an extremely long tongue—up to 41cm (16 in.), almost the same length as the animal itself—that retracts back into a sheath in the chest cavity. Like the anteater, the pangolin eats termites by digging a shallow hole in a termite mound into which it extends its long, sticky tongue. It can curl up into a ball when threatened, with its overlapping scales acting as armor and its face tucked under its tail. Pangolins can also secrete a noxious smell from glands near the anus, similar to the spray of a skunk. Gestation is 5 months; females give birth to one young. They can live 20 years.

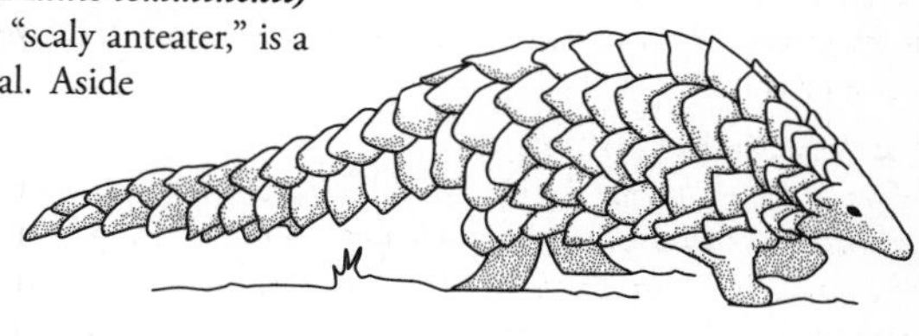
Pangolin

Serval, or *Mondo (Felis serval)*
Almost as elusive as the leopard, the pretty serval is another spotted cat with a similar build but is easily identified by its much smaller size (91–135cm/35–53 in.) and larger, almost bat-like ears. It is, like most felines, a loner, though it

Serval

is sometimes seen in pairs or small family groups. A very efficient hunter with a high kill-to-strike ratio, the serval has a distinctive hunting style: High bounding leaps help them land down onto prey, which they kill with strikes of the claws. The serval's long legs (proportionally the longest of any cat) are ideal for hunting in long grass, and it uses its large ears to locate otherwise hidden prey. It also excavates nesting birds and rodents out of burrows or holes in trees. If lucky, the serval will live to the ripe old age of 15 years, but is listed in *CITES Appendix 2,* indicating that it is "not necessarily now threatened with extinction, but may become so."

Small-Spotted Genet, or *Kanu (Genneta gennata)*

About the size of a large cat, with leopard spots and very feline behavior (back arching, grooming, purring), the genet is, surprisingly enough, more closely related to the mongoose. Genets also have semi-retractable claws adapted to climbing and catching prey—they spend most of their time in trees but also hunt on the ground and take shelter in escarpments and rocky outcrops, as well as unused aardvark burrows. Female genets are thought to be more territorial than males, marking their territory with cheek and anal secretions. The large-spotted genet is very similar in appearance to the small-spotted genet—the latter is slightly grayer with a white-tipped tail, and the spots are, of course, smaller. Genets gestate for 77 days, giving birth to two to four kittens, each of which may live for up to 13 years.

Small-Spotted Genet

Striped and Spotted Hyena, or *Fisi* (*Hyena hyena* and *Crocuta crocuta*)

The hyena family comprises the spotted, striped, and brown hyena (the latter not occurring in East Africa), as well as the smaller, atypical aardwolf (see above). All are easily identified by their sloping backs—their front legs are longer than their back legs—and their peculiar bear-like gait. Hyenas are much maligned by humans, perhaps because of their ability to eat carrion—their powerful jaws and digestive system allow them to extract nutrients from every part of their prey, including skin and bone, as well as animal droppings. Their menacing appearance and the eerie call of the spotted hyena (also aptly known as the "laughing hyena") are no doubt further contributing factors. Hyenas do not only scavenge, however. The spotted hyena (the most common hyena) is a very efficient predator; its innate intelligence is evident in its strategic hunting methods. One unusual feature of the spotted hyena is the enlarged clitoris, or "pseudo-penis" of the female—this, along with similarity in size, makes it hard to distinguish gender in this matriarchal society. Gestation is 90 days, and cubs are then suckled for a lengthy 12 to 18 months.

Striped Hyena

Spotted Hyena

Wild Dog, or *Mbwa Mwitu (Lycaon pictus)*

Wild Dog

If you spot these rounded, large ears and the irregular patterned coat of black, yellow, and white (distinctive for each individual), you can count yourself very lucky, for the wild dog is Africa's most endangered carnivore (total population on the continent is around 2,000–3,000), with numbers diminishing mainly due to range contraction over a very short time. The diseases brought by domestic dogs (rabies and distemper) have also contributed to the reduction in numbers. Wild dogs have the highest hunting success rate (about 70%) of all the large carnivores. They are specialized pack hunters and can chase down their prey—usually medium-size antelope—over a distance of up to 5km (3 miles), with the pack averaging just under 50kmph (31 mph). They are also capable of shorter bursts, attaining 60kmph (37 mph) over a 2km (1¼-mile) distance. Although the hyena is generally considered to have the most powerful bite, the African wild dog has a Bite Force Quotient (the strength of bite as measured against the animal's mass) of 142, the highest of any carnivore. The wild dog is the most social member of the dog family, able to take care of its old, sick, and disabled, and bonds are continually reinforced with greeting ceremonies. They have a submission-based hierarchy instead of a dominance-based one; they will beg energetically instead of fight, and will lick the mouth of the alpha member (which may explain their vulnerability to infectious diseases). Normally, only the alpha pair breeds (unless food is plentiful, when other females may give birth), but the whole pack is involved in raising the litter. Unusual for social mammals, in which related females form the core pack, males typically do not leave the pack and females will disperse at 14 to 30 months of age and join other packs that lack sexually mature females.

2 PRIMATES

Bushbaby, or *Komba (Galago senegalensis)*

Bushbaby

Bushbabies—so called because their nocturnal cry sounds like that of a distressed baby (and perhaps also because of its endearingly huge eyes)—are primates, though more closely related to the lemurs of Madagascar than the distantly related higher primates such as chimpanzees. Though they call to announce their location, most communication is done via scent: Aside from glands in their skin that imbue each bushbabies' fur with a musky scent, they mark their territory by urinating on their hands, wiping their hands on their feet, and then walking over branches (this may be why they do not make great pets, despite scoring high on the "oh gosh, how cute" scale). Bushbabies live in loose troops ruled by a dominant female, while dominant males travel among several troops; young males live on the periphery of troops. Preferring riverine thickets and forests, bushbabies are highly mobile—a single animal can cover up to 2km (1¼ miles) per night, visiting about 500 trees in only 6 hours of foraging time. They do not eat tree leaves, but live on a diet of tree sap, flowers, fruits, and insects. Scientists have identified about 16 to 18 species of bushbaby in Africa; there are thought to be more. Bushbabies live for about 8 years.

498 **Chimpanzee, or *Sokwe Mtu (Pan troglodytes)***

Chimpanzee

The chimpanzee is not only more closely related to man than any other living creature (sharing around 93% of DNA sequences), but it is also the most studied primate to date: Jane Goodall's study of the chimps at Gombe Stream on Lake Tanganyika in Tanzania—going for more than 40 years now—is the longest-standing animal research project in the wild. Chimps live in large troops—up to 100 individuals—dominated by an alpha male, sometimes subdivided into smaller sub-troops. They are primarily frugivorous, but males also hunt opportunistically, killing colobus monkeys, baboons, young antelope, guinea fowl, and pigs in well-organized hunting parties characterized by rapid mobilization and cooperation between the males who play different roles such as blockers, chasers, and ambushers. Chimpanzees use tools, showing their innate intelligence and abilities by "fishing" for termites, ants, and bees with grass stems that they insert into nests; they also use clubs and rocks to break open nuts. Chimps communicate in a manner similar to human nonverbal communication, using vocalizations, hand gestures, and facial expressions; captive chimps have been taught sign language. Scientists have documented mourning displays, humor (especially when tickled), and empathy toward other species (like feeding turtles). Gestation is 8 months and produces a single baby (occasionally twins)—if the baby is a daughter, the mother-daughter bond will last a lifetime (usually 40–50 years).

Olive Baboon, or *Nyani (Papio cynocephalus anubis)*

Africa's largest and most widespread baboon (found in 25 countries throughout Africa) is also its most confident, and the chances are very high that you'll encounter it. Named for its green-gray coat, the baboon is immediately recognized by its tail (held up and bent down in the opposite direction to that of a monkey) and doglike muzzle, which is why it is also known as Anubis (after the Egyptian god Anubis, often represented by a dog head). Living in big troops of up to 130, baboons are active during the day, when they forage, play, groom, nurse, and spar in full view of any onlookers. The olive baboon troop has a rigid social structure with complex communication comprising aural and visual means (what looks like a big yawn to a human onlooker is perhaps the need to show off a full set of canines to an approaching rival), as well as tactile means such as social grooming and nose-to-nose greetings. Part of its success is that it is omnivorous, resourceful, and at home in various habitats, therefore able to find nutrition in almost any environment, whether within the tree canopy or beneath the ground. Gestation is 6 months; the female produces one offspring at a time, which may live up to 20 years.

Olive Baboon

Vervet Monkey, or *Tumbili* (*Cercopithecus aethiops*)

This medium-size monkey is a common sight throughout East Africa and, like the olive baboon, adapts easily to many environments. There are several subspecies, but the body is generally silvery gray, whereas the face, ears, hands, feet, and tip of the tail are black; males are easily recognized by a turquoise blue scrotum and red penis. Vervets live in troops of 10 to 50 individuals comprising mainly adult females and their offspring. There is a strict social hierarchy, and a mother's social standing predetermines her offspring's, with even adults submitting to juveniles of families with higher social status, who will also be on the receiving end of the most grooming. Gestation lasts 7 months and produces a single offspring with a lifespan of up to 20 years.

Vervet Monkey

3 ANTELOPES & OTHER RUMINANTS

African Buffalo, or *Nyati (Syncerus caffer)*

The barrel-chested African buffalo is the second-largest animal in the bovid class (second only to the North American plains buffalo), weighing between 500 and 900kg (1,100–2,000 lb.). While it looks placid and bovine, it has one of the most fearsome, aggressive temperaments, and will engage in mobbing behavior to fight off predators. A startled or angry buffalo will make a loud, explosive grunt; this is usually a signal to climb the nearest tree! The savannah buffalo has a sparse coat of short black hair, with males typically darker than females (forest buffalo are more red in hue); both males and females bear the buffalo's distinguishing horns. Buffalo are ruminants (they have anaerobic bacteria in a specially segmented stomach that breaks down rough and otherwise inedible food). This makes it one of the most successful grazers in Africa, as it is able to survive in almost any habitat, though it does need regular access to water. African buffalo are sociable, living in large herds; the biggest of these can grow 1,000-strong, though the introduction of the cattle disease rinderpest decimated numbers (it was the hardest hit animal) in the Serengeti at the turn of the century. The basic herds consist of related females and their offspring; these are surrounded by sub-herds of bachelor males, high-ranking males and females, and old or invalid animals. With very few predators (predominantly man and lions), the buffalo often lives to 18 years; aging males are displaced by new dominant males, and are forced to leave the herd and live on their own; these are prized by hunters for their thick horns.

African Buffalo

Coke's Hartebeest, or *Kongoni (Alcephalus busephalus cokei)*

Similar in outline to the topi, but larger and not as variegated in markings, the fawn- to reddish-hued Coke's hartebeest has medium-size horns, reaching up to 70cm (27 in.). Coke's hartebeest, also commonly known as *kongoni* (tough ox), is the most widespread of the hartebeest. Its preferred grazing grounds are medium and tall grasslands; it tends to migrate between short, well-drained pastures in the wet season to long grasslands in the dry. Unlike wildebeest, *kongoni* do not give birth at a certain time of year or in the midst of the herd, but in isolation, well hidden in the scrub; the female will leave her young calf hidden there for a fortnight, visiting it briefly to suckle. Even more unusual, adult females have long relationships with their offspring and seemingly prefer their company to that of other adults; they are often accompanied by up to four generations of their young, with female offspring remaining close to their mothers up to the time they give birth to calves of their own; even male offspring often remain with their mothers for as long as 3 years. Gestation is 8 months; lifespan can be up to 20 years.

Coke's Hartebeest

Eland, or *Pofu (Taurotragus oryx pattersoni)*

The largest antelope in Africa (weighing 300–1,000kg [660–2,200 lb.], depending on sex, and up 180cm [6 ft.] at the shoulder) is identified by its twisted horns: about 65cm (26 in.) long, with a steady spiral ridge. It is also the slowest antelope and tires quickly. When the eland moves, it makes a clicking noise—this is from overlapping hoof tips, not from the ankle or knee joint, as popularly believed. Herds usually have 30 to 80 individuals but are known to exceed 400; the eland has an unusual social structure, in that individuals leave or join herds as necessary without forming close ties. It has been held in high esteem in tribal mythology throughout Africa; in East Africa, the Maasai believe they are "God's cattle," and this is then the only wild meat that they will eat. Gestation is 9 months; lifespan is up to 20 years.

Eland

Greater Kudu, or *Tandala Mkubwa (Tragelaphus strepsiceros)*

Along with the sable and the oryx, the male kudu—identifiable not only by its horns, but also by the long fringe or "beard" of hair running down his throat and chest—is the antelope with the most magnificent horns: A long, elegant spiral that, when fully grown, reaches 2½ twists, these can sometimes become entangled when jousting with another male, which may result in both animals starving to death. Males are typically loners or live in small bachelor herds, joining the female only during mating season. The female is smaller and has no horns. Both males and females have 6 to 12 thin vertical white stripes on each flank, and an equally white chevron across the forehead. When pregnant, the female will leave the herd to give birth and leave the newborn hidden for 4 to 5 weeks. The kudu is a browser, feeding on seeds, leaves, and shoots. Gestation is 8 to 9 months; lifespan can be up to 20 years.

Greater Kudu

Maasai Giraffe, or *Twiga (Giraffa camelopardalis tippelskirchi)*

The graceful Maasai giraffe is one of six different species of the family *Giraffidae,* tallest of all land mammals (the height of a double-decker bus), with the Maasai giraffe typified by its large irregular jagged patches, which look rather like giant snowflakes. You may find huge individual variation in a single herd, with markings for each individual as distinctive as a fingerprint. The Maasai giraffe is gregarious and non-territorial, appearing in loose, fluid herds that can number between 2 and 50. Calving happens throughout the year; following a 15-month gestation, the giraffe will give birth to one calf. The embryonic sack usually bursts when the baby falls to the ground, and within 5 minutes, the 1.8m (6-ft.) calf can stand. It nearly doubles its height in the first year. Despite its weight and almost cumbersome height (the record-size bull, shot in Kenya in 1934, was 5.9m/19 ft. tall and weighed approximately 2,000kg/4,400 lb.), the giraffe is surprisingly agile, reaching top speeds of up to 60kmph (37 mph) and moving with an endearing loping gait (unlike most four-legged species, legs on the same side move in unison to propel the animal forward). Giraffe can inhabit savannahs, grasslands, or open woodlands. They have specially adapted tongues and lips to nibble acacia leaves, avoiding (and even consuming) the trees' ferocious thorns. They drink large quantities of water and, as a result, can spend long periods of time in arid areas. Tanzania's national animal, the giraffe may not be hunted in Tanzania; anyone caught with any parts or products made from a giraffe faces up to 15 years' imprisonment.

Maasai Giraffe

Oryx, or *Choroa (Oryx beisa)*

East Africa has two types of oryx—the common beisa oryx (*Oryx gazella beisa*) and the fringe-eared oryx (*Oryx g. callotis*). Though it is difficult to distinguish between the two, there is no mistaking this beautiful antelope, with its attractive black-and-white markings on a horse-like head, from which grow straight, narrow, rapier-like horns reaching 75 to 80cm (around 30 in.) long. Both males and females have horns, and they are lethal—capable of killing a lion. Some say that if seen from the side, the horns appear as one, and therein lies the origin of the fabled unicorn. The oryx is perfectly adapted to near-desert conditions, able to survive without water for long periods and to store water by raising their body temperature, thereby avoiding perspiration. It also feeds on plants late at night or early in the morning, times when the desert-adapted foliage retains the most water, thereby providing the oryx with both nutrients and moisture. A female leaves the herd to give birth and hides the calf for 2 or 3 weeks, visiting a few times a day to nurse it. After that time, calves are able to run with the herd. Lifespan is up to 20 years.

Oryx

Sable Antelope, or *Mbarapi* (*Hippotragus niger*)

One of the most impressive-looking antelopes, the sable has majestic, backward-sweeping, scimitar-shaped horns that can reach more than 1m (3.3 ft.); the males have a glossy, jet-black coat with striking white facial markings and underbelly. Listed as rare by the International Union for Conservation of Nature

Sable Antelope

(IUCN), the most important populations are found in wooded savannahs of Zimbabwe, Zambia, and East Africa. Sable antelope form herds of 10 to 30 strictly hierarchical females and their calves, led by a single bull; when males fight, they drop to their knees and use their horns. Adult males often reach 1.5m (5 ft.) at the shoulder and can weigh more than 270kg (595 lb.); males are about 20% larger and heavier than females. Lifespan is up to 17 years.

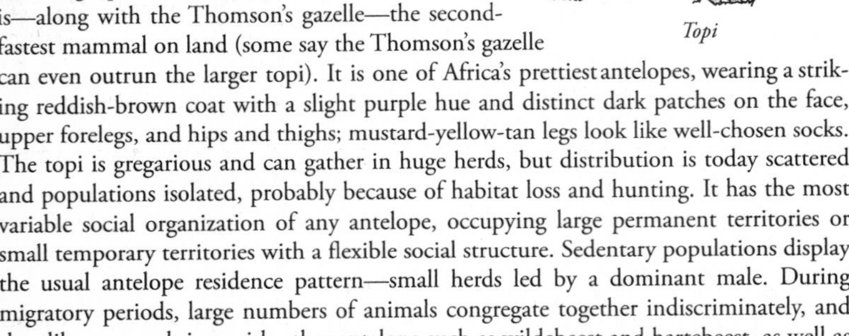

Topi

Topi, or *Nyamera (Damaliscus lunatus jimela)*

Reaching speeds of 70kmph (43 mph), the topi is—along with the Thomson's gazelle—the second-fastest mammal on land (some say the Thomson's gazelle can even outrun the larger topi). It is one of Africa's prettiest antelopes, wearing a striking reddish-brown coat with a slight purple hue and distinct dark patches on the face, upper forelegs, and hips and thighs; mustard-yellow-tan legs look like well-chosen socks. The topi is gregarious and can gather in huge herds, but distribution is today scattered and populations isolated, probably because of habitat loss and hunting. It has the most variable social organization of any antelope, occupying large permanent territories or small temporary territories with a flexible social structure. Sedentary populations display the usual antelope residence pattern—small herds led by a dominant male. During migratory periods, large numbers of animals congregate together indiscriminately, and they like to spend time with other antelope such as wildebeest and hartebeest, as well as zebra. Gestation is 8 months. Lifespan is usually 15 years.

Thomson's and Grant's Gazelle, or *Swala Tomi* and *Swala Granti* (*Gazella rufifrons thomsoni* and *Gazella granti robertsi*)

Thomson's Gazelle

The pale, sandy-color gazelle—all occurring with ribbed, S-shaped horns—is the most widespread of all antelope and is characterized by its ability to survive in arid areas by allowing its own body temperature to rise by as much as 10°F. Curiously, they regulate their temperature by panting rapidly: As blood passes through the vessels of the moist nasal mucous, it is cooled by evaporation. The Thomson's gazelle is, along with the topi, also the second-fastest land mammal on Earth, reaching 70 to 80kmph (around 45 mph). Producing two lambs per year, the dainty Thomson's (55–65cm/15–30kg [25 in./33–66 lb.]) is also the most abundant gazelle, numbering 360,000 in the migration alone. Easily identified from the Grant's by the black stripe that separates the fawn from the white on its flank (not to mention size and horns), the "Tommies" tend to follow behind the big herds, grazing on the short-cropped shoots in heavily grazed grassland, thereby avoiding competition for limited resources. Almost twice the size of the Thomson's, the Grant's gazelle (80–95cm/35–80kg [31–37 in./77–176 lb.]) has elegantly shaped divergent horns, with tips pointed to the side and backward. The Grant's selects different food plants from the Tommies and is believed to be completely water independent (able to derive all its moisture from plant materials grazed).

Grant's Gazelle

White-Bearded Wildebeest, or *Nyumbu (Connochaetes taurinus)*

Also known as the white-bearded gnu, the wildebeest is Africa's most abundant antelope, appearing in super-herds numbering up to 1.5 million in the Serengeti and Masai Mara. The wildebeest is relatively hardy but prefers sweet young grasses, which it will graze day and night until depleted, and will commute many miles to find water and fresh pasture, hence the annual Migration that takes place in East Africa. Calving is synchronized to happen when they are in freshly laundered open-plain savannahs, where they are safest from approaching predators—an estimated 80% of the females calve within the same 2- to 3-week period, and calves can run within minutes of being born. Gestation is 8 to 8.5 months; lifespan is up to 20 years.

White-Bearded Wildebeest

4 OTHER HOOFED MAMMALS/ NONRUMINANTS

African Elephant, or *Tembo (Loxondonta Africana)*

The elephant is the largest land mammal, weighing up to 6 tons. Aside from their sheer size, the characteristic that sets most elephants apart is what one might call their emotional intelligence; elephants grow up in close-knit family groups (with adolescent males moving to bull herds) and show visible and prolonged signs of distress when one of the herd is injured or killed. Breeding herds are led and dominated by a matriarch, and when males reach a certain age (around 12–15 years), they are encouraged to join bull herds. Mature bulls (usually over age 25, when they weigh 5–6 tons) join female breeding herds during mating only; if conception is successful, gestation is 22 months, and babies are dependent on the mother and weaned only at 4 years or more. Elephants eat up 250kg (550 lb.) of food and drink up to 150 liters (40 gallons) of water every day; given that they live 50 to 60 years, they have a huge impact on the environment. Elephants flap their ears continuously; this is to keep the animal cool as warm blood is pumped from the body into the rich network of blood vessels in the ears—which account for 20% of the surface area—at a rate of 12 liters (3 gallons) per minute per ear. Elephants communicate using infrasound, meaning it is below our range of hearing; new studies suggest there may be also be sub-terrain communication, with messages received through their feet. Elephants are estimated to cover more than 20km (12 miles) per day. Their trunk, probably nature's most versatile tool, has more than 150,000 muscle fascicles in it. Unusual for a family, *Elephantidae* comprises only two species (the other being the Indian elephant).

African Elephant

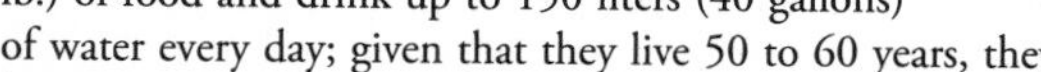

Black Rhinoceros, or *Kifaru (Diceros bicornis)*

Africa's most primitive-looking mammal dates from the Miocene era and survived pretty much unchanged for millions of years. Then in the 1970s, the explosion in poaching reduced the world rhino population by an estimated 90%. Having been poached almost to extinction in East Africa, there are only isolated populations of the critically endangered black rhino (which is actually gray and is also known as the "hook-lipped rhino"), predominantly in the Masai Mara in Kenya, Moru Koppies in Serengeti, and nearby Ngorongoro Crater. The black rhino is a solitary animal and is usually spotted at waterholes or in savannah with thickets; its ominous hulk (weighing upward of 1 ton) is fed by the leaves of a huge variety of plants (more than 200 different species), which are nimbly devoured with the use of its muscular upper lip and molar and premolar teeth. An odd-toed ungulate (three toes on each foot), the rhino is easily irritated, despite the fact that it has a remarkably thick skin (15–50mm/½–2 in. thick; human skin is 1.5mm/.05 in.). Despite its bulk (700–1,400kg/1,500–3,000 lb.), it is surprisingly nimble and can reach speeds of up to 48kmph (30 miles). The rhino can inflict a lot of damage with its horn. It has a relatively small brain, given its overall size, and very poor eyesight (the latter made up for by good senses of smell and hearing). In an ideal world, the black rhino will live to about 50, but its horns—actually thickly matted hair that grows from the skin—are literally worth their weight in gold in Asian markets; authorities suspect heavily armed gangs of Somali bandits of being responsible for most of the continued poaching. After a 15-month gestation, calves will stay with the mother for 2 to 4 years. You will often see the bird known as an oxpecker (or *askari wa kifaru,* literally "the rhino's security guard") sitting on the rhino, feeding on ticks and alerting the rhino to danger—with no known predators, this is invariably the presence of man.

Black Rhinoceros

Hippopotamus, or *Kiboko (Hippopotomus amphibious)*

One of the three largest mammals on land (males weigh an average 1.5 tons, females 1.3 tons), the gregarious hippo is found in herds of 10 or more, submerged up to its nostrils in the waters of tropical rivers, as it has sensitive skin and is highly susceptible to sunburn. The hippo has no sweat glands; when unable to fully submerge, or when basking on the sand bank, sub-dermal glands release a secretion that keeps the skin moist and protects the hippo from U.V. damage. Due to the reddish color of this secretion, it was originally thought that hippos sweated blood (see box on p. 423). It has been suggested

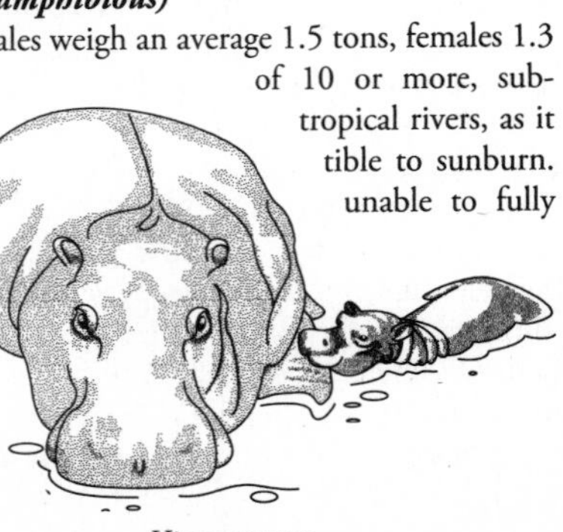

Hippopotamus

that these secretions have extremely effective antibiotic properties, given that the wounds inflicted during fights seldom become infected despite the conditions of the water it will immerse itself in. Hippos are able to hold their breath for 5 to 6 minutes but usually spend much less time under water. Mating takes place in the water. Calving takes place either in shallow water or on land; gestation is 8 months, and hippos can live up to 40 years. Despite being herbivores, they are said to be responsible for more human deaths than any other African mammal—this is largely due to the fact that they are fiercely territorial and not confined to nature reserves. They are nocturnal grazers: At sunset they leave the water to follow well-worn pathways to pasture, returning to their water sanctuaries at dawn; humans using the same tracks to access rivers do so at their peril.

Plains Zebra, or *Punda Milia (Equus burchellii)*

Each zebra's stripe pattern is as unique as a fingerprint—zebras are thought to recognize these stripes, using them to identify each other in big herds (young foals, in particular, are said to "imprint" their mother's pattern). Zebras will mate freely (and successfully) with donkeys to form a hybrid (although the offspring are infertile; these animals are known as zebdonks and were unsuccessfully bred as beasts of burden in the early to mid-1900s). Gestation is 12 months. Young zebra foals need to consume their mother's feces to ingest the micro-organisms (gastric fauna) necessary for digestion in their stomachs. Zebras have never successfully been domesticated or used by man—they are said to lack the stamina of a horse, have a weak spine, and are incredibly cantankerous and stubborn. They live up to 20 years.

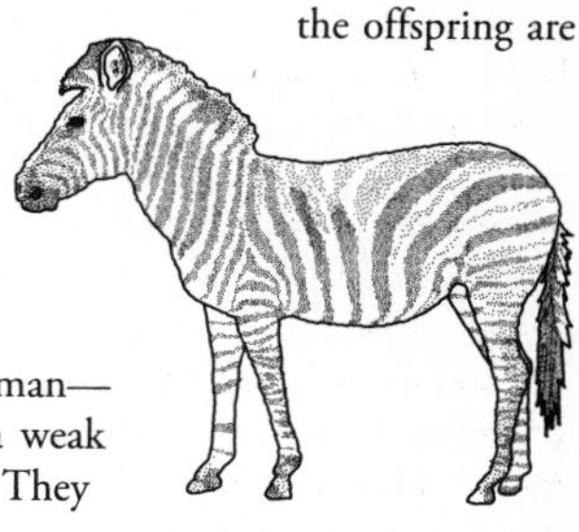

Plains Zebra

Warthog, or *Ngiri (Phacochoerus aethiopicus)*

The name for this wild pig is derived from the huge wart-like protrusions found on the head (males have two pairs, females one), but the warthog is identifiable by the two pairs of curving tusks protruding from the mouth, which are used for digging and as weapons to protect the face during fighting (swept sideways). The smaller lower tusks do most of the damage and are kept knife-sharp by constant rubbing (during chewing) against the larger top tusks. The warthog is omnivorous but more of a vegetarian, mainly grazing grass in the wet season, while the dry season sees them "rooting" on their knees, using their nose disc or snout to dig out roots, bulbs, tubers, and rhizomes. They will, if the opportunity or need arises, settle for carrion and, occasionally, fallen fruits. They also regularly eat soil, which supplements their diet with minerals and trace elements. When they run, they keep their tails upright like antennae—in long grass, this is thought to help alert other members of the family, particularly young, to their location. Gestation is 5 to 6 months; litter comprises one to eight piglets. Warthogs can live up to 18 years.

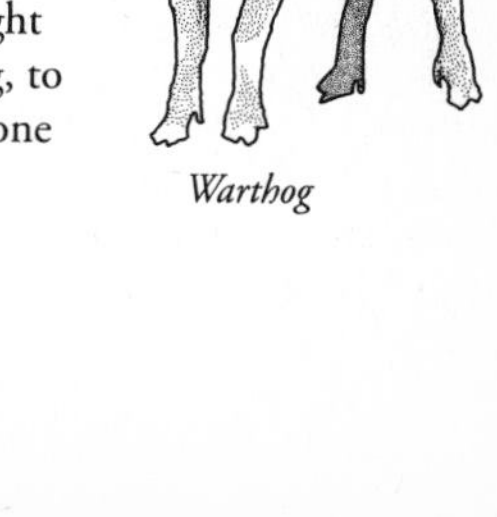

Warthog

5 INTERESTING RODENTS

African Dormouse (*Graphiurus spp*)

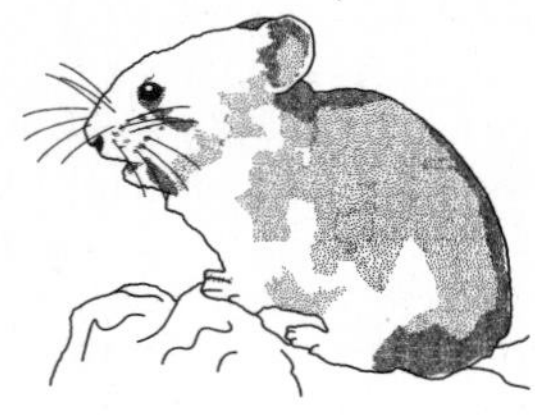

African Dormouse

These are some of the cutest rodents around, with soft bushy tails, big ears, and endearing faces. There are about 14 species of African dormouse, and all are very good climbers. At only 85g (3 oz.), these small omnivores are very agile and are exceptionally quick when hunting. They pounce very quickly onto sleeping birds, as well as lizards, eggs, and carrion, and can easily overpower prey the same size as them. Fat deposits and nest-building abilities allow these mice to tolerate seasonal food shortages. They are also very vocal, especially during mating, when both sexes click, growl, and whistle.

North African Crested Porcupine, or *Nungunungo (Hystrix cristana)*

Meaning "quill pig" in Latin and appearing somewhat like a hedgehog, the porcupine is, in fact, a rodent (the third-largest rodent after the capybara and the beaver), with a coat of "hair" modified into sharp spines that it uses rather successfully to defend itself from predators. The African porcupine can grow to well over 15 to 27kg (33–60 lb.), and the quills that run along the head, nape, and back can be raised into a crest to make itself appear even larger. If threatened, the porcupine will charge—in reverse—to stab the enemy with its quills (it cannot *shoot* its quills, as is commonly believed). The crested porcupine is, for the most part, herbivorous—eating roots, bulbs, crops—but will also occasionally consume carrion (it gnaws on bones for calcium). Nocturnal and monogamous, the crested porcupine lives in small family groups consisting of an adult pair and young of various ages. Gestation is 94 days; litter comprises one to three; lifespan is 15 years.

North African Crested Porcupine

Savanna Cane Rat, or *Ndezi (Thryonomys gregorianus)*

This robust rodent, weighing in at 7.5kg (17 lbs.), is seldom seen, due to its preferred habitat of long rank grasslands and nocturnal habits. These rats are surprisingly vocal, and their repertoire includes grunts, whistles, and hoots. When alarmed, they thump their back legs on the ground, in an attempt to deter their potential predator. They need to be on the lookout for man, who prizes their meat as a delicacy, as well as most carnivores and eagles. They have specially adapted large cutting teeth and manipulative hands that allow to them feed on mature grasses and reeds. They also feed on fruits, bark, and roots. They usually produce two litters a year, of an average size of four youngsters. The young are born very well developed and are sexually mature, producing their own offspring at 6 months of age.

Savanna Cane Rat

Spring Hare, or *Kamendegere (Pedetes capensis surdaster)*

Bouncing across the plains on its well-developed hind legs, reaching heights of almost 2m (6½ ft.), the spring hare looks like a tiny kangaroo, but it is neither rabbit nor marsupial, but rodent. Spring hares are very common but seldom seen during the day, as they tend to rest in their warrens, emerging primarily at night to feed. Spring hares live and graze in groups of up to nine and build burrows that can extend up to 50m (164 ft.). Burrows may have a series of escape holes that do not open above the ground; instead, entrances are plugged with soil from the inside of the tunnel. Spring hares are primarily grazers favoring overgrazed grasslands but will also eat roots and fruit. Gestation is 77 days; females will produce around three young in 1 year. Lifespan is around 7 years.

Spring Hare

20

Useful Swahili Terms & Phrases

Considered one of the world's easiest languages to pick up, Swahili developed to make communication between Arab and coastal African traders simpler. There are regional variations and dialects, with the standard format evolving from Zanzibar Swahili—this was the form of the language Christian missionaries first transcribed using the Roman alphabet. The trick with Swahili is to sound out all the syllables that you see in the written form (which may vary from place to place, so take spelling variants with a pinch of salt)—there are no silent letters or syllables. Bear in mind, too, that Swahili is not necessarily the first language for many of the people you will meet in East Africa. Many people, particularly outside Tanzania and away from the coast, speak only an informal or passable version of the language (in addition to their home tongue), and this may lack correct grammar, have a simplified vocabulary, and, ultimately, be no better than your own practiced attempts at blending in.

1 BASIC VOCABULARY

English	Swahili	Pronunciation
Hello (*lit:* Problems?)	**Jambo/Hujambo?**	Jum-boh/Who-jum-boh
Good morning	**Habari ya asubuhi**	Huh-hab-ree ah-soo-boo-hee
Good afternoon	**Habari ya mchana**	Huh-hab-ree yah mm-cha-nah
Good evening	**Habari ya jioni**	Huh-hab-ree yah gee-oh-nee
Good night	**Usiku mwema**	Oo-see-koo mm-weh-mah
Sleep well (Good night)	**Lala salama**	Lah-lah sah-lah-mah
No problems	**Jambo/Sijambo**	Jum-boh/*Si*-jum-boh
How are you?	**Habari yako?**	Huh-hab-ree yah-koh?
Fine	**Mzuri**	Mm-zoo-ree
I'm fine, thank you	**Habari mzuri, asante**	Huh-bah-ree mm-zoo-ree, ah-sun-tay
And you?	**Na wewe?**	Nah weh-weh?
How's it going? (*lit:* Now?)	**Sasa?**	Sah-sah?
Hi! (lit: Things? or Issues?)	**Mambo?**	Mum-boh?
How're things? (*lit:* News?)	**Habari?**	Huh-bah-ree?

English	Swahili	Pronunciation
Hey, what's happening? *(coll.)*	**Vipi?**	Vee-pee?
What's up?	**Namna gani?**	Numm-nah gah-nee?
Very good, cool (*lit:* fit)	**Fiti**	Fee-tee
Cool (*lit:* pure)	**Safi**	Sah-fee
Absolutely/completely	**Kabisa**	Kah-bee-sah
Please	**Tafadhali**	Tuff-ah-duh-lee
Thank you	**Asante**	Ah-sun-tay
Thank you very much	**Asante sana**	Ah-sun-tay sah-nah
You're welcome	**Asante kushukuru**	Ah-sun-tay koo-shoo-koo-roo
Welcome/You're welcome	**Karibu**	Kar-ee-boo
Hello? Anyone home?	**Hodi!**	Hoh-dee!
Good-bye	**Kwaheri**	Qua-hair-ee
See you! (*lit:* We shall meet!)	**Tutaonana!**	Too-tah-oh-nah-nah!
Good luck	**Bahati njema!**	Bah-hah-tee nn-gem-ah
Have a good day!	**Nakutakia siku njema!**	Nah-koo-tuckia see-koo nn-gem-ah
Cheers!/Good health!	**Maisha marefu! Afya! Vifijo!**	May-ee-shah mah-reh-foo! Uff-yah! vee-fee-joh!
What's your name?	**Jina lako nani?**	Gee-nah lah-koh nah-nee?
My name is . . .	**Jina langu ni . . .**	Gee-nah lung-goo nee . . .
I am called . . .	**Nina itwa . . .**	Nee-nah eet-wah . . .
I/me	**Mimi**	mee-mee
we/us	**sisi**	see-see
you	**wewe** *(sing.)*/**ninyi** *(pl.)*	weh-weh/neen-yee
him/her/he/she	**yeye**	yeah-yeah
them/they	**wao**	wah-ah
yes	**ndiyo**	nn-dee-yah
no	**hapana/siyo**	Ha-pah-nah/See-yah
No, thanks	**La, asante**	Lah, ah-sun-tay
Where are you from?	**Unatoka wapi?**	Una-toh-kah wah-pee?
I'm from . . .	**Natoka . . .**	Nah-toh-kah . . .
Pleased to meet you	**Nafurahi kukuona**	Nah-foo-ra-hee koo-koo-oh-nah
Madam *(married/adult woman)*	**Mama**	Mad-mwa-*zel*
Mister	**Bwana**	Bwah-nah
White person	**Mzungu**	Mm-zoon-goo

(***Note:*** This will often be used as an interjection, yelled out by locals while pointing at you. It's not meant to offend, but is typically an excited observation.)

English	Swahili	Pronunciation
I'm fine, thank you	**Habari mzuri, asante**	Huh-bah-ree mm-zoo-ree ah-sun-tay
Fine, okay, right, ready	**Sawa**	Suh-wah
No problem	**Hakuna matata/Hakuna wasiwasi**	Huh-coo-nah mah-tah-tah/ Huh-coo-nah wah-see-wah-see
Excuse me, let me pass *(informal)*	**Hebu/Samahani nipishe**	Heh-boo/Sah-mah-huh-nee nee-pee-she-eh
Excuse me *(getting attention)*	**Samahani**	Suh-mah-huh-nee
I am sorry	**Nasikitika**	Nah-see-kee-tee-kah
No problem	**Hakuna matata**	Huh-coo-nah mah-tah-tah
There is	**Kuna**	Coo-nah
There is not	**Hakuna**	Huh-coo-nah
I'm sick	**Mimi mgonjwa**	Mee-mee mm-gon-jwah
I'm hungry	**Nina njaa**	Nee-nah nn-jah-ah
I'm thirsty	**Nina kiu**	Nee-nah kee-oo
Toilet/bathroom	**Choo/bafu**	cho/bah-foo
Where's the toilet?	**Choo kiko wapi?**	Cho kee-koh wah-pee?
Help!	**Msaada!**	Mm-sah-aa-dah!

STREET SMARTS

English	Swahili	Pronunciation
Do you speak English?	**Unasema Kiingereza?**	Oo-nah-seh-mah kee-een-geh-reh-zah
Do you speak Swahili?	**Unazungumza kiSwahili?**	Oo-nah-zuhn-goom-zah kee-swah-hee-lee
Yes, a little	**Ndiyo, kidogo tu**	Nn-dee-yoh, kee-doh-go too
I don't speak Swahili	**Sisemi Kiswahili**	See-seh-mee kee-swah-hee-lee
Where am I?	**Niko wapi?**	Nee-koh wah-pee?
I don't understand	**Sifahamu/Sielewi**	See-fah-hah-moo/See-eh-leh-wee
Please write it down for me	**Wawexa kuiandika?**	Wah-weh-ksa coo-ee-un-dee-kah?
I understand	**Naelewa**	Nah-eh-leh-wah
How do you say . . . in Swahili?	**Unasemaje kwa kiswahili . . . ?**	Oo-nah-seh-mah-jeh qua kee-swah-hee-lee
Could you speak slowly?	**Sema pole pole**	Seh-mah poh-leh poh-leh
Could you repeat that?	**Sema tena?**	She-mah teh-nah
I want . . .	**Nataka . . .**	Nah-tah-kah
a room	**chumba**	choom-bah
I don't want . . .	**Sitaki . . .**	See-tah-kah
Yes, correct	**Ndiyo**	Nn-dee-yoh

Dealing with Drivers

You'll inevitably be driven around for much of your time in Kenya and Tanzania, and there will be times when the style, pace, or attitude of your driver will make you nervous or uneasy. Here are a few essential terms that will help you get your point across—firmly and in absolute terms—when you need to modify your travel experience:

Simana! (Stop!)
Pole pole (Slowly)
Unaenda wapi? (Where are you going?)
Twende (Let's go)
Ngoja kidogo! (Hang on a moment!)

English	Swahili	Pronunciation
and/with	**na**	nah
or	**au**	ah-oo
How do you say . . . ?	**Unasemaje . . . ?**	Oo-nah-seh-mah-jeh . . . ?
What?	**Nini?**	Nee-nee?
When?	**Lini?**	Lee-nee?
Now	**Sasa**	Sah-sah
Where is . . . ?	**Wapi . . . ?**	Wah-pee . . . ?
telephone	**simu**	see-moo
toilet/washroom	**choo/bafu**	cho/bah-foo
Which?	**Gani?**	Gah-nee?
Who?	**Nani?**	Nah-nee?
Why?	**Kwa nini?**	Kwah nee-nee
Because . . .	**Kwa sababu . . .**	Kwah sah-baa-boo
I don't know	**Sijui**	See-jew-ee
How much?	**Ngapi?**	Nn-gah-pee?
How much is this?	**Hii ni bei gani?**	Hee-ee nee bay-ee gah-nee?
Money	**Pesa**	Peh-sah
I'm American	**Mimi ni mwamerika**	Mee-mee nee mmwah-merica
. . . Canadian	**. . . mkanada**	. . . mm-kun-ah-dah
. . . British	**. . . mwingereza**	. . . mm-win-geh-reh-zah
police	**polisi**	police-ee
Bring me . . . /	**Niletee . . . /**	Nee-leh-tee . . . /
Give me . . .	**Nipe . . .**	Nee-pah . . .
hot water	**maji moto**	mah-gee mo-toh
cold water	**maji baridi**	mah-gee bah-ree-dee

English	Swahili	Pronunciation
big	**kubwa**	coo-bwah
small	**kidogo**	key-doh-go

GETTING AROUND

English	Swahili	Pronunciation
journey	**safari**	suh-fah-ree
Bon voyage!	**Safari njema!**	Suh-fah-ree nn-gem-ah
travel	**kusafiri**	koo-suh-fah-ree
road	**njia**	nn-gee-ah
highway	**barabara**	bah-rah-bah-rah
here/there	**hapa**	hah-pah
left/right	**kushoto**	koo-shoh-toh
right	**kulia**	koo-lee-ah
straight ahead	**moja kwa moja**	moh-jah qua moh-jah
up	**juu**	jew-oo
down	**chini**	chee-nee
petrol (gas/fuel)	**petroli**	petrol-ee
I'm going to . . .	**Nenda . . .**	Nen-dah . . .
river	**mto**	mm-toh
lake	**ziwa**	zee-wah
hill	**kilima**	kill-eema
I want to get off here	**Nataka kushuka hapa**	Nah-tah-kah coo-shoo-kah huh-pah
fast	**haraka**	huh-rah-kah
open	**fungua**	foon-goo-ah
closed	**funga**	foon-gah
on foot	**kwa miguu**	qua mee-goo-oo
plane	**ndege**	nn-deh-geh
airport	**uwanga wa ndege**	oo-wahn-gah wah nn-deh-geh
boat	**chombo/mashua**	chom-boh/mash-oo-ah
bus	**basi/buu**	bus-ee/boo-oo
minibus	**daladala**	duller duller
bus station	**basi kituo**	bus-ee kee-too-oh
by bicycle	**kwa baiskeli**	qua bi-ees-keh-lee
by car	**kwa gari**	qua gah-ree
taxi	**teksi**	tek-see
train	**treni**	tren-ee
When does it depart?	**Inaondoka lini?**	Een-ah-oh-nn-dork-ah lee-nee?
When will we get there?	**Tutafika lini?**	Too-tah-fee-kah lee-nee

TIME

English	Swahili	Pronunciation
What time is it?	**Saa ngapi?**	Sah-ah nn-gah-pee?
morning	**asubuhi**	ah-sue-boo-hee
early	**mapema**	mah-peh-mah
daytime	**mchana**	mm-chah-nah
nighttime	**usiku**	oo-see-coo
dusk	**magharibi**	mah-gghah-ree-bee
day	**siku**	see-coo
week	**wiki**	wee-kee
month	**mwezi**	mm-weh-zee
year	**mwaka**	mm-wah-kah
now	**sasa**	sah-sah
yesterday	**jana**	jah-nah
today	**leo**	lee-oh
tomorrow	**kesho**	keh-show

NUMBERS

0 **sifuri** (si-furi)
1 **moja** (moh-jah)
2 **mbili** (mmbee-lee)
3 **tatu** (tah-too)
4 **nne** (nn-neh)
5 **tano** (tah-noh)
6 **sita** (see-tah)
7 **saba** (saa-bah)
8 **nane** (nah-neh)
9 **tisa** (tee-sah)
10 **kumi** (koo-mee)
20 **ishirini** (ish-eer-ee-nee)
30 **thelathini** (tell-lah-teeny)
40 **arobaini** (ah-roh-bah-ee-nee)
50 **hamsini** (hah-um-see-nee)
60 **sitini** (see-teeny)
70 **sabini** (sah-bee-nee)
80 **themanini** (teh-mah-nee-nee)
90 **tisini** (tee-see-nee)
100 **mia moja** (mee-ah moh-jah)
1,000 **elfu** (el-foo)

DAYS OF THE WEEK

Monday	**jumatatu**	jew-mah-tah-too
Tuesday	**jumanne**	jew-mah-nn-neh
Wednesday	**jumatano**	jew-mah-tah-noh
Thursday	**alhamisi**	al-hah-mee-see
Friday	**ijumaa**	ee-jew-mah-ah
Saturday	**jumamosi**	jew-mah-moh-see
Sunday	**jumapili**	jew-mah-pee-lee

NECESSITIES/SHOPPING

English	Swahili	Pronunciation
bank	**benki**	benk-ee
shop	**duka**	doo-kah
post office	**posta**	pos-tah
hospital	**hospitali**	hos-pee-tah-lee

English	Swahili	Pronunciation
pharmacy (drug store)	**duka la dawa**	dookah lah dah-va
restaurant/cafe	**hoteli**	hotel-ee
I'm just looking	**Mimi na angalia tu**	Mee-mee nah ah-nn-gull-ee-ah too
Is there any . . . ?	**Iko . . . ?/Kuna . . . ?**	Ee-koh . . . ?/Koo-nah . . . ?
What's the price…?	**Bei gani…?**	Beh-ee gah-nee…?
Bring down the price a bit!	**Punguza kidogo!**	Poon-goo-zah kee-doh-go
cheap	**rahisi**	rah-hee-see
(too) expensive	**ghali (sana)**	gg-halli (sah-nah)

2 DINING

English	Swahili	Pronunciation
What would you like to drink?	**Utapenda kunywa nini?**	Oo-tah-pen-dah coo-nyah-wah nee-nee?
I'll drink tea with milk and a little sugar.	**Nitakunywa chai na maziwa na sukari kidogo.**	Nee-tah-coo-nyah-wah tchai nah mah-zee-wah nah soo-kah key-doh-go.
What would you like to eat?	**Utapenda kula nini?**	Oo-tah-pen-dah coo-lah nee-nee?
I want . . .	**Nataka . . .**	Nah-tah-kah . . .
food	**chakula**	cha-coo-lah
water	**maji**	mah-gee
a table	**meza**	meh-zah
a knife	**kisu**	kee-sooh
a fork	**uma**	oo-mah
the bill	**hesabu**	heh-sah-boo
another one	**ingine**	in-geen-ee
Bon appétit *(singular)*	**Ufurahie chakula chako**	Oo-foo-rah-hee-eh cha-coo-lah cha-koh
Bon appétit *(plural)*	**Msifurahie chakula chenu**	Mm-see-foo-rah-hee-eh cha-coo-lah cheh-noo

BASICS

baridi	cold	**mkate**	bread
bia/tembo	beer	**molo**	hot (temperature)
chai	tea	**na . . . / bila . . .**	with . . . / without . . .
chumvi	salt	**siagi**	butter
kahawa	coffee	**sukari**	sugar
kali	hot (spicy)	**unga**	flour
mayai	eggs	**wali**	rice
maziwa	milk		

MEAT

kondo	lamb	**nguruwe**	pork
kuku	chicken	**nyama**	meat
mbuzi	goat	**samaki**	fish
ng'ombei	beef	**steki**	steak

FRUITS & VEGETABLES

machungwa	oranges	**ndimu**	lemon
maembe	mangoes	**nyanya**	tomatoes
mahindi	corn	**papai**	papaya
matunda	fruit	**parachichi**	avocado
mboga	vegetables	**pera**	guava
nanasi	pineapple	**viazi**	potatoes
nazi	coconuts	**vitunguu**	onions
ndizi	bananas		

3 WILDLIFE

THE BIG FIVE

chui	leopard	**nyati**	buffalo
faru	rhinoceros	**samba**	lion
ndovu	elephant		

PREDATORS, SCAVENGERS & MEAT-EATERS

bweha	jackal	**mamba**	crocodile
bweha masigio	bat-eared fox	**mbwa mwitu**	wild dog/ hunting dog
duma	cheetah	**mondo**	serval
fisi	hyena	**paka pori**	wild cat
fungo	civet	**papa**	shark
kanu	genet	**simbamangu**	caracal

BUCK, ANTELOPE & PLAINS GAME

choroa	oryx	**punda milia**	zebra
kuru	waterbuck	**swala granti**	Grant's gazelle
mbuzi mawe	klipspringer	**swala pala**	impala
ngiri	warthog	**swala tomi**	Thomson's gazelle
nsya	duiker	**swala twiga**	gerenuk
nyamera	topi	**tandala**	kudu
paa	suni	**taya**	oribi
pala hala	sable antelope	**tohe**	reedbuck
pofu	eland	**twiga**	giraffe

"Hatari!"

While you may want to memorize the Big Five (named because they were traditionally, in the early days of safari-era hunting, the animals responsible for the largest number of human deaths in the bush), the words you'll be screaming from your tent to attract the attention of assistance will more likely be ***mdudu*** if there is an insect or bug, and—more specifically—***mbu,*** when you're threatened by a mosquito, which is absolutely the biggest killer in Africa. The other creature you really don't want to find curled up in your tent—or, indeed, slithering across your path—is an ***nyoka,*** or snake. And if you come between a ***kiboko*** (hippopotamus) and the water, there's not very much use remembering how to pronounce its name. Incidentally, take heed of signs bearing the slogan ***Hakuna njia,*** as it means **"No entry,"** while the Swahili word for danger is ***hatari*** and is likely to be accompanied on signboards by a fierce-looking skull and crossbones.

APES & MISCELLANEOUS OTHERS

kakukuona	pangolin	**ndege**	bird
kalasinga	De Brazza's monkey	**ng'ombe**	cow
		nguchiro	mongoose
kalunguyeye	hedgehog	**nguruwe**	pig
kamandegere	springhare	**nungu**	porcupine
kima	monkey	**nyani**	baboon
kindi	ground squirrel	**nyegere**	ratel
kobe	tortoise	**paka**	cat
komba	bushbaby	**pembere**	tree hyrax
kuku	chicken	**pimbi**	rock hyrax
mbega	Colobus monkey	**punda**	horse/donkey
mbuni	ostrich	**sange**	elephant shrew
mbuzi	goat	**soko**	chimpanzee
mbwa	dog	**sokwe**	ape/chimpanzee
mjusi	lizard	**sunguru**	rabbit/hare
muhanga	aardvark	**tumbili**	vervet monkey

INDEX

See also Accommodations and Restaurant indexes, below.

General Index

Accommodations—Kenya

Accommodations—Tanzania

Restaurants—Kenya

Restaurants—Tanzania